Health
The Basics

FOURTH EDITION

REBECCA J. DONATELLE

Oregon State University

ALLYN AND BACON

Boston • London • Toronto • Sydney • Tokyo • Singapore

Publisher: *Joseph E. Burns*
Vice President and Editor-in-Chief: *Paul Smith*
Senior Developmental Editor: *Mary Kriener*
Marketing Manager: *Richard Muhr*
Production Administrator: *Deborah Brown*
Series Editorial Assistant: *Annemarie Kennedy*
Editorial-Production Service: *Colophon*
Composition and Prepress Buyer: *Linda Cox*
Manufacturing Buyer: *Megan Cochran*
Photo Researcher: *Iquest*
Text Design: *The Davis Group, Inc.*
Electronic Composition: *Omegatype Typography, Inc.*
Cover Administrator: *Linda Knowles*

Library of Congress Cataloging-in-Publication Data
Donatelle, Rebecca J., 1950–
   Health: The Basics / Rebecca J. Donatelle. —
4th ed.
    p. cm.
   Includes bibliographical references and index.
   ISBN 0-205-32215-8 (alk. paper)
   1. Health.   II. Title.
RA776.D663 2000
613—dc21
                           99-32285
                             CIP

Between the time website information is gathered and then published, it is not unusual for some sites to have been closed. Also, the transcription of URLs can result in unintended typographical errors. The publisher would appreciate being notified of any problems with URLs so that they may be corrected in subsequent editions. Thank you.

Printed in the United States of America

10 9 8 7 6 5 4 3 2   WC   04 03 02 01 00

Photo Credits

Chapter 1   1: Corbis/Digital Stock; 3: Hugh Rogers/Monkmeyer; 8: Bob Daemmrich/The Image Works; 23: Bill Bachmann/The Image Works.

Chapter 2   27: "In the Mirror" by Linda Clave, © Linda Clave; 31: C. J. Allen/Stock Boston; 35: Dana White/PhotoEdit; 42: Dion Ogust/The Image Works; 45: Myrleen Ferguson/PhotoEdit.

Chapter 3   51: Corbis/Digital Stock; 55: Mike Greenlar/The Image Works; 61: Bob Daemmrich/Stock Boston; 66: Myrleen Ferguson Cate/PhotoEdit.

Chapter 4   71: "Through the Fire" by Ray, Gayle Ray/Superstock; 77: AP/Wide World Photos; 79: Steven D. Starr/Stock Boston; 84: Zed Nelson/IPG/Matrix.

Chapter 5   95: "Man and Woman Embracing with House" by Alexandra Maldonado, © Alexandra Maldonado/Stock Illustration Source; 97: Jeff Greenburg/Stock Boston; 100: Lori Adamski Peek/Stone; 122: T. J. Florian/Rainbow.

Chapter 6   125: "Mother and Child (digital)" by Jose Ortega, © Jose Ortega/Stock Illustration Source; 141: Will Hart; 147: Myrleen Ferguson Cate/PhotoEdit.

Chapter 7   155: "Bigma" 1998 by Robert Chambers (c) Robert Chambers/Museum of Contemporary Art, N. Miami, FL; 160: Tony Freeman/PhotoEdit; 171: Michael Newman/PhotoEdit; 179: AP/Wide World Photos.

Chapter 8   185: Corbis/Digital Stock; 195: Judy Gelles/Stock Boston; 198: Richard Hutchings/Photo Researchers; 207: Bob Daemmrich/Stock Boston; 213: David Weintraub/Stock Boston.

Chapter 9   217: "Falling Fruits" by Mary Lou Nye, © Mary Lou Nye; 235: PhotoDisc.

Chapter 10   247: Corbis/Digital Stock; 248: AP/Wide World Photos; 257: Charles Gupton/Stock Boston.

Chapter 11   265: "Party People" by Ong, Diana Ong/Superstock; 269: Topham/The Image Works; 275: Mitch Wojnarowicz/The Image Works; 280: Gary A. Connor/PhotoEdit.

Chapter 12   285: Corbis/Digital Stock; 292: Fotopic/Omni—Photo Communications, Inc.; 307: American Academy of Dermatology; 309: Courtesy of the Dana Farber Institute.

Chapter 13   315: "People Shaking Hands" by Campbell Laird, Campbell Laird/Stock Illustration Source; 317: Mary Kate Denny/PhotoEdit; 335: Dan McCoy/Rainbow; 338: Stone; 345: Bonnie Kamin.

Chapter 14   351: "Women Laughing" by Michael Collier, © Michael Collier/Stock Illustration Source; 353: Robert Harbison; 362: Merritt Vincent/PhotoEdit; 367: Mark Reinstein/The Image Works; 370: AP/Wide World Photos.

Chapter 15   375: "Ebben's Eden" by Saira Elizabeth Austin, © Saira Elizabeth Austin; 377: AP/Wide World Photos; 386: Bonnie Kamin/PhotoEdit; 391: Kaz Chiba/Stone.

Chapter 16   395: "Laughter is the Best Medicine" by Mary Lou Nye, © Mary Lou Nye; 397: © Esbin/Anderson/The Image Works; 404: Nick Lammers/Liaison Agency; 406: Andy Levin/Photo Researchers.

Brief Contents

Contents

Chapter 3

MANAGING STRESS: COPING WITH LIFE'S CHALLENGES   51

Chapter 4

INTENTIONAL AND UNINTENTIONAL INJURIES: STAYING SAFE IN A VIOLENT WORLD   71

PART II
CREATING HEALTHY AND CARING RELATIONSHIPS

Chapter 5

HEALTHY RELATIONSHIPS AND SEXUALITY: MAKING COMMITMENTS   95

PART IV
BUILDING HEALTHY LIFESTYLES

Chapter 9
NUTRITION: EATING FOR OPTIMUM HEALTH   217

Chapter 10
MANAGING YOUR WEIGHT: FINDING A HEALTHY BALANCE   247

Chapter 11
PERSONAL FITNESS: IMPROVING YOUR HEALTH THROUGH EXERCISE   265

PART V
PREVENTING AND FIGHTING DISEASE

Chapter 12
CARDIOVASCULAR DISEASE AND CANCER: REDUCING YOUR RISKS 285

Chapter 13
INFECTIOUS DISEASES AND NONINFECTIOUS CONDITIONS: RISKS AND RESPONSIBILITIES 315

PART VI
FACING LIFE'S CHALLENGES

Chapter 14
LIFE'S TRANSITIONS: THE AGING PROCESS   351

Chapter 15
ENVIRONMENTAL HEALTH: THINKING GLOBALLY, ACTING LOCALLY   375

Preface

As we enter a new millennium, health challenges once considered unimaginable to our ancestors have emerged. Try to imagine what the greatest health challenges were to your parents when they were your age. Or your grandparents. Or even your great-grandparents. We live in an ever-changing world and nowhere is this more evident than in public and personal health. Today brings with it issues of violence, new threats from emerging infectious diseases, remarkable insights into chronic diseases, and concerns over global health and the degradation of the environment.

Juxtaposed against the threats to health, are new knowledge, opportunities, policies, and strategies for promoting health and preventing premature disease and disability. The new millennium also brings with it increased longevity and greater understanding of psychological stressors, mental health, and all forms of addictions. Advancing technologies will continue to change the face of health care diagnosis and treatment, groundbreaking research will overturn many of the "truths" that we take for granted today, and each of us will become increasingly more responsible for our own health and well-being. Already today an astounding, contradictory, and confusing array of health information is available to us through the simple click of a "mouse." Each new class of college students offers health instructors a more savvy group of health "connoisseurs." With that added arsenal of information, students should be better prepared to examine, to think, and to make health decisions. Using yesterday's information to stimulate tomorrow's student is no longer appropriate in today's techno-driven, health conscious world.

Needless to say, writing an introductory health text presents an interesting challenge. As quickly as the last words are written for one edition, a new discovery is announced that probably should have been included in the book. So today's *texts* have gone high *tech,* linking you to the latest developments in disease prevention, health promotion, and policy change. There is no better evidence of this than the companion website for *Health: The Basics* on the Allyn and Bacon website (http://www.abacon.com) and the special PIN-coded Interactive Companion website linked to this text. Each allows us the opportunity to provide new information as it occurs.

Trying to keep up with the emerging health market and health news in general can be frustrating; but as health educators and practitioners, it also can be very exciting. We have the opportunity to assist a new generation of students to become future "change" agents for health—not just in the arena of personal health behaviors, but in the larger realm of policy changes that can assist the global population as a whole. In short, this text is designed not just to help teach you health facts, but to help you think of health as a much broader concept, *desired by all and deserved by all.* Each of you provides a starting place for a better health future. By understanding the factors that contribute to your health risk and the health risks of those around you, exploring concepts provided in this text and contemplating action plans that might serve to reduce risk, and by utilizing the technological tools that we've provided, you take the first step in *accessing* better health. The decisions you make today become the building blocks for your future health as well as the health of future generations.

NEW TO THIS EDITION

This edition of *Health: The Basics* maintains many of the strong features it is known for while focusing on new trends and concepts that make *Health: The Basics* one of the most contemporary books for the 21st century. The 4th edition includes a major update of all pertinent information as well as the following specific changes:

- The special focus on consumer health issues is broadened with a **special appendix, entitled** *Complementary and Alternative Medicine: New Choices, New Responsibilities,* that is dedicated to understanding complementary and alternative medicine, its practical uses, and its appeal to the masses.
- With unintentional injuries one of the leading causes of premature death among young people, **Chapter 4 on violence has been reorganized** to explore both intentional and unintentional injuries.
- A broadened look at diversity that is more global in nature recognizes that the understanding of health and health concepts can no longer be limited to the influences of cultures inside American borders but rather to those that are greatly affected by international occurrences. This perspective is emphasized in a **NEW box, "Health in a Diverse World,"** which appears in every chapter.
- **NEW Health Headline boxes** allow for in-depth looks at pertinent health issues prominent in today's news.
- **NEW Reality Check boxes** offer students data about trends on campus and about health issues that affect them personally and immediately.
- A **minor reorganization** of the book now places the Substance Abuse part earlier.
- **NEW PIN-protected Interactive Companion** website linked free with each text represents an exciting new study tool that uses the latest in multimedia to review, enrich, and expand upon key concepts presented in its companion textbook.

Maintaining a Standard of Excellence

In addition to the major changes noted above, this edition of *Health: The Basics* maintains and builds off the solid pedagogical standards established in previous editions:

- Chapter 1 establishes a strong decision-making strand that weaves its way throughout the book, **incorporating the best-known models in behavior change.** Decision making through critical thinking continues to form the cornerstone of every chapter, from the "What Do You Think?" scenarios and reflective questions throughout the chapter to the boxed features and the "Taking Charge" section at the end of the chapter.
- **The role of community in disease prevention and health promotion** is integrated throughout the text and in a special "Checklist for Change: Making Community Decisions" section within the "Taking Charge" wrap-up feature at the end of each chapter.
- **Expanded coverage of multicultural and global issues** will enhance your understanding of the diversity of the human experience and will help you to realize the interconnectedness of people throughout the world and the impact that has upon personal health.
- With a **strong pedagogical framework,** emphasis on building health skills is integrated consistently through-

out the text. You'll learn specific applications in every chapter through "Skills for Behavior Change" boxes, "Consumer Health" boxes, and in the "Taking Charge" section at the end of the chapter.

SPECIAL FEATURES

Each chapter of *Health: The Basics* includes the following special feature boxes designed to help you build health behavior skills as well as think about and apply the concepts. Three boxes complement the chapter information by providing further depth to specific topics. These include:

- **"Health Headlines"** boxes look at health "In the News." Health is an ever-changing field that makes the news in one way or another each and every day. Health Headlines boxes take a look at some of these hot discussions.
- **"Reality Check"** boxes focus attention on potential risks and safety issues, often as they relate to college-age students. Statistical information and occurrence rates help you recognize your own risks as they relate to particular subjects.
- **"Health in a Diverse World"** boxes promote acceptance of diversity on college campuses and assist you in adjusting to an increasingly diverse world. These boxes encourage an understanding of the global perspectives on health as they relate to current health issues.

In addition to these three conceptual boxes, two boxes focus on the development of skills necessary in obtaining optimum health. These include:

- **"Consumer Health"** boxes appear in each chapter and focus on health issues as they relate to consumer skills. This feature broadens the scope of awareness about consumer health while focusing on contemporary consumer issues.
- **"Skills for Behavior Change"** boxes offer specific skills that you can use in improving your health behavior. Topics include self-esteem building, cutting fat from your diet, and the positive relationship between diet and exercise, to name a few.

LEARNING AIDS

▶ *Chapter Objectives*   Each chapter begins with a list of objectives tied to the major sections of the chapter to emphasize important topics. These objectives can serve as a helpful tool for you to use when learning the key concepts presented in the chapter.

▶ *"What Do You Think?" chapter opening scenarios*   These scenarios prompt stimulating discussions that quickly involve you in the concepts to be presented in the chapters.

▶ *"What Do You Think?" reflective questions*   These questions appear in major sections of every chapter to encourage you to think critically about important concepts as you read through the chapter.

▶ *Margin Glossary of Key Terms*   For convenience and added emphasis, key terms are boldfaced in the text and defined in the margin close to the page where they are first introduced.

▶ *"Accessing Health on the Internet"*   This special feature provides listings and addresses of Internet websites related to the subject matter of each chapter. Link directly into major health sites from around the world, such as the World Health Organization, the Centers for Disease Control and Prevention, and the National Institutes for Health, and discover what these major organizations are currently working on. A link to such sources brings you the latest information in a matter of seconds. Hundreds of additional links can be found on the Interactive Companion website, as well as on the *Health: The Basics* website.

▶ *"Taking Charge"*   This special feature at the end of each chapter serves as a "wrap-up" to the entire chapter. This highly acclaimed feature directs you to review your personal attitudes and offers *Checklists for Change,* which outline specific actions you can take to change unhealthy behaviors, on both a personal and community level. In addition, this end-of-chapter section provides you with the opportunity to explore key concepts with the following study tools:

> ▶ *Chapter Summary*   Linked to the chapter opening learning objectives, these summaries provide a quick, at-a-glance review of key points presented in each chapter.

> ▶ *Discussion Questions*   Tied to major sections of the chapter, these questions encourage you to consider important concepts from varying angles.

> ▶ *Application Exercises*   These exercises are linked to the chapter opening "What Do You Think?" scenarios and expand class discussion on these points.

▶ *References*   Extensive listings of major sources used in researching each chapter are provided in the Reference section at the end of the text.

STUDENT SUPPLEMENTS

Available with *Health: The Basics, Fourth Edition,* is a comprehensive set of ancillary materials designed to enhance your learning.

▶ Health: The Basics *Interactive Companion Website*   Using chapter highlights as the organizing structure of the website, the IC encourages you to apply what you have learned by presenting you with hundreds of links to audio and video clips, web sites, activities, and practice tests. These links are annotated with brief descriptions that help you understand the value and purpose of each media asset in the context of the chapter. The IC makes use of proven pedagogical techniques to guide you through your studies and help you reach beyond the covers of the printed text. This site can only be accessed by using the specially-assigned PIN code provided on the inside front cover.

▶ *Thinking About Health: A Student Resource Manual*   This study guide includes language-enrichment sections for those of you who need special language assistance or who have difficulty with health vocabulary. A valuable study tool, it also provides a wealth of learning objectives, critical thinking exercises and activities, chapter summaries, key terms, review questions, and practice tests.

▶ *Newly Revised! Take Charge of Your Health! Self-Assessment Workbook with Practice and Review Tests*   Using this self-assessment workbook along with *Health: The Basics* will assist you in acquiring a broader understanding of health issues, evaluating your attitudes and behaviors, and gaining a clearer picture of your overall health. Also included are general review questions and two practice tests for each chapter.

▶ *Health Assessment Website*   You can further assess your individual health behaviors and plan a risk-reduction program by visiting this special site linked directly to the *Health: The Basics* website at www.abacon.com. This special assessment site link provides a number of customized assessment tools as well as links to numerous other health assessments provided by agencies from around the world.

▶ Health: The Basics *Companion Website*   Log onto the *Health: The Basics* website at http://www.abacon.com to read about changing events in health and to test your knowledge further as you study for class using the Online Study Guide, containing numerous essay, multiple choice, matching, and true/false items for each chapter.

INSTRUCTOR SUPPLEMENTS

A full resource package accompanies *Health: The Basics* to assist the instructor with classroom preparation and presentation. The package includes an Instructor's Resource Manual with an array of suggested resources for enhancing learning. A Test Item File containing over 1,600 items, all of which are also available in its computerized version. The Allyn and Bacon Test Manager is an integrated suite of testing and assessment tools for Windows and Macintosh. You can use Test Manager to create professional-looking exams in just minutes by building tests from the existing database of questions, editing questions, or writing your own. Course management features include a class roster, gradebook, and item analysis. Test Manager also has everything you need to create and administer online tests. For first-time users, there is a guided tour of the entire Test Manager system, and screen wizards to walk you through each area.

Classroom presentations can be enhanced using Powerpoint outline for instruction, the Digital Image Archive CD-ROM containing 200 images that can be incorporated into any electronic presentation program or onto overheads, the Digital Media Archive of digitized images and audio and video clips. The teaching package also includes a revised Health Transparency package containing over 180 images, many of which are NEW for this package.

In addition, instructors can obtain copies of individual videos or the entire set of the Allyn and Bacon *Total Health: Achieving Your Personal Best* video series that provides interactive critical thinking opportunities within the health classroom. This multidimensional package allows for distance learning, classroom discussion, remedial instruction, and tutorials for students.

ACKNOWLEDGMENTS

After writing four editions of *Health: The Basics*, there is only one thing we are certain of . . . it NEVER gets any easier. The complexities and considerations of publishing a book are too numerous to detail here. Fortunately, we've always had wonderful and competent people with whom we've worked on each book. From the excellent initial efforts of Joe Heider and Ted Bolen of Prentice Hall to continued professionalism of Allyn and Bacon editors Suzy Spivey and Joe Burns, I have always been pleased and grateful for the efforts of our publishing teams. As with any such work, the expertise of many are necessary to pull off a finished work that represents the best available health information source for college level students. In particular, we would like to thank Mary Kriener, senior developmental editor with the Allyn and Bacon group. It is somewhat unusual to have someone working in this capacity who has actual expertise in the area, and who is so enthusiastic about putting together a book that surpasses the competition. Her patience, wisdom, and painstaking attention to detail provided the foundation that ensures the continued success of *Health: The Basics* in the marketplace. To Mary and the countless other Allyn and Bacon staff members who worked overtime to help us meet ever-pressing deadlines without sacrificing the quality that readers have come to expect . . . thank you. With your help and direction, *Health: The Basics* continues to be among the leading texts in the health market today!

In addition to the Allyn and Bacon staff, many colleagues, students, and staff members have provided the feedback, reviews, extra time and assistance, and encouragement that have helped meet the demands of rigorous publishing deadlines over the years. With each edition of the book, your assistance has helped my vision for *Health: The Basics* become a reality. Rather than just being an up-scale version of a high school text, I have worked diligently to provide a text that is "alive" for readers. With each edition, I could not have developed a book like this one without the outstanding contributions of several key people. Whether acting as reviewers, generating new ideas, providing expert commentary, or writing chapters, these professionals have added their skills to a collective endeavor.

Contributors to the Fourth Edition

Dr. Patricia Ketcham (*University of Iowa*) for her work on Part III on substance abuse and the First Aid appendix since the inception of this project.

Sarah Hansen (*University of Iowa*)—Addictions and Addictive Behavior

Dr. Peggy Pederson (*University of Northern Illinois*)—Sexuality

Donna Champeau (*Oregon State University*)—Death and Dying

Dr. Rod Harter (*Oregon State University*)—Personal Fitness

Dr. Susan Prows (*Oregon State University*)—Consumerism

In addition, Jessica Henderson provided much needed updating of the environmental health chapter and the HIV/AIDS section of the Infectious Disease material in this edition. We would also be remiss in not thanking Chris Eisenbarth, a doctoral student at Oregon State who has provided exceptional levels of assistance with library research, organization of key concepts, and materials acquisition in writing this text.

Individuals who have provided their expertise and assistance with previous editions include Cathy Barnett, University of Iowa; Cheryl Graham, Oregon State University; Chris Hafner-Eaton, the RAND Corporation; Tomina Torey, Western Oregon State University; Tom Thomas, University of Missouri; Marion Micke, Illinois State University; Anna Harding, Oregon State University; and Carolyn Hoover, Alaska Public Schools.

Clearly, *Health: The Basics* continues to be an evolving "work in progress." With each new edition, we have built on the combined expertise of many colleagues throughout the country who are dedicated to the education and behavioral changes of students. Reviewers who have helped us with this fine tradition of excellence include:

Reviewers for the Fourth Edition of Health: The Basics

Judy B. Baker, East Carolina University; Robert Bensley, Western Michigan University; Susan Butler, Emory University; Kim Clark, California State University-San Bernadino; Carl Fertman, University of Pittsburgh; Matthew Garrett, Blackburn College; Marty Mahieu, Augustana College; Jack Osman, Towson University; Mike Perko, University of North Carolina-Wilmington; Marianne Zeanah, University of Montevallo

1

Promoting Healthy Behavior Change

OBJECTIVES

▶ Define health and wellness, and explain the interconnected roles of the physical, social, mental, emotional, environmental, and spiritual dimensions of health.

▶ Discuss the health status of Americans, the factors that contribute to health, and the importance of *Healthy People 2000*, *Healthy People 2010*, and the AHCPR guidelines in establishing national goals for promoting health and preventing premature death and disability.

▶ Discuss the importance of health promotion and disease prevention and differentiate among the major prevention types.

▶ Evaluate the role of gender in health status, health research, and health training.

▶ Provide a rationale for focusing on current risk behaviors as a means of influencing current and future health status.

▶ Identify the leading causes of death and the lifestyle patterns associated with the reduction of risks.

▶ Examine how predisposing factors, beliefs, attitudes, and significant others affect your behavior changes.

▶ Survey behavior change techniques, and learn how to apply them to personal situations.

▶ Apply decision-making techniques to behavior changes.

Peggy, aged 24, is a compulsive exerciser. She talks incessantly about her latest workouts, brags about her performances in minor races, and seldom engages in meaningful conversations about anything beyond her latest exercise injury, physical functioning, or next fitness event. She has few friends and doesn't notice when people quickly brush her off in conversations or walk away. Kathy, aged 22, is a highly competitive athlete who trains vigorously but seldom discusses her dietary habits, rigorous training, or outstanding successes in the field. She is quiet and well-liked, and others seek her advice on their own attempts to be healthy. Mary, aged 24, is a straight-A student in biochemistry, whose only exercise consists of daily walks and routine performance of daily activities. She does nothing extra to lose weight or become more fit, but consciously tries to stay active during the day and avoids watching TV at night. She is prone to perfectionism and is against wasting time at the gym or paying for special classes to be healthier.

Which of these individuals displays the most indicators of health/wellness? Which of these individuals appears to be the most unhealthy? Before making judgments about health or the lack of health, what else would you need to know? Describe one of your friends who you think provides an excellent example of positive health behaviors. What one characteristic about this person would you like to improve in your own health activities?

CONCERNED ABOUT YOUR HEALTH? You are not alone. At no time in U.S. history have so many government agencies, educational systems, community groups, businesses, and health care organizations been so concerned about your health or sought to influence your daily health habits. Billboards graphically display the dangers of drinking and driving. Television ads warn of the dangers of sexual promiscuity, drugs, high-fat diets, and other "unhealthy" behaviors. On a daily basis, you are challenged to "Just do it," "Be all you can be," "Drink your milk," "Eat cruciferous vegetables," "Save the environment," and to exercise, exercise, exercise! Policymakers restrict smoking in public, require detailed labeling on the foods you eat, and legislate a host of other policies designed to protect your health. Friends and family members probe your health status with inquiries about your health and comments about your weight. For some, a seeming need to be thought of as healthy prompts an endless stream of chatter about their latest workout. All this leaves us wondering whether we have gone too far in "hyping" health. Has the steady bombardment of conflicting information left us confused and misguided in our attempts to improve our health?

Our preoccupation with health should make it easy for us to get healthy, to stay healthy, and to live a long and productive life. However, many indicators provide evidence of our collective difficulties in achieving health goals. Consider this:

- Several national studies indicate that our citizens are becoming more obese and more unfit each year.[1]

- Sales of high-fat foods, red meats, butter, and other products that were on the decline are seeing an unprecedented rise in consumption.[2]
- Salad bars, low-fat grilled items, and portion control are on the decline, as consumers opt for the SUPER-sized burgers and MONSTER meals at popular restaurant chains.
- Cigarette smoking among our nation's young is at an all time high, especially among young women.[3]
- Depression, diabetes, hypertension, homicide, suicide, certain infectious diseases, and other preventable ailments are on the rise.[4]
- Increasing numbers of Americans lack access to basic health care.[5]

Why is being healthy so challenging for so many of us? What can we do to overcome the many challenges to our health, to make better decisions about our health-related behaviors, and to be wiser, more responsible health consumers? There are no easy answers, because health is influenced by myriad factors—some that we can control and some that we can't control. But the good news is that many people have found the skills and motivation to look objectively at where they are, to plan carefully, and to make the decisions that will lead to an improved life and health status. Have you ever wondered how one of your friends managed to lose weight and is now out kayaking and running in triathlons, when you can't seem to lose an ounce, and the latest trip up the stairs to class leaves you panting for breath? Or, why another

Today, health and wellness mean taking a positive, proactive attitude toward life and living it to its fullest.

PUTTING HEALTH IN PERSPECTIVE

Although we use the term **health** almost unconsciously, few people understand the complex nature of the term or what it really means. For some, *health* is the antithesis of sickness. To others, *health* means being in good physical shape and being able to resist illness. Still others use terms like **wellness,** or *well-being* to include a wide array of factors that seem to lead to positive health status. Why all of these variations? In part, the differences are due to a more enlightened way of viewing health. In addition, as our collective understanding of illness has increased, so has our ability to understand the many nuances of health. Our progression to current understandings about health has evolved over the centuries, and it is increasingly clear that we have a long way to go.

friend is calm under pressure and seems to thrive on it, while you are just as likely to break down into a screaming fit or tears? Why have so many of your good health intentions remained only intentions, rather than moving to the action phase?

This text is not designed to provide you with a foolproof recipe for achieving health or to answer all of your questions. It *is* designed to provide you with fundamental knowledge about many health topics, to help you develop the skills to utilize personal and community resources to create your own health profile, and to challenge you to think more carefully before making decisions that will ultimately affect your health. Health decisions should be based on the best available research and should be consistent with who you are, your values and beliefs, and who you want to become. Although health is not always totally within your control, there are changes that you can make in your behavior that will affect you today, as well as reduce future health risks. For those risk factors that are beyond your control, you must learn to react, adapt, respond appropriately, and use a reasoned, rather than purely emotional, rationale for your choices. By making informed, rational decisions, you will be able to improve both the quality and the length of your life and perhaps have a positive influence on those around you.

Health   Dynamic, ever-changing process of trying to achieve your individual potential in the physical, social, emotional, mental, spiritual, and environmental dimensions.

Wellness   The achievement of the highest level of health possible in each of several dimensions.

Health: Yesterday and Today

Prior to the 1800s, if you weren't sick, you were not only regarded as lucky, but also regarded as healthy. When deadly epidemics such as bubonic plague, pneumonic plague, influenza, tuberculosis, and cholera killed millions of people, survivors were believed to be of hearty, healthy stock, and congratulated themselves on their good fortune. Poor health was often associated with poor hygiene and unsanitary conditions, and certain stigmas were attached to households that harbored any of these illnesses. It wasn't until the late 1800s and early 1900s that researchers slowly began to discover that victims of these epidemics were not simply unhealthy or dirty people. Rather, they were victims of environmental factors that made them sick and over which they often had little control (microorganisms found in contaminated water, air, and human waste). Public health officials moved swiftly to address these problems, and as a result, the term *health* became synonymous with *good hygiene.* Colleges offered courses in "Health and Hygiene" or "Hygiene" that were the predecessors of the course you are in today.

Investigation into the environment as the primary cause of diseases continued well into the early 1900s, as diseases such as tuberculosis, pneumonia, and influenza surged in many regions of the world. If people made it through the first few years of life without succumbing to an infectious disease, they usually were able to survive to "old age." Keep in mind, however, that the average life expectancy in 1900 was only 47 years. Continued improvements in sanitation brought about dramatic changes in life expectancy, and the development of vaccines and antibiotics added even more years to the average life span.

By the 1940s, progressive thinkers in public health began to note that there was more to health than the early associations with hygiene or the focus on disease had indicated. At

HEALTH
HEADLINES

Achievements in Public Health: Where We've Been and Where We're Heading

To those of us in the field of public health, the saying "we've come a long way, baby" accurately reflects the health achievements of the last 100 years. In a review of advancements in public health, the Centers for Disease Control and Prevention (CDC) cited what they consider to be the ten greatest public health achievements of the twentieth century, a timespan in which the average lifespan of the U.S. population lengthened by more than 30 years.

- *Vaccinations:* Vaccinations have resulted in eradication of smallpox, elimination of poliomyelitis, and control of a number of infectious diseases, including measles, rubella, tetanus, diphtheria, and *Haemophilus influenzae* Type B, all of which once claimed the lives of large numbers of people in the early 1900s, many before they had reached the age of five.
- *Motor Vehicle Safety:* Improvements in motor vehicle safety have been the result of engineering efforts to make both vehicles and highways safer and successful efforts to change personal behavior, such as the use of

safety belts, child safety seats, and motorcycle helmets and the discouragement of drinking and driving.
- *Workplace Safety:* Work-related health risks common at the beginning of the century are now either under better control or completely eliminated. Since 1980 alone, safer workplaces have resulted in a 40 percent reduction in the rate of fatal occupational injuries.
- *Control of Infectious Diseases:* Clean water and improved sanitation have greatly reduced the development and transmission of infectious diseases since 1900. In addition, antimicrobial therapy, such as the discovery of and treatment with antibiotics, has greatly reduced the risk of diseases such as tuberculosis and sexually transmitted infections.
- *CVD and Stroke Deaths:* Efforts to educate the public on how to modify health risk factors, such as smoking cessation and blood pressure control, coupled with improved access to early detection and better treatment, have resulted in declines in incidences of CVD and stroke.
- *Safe and Healthy Foods:* Since 1900, technology for eradicating microbial contaminants from foods has increased drastically. In addition, identification of essential micronutrients and establishment of food-fortification programs have almost eliminated major nutritional deficiency diseases such as rickets, goiter, and pellagra.
- *Maternal and Infant Care:* Better hygiene and nutrition, improved avail-

ability of antibiotics, greater access to health care, and technologic advances in medicine have greatly reduced the risks to infants and mothers. Since 1900, infant mortality has decreased 90 percent, and maternal mortality has decreased 99 percent.
- *Family Planning:* Access to family planning and contraceptive services has altered social and economic roles of women. Family planning has provided health benefits that have helped reduce the number of infant, child, and maternal deaths; increased opportunities for preconceptional counseling and screening; and increased the use of barrier contraceptives to prevent unwanted pregnancies and transmission of sexually transmissible infections.
- *Fluoridation of Drinking Water:* Fluoridation of drinking water began in 1945 and in 1999 reached an estimated 144 million persons in the United States. Fluoridation safely and inexpensively benefits both children and adults by effectively preventing tooth decay, regardless of socioeconomic status or access to health care. Fluoridation has played an important role in the reductions in tooth decay in children and tooth loss in adults.
- *Recognition of Tobacco Use as a Health Hazard:* This recognition and subsequent public health antismoking campaigns have resulted in changes in social norms to prevent initiation of tobacco use, promote cessation of use, and reduce exposure to envi-

an international conference in 1947 focusing on global health issues, the World Health Organization (WHO) took the landmark step of trying to clarify what *health* truly meant: "Health is the state of complete physical, mental, and social-well-being, not just the absence of disease or infirmity."[6] For the first time, health came to mean more than "the absence of disease." However, it still wasn't clear how much more.

It wasn't until the 1960s and 1970s that critics successfully argued that health included much more than physical, social, or mental elements of life, and that other elements, such as environmental, spiritual, emotional, and intellectual aspects, helped define whether a person was truly capable of optimal functioning in typical daily settings. In addition, critics argued that it wasn't just how long you lived or the number of years you were disease-free that really mattered,

ronmental tobacco smoke. Since the 1964 Surgeon General's report on the health risks of smoking, millions of smoking-related health issues have been prevented and lives have been saved.

While past achievements are indeed remarkable, they also raise questions about where we're going in the next century. Will the future of our health rest solely in the hands of researchers, technological wizardry, and pharmaceutical houses? What roles will public health practitioners and the health care system play? What will our own role be in health promotion and disease prevention in the twenty-first century? Interviews with leading experts in health-related fields offer some clues.

- *New Drugs:* By 2010, experts predict a whole new arsenal of medicines for diseases such as Alzheimer's and multiple sclerosis, which defy treatment today. Genetically targeted drugs will home in on certain conditions, and new, slow-release vaccinations will control diseases such as diabetes.
- *Cancer:* By the year 2015, cancer deaths are expected to drop by 21 percent, with 13 percent fewer people ever getting cancer. Although many of our cancer-producing behaviors, such as smoking, will persist, we will have better methods of genetic screening for risk, targeted vaccines that control certain cancers, and less invasive treatments. Cancer treatment will be less debilitating.

- *Bacteria and Infectious Diseases:* Infectious diseases are the number one cause of death worldwide, with emergent/resurgent diseases on the increase. By 2010, a new strain of antibiotics will provide improved prognosis for resistant diseases, but an as-yet-to-be-discovered virus may have the potential to wipe out over one-third of the world's population.
- *Spirituality:* Spirituality training will become a common element of traditional medical training. Insurers will reimburse it, and medical schools will teach alternative medicine.
- *Heart Disease:* As baby boomers age, heart disease will boom, but better diagnostic tests will exist and better drug treatment will be developed, including proteins that create small arteries when main arteries are blocked.
- *Colds and Flu:* Although there won't be a cure for the cold in 2010, new vaccines will cut the cost of inoculating a child in a developing country from $100 to 10 cents, and drugs will provide great relief for many. However, a pandemic flu also is projected.
- *Foods:* In the year 2010, we'll have more "medical" foods that combine supplements, micronutrient additives, and medicines to boost food content, protect against disease, and bolster the immune system.
- *Aging:* By 2010, advances in medicine will include a "Methuselah" gene, which currently doubles or triples lifespan in roundworms;

calorie-restricted meals that increase longevity; and proteins that might halt the brain declines found in Alzheimer's disease.

While it's clear that we've come a long way, the possibilities for health and well-being in the future defy the imagination. Living longer, living more disease-free years, and injecting more quality into the extra years of life will be major goals of the future. The more we learn about the remarkable resilience of the human body and spirit, and the more technology stretches our imagination and enlarges our possibilities, the more likely that the twenty-first century will rival the twentieth century for major health-related achievements.

STUDENTS SPEAK UP:

What do *you* consider the greatest achievements in public health in the twentieth century? Do you think we will become more and more reliant on technology for better health in the future?

Sources: Adapted from "Ten Great Public Health Achievements—United States, 1900–1999." MMWR Weekly, April (1999), 48(12):241–243. Web site: www.cdc.gov/epo/mmwr/preview/mmwrhtml/00056796.htm and Strohl, Linda, "A Special Health Report: A Look at the Future of Medicine." *USA Weekend,* October 1–3, 1999. Pp. 6–9.

but whether you were able to live life to the fullest and reach your optimum potential for a happy, healthy, and productive life.

Mortality   Death rate.
Morbidity   Illness rate.

Today, because most childhood diseases are preventable or curable and because massive public health efforts are aimed at reducing the spread of infectious diseases, many people are living well into their 70s and 80s. According to **mortality** (death rate) statistics, people are now living longer than at any previous time in our history. **Morbidity** (illness) rates also indicate that people are sick less often from the common infectious diseases that devastated previous generations. However, just because we're living longer and not getting sick as often doesn't mean we're healthier.

The Evolution toward Wellness

René Dubos, biologist and philosopher, aptly summarized the thinking of his contemporaries by defining *health* as: "A quality of life, involving social, emotional, mental, spiritual, and biological fitness on the part of the individual, which results from adaptations to the environment."[7] The concept of adaptability, or the ability to successfully cope with life's ups and downs, became a key element of the overall health definition. Eventually the term *wellness* became popular and not only included the previously mentioned elements, but also implied that there were levels of health in each category. To achieve *high-level wellness,* a person would move progressively higher on a continuum of positive health indicators. Those who fail to achieve these levels may move to the illness side of the continuum. Today, the terms *health* and *wellness* are often used interchangeably to mean the dynamic, ever-changing process of trying to achieve one's individual potential in each of several inter-related dimensions. These dimensions typically include those presented in Figure 1.1.

- **Physical Health.** Includes characteristics such as body size and shape, sensory acuity and responsiveness, susceptibility to disease and disorders, body functioning, physical fitness, and recuperative abilities. Newer definitions of physical health also include our ability to perform normal **Activities of Daily Living (ADLs),** or those tasks that are necessary to our normal existence in today's society. Being able to get out of bed in the morning, being able to bend over to tie your shoes, or other usual daily tasks are examples of ADLs.
- **Intellectual Health.** Refers to your ability to think clearly, to reason objectively, to analyze critically, and to use your "brain-power" effectively to meet life's challenges. It means learning from your successes and mistakes and making sound, responsible decisions that take into consideration all aspects of a situation.
- **Social Health.** Refers to the ability to have satisfying interpersonal relationships: interactions with others, the ability to adapt to various social situations, and daily behaviors.
- **Emotional Health.** Refers to the feeling component; to express emotions when appropriate and to control expressing emotions either when it is inappropriate to do so or in an inappropriate manner. Feelings of self-esteem, self-confidence, self-efficacy, trust, love, and many other emotional reactions and responses are all part of emotional health.
- **Environmental Health.** Refers to an appreciation of the external environment and the role individuals play

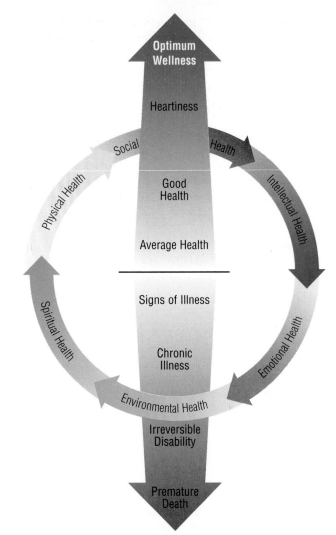

Figure 1.1

The Dimensions of Health and the Wellness Continuum

in preserving, protecting, and improving environmental conditions.

- **Spiritual Health.** May involve a belief in a supreme being or a specified way of living prescribed by a particular religion. Spiritual health also includes the feeling of unity with the environment—a feeling of oneness with others and with nature—and a guiding sense of meaning or value in life. It also may include the ability to understand and express one's purpose in life; to feel a part of a greater spectrum of existence; to experience love, joy, pain, sorrow, peace, contentment, and wonder over life's experiences; and to care about and respect all living things.

A well individual might display the following characteristics:

- A realistic sense of self, including personal capabilities and limitations

- An appreciation of all living things, no matter how ugly or beautiful, how unique or different, or how great or small
- A willingness to understand imperfection, to forgive other's mistakes, and to learn to grow from personal mistakes or shortcomings
- The ability to laugh, to cry, and to genuinely "feel" emotions without getting lost in emotional upsets
- The ability to function at a reasonable level physiologically
- The ability to maintain and support healthy relationships with family, friends, intimate partners, and strangers
- An appreciation for one's role in preserving and protecting the environment
- A sense of satisfaction with life and an appreciation for the stages of the life experience
- A zest for living, coupled with a curiosity about what each new encounter, each new day will bring
- A respect for self, as well as a respect for others
- A realistic perspective about life's challenges and the skills to cope with life's stresses and challenges
- A balance in all things

Many people believe that wellness can best be achieved by adopting a *holistic* approach, in which a person emphasizes the integration of and balance among mind, body, and spirit. Persons on the illness and disability end of the continuum may have failed in one or more of these areas. This does not mean, however, that someone who is physically disabled can never achieve wellness. Rather, wellness implies that each person is able to achieve the optimum level of wellness for their unique set of limitations or strengths. A physically disabled person may be functioning to their optimum level of performance; have satisfying interpersonal relationships; work to maintain emotional, spiritual, and intellectual health; and have a strong interest in environmental concerns. In contrast, those who spend hours lifting weights to perfect the size and shape of each muscle but pay little attention to nutrition may *look* healthy but may not have a healthy balance in all areas of their health. Although we often place a premium on the physical attractiveness and external trappings of a person, appearance and physical performance indicators are actually only two signs of physical health, indicating little about the other dimensions.

NEW DIRECTIONS FOR HEALTH

With so much attention focused on health and so many indications that Americans were not as healthy as they should be, the Surgeon General of the United States proposed in 1990 a national plan for promoting health among individuals and groups.

Healthy People 2000 and 2010

Known as *Healthy People 2000,* the Surgeon General's plan outlined a series of long- and short-range goals and objectives.[8] Essentially, these goals included features such as improving the life span of all Americans by three years, reducing disparities in life expectancy, and improving access to health care for all Americans regardless of sex, race, socioeconomic status, and other variables. To realize these broad-based goals, *Healthy People 2000* provided hundreds of specific objectives for the nation to reach by the year 2000. For example, one goal was to reduce the average dietary-fat intake to 30 percent of calories consumed from the 40 percent average of the time. Other goals focused on specific priority areas relating to diet, smoking, exercise, immunizations, homicides, and other areas of concern. While *Healthy People 2000* was viewed as a landmark public health measure, the document also was criticized by many in the field for what were perceived as unreachable goals and a lack of national financial support and a plan for achieving the goals. While many communities began working vigorously toward these goals soon after their initiation, as a nation, we still had a long way to go by as late as 1998. In an effort to continue working toward common goals, a new document, *Healthy People 2010,* took the initiative to the next level.[9] In the public sector, the Agency for Health Care Policy and Research (AHCPR) added additional direction for national health care efforts through its *AHCPR Guidelines,* a set of objectives for health care providers to meet in specific areas of their practices.[10] For example, AHCPR guidelines for tobacco specifically indicate what doctors should do when a smoking patient visits them. Complete listings of the *Healthy People 2000* and *2010* documents, as well as area-specific AHCPR Guidelines can be accessed through their respective websites. Visit the *Access to Health* web site for a direct link.

Health Promotion

As the *Objectives of the Nation* from the *Healthy People* documents prompted action toward the promotion of health and the prevention of premature disability through social, policy, environmental, and community-based programming, a new emphasis on individual behavioral change began to emerge. However, making behavioral changes without help is not easy. The term **health promotion** began to be used to describe the educational, organizational, procedural, environmental, social, and financial supports that help individuals and groups reduce negative health behaviors and promote positive change. Persons who engage successfully in health-promoting behaviors actively utilize services and supports that can help them improve or maintain good health. Health promotion programs, for instance, don't simply say, "Just do it," when providing advice to quit smoking. Instead, they provide information about risk behaviors and possible consequences to smokers and their sidestream smoke victims (educational supports); they encourage smokers to participate in smoking cessation classes and allow time off for worker attendance or they set up buddy systems of social supports to help them (organizational supports); they establish rules governing their behaviors and supporting their decisions to change, such as bans on smoking in the workplace and removal of cigarettes from vending machines (environmental supports); and they provide monetary incentives to motivate people to participate (financial supports).[11]

Health promotion programs identify healthy people who are engaging in **risk behaviors,** or behaviors that increase their susceptibility to negative health outcomes, and attempt to motivate them to change their behaviors. They encourage those whose health and wellness behaviors are already sound to maintain and improve them. By attempting to modify behaviors, increase skills, change attitudes, increase knowledge, influence values, and improve on health decision making, health promotion goes well beyond the simple information campaign to help your chances for success. By emphasizing health promotion programs and services in communities, organizations, schools, and other places where most people spend their time, the likelihood of long-term success on the road to health and wellness will be more realistic.

Whether we use the term *health* or *wellness,* we are talking about a person's overall responses to the challenges of living. Occasional dips into the ice cream bucket and other dietary slips, failures to exercise every day, flare-ups of anger, and other deviations from optimal behavior should not be viewed as major failures on the wellness scales. Actually, an ability to recognize that each of us is an imperfect being attempting to adapt in an imperfect world signals individual well-being.

We must also remember to be tolerant of others who are attempting to improve their health. Rather than being warriors against pleasure in our zeal to change the health behaviors of others, we need to be supportive, understanding, and nonjudgmental in our interactions with them. *Health bashing*—intolerance or negative feelings, words, or actions aimed at people who fail to meet our own expectations of health—may indicate our own deficiencies in the psychological, social, and/or spiritual dimensions of the health continuum.

Disease Prevention

Most documents that talk about health promotion typically include **disease prevention** as part of the health promotion

Having the motivation to improve the quality of your life within the framework of your unique capabilities is crucial to achieving health and wellness.

terminology. But what are we really talking about when we talk about disease prevention? Historically, three major types of prevention have been described in the health literature. In a general sense, *prevention* means taking positive actions now to avoid becoming sick later. Getting immunized against diseases such as polio, never starting to smoke cigarettes, practicing safer sex, and similar preventive actions constitute **primary prevention**—actions designed to reduce risk and avoid health problems before they start. **Secondary prevention** (also referred to as **intervention**) is the recognition of health risks or early problems before they lead to actual illness and taking action to prevent, or intervene, to stop the behavior or reduce risk before the disease gets a foothold. Getting a young smoker to quit or reduce the number of cigarettes smoked during the early stages of smoking behavior through some form of behavioral program is an example of an intervention or secondary prevention. Because two of every three deaths and one of every three hospitalizations in the United States are linked to preventable lifestyle behaviors, such as tobacco use, sedentary lifestyle, alcohol consumption, and overeating, primary and secondary prevention offer our best hope for reducing the **incidence** (number of new cases) and **prevalence** (number of existing cases) of disease and disability.[12]

As we approach the deadline for the 2000 objectives and move on to the 2010 Objectives of the Nation, it is clear that we need to move from a mindset of **tertiary prevention** (treatment and/or rehabilitation after the person is already sick and typically offered by medical specialists) and focus more on the role of prevention specialists and prevention programs. Health educators in U.S. schools and communities offer affordable and effective prevention and intervention programs. **Certified Health Education Specialists (CHES)** make up a trained cadre of public health workers with special credentials that indicate their competencies to plan, implement, and evaluate prevention programs that offer scientifically sound, behaviorally based methods to help you and members of the community increase the likelihood of success.[13] As a nation that historically spends little on prevention (less than 5 percent of our total national funding for health goes to prevention), however, such a shift has been and will continue to be difficult.

Preparing for the Future

As you can see, our definition of *health* has truly evolved over the years. Today, healthy people should have a sense of both individual and social responsibility. Rather than focusing solely on their own personal health, healthy people are concerned about others and the greater environment. This concern translates into taking actions designed to help themselves as well as to help others. It also means taking the time to understand the vast differences in health status between various social groups and actively promoting community actions that erase disparities (see Health in a Diverse World box on page 10).

Risk behaviors Behaviors that increase your susceptibility to negative health outcomes.

Disease prevention Actions or behaviors designed to keep you from getting sick.

Primary prevention Actions designed to stop problems before they start.

Secondary prevention (intervention) Intervention early in the development of a health problem.

Incidence The number of new cases.

Prevalence The number of existing cases.

Tertiary prevention Treatment and/or rehabilitation efforts.

Certified Health Education Specialists (CHES) Academically trained health educators who have passed a national competency examination for prevention/intervention programming.

While the definitions are clearer than ever before, the focus of many of our health promotion efforts, particularly for young adults, remains clouded. We have tended to focus almost exclusively on the leading causes of death in our society rather than focusing on those things that sap the life from young Americans. To a 20-year-old, death usually is not an imminent threat; thus, the motivation for behavior change is not as great as it perhaps should be. It is very important to look at how what you do now affects you right now *and* in the immediate future. For example, do you have days when you're tired all of the time or find yourself feeling disinterested in what is going on around you? Or perhaps you are a bit dissatisfied with yourself, your friends, your career choices, or other things in your life? In contrast, you probably also have days when you are full of zest first thing in the morning, when you look forward to the next fun event, and fall into bed exhausted at night, yet excited about the next day. What is the difference between the "blah" version of you and the "actively engaged" version? It is probably greatly dependent on what you eat, the exercise you get, the amount of sleep you get, the excitement you feel in meeting your challenges and being rewarded, and whether you take time to refresh the spiritual side of your life. In short, your investment in healthy behaviors contributes to how you are able to live each day.

By focusing on those factors that will get you "up" for living life, you can become actively engaged in life. If you don't go for that early morning walk because you can't drag yourself out of bed, if you don't socialize with friends because you are worried about how "fat" you look, if you find that your interactions with others cause you increasing levels of stress, it may be time to reexamine your health status. What are your current health risks? Future health risks? What can you do to improve your current status? What are you doing right that you need to spend more time on? While ADLs are performance-based measures typically used to assess functioning in the later years of life, perhaps we need to focus on them earlier. In addition, rather than rating ourselves based on what everyone else is doing, we need to consider potential differences based on race, socioeconomic opportunity, gender, age, and other variables. We all need to seek out our personal best.

·········· WHAT DO YOU THINK?

Think about your own performance abilities in each of the dimensions of wellness discussed here. What are some of your strengths in each dimension? What are some of your deficiencies in each dimension? What are one or two things you can do to enhance both your strengths and weaknesses?

HEALTH IN A DIVERSE WORLD

Global Burden of Disease: Changing Risk Profile for the Future

With all of the concern over personal health or public health in the United States, it is often easy to overlook health-related issues and problems in other regions of the world. As we move to a global economy, as transportation to the most remote regions of the world can occur within a matter of hours, and as our ability to deal with international health crises becomes more of a challenge, we must all learn more about international risk factors and the implications of these risks to the global population. It is likely that the next two decades will see dramatic changes in the health needs of the world's population. In the developing regions, where four-fifths of the planet's people live, noncommunicable diseases such as depression and heart disease are fast replacing the traditional enemies, such as infectious disease and malnutrition, as the leading causes of disability and premature death. By the year 2020, noncommunicable diseases are expected to account for seven out of every ten deaths in the developing regions, compared with less than half today. Injuries, both unintentional and intentional, are also growing in importance, and by 2020 could rival infectious diseases worldwide as a source of ill health.

According to a new body of research compiled by researchers at the Harvard School of Public Health and the World Health Organization (WHO) and colleagues throughout the world, a projection for ranking major threats to health, called the Global Burden of Disease, indicates massive shifts in health threats. Using a unique new method of rating, researchers attempted to assess the impact of risk on years of healthy life lost, a round-about way of building quality of life into an age-old formula that looks at risk only in terms of death rates. Thus, a risk factor that causes you to be disabled or function at less than optimal capacity is shown to have an immediate impact even though you may not die from it. Using this new formula, the following comparisons in rank orders of disease burden for the fifteen leading causes were computed. This is an approximate listing of comprehensive health risks for the global population.

Based on this information, what are the major differences in global health threats between 1990 and 2020? What factors contribute to these changes? Are there any areas of improvement? Decline? Based on current knowledge, what future role might tobacco use play in the 2020 statistics?

1990	2020 Projections
1. Lower respiratory infections	1. Ischemic heart disease
2. Diarrheal diseases	2. Unipolar major depression*
3. Perinatal conditions	3. Road traffic accidents
4. Unipolar major depression	4. Cerebrovascular diseases
5. Ischemic heart disease	5. Chronic obstructive pulmonary disease
6. Cerebrovascular disease	6. Lower respiratory infections
7. Tuberculosis	7. Tuberculosis
8. Measles	8. War
9. Road traffic accidents	9. Diarrheal diseases
10. Congenital abnormalities	10. HIV disease
11. Malaria	11. Perinatal conditions
12. Chronic obstructive pulmonary disease	12. Violence
13. Falls	13. Congenital abnormalities
14. Iron deficiency anemia	14. Self-inflicted injuries
15. Protein-energy malnutrition	15. Trachea, bronchus, and lung cancers

*In females and developing countries, unipolar major depression is projected as becoming the leading cause of disease burden.

Source: Murray, Christopher, and D. Lopez. *The Global Burden of Disease: Summary.* Harvard University Press, 1996.

GENDER DIFFERENCES AND HEALTH STATUS

You don't have to be a health expert to know that there are physiological differences between men and women. Although much of male and female anatomy is identical, it's clear that many major medical differences exist. Many diseases—osteoporosis, multiple sclerosis, and Alzheimer's disease, for example—are far more common in women than in men. Finally, although women live longer than men, they don't necessarily have a better quality of life.[14]

Much of the current interest in exploring women's health came after a highly publicized 1990 government study raised concern about the uneven numbers of women included in clinical trial research conducted by the *National Institutes of Health* (NIH). The NIH established the Office of Research on Women's Health (ORWH) in 1990 to oversee the representation of women in NIH studies. According to Vivian Pinn, ORWH's director, "For too long, medicine has viewed women as 'abnormal men' when considering health problems."[15]

Researchers excluded women from clinical trials of new drugs for several reasons. The Food and Drug Administration (FDA) issued rules in the 1970s stating that women with "childbearing potential" should be excluded from most studies, due largely to the disastrous results of a study of the drug thalidomide—a large number of the pregnant women in the study went on to have deformed babies. Moreover, in order to determine the precise effects of a drug or treatment, researchers have not wanted to deal with variations caused by women's menstrual cycles.

Of course, men and women do vary physiologically, and the elimination of women from many studies means that the results from these studies cannot be applied to women directly. According to social psychologist Carol Tavris, "If you want to know the effects of Drug X and you throw women out of your study because the menstrual cycle affects their responses to medication, you cannot then extrapolate from your study of men to women, precisely because the menstrual cycle affects their responses to medication."[16]

To address concerns about women's health, the NIH launched the **Women's Health Initiative (WHI)**, a 15-year, $625 million study focusing on the leading causes of death and disease in more than 140,000 postmenopausal women. WHI researchers hope to find out how a healthful lifestyle and increased medical attention can help prevent women's cancers, heart disease, and osteoporosis. In addition, the NIH has specified that equal amounts of money and time must be spent on men's and women's health research.[17]

········· **WHAT DO YOU THINK?**

What factors do you think may contribute the disparities in men's and women's health status? What actions should be taken to reduce these disparities?

Women's Health Initiative (WHI)   National study of postmenopausal women and which mandates equal research priorities for women's health issues.

IMPROVING YOUR HEALTH
Benefits of Optimal Health

Table 1.1 on pages 12–13 provides an overview of the leading causes of death in the United States by age. Risks for each of these leading killers can be reduced significantly by the practice of specific lifestyle patterns—for example, consuming a diet low in saturated fat and cholesterol, exercising regularly, not smoking or consuming alcohol, and managing stress. Individual behavior is believed to be a major determinant of good health, but heredity, access to health care, and the environment are other factors that influence health status (see Figure 1.2 on page 14). When these factors are combined, the net effect on health can be great.

For example, you may be predisposed to a less healthy lifestyle if you are unable to access the health-care system because you have no health insurance, if your family doesn't believe in traditional medicine, or if family members or friends smoke, drink heavily, and/or take drugs. While you can't change your genetic history, and while improving your environment and the health-care system can be difficult, you can influence your current and future health status by the behaviors you choose today.

Health Behaviors

Although mounting evidence indicates that there are significant benefits to being healthy, many people find it difficult to become and remain healthy. Most experts believe that there are several key behaviors that will help people live longer, such as:

- getting a good night's sleep (minimum of seven hours)
- maintaining healthy eating habits
- weight management
- physical recreational activities
- avoiding tobacco products
- practicing safe sex
- limiting intake of alcohol
- scheduling regular self-exams and medical check-ups

Although health professionals can statistically assess the health benefits of these behaviors, there are several other actions that may not cause quantifiable "years added to life," but may significantly result in "life added to years," such as

- controlling the real and imaginary stressors in life
- forming and maintaining meaningful relationships with family and friends
- making time for oneself
- participating in at least one fun activity each day
- respecting the environment and the people in it

TABLE 1.1

Leading Causes of Death in the United States by Age (Years)

RANK	ALL AGES		1–4		5–14		15–24	
1	Diseases of the heart	880.0	Accidents and adverse effects	40.6	Accidents and adverse effects	22.5	Accidents and adverse effects	95.3
2	Malignant neoplasms	204.9	Congenital anomalies	4.4	Malignant neoplasms	2.7	Homicide and legal intervention	20.3
3	Cerebrovascular disease	60.1	Malignant neoplasms	3.1	Homicide and legal intervention	1.5	Suicide	13.3
4	Chronic obstructive disease	39.2	Homicide and legal intervention	2.9	Congenital anomalies	1.2	Malignant neoplasms	4.6
5	Accident and adverse effects	35.5	Diseases of the heart	1.6	Suicide	0.9	Diseases of the heart	2.9
6	Pneumonia and influenza	31.6	Human immuno-deficiency virus	1.4	Diseases of the heart	0.8	Human immuno-deficiency virus	1.7
7	Diabetes mellitus	22.6	Pneumonia and Influenza	1.0	Human immuno-deficiency virus	0.5	Congenital anomalies	1.3
8	Human immuno-deficiency disease	16.4	Condition of perinatal period	0.6	Chronic obstructive pulmonary disease	0.4	Chronic obstructive pulmonary disease	0.7
9	Suicide	11.9	Septicemia	0.4	Pneumonia and influenza	0.3	Pneumonia and influenza	0.6
10	Chronic liver disease	9.6	Cerebrovascular disease	0.4	Benign neoplasms and other	0.3	Cerebrovascular disease	0.5

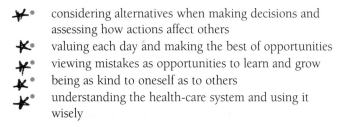

- considering alternatives when making decisions and assessing how actions affect others
- valuing each day and making the best of opportunities
- viewing mistakes as opportunities to learn and grow
- being as kind to oneself as to others
- understanding the health-care system and using it wisely

While it's easy to list things that one should do, change is not easy. All people, no matter where they are on the health/wellness continuum, have to start somewhere. All people have faced personal and external challenges to their attempts to change their health behaviors—some have not done so well, some have been extremely successful, and some have made only small changes that may add up to significant improvements in how they feel and how they live their lives. The key is to identify the behaviors most in need of change, determine the major actions necessary for the accomplishment of goals, set up a plan of action, and get started. But first, it is important to take a close look at those factors that may contribute to current behaviors.

PREPARING FOR BEHAVIOR CHANGE

Mark Twain said that "habit is habit, and not to be flung out the window by anyone, but coaxed downstairs a step at a time." The chances of successfully changing negative behavior problems improve when you make gradual changes that give you time to unlearn negative patterns and to substitute positive ones. To understand how the process of behavior change works, we must first identify specific behavior patterns and attempt to understand the reasons for them. A number of theories/models help explain why some people are successful at their attempts at behavior change and others are not. Several of these are discussed here, including Prochaska and DiClemente's Stages of Change or Transtheoretical model, which has gained considerable attention in recent years (see Skills for Behavior Change on page 15).[18]

The reasons why people behave in unhealthy ways, despite known risks, are complex and not easily understood. Health researchers have studied health behaviors for decades

25–44		45–65		65+	
Human immunodeficiency virus	36.9	Malignant neoplasms	253.0	Diseases of the heart	5,052.8
Accidents and adverse effects	33.2	Diseases of the heart	196.8	Malignant neoplasms	1,136.6
Malignant neoplasms	26.4	Accident and adverse effects	31.3	Cerebrovascular diseases	413.8
Diseases of the heart	20.5	Cerebrovascular diseases	29.1	Chronic obstructive pulmonary disease	263.9
Suicide	15.3	Chronic obstructive pulmonary disease	24.4	Pneumonia and influenza	221.6
Homicide and legal intervention	12.3	Diabetes mellitus	23.3	Diabetes mellitus	132.6
Chronic liver disease	5.2	Chronic liver disease	20.3	Accident and adverse effects	64.0
Cerebrovascular disease	4.2	Human immunodeficiency virus	20.1	Alzheimer's disease	60.3
Diabetes mellitus	2.9	Suicide	14.1	Nephritis etc.	60.2
Pneumonia and influenza	2.5	Pneumonia and influenza	10.6	Septicemia	50.4

*Rates per 100,000 population in a specific group.
Sources: Anderson, R. N., K. D. Kochanek, and S. L. Murphy. Report of Final Mortality Statistics. 1996. Monthly Vital Statistics Report, Vol. 45 No. 11, Supp 2, Table 7, pp. 22–33. Hyattsville, Maryland: National Center for Health Statistics, 1997.
Web site for latest data: http://www.cdc.gov/nchswww/fastats/lcod.htm

and continue to analyze the reasons why one person chooses to act responsibly while another ignores obvious health risks.

Factors Influencing Behavior Change

Figure 1.3 on page 16 identifies the major factors that influence behavior and behavior-change decisions. These factors can be divided into three general categories: predisposing, enabling, and reinforcing factors.

▶ *Predisposing Factors*   Our life experiences, knowledge, cultural and ethnic inheritance, and current beliefs and values are all *predisposing factors* influencing behavior and behavior change. Factors that may predispose us to certain conditions include our age, sex, race, income, family background, educational background, and access to health care. For example, if your parents smoked, you are 90 percent more likely to start smoking than someone whose parents didn't. If your peers smoke, you are 80 percent more likely to smoke than someone whose friends don't.

▶ *Enabling Factors*   Skills or abilities; physical, emotional, and mental capabilities; and resources and accessible facilities that make health decisions more convenient or difficult are *enabling factors.* Positive enablers encourage you to carry through on your intentions. Negative enablers work against your intentions to change. For example, if you would like to join a local fitness center but discover that the closest one is 4 miles away and that the membership fee is $500, those negative enablers may convince you to stay home. On the other hand, if your school's fitness center is two blocks away, is open until midnight, and has a special student membership deal, those positive enablers will probably convince you to join the center. Identifying these positive and negative enabling factors and devising alternative plans when the negative factors outweigh the positive are part of a necessary planning strategy for behavioral change.

▶ *Reinforcing Factors*   The presence or absence of support, encouragement, or discouragement that significant people in your life bring to a situation is a *reinforcing factor.* For example, if you decide to stop smoking and your family and friends

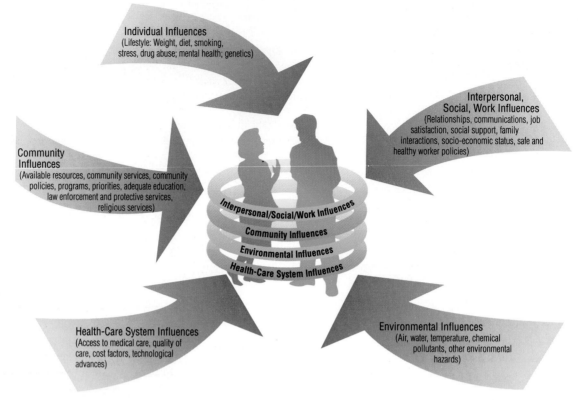

Figure 1.2

Factors That Influence Your Health Status

smoke in your presence, you may be tempted to start smoking again. In other words, your smoking behavior was reinforced. Reinforcing factors also include policies and services that make it easier for you to maintain a particular behavior. If, however, you are overweight and you lose a few pounds and all your friends tell you how terrific you look, your positive behavior will be reinforced and you will be more likely to continue to diet. Reinforcing factors, which may influence you toward positive and/or negative behaviors, include money, popularity, social support and appreciation from friends, and family interest and enthusiasm for what you are doing.[19,20]

The manner in which you reward or punish yourself for your own successes and failures may affect your chances of adopting healthy behaviors. Learning to accept small failures and to concentrate on your successes may foster further successes. Berating yourself because you binged on ice cream, argued with a friend, or didn't jog because it was raining may create an internal environment in which failure becomes almost inevitable. Telling yourself that you're worth the extra time and effort and giving yourself a pat on the back for small accomplishments is an often overlooked factor in positive behavior change.

Motivation

Wanting to change is a prerequisite of the change process, but there is much more to the process than motivation.

Motivation must be combined with common sense, commitment, and a realistic understanding of how best to move from point A to point B.[21] *Readiness* is the state of being that precedes behavior change. People who are ready to change possess the knowledge, attitudes, skills, and internal and external resources that make change a likely reality. For someone to be ready for change, certain basic steps and adjustments in thinking must occur.

WHAT DO YOU THINK?

Who do you think you could ask to help support you in your behavior change effort? What factors could make this change difficult? Why do you think you weren't successful before in changing a key behavior? What skills will you need to be successful? How ready are you?

Your Beliefs and Attitudes

Even if you know why you should make a specific behavior change, your beliefs and attitudes about the value of your actions in making a difference will significantly affect what you do. We often assume that when rational people realize there is a risk in what they are doing, they will act to reduce that risk. But this is not necessarily true. Consider

Staging for Change

On any given day, countless numbers of us get out of bed and resolve to begin to change a given behavior "today." Whether it be losing weight, drinking less, exercising more, being nicer to others, managing time better, or some other change in a negative behavior, we start out with high expectations. In a short time, however, a vast majority of people fail and are soon back doing whatever it was they thought they shouldn't be doing.

Why do so many good intentions end up as failures? According to Dr. James Prochaska, psychologist and head of the Health Promotion Partnership at the University of Rhode Island, and Dr. Carlos DiClimente these failures occur because we are going about things in the wrong way. According to Prochaska and DiClimente, fewer than 20 percent of us are really prepared to take action. Yet, prevention specialists, doctors, and other professionals continue to force us to "Just Do It! and do it *now!*" After considerable research, Prochaska and DiClimente believe that behavior changes usually do not succeed if they start with the change itself. Instead, they believe that we must go through a series of "stages" to adequately prepare, or ready, ourselves for that eventual change. They insist that through proper reinforcement and help during each of the following stages, our chances of making and keeping those New Year's resolutions will be greatly enhanced.

1. Precontemplation: People in the precontemplation stage have no current intention of changing. They may have tried to change a behavior before and may have all but given up, or they may just be in denial and unaware of any problem. People in this stage don't have to worry about failure and have no intention of taking any actions.

Strategies for Change: Although a very touchy area, sometimes a few frank, yet kind words from friends may be enough to make the precontemplator take a closer look at him- or herself. This is not to say that you should become a "warrior against pleasure" or that you should feel justified in telling people what to do when they haven't asked for advice. Recommended readings or tactful suggestions, however, can be useful.

2. Contemplation: In the contemplation stage, the person recognizes that he or she has a problem and begins to think about the need to change. Acknowledgment usually results from increased awareness, often due to feedback from family and friends or access to information. Despite this acknowledgment, people can languish in this stage for years, knowing that they have a problem but never finding the time or energy to make the change.

Strategies for Change: Often, contemplators need a little push to get them started. This may come in the form of helping them set up a change plan (e.g., an exercise plan), buying them a gift that helps with the plan (i.e., a low-fat cookbook), giving them articles about a particular problem, or inviting them to go with you to hear a speaker on a related topic. In this stage, they often are in need of skill building or time to think about what they might want to do. Your assistance can help them move off the point of indecision.

3. Preparation: Most people in this stage are close to taking action. They've thought about several things they might do and may even have come up with a plan. Rather than thinking only about the reasons why they *can't* begin action, they have started to focus on what they could do to start action.

Strategies for Change: Successful change requires following some standard guidelines at this stage: set realistic goals (large and small), take small steps toward change, change only a couple of things at once, reward small milestones, and seek support from friends. Identify those factors that have predisposed, enabled, or served as a barrier to success in the past and

change or modify those conditions where possible.

4. Action: In the action stage, the individual begins to follow the action plan he or she has put together. People who have prepared for change, thought about alternatives, engaged social support, and made a plan of action are more ready for action than those who have given it little thought. Unfortunately, too many people start behavior change here rather than going through the first three stages. Without a plan, without enlisting the help of others, or without a realistic goal, failure is likely.

Strategies for Change: Publicly stating the desire to change often helps ensure success. Encourage a friend making a change to share his or her plan with you. Whenever possible, offer to help, and try to remove potential obstacles. Social support and the buddy system often help motivate even the most reluctant person.

5. Maintenance: Maintenance requires vigilance, attention to detail, and long-term commitment. Many people reach their goals, only to relax and slip back into the undesired behavior. In this stage, it is important to be aware of the potential for relapses and develop strategies for dealing with such challenges. Common causes of relapse include overconfidence, daily temptations, stress or emotional distractions, and self-deprecation for failure.

Strategies for Change: During maintenance, you must continue doing the same things that led to success in the first place. Find fun and creative ways to maintain the positive behaviors. This is where a willing and caring support group can be vital. Knowing where to turn on your campus for help when you don't have a close support network also can be helpful.

6. Termination: In this stage, the behavior is so ingrained that the current level of vigilance may be unnecessary. The new behavior has become an essential part of daily living. Can you think of someone you know who has made a major behavior change that has now become an essential part of them?

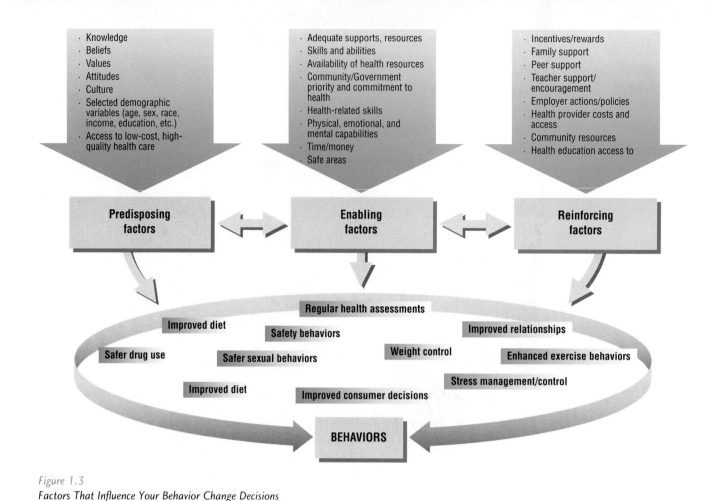

Figure 1.3
Factors That Influence Your Behavior Change Decisions

the number of physicians and other health professionals who smoke, fail to manage stress, consume high-fat diets, and act in other unhealthy ways. They surely know better, but their "knowing" is disconnected from their "doing." Why is this so? Two strong influences on our actions are beliefs and attitudes.

A **belief** is an appraisal of the relationship between some object, action, or idea (for example, smoking) and some attribute of that object, action, or idea (for example, smoking is expensive, dirty, and causes cancer—or it is relaxing). Beliefs may develop from direct experience (for example, if you have trouble breathing after smoking for several years) or from secondhand experience or knowledge conveyed by other people (for example, if you see your grandfather die of lung cancer after he has smoked for years).[22] Although most of us have a general idea of what constitutes a belief, we may be a bit uncertain about what constitutes an attitude. We often hear or make such comments as, "He's got a rotten attitude," or, "She needs an attitude adjustment," but may still be unable to define *attitude*. An **attitude** is a relatively stable set of beliefs, feelings, and behavioral tendencies in relation to something or someone.

Do Beliefs and Attitudes Influence Behavior?

It seems logical to conclude that your beliefs will influence your behavior. If you believe (make the appraisal) that taking drugs (an action) is harmful for you (attribute of that action), you will not use drugs. If you believe that drinking and driving are incompatible, you will never drink and drive. Or will you?

Psychologists studying the relationship between beliefs and health behaviors have determined that although beliefs may subtly influence behavior, these beliefs may not actually cause people to change behavior. In 1966, psychologist I. Rosenstock developed a model for explaining how beliefs may or may not influence subsequent behaviors.[23] His **Health Belief Model (HBM)** provides a means to show when beliefs affect behavior change. Although many other models attempt to explain the influence of beliefs on behaviors, the HBM is one of the most widely accepted models. According to the HBM, several factors must support a belief in order for change to be likely to occur:

- *Perceived seriousness of the health problem.* First, a person needs to consider how severe the medical and social consequences would be if the health problem was to develop or was left untreated. The more serious a person believes the effects will be, the more likely he or she is to take action.
- *Perceived susceptibility to the health problem.* Next, a person needs to evaluate the likelihood of developing the health problem. Those who perceive themselves as more likely to develop the health problem are more likely to take preventive action.
- *Cues to action.* Those who are reminded or alerted about a potential health problem are more likely to take preventive action.

Three other factors are linked to perceived risk for health problems: *demographic variables,* including age, gender, race, and ethnic background; *sociopsychological variables,* including personality traits, social class, and social pressure; and *structural variables,* including knowledge about or prior contact with the health problem.

The Health Belief Model is followed many times every day. Take, for example, smokers. Older smokers are likely to know other smokers who have developed serious heart or lung problems as a result of smoking. They are thus more likely to perceive a threat to their health connected with the behavior of smoking than is a young person who has just begun smoking. The greater the perceived threat of health problems caused by smoking, the greater the chance a person will quit smoking. However, many chronic smokers know that they may develop serious health problems, yet they continue to smoke. Why do people fail to take actions to avoid further harm? According to Rosenstock, some people do not believe that they will be affected by a severe problem—they act as if they believe they have some kind of immunity—and are unlikely to change their behaviors. In some cases, they may think that, even if they get cancer or have a heart attack, the health-care system will cure them. They also may feel that the immediate costs outweigh the long-range benefits.

Belief   Appraisal of the relationship between some object, action, or idea and some attribute of that object, action, or idea.

Attitude   Relatively stable set of beliefs, feelings, and behavioral tendencies in relation to something or someone.

Health Belief Model (HBM)   Model for explaining how beliefs may influence behaviors.

Theory of Reasoned Action   Model for explaining the importance of our intentions in determining behaviors.

ACCESSING YOUR HEALTH ON THE INTERNET

Check out the following Internet sites related to the topics discussed in this chapter.

1. *CDC Wonder.*   Outstanding reference for comprehensive information from the Centers for Disease Control and Prevention (CDC), including special reports, guidelines, and access to national health data.

   http://wonder.cdc.gov/

2. *National Center for Health Statistics.*   Definitive reference for vast array of national health statistics.

   http://www.cdc.gov/nchswww/

3. *National Health Information Center.*   Great resource for consumer information about health.

   http://nhic-nt.health.org/

4. *Healthy People 2000 Home Page.*   This page links to progress reviews on how far we have come in meeting these objectives and to the 2010 objectives to show where we're going.

   http://odphp.osophs.dhhs.gov/pubs/hp2000

WHAT DO YOU THINK?

What is one major health behavior that you believe you should change? How serious a threat to your health is this behavior right now? Do you worry much about what will happen if you don't make the change? What can you do right now to reduce your risks for the above health threat? List the steps that you intend to take. Is anyone influencing you to make this decision?

Your Intentions to Change

Our attitudes tend to reflect our emotional responses to situations and also tend to follow from our beliefs. According to the **Theory of Reasoned Action,** our behaviors result from our intentions to perform actions. An intention is a product of our attitude toward an action and our beliefs about what others may want us to do.[24] A behavioral intention, then, is a written or stated commitment to perform an action.

In brief, the more consistent and powerful your attitudes about an action are and the more you are influenced by others to take that action, the greater will be your stated intention to do so. The more you verbalize your commitment to change, the more likely it is that you will be successful.

CONSUMER HEALTH

Health on the Internet: A Prescription to Lessen the Confusion

Looking for health-related information? Always consult your doctor first. However, to get additional information, there are innumerable resources right at your fingertips on the Internet. But how do you know how reliable the information is? Which of the thousands of web sites should you click onto first? Before you start your search, bear in mind that not all health Web sites are created equal.

If you have never researched a health site and don't know where to begin, here are some hints to help you recognize those that are likely to be reliable.

- Web sites sponsored by an official government agency, a college or university, or a hospital tend to have accurate, up-to-date information about a wide range of health topics. Government sites are easily identified by their .gov extensions; college and university sites typically have .edu extensions. Hospitals often have a .org extension, although some may have other extensions as well. For example, notice the extension on the National Institute of Mental Health: http://www.nimh.nih.gov/; or John Hopkins University: http://www.jhu

.edu/; or Mayo Clinic: http://www.mayohealth.org/

- Links provided within proven web sites are often valuable resources.
- Many medical journal web sites, such as *The New England Journal of Medicine*, http://www.nejm.org/; or the *Journal of the American Medical Association* (JAMA), http://www.ama-assn.org/public/journals/jama/jamahome.htm, are good sources of current breakthroughs in research. (While some of these sites may require a fee for access, often you can access some basic information, such as a weekly Table of Contents, that can help you conduct a library search.) However, not all medical journals are of this caliber. If you have questions about a journal's reputation, ask your doctor or another qualified medical professional.
- In most cases, it is important that Web sites include fresh content; however, beware of information that is trendy or based on fads. This information is not always the most accurate or useful. Also, if a site contains encyclopedic information, such as definitions of diseases and other health-related issues, it is not necessary that they be updated as frequently as those sites containing current research.
- When frequenting health web sites, use discretion. Don't believe everything you read. If you notice grammatical or spelling errors, that should raise a red flag. If the site you're using is sponsored by a pharmaceutical company or a retail medical operation, consider whose best interests are being considered.

As in everyday practice, quackery runs rampant on the Internet. This is particularly true if you visit certain health Usenet groups or bulletin boards. Just because some claim to be physicians or experts does not mean that they are, in fact, telling the whole truth. In the same vein, if you are seeking information pertaining to a personal health issue, make sure you have checked your source's credentials. Privacy on the Internet is a valuable and rare commodity that you want to preserve.

In addition to the many government and education-based sites, there are also many useful sites that are independently sponsored. The following are just a sample of the many that exist on the Internet.

1. Adam: www.adam.com
2. HealthAnswers.com: www.healthanswers.com
3. Dr. Koop.com: www.drkoop.com
4. ThriveOnline: www.thriveonline.com
5. Better Health: www.betterhealth.com
6. InteliHealth: www.intelihealth.com
7. HealthAtoZ.com: www.healthatoz.com
8. OnHealth: www.ohhealth.com
9. America's Doctor: www.americasdoctor.com
10. Drug Infonet: www.druginfonet.com

Throughout this book, you will find some of these sites among the many that are provided in each chapter. These sites are related to each of the health areas presented so that you can further enhance your knowledge base. Use good judgment; be a health-wise consumer of information.

Source: Use Today, Special Report, July 14, 1999, pgs. 1D, 2D, 4D, and 5D.

Significant Others as Change Agents

Many people are highly influenced by the approval or disapproval (real or imagined) of close friends and loved ones and of the social and cultural groups to which they belong. Such influences can offer support for health actions, making healthy behavior all the more possible to attain; they can also affect behavior negatively, interfering with even the best intentions of making a positive change.

▶ *Your Family* From the time of your birth, your parents have influenced your behaviors by giving you strong cues about which actions are socially acceptable and which are not. Brushing your teeth, bathing, wearing deodorant, and chewing food with your mouth closed are probably all behaviors that your family instilled in you long ago. Your family culture influenced your food choices, your religious beliefs, your political beliefs, and all your other values and actions. If you deviated from your family's norms, your mother or father probably let you know fairly quickly. What good family units have in common is a dedication to the healthful development of all family members, unconditional trust, and a commitment to work out difficulties.

When the loving family unit does not exist, when it does not provide for basic human needs, or when dysfunctional, irresponsible individuals try to build a family under the influence of drugs or alcohol, it becomes difficult for a child to learn positive health behaviors. Healthy behaviors get their start in healthy homes; unhealthy homes breed unhealthy habits. Healthy families provide the foundation for a clear and necessary understanding of what is right and wrong, what is positive and negative. Without this fundamental grounding, many young people have great difficulties.[25]

▶ *Social Bonds*   Like family, personal environments also mold behaviors. If you deviated from the actions expected in your hometown, you probably suffered strange looks, ostracism by some high school cliques, and other negative social reactions. The more you value the opinions of other people, the more likely you are to change a behavior that offends them. If you couldn't care less what they think, you probably brush off their negative reactions or suggested changes. How often have you told yourself, "I don't care what so-and-so thinks. I'll do what I darn well please"? Although most of us have thought or said these words, we in fact all too often care too much about what even the insignificant people in our lives think. We say certain things, act in a prescribed manner, and respond in a specific way because our culture, our upbringing, and our need to be liked by others pressure us to do what we believe they think is the right thing. In general, the lower your level of self-esteem and self-efficacy, the higher the chances that others will influence your actions.

Sometimes, the influence of others can be a powerful social support for our positive behavior changes.[26] At other times, we are influenced to drink too much, party too hard, eat too much, or engage in some other negative action because we don't want to be left out or because we fear criticism. Learning to understand the subtle and not-so-subtle ways in which our families, friends, and other people have influenced and continue to influence our behaviors is an important step toward changing our behaviors.

Shaping   Using a series of small steps to get to a particular goal gradually.

Imagined rehearsal   Practicing through mental imagery, to become better able to perform an event in actuality.

CHOOSING A BEHAVIOR CHANGE STRATEGY

Once you have analyzed all the factors influencing your current behavior and all the factors that may influence the direction and potential success of the behavior change you are considering, you must decide which of several possible behavior change techniques will work best for you.

Shaping

Regardless of how motivated and committed you are to change, some behaviors are almost impossible to change immediately. To reach your goal, you may need to take a number of individual steps, each designed to change one small piece of the larger behavior. This process is known as **shaping.** For example, suppose that you have not exercised for a while. You decide that you want to get into shape and your goal is to be able to jog 3 to 4 miles every other day. You realize that you'd face a near-death experience if you tried to run even just a few blocks in your current condition. So you decide to start slowly and build up to your desired fitness level gradually. During week 1, you will walk for one hour every other day at a slow, relaxed pace. During week 2, you will walk the same amount of time but will speed up your pace and cover slightly more ground. During week 3, you will speed up even more and will try to go even farther. You will continue taking such steps until you reach your goal.

Whatever the desired behavior change, all shaping involves

- starting slowly and trying not to cause undue stress during the early stages of the program
- keeping the steps small and achievable
- being flexible and ready to change if the original plan proves uncomfortable
- refusing to skip steps or to move to the next step until the previous step has been mastered. Behaviors don't develop overnight, so they won't change overnight.

Visualization

Mental practice and rehearsal can help change unhealthy behaviors into healthy ones. Athletes and others have used a technique known as **imagined rehearsal** to reach their goals. By visualizing their planned action ahead of time, they were better prepared when they put themselves to the test.

For example, suppose you want to ask someone out on a date. Imagine the setting (walking together to class) for the action. Then practice exactly what you're going to say ("Minh, there's a great concert this Sunday and I was wondering if . . .") in your mind and out loud. Mentally anticipate different responses ("Oh, I'd love to but I'm busy that evening.") and what you will say in reaction ("How about if I call you sometime this week?"). Careful mental and verbal rehearsal (you could even try your scenario out on a good friend) will greatly improve the likelihood of successful behavioral consequences because you will be less likely to be flustered or to be taken by surprise.

Modeling

Modeling, or learning behaviors through careful observation of other people, is one of the most effective strategies for changing behavior. For example, suppose that you have great difficulty talking to people you don't know very well. Effective communication is essential to achieving optimal health. One of the easiest ways to improve your communication skills is to select friends whose "gift of gab" you envy. Observe their social skills. What do they say? How do they act? Do they talk more or listen more? How do people respond to them? Why are they such good communicators? If you carefully observe behaviors you admire and isolate their components, you can model the steps of your behavior change strategy on a proven success.

Controlling the Situation

Sometimes, putting yourself in the right setting or with the right group of people will positively influence your behaviors directly or indirectly. Many situations and occasions trigger similar behaviors by different people. For example, in libraries, churches, and museums, most people talk softly. Few people laugh at funerals. The term **situational inducement** refers to an attempt to influence a behavior by using situations and occasions that are structured to exert control over that behavior.

For example, you may be more apt to stop smoking if you work in a smoke-free office, a positive situational inducement. But a smoke-filled bar, a negative situational inducement, may tempt you to resume smoking. Your careful consideration of which settings will help and which will hurt your effort to change, and your decision to seek the first and avoid the second, will improve your chances for successful behavior change.

Reinforcement

A **positive reinforcement** seeks to increase the likelihood that a behavior will occur by presenting something positive as a reward for that behavior. Each of us is motivated by different reinforcers. While a special T-shirt may be a positive reinforcer for young adults entering a race, it would not be for a 40-year-old runner who dislikes message-bearing T-shirts.

Most positive reinforcers can be classified under five headings: consumable, activity, manipulative, possessional, and social reinforcers.

- *Consumable reinforcers* are delicious edibles such as candy, cookies, or gourmet meals.
- *Activity reinforcers* are opportunities to watch TV, to go on a vacation, to go swimming, or to do something else enjoyable.
- *Manipulative reinforcers* are such incentives as lower rent in exchange for mowing the lawn or the promise of a better grade for doing an extra-credit project.
- *Possessional reinforcers* are tangible rewards such as a new TV or a sports car.
- *Social reinforcers* are such things as loving looks, affectionate hugs, and praise.

When choosing reinforcers to help you maintain a healthy behavior or change an unhealthy behavior, you need to determine what would motivate you to act in a particular way. Your rewards or reinforcers may initially come from others (extrinsic rewards), but as you see positive changes in yourself, you will begin to reward and reinforce yourself (intrinsic rewards). Keep in mind that reinforcers should immediately follow a behavior. But beware of overkill. If you reward yourself with a movie on the VCR every time you go jogging, this reinforcer will soon lose its power. It would be better to give yourself this reward after, say, a full week of adherence to your jogging program.

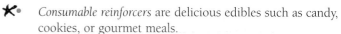

WHAT DO YOU THINK?

What type of consumable reinforcers (food or drink) would be a healthy reward for your new behavior? If you could choose one activity reinforcer with which to reward yourself after you've been successful for one day in your new behavior, what would it be? If you could obtain/buy something for yourself (possessional reinforcer) after you reach your goal, what would it be? If you maintain your behavior for one week, what type of social reinforcer would you like to receive from your friends?

Changing Self-Talk

Self-talk, or the way you think and talk to yourself, can also play a role in modifying your health-related behaviors. Here are some cognitive procedures for changing self-talk.

▶ *Rational-Emotive Therapy* This form of cognitive therapy or self-directed behavior change is based on the premise that there is a close connection between what people say to themselves and how they feel. According to psychologist Albert Ellis, most everyday emotional problems and related behaviors stem from irrational statements that people make to themselves when events in their lives are different from what they would like them to be.[27]

For example, suppose that after doing poorly on an exam, you say to yourself, "I can't believe I flunked that easy exam. I'm so stupid." By changing this irrational, "catastrophic" self-talk into rational, positive statements about what is really going on, you can increase the likelihood that positive behaviors will occur. Positive self-talk could be, "I really didn't study enough for that exam, and I'm not surprised I didn't do very well. I'm certainly not stupid. I just need to prepare better for the next test." Such self-talk will help you to recover quickly from your disappointment and to take positive steps to correct the situation.

▶ *Meichenbaum's Self-Instructional Methods* In Meichenbaum's behavioral therapies, clients are encouraged to give "self-instructions" ("Slow down, don't rush") and "positive affirmations" ("My speech is going fine—I'm almost done!") to themselves instead of thinking self-defeating thoughts ("I'm talking too fast—my speech is terrible") whenever a situation seems to be getting out of control. Meichenbaum is perhaps best known for a process known as stress inoculation, in which clients are subjected to extreme stressors in a laboratory environment. Before a stressful event (e.g., going to the doctor), clients practice individual coping skills (e.g., deep breathing exercises) and self-instructions (e.g., "I'll feel better once I know what's causing my pain"). Meichenbaum demonstrated that clients who practiced coping techniques and self-instruction were less likely to resort to negative behaviors in stressful situations.

▶ *Blocking/Thought Stopping* By purposefully blocking or stopping negative thoughts, a person can concentrate on taking positive steps toward necessary behavior change. For example, suppose you are preoccupied with your ex-partner, who has recently deserted you for someone else. In blocking/thought stopping, you consciously stop thinking about the situation and force yourself to think about something more pleasant (e.g., dinner tomorrow with your best friend). By refusing to dwell on negative images and by forcing yourself to focus elsewhere, you can save wasted energy, time, and emotional resources and move on to positive change.

Modeling Learning specific behaviors by watching others perform them.

Situational inducement Attempt to influence a behavior by using situations and occasions that are structured to exert control over that behavior.

Positive reinforcement Presenting something positive following a behavior that is being reinforced.

MAKING BEHAVIOR CHANGE

Self-Assessment: Antecedents and Consequences

Behaviors, thoughts, and feelings always occur in a context—the situation. Situations can be divided into two components: the events that come before and those that come after a behavior. *Antecedents* are the setting events for a behavior; they cue or stimulate a person to act in certain ways. Antecedents can be physical events, thoughts, emotions, or the actions of other people. *Consequences*—the results of behavior—affect whether a person will repeat a behavior.[28] Consequences can also be physical events, thoughts, emotions, or the actions of other people.

For example, suppose you are shy and must give a speech in front of a large class. The antecedents are walking into the class, feeling frightened, wondering if you are capable of doing a good job, and being unable to remember a word of your speech. If the consequences are negative—if your classmates laugh and you get a low grade—your terror about speaking in public will be reinforced and you will continue to dread this kind of event. In contrast, if you receive positive feedback from the class or instructor, you may actually learn to like speaking in public.

Learning to recognize the antecedents of a behavior and acting to modify them is one method of changing behavior. A diary noting your undesirable behaviors and identifying the settings in which they occur can be a useful tool. Figure 1.4 on the next page identifies several factors that can make behavior change more difficult.

Analyzing Personal Behavior

Successful behavior change requires a careful assessment of exactly what it is that you want to change. All too often we berate ourselves by using generalities: "I am not a good person, I'm lousy to my friend, I need to be a better person." Before you can begin to change a negative behavior, you must take a hard look at its specifics. Determining the specific behavior you would like to change—in contrast to the general problem—will allow you to set clear goals for change. What are you doing that makes you a lousy friend? Are you gossiping about your friend? Are you lying to your friend? Have you been a "taker" rather than a "giver" in the friendship? Or are you really a good friend most of the time?

Let's say the problem is gossiping. You can now analyze this behavior by examining the following components:

- *Frequency.* How often are you gossiping? All the time, or only once in a while?

Figure 1.4

Obstacles to Behavior Change. Psychologists offer a number of explanations for why you may fail in your efforts to change your behavior and strategies for overcoming these obstacles.

Source: From *Self-Directed Behavior: Self-Modification for Personal Adjustment,* by D. L. Watson and R. G. Tharp, Copyright 1997, 1993, 1989, 1985, 1981, 1977, 1972 Brooks/Cole Publishing Company, Pacific Grove, CA 93950, a division of Thomson Publishing Inc. By permission of the publisher.

OBSTACLE	STRATEGY
Stress	Identify potential sources of stress, and find constructive ways to lower your stress level.
Social pressures to repeat old habits	Enlist the support of friends.
Not expecting mistakes	Accept that slips are inevitable, but maintain control.
Blaming yourself for poor coping or a weak personality	Blame pressures from the environment or your own lack of skills rather than innate weakness.
Lack of effort	Assess your effort and make sure you are giving your full effort.
Faulty beliefs/low self-efficacy	Develop new skills, focus on your successes, and plan ahead for difficult situations.

- *Duration.* Have you been gossiping about your friend for a long period of time? How long?
- *Seriousness.* Is your gossiping just idle chatter, or are you really getting down and dirty and trying to injure the other person? What are the consequences for you? For your friend? For your friendship?
- *Basis for problem behavior.* Is your gossip based on facts, on your perceptions of facts, or on deliberate embellishments of facts?
- *Antecedents.* What kinds of situations trigger your gossiping? Do some settings or people bring out the gossip in you more than other settings and people? What triggers your feelings of dislike for or irritation toward your friend? Why are you talking behind your friend's back?

Decision Making: Choices for Change

Once you have assessed your risks, looked at potential contributors to your risks, examined possible strategies for change, and thought about community or social supports that might help you be successful, it is largely up to you to make the decisions that will lead to positive health outcomes. Choosing among alternatives isn't easy, particularly when there are friends, family, media influences, and pleasurable options to tempt you. "Just saying no" is usually easier said than done. However, if you are trying to fit in, be liked, feel desirable, or have other needs met, decision making becomes more difficult. That's why trying to anticipate a given set or

setting and thinking through all the possible safe alternatives is important. For example, knowing that you are likely to be offered a drink when you go to a party, what kind of response could you make that would be okay in your social group? If someone is flirting with you and the situation takes on a distinct sexual overtone, what might you do to prevent the situation from turning bad?

It is important to remember that things typically don't "just happen." By being alert to potential problems, being aware of your alternatives and all potential consequences, and having a good sense of your own values and beliefs, and sticking to your beliefs under pressure, you will have a good start toward gaining control over many health-related situations in your life.

Setting Realistic Goals

Making a change in behavior is not easy, but sometimes we make it even harder on ourselves by setting unrealistic goals. This, in turn, can adversely affect decisions you make as you strive to reach a goal that may have been unattainable from the beginning. To start making positive changes, there are a few simple questions you can ask yourself that will give you valuable insights into your behaviors.

- **What do I want?** What is your ultimate goal? To lose weight? Exercise more? Reduce stress? Have a lasting relationship? Whatever it is, you need to have a clear picture of the eventual target outcome.

- **Which change is of greatest priority at this time?** All too often people take a look at several things about themselves they want to change and decide to change them all at once. They want to be better students, be more fit, eat more fruits and vegetables, socialize more, recycle, and so on. Pick the behavior that you think is your greatest risk or problem and tackle that first. You can always work on something else later. Take small steps, experiment with alternatives, and find the best way to meet your unique goals.
- **Why is this important to me?** Think through exactly why you want to make a change. Are you doing it because of your health? To look better or feel better? To win someone else's approval? Usually, doing things because it's right for you rather than to win other's approval is a sound strategy. If you are doing it for someone else, what happens when that other person isn't around, or if they become less important to you?
- **What are the potential positive outcomes?** What do you hope to accomplish with this change?
- **What health-promoting programs and services are available to help me get started?** Nearly all campuses and communities have programs and services designed to help you be successful in your behavioral change. It may mean getting self-help books to guide you, speaking to a counselor or some other expert, or enrolling in an aerobics class at the local fitness center. Depending on the change you wish to make, each of these extra services or programs can help you stay motivated.
- **Are there family or friends whose help I can enlist?** Social support is one of your most powerful allies. Getting a friend to walk with you on a regular basis, asking your partner to help you stop smoking by stopping his or her own smoking, and making a commitment with a friend to never let each other drive if you've had something to drink are all examples of how people can help each other make positive changes.

Once you've identified what it is you want to change, there are several steps you can take to develop behavior change goals that are realistic for you.

1. *Be specific about your current behavior.* Suppose that you are gaining unwanted weight. Rather than saying, "I eat too much and my goal is to not eat so much," you need to be specific about your current behavior. Are you eating too many sweets? Are you eating too many foods high in fat? Perhaps a better statement of the problem would be, "I eat too many high-fat foods, particularly during dinner." A realistic goal, therefore, would be, "I am going to try to eat less fat during dinner every day."
2. *Develop strategies and intermediate goals* that will help you reach the ultimate goal. Recording all the foods you eat

Each individual's personal support group plays a key role in influencing the decisions we all make and developing positive health behaviors.

every day may show, for instance, that the greatest source of fat in your meals is condiments. You could reach your goal by buying low-fat dressings and other condiments, by limiting high-fat condiments, or by finding fat-free substitutes. You may find that you eat too many fried and sauteed foods. In that case, your goal would be to bake or broil as many foods as possible, thereby reducing your fat intake. In addition, establishing intermediate stepping stones helps you maintain your motivation and can give you a sense of accomplishment. Rather than aiming for that 30-pound loss, thinking of weight loss in 3-pound increments could be more encouraging.

3. *Identify the situations* that may make you more susceptible to the undesired behavior. Do you tend to eat more fatty foods when you're with certain people or in certain situations? (There's nothing quite like that buttered popcorn at the movies, is there?) Do you tend to snack more when you're alone?

WHAT DO YOU THINK?

Why is it sometimes hard for you to make decisions? What influences your decisions? Select one behavior that you want to change. Using the goal-setting elements discussed here, how would you respond to the questions posed and what would be your strategy for change?

Taking Charge ....
Managing Your Behavior Change Strategies

Behavior change is not easy. Many attempts will fail. Some will succeed. The key to having your successes outnumber your failures is recognizing that you are a unique individual, with your own emotional makeup, physical characteristics, and values and beliefs. Finding the right behavioral change strategy involves a great amount of perseverance, introspection, careful planning, and motivation. Regardless of the model, or the strategies employed, each person has a unique road to follow. As you read this book, you will find that each chapter lists specific activities and choices that enable you to adopt or maintain healthy behaviors.

CHECKLIST FOR CHANGE

MAKING PERSONAL CHOICES

✓ Are you ready to make this change? Are you in a healthy emotional state? Are you doing it for you or to please someone else?

✓ Have you completed a personal health history to assess your risks from various sources?

✓ Have you developed an action plan with short- and long-term goals? Have you set priorities?

✓ Have you assessed your personal resources? Where can you go for support and advice?

✓ Have you planned alternative actions in case you run into obstacles or begin to self-sabotage?

✓ Have you set up a list of reinforcers and supports that will keep you motivated along the way?

✓ Have you established a set of guidelines for success? Will you have small goals to achieve at selected intervals or will you only consider yourself successful if you have met your ultimate goal?

MAKING COMMUNITY CHOICES

✓ Have you taken time to become educated about issues/concerns affecting others in your community?

✓ Have you prioritized the actions that you can take to make a difference in changing community behaviors? Do you have a particular goal?

✓ Do you analyze what is happening in your school, community, state, and nation by reading about issues, actively discussing problems and possible solutions, and developing personal opinions?

✓ Do you listen carefully to what your elected officials say and take constructive action if you disagree with them?

✓ Do you vote for elected officials whose policies, rhetoric, and past histories have indicated that they support improvements in health care, the environment, education, and minority health?

✓ Do you volunteer your time to help others who are less fortunate at least once during every term?

✓ Do you purchase products and services from companies that have proven records of supporting the health and well-being of others through their organizational practices?

SUMMARY

- *Health* is defined as a dynamic process of trying to achieve your individual potential in the physical, social, emotional, spiritual, intellectual, and environmental dimensions. *Wellness* means achieving the highest level of health possible along several dimensions.

- Although Americans have increased average lifespan, we need to increase our span of quality life. *Healthy People 2000, 2010,* and documents such as the AHCPR guidelines establish a national set of objectives for achieving improved life span and quality of life for all Americans through health promotion and prevention.

- There are three major types of disease prevention: Primary prevention refers to actions designed to reduce risk. Secondary prevention, or intervention, refers to the recognition of health risks and actions taken to intervene, to reduce the risk. Tertiary prevention refers to treatment or rehabilitation after the person is already ill.

- Gender continues to play a major role in health status and care. Women have longer lives but more medical problems than do men. The recent inclusion of women in medical research and training attempts to close the gap in health care.

- The leading causes of death are heart disease, cancer, and stroke. But in the 15- to 24-age group, the leading causes are accidents, homicide, and suicide. Many of the risks associated with the leading killers can be reduced through lifestyle changes. Many of the risks associated with the 15- to 24-age-group killers can be reduced through preventive measures.

- We "die" or lose quality in life-years from very different things in the United States than in other regions of the world. By 2020, the leading contributors to global ill health are projected to be heart disease, depression, and traffic accidents.

- Several factors contribute to your health status, but not all of them are within your control. Your beliefs and attitudes, your intentions to change, support from significant others, and your readiness to change are all factors over which you have some degree of control. Access to health care, genetic predisposition, health policies that are supportive of your actions, and other factors are all potential reinforcing, predisposing, and enabling factors that may influence your health decisions.

- Applying behavior change techniques such as shaping, visualizing, modeling, controlling the situation, reinforcing, and changing self-talk to your personal situations will help you to be successful in making behavior changes.

- Decision making has several key components: Each person must explore his or her own problems, the reasons for making change, and expected outcomes and plan a course of action best suited for individual needs.

DISCUSSION QUESTIONS

1. How are the terms *health* and *wellness* similar? What, if any, are important distinctions between these terms? What is health promotion? Disease prevention?

2. How healthy are Americans today? How will health promotion and illness and accident prevention improve both life span and quality of life right now? In the future?

3. What are some of the major differences in the way males and females are treated in the health-care system? Why do you think these differences exist?

4. What are the leading causes of death when you look at all ages and races? What are the leading causes of death for people aged 15 to 24? Why are these statistics so different? Explain why it is important to look at these statistics by age rather than just in total. What lifestyle changes can you make to lower your risks for major diseases?

5. What are the biggest differences in the leading causes of death for Americans and other people in other regions of the world?

6. What is the Health Belief Model? The Theory of Reasoned Action? How may each of these models be working when a young woman decides to smoke her first cigarette? Her last cigarette?

7. Explain the predisposing, reinforcing, and enabling factors influencing the decision of a young welfare mother who is deciding to sell drugs to support her children.

8. Using the Stages of Change model, discuss what you might do (in stages) to help a friend stop smoking.

9. Why is it important that you be ready to change before you try to start changing?

APPLICATION EXERCISE

Reread the *What Do You Think?* scenario at the beginning of the chapter and answer the following questions.

1. From what you learned in this chapter, why are young people at high risk for things like accidents, homicide, and suicide? Why do these risks decline with age?

2. On your campus, or in your community, what programs, services, or policies are in place to reduce risk from these types of problems?

2

Psychosocial Health

Being Mentally, Emotionally, Socially, and Spiritually Well

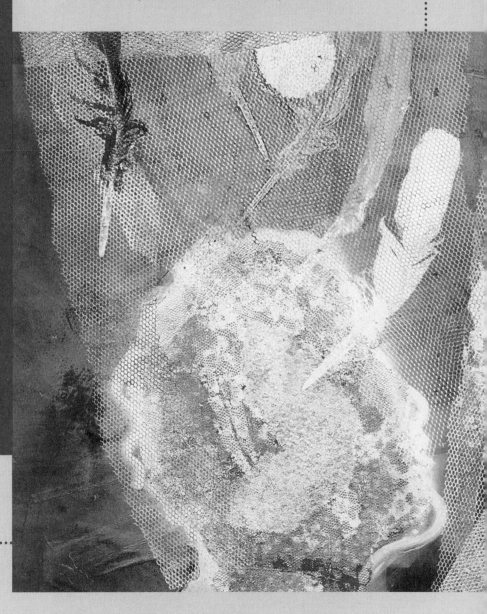

Marlene is a 20-year-old junior majoring in health education. She is chronically tired and tends to be highly "reactive" with her friends, often blasting them with verbal outbursts when she is angry. She is cynical, hostile, and often, just plain "mean" to others when stressed. Many times when she is alone, she feels like crying, but the tears never come. She used to dress up a bit for classes but now rarely gets out of her sweat pants and sloppy sweatshirts during the day. She can't sleep, she is gaining weight, and she doesn't care about much that is going on around her. Even her closest friends are starting to get fed up with her actions, and few of them call her to ask her to do things with them anymore.

If you were one of Marlene's friends, what would you do to help her? What programs and or services on your campus might be of use to her? Why is it often so difficult to confront someone who is acting like Marlene? Do you know anyone right now that is displaying some of these same symptoms? What might contribute to them?

*I*N INCREASING NUMBERS, young adults today report being tired, unhappy, drained of energy, and/or depressed on a regular basis. Life becomes one continuous hassle, punctuated by few good moments and all too many bad, monotonous, or mundane moments. For some of us, these skirmishes with the blues become persistent, nagging experiences that vary from being small "downers" to full-scale tumbles into "black holes" that are increasingly more difficult to emerge from without assistance. For many of us, although we aren't quite down enough to need a therapist, we probably aren't totally healthy in our mental, emotional, social, or spiritual lives either.[1]

Whatever the cause for the "lows" in our lives, they have the power to sap our energy, drain our emotions, and break our spirits. When these low points become a chronic way of life, they can lead to a joyless existence—one filled with emotional problems, difficulties in relationships, and physical illness. Over the long haul, they can even shorten our life expectancy. Why some people remain in a continuous downward spiral while others seem to possess a resiliency that allows them to cope, adapt, and even thrive, regardless of life's challenges, remains a mystery.

Noted biologist, Renee Dubois, has stated that we should "measure our health by our sympathy with morning and with spring." Inherent in this way of thinking is the fact that when we are healthy, we are able to fully appreciate the finer nuances of life rather than dwell on life's negatives. Noticing the beauty of a sunset, listening to the quiet lapping of the waves against the rocks on the beach, and taking time to smell the first flowers of spring or hear the birds chirping at dawn are all signs that our senses are alive and that we are not numbed by the problems we may face. How we feel and think about ourselves, those around us, and our environment can tell us a lot about our psychosocial health and whether we are healthy emotionally, spiritually, and mentally.

Although often overlooked while in pursuit of a fit and firm body, a fit mind can be equally important in determining not only the number of years we live, but also the *quality* of those years. Increasingly, health professionals have come to recognize that having a solid social network, being emotionally and mentally healthy, and acknowledging and developing our spiritual capacity may put life into years, as well as add years to life.

DEFINING PSYCHOSOCIAL HEALTH

Psychosocial health encompasses the mental, emotional, social, and spiritual dimensions of health (Figure 2.1). It is the result of a complex interaction between a person's history and conscious and unconscious thoughts about and interpretations of the past. Psychosocially healthy people are emotionally, mentally, socially, and spiritually *resilient* and are able to draw on deep reserves in times of crisis. They have experienced pain and pleasure, and they have learned from these experiences and grown as individuals. They know when to call on friends for help, when to give help to others, and when it is okay to just be alone. They respond to challenges, disappointments, joys, frustrations, and pain in appropriate ways most of the time, even though they may have occasional slips in their actions or behaviors. Although definitions of psychosocial health vary, most authorities identify several basic elements shared by psychosocially healthy people.[2]

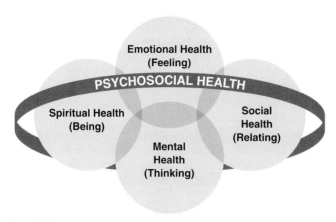

Figure 2.1

Psychosocial health is a complex interaction of your mental, emotional, social, and spiritual health.

* *They feel good about themselves* and are not typically overwhelmed by fear, love, anger, jealousy, guilt, or worry. They know who they are and have a realistic sense of their capabilities. They respect themselves even though they realize they aren't perfect.
* *They feel comfortable with other people* and have satisfying and lasting personal relationships and do not take advantage of others, nor do they allow others to take advantage of them. They can give love, respect personal differences, and feel responsible for their fellow human beings.
* *They control tension and anxiety* by recognizing the underlying causes and symptoms of stress and anxiety in their lives. They struggle to avoid illogical or irrational thoughts, unnecessary aggression, hostility, excessive excuse making, and blaming others for their problems.
* *They are able to meet the demands of life* by solving problems as they arise. They set realistic goals, think for themselves, and make independent decisions. Acknowledging that change is inevitable, they welcome new experiences.
* *They curb hate and guilt* by acknowledging and combating their tendencies to respond with hate, anger, thoughtlessness, selfishness, vengeful acts, or feelings of inadequacy. They do not try to knock others aside to get ahead but rather reach out to help others—even those they don't particularly care for. Rather than responding "in kind" to other people's negativity, they make honest attempts to listen, hear, and understand before jumping into the fray themselves.
* *They maintain a positive outlook* and try to approach each day with a presumption that things will go well. Since

they believe that life is a gift, they are determined to enjoy it on a moment-to-moment basis rather than wander through it aimlessly. They block out most negative and cynical thoughts and give the good things in life star billing. They look to the future with enthusiasm rather than dread.

* *They enrich the lives of others* and recognize that there are others whose needs are greater than their own. They seek to ease these others' burdens by doing such simple things as making dinner for someone who's too grief-stricken to cook, volunteering at a community agency, and making charitable donations.
* *They cherish the things that make them smile,* such as memories of the past. Family pictures, high school mementos, souvenirs of past vacations, and other reminders of good experiences brighten their day. Fun is an integral part of their lives. So is making time for themselves.
* *They value diversity* and do not feel threatened by people who are of a different race, gender, religion, sexual orientation, ethnicity, or political party. They appreciate creativity in others as well as in themselves.
* *They appreciate nature* and respect natural beauty and wonders. They take the time to enjoy their surroundings and are conscious of their place in the universe.

Of course, few of us ever achieve perfection in these areas. Attaining psychosocial health and wellness involves many complex processes. The following sections of this chapter will help you understand not only what it means to be psychosocially well, but also why we often run into problems.

WHAT DO YOU THINK?

What areas of psychosocial health do you have the most trouble with? What are your greatest challenges? Why are these areas problematic for you? Do your friends or other people you associate with demonstrate the qualities of psychosocially healthy people?

Mental Health: The Thinking You

The term **mental health** is often used to describe the "thinking" part of psychosocial health. As a thinking being, you have the ability to reason, interpret, and remember events from a unique perspective; to sense, perceive, and evaluate what is happening; and to solve problems. In short, you are intellectually able to sort through the clutter of events, contradictory messages, and uncertainties of a situation and attach meaning (either positive or negative) to it. Your values, attitudes, and beliefs about your body, your family, your relationships, and life in general are usually—at least in part—a reflection of your mental health.

A mentally healthy person is likely to respond in a positive way even when things do not go as expected. For example, a mentally healthy student who receives a *D* on an exam

Psychosocial health The mental, emotional, social, and spiritual dimensions of health.

Mental health The "thinking" part of psychosocial health. Includes your values, attitudes, and beliefs.

may be very disappointed, but she will try to assess why she did poorly. Did she study enough? Did she attend class and ask questions about the things she didn't understand? Even though the test result may be very important to her, she will find a constructive way to deal with her frustration: She may talk to the instructor, plan to devote more time to studying before the next exam, or hire a tutor. In contrast, a mentally unhealthy person may take a distorted view and respond in an irrational manner. She may believe that her instructor is out to get her or that other students cheated on the exam. She may allow her low grade to provoke a major crisis in her life. She may spend the next 24 hours getting wasted, decide to quit school, try to get back at her instructor, or even blame her roommate for preventing her from studying.

When a person's mental health begins to deteriorate, he or she may experience sharp declines in rational thinking ability and increasingly distorted perceptions. The person may become cynical and distrustful, experience volatile mood swings, or choose to be isolated from others. The person's negative reactions to events may threaten the life and health of others (see Chapter 4). People showing such signs of extreme abnormal behavior or mental disorders are classified as having *mental illnesses,* discussed later in this chapter.

Emotional Health: The Feeling You

The term **emotional health** is often used interchangeably with *mental health.* Although emotional and mental health are closely intertwined, emotional health more accurately refers to the "feeling," or subjective, side of psychosocial health. **Emotions** are intensified feelings or complex patterns of feelings that we experience on a minute-by-minute, day-to-day basis. Loving, caring, hating, hurt, despair, release, joy, anxiety, fear, frustration, and intense anger are some of the many emotions we experience. Typically, emotions are described as the interplay of four components: physiological arousal, feelings, cognitive (thought) processes, and behavioral reactions. Each time you are put in a stressful situation, you react physiologically while your mind tries to sort things out. You consciously or unconsciously react based on how rationally you interpret the situation.

Psychologist Richard Lazarus believes that there are four basic types of emotions: (1) emotions resulting from harm, loss, or threats; (2) emotions resulting from benefits; (3) borderline emotions, such as hope and compassion; and (4) more complex emotions, such as grief, disappointment, bewilderment, and curiosity.[3] Each of us may experience any of these emotions in any combination at any time. As rational beings, it is our responsibility to evaluate our individual emotional responses, the environment that is causing these responses, and the appropriateness of our actions.

Emotionally healthy people are usually able to respond in a stable and appropriate manner to upsetting events. When they feel threatened or emotionally wounded, they are not likely to react in an extreme fashion, behave inconsistently, or adopt an offensive attack mode.

Emotionally unhealthy people are much more likely to let their feelings overpower them. They may be highly volatile and prone to unpredictable emotional outbursts and to inappropriate, sometimes frightening responses to events. An ex-boyfriend who becomes so angry that he begins to hit you and push you around in front of your friends because he is jealous of your new relationship is showing an extremely unhealthy and dangerous emotional reaction. Violent responses to situations have become a problem of epidemic proportions in the United States (see Chapter 4).

Emotional health also affects social health. People in the midst of emotional turmoil may be grumpy, nasty, irritable, or noncommunicative; they may cry easily or demonstrate other disturbing emotional responses. Since they are not much fun to be around, their friends may avoid them at the very time they are most in need of emotional support. Social isolation is just one of the many potential negative consequences of unstable emotional responses.

For students, a more immediate concern is the impact of emotional trauma or turmoil on academic performance. Have you ever tried to study for an exam after a fight with a close friend or family member? Emotional turmoil may seriously affect your ability to think, reason, or act in a rational way. Many otherwise rational, mentally healthy people do ridiculous things when they are going through a major emotional upset. Mental functioning and emotional responses are indeed intricately connected.

Social Health: Interactions with Others

Social health is the part of psychosocial health dealing with our interactions with others and our ability to adapt to social situations. Socially healthy individuals have a wide range of social interactions with family, friends, acquaintances, and individuals with whom they may only occasionally come into contact. They are able to listen, to express themselves, to form healthy relationships, to act in socially acceptable and responsible ways, and to find a best fit for themselves in society.

Numerous studies have documented the importance of our social life in achieving and maintaining health, and two factors of social health have proven to be particularly important:[4,5]

- *Presence of strong social bonds.* **Social bonds,** or social linkages, reflect the general degree and nature of our interpersonal contacts and interactions. Social bonds generally have six major functions. They provide (1) intimacy, (2) feelings of belonging to or integration with a group, (3) opportunities for giving or receiving nurturance, (4) reassurance of one's worth, (5) assistance and guidance, and (6) advice. In general, people who are more "connected" to others manage stress more effectively and are much more resilient when they are bombarded by life's crises.

The social bonds you form can become valuable resources for reducing personal stress and strengthening your sense of social support during times of trouble.

• *Presence of key social supports.* **Social supports** refer to relationships that bring positive benefits to the individual. Social supports can be either *expressive* (emotional support, encouragement) or *structural* (housing, money). Families provide both structural and expressive support to children. Adults need to develop their own social supports. Psychosocially healthy people create a network of friends and family to whom they can give and receive support.

Social health also reflects the way we react to others around us. In its most extreme forms, a lack of social health may be represented by aggressive acts of prejudice and bias toward other individuals or groups. **Prejudice** is a negative evaluation of an entire group of people that is typically based

Emotional health The "feeling" part of psychosocial health. Includes your emotional reactions to life.

Emotions Intensified feelings or complex patterns of feelings we constantly experience.

Social health Deals with our interactions with others and our ability to adapt to social situations.

Social bonds Degree and nature of our interpersonal contacts.

Social supports Structural and functional aspects of our social interactions.

Prejudice A negative evaluation of an entire group of people that is typically based on unfavorable and often wrong ideas about the group.

Spiritual health Possessing a belief in a unifying force that gives purpose or meaning to life.

on unfavorable (and often wrong) ideas about the group. In its most obvious manifestations, prejudice is reflected in acts of discrimination against others, in overt acts of hate and bias, and in purposeful intent to harm individuals or groups.

Spiritual Health

Although mental and emotional health are key factors in your overall psychosocial functioning, it is possible for you to be mentally and emotionally healthy and still not achieve optimal levels of psychosocial well-being. What is missing? For many people, that difficult-to-describe element that gives zest to life is the spiritual dimension. What does it mean to be spiritually healthy? **Spiritual health** refers to possession of a belief in some unifying force that gives purpose or meaning to life or to a sense of belonging to a scheme of existence greater than the merely personal. Dr. N. Lee Smith, internist and Associate Professor of Medicine at the University of Utah, defines spiritual health as:[6]

- the quality of existence in which one is at peace with him- or herself and in good stead with the environment
- a sense of empowerment and personal control that includes feeling heard and valued, feeling in control over one's responses (but not necessarily in control of one's environment)
- a sense of connectedness to one's deepest self, to other people, and to all regarded as good
- a sense of meaning and purpose, which provides a sense of mission, finding meaning and wisdom in here-and-now difficulties, enjoying the process of growth, and having a vision of one's potential
- hope—having positive expectations

Many of us live on a rather superficial material plane throughout the formative years of our lives. We have basic human needs that must be satisfied according to a set hierarchical order. We tend to be rather egocentric, or self-oriented, during these formative years and seek immediate material and emotional gratification while denying or ignoring the spiritual aspect of our selves. Worrying about the clothes you wear, the car you drive, the appearance of your apartment, and other material possessions are examples of this type of preoccupation. According to psychologists and psychoanalysts such as Carl Jung, our materialistic Western civilization leads us to deny our spiritual needs for much of our lives. But there comes a point, usually around midlife, when we discover that material possessions do not automatically bring a sense of happiness or self-worth[7] (see Figure 2.2 on page 33). Crisis may move us to this realization earlier. A failed relationship, the death of a close friend or family member, or other loss often prompts us to look for meaning in what is happening around us. We recognize that material things, prestige, money, power, and fame count for little in the larger scheme of existence, and that if we were to die tomorrow these would not give meaning to our lives. At this point,

Recipes for Happiness: Keys to Improving Psychosocial Health

How many times have you heard someone say, "I just want to be happy"? While this would appear to be a relatively simple wish to obtain, it seems to elude more and more of us all the time. For years, the field of psychoneuroimmunology has studied how our mental and emotional states may influence our immune system by bolstering it during times of positive emotion and stress and weakening it during times of negative emotion or a persistent negative outlook on life. Now experts are taking this a step further by focusing on ways that individuals can help themselves get out of negative self-talk, find simple joys in life, and try to live life more optimistically. As part of a relatively new movement known as *Positive Psychology,* experts increasingly point to the importance of achieving, nurturing, and maintaining happiness as a panacea for much of what ails us.

In a January 1999 *Los Angeles Times* interview, author and researcher Martin Seligman defined *Positive Psychology* as "based on the idea that if young people are taught to be resilient and optimistic, they'll be less likely to suffer from depression and will lead happier, more productive lives." By taking a positive approach to life, and by working at building on our strengths, we can begin to unlock the secrets to happiness, and as a result realize overall health benefits. A recent summit focusing on Positive Psychology and its importance to health examined the key elements of happiness and the steps that each of us might take to be happier. Experts from throughout the United States shared some of their findings.

- According to Dr. Rick Snyder of the University of Kansas, you can determine whether you are generally a negative or a positive person by assessing your level of "hope," a major factor in optimism. Hope helps you define how you can get what you want out of life, the pathways you take to reaching those goals, as well as your motivations in choosing particular paths. As part of his work, Dr. Snyder has developed a Hope Scale for measuring levels of hope. His research indicates that people who have high hope and are generally positive tend to tolerate pain and suffering more readily than others. They are also more likely to take the "high" road to getting what they want in life.

- Dr. Martin Seligman, famous for his historic studies of learned helplessness and author of *The Optimistic Child,* has introduced the idea of the existence of a genetic predisposition to negativity and depression in humans. He has developed a test to measure risk factors for depression and advocates learning new "self-talk" that minimizes the negatives and focuses instead on learning to look at a bad situation and ask, "Where is the evidence that this is so bad? What is the worst thing that could possibly happen?" Rather than catastrophizing about life, Dr. Seligman encourages people to challenging their negative beliefs and substitute positive self-talk in its stead.

- Sport psychologist Dr. Doug Newberg focuses his research on finding the *fun* in life and trying to make time for things you really enjoy. Finding your own joy in life aids in reducing stress and helping you find more energy to get through the more difficult times that occur during the day.

- Through his extensive work with patients recovering from by-pass surgery, Dr. Michael Scheir at Carnegie Mellon suggests that those patients who are most optimistic about their outcomes from surgery tend to do better and live longer, in addition to having fewer complications during surgery itself.

- The longtime work of Dr. Norman Cousins has explored the role of laughter in health and has found that laughter is a factor in longevity and survivability after cancer.

Collectively, researchers in Positive Psychology suggest the following points about obtaining happiness:

- If you are looking to achieve happiness, the following elements must be part of your general conditioning: courage, hope, optimism, and wisdom. People who practice these behavioral patterns, and who consciously work on achieving these elements of behavior, tend to be happiest and most able to deal with life's little ups and downs.

- It's unrealistic to expect to be happy every minute of every day. We should really be happy only for a reason, but the reasons can be quite simple.

- You need to ask yourself what you do well and focus on that rather than obsess over things in life that haven't worked out well for you.

- You need to study people who are strong in your field of interest and imitate them; watch them carefully; try to analyze what works for them and why.

- Remember that generosity and enthusiasm are keys to success. Do you tend to focus on the barriers or benefits? Examine what kinds of things you focus on and how you can make sure your approach is a positive one?

- Experts believe that wisdom, spirituality, compassion, and the ability to step outside of yourself to think of others are key to happiness. Although life sometimes "gives us lemons," they support the notion that tragedy can bring growth and new directions.

Increasingly, the role that positive emotions, spirituality, faith, and happiness play in daily living is being examined more thoroughly today than ever before. Although the entire body of Positive Psychology research is in its infancy, it has gained increasing credibility as more scientific investigations whittle away at the mechanisms that may serve to bolster the immune system or make it vulnerable.

STUDENTS SPEAK UP:

Do you think there is merit to Positive Psychology? Why might people be skeptical of this movement?

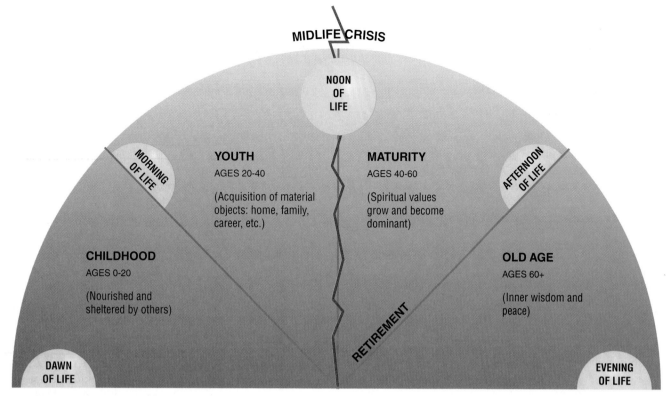

Figure 2.2
Jung's View of Personal Growth and Spiritual Development

many people reach what is often called a midlife crisis, which is characterized by a sense of spiritual bankruptcy.[8]

As we develop into spiritually healthy beings, we begin to recognize who we are as unique individuals. We reach a better understanding of our strengths and shortcomings and of our place in the universe. Many of us find that our families, the environment, animals, friends, strangers who are suffering, and religion assume greater significance in our lives. Spiritual health takes time and experience to acquire. The longer you live, the more you experience, and have the potential for growth. The more you ponder the meaning of your experiences, the greater your chances of achieving psychosocial health.

················ **WHAT DO YOU THINK?**

What are your strengths in the area of psychosocial heath? Your weaknesses? What can you do to enhance your strengths? What does spiritual health mean to you? What could you do to enhance your spiritual health?

Dysfunctional families   Families in which there is violence; physical, emotional, or sexual abuse; parental discord; or other negative family interactions.

FACTORS INFLUENCING PSYCHOSOCIAL HEALTH

Most of our mental, emotional, and spiritual reactions to life are a direct outcome of our experiences and social and cultural expectations. Each of us is born with the innate capacity to experience emotions. These interpretations are often learned reactions to certain environmental and social stimuli.

External Factors

Our psychosocial health is based on how we perceive our life's experiences. While some experiences are under our control, others are not. External influences are factors in our life that we do not control, such as who raised us and the physical environment in which we live.

▶ *The Family*   Our families are a significant influence on our psychosocial development. Children raised in healthy, nurturing, happy families are more likely to become well-adjusted, productive adults. Children raised in families in which violence, sexual, physical, or emotional abuse, negative behaviors, distrust, anger, dietary deprivation, drug abuse, parental discord, or other characteristics of **dysfunctional families** are present may have a harder time adapting to life. In dysfunctional families, love, security, and unconditional trust are so lacking that the children are often confused and psychologically bruised. Yet, not all people raised in dysfunctional families become psychosocially unhealthy. Conversely, not all people from healthy family environments become well-adjusted. There are obviously more factors involved in our "process of becoming" than just our family.

The Greater Environment   While isolated negative events may do little damage to psychosocial health, persistent stressors, uncertainties, and threats may cause significant problems. Children raised in environments where crime is rampant and daily safety is in question, for example, run an increased risk of psychosocial problems. Drugs, crime, violent acts, school failure, unemployment, and a host of other bad things can happen to good people. But it is believed that certain protective factors, such as having a positive role model in the midst of chaos or a high level of self-esteem, may help children from even the worst environments remain healthy and well adjusted.

Another important influence on psychosocial health is access to health services and programs designed to support psychosocial health. Going to a support group or seeing a trained counselor or therapist is often a crucial first step in prevention and intervention efforts. Individuals from poor socioeconomic environments who cannot afford such services, however, often find it difficult to secure such help.

Social Supports/Social Bonds   Although often overlooked, a stable, loving support network of family and friends is key to psychosocial health. *Social supports* and the *social bonds* that come from close relationships help us get through even the most difficult times. Having those with whom we can talk, share thoughts, and practice good and bad behaviors without fear of losing their love is an essential part of growth.

Internal Factors

We each have many internal factors at work shaping who we are and who we become. Some of these factors include hereditary traits, hormonal functioning, physical health status (including neurological functioning), physical fitness level, and selected elements of our mental and emotional health. If problems occur with any of these factors, overall psychosocial health declines.

During our formative years, our successes and failures in every aspect of life, such as school, sports, and relationships, subtly shape our perceptions and beliefs about our personal worth and ability to help ourselves. These perceptions and beliefs in turn influence our psychosocial health. Psychologist Albert Bandura used the term **self-efficacy** to describe a person's belief about whether he or she can successfully engage in and execute a specific behavior. If one has already been successful in academics, athletics, or achieving popularity, one will undoubtedly expect to be successful in these events in the future. If one has always been the last chosen to play

basketball or volleyball or has never been able to make friends easily, one may tend to believe that failure is inevitable. In general, the more self-efficacious a person is and the more his or her past experiences have been positive, the more likely he or she will be to keep trying to execute a specific behavior successfully. A person having low self-efficacy may give up easily or never even try to change a behavior. People who have a high level of self-efficacy are also more likely to feel that they have **personal control** over situations, or, in other words, their own internal resources allow them to control events.

Psychologist Martin Seligman has proposed that people who continually experience failure may develop a pattern of responding known as **learned helplessness** in which they give up and fail to take any action to help themselves. More recently, Seligman's theory has been expanded; just as we may learn to be helpless, so may we learn to be optimistic. His learned optimism research provides growing evidence for the central place of mental health in overall positive development.[9]

Personality   Our personality is the unique mix of characteristics that distinguishes us from others. Hereditary, environmental, cultural, and experiential factors influence how we develop. For each of us, the amount of influence exerted by any of these factors differs. Our personality determines how we react to the challenges of life. It also determines how we interpret the feelings we experience and how we resolve the conflicts we feel on being denied the things we need or want.

Most of the later schools of psychosocial theory promote the idea that we have the power not only to understand our behavior but also to actively change it and thus to mold our own personalities. An accurate picture of personality development probably requires combining aspects of all the personality theories.

Life Span and Maturity   Although the exact determinants of personality are impossible to define, researchers do know that our personalities are not static. Rather, they change as we move through the stages of our lives. Our temperaments also change as we grow, as is illustrated by the extreme emotions experienced by many people in early adolescence. Most of us learn to control our emotions as we advance toward adulthood.

The college years mark a critical transition period for young adults. For most, this step toward maturity entails changing the nature of your relationship with your parents. The transition to independence will be easier if you have successfully accomplished earlier developmental tasks such as learning how to solve problems, to make and evaluate decisions, to define and adhere to personal values, and to establish both casual and intimate relationships. If you have not fulfilled earlier tasks, you will continue to grow, but may find your life interrupted by recurrent "crises" left over from earlier stages. For example, if you did not learn to trust others in childhood, you may have difficulty establishing intimate relationships in late adolescence or early adulthood.

Which of the foregoing external factors does an individual have the most control over? Which factors do you think had the greatest impact on making you who you are today?

ENHANCING PSYCHOSOCIAL HEALTH

You may believe that your psychosocial health is fairly well developed by the time you reach college. However, you can always take steps to change your behavior and to improve your psychosocial health. Your well-being is largely determined by your ability to respond to life's challenges and can be defined by your level of self-fulfillment or self-actualization. Attaining self-fulfillment is a lifelong, conscious process that involves building self-esteem, understanding and controlling emotions, and learning to solve problems and make decisions.

Maintaining a nutritious diet and establishing an exercise routine helps a person develop a sense of self-control, thereby enhancing psychosocial health as well.

Self-Esteem and Self-Efficacy

Self-esteem refers to one's sense of self-respect or self-confidence. It can be defined as how much one likes oneself and values one's personal worth. People with high self-esteem tend to feel good about themselves and have a positive outlook on life. People with low self-esteem often do not like themselves, constantly demean themselves, and doubt their ability to succeed.

Our self-esteem is a result of the relationships we have with our parents and family during our formative years, our friends as we grow older, our significant others as we form intimate relationships, and with our teachers, co-workers, and others throughout our lives. If we felt loved and valued as children, our self-esteem may allow us to believe that we are inherently "lovable individuals" as we reach adulthood.

▶ **Finding a Support Group** The best way to maintain your self-esteem is through a support group. You need peers who share your values and offer you the nurturing that your family can no longer provide. The prime prerequisite for a support group is that it makes you feel good about yourself and forces you to take an honest look at your actions and the choices that you make. Although finding a support group seems to imply that this is always a new group, it is important to remember that old ties are often among the strongest that you will make. Keeping in contact with these friends and with important family members can provide a foundation of unconditional love that may help you through the many life transitions ahead.

▶ **Completing Required Tasks** A way to boost your self-efficacy is to complete required tasks successfully and develop a history of success. You are not likely to succeed in your studies if you leave term papers until the last minute, fail to keep up with the reading for your courses, and do not ask for clarification of points that are confusing to you. Most college campuses provide study groups for various content areas. These groups offer tips for managing time, understanding assignments, dealing with professors, and preparing for tests. Poor grades, or grades that do not meet a student's expectations, are major contributors to diminished self-esteem and self-efficacy and to emotional distress among college students.

▶ **Forming Realistic Expectations** Having realistic expectations of yourself is another method of boosting self-esteem. College is a time to explore your potential. The stresses of college life may make your expectations for success difficult to meet. If you expect perfect grades, a steady stream of Saturday-night dates and a soap-opera-type romantic involvement, and the perfect job, you may be setting yourself up for

---

Self-efficacy Belief in your ability to perform a task successfully.

Personal control Belief that your internal resources can allow you to control a situation.

Learned helplessness Pattern of responding to situations by giving up because you have always failed in the past.

Self-esteem Sense of self-respect or self-confidence.

failure. Assess your current resources and the direction you are heading. Set small, incremental goals that are possible for you to meet.

▶ *Taking and Making Time for You* Taking time to enjoy yourself is another way to boost your self-esteem and psychosocial health. Viewing each new activity as something to look forward to and an opportunity to have fun is an important part of keeping the excitement in your life.

▶ *Maintaining Physical Health* Maintaining physical health also contributes to self-esteem and self-efficacy. Regular exercise fosters a sense of well-being. Nourishing meals can help you avoid the weight gain experienced by many college students. (See Chapter 11 for more information on the role of exercise on health.)

▶ *Examining Problems and Seeking Help* Knowing when to seek help from friends, support groups, family, or professionals is another important factor in boosting one's self-esteem. Sometimes life's problems are insurmountable; sometimes you can handle them alone. Recognizing your strengths and acting appropriately are keys to psychosocial health.

··········· **WHAT DO YOU THINK?**

Based on how self-esteem and self-efficacy develop, which do you think it would be easier to improve on in adulthood? What do you think might work to improve self-esteem in young people?

Getting adequate sleep is a key contributor to positive physical and psychosocial functioning. Many of us never seem to get enough sleep. Either we don't have time to sleep or we can't seem to fall asleep once our heads hit the pillow. An estimated 20 to 40 percent of all adults have trouble sleeping. Known as *insomnia*, this sleep disorder afflicts almost everyone at one time or another. Insomnia is more common in women than in men, and its prevalence correlates with age and socioeconomic class. Though many people turn to over-the-counter sleeping pills, barbiturates, or tranquilizers to get some sleep, the following methods for conquering sleeplessness are less harmful:[10] 7 hrs.

Don't drink alcohol or smoke before bedtime. Alcohol can disrupt sleep patterns and make insomnia worse. Nicotine also makes you wakeful.

Avoid eating a heavy meal in the evening, particularly at bedtime. Don't drink large amounts of liquids before retiring, either.

Eliminate or reduce consumption of caffeinated beverages except in the morning or early afternoon.

Avoid daytime naps, even if you're tired.

Spend an hour or more relaxing before retiring. Read, listen to music, watch TV, or take a warm bath.

If you're unable to fall asleep, get up and do something rather than lie there. Don't bring work to bed. If you wake up in the middle of the night and can't fall asleep again, try reading for a short time. Counting sheep or reconstructing a happy event or narrative in your mind may lull you to sleep.

Avoid reproaching yourself. Don't make your sleeplessness a cause for additional worry. Insomnia is not a crime. Not everyone needs eight hours of sleep. You can feel well—and be quite healthy—on less. Don't worry that you have to make up lost sleep. One good night's sleep will reinvigorate you.

Don't watch the clock at night. Turn it to the wall to avoid the temptation to worry about the night slipping away.

Go to bed and rise on a regular schedule. Keep this schedule no matter how much you have or haven't slept in the recent past.

THE MIND-BODY CONNECTION

Can negative emotions make a person physically sick? Can positive emotions boost the immune system? Researchers have explored the possible interaction between emotions and health, especially in conditions of uncontrolled, persistent stress. According to the simplest theory of this interaction, the brain of an emotionally overwrought person sends signals to the adrenal glands, which respond by secreting *cortisol* and *epinephrine* (adrenaline), the hormones that activate the body's stress response. These chemicals are also known to suppress immune functioning, so it has been surmised that the persistently overwrought person undergoes subtle immune changes. What remains to be shown is how these changes affect overall health, if they do at all. According to Marvin Stein, a professor of psychiatry at the Mount Sinai School of Medicine in New York City, "Work thus far on emotions and health adds up to little more than findings in search of meaning."[11] We still do not have conclusive proof of a relationship between emotions and health, he argues, but evidence for such a relationship is accumulating.[12]

Evidence of Support

In the 1970s and 1980s, a number of widely publicized studies of the health of widowed and divorced people showed that their rates of illness and death were higher than those of married people. Moreover, their lab tests revealed below-normal immune-system functioning. Several follow-up studies have shown unusually high rates of cancer among depressed people.[13] But are these studies conclusive evidence of the mind-body connection? Probably not, because they do not account for many other factors known to be relevant to health. For example, some researchers suggest that people who are divorced, widowed, or depressed are more likely to drink and smoke, to use drugs, to eat and sleep poorly, and to fail to exercise—all of which may affect the immune system. Another possibly relevant factor is that such people may be less tolerant of illness and more likely to report their problems.

Among the work most widely cited as proof that psychosocial treatment can help patients fight disease is an experiment involving women with advanced breast cancer. David Spiegel, professor of psychiatry at Stanford University, reported in 1989 that 50 women randomly assigned to a weekly support group lived an average of 18 months longer than 36 similarly afflicted women not in the support group. The implication of this finding is that the women in the support group cheered each other on while they endured agonizing therapy and that this allowed them to sleep and eat better, which promoted their survival. But a significant flaw in Spiegel's study was his failure to specifically measure immune functioning.[14]

In fact, the immune system changes measured in various other studies of the mind-body connection are relatively small. (They are nowhere near as large as the disruptions that occur in people with AIDS, for example.) The health consequences of such minute changes are difficult to gauge because the body can tolerate a certain amount of reduced immune function without illness resulting. The exact amount it is able to tolerate and under what circumstances are still in question.[15]

Probably the boldest theory put forward in mind-body research is the notion that certain psychosocial behaviors actually make people vulnerable to cancer. In her book on the mind-cancer link, *The Type C Connection*, psychologist Lydia Temoshok reported that among the patients she studied who had malignant melanoma (a potentially deadly skin cancer), 75 percent shared common traits. They tended to be unfailingly pleasant, to repress their negative feelings and emotions, to put others' needs ahead of their own, and to make extraordinary attempts to accommodate others. She hypothesized that this "Type C" personality signals emotional repression, which may work to suppress the immune system.[16]

Laughter: Medicine for the Soul?

The notion that laughter can save your life gained wide acceptance with the 1979 publication of *Anatomy of an Illness*, by magazine editor Norman Cousins. In this book, Cousins recounted his recovery from a rheumatic disease of the spine—ankylosing spondylitis—with the aid of Marx Brothers movies and *Candid Camera* videos that made him laugh.[17] Similarly, in his 1988 best-seller, *Love, Medicine and Miracles*, surgeon Bernie Siegel argued that a fighting spirit and the determination to survive are vital adjuncts to standard cancer

ACCESSING YOUR HEALTH ON THE INTERNET

Check out the following Internet sites related to psychosocial health:

1. *MEDWEB.* Search "Mental Health" for an extensive list of sites and resources for many aspects of mental health information.

    http://www.emory.edu/

2. *Mental Health Net.* Easy to use, friendly resource in which to access all the mental health topics available on the net.

    http://www.cmhc.com/

3. *American Psychological Association.* Includes APA newsletters, links to other sites, information on books, journals, employment, and public, practical, and educational materials.

    http://www.apa.org

therapy.[18] Other researchers, such as Lee Berk, M.D., and Stanley Tan, M.D., have noted that laughter sharpens our immune systems by activating T cells and natural killer cells and increasing production of immunity-boosting interferon.[19] It also reduces levels of the stress hormone, cortisol.

As one of our common mood indicators, scientists are just beginning to understand the role of humor in our lives and on our health. Some emerging pieces of the laughter–mental health puzzle include the following:

-   Stressed out people with a strong sense of humor become less depressed and anxious than those whose sense of humor is less well developed.
-   Students who use humor as a coping mechanism report being more likely to be in a positive mood.
-   In a study of depressed and suicidal senior citizens, patients who recovered were the ones who demonstrated a sense of humor.
-   Telling a joke, particularly one that involves a shared experience, increases our sense of belonging and social cohesion.

While laughter may not be a panacea for happiness, it helps us in so many ways. People like to be around people who are fun-loving and laugh easily. Learning to laugh and laugh often will help put more joy into our everyday experiences as well as increasing the likelihood of having fun people around us to enjoy life with. Clearly, we still have a lot to learn in this area. In the meantime, however, maintaining an optimistic mindset is probably sound advice.

COMMON PSYCHOSOCIAL PROBLEMS

In spite of our own best efforts to remain psychosocially healthy, circumstances and events in our lives sometimes prove to be more than we can handle. If we have the financial and educational resources to seek help, some of these difficulties can be prevented. But in the case of other difficulties, the road to recovery may be long.

Depression

Depression: It's a shell of a word, drained of its meaning through overuse. Missing your morning bus is depressing. The evening news is depressing. The word doesn't even begin to communicate the reality of the clinical disorder that affects millions of Americans each day. This isn't the blues, the occasional sadness that visits every life; this is the dark swamp of despair. It can be life threatening: 15 percent of people who are clinically depressed kill themselves. And it is a woman's disease, striking one out of every five women—twice as many women as men. If you're a typical woman today, your risk of becoming clinically depressed is double your risk of developing breast cancer, yet most women ignore this problem as if it was a petty annoyance to be borne by all. ("If drugs cure depression, why don't I feel better?" by Kim Pittaway. *Chatelaine,* March 1997 v70 n3, p46)   2/3 - women

There are two acknowledged forms of depression: endogenous and exogenous depression. Endogenous depression is of biochemical origin. Neurotransmitters (chemicals that transmit nerve impulses across synapses) in the brain that are responsible for mood elevation become unbalanced for unknown reasons. A decrease in the amount of these neurotransmitters gives rise to outward expressions of depression. If not treated, endogenous depression may become chronic. Exogenous depression, on the other hand, is usually caused by an external event such as the loss of something or someone of great value. Victims of exogenous depression can slide into chronic depression if they are unable to work through the grieving process necessary for overcoming event-related depression.

▶ *Are You Depressed?*   Sadness and despair are the main indicators of depression. The following are among the more common symptoms that a person may experience.

- Loss of motivation or interest in pleasurable activities
- Preoccupation with failures and inadequacies; concern over what others are thinking
- Difficulty concentrating; indecisiveness; memory lapses
- Loss of sex drive or interest in close interactions with others
- Fatigue and loss of energy; slow reactions
- Sleeping too much or too little; insomnia
- Feeling agitated, worthless, or hopeless
- Withdrawal from friends and families
- Diminished or increased appetite

- Recurring thoughts that life isn't worth living, thoughts of death or suicide
- Significant weight loss or weight gain

A person who is depressed may display any or all of these symptoms. Sometimes he may mask his symptoms with a forced, upbeat sense of humor or high energy levels that are deceptive. Usually, the depressed person suffers from low self-esteem, loneliness, or detachment. Communication may cease or seem frantic at times. After a while, depression becomes a vicious cycle in which a person may feel helpless or trapped. Sometimes she believes that the only way out is through death.

▶ *Facts and Fallacies about Depression*   Depression among young Americans has come to be known as the common cold of mental illnesses. It is one of the fastest growing problems in U.S. culture, yet it is among the most misunderstood of the mental disorders. Myths and misperceptions about the disease abound. Consider these:[20]

1. *True depression is not a natural reaction to crisis and loss.* Depression is a pervasive and systemic biological problem that results in deep-seated pessimism and feelings of helplessness, despair, and lethargy, sometimes coupled with agitation. Victims may have problems at work or difficulties in relationships. Symptoms may come and go, and the severity will fluctuate, but they do not simply go away. Depressed people forget what being normal feels like. Crisis and loss can lead an already depressed person over the edge to suicide or other problems, but crisis and loss do not inevitably result in depression.

2. *People will not snap out of depression by using a little willpower.* Telling a depressed person to snap out of it is like telling a diabetic to produce more insulin. Medical intervention in the form of antidepressant drugs and therapy is often necessary for recovery. Remember that depression is the leading cause of suicide in the United States, and even with treatment, more than half of those who have it will eventually get it again. Understanding the seriousness of the disease and supporting victims in their attempts to recover are key elements of support.

3. *Frequent crying is not a hallmark of depression.* Some people who are depressed bear their burdens in silence, or may even be the life of the party. Some depressed individuals don't cry at all. Rather, biochemists theorize that crying may actually ward off depression by releasing chemicals that the body produces as a positive response to stress.

Endogenous depression   A type of depression that has a biochemical basis, such as neurotransmitter imbalances.

Exogenous depression   A type of depression that has an external cause, such as the loss of a loved one.

Depression Strikes Increasing Numbers of Young People

Based on recent statistics, depression and a host of other psychological problems are extremely common in the United States, affecting large numbers of people at any given time. While some statistics indicate a rising incidence of depression among all age groups, the most alarming aspect of these numbers is that they are probably gross "underestimations" of the true problem. Many people suffer silently; others are totally unaware that their cynical, unhappy attitudes are really part of a much greater problem. Consider the following:

✓ The known suicide rate among 15- to 19-year-olds has more than doubled since 1950. In the United States, suicide rates are higher among Whites than Blacks, and higher among males than females. Rates for suicide among Black women are very low.

✓ Suicide rates among elementary school children and high school students and on college campuses have increased dramatically in the last decade, forcing educational institutions to take significant steps to improve counseling services, teach teachers to recognize and refer high-risk students, and include communities and families in suicide prevention and intervention programs.

✓ Depression strikes over 17 million Americans each year, with less than half of those who suffer from it receiving the treatment they need.

✓ Many of the drug and alcohol problems facing Americans have their roots in a hopeless, depressed psychological state in which victims turn to drugs to ease their suffering. In addition, many drugs cause victims to be depressed.

✓ More than 80 percent of people with depression can be treated successfully with medication, therapy, or a combination of both; however, most people never go for treatment.

✓ Nearly 20 percent of Americans will seek psychological help from trained professionals during their lifetimes. Many of those who seek help will be suffering from depression-related problems.

✓ The risk of depression increases if you have a parent or sibling who suffered from depression before age 30.

✓ Suicide is one of the leading causes of death in the United States, and more than 40,000 depressed people in the United States kill themselves every year.

✓ Antidepressant medications are among the most-prescribed drugs in the United States, with dramatic increases in the numbers of prescriptions filled and the length of time that patients are on these medications.

Sources: Health, U.S. 1998. U.S. Department of Health and Human Services. M. Clements, and D. Hales. "How Healthy are We?" *Parade Magazine,* September 7, 1997, pp. 4–7. U.S. Bureau of the Census, 1996.

---

4. *Depression is not "all in the mind."* Depression isn't a disease of weak-willed, powerless people. In fact, research has shown that genetics plays a critical role in the development of severe depression. Data suggest that depressive illnesses originate with an inherited chemical imbalance in the brain. In addition, some physiological conditions, such as thyroid disorders, multiple sclerosis, chronic fatigue syndrome, and certain types of cancer, often have depressive side effects. Certain medications also are known to prompt depressive-like symptoms.

5. It is not *true that only in-depth psychotherapy can cure long-term clinical depression.* No single psychotherapy method works for all cases of depression.

▶ **Depression and Gender** For reasons that are not well understood, two-thirds of all people suffering from depression are women. Researchers have proposed biological, psychological, and social explanations for this fact. The biological explanation rests on the observation that women appear to be at greater risk for depression when their hormone levels change significantly, as during the premenstrual period, the period following the birth of a child, and the onset of menopause.

Men's hormone levels appear to remain more stable throughout life. Researchers therefore theorized that women were inherently more at risk for depression. Yet evidence to support this theory is either inconsistent or contrary.

Although adolescent and adult females have been found to experience depression at twice the rate of males, the college population seems to represent a notable exception, with equal rates experienced by males and females. Why? Several theories have been suggested for this anomaly.[21]

✗ The social institutions of the college campus provide a more egalitarian sex role status for men and women.

✗ College women have fewer negative events than do high school females. Males in college report more negative events than in high school.

✗ College women report smaller and more supportive social networks.

Depression is often preceded by a stressful event. Some psychologists therefore theorized that women might be under more stress than are men and thus more prone to become depressed. However, women do not report a greater occurrence of more stressful events than do men.

Finally, researchers have observed gender differences in coping strategies, or the response to certain events or stimuli, and have proposed the explanation that women's strategies put them at more risk for depression than do men's strategies. Presented with "a list of things people do when depressed," college students were asked to indicate how likely they were to engage in the behavior outlined in each item on the list. Men were more likely to assert that, "I avoid thinking of reasons why I am depressed," "I do something physical," or "I play sports." Women were more likely to assert that, "I try to determine why I am depressed," "I talk to other people about my feelings," and "I cry to relieve the tension." In other words, the men tried to distract themselves from a depressed mood whereas the women tended to focus attention on it. If focusing on depressed feelings intensifies these feelings, women's response style may make them more likely than men to become clinically depressed. This hypothesis has not been directly tested, but some supporting evidence suggests its validity.[22]

▶ *Treating Depression* Different types of depression require different types of treatment. Selecting the best treatment for a specific patient involves determining his or her type and degree of depression and its possible causes. Both psychotherapeutic and pharmacological modes of treatment are recommended for clinical (severe and prolonged) depression. Drugs often relieve the symptoms of depression, such as loss of sleep or appetite, while psychotherapy can improve a depressed person's social and interpersonal functioning. Treatment may be weighted toward one or the other mode depending on the specific situation. In some cases, psychotherapy alone may be the most successful treatment. The two most common psychotherapeutic therapies for depression are cognitive therapy and interpersonal therapy.

Cognitive therapy aims to help a patient look at life rationally and to correct habitually pessimistic thought patterns. It focuses on the here and now rather than analyzes a patient's past. To pull a person out of depression, cognitive therapists usually need 6 to 18 months of weekly sessions comprising reasoning and behavioral exercises.

Interpersonal therapy has also proved successful in the treatment of depression and is sometimes combined with cognitive therapy. It also addresses the present but differs from cognitive therapy in that its primary goal is to correct chronic human relationship problems. Interpersonal therapists focus on patients' relationships with their families and other people.

Antidepressant drugs relieve symptoms in nearly 80 percent of people with chronic depression. Several types of the antidepressant drugs known as **tricyclics** are available and work by preventing the excessive absorption of mood-lifting neurotransmitters. Tricyclics can take from six weeks to three months to become effective. Newer antidepressant drugs, called **tetracyclics,** work in one or two weeks.

In recent years, words like *Zoloft* and *Prozac* have become such a part of our vocabulary that it doesn't seem at all unusual to know someone who is taking an antidepressant. Such frequency of use could lead one to think that antidepressants can be taken like aspirin. However, countless emergency room visits occur as a result of people who misuse their antidepressants, decide to quit using them "cold turkey," or have reactions to the type of antidepressant they are taking. The potency and dosage of each varies greatly. Antidepressants should be prescribed only after a thorough psychological and physiological examination.

Electroconvulsive therapy (ECT) is another treatment for depression. A patient given ECT is sedated under light general anesthesia and electric current is applied to the temples for five seconds at a time for a period of about 15 or 20 minutes. Between 10 and 20 percent of depressives who do not respond to drug therapy are responsive to ECT, but because a major risk associated with ECT is permanent memory loss, some therapists do not recommend its use under any circumstances.

Obsessive-Compulsive Disorders

Approximately 5 million Americans suffer from obsessive-compulsive disorders. An **obsessive-compulsive disorder (OCD)** is an illness in which people have obsessive thoughts or perform habitual behaviors that they cannot control. People with obsessions have recurring ideas or thoughts that they cannot control. People with compulsions feel forced to engage in a repetitive behavior, almost as if the behavior controls them. Feeling an obsessive need for cleanliness and washing one's hands 20 times before eating, counting to a certain number while using the toilet, and checking and rechecking all the light switches in the house before leaving or going to bed are examples of compulsive behaviors.

Cognitive therapy Helps patients look at life rationally and to correct habitually pessimistic thought patterns. Focuses on the here and now.

Interpersonal therapy Addresses the present, with the primary goal being to correct chronic relationship problems.

Tricyclics Antidepressant drugs that prevent the excessive absorption of mood-lifting neurotransmitters.

Tetracyclics Antidepressant drugs that are newer and faster acting than tricyclics.

Obsessive-compulsive disorder (OCD) A disorder characterized by obsessive thoughts or habitual behaviors that cannot be controlled.

Anxiety disorders Disorders characterized by persistent feelings of threat and anxiety in coping with the everyday problems of living.

Phobia A deep and persistent fear of a specific object, activity, or situation that results in a compelling desire to avoid the source of the fear.

Panic attack The sudden, rapid onset of disabling terror.

SKILLS FOR BEHAVIOR CHANGE

Understanding Your Options

Opting to begin an antidepressant regimen is a serious decision that you must investigate thoroughly. If you have been feeling depressed, anxious, sad, or isolated, or have been suffering any other symptoms of depression, and you have exhausted all avenues, such as therapy and self-help groups, then medication may be the best solution. However, be-

fore filling any prescriptions, make sure to ask your physician the following questions:

- What biological indicators am I using to determine whether I really need this drug? (*Beware of the health professional who gives you a 5-minute exam, asks you if you are feeling down or blue, and prescribes an antidepressant to fix your problems.*)
- What is the action of this drug? What will it do and when will I start to feel the benefits?
- What is my rationale for selecting this antidepressant treatment over any of the other antidepressants that are available?
- What are the side effects of using this drug?

- How long can I be on this medication without significant risk to my health?
- What happens if I stop taking this medication?
- How will I follow-up or monitor the levels of this drug in my body? How often will I need to be checked?
- Since this is a drug that I'll be taking on a long-term basis, are there any drug interactions of which I should be aware? (*Bear in mind that the use of alcohol intensifies the effects of most antidepressants, so modify your consumption, as necessary.*)

Once you feel your questions have been answered to your satisfaction, you can rest assured that you have made an informed decision and are ready to take the next step.

The causes of obsessive-compulsive disorders are difficult to isolate. Some theorists believe that sufferers engage in compulsive behaviors to distract themselves from more pressing problems. Research now suggests, however, that some of these disorders may be caused by a lack of the neurotransmitter serotonin in the limbic system (an area of the brain concerned with emotion and motivation), with drug therapy providing some help.

Anxiety Disorders

Between 20 and 30 million Americans suffer from anxiety disorders. **Anxiety disorders,** in which people are plagued by persistent feelings of threat and of anxiety about everyday problems of living, are characterized by fatigue, back pains, headaches, feelings of unreality, a sensation of weakness in the legs, and fear of losing control. Generalized anxiety disorders can last for more than six months and typically result in excessive worry about two or more personal problems. Three major types of anxiety disorders are phobias, panic attacks, and posttraumatic stress disorder.

▶ *Phobias* A **phobia** is a deep and persistent fear of a specific object, activity, or situation, and results in a compelling desire to avoid the source of fear. Experts estimate that one of eight American adults suffers from phobias. Phobias are also thought to be more prevalent in women than in men. Simple phobias, such as fear of spiders, fear of flying, and fear of

heights, can be treated successfully with behavioral therapy. Social phobias (fears that are related to interaction with others), such as fear of public speaking, fear of inadequate sexual performance, and fear of eating in public places, require more extensive therapy.

▶ *Panic Attacks* A **panic attack** is the sudden onset of disabling terror. Symptoms include shortness of breath, dizziness, sweating, shaking, choking, trembling, and heart palpitations. A victim of a panic attack may feel that he or she is having a heart attack. Panic attacks may have no obvious link to environmental stimuli, or they may be learned responses to environmental stimuli. Researchers believe that panic attacks are caused by some physiological change or biochemical imbalance in the brain and are still searching for the mechanisms that trigger such attacks.[23]

▶ *Posttraumatic Stress Disorder* Posttraumatic stress disorder (PTSD) afflicts some victims of severe traumas such as rape, assault, war, or airplane crashes. PTSD manifests itself in terrifying flashbacks to the sufferer's trauma.

When correctly diagnosed, anxiety disorders are treatable, usually through a combination of methods. Because undiagnosed diabetes, heart conditions, and endocrine disorders can mimic anxiety disorders, doctors recommend a thorough physical examination to rule out physical causes. If it is established that the causes are not physical, treatment usually consists of psychotherapy combined with medication.

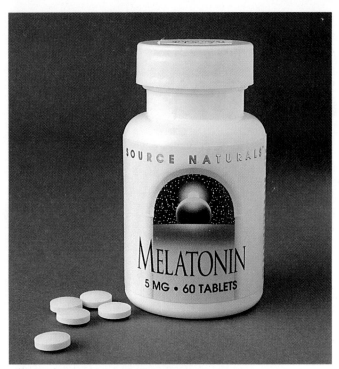

With the success of prescription antidepressant drugs, a number of related natural supplements have attained equal success. One such supplement, melatonin, has grown in popularity in recent years.

Seasonal Affective Disorder

An estimated 6 percent of Americans suffer from **seasonal affective disorder (SAD),** a type of depression, and an additional 14 percent experience a milder form of the disorder known as the winter blues. SAD strikes during the winter months and is associated with reduced exposure to sunlight. People with SAD suffer from irritability, apathy, carbohydrate craving and weight gain, increases in sleep time, and general sadness. Researchers believe that SAD is caused by a malfunction in the hypothalamus, the gland responsible for regulating responses to external stimuli. Stress may also play a role in SAD.

Certain factors seem to put people at risk for SAD. Women are four times more likely to suffer from SAD than are men. Although SAD occurs in people of all ages, those between 20 and 40 appear to be most vulnerable. Certain families appear to be at risk. And people living in northern states in the United States are more at risk than are those living in southern states. During the winter, there are fewer hours of sunlight in northern regions than in southern areas. An estimated 10 percent of the population in northern states such as Maine, Minnesota, and Wisconsin experience SAD, whereas fewer than 2 percent of those living in southern states such as Florida and New Mexico suffer from the disorder.

There are some simple but effective therapies for SAD. The most beneficial appears to be light therapy, in which a patient is exposed to lamps that mimic sunlight. After being exposed to this lighting each day, 80 percent of patients experience relief from their symptoms within four days. Other forms of treatment for SAD are diet change (eating more foods high in complex carbohydrates), increased exercise, stress management techniques, sleep restriction (limiting the number of hours slept in a 24-hour period), psychotherapy, and antidepressants.

Schizophrenia

Perhaps the most frightening of all mental disorders is **schizophrenia,** a disease that affects about 1 percent of the U.S. population. Schizophrenia is characterized by alterations of the senses (including auditory and visual hallucinations); the inability to sort out incoming stimuli and to make appropriate responses; an altered sense of self; and radical changes in emotions, movements, and behaviors. Victims of this disease often cannot function in society.

For decades, scientists believed that schizophrenia was an environmentally provoked form of madness. They blamed abnormal family interactions or early-childhood traumas. Since the mid-1980s, however, when magnetic resonance imaging (MRI) and positron emission tomography (PET) began to allow scientists to study brain function more closely, scientists have recognized that schizophrenia is a biological disease of the brain. It has become evident that the brain damage involved occurs very early in life, possibly as early as in the second trimester of fetal development. However, the disease most commonly has its onset in late adolescence.

Schizophrenia is treatable but not curable at present. Treatments usually include some combination of hospitalization, medication, and supportive psychotherapy. Supportive psychotherapy, as opposed to psychoanalysis, can help the patient acquire skills for living in society.

Even though the environmental theories of schizophrenia have been discarded in favor of biological theories, a stigma remains attached to the disease. Families of schizophrenics often experience anger and guilt associated with misunderstandings about the causes of the disease. They often need help in the form of information, family counseling, and advice on how to meet the schizophrenic's needs for shelter, medical care, vocational training, and social interaction.

Seasonal affective disorder (SAD)   A type of depression that occurs in the winter months, when sunlight levels are low.

Schizophrenia   A mental illness with biological origins that is characterized by irrational behavior, severe alterations of the senses (hallucinations), and, often, an inability to function in society.

Gender Issues in Psychosocial Health

Studies have shown that gender bias often gets in the way of correct diagnosis of psychosocial disorders. In one study, for instance, 175 mental health professionals, of both genders, were asked to diagnose a patient based upon a summarized case history. Some of the professionals were told that the patient was male, others that the patient was female. The gender of the patient made a substantial difference in the diagnosis given (though the gender of the clinician did not). When subjects thought the patient was female, they were more likely to diagnose hysterical personality, a "women's disorder." When they believed the patient to be male, the more likely diagnosis was antisocial personality, a "male disorder."

▶ *PMS: Physical or Mental Disorder?*   A major controversy regarding gender bias has been the inclusion of a "provisional" diagnosis for premenstrual syndrome (PMS) in the American Psychiatric Association's *Diagnostic and Statistical Manual of Mental Disorders* (fourth edition; known as *DSM-IV*). The provisional inclusion, in an appendix to *DSM-IV*, signals that PMS should come in for further study and may be included as an approved diagnosis in future editions of the *DSM*. In other words, PMS could be considered a mental disorder in the future.

PMS is characterized by depression, irritability, and other symptoms of increased stress typically occurring just prior to menstruation and lasting for a day or two. A more severe case of PMS is known as *premenstrual dysphoric disorder,* or PMDD. The distinction between these disorders is that while PMS is somewhat disruptive and uncomfortable, it does not interfere with the way a woman functions from day to day; PMDD does. To be diagnosed with PMDD, a woman must have at least five symptoms of PMS for a week to 10 days, with at least one symptom being serious enough to interfere with her ability to function at work or at home. In these more severe cases, antidepressants may be prescribed. The point of contention lies in whether administering this treatment indicates that PMDD is viewed as a mental disorder as opposed to a physical disorder.[24] The controversy involves the legitimacy of attaching a label indicating dysfunction and disorder to symptoms experienced only once or twice a month. Further controversy stems from the possible use (or misuse) of the diagnostic label to justify systematic exclusion of women from certain desirable jobs.

SUICIDE
Giving Up on Life

There are over 35,000 reported suicides each year in the United States. Experts estimate that there may actually be closer to 100,000 cases; due to the difficulty in determining many causes of suspicious deaths, many suicides are not re-flected in the statistics. More lives are lost to suicide than to any other single cause except cardiovascular disease and cancer. Suicide is often a consequence of poor coping skills, lack of social support, lack of self-esteem, and the inability to see one's way out of a bad or negative situation.

College students are more likely than the general population to attempt suicide; suicide is the third leading cause of death in people between the ages of 15 and 24. In fact, this age group now accounts for nearly 20 percent of all suicides.[25] The pressures, joys, disappointments, challenges, and changes of the college environment are believed to be in part responsible for these rates. However, young adults who choose not to go to college but who are searching for the directions to their career goals, relationship goals, and other life aspirations are also at risk for suicide.

Risk factors for suicide include a family history of suicide, previous suicide attempts, excessive drug and alcohol use, prolonged depression, financial difficulties, serious illness in the suicide contemplator or in his or her loved ones, and loss of a loved one through death or rejection. Although women attempt suicide at four times the rate of men, more than three times as many men as women actually succeed in ending their lives. The elderly, divorced people, former psychiatric patients, and Native Americans have a higher risk of suicide than others. In fact, the elderly make up 23 percent of those who commit suicide. Alcoholics also have a high rate of suicide.

Depression is often a precursor of suicide. People who have been suffering from depression are more likely to attempt suicide while they are recovering, when their energy level is higher, than while they are in the depths of depression. Although only 15 percent of depressed people are suicidal, most suicide-prone individuals are depressed.[26]

Due to the growing incidence of suicide, many of us will be touched by a suicide at some time. In most cases, the suicide does not occur unpredictably. In fact, between 75 and 80 percent of people who commit suicide give a warning of their intentions.

Recognizing the signs of depression and possible suicide risks is an important aspect of prevention. Common signs include:[27]

- recent loss and a seeming inability to let go of grief
- change in personality—sad, withdrawn, irritable, anxious, tired, indecisive, apathetic
- change in behavior—inability to concentrate, loss of interest in classes
- diminished sexual interest—impotence, menstrual abnormalities
- expressions of self-hatred
- change in sleep patterns
- change in eating habits
- a direct statement about committing suicide, such as "I might as well end it all."

**H E A L T H
I N   A
D I V E R S E
W O R L D**

Suicide: A Neglected Problem among Diverse Populations

One of the most underrated public health problems facing Americans today, suicide accounts for more than 35,000 preventable deaths each year, nearly 10,000 more than the deaths from homicide. It touches all ages, all races, and all social groups, and is on the rise in many segments of the population.

- Overall, suicide is the ninth leading cause of death for all Americans and the third leading cause of death for young people aged 15 to 24, for whom suicide rates have tripled since 1950.

- Depression, substance abuse, a history of family violence, social isolation, and other factors increase the risk.
- Young White males are the most frequent victims. Nonetheless, from 1979 to 1992, suicide rates for Native Americans were about 1.5 times the national average. In addition, a recent report from the Centers for Disease Control showed the rate of suicides among Black teens aged 15 to 19 more than doubled between 1980 and 1995.
- For every successful suicide, another 17 are attempted.
- Elderly men use the most violent means of suicide and are the most likely to be successful.
- After age 75, suicide rates are three times the national average, and after age 80, six times the national average.
- The average teen suicide is a White male who uses a firearm to kill himself. Males outnumber females five to one in completed suicides, while females are two times more likely to attempt suicide, often by using less

lethal means, such as drugs or alcohol. Native Americans have a higher suicide rate than Whites of all ages.
- Teen suicides often occur in clusters, particularly when friends or prominent national figures, such as rock stars, commit suicide.
- Rates of suicide are considerably higher in the western states, followed by the South, Midwest, and Northeast.
- People who have never been married are twice as likely to commit suicide as currently married people; the highest rates of all occur among the divorced or widowed.
- Suicide rates are lower in rural areas than in cities.
- Suicide rates are highest in German-speaking countries, Switzerland, Scandinavia, Eastern Europe, and Japan, and lowest in Greece, Italy, and Spain.

Sources: Stephanie Stapleton. "The Surgeon General Calls for Suicide Prevention," *American Medical News,* 41 (1998): 9; "Suicide Among Black Youth, 1980–1995," *JAMA,* 279 (1998): 1431.

- an indirect statement about committing suicide, such as, "You won't have to worry about me anymore."
- "final preparations," such as writing a will, repairing poor relationships with family or friends, giving away prized possessions, or writing revealing letters
- a preoccupation with themes of death
- a sudden and unexplained demonstration of happiness following a period of depression
- marked changes in personal appearance
- excessive risk taking and an "I don't care what happens to me" attitude

Taking Action

If someone you know threatens suicide or displays any of the above warnings, take the following actions:

- *Monitor the warning signals.* Try to keep an eye on the person involved, or see that there is someone around the person as much as possible.
- *Take any threats seriously.*

- *Let the person know how much you care about him or her.* State that you are there if he or she needs help.
- *Listen.* Try not to be shocked by or to discredit what the person says to you. Empathize, sympathize, and keep the person talking.
- *Ask the person directly, "Are you thinking of hurting or killing yourself?"*
- *Do not belittle the person's feelings or say that he or she doesn't really mean it or couldn't succeed at suicide.* To some people, these comments offer the challenge of proving you wrong.
- *Help the person think about other alternatives.* Be ready to offer choices. Offer to go for help with the person. Call your local suicide hotline and use all available community and campus resources.
- *Remember that your relationships with others involve responsibilities.* If you need to stay with the person, take the person to a health-care facility, or provide support, give of yourself and your time.
- *Tell your friend's spouse, partner, parents, brothers and sisters, or counselor.* Do not keep your suspicions to yourself. Don't let a suicidal friend talk you into keeping your dis-

cussions confidential. If your friend is successful in a suicide attempt, you will have to live with the consequences of your inaction.

······· WHAT DO YOU THINK?

If your roommate showed some of the warning signs of suicide, what action would you take? Who would you contact first? Where on campus might your friend get help? What if someone in your class that you hardly knew gave some of the warning signs? What would you then do?

SEEKING PROFESSIONAL HELP

Many Americans feel that seeking professional help for psychosocial problems is an admission of personal failure they cannot afford to make. Typically, any physical health problem, such as abscessed tooth or prolonged severe pain, sends us to the nearest dentist or physician. On the other hand, we tend to ignore psychosocial problems until they pose a serious threat to our well-being—and even then, we may refuse to ask for the help we need. Despite this tradition, an increasing number of Americans are turning to mental health professionals for help, and in 1996, nearly one in five Americans sought such help. Researchers believe that more people want help today because "normal" living has become more hazardous. Breakdown in support systems, high expectations of the individual by society, and dysfunctional families are cited as the three major reasons more people are asking for assistance than ever before.

You should consider seeking help under the following circumstances:

- If you think you need help.
- If you experience wild mood swings.
- If a problem is interfering with your daily life.
- If your fears or feelings of guilt frequently distract your attention.
- If you begin to withdraw from others.
- If you have hallucinations.
- If you feel that life is not worth living.
- If you feel inadequate or worthless.
- If your emotional responses are inappropriate to various situations.
- If your daily life seems to be nothing but repeated crises.
- If you feel you can't "get your act together."
- If you are considering suicide.
- If you turn to drugs or alcohol to escape from your problems.
- If you feel out of control.

Psychiatrist   A licensed physician who specializes in treating mental and emotional disorders.

Psychoanalyst   A psychiatrist or psychologist having special training in psychoanalysis.

More and more studies indicate that the unconditional love of a pet can do wonders for a person's psychosocial health.

Mental Health Professionals

Several types of mental health professionals, or providers, are available to help you. Most insurance companies have some type of psychiatric care provision, although the amount of coverage varies based on the policy plan and the credentials of the provider. The most important criterion when choosing a provider is whether you feel you can work well with that person, not how many degrees he or she has.

▶ *Psychiatrist*   A **psychiatrist** is a medical doctor. After obtaining an M.D. degree, a psychiatrist spends up to 12 years studying psychosocial health and disease. As a licensed physician, a psychiatrist can prescribe medications for various mental or emotional problems and may have admitting privileges at a local hospital. Some psychiatrists are affiliated with hospitals, while others are in private practice.

▶ *Psychoanalyst*   A **psychoanalyst** is a psychiatrist or a psychologist having special training in psychoanalysis. Psychoanalysis is a type of therapy in which a patient is helped to remember early traumas that have blocked personal growth. Facing these traumas helps the patient to resolve the conflicts and to begin to lead a more productive life.

TABLE 2.1
Traditional Forms of Psychotherapy: Assumptions, Goals, and Methods

TYPE OF THERAPY	BASIC ASSUMPTIONS	GOALS AND METHODS
Psychoanalysis	Behavior is motivated by intrapsychic conflict and biological urges.	Discover the sources of conflict and resolve them through insight.
Psychodynamic	Behavior is motivated by both unconscious forces and interpersonal experiences.	Understand and improve interpersonal skills by modifying the client's inappropriate schemas about interpersonal relationships.
Humanistic and Gestalt	People are good and have innate worth.	Use techniques to enhance personal awareness and feelings of self-worth to promote personal growth and self-actualization and to enhance clients' awareness of bodily sensations and feelings.
Behavior and cognitive-behavior	Behavior is largely controlled by environmental contingencies, people's perception of them, or their combination.	Change maladaptive behavior and thinking patterns; done by manipulating environmental variables, restructuring thinking patterns, and correcting faulty thinking or irrational beliefs.
Family/couples	Problems in relationships entail everybody involved in them.	Analyze relationship patterns and others' roles in order to discover how interactions influence problems in individual functioning.

Source: Adapted from Neil R. Carson and William Buskist, Psychology: The Science of Behavior, 5th ed., p. 629. Copyright © 1997 Allyn & Bacon. Reprinted by permission.

▶ *Psychologist* A **psychologist** usually has a Ph.D. degree in counseling or clinical psychology. In addition, many states require licensure. Psychologists are trained in various types, including behavior and insight therapy. Most are trained to conduct both individual and group counseling sessions. Psychologists may also be trained in certain specialties, such as family counseling, sexual counseling, or counseling related to compulsive behaviors.

▶ *Clinical/Psychiatric Social Worker* A **social worker** has at least a master's degree in social work (M.S.W.) and two years of experience in a clinical setting. Many states require an examination for accreditation. Some social workers work in clinical settings, whereas others have private practices.

▶ *Counselor* The **counselor** often has a master's degree in counseling, psychology, educational psychology, or a related human service. Professional societies recommend at least two years of graduate coursework or supervised practice as a minimal requirement. Many counselors are trained to do individual and group counseling. They often specialize in one type of counseling, such as family, marital, relationship, children, drug, divorce, behavioral, or personal counseling.

▶ *Psychiatric Nurse Specialist* Although all registered nurses can work in psychiatric settings, some have chosen to continue their education and specialize in psychiatric practice. The psychiatric nurse specialist can be certified by the American Nursing Association in either adult, child, or adolescent psychiatric nursing.

Remember that, in most states, anyone can use the title of therapist or counselor. Before you begin treatment, you should consider the credentials of your counselor, your desired outcomes, and the expectations of you and your counselor. The Consumer Health box identifies key factors to consider when seeking help.

When working with a client, therapists often subscribe to a primary philosophy of treatment based on their educational background and experiential training. Most, however, employ a variety of methods when helping a client, depending on the client's needs and the therapist's experiences in the field. Many different types of therapy exist, ranging from individual therapy, which involves one-on-one work between therapist and the client, to group therapy, in which two or more clients meet with a therapist to discuss problems. Table 2.1 identifies some of the more traditional forms of psychotherapy.

Psychologist A person with a Ph.D. degree and training in psychology.

Social worker A person with an M.S.W. degree and clinical training.

Counselor A person having a variety of academic and experiential training who deals with the treatment of emotional problems.

Choosing a Therapist: Key Factors to Consider

When you are in emotional or psychological trouble, you are often in the most vulnerable of situations. The choices you make in times of desperation are often critical to your eventual health; yet, many people choose their therapists at random, or pick a name out of the phone book at their lowest emotional point. Like auto mechanics, physicians, and college professors, all therapists are not created equal and are not equally skilled at what they do. A degree or credential does not ensure compatibility with you or general competence. Taking some time to check out the person you are going to see and evaluating that person during your first session are important first steps in taking care of yourself. While even the most thorough check does not guarantee satisfaction, assessing the following may help make your experience a positive and fulfilling one.

Does the Therapist Have Qualities You Would Want in a Close Friend?
Early in your interaction with the therapist, you should find that the therapist is someone you like, admire, and respect and is someone with whom you relate well and would be willing to trust with your most intimate thoughts. According to Russ Newman, Ph.D., J.D., executive director of professional practice for the American Psychological Association, "The best-trained, best credentialed psychotherapist in the world is not going to be a big help to you if there is something about the way that you interact with him or her that doesn't feel right." The therapist should convey a genuine interest in you and your problems, rather than be watching the clock or looking in his or her book to schedule your next appointment. You should enjoy sitting in the room with this person and talking, rather than talking with someone who seems detached, cool, or arrogant. In short, you need to "connect" with your therapist on some very basic levels.

Does the Therapist Act Professionally?
Most therapists adhere to a very basic code of ethics. They set boundaries around their relationships with clients to ensure the clients' safety, to foster a feeling of trust, and to encourage confidence in their ability to help. There are exceptions, however. Signs of unprofessional behavior include:

- suggestions of meetings or social interactions outside of your sessions; particularly if they appear to be trying to be a personal friend or lover rather than maintaining a professional role.
- agreeing to counsel someone with whom there is a conflict of interest in the counseling situation. Former partners, business relationships, friends, and other clients should be off limits in most cases.
- continually being late for sessions, seeming distracted in sessions, forgetting what you have told them before and needing you to repeat things.
- spending too much time talking about him- or herself during the session rather than listening to you; identifying too much of what you are saying with him- or herself rather than your own situation.
- questionable billing practices, such as discrepancies in billing, billing errors to insurance companies, or seeming to want your business and the money rather than displaying a sincere desire to help.
- locking you into their own specialty; for example, a counselor who specializes in alcoholism and adult children of alcoholics who continually tries to force you into the adult child of alcoholic box, even though this has little to do with your unique situation.
- continual interruptions of your session with phone calls, talking to the receptionist, or other diversions so that you do not get your full amount of time.
- never seeming to want to release you from therapy or encouraging an indefinite dependence on their help. Although the length of treatment varies with each client and his or her respective problems, one of the goals of therapy should be *to get out of therapy.*

Does the Therapist Work with You to Set Your Own Goals, Thereby Empowering You to Get Better at Your Pace?
Good therapists will assess your general problem fairly early and set at least some provisional goals on which to work. These usually take the form of small steps that you can tackle each week between sessions, or things that you can do to help you think about your issues and problems. If therapy takes place only in the office, the therapist is not moving you toward recovery. A good therapist is not a detective who is there to solve your problem per se, but rather to provide insight into the things you are doing or to help you understand how your situation and personal actions are contributing to your problems. A good therapist should serve as a catalyst for you helping yourself, rather than serve as your savior. Good therapists help you find your own answers and build on your own strengths, rather than just focussing on getting rid of your weaknesses.

Is the Therapist Willing to Let You Conduct an Interview Before Committing to His or Her Services?
Good therapists will allow you at least one "meeting" (often at a minimal or reduced charge) to check out the aforementioned information and to find out about their credentials, their counseling style, their personality, and the general "fit."

Most therapy should result in at least minor improvements in 6 to 8 weeks. If you find that you are getting nowhere, if you are repeating the same things over and over, or if you find problems with any of the above, do not be afraid to find another therapist.

Sources: "How to Choose a Therapist," *CBS This Morning,* July 24–26, 1996; David Meyers, *Psychology.* Chapter 16—"How to Choose a Therapist." Worth Publishing, pp. 537–572. James W. Kalat, "Treatment of Psychologically Troubled People," in *Introduction to Psychology,* Fourth Edition, eds. Brooks/Cole (1996), pp. 648–678.

What to Expect in Therapy

The first trip to a therapist can be extremely difficult. Most of us have misconceptions about what therapy is and about what it can do. That first visit is a verbal and mental sizing up between you and the therapist. You may not accomplish much in that first hour. If you decide that the therapist is not for you, you will at least have learned how to present your problem and what qualities you need in a therapist.

1. Before meeting a therapist, briefly explain your needs. Ask what the fee is. Arrive on time. Wear comfortable clothing. Expect to spend about an hour with the therapist during your first visit.
2. The therapist will want to take down your history and details about the problems that have brought you to therapy. Answer as honestly as possible. Many therapists will ask how you feel about aspects of your life. Do not be embarrassed to acknowledge your feelings.
3. Therapists are not mind readers. They cannot tell what you are thinking. It is therefore critical to the success of your treatment that you have enough trust in your therapist that you can be open and honest.
4. Do not expect the therapist to tell you what to do or how to behave. The responsibility for improved behavior lies with the individual.
5. Find out if the therapist will allow you to set your own therapeutic goals and timetables. Also, find out if, later in therapy, your therapist will allow you to determine what is and what is not helping you.
6. If, after your first visit (or even after several visits), you feel you cannot work with a therapist, you must say so. Do not worry about hurting the therapist's feelings. If there is a personality conflict or if you do not feel comfortable, the therapy will not be effective.

WHAT DO YOU THINK?

Have you ever thought about seeing a therapist? What made you decide to go—or not to go? If you didn't go, did things get better quickly? Do you think you might have worked out your problem faster if you saw a therapist?

Taking Charge
Managing Your Psychosocial Health

Psychosocial health is a complex concept. Finding the best way to help yourself achieve optimal psychosocial health requires careful introspection and planned action. Remembering the following points and acting upon them whenever possible may help you along the way.

CHECKLIST FOR CHANGE

✓ Consider life a constant process of discovery.

✓ Accept yourself as the best that you are able to be right now.

✓ Remember that nobody is perfect.

✓ Remember that the most difficult times in life occur during transitions and can be opportunities for growth even when they are painful.

✓ Be open to other perspectives.

✓ Recognize the sources of your own anxiety and act to reduce them.

✓ Ask for help when you need it; discuss your problems with others.

✓ Become sensitive to and aware of your own body's signals—take care of yourself.

✓ Find a meaning for your life and work toward achieving your goals.

✓ Develop strategies to get through problem situations.

✓ Remain open to emotional experiences—give yourself to today rather than always reserving yourself for tomorrow.

✓ Even when you fail, be proud of yourself for trying.

✓ Keep your sense of humor—learn to laugh at yourself.

✓ Never quit trying to grow, to experience, to love, and to live life to its fullest.

SUMMARY

- Psychosocial health is a complex phenomenon involving mental, emotional, social, and spiritual health.

- Many factors influence psychosocial health, including life experiences, family, the environment, other people, self-esteem, self-efficacy, and personality. Some of these are modifiable; others are not.

- Social bonds and social support networks contribute to the ability to cope with life's challenges.

- The mind-body connection is an important link in overall health and well-being.

- Common psychosocial problems include depression, obsessive-compulsive disorders, anxiety disorders

(including phobias, panic attacks, and posttraumatic stress syndrome), seasonal affective disorder, and schizophrenia.

- Suicide is a result of negative psychosocial reactions to life. People intending to commit suicide often give warning signs of their intentions. Such people can often be helped.

- Mental health professionals include psychiatrists, psychoanalysts, psychologists, clinical/psychiatric social workers, counselors, and psychiatric nurse specialists. Major types of therapy include behavioral, cognitive, family, and psychodynamic therapies.

DISCUSSION QUESTIONS

1. What is psychosocial health? What indicates that you either are or aren't psychosocially healthy? Why do you think the college environment may provide a real challenge to your psychosocial health?

2. Discuss the factors that influence your overall level of psychosocial health. What factors can you change? Which ones may be more difficult to change?

3. What steps could you take today to improve your psychosocial health? Which steps require long-term effort?

4. What factors appear to contribute to psychosocial difficulties and illnesses? Which of the more common psychosocial illnesses is likely to affect people in your age group?

5. What are the warning signs of suicide? Of depression? Why is depression so pervasive among young Americans

today? Why are some groups more vulnerable to suicide and depression than are others? What would you do if you heard a friend in the cafeteria say to no one in particular that he was going to "do the world a favor and end it all"?

6. Discuss the different types of health professionals and therapies. If you felt depressed about breaking off a long-term relationship, which professional and therapy do you think would be most beneficial? Explain your answer. What services are provided by your student health center? What fees are charged to students?

7. What psychosocial areas do you need to work on? Which are most important? Why? What actions can you take today?

APPLICATION EXERCISE

Reread the *What Do You Think?* scenario at the beginning of the chapter and answer the following questions.

1. How psychosocially healthy do you consider Marlene to be? As a friend, what could you do to help Marlene?

2. What factors may have contributed Marlene's behavior? Why might her friends be hesitant about reaching out to help her?

3. What services on your campus would be available to help Marlene improve her psychosocial health? What community services are available to nonstudents who have limited incomes?

OBJECTIVES

▶ Define stress and examine how stress may have direct and indirect effects on your immune system and on your overall health status.

▶ Explain the three phases of the general adaptation syndrome and describe what happens physiologically when you experience a real or perceived threat.

▶ Examine the health risks that may occur with chronic stress.

▶ Discuss psychosocial, environmental, and self-imposed sources of stress. Examine ways in which you might reduce risks from these stressors or inoculate yourself against stressful situations.

▶ Examine how evolving societal expectations may cause new kinds of stress.

▶ Examine the special stressors that affect college students and strategies for reducing risk.

▶ Explore techniques for coping with unavoidable stress, reducing exposure to stress, and making optimum use of positive stressors to promote growth and enrich life experiences.

3

Managing Stress

Coping with Life's Challenges

Mary and DeWayne have been dating for over two years, and they have discussed their eventual marriage. Mary's whole world centers on DeWayne and she thinks about him constantly. But DeWayne has seemed less interested in the relationship recently and has broken several dates, saying he has too much work to do. But on one occasion when he is supposedly studying, Mary spots DeWayne strolling into a restaurant with another woman. When she confronts him, DeWayne tells her that the relationship is over and that he's met someone else. Mary is devastated. She stops eating, starts skipping classes, and begins to drink heavily in the early afternoon. Her friends worry that she appears listless and depressed.

What thoughts does Mary probably have about the significance of her relationship with DeWayne? Are her perceptions valid? If you were Mary's friend, what would you do to help her cope with her loss? Why are changes in relationships so stressful for people? Is there a way to reduce the impact of these changes? If you were to experience a painful breakup, where on your campus could you go for help?

STRESS! There's no way to run or hide from it. It is a part of modern life. Whether stretched too thin by the demands of school, financial shortcomings, or the ever-changing world, each of us experiences the grip of stress in our own way.

Stress is a constant. Even as we sleep it encroaches on our psyche through noise, temperature changes, someone rustling around next to us in bed, or through incessant worries over things that need to be done. While the exact toll stress exacts from us during a lifetime is unknown, increasing evidence points to the fact that it is much more than a contemporary annoyance. Rather, it is a significant health hazard that can rob the body of nutrients, damage the cardiovascular system, raise blood pressure, and dampen the immune system's defenses, leaving us vulnerable to infections and a host of diseases. In addition, it can drain our emotional reserves, contribute to depression, anxiety, and irritability, and cause our social interactions to be punctuated with hostility, anger, and problem interactions.[1] Stress and stress-related mental disorders constitute areas of major concern in the United States.[2] Although much has been written about stress and nearly everyone talks about being "stressed," we have probably only just begun to understand the multifaceted nature of the stress response and its tremendous potential for harm or benefit.

Stress itself is neither positive nor negative. Rather, the difference lies in each individual's reaction to stress. One person's motivation can be another's nightmare. In this chapter, we will explore why and how we respond to stress as we do and the long- and short-term consequences of those reactions.

WHAT IS STRESS?

Many things that have contributed to making you who you are also have influenced how you respond to stressful events in your life. Stress reactions such as breaking out in a cold sweat before getting up in front of the class to speak, becoming anxious around people who speak too slowly or drive too cautiously, feeling nervous when meeting new people are all unique by-products of past experiences. Your family, friends,

Stress   Our mental and physical responses to change.

Stressor   A physical, social, or psychological event or condition that causes us to have to adjust to a specific situation.

Adjustment   Our attempt to cope with a given situation.

Strain   The wear and tear our bodies and minds sustain as we adjust to or resist a stressor.

Eustress   Stress that presents opportunities for personal growth.

Distress   Stress that can have a negative effect on health.

Homeostasis   A balanced physical state in which all the body's systems function smoothly.

Adaptive response   Form of adjustment in which the body attempts to restore homeostasis.

General adaptation syndrome (GAS)   The pattern followed by our physiological responses to stress, consisting of the alarm, resistance, and exhaustion phases.

environmental conditions, general health status, personality, and support systems affect how you respond to a given event.

But, actually, most stress is self-imposed and is usually the result of an internal state of emotional tension that occurs in response to the various demands of living. Stress may manifest itself in physiological responses to the demands placed upon us, and many researchers define *stress* as these responses.[3] Most current definitions state that **stress** is the mental and physical response of our bodies to the changes and challenges in our lives. Inherent in these definitions is the idea that we sometimes take ourselves and our lives too seriously; that we should loosen up, worry less, and gain greater control over our minds as well as our bodies.

★ A **stressor** is any physical, social, or psychological event or condition that causes our bodies to have to adjust to a specific situation. Stressors may be tangible, such as an angry parent or a disgruntled roommate, or intangible, such as the mixed emotions associated with meeting your significant other's parents for the first time. **Adjustment** is our attempt to cope with a given situation. As we try to adjust to a stressor, strain may develop. **Strain** is the wear and tear our bodies and minds sustain during the process of adjusting to or resisting a stressor.

Stress and strain are associated with most of our daily activities. Generally, positive stress, or stress that presents the opportunity for personal growth and satisfaction is called **eustress.** Getting married, starting school, beginning a career, developing new friendships, and learning a new physical skill all give rise to eustress. **Distress,** or negative stress, is caused by those events, such as financial problems, injury or illness, the death of a loved one, trouble at work, academic difficulties, and the breakup of a relationship, that result in debilitative stress and strain.

In many cases, we cannot prevent the occurrence of distress: like eustress, it is a part of life. However, we can train ourselves to recognize the events that cause distress and to anticipate the reactions we have to them. We can learn to practice prestress coping skills and to develop poststress management techniques. Development of both skills depends on our understanding of the major components of stress.

STRESS AND YOUR BODY

We all respond to stress with similar physiological bursts. Whenever we're surprised by a sudden stressor, such as someone swerving into our lane of traffic, the adrenal glands jump into action. These two almond-sized glands sitting atop our kidneys secrete adrenaline and other hormones into the bloodstream. As a result, the heart jumps into action with a burst of speed, breathing rate increases, blood pressure elevates, and the flow of blood to our muscles increases with a rapid release of blood sugars into the bloodstream. This sudden burst of energy and strength is believed to provide the extra edge that has helped generations of humans survive during adversity. Known as the *fight-or-flight response,* this physiological reaction is believed to be one of our most basic, innate survival instincts. It is a point at which our bodies go on the alert either to fight or to flee.

The General Adaptation Syndrome

What has just been described in very general terms is a complicated physiological response to stress in which our bodies move from **homeostasis,** a level of functioning in which systems operate smoothly and equilibrium is maintained, to one of crisis, in which the body attempts to return to homeostasis. This adjustment is referred to as an **adaptive response.** First characterized by Hans Selye in 1936, this internal fight to restore balance when upset is known as the **general adaptation syndrome (GAS)** (see Figure 3.1), which has three distinct phases: alarm, resistance, and exhaustion.[4]

Alarm Phase Whether real or perceived, when exposed to a stressor, the fight-or-flight reaction kicks into gear. Stress hormones flow into the body and it prepares to do battle with whatever is causing you to be upset. The subconscious perceptions and appraisal of the stressor stimulate the areas in the brain responsible for emotions. Emotional stimulation, in turn, starts the physical reactions that we associate with stress (see Figure 3.2 on the next page). This entire process takes but a few seconds.

Consider the following: Suppose that you are walking to your car after a late-night class on a dimly lit campus. As you pass a particularly dark area, you hear someone cough behind

Initial phase

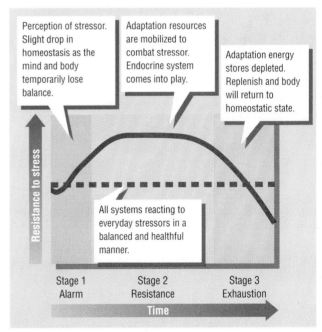

Perception of stressor. Slight drop in homeostasis as the mind and body temporarily lose balance.

Adaptation resources are mobilized to combat stressor. Endocrine system comes into play.

Adaptation energy stores depleted. Replenish and body will return to homeostatic state.

All systems reacting to everyday stressors in a balanced and healthful manner.

Resistance to stress

Stage 1 Alarm

Stage 2 Resistance

Stage 3 Exhaustion

Time

Figure 3.1
The General Adaptation Syndrome

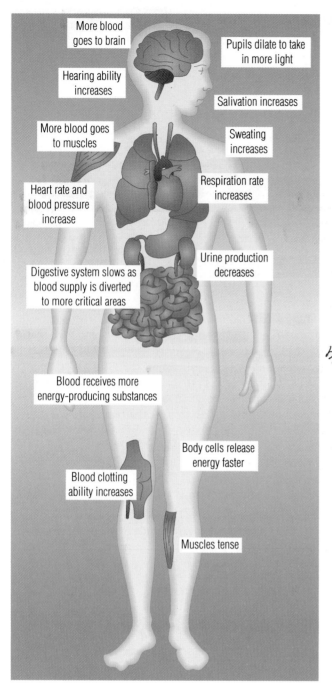

Figure 3.2

The General Adaptation Syndrome: Alarm Phase

More blood goes to brain

Pupils dilate to take in more light

Hearing ability increases

Salivation increases

More blood goes to muscles

Sweating increases

Heart rate and blood pressure increase

Respiration rate increases

Digestive system slows as blood supply is diverted to more critical areas

Urine production decreases

Blood receives more energy-producing substances

Body cells release energy faster

Blood clotting ability increases

Muscles tense

is Mrs. Fletcher, a woman in your class, who has been trying to stay close to you out of her own anxiety about walking alone in the dark. She screams and jumps back off the street, only to trip and fall. You look at her in startled embarrassment, help her to her feet, and nervously laugh about your reaction. You have just experienced what is commonly known as the *alarm* phase of stress response.

When the mind perceives a stressor (either real or imaginary), such as a potential attacker, the *cerebral cortex,* the region of the brain that interprets the nature of an event, is called to attention. If the cerebral cortex consciously or unconsciously perceives a threat, it triggers an instantaneous **autonomic nervous system (ANS)** response that prepares the body for action. The ANS is the portion of the central nervous system that regulates bodily functions that we do not normally consciously control, such as heart function, breathing, and glandular function. When we are stressed, the rate of all these bodily functions increases dramatically to give us the physical strength to protect ourselves against an attack, or to mobilize internal forces. The ANS has two branches. The **sympathetic nervous system,** one branch, begins to energize the body for either fight or flight by signaling the release of several stress hormones that speed the heart rate, increase the breathing rate, and trigger many other stress responses. The **parasympathetic nervous system,** the other branch, functions to slow all the systems stimulated by the stress response. Thus, the parasympathetic branch of the ANS serves as a system of checks and balances on the sympathetic branch. In a healthy person, these two branches work together in a balance that controls the negative effects of stress. However, long-term stress can cause this balance to become strained, and chronic physical problems can occur as stress reactions become the dominant forces in a person's body.

The responses of the sympathetic nervous system to stress involve a complex series of biochemical exchanges between different parts of the body. The **hypothalamus,** a section of the brain, functions as the control center of the sympathetic nervous system and determines the overall reaction to stressors. When the hypothalamus perceives that extra energy is needed to fight a stressor, it stimulates the adrenal glands, located near the top of the kidneys, to release the hormone **epinephrine,** also called **adrenaline.** Epinephrine causes more blood to be pumped with each beat of the heart, dilates the bronchioles (air sacs in the lungs) to increase oxygen intake, increases the breathing rate, stimulates the liver to release more glucose (which fuels muscular exertion), and dilates the pupils to improve visual sensitivity. The body is then poised to act immediately.

As epinephrine secretion increases, blood is diverted away from the digestive system, possibly causing nausea and cramping if the distress occurs shortly after a meal, and drying of nasal and salivary tissues, producing a dry mouth.

The stress response occurring during the alarm phase also provides for longer-term reaction to stress. The hypothalamus triggers the pituitary gland, which in turn releases another powerful hormone, **adrenocorticotrophic hormone (ACTH).** ACTH signals the adrenal glands to release **cortisol,** a hor-

release hormones

you and sense that this person is fairly close. You walk faster, only to hear the quickened footsteps of the other person. Your senses become increasingly alert as you note that there are no other people in the area. Your breathing quickens, your heart races, and you begin to perspire. The stranger is getting closer and closer. In desperation you stop, clutching your book bag in your hands, determined to use force if necessary to protect yourself. You turn around quickly and let out a blood-curdling yell. To your surprise, the only person you see

★ endorphins: released to relive pain and in exercise

mone that makes stored nutrients more readily available to meet energy demands. Finally, other parts of the brain and body release endorphins, the body's naturally occurring opiates, which relieve pain that may be caused by a stressor.

▶ *Resistance Phase*   The resistance phase of the GAS begins almost immediately after the alarm phase starts. In this phase, the body has reacted to the stressor and adjusted in a way that begins to allow the system to return to homeostasis. As the sympathetic nervous system is working to energize the body via the hormonal action of epinephrine, norepinephrine, cortisol, and other hormones, the parasympathetic nervous system is helping to keep these energy levels under control and returns the body to a normal level of functioning.

▶ *Exhaustion Phase*   In the exhaustion phase of the GAS, the physical and emotional energy used to fight a stressor has been depleted. The toll it takes on the body depends on the type of stress we experience or the period of time we're under stress. Short-term stress probably would not deplete all of a person's energy reserves, but chronic stress experienced over a period of time can create continuous states of alarm and resistance, resulting in total depletion of energy and susceptibility to illness. The key to warding off the effects of stress lies in what many researchers refer to as our *adaptation energy stores,* the physical and mental foundations of our ability to cope with stress.

Two levels of adaptation energy stores exist: deep and superficial. We apparently have little control over the deep adaptation energy stores, as their size appears to be preset by heredity. Superficial adaptation energy stores, however, are renewable and present the first line of defense against stress, as they are tapped into initially as the body fights stress. Only when the superficial energy stores are exhausted does the body tap into the deep energy stores. As our adaptation energy stores are depleted, we tire more quickly and require more rest. Without this replenishing sleep, the alarm and resistance phases eventually will limit our ability to rebound properly.

When stress is unresolved and our body adjusts to chronic stress, another hormone is released to provide assistance. Also released by the adrenal glands, cortisol remains in the bloodstream for longer periods of time due to a slower metabolic responsiveness. Over time, without relief, cortisol can con-

Many people enjoy the adrenaline rush of a strenuous and challenging workout. Such a workout also can help replenish the energy stores the body uses in adapting and adjusting to negative stressors.

tribute to reductions in immunocompetence, or the ability of the immune system to respond to various onslaughts, blood pressure can remain dangerously elevated, and our body systems become unable to respond with the same vigor as they once did. The net effect? Greater chance of minor illnesses at

---

Autonomic nervous system (ANS)   The portion of the central nervous system that regulates bodily functions that we do not normally consciously control.

Sympathetic nervous system   Branch of the autonomic nervous system responsible for stress arousal.

Parasympathetic nervous system   Part of the autonomic nervous system responsible for slowing systems stimulated by the stress response.

Hypothalamus   A section of the brain that controls the sympathetic nervous system and directs the stress response.

Epinephrine   Also called adrenaline, a hormone that stimulates body systems in response to stress.

Adrenocorticotrophic hormone (ACTH)   A pituitary hormone that stimulates the adrenal glands to secrete cortisol.

Cortisol   Hormone released by the adrenal glands that makes stored nutrients more readily available to meet energy demands.

Immunocompetence   The ability of the immune system to respond to assaults.

The Consequences of Stress

No matter how we try to control it, manage it, or avoid it, stress is an inevitable part of our daily lives. It is generally accepted that stress is pervasive and insidious, and can lead to a wide array of negative health consequences. While nearly everyone knows that stress has negative effects on health, few really know just how damaging too much stress over too long a time can really be. Consider the following:

✓ According to the National Mental Health Association, between 75 and 90 percent of all visits to physicians are stress related.

✓ Job stress is a major health factor, costing businesses an estimated $150 billion annually. Stress-related disorders are a major cause of rapidly increasing health-care costs. This compares with approximately $104 million for cancer, $99 million for respiratory diseases, and $43 million for AIDS.

✓ Taken together, the estimated 27 million adults and more than eight million children and youth with a diagnosable mental or emotional disorder outnumber those with cancer, heart disease, and lung disease combined.

✓ Nearly half of all Americans suffer from a mental or addictive disorder; many of which are stress related.

✓ According to the National Institutes of Mental Health, the top sources of stress include:
Overscheduled daily calendars
Job stress/demands
Lack of play/down time
Lack of time with family/friends
Insufficient funds

✓ Stress and stress-related mental disorders (specifically, clinically relevant depression, anxiety, anger, and substance abuse) constitute areas of major concern in the United States and are the topic of *Healthy People 2000* and *2010* as well as other national initiatives.

Source: Glenn R. Schiraldi, Thomas Spalding, and Craig Hofford. "Expanding Health Educators' Roles to Meet Critical Needs in Stress Management and Mental Health." *Journal of Health Education.* 29 (2) (1998):68–74.

one end of the continuum; greater risk of life-threatening disease at the other end.

Stress management, therefore, is dependent on an ability to replenish superficial stores and conserve deep stores. Besides getting adequate amounts of rest, adaptation energy stores can be replenished by aerobic exercise, finding a balance between work and relaxation, practicing good nutritional habits, setting realistic goals, and establishing and maintaining supportive relationships.

WHAT DO YOU THINK?

What are the greatest sources of stress for you right now? What can you do to keep your superficial adaptation energy stores high and reduce your risks of becoming run down? Have you ever noticed that you tend to get sick more often during certain times? Why might this occur?

STRESS AND YOUR HEALTH

Although much has been written about the negative effects of stress, researchers have only recently begun to untangle the complex web of physical and emotional interactions that actually cause the body to break down over time. As a result, stress is often described generically as a "disease of prolonged arousal" that often leads to other negative health effects. Nearly all systems of the body become potential targets for this onslaught, and the long-term effects may be devastating.

Much of the initial impetus for studying the health effects of stress came from indirect observations. Cardiologists in the Framingham Heart Study and other research projects noted that highly stressed individuals seemed to experience significantly greater risks for cardiovascular disease and hypertension.[5] Monkeys exposed to high levels of unpredictable stressors in studies showed significantly increased levels of disease and mortality.[6] In a landmark study, Jeremko (1984) observed that chronic stress activation can result in headaches, asthma, hypertension, ulcers, lower back pain, and other medical conditions, a finding substantiated by a meta-analysis of over one hundred similar studies during the 1980s.[7,8] This work supports an earlier Harvard study, which concluded that mental health was the most important predictor of physical health.[9] While the battle over the legitimacy of these observations continues to be waged in research labs across the country, the theory that chronic stress leads to increased susceptibility to certain ailments has gained credibility.

Stress and CVD Risks

Since Friedman and Rosenman's classic study of Type A and Type B personalities and heart disease in the late 1960s and early 1970s (discussed later in this chapter), researchers have tried time and time again to definitively link personality, toxic core, anger, depression, and a host of other variables to heart disease.[10–12] Although the results are compelling, it is generally assumed that too much stress contributes to (1) increased plaque buildup in the arteries due to elevations in cholesterol levels, (2) hardening of the arteries, (3) alterations in heart rhythms, (4) increased blood pressure, and (5) difficulties in cardiovascular system responsiveness due to all of the above.

Stress and Impaired Immunity

Although the health effects of prolonged stress provide dramatic evidence of the direct and indirect impact of stress on body organs, researchers continue to seek more definitive answers about the exact physiological mechanisms that lead to specific diseases. The science of **psychoneuroimmunology (PNI)** attempts to analyze the relationship between the mind's response to stress and the ability of the immune system to function effectively.

Much of the preliminary PNI data on stress and immune functioning have focused on the idea that during periods of prolonged stress, elevated levels of adrenal hormones destroy or reduce the ability of the white blood cells known as *natural killer T cells* to aid in the immune response. When killer T cells are suppressed, illnesses have a greater chance of gaining a foothold in the body. In addition to killer T-cell suppression, many other body processes are disrupted and overall disease-fighting capacity is reduced. Several studies have supported the relationship between increased stress levels and greater risk of infectious and chronic diseases. Many of these early studies are summarized as follows:[13]

- Accumulating evidence shows that stress lowers the body's resistance to upper respiratory infections as well as to herpes.[14]
- Several studies have shown increased risk for cancer and other chronic ailments after significant loss, grief, and depressive episodes, as well as after significant "other" stressors. Those who seek support from others, rather than bottling up their fears, tended to survive longer than their isolated counterparts.[15]
- Other studies show that students' disease-fighting mechanisms are weaker during high stress times, such as exam weeks and on days when they are upset. In one experiment, a stress experience increased the severity of symptoms by volunteers who were knowingly infected with a cold virus. In another, 47 percent of subjects living stress-filled lives developed colds after a virus was dropped into their noses, but only 27 percent of those living relatively stress-free lives caught colds.[16]

Psychoneuroimmunology (PNI) Science of the interaction between the mind and the immune system.

Although several studies have supported the hypothesis of a relationship between increased stress levels and greater risk of disease in times of grief, social disruption, poor mood, and so forth, there is much to be learned about possible mediating factors in this process.[17] Other studies have shown no increased risk for disease among people suffering from prolonged arousal by stressors.[18]

Stress and Your Mind

When people are stressed, it is difficult for them to think straight, concentrate, or control certain emotional reactions. Although difficult to measure directly, stress may be one of the single greatest contributors to mental disability and emotional dysfunction in the United States. Whether it be from lost work productivity, difficulties in relationships, substance abuse, displaced anger, or a host of other problems, stress overload does much more than cause heart rate to soar. In fact, the cumulative evidence suggests a strong relationship between stress and the potential for negative mental health reactions. Consider the following:[19]

- Numerous researchers have demonstrated that provoking stressors, interacting with low self-esteem and/or maladaptive coping styles, predict depression and/or anxiety.
- Dysfunctional anger results from the interaction between exposure to stressors and maladaptive thoughts and behaviors.
- Depression and drug abuse are highly correlated with excessive exposure to stress.
- Among college students, low self-esteem or depression and concerns about stress and health were identified as unresolved problems for 35 percent and 20 percent of the respondents, respectively.
- Persons with high nervous tension have increased risk for mental illness, suicide, and coronary heart disease.
- A recent national study of comorbidity in the United States among persons aged 15 to 54 found that almost half of all Americans will suffer a mental and addictive disorder during their lifetime. Many of these disorders are believed to be stress related.
- Mental illness is on the increase in almost all segments of U.S. society.

SOURCES OF STRESS

Both eustress and distress have many sources. These include psychosocial factors, such as changes, hassles, pressure, inconsistent goals and objectives, conflict, overload, and burnout; environmental stressors, such as natural and human-made disasters; and self-imposed stress. We'll look at each factor in more detail in this section.

Psychosocial Sources of Stress

As you learned in the previous chapter, psychosocial health relates to the mental, emotional, social, and spiritual dimensions of health. These dimensions define how we perceive our lives, relate to one another, and react to stress. Psychosocial stress refers to the factors in our daily lives that cause stress, such as our interactions with others, the expectations we and others have of ourselves, and the social conditions we work in and play in. Some of these stressors present very real threats to our mental and/or physical well-being; others cause us to worry about things that may never happen. Still other stressors result from otherwise good psychosocial events—being around someone you're attracted to, meeting new friends, or moving to a new and better apartment.

▶ **Change** Any time there is change in your normal daily routine, whether good or bad, you will experience stress. The more changes you experience and the more adjustments you must make, the greater the degree of stress. In 1967, Drs. Thomas Holmes and Richard Rahe analyzed the social readjustments experienced by over 5,000 patients, noting which events seemed to occur just prior to disease onset.[20] They determined that certain events (both positive and negative) were predictive of increased risk for illness. They called their scale for predicting stress overload and the likelihood of illness the Social Readjustment Rating Scale (SRRS).[21] The

SRRS has since served as the model for the development of scales for certain groups, including college-aged students, as shown in Table 3.1. Although many other factors must be considered, it is generally believed that the more of these you have, the more you need to change your behaviors or situation before problems occur.

▶ **Hassles** While Holmes and Rahe focused on such major sources of stress as a death in the family, psychologists such as Richard Lazarus have more recently focused on petty annoyances, irritations, and frustrations, collectively referred to as hassles, as sources of stress.[22] Minor hassles—losing your keys, having the grocery bag rip on the way to the door, or slipping and falling in front of everyone as you walk to your seat in a new class—may seem unimportant, but the cumulative effects of these minor hassles may be harmful in the long run.

▶ **Pressure** Pressure occurs when we feel forced to speed up, intensify, or shift the direction of our behavior to meet a higher standard of performance.[23] Pressures can be based on our personal goals and expectations or on a concern about what others may think of us. Pressure can also come from outside influences. Among the most significant and consistent of these are seemingly relentless demands from society that we compete and that we be all that we can be, particularly in

---

TABLE 3.1
Chronic Stressors for College Students

Here are several chronic stressors often experienced by college students. Each has the potential to cause serious health problems, particularly if experienced on a fairly regular basis (i.e., at least two or three times per week for the last month).

1. Roommate conflict	19. Friends with problems
2. Homesickness	20. Parental problems/family problems
3. Friend conflict	21. Not enough sex/intimacy
4. Writing major papers	22. Behind in schoolwork
5. Dieting	23. Problem with lover
6. Money/financial problems	24. Not enough exercise
7. Long-distance relationship	25. Conflict with parents
8. Juggle school/job	26. Academic performance
9. Time management	27. Overweight
10. Noisy dorm or apartment	28. Don't fit in; no friends
11. No car or car not working	29. Living/housing situations
12. Underweight	30. Tuition bills/book costs
13. Uncertainty over whether you are in the right major	31. Health problems/not feeling well
14. Miss distant friends	32. Difficult class or instructor
15. Family illness	33. Unsure of job future
16. Loneliness	34. Not enough sleep
17. Job pressures	35. Problem with drugs/alcohol
18. Privacy (lack of)	

Source: Adapted from L. Towbes and L. Cohen, "Chronic Stress in the Lives of College Students: Scale Development and Prospective Predictions of Distress." Journal of Youth and Adolescence 25, no. 2 (1996): 202–203. By permission of Plenum Publishing Corporation.

meeting our parents' expectations.[24] The forces that push us to compete for the best grades, the nicest cars, the most attractive significant others, and the highest paying jobs create significant pressure to be the personification of American success. When we are pressured into doing something we don't want to do (for example, studying when everyone else is going to a movie), significant frustration can occur.

▶ **Inconsistent Goals and Behaviors**   For many of us, negative stress effects are magnified when there is a disparity between our goals (what we value or hope to obtain in life) and our behaviors (actions or activities that may or may not lead us to achieving these goals). For instance, you may want good grades, and your family may expect them. But if you party and procrastinate throughout the term, your behaviors are inconsistent with your goals, and significant stress in the form of guilt, last-minute frenzy before exams, and disappointing grades may result. On the other hand, if you want to dig in and work, and are committed to getting good grades, much of your negative stress may be eliminated or reduced. Thwarted goals may lead to frustration, and frustration has been shown to be a significant disrupter of homeostasis. Determining whether our behaviors are consistent with goal attainment is an essential component of our efforts to maintain a balance in our lives.

▶ **Conflict**   Conflict occurs when we are forced to make difficult decisions concerning two or more competing motives, behaviors, or impulses or when we are forced to face two incompatible demands, opportunities, needs, or goals.[25] What if your best friends all choose to smoke marijuana and you don't want to smoke but fear rejection? Conflict often occurs as our values are tested. College students who are away from home for the first time often face conflict between parental values and their own set of developing beliefs.

(handwritten: ++ +- --) → paper due and test (no positive option)

▶ **Overload**   Overload occurs when you suffer from excessive time pressure, excessive responsibility, lack of support, or excessive expectations of yourself and those around you. Have you ever felt that you had so many responsibilities that you couldn't possibly begin to fulfill them all? Have you longed for a weekend when you could just curl up and read a good book or take time out with friends and not feel guilty? These feelings typically occur when a person has been under continued stress for a period of time and is suffering from overload. Students suffering from overload may experience anxiety about

(handwritten: △ growth → short lived)
(handwritten: △ conflicting interests going out vs. homework)

Overload   A condition in which we feel overly pressured by demands made on us.

Burnout   Physical and mental exhaustion caused by excessive stress.

Background distressors   Environmental stressors that we may be unaware of.

tests, poor self-concept, a desire to drop classes or to drop out of school, and other problems. In severe cases, in which they are unable to see any solutions to their problems, students may suffer from depression or turn to substance abuse.

▶ **Burnout**   People who regularly suffer from overload, frustration, and disappointment may eventually begin to experience **burnout, a state of physical and mental exhaustion caused by excessive stress.** People involved in the "helping professions," such as teaching, social work, drug counseling, nursing, and psychology, appear to experience high levels of burnout, as do people such as police officers and air-traffic controllers who work in high-pressure, dangerous jobs.

▶ **Other Forms of Psychosocial Stress**   Other forms of psychosocial stress include problems with overcrowding, discrimination, and such socioeconomic events as inflation, unemployment, or poverty. People of different ethnic backgrounds may face disproportionately heavy impact from these sources of stress (see Health in a Diverse World box on page 60).

Environmental Stress

Environmental stress results from events occurring in our physical environment as opposed to our social environment. Environmental stressors include natural disasters, such as floods, earthquakes, hurricanes, forest fires, and industrial disasters, such as chemical spills, accidents at nuclear power plants, and explosions. Often as damaging as one-time disasters are **background distressors,** such as noise, air, and water pollution, although we may be unaware of them and their effects may not become apparent for decades. As with other distressors, our bodies respond to environmental distressors with the general adaptation syndrome. People who cannot escape background distressors may exist in a constant resistance phase, which may contribute to the development of stress-related disorders.

·········· **WHAT DO YOU THINK?**

What are two things that currently cause you significant stress? Can you make changes to reduce stress levels? Are others affected by these same problems?

Self-Imposed Stress

▶ **Self-Concept and Stress**   How we feel about ourselves, our attitudes toward others, and our perceptions and interpretations of the stressors in our lives are all part of the psychological component of stress. Also included are the defense or coping mechanisms we have learned to use in various stressful situations.

Tibetan Medicine Strikes a Balance

As society becomes faster paced, more technological, and ever-more competitive, we are bombarded by daily stressors. As we get older and take on increasing amounts of responsibility, expectations for us increase by leaps and bounds. We are told time and again to make sure to "stop and smell the roses," but who has time?

According to Tibetan medicine, our health depends on finding balance in our lives—specifically, finding a balance among our three bodily "humors." These refer to the water humor (*bad-kan*), responsible for support and cohesion; the fire humor (*mkhris-pa*), responsible for heat and digestion; and the wind humor (*rlung*), responsible for breath and mobility. When these humors fall out of balance, disease results. To maintain balance, Tibetan physicians look to our be-

havior as a catalyst for health or disease. Their belief that the mind and body are one makes it mandatory that our behavior is such that it encourages equilibrium. For example, doctors prescribe changes in lifestyle and diet to effect change in the body. Behaviors considered unhealthy may be evil deeds in present or past lives, sexual indiscretions, or unhealthy diets. In fact, in a recent art exhibit on Tibetan medicine held in Washington, D.C., one of the paintings illustrating the general rules of healthy conduct specified: "Do not take what is not yours," "Do not lie," "Do not gossip," and "Do not be covetous."

The information process that takes place when a Tibetan physician diagnoses an illness differs from that utilized in the United States. State-of-the-art diagnostic tools are absent, superseded only by the physician's keen sense of observation and conversation. Tibetan physicians use their senses of smell, touch, sight, and hearing to draw their conclusions.

Tibetan physicians begin learning the process at about 13 years of age and continue for the next 11 years, following a strict daily regimen that starts at 4 A.M. and ends at 10 P.M. Special training is provided in subjects such as pulse diagnosis and herb identification, as herbs

are key in Tibetan medicines. Four-year internships are then required before one becomes a full-fledged physician.

In the United States there is an increased interest in Tibetan medicine, just as there is in all forms of alternative medical care. Our newspapers, magazines, medical journals, and even yearly visits to doctors point to the importance of finding a balance. More than ever, the American medical community is urging the general public to eat a balanced diet, to exercise, and to avoid harmful habits such as smoking, drinking irresponsibly, and abusing substances. Like the Tibetan physicians, we are being urged to use our senses, and common sense, to glean the healthiest results. Although the alternative approach of Tibetan medicine may be seen as too extreme by many, the message of *balance* as the central theme of care appeals to others. Above all else, the arrival of Tibetan medicine in the United States serves as another indication of the growth of alternative care and the blending of cultures within this country.

Source: Susan Okie, "The Washington Post," *Health Supplement,* October 27, 1998, pp. 15–19.

The psychological system that governs our responses to stressors is called the **cognitive stress system.**[26] Our cognitive stress system serves to recognize stressors, evaluate them on the basis of self-concept, past experiences, and emotions; and make decisions regarding how to cope with them.

Our sensory organs serve as input channels for any information reaching the brain. From that point on, attention to the problem, memory, reasoning processes, and problem solving are organized in various parts of the brain before we act on the stressor. Because learning and memory involve the changing of various proteins in brain neurons, the emotions experienced during the stress response also "tickle" the memory storage neurons and contribute to our responses. Behaviorally, we will respond to the stressor in ways consistent with our memories of similar situations.

Self-esteem is closely related to the emotions engendered by past experiences. People with low self-esteem are more likely to become victims of helpless anger, an emotion experi-

enced by people who have not learned to express anger in appropriate ways. People suffering helpless anger have usually learned that they are wrong to feel anger; therefore, instead of learning to express their anger in healthy ways, they turn it inward. They may "swallow" their anger in food, alcohol, or other drugs, or may act in other self-destructive ways. A recent national priority of the former Secretary of Health and Human Services of the United States, Donna Shalala, is a program called "Girl Power," designed to improve the self-esteem of young women between the ages of 9 and 14, a time when low self-esteem is thought to trigger a host of negative health behaviors.

Research indicates that self-esteem significantly affects various disease processes. People with low self-esteem create a self-imposed distressor that can impair the immune system's ability to combat disease. Some researchers believe that chronic distress can depress the immune system and thus increase the symptoms of such diseases as acquired immune deficiency syndrome (AIDS), herpes, multiple sclerosis, and Epstein-Barr syndrome.

▶ *Personality Types and Hardiness* A person's personality may contribute to the kind and degree of self-imposed stress he or she experiences. The coronary disease-prone personality was first described in 1974 by physicians Meyer Friedman and Ray Rosenman in their book *Type A Behavior and Your Heart.*[27] Although their 9-year project is now considered controversial, it is the basis for much current research.

Friedman and Rosenman identified two stress-related personality types: Type A and Type B. Type A personalities are hard-driving, competitive, anxious, time-driven, impatient, angry, and perfectionist. Type B personalities are relaxed and noncompetitive. According to Rosenman and Friedman, people with Type A characteristics are more prone to heart attacks than are their Type B counterparts.

Researchers today believe that more needs to be discovered about Type A and Type B personalities before we can say that all Type As will have greater risks for heart disease than will Type Bs. First of all, most people are not one personality type or the other all of the time. Second, there are many other unexplained variables that must be explored, such as why some Type A personalities seem to thrive in stress-filled environments. Now labeled Type C personalities, these individuals appear to succeed more often than Type B personalities and have good health even while displaying Type A patterns of behavior.

Critics of these categories for stress risk argue that attempts to explain ill health by means of personal behavioral patterns have so far been crude. For example, researchers at Duke University contend that the Type A personality may be more complex than previously described. They have identified a "toxic core" in some Type A personalities. People who have this toxic core are angry, distrustful of others, and have above-average levels of cynicism. People who are angry and hostile often have below-average levels of social support and other increased risks for ill health. It may be this toxic core rather than the hard-driving nature of the Type A personality that makes people more prone to self-imposed stress and its consequences.[28]

Psychologist Susanne Kobasa has identified **psychological hardiness** as a characteristic that has helped some people negate self-imposed stress associated with Type A behavior. Psychologically hardy people are characterized by *control, commitment,* and *challenge.*[29] People with a sense of control are able to accept responsibility for their behaviors and to make changes in behaviors that they discover to be debilitating. People with a sense of commitment have good self-

Achieving a sense of accomplishment at a young age encourages the development of positive self-esteem, which can alleviate some of the self-imposed pressures experienced later in life.

esteem and understand their purpose in life. People with a sense of challenge see changes in life as stimulating opportunities for personal growth.

Modification of Type A behavior is possible because some of this behavior is "learned." Some Type A people are able to reduce their hurried behavior and become more tolerant, more patient, and better humored. Unfortunately, many people do not decide to modify their Type A habits until after they have become ill or suffered a heart attack or other circulatory system distress. Prevention of heart and circulatory disorders resulting from stress entails recognizing and changing dangerous behaviors before damage is done.

▶ *Self-Efficacy and Control* Whether people are able to cope successfully with stressful situations often depends on their level of self-efficacy, or belief in their skills and performance abilities.[30] If people have been successful in mastering similar problems in the past, they will be more likely to believe in their own effectiveness in future situations. Similarly, people who have repeatedly tried and failed may lack confidence in their abilities to deal with life's problems. In some cases, this insecurity may prevent them from trying to cope.

In addition, people who believe they lack control in a situation may become easily frustrated and give up. Those

Cognitive stress system The psychological system that governs our emotional responses to stress.

Psychological hardiness A personality characteristic characterized by control, commitment, and challenge.

who feel they have no personal control over anything tend to have an *external locus of control* and a low level of self-efficacy. People who are confident their behavior will influence the ultimate outcome of events tend to have an *internal locus of control*. People who feel that they have limited control over their lives tend to have higher levels of stress.

STRESS AND THE COLLEGE STUDENT

Stress related to college life is not caused only by pressure to excel academically. College students experience numerous distressors, including changes related to being away from home for the first time, climatic differences between home and school, pressure to make friends in a new and sometimes intimidating setting, the feeling of anonymity imposed by large classes, test-taking anxiety, and pressures related to time management. (See Skills for Behavior Change box.)

College students may be especially vulnerable because they are in a period of developmental transition, facing several key developmental tasks: (1) achieving emotional independence from family; (2) choosing and preparing for a career; (3) preparing for a relationship, commitment, and/or family life; and (4) developing an ethical system. These tasks require that college students develop new social roles and modify old ones, changes that can result in role strain, a major aspect of chronic stress.

In a large study of chronic stressors, male and female college students differed significantly in the things they perceived to be significant stressors.[31,32] Women indicated that (1) trying to diet, (2) being overweight, (3) having an overload of school work, and (4) gaining weight were among their most frequent stressors. Men, on the other hand, tended to list the following items as major stressors much more

SKILLS FOR BEHAVIOR CHANGE

Overcoming Test-Taking Anxiety

Doing well on a test is an ability needed far beyond your college days. Many careers require special exams. Tests are a fact of life in government, insurance, medicine, and other fields. And stress is a fact of tests!

Here are some helpful hints that you will find useful now and in the future. Give them a try on your next exam.

BEFORE THE EXAM:

1. Manage your time. Plan to study beginning a week before your test (longer if a career exam). The more advance studying, the less anxiety you will feel. The final night should be limited to review. Arrive at the test a half hour early for a final run through. You will find that this will ease your anxiety and increase your confidence.
2. Get adequate sleep. You need to be alert, so try to get a little extra sleep for a few nights before your exam.
3. Eat well before the exam. Avoid all sugary foods the day before the test and also those foods that might upset your stomach. You want to be feeling your best.
4. Take caffeine about an hour before the test. Research shows that caffeine promotes alertness, motor performance, and the capacity for work, as well as a decrease in fatigue. A cup or two of coffee, tea, or a cola drink is sufficient. Some people shouldn't use caffeine. Avoid it if you are one of the small percentage that it leaves feeling shaky and on edge for hours or if you regularly do not use caffeinated products. Test day is not the day to find out how your body reacts to caffeine.

DURING THE TEST:

1. Use time management during the test. If you have 60 minutes to answer 30 multiple choice questions, you might decide to spend the first 45 minutes taking the test (1½ minutes per question) and 15 minutes reviewing your answers (30 seconds per question). Hold yourself to this schedule. After 15 minutes, you should have completed the first 10 questions, etc. If you don't know an answer, or the question is taking too long, skip it and move on. Since you allotted yourself time at the end to review, you will have the time to go back.

    Test-makers usually allow sufficient time to complete and review a test. However, if you feel that you are a slow reader and may need more time, talk to your teacher or the test administrator *before* the exam.
2. Slow down. When you open your test book, always write RTFQ (Read the Full Question) at the top. Make sure you understand the question.

frequently than their female counterparts: (1) being underweight, (2) problems relating to commuting to school, (3) not having someone to date, (4) not enough sex, (5) being behind in schoolwork, (6) not enough friends, and (7) concerns about drug or alcohol use.[33]

Most colleges offer stress management workshops through their health centers or student counseling departments. You should not ignore the symptoms of stress overload. If you experience one or more of the following symptoms, you should act promptly to reduce their impact.

- Difficulty keeping up with classes or difficulty concentrating on and finishing tasks
- Frequent clashes with close friends, family, or intimate partners about trivial issues such as housekeeping
- Persistent hostile or angry feelings; increased frustration with minor annoyances
- Increased boredom and fatigue; a general sense of "the blahs"
- Disinterest in social activities or tendency to avoid others
- Increased use of alcohol or other drugs
- Sleep disturbances, problems with eating
- Difficulty in maintaining an intimate relationship
- Disinterest in sexual relationships or inability to participate in satisfactory sexual relationships
- Frequent headaches, backaches, muscle aches, or tightness in the stomach
- Problems making decisions; increased procrastination
- Frequent indigestion, diarrhea, or urination
- Frequent colds and infections
- Tendency to be intolerant of minor differences of opinion
- Hunger and cravings or tendency to overeat or to eat while thinking of other things
- Inability to listen or tendency to jump from subject to subject in conversation
- Stuttering or other speech difficulties
- Becoming prone to accidents

········ WHAT DO YOU THINK?

How many of these psychological and emotional reactions have you experienced? Which reactions do you think are the most damaging to you and to your relationships with others? Which ones would be the easiest to change? What actions could you take immediately to cope with these problems? What could you do to cope with these problems in the long run?

STRESS MANAGEMENT

In addition to creating potentially stressful situations, college can give you the opportunity to evaluate and change how you manage stress. Stress can be challenging or debilitating depending upon how we learn to view it. The most effective way to avoid problems is to learn a number of skills known collectively as stress management. Stress management consists primarily of finding balance in our lives. We balance rest, relaxation, exercise, nutrition, work, school, family, finances, and social activities. As we balance our lives, we make the choice to react constructively to our stressors. Robert Eliot, a cardiologist and stress researcher, offers two rules for people trying to cope with life's challenges: (1) "Don't sweat the small stuff," and (2) Remember that "it's all small stuff."[34]

Dealing with Stress

Dealing with stress involves examining how you are currently responding to stressors and evaluating various methods of coping with these stressors. Often we cannot change the requirements at our college, assignments in class, or unexpected distressors. Although the facts cannot be changed, our reactions to the distressors in our lives can be.

▶ *Assessing Your Stressors* After recognizing a stressor, you need to assess it. Can you alter the circumstances in any way to reduce the amount of distress you are experiencing, or must you change your behavior and reactions to the stressor to reduce your stress levels? For example, if five term papers for five different courses are due during the semester, your professors are unlikely to drop their requirements. You can, however, change your behavior by beginning the papers early and spacing them over time to avoid last-minute stress.

▶ *Changing Your Responses* Changing your responses requires practice and emotional control. If your roommate is habitually messy and this causes you stress, you can choose among several responses. You can express your anger by yelling, you can pick up the mess and leave a nasty note, or you can defuse the situation with humor. The first response that comes to mind is not always the best response. Stop before reacting to gain the time you need to find an appropriate response. Ask yourself, "What is to be gained from my response?"

Many people change their responses to potentially stressful events through *cognitive coping strategies*. These strategies help them prepare for stressors through gradual exposure to increasingly higher stress levels.

▶ *Learning to Cope* Everyone copes with stress in different ways. For some people, drinking and taking drugs helps them to cope. Others choose to get help from counselors. Still others try to keep their minds off stress or to engage in positive activities such as exercise or relaxation techniques. Stress inoculation is one of the newer techniques for helping people prepare for stressful events. Through stress inoculation, people are able to prepare for potential stressful events ahead of time. For example, if you were petrified over speaking in front of a class, practicing in front of friends, in front of a video camera,

Yearning for Peace and Quiet

Do you ever find yourself yearning for peace and quiet? Fewer hours lost waiting in traffic? Fewer bodies to bump into while shopping at the local mall? Does it seem as though "getting away from it all" is more and more difficult to attain? This "press of humanity" is not just your imagination. Of all the challenges of the twenty-first century, none is more far-reaching than the explosion of the human population, all pushing and shoving for increasingly scarce "pieces of the global pie." One hundred years ago, 1.6 billion people lived on the earth. In 1999, our planetary population grew to over 6 billion. In 50 years that number is expected to climb to 8.9 billion. While environmentalists point to the obvious implications this trend has on dwindling resources, some researchers have started to examine the stressful side effects a growing population may have on us individually.

According to Gordon Hempton, a professional sound tracker, the crush of humanity poses threats to our psyche and physical health that may well go undetected. He points to the stress from constant, intrusive noise, and the fact that there are few places to which we can run to hide from it all. Whether it's the smoke stacks of coal-fired electric plants dotting the Southeastern landscape; the rhythmic booming of oil well pumps in the west; or the rumblings from the nearest cities, highways, power transmission lines, industry, and mining that interrupt the solitude of the Southwestern deserts, Hempton finds no peace. Fifteen years ago, he documented twenty-one spots in Washington state where he could reliably capture 15 minutes of natural sounds, uninterrupted by the likes of roaring jets, humming trucks, and barking dogs. Now he finds only three. Numerous news reports on vacation destinations in recent summers indicate that visits to our National Parks have increased so significantly that the walking trails in the wilderness today now resemble more closely the waiting lines at a theme park than they do the pristine paths of solitude sought by the overworked seeking a serene escape.

What this means is that it is becoming more and more difficult for people to "escape" the pressures and trappings of their daily routines, which leaves them vulnerable to burnout and other stress-related illnesses. While the global population compromises the planet's ability to sustain itself, the day-to-day impact of too many people in our cities, on our roads, in our schools, and in our recreation areas may also result in more individualized stress responses. As our resources dwindle and the population grows, such things as road rage and other displays of intolerance will likely become more pervasive.

Tomorrow's stressors may, in fact, be of the human kind. Already we see signs of unrelenting stimuli and the accommodations we have to make to adjust: cell phones going off at dinner or at the theatre, long lines at stores, more people invading our personal spaces, more crowded cubicles at work, more difficulty getting a quiet place for a break, and medical appointments that have to be made four months in advance because that's the only next available opening. Sound imposing?

For persons like Hempton and others who crave solitude and quiet, the press of humanity and its trappings can be overwhelming. The larger question, though, concerns not so much whether 6 billion or 16 billion people can be crammed onto the planet, but rather, the quality of life they will have. Imagine fewer and fewer birds singing and fewer and fewer quiet summer nights when you can hear frogs croaking or crickets chirping.

STUDENTS SPEAK UP:

What signs of population overload have you experienced? Where do you go to escape the stressors of daily life?

Source: Adapted from David Foster, "It's Getting Pretty Noisy on Earth," Associated Press, June 27, 1999. Section 1, p. 1.

---

or other strategies may *inoculate* or prevent the chances of your freezing up on the day of the presentation. Some health experts compare stress inoculation to a vaccine given to protect against a disease. Regardless of how you cope with a given situation, your conscious effort to deal with this situation is an important step in stress management.

▶ *Downshifting*   More and more people recognize that today's lifestyle is more hectic and pressure-packed than ever before, and that much of the stress in their lives is due in great part to trying to keep up with this lifestyle. Many of these people are also questioning whether "having it all" is worth it anymore. In recent years, a number of top executives have said "enough" and have voluntarily left their high-paying jobs to lead a simpler life. While you may argue that it is easy to lead a simple life with a large bank account, the truth is that people of all walks of life and vastly different financial statuses are taking a step back and simplifying their lives. They are following a trend known as **downshifting.** Moving from a large urban area to the country or to small towns,

> **Downshifting**   Conscious attempt to simplify life in an effort to reduce the stresses and strains of modern living.

CONSUMER HEALTH

Avoiding the Dark Side of the Media

Writer Andrew Weil suggests that as part of our strategy to improve our health we should all take a break from the mass media for a while, or "news fast." Underlying his message is the theme that too much bad news and negativity in any given day can sap our strength, diminish our spirit, and stress us out without our even knowing it is happening.

While our techno-driven world has forced many advances, the net effect of 24-hour cable stations, up-to-the second Internet sites, and all-day talk radio may be stimulus overload. Sitting down to dinner in front of the TV may be the best way to diet, as many of us are left nauseated and shaken from yet another atrocity in the world. What is the net effect on our mental, emotional, spiritual, and physical health? Consider the findings of various studies:

- According to a study by the Center for Media and Public Affairs, network coverage of murder tripled during the first half of this decade, while real-life homicides actually dropped 13 percent.
- British researchers at the University of Sussex had separate groups watch news programs that had been edited to be upbeat, neutral, or negative. The people who watched the downbeat shows became not only sadder and more anxious about the larger world, but significantly more likely to blow their personal worries out of proportion.
- Researchers know that having a sense of control over your world is good for your health, while believing that you have no control can raise your vulnerability to disease. One analysis found that 71 percent of network news time was devoted to stories that showed their central characters as having little or no control in their lives.

Christopher Peterson, a professor of psychology at the University of Michigan, summarized this best when he said, "What the evening news is telling you is that bad things happen, they hit at random, and there's nothing you can do about it." Not necessarily. Here are some actions that you can take to reduce your negative *hits* from the media.

- Limit your news time each day to only a predetermined amount. Try to find debates of issues that focus on both sides of a problem rather than on one-sided, negative approaches.
- Let media producers know when you object to something that is particularly offensive, such as focusing on gore or outrageous actions. Better yet, contact the companies who purchase ad time during the program. Let your actions speak volumes.
- Redford Williams, professor of Psychiatry at Duke University Medical Center in Durham, North Carolina, suggests that you ask yourself: (1) Is this important to me? (2) Is there anything I can do about it? If the answer to either of these is "no," shut off the TV or put down the paper and force yourself to focus on something else. Read a book or magazine during the period you would normally do the activity. If you answer "yes" to either question, the least you can do is write to someone in public office, or to the persons responsible for the information.
- Limit your contact with others who focus on the latest negative event seen on the television. These stress "carriers" may exacerbate your own stress response.
- Search for at least one positive thing in the news each day. Try to stay focused on that and tell others about it.
- Try to focus on who is delivering the message. Are they doing it for effect? Are they doing it to point out the injustice so that people can change it? Or is the "dirt" better news than the positive slant? Buy papers that have more good journalism and less sensationalism. And, if you ever get the chance to rate television broadcasts, express your opinions by voting for substantive, meaningful programming, rather than what you consider smut, stereotypes, and sensational flickers on the screen.

Source: David Jacobson, "Protecting Your Peace of Mind," *Health* 12 (1998): 64–58.

---

buying a smaller house, exchanging the expensive SUV for a run-of-the-mill four-door sedan, and a host of other patterns typify this move. Some dedicated downshifters have given up television, microwaves, phones, and even computers in order to learn to live more simply and avoid the jarring intrusions of the outside world. (See Consumer Health box.)

This trend toward simplicity was promoted by Henry David Thoreau in the nineteenth century, but for years it has been seen as an eccentric battle against machines or part of a back-to-nature movement. In the 1990s, however, the idea started to become more mainstream. In a 1997 study, nearly 32 percent of those surveyed indicated that they would give up their lifestyles for a return to simpler times.[35] According to researchers at Trends Institute, as many as 25 percent of all Americans will scale back their lives to some degree in the next 10 years. In fact, the practice is so common that

Taking the time to "smell the roses" allows a person the opportunity to gain perspective on life and identify true priorities.

consultants who once coached clients on getting ahead now run programs that teach clients how to be satisfied with less. Self-help books, newsletters, and networking groups all pitch the simpler life.

As with most trends, downshifting is not without its critics, because the change can be jarring on the family unless everyone is part of the decision and has bought into it fully. It involves a fundamental values shift and honest introspection about what is important in life. When considering any form of downshift or perhaps even starting out your career this way, it's important to move slowly and consider the following:

- *Determine your ultimate goal.* What is most important to you, and what will you need to reach that goal? What can you do without? Where do you want to live?
- *Make a short-term and long-term plan for simplifying your life.* Set up your plan in doable steps, and work slowly toward each. Begin saying "no" to requests for your time, and determine those people with whom it is important for you to spend time.
- *Complete a financial inventory.* How much money will you need to do the things you want to do? Pay off credit cards and eliminate existing debt, or consider debt consolidation. Get used to paying with cash. If you don't have the cash, don't buy. Will you rent or buy a home? With what kind of car could you get by?
- *Plan for health-care costs.* Make sure that you budget for health insurance and basic preventive health services. This should be a top priority.

- *Select the right career.* Look for work that you enjoy and that isn't necessarily driven by salary. Can you be happy taking a lower paying job that is less stressful and allows you the opportunity to have a life?
- *Consider options for saving money.* Downshifting doesn't mean you renounce money; for the most part, it simply means you choose not to let money dictate your life. It's still important to save. If you're just getting started, you need to prepare for emergencies and for future plans. Avoid compulsive buying, and consider living with others to share the costs.
- *Clear out/clean out.* A cluttered life can be distressing. Take an inventory of material items and get rid of things you haven't worn or used in the last year. Donate items to charity groups. Clean as you go, and get rid of the frills.
- *Stop junk mail from entering your home.* Get your name off of mailings lists, and avoid letting extra mail pile up in your living space.
- *Take time each week to "smell the roses."* Take a walk in the woods, in the park, by the lake, or by the ocean. Make a point of taking notice of the world around you.

Managing Emotional Responses

Have you ever gotten all worked up about something you thought was happening only to find that your perceptions were totally wrong? We often get upset not by realities but by our faulty perceptions. For example, suppose you found out that everyone except you is invited to a party. You might easily begin to wonder why you were excluded. Does someone dislike you? Have you offended someone? Such thoughts are typical. However, the reality of the situation may have absolutely nothing to do with your being liked or disliked. Perhaps you were sent an invitation and it didn't get to you.

Stress management requires that you examine your self-talk and your emotional responses to interactions with others. With any emotional response to a distressor, you are responsible for the emotion and the behaviors elicited by the emotion. Learning to tell the difference between normal emotions and those based on irrational beliefs can help you either to stop the emotion or to express it in a healthy and appropriate way.

Taking Mental Action

Stress management calls for mental action in two areas. First, it involves mentally developing and practicing self-esteem skills. Second, because you can't always anticipate what the next distressor will be, you need to develop the mental skills necessary to manage your reactions to stresses after they have occurred. The ability to think about and react quickly to stress comes with time, practice, experience with a variety of stressful situations, and patience.

▶ **Changing the Way You Think** Once you realize that some of your thoughts may be irrational or overreactive, making a

laughing
crying

conscious effort to reframe or change the way you've been thinking and focus on more positive ways of thinking is a key element of stress management. Here are some specific actions you can take to develop these mental skills.

- *Worry constructively.* Don't waste time and energy worrying about things you can't change or things that may never happen.
- *Look at life as being fluid.* If you accept that change is a natural part of living and growing, the jolt of changes may hold much less stress for you.
- *Consider alternatives.* Remember that there is seldom only one appropriate action. Anticipating options will help you plan for change and adjust more rapidly.
- *Moderate expectations.* Aim high, but be realistic about your circumstances and motivation.
- *Weed out trivia.* Don't sweat the small stuff, and remember that most of it is small stuff.
- *Don't rush into action.* Think before you act.

Taking Physical Action

Adopting the attitudes necessary for effective stress management may seem to have little effect. However, developing successful emotional and mental coping skills is actually a satisfying accomplishment that can help you gain confidence in yourself. Learning to use physical activity to alleviate stress helps support and complement the emotional and mental strategies you employ in stress management.

▶ **Exercise** Exercise reduces stress by raising levels of endorphins, mood-elevating, pain-killing hormones, in the bloodstream. As a result, exercise often increases energy, reduces hostility, and improves mental alertness.

Most of us have experienced relief from distress at one time or another by engaging in some aggressive physical activity. Exercise performed as part of an immediate response to a distressor can help alleviate stress symptoms. However, a regular exercise program usually has more substantial stress management benefits than does exercise performed as an immediate reaction to a distressor. Engaging in 25 minutes of aerobic exercise three or four times a week is the most beneficial plan of action. But even simply walking up stairs, parking farther away from your destination or standing rather than sitting helps to conserve and replenish your adaptive energy stores. Plan walking breaks with friends. Stretch after prolonged periods of sitting at your desk studying. A short period of physical exercise may provide the stress break you really need.

▶ **Relaxation** Like exercise, relaxation can help you to cope with stressful feelings, to preserve adaptation energy stores, and to dissipate the excess hormones associated with the GAS. Relaxation also helps you to refocus your energies and should be practiced daily until it becomes a habit.

ACCESSING YOUR HEALTH ON THE INTERNET

Check out the following Internet sites related to the topics discussed in this chapter.

1. **Center for Anxiety and Stress Treatment.** Provides resources and services regarding a broad range of stress-related topics.

    http://stressrelease.com

2. **National Center for Post-Traumatic Stress Disease.** Research and education on PTSD, offering a variety of links to fact sheets and help sites.

    http://www.dartmouth.edu/dms/ptsd/

3. **Hampden-Sydney College.** Links to helpful tips for dealing with stressful issues commonly experienced by college students.

    http://www.hsc.edu/admin/counsel/index.html

Once you have learned some relaxation techniques, you can use them at any time. If you're facing a tough exam, for example, you may choose to relax before it or at intervals during it. You can also use relaxation techniques when you face stressful confrontations or assignments. When you begin to feel your body respond to distress, make time to relax, both to give yourself added strength and to help alleviate the negative physical effects of stress. As your body relaxes, your heart rate slows, your blood pressure and metabolic rate decrease, and many other body-calming effects occur, allowing you to channel energy appropriately.

▶ **Eating Right** Have you ever sat down with a glass of warm milk or a cup of hot chocolate to try to relax? Have you ever been told, "Eat—you'll feel better"? Is food really a destressor? Whether foods can calm us and nourish our psyches is a controversial question. Much of what has been published about hyperactivity and its relation to the consumption of candy and other sweets has been shown to be scientifically invalid. High-potency stress-tabs that are supposed to provide you with resistance against stress-related ailments are nothing more than gimmicks. But what is clear is that eating a balanced, healthful diet will help provide you with the stamina needed to get through problems and may stress-proof you in ways that are not fully understood. It is also known that undereating, overeating, and eating the wrong kinds of foods can create distress in the body. For more information about the benefits of sound nutrition in overall health and wellness, see Chapter 9.

Time. Everybody needs more of it, especially students trying to balance the demands of classes, social life, earning money for school, family obligations, and time needed for relaxation. The following should become a part of your stress management program:

- *Clean off your desk.* According to Jeffrey Mayer, author of *Winning the Fight Between You and Your Desk,* most of us spend many stressful minutes each day looking for things that are lost on our desks or in our homes. Go through the things on your desk, toss the unnecessary papers, and put papers for tasks that you must do in folders.
- *Never handle papers more than once.* When bills and other papers come in, take care of them immediately. Write out a check and hold it for mailing. Get rid of the envelopes. Read your mail and file it or toss it. If you haven't looked at something in over a year, toss it.
- *Prioritize your tasks.* Make a daily "to do" list and try to stick to it. Categorize the things you must do today, the things that you have to do but not immediately, and the things that it would be nice to do. Prioritize the Must Do Now and Have to Do Later items and put deadlines next to each. Only consider the Nice to Do items if you finish the others or if the Nice to Do list includes something fun for you. Give yourself a reward as you finish each task.
- *Avoid interruptions.* When you've got a project that requires your total concentration, schedule uninterrupted time. Unplug the phone or let your answering machine get it. Close your door and post a Do Not Disturb sign. Go to a quiet room in the library or student union where no one will find you.
- *Reward yourself for being efficient.* If you've planned to take a certain amount of time to finish a task and you finish early, take some time for yourself. Have a cup of coffee or hot chocolate. Go for a walk. Differentiate between rest breaks and work breaks. Work breaks simply mean that you switch tasks for awhile. Rest breaks get you away for yourself.
- *Reduce your awareness of time.* Try to ignore the clock. Get rid of your watch, and try to listen to your body when deciding whether to eat, sleep, and so on. When you feel awake, do something productive. When you are too tired to work, take time out to sleep or to relax to try to energize yourself.
- *Remember that time is precious.* Many people learn to value their time only when they face a terminal illness. Try to value each day. Time spent not enjoying life is a tremendous waste of potential.
- *Become aware of your own time patterns.* Chart your daily schedule, hour by hour, for one week. Assess how you could be more productive and make more time for yourself.
- *Manage your anger.* Rather than *reacting* to life's frustrations with your own outbursts, try to "talk yourself out of anger." Calm yourself through deep breathing. Take time out, or try to *diffuse* your negative hostility by blocking out thoughts and forcing other images into your head.[36,37]

Making the Most of Support Groups

Support groups are an important part of stress management. Friends, family members, and co-workers can provide us with emotional and physical support. Although the ideal support group differs for each of us, you should have one or two close friends in whom you are able to confide and neighbors with whom you can trade favors. You should take the opportunity to participate in community activities at least once a week. A healthy committed relationship can also provide vital support.

If you do not have a close support group, you should know where to turn when the pressures of life seem overwhelming. Family members are often a steady base of support on which you can rely. But if friends or family are unavailable, most colleges and universities have counseling services available at no cost for short-term crises. Clergy members, instructors, and dorm supervisors may also be excellent resources. If university services are unavailable or if you are concerned about confidentiality, most communities offer low-cost counseling through mental health clinics.

Alternative Stress Management Techniques

The popularity of stress management as a media topic has increased the amount of advertising for various "stress fighters." We have been made aware of consumer products and services designed to fight stress: hypnosis, massage therapies, meditation, and biofeedback.

▶ *Hypnosis* **Hypnosis** is a process that requires a person to focus on one thought, object, or voice, thereby freeing the right hemisphere of the person's brain to become more active. The person is then unusually responsive to suggestions. Whether self-induced or induced by another person, hypnosis can reduce certain types of stress.

▶ *Massage* If you have ever had someone massage your stiff neck or aching feet, you know that massage is an excellent means of relaxation. Massage therapists use techniques that vary from the more aggressive methods typical of Swedish massage to the more gentle methods associated with acupressure and Esalen massage. Before selecting a massage therapist, check his or her credentials carefully. He or she should have training from a reputable program that teaches scientific principles for anatomic manipulation.

Hypnosis A process that allows people to become unusually responsive to suggestion.

Meditation A relaxation technique that involves deep breathing and concentration.

Biofeedback A technique involving self-monitoring by machine of physical responses to stress.

▶ _Meditation_   **Meditation** generally focuses on deep breathing, allowing tension to leave the body with each exhalation. There is no "right" way to meditate. Although there are several common forms of meditation, most involve sitting quietly for 15 to 20 minutes, focusing on a particular word or symbol, controlling breathing, and getting in touch with your inner self.

▶ _Biofeedback_   **Biofeedback** involves self-monitoring by machine of physical responses to stress and attempts to subsequently control these responses. Perspiration, heart rate, respiration, blood pressure, surface body temperature, muscle tension, and other stress responses are monitored. Then, by trial and error, the person using biofeedback techniques learns to lower his or her stress responses through conscious effort. Eventually, the person develops the ability to lower his or her stress responses at will without using the machines.

Taking Charge
Managing Stress Behaviors

Stress is not something that you can run from or wish into nonexistence. To control stress, you must meet it head on and use as many resources as you can to ensure that your coping skills are fine-tuned and ready to help you. In planning your personal strategy for stress success, following a few simple guidelines can help you enjoy more guilt-free time and become more productive.

• _Plan life, not time._ Evaluate all your activities, even the most trivial, to determine whether they add to your life. If they don't, get rid of them.

• _Decelerate._ When rushed, ask yourself if you really need to be. What's the worst that could happen if you slow down? Tell yourself at least once a day that failure seldom results from doing a job slowly or too well.

• _Learn to delegate and share._ Don't be afraid to ask others to help or to share the work load and responsibilities.

• _Learn to say no._ Decide what things you can do, what things you must do, and what things you want to do, and delegate the rest to someone else either permanently or until you complete some of your priority tasks. Before you take on a new responsibility, finish or drop an old one.

• _Schedule time alone._ Find time each day for quiet thinking, reading, exercising, or other enjoyable activities.

CHECKLIST FOR CHANGE

ASSESSING YOUR LIFE STRESSORS

✓ Have you assessed the major stressors in your life? Are they people, events, or specific activities?

✓ Do you often worry about things that never happen? Are you often anxious about nothing?

✓ Have you thought about what you could change to reduce your stress levels?

✓ Do you have a network of friends and family members who can help you reduce your stress levels? Do you know where you could go to get professional advice about how to start reducing them?

✓ Have you thought about what changes you'd like to work on first? Have you developed a plan of action? When do you want to start?

ASSESSING COMMUNITY STRESSORS

✓ Have you considered what in your environment may cause stress for you and the people around you?

✓ Could these stressors be changed? How could they be changed? Why would changing them make a difference?

✓ What on your campus or in your living situations causes undue stress for you or your friends? What could you do to change these stressors?

✓ What advice might you give to your school administrators to help them reduce unnecessary stress among students?

SUMMARY

- Stress is an inevitable part of our lives. Eustress refers to stress associated with positive events, distress to negative events. Psychoneuroimmunology is the science that attempts to analyze the relationship between the mind's reaction to stress and the function of the immune system. While increasing evidence links disease susceptibility to stress, much of this research is controversial. Stress has been linked to numerous health problems including CVD, cancer, and increased susceptibility to infectious diseases.

- The alarm, resistance, and exhaustion phases of the general adaptation syndrome involve physiological responses to both real and imagined stressors and cause a complex cascade of hormones to rush through the body. Prolonged arousal may be detrimental to your health.

- Undue stress for extended periods of time can compromise the immune system and result in serious health consequences.

- Multiple factors contribute to stress and to the stress response. Psychosocial factors include change, hassles, pressure, inconsistent goals and behaviors, conflict, overload, and burnout. Other factors are environmental stressors, and self-imposed stress.

- College can be an especially stressful time. Recognition of the signs of stress is the first step in helping yourself toward better health. Learning to reduce test anxiety and to cope with multiple stressors are also important.

- Managing stress begins with learning simple coping mechanisms: assessing your stressors, changing your responses, and learning to cope. Finding out what works best for you—probably some combination of managing emotional responses, taking mental or physical action, downshifting to simplify your life, learning time management, or using alternative stress management techniques—will help you better cope with stress in the long run.

DISCUSSION QUESTIONS

1. Compare and contrast distress and eustress. Are both types of stress potentially harmful?
2. Describe the alarm, resistance, and exhaustion phases of the general adaptation syndrome and your body's physiological response to stress. Does stress lead to more irritability or emotionality, or does emotionality lead to stress? Provide examples.
3. What are the major factors that seem to influence the nature and extent of a person's stress susceptibility? Explain how social support, self-esteem, and personality may make you more or less susceptible to stress.
4. Why are some students more susceptible to stress than are others? What services are available on your campus to help you deal with excessive stress?
5. What can college students do to inoculate themselves against negative stress effects? What actions can you take to manage your stressors? How can you help others to manage their stressors more effectively?

APPLICATION EXERCISE

Reread the *What Do You Think?* scenario at the beginning of the chapter and answer the following questions:

1. What could Mary have done to help inoculate herself against this stressful event in her life? What services on your campus could she have used to help her through her troubles?
2. What direct and indirect health effects of stress might Mary experience? What symptoms of stress should particularly concern her?
4. What strategies should Mary use to reduce the stress she is experiencing?

OBJECTIVES

▶ Differentiate between intentional and unintentional injuries and discuss societal and personal factors that contribute to violence in American society.

▶ Identify those factors that contribute to homicide, domestic violence, sexual victimization, and other intentional acts of violence.

▶ Identify strategies for prevention and risk reduction of intentional injuries.

▶ Identify major areas of crime that are common on college campuses and explain ways in which the campus community, law enforcement officials, and individuals can prevent crime from occurring.

▶ Discuss the impact of unintentional injuries on American society and explain actions that might contribute to personal risks from injuries of all types.

4

Intentional and Unintentional Injuries

Staying Safe in a Violent World

During the 1997–1999 school years, a number of shootings of school children by gun-toting classmates sent a chill through everyone in the country, particularly parents of school-age children. Since all the shootings took place on school grounds, they left people wondering whether any place was safe and questioning the pervasiveness of violence in our society.

In 1998, in a quiet town in Wyoming, Matthew Shepard, a young gay student was approached by two men at a local bar. Before the evening ended, his battered body was left tied to a wooden rail fence in a desolate area outside of town. When someone finally noticed the scarecrow-like figure hanging limply on the fence, it was too late to save Matthew's life.

In each case, what type of violence was perpetrated? What is the potential nature and extent of the impact on the victims? Do you consider either incident to be more serious than the other? Why? Are certain values, beliefs, and attitudes pervasive in the United States that make such behaviors more acceptable today than they used to be? What policies, programs, and/or personal actions would help prevent these events from occurring?

"Across the land, waves of violence seem to crest and break, terrorizing Americans in cities and suburbs, in prairie towns and mountain hollows."

"To millions of Americans few things are more pervasive, more frightening, more real today than violent crime. . . . The fear of being victimized by criminal attack has touched us all in some way."

"Among urban children ages 10–14, homicides are up 150 percent, robberies are up 192 percent, assaults are up 290 percent."

ON FIRST READING these quotations, you might think they are statements from current public officials or perhaps headlines of today's newspapers or television news. But they're not. The first quote comes from President Herbert Hoover's 1929 inauguration speech. The next comes from the 1860 Senate report on crime. The final quote comes from a 1967 report on children's violence.[1] Clearly, violence and our concern over its rising rates are not new concepts. Violence can strike any of us, rich or poor, young or old, educated or uneducated. It can strike in our homes, our schools, on the streets, at our jobs, or just about any place where people can come together formally or informally.

The term **violence** is used to indicate a set of behaviors that produces injuries, regardless of whether they are **intentional** (committed with intent to harm) or **unintentional** (committed without intent to harm, often accidentally). Any definition of *violence* implicitly includes the use of force, regardless of the intent, but as you'll see, some forms of violence are also extremely subtle. In this chapter, we focus on the various types of intentional and unintentional violence, the underlying causes or contributors to these problems, strategies to reduce your risk, and possible methods for

preventing violence from occurring. Before we begin, it is important to recognize that although certain indicators of violence, such as murders and deadly assaults, seem to be on the decline, other forms of violence, such as rape and hate crimes, are on the increase. Even more important is that for all we know about violence incidence and prevalence, there is a great deal that remains unknown. Just how many people suffer in silence, failing to report violent acts due to fear of repercussions or accepting violence as "the way it is," remains unknown. Estimates suggest that the known statistics reflect only the tip of the iceberg.

VIOLENCE IN THE UNITED STATES

Even though violence has been a major issue in American society since this country's earliest beginnings, it wasn't until 1985 that the U.S. Public Health Service formally identified violence as a leading public health problem that was con-

---

Violence Refers to a set of behaviors that produce injuries, as well as the outcomes of these behaviors (the injuries themselves).

Intentional injuries Injuries done on purpose with intent to do harm.

Unintentional injuries Injuries done without intent to harm.

tributing to significant death and disability rates among its citizenry. In response to the spiraling increases in reported homicides, the Centers for Disease Control and Prevention (CDC) created an entire section devoted to the prevention of violence, listing violence as a form of chronic disease that is pervasive at all levels of American society. Vulnerable populations, such as children, women, black males, and the elderly, were listed as being at high risk.

Is violence in the United States getting worse? Recent numbers indicate that we have made dramatic improvements in certain areas. Since 1991, FBI statistics show that overall crime and certain types of violent crime have actually decreased each year. In addition, a recent Department of Justice report on crime and safety on college campuses suggests that colleges and universities are relatively safe.[2] However, although your chances of being murdered or violently assaulted may have gone down, the odds of being a victim of crime in general are on the increase.

Unfortunately, violence affects everyone directly or indirectly. While the direct victims of violence and those close to them obviously suffer the most, others suffer in various ways because of the climate of fear that violence generates. Women are afraid to walk the streets at night. The elderly are often afraid to go out even in the daytime. Tourists are afraid of being brutalized in many of our nation's cities. We hear of children dodging bullets while playing in many of our major cities. Even people who live in "safe" areas often become victims of violence within their own homes or at the hands of family members. At the very least, everyone pays higher tax bills for law enforcement and prisons and higher insurance premiums for damage done to others' or their own property. Although the greatest cost of violence is in human suffering and loss, the financial cost of homicide, suicide, and related injuries is estimated at more than $224 billion, an increase of nearly 42 percent in the last decade.[3]

Although the underlying causes of violence and abuse are as varied as the individual crimes and people involved, several social, cultural, and individual factors seem to increase the likelihood of violent acts. Those factors most commonly listed are presented in Table 4.1. While these are broad, societally based factors that contribute to violence, there are many personal factors that also can lead us to act out violently.

WHAT DO YOU THINK?

Why do you think there is so much violent behavior in the United States? What personal actions can you take personally to prevent violent events from occurring? What actions could be taken on your campus to reduce risk? In your community?

TABLE 4.1
Societal Causes of Violence

SOCIETAL CONDITIONS	REACTIONS TO THESE CONDITIONS
Poverty	Low socioeconomic status and poor living conditions can create an environment of hopelessness. Violence becomes the way of obtaining what is needed or wanted.
Unemployment	When the economy goes sour, violent crime, suicide, assault, and other crimes increase.
Parental influence	Children raised in environments in which shouting, slapping, hitting, and other forms of violence are commonplace are more apt to "act out" these behaviors as adults.
Cultural beliefs	Cultures that objectify women and empower men to be tough and aggressive tend to have increased rates of violence in the home.
Media	Public airing of murder and mayhem can elicit violent reactions and imitators.
Discrimination/oppression	Whenever one group is oppressed by another, the seeds of discontent are spawned and hate crimes arise.
Religious differences	Religious persecution has been a part of the human experience since the earliest times; the dispute over the right to impose the beliefs on each other continues.
Breakdowns in the criminal justice system	Overcrowded prisons, lenient sentences, early releases from prison, and trial errors subtly encourage violence in a number of ways.
Stress	People who suffer from an inordinate amount of stress or who are in crisis are more apt to be highly reactive and strike out at others.

Sources: Larry Cohen and Susan Swift, "A Public Health Approach to the Violence Epidemic in the United States," Environment and Urbanization, October, 1993, 1–12; Lynn Lamberg, "Prediction of Violence Both Art and Science," Journal of the American Medical Association, 275 (1996): 1712–1715.

PERSONAL PRECIPITATORS OF VIOLENCE

For many people, the thought of being violent is repugnant; for others, violent behavior is a "rush." If you are like most people, you probably acted out your anger much more readily as a child than you do today. You might have fought, kicked, and screamed when you didn't get your way. However, even the worst behaved children usually grow up. As we mature, we learn to control our outbursts of anger. We learn to approach conflict rationally rather than use aggression.

Yet, others go through life acting out their aggressive tendencies in much the same ways they did as children or as they saw modeled in their homes. Why do two children from the same neighborhood, from the same school, in the same small town go in different directions when it comes to violence? For that matter, what causes two children raised in the same household by the same parent to go in such different directions? Parents of violent perpetrators across the country ask that question every day. Clearly, there are no simple answers. There are, however, some antecedents or predictors of future aggressive behavior.

Anger

Anger is a spontaneous, usually temporary, biological feeling or emotional state of displeasure that occurs most frequently during times of personal frustration. Since life is stressful, anger becomes a part of daily life experiences. Anger can range from slight irritation to rage, a violent and extreme form of anger.[4] When it is acted out in our homes or on the road or in airplanes, the consequences can be deadly. (See Skills for Behavior Change box.)

What makes some people get angry or flare at the slightest provocation? Often, people who anger quickly are individuals who have a low tolerance for frustration, believing that they should not have to put up with inconvenience or petty annoyances. The cause may be genetic or physiological; there is evidence that some people are born unstable, touchy, or easily angered.[5] Another cause of anger is sociocultural. Because we are taught not to express anger or to "bury" it in public, many of us do not know how to handle it when it begins to be more than we can hide. Perhaps most important, family background plays a role in anger-prone individuals. Typically, people who are easily angered come from families that are disruptive, chaotic, and not skilled in emotional expression.[6] In fact, the single largest predictor of future violence is past violence.[7]

Aggressive behavior is often a key aspect of violent interactions. **Primary aggression** is goal-directed, hostile self-assertion that is destructive in nature. **Reactive aggression** is more often part of an emotional reaction brought about by frustrating life experiences. Whether aggression is reactive or primary in nature, it is usually most likely to flare in times of acute stress, during relationship difficulties or loss, or when a person is so frustrated that the only recourse is to fight back or strike out at others.

WHAT DO YOU THINK?

What are some examples of primary aggression? Reactive aggression? Can both of these aggressive patterns result in the same degree of harm? Do you think our laws are more lenient when violent acts are the result of reactive aggression? If yes, why do you think this is so?

Substance Abuse

There are situations in which some psychoactive substances appear to be a form of "ignition" for violence. Research examining possible relationships between substance abuse and violence indicates that:

- Consumption of alcohol—by perpetrators of the crime, the victim of the crime, or both— immediately preceded over half of all violent crimes, including murder.[8]
- Chronic drinkers are more likely than others to have histories of violent behavior.[9]
- Criminals using illegal drugs commit robberies and assaults more frequently than nonusing criminals, and especially during periods of heavy drug use.[10]
- In domestic assault cases, more than 86 percent of the assailants and 42 percent of domestic violence victims reported using alcohol at the time of the attack. Nearly 15 percent of victims and assailants reported using cocaine at the time of the attack.[11]
- Ninety-two percent of assailants and 42 percent of victims reported having used alcohol or other drugs on the day of the assault.[12]
- Mentally ill patients who fail to adhere to prescription drug regimens and abuse alcohol and/or other drugs are significantly more likely to be involved in a serious violent act in the community.[13]
- Substance abuse markedly increases the risk of both homicide and suicide. Being in trouble at work due to drinking, being hospitalized for a drinking problem, use of illicit drugs, and arrest for use of illicit drugs all placed subjects at risk for violent death by homicide. The combination of depression and use of alcohol or other drugs increased homicide and suicide rates threefold.[14]

Primary aggression   Goal-directed, hostile self-assertion, destructive in character.

Reactive aggression   Emotional reaction brought about by frustrating life experiences.

Road Rage!

"We pulled out into traffic and immediately were serenaded by the sound of a blaring horn from a car speeding by in the next lane. Apparently we had pulled out in front of the car, causing the driver to swerve quickly to the left lane to avoid hitting us. We felt badly and were thankful that nothing serious had happened, however, the other driver wasn't so quick to forgive. For several miles she maneuvered in an effort to cause us to pull over, or slowed down in the neighboring lane in order to pull alongside our car. I wanted nothing to do with this and slowed down as well to avoid having to face her. I had no idea what to expect if we pulled alongside. Finally, she pulled over as she approached a right-hand turn, and as we went by, she stuck her head out the window and screamed venomous slurs our way. I'll never forget the expression on the woman's face as we went by. It was filled with such hatred and anger, such rage."

—From the author's files

Rage indeed. If you haven't heard or seen anything about Road Rage in the last few months, you've probably been avoiding the media. There have been countless stories about this new and scary phenomenon, considered a type of aggressive driving. You have most likely encountered aggressive driving and/or Road Rage recently if you drive at all.

While drunk driving remains a critical problem, the facts about aggressive driving are surely as ominous. For instance, according to the National Highway Transportation Safety Association, 41,907 people died on the highways last year. Of those fatalities, the agency estimates that about two-thirds were caused at least in part by aggressive driving behavior.

Why is this phenomenon occurring more than ever now, and why is it something that seemed almost nonexistent a few short years ago? Experts have several theories, and all are probably partially correct. One suggestion is sheer overcrowding. In the last decade, the number of cars on the roads has increased by more than 11 percent, and the number of miles driven has increased by 35 percent; however, the number of new road miles has only increased by 1 percent. That means more cars in the same amount of space; and the problem is magnified in urban areas. Also, people have less time and more things to do. With [people working and] trying to fit extra chores and activities into the day, stress levels have never been higher. Stress creates anxiety, which leads to short tempers. These factors, when combined in certain situations, can spell Road Rage.

ARE YOU IMMUNE TO ROAD RAGE?

You may think you are the last person who would drive aggressively, but you might be surprised. For instance, have you ever tailgated a slower driver, honked long and hard at another car, or sped up to keep another driver from passing? If you recognize yourself in any of these situations, watch out!

AVOID THE "RAGE" (YOURS AND OTHER DRIVERS')

Whether you are getting angry at other drivers, or another driver is visibly upset with you, there are things you can do to avoid any major confrontations. If you are susceptible to Road Rage, the key is to discharge your emotion in a healthy way. [I]f you are the target of another driver's rage, do everything possible to get away from the other driver safely, including avoiding eye contact and getting out of their way. The following safety tips can help you avoid Road Rage.

- Avoid eye contact!
- If you need to use your horn, do it sparingly.
- Get out of the way. Even if the other guy is speeding, it's safest to not make a point by staying in your lane.
- If someone is following you after an on-the-road encounter, drive to a public place or the nearest police station.
- Report any aggressive driving incidents to the police department immediately. You may be able to prevent further occurrences by the same driver.
- Above all, always use your seat belt! Seat belt use saves 9,500 lives annually.

Even though the problem of Road Rage may seem daunting, there are large-scale preventative measures currently underway to reduce the risk of aggressive driving and related fatalities. For instance, there is a major push to inform and educate the public about the problem, to improve enforcement techniques designed to punish and deter aggression, and to design safer roads.

According to the Coalition for Consumer Health and Safety, unsafe driving reflects not only the irresponsible behavior of a small minority of all drivers, but also the slow erosion of safe, courteous driving standards among the majority of all drivers. By disseminating information about the dangers of aggressive driving and emphasizing courteous driving, the Coalition hopes to teach drivers about the value of driving carefully and courteously, and cool Road Rage.

Source: Reprinted with permission of Allstate Insurance Co. "Don't Be Blinded by Road Rage," Allstate Insurance website, http://www.allstate.com/safety/auto/rage.html

INTENTIONAL INJURIES

Anytime someone sets out to do harm to another person or to his or her property, the incident may be referred to as one of intentional violence. Such incidents often result in intentional injuries, which come in many forms. Whether it be a simple outburst of anger or a fatal attack with a weapon, intentional injuries result in pain and suffering at the very least, and death and disability at their worst.

Gratuitous Violence

Violence can manifest itself in many different ways, and often that crime that is the most shocking or gratuitous gains the greatest amount of attention. Stories of innocent victims of drive-by shootings, or of a man dragged to his death tied to the back of a pickup, or of a simple disagreement that took a turn for the worst. Or perhaps it's a story of a young student who turns his internal rage outward on his family, classmates, and teachers, or a story of a man raging against his religion and killing members of a church congregation. It is such acts that often send shudders of fear and trepidation among society as a whole.

▶ *Homicide*   **Homicide,** death that results from intent to injure or kill, accounts for nearly 21,000 premature deaths every year in the United States. Although these numbers are down slightly from 1992, they still represent a significant contributor to life lost in certain segments of the population. Although homicide was the fourteenth leading cause of death in the United States among all age groups in 1996, it was the second leading cause of death for persons aged 15 to 24; and it exacted a heavy toll among other groups (see Table 4.2). Homicide continues to be the leading cause of death among black males aged 15 to 34, with rates that are five to ten times higher than those of white men in the same age range. Young Hispanic Americans, both male and female, also experience disproportionately high homicide rates.[15]

For every violent death, there are at least one hundred nonfatal injuries caused by violence. In 1996, there were an estimated 35,000 firearm-related deaths, including large numbers of homicides, suicides, and hospitalizations due to firearm-related injuries. For every person shot and killed by a firearm, there were almost three others treated annually for nonfatal shootings, large numbers of whom were children under the age of 10.[16]

For the average American, the lifetime probability of being murdered is 1 in 153. For white women, the risk is 1 in 450; for black men, it is 1 in 28. For a black man in the 20- to 22-year age group, the risk is 1 in 3. Combined across races, males represent 77 percent of all murder and nonnegligent manslaughter victims. Black males are 1.14 times more likely than white males to be murder victims; white females

were 1.5 times more likely than black females to be victims.[17] Over half of all homicides occur among people who know one another. In two-thirds of these cases, the perpetrator and the victim are friends or acquaintances; in one-third, they belong to the same family.[18]

While there appears to be a strong correlation between homicide and age, gender, and race, living in certain regions of the country also seems to increase one's risk for homicide. Reports suggest that the most violent region of the country is the South, accounting for approximately 40 percent of the nation's murders, rapes, and fatal assaults. The Midwest and West account for nearly 25 percent of the violence in these categories, with the Northeast accounting for just over 15 percent of these crimes.[19]

▶ *Bias and Hate Crimes*   As the population of the United States becomes more diverse, and people of color and differing cultures and lifestyles become more visible, there has been a corresponding rise in intolerance of those differences. Continuing anti-Semitic acts, gay bashing, and racially motivated hate crimes indicate that intolerance continues to smolder in our nation. In 1996, there were nearly 8,000 hate crimes reported in the United States, with over 1,000 of these being sex-bias crimes.[20] Hatred and bigotry divide communities and

---

TABLE 4.2
Rates and Rankings of Violent Deaths in the United States: 1996

Firearm Mortality	
Annual deaths	34,234
Age-adjusted death rates	13/100,000
Death rates: males, ages 15–24 years	47.6/100,000
Death rates: black males, ages 15–24 years	140/100,000
Firearm deaths: accidental	3.4%
Firearm deaths: suicide	51%
Firearm deaths: homicide	44%
Homicide Mortality	
Annual deaths	20,738
Age-adjusted death rate	8.4/100,000
Cause of death rank: overall	14th
Cause of death rank: ages 5–14 years	3rd
Cause of death rank: ages 15–24 years	2nd
Cause of death rank: ages 25–44 years	6th

Source: National Center for Health Statistics, Centers for Disease Control and Prevention. FASTATS: http://www.cdc.gov/nehswww/FASTATS/homicide.htm, June 6, 1998.

Homicide   Death that results from intent to injure or kill.

Ethnoviolence   Violence directed randomly at persons affiliated with a particular group.

shatter the social, educational, legal, political, and economic bonds between people and cause untold amounts of fear, pain, and suffering.

Hate crimes, in general, vary widely along two dimensions: (1) in the way they are carried out and (2) in their effects on victims. Recent studies have identified three additional characteristics of hate crimes.[21] They tend to be

- excessively brutal
- perpetrated at random on total strangers
- perpetrated by multiple offenders

The murder in Wyoming of Matthew Shepard, a young gay student, served as another reminder of the emotions that lie simmering beneath the surface of some people. The incident shocked the nation on a number of levels, but not because it was a hate crime against a gay person. The attack was shocking because of its gruesome nature and because of where it took place, in a college community—an environment often seen as a bastion of liberalism and tolerance. But academic settings are not immune to hatred and bias. According to a report in the *Chronicle of Higher Education*, nearly one-third of our nation's campuses reported incidents of hate crimes in 1997. Another study of four campuses found that victimization rates varied widely, from 12 percent of Jewish students to as high as 60 percent of Hispanic students. White students were victimized at rates ranging from 5 to 15 percent.[22] The sad truth is, however, that many minor assaults go unreported; so, like many crimes, what is known is likely to be only part of the total picture. (See Health in a Diverse World box on page 78.)

The grisly 1998 murders of Matthew Shepard and James Byrd served as grim reminders of the power and senselessness of hatred.

The tendency toward violent acts on campus might best be defined as campus **ethnoviolence,** a term that reflects relationships among groups in the larger society and is based on prejudice and discrimination. Although ethnoviolence often is directed randomly at persons affiliated with a particular group, the group itself is specifically differentiated and targeted apart from other groups, and that differentiation is usually ethnic in nature. Typically, there is consensus or at least strong agreement among perpetrators that "the group is an acceptable target." For example, in a largely Christian community, Jews and Muslims may be considered acceptable targets.[23] Students bring with them attitudes and beliefs from past family and life experiences and integrate them within their college community as a whole.

Prejudice and discrimination are always at the base of ethnoviolence. *Prejudice* is a reflection of attitudes toward a group of people. To say that a person is prejudiced against some group is to say that the person holds a set of beliefs about the group, has an emotional reaction to the group, and is motivated to behave in a certain way toward the group. *Discrimination* is the behavioral corollary of prejudice. It constitutes actions that deny equal treatment or opportunities to a group of people, often based on prejudice and bias. Acts of ethnoviolence also are often situational and opportunistic. In 1989 a group of young black men in Kenosha, Wisconsin, viewed the film *Mississippi Burning* and, incensed by the film's depiction of injustice toward blacks, decided to get even with Whites by finding the first solitary white male they came upon and viciously beating him.[24]

It is believed that much of the violence stems from a fear of change and a desire to blame others when forces such as the economy and crime seem to be out of control. How can you be part of the solution rather than part of the problem?

- Support educational programs designed to foster understanding and appreciation for differences in people. Many colleges now require diversity classes as part of their academic curriculum.
- Examine your own attitudes and behaviors. Are you intolerant of others? Do you engage in racist, sexist, ethnic, or similar behaviors meant to demean any group of individuals? Have you thought about the reasons why you have problems with a particular group?
- Do you discourage jokes and other forms of social or ethnic bigotry? Do not participate in such behaviors and express your dissatisfaction with others who do.
- Vote for community leaders who respect the rights of others, who value diversity, and who do not have racially or ethnically motivated hidden agendas. Vote against intolerant candidates who are attempting to control our school boards and local government through planned infiltration.
- Educate yourself. Read, interact with, and attempt to understand people who may appear to be different from you. Remember that you do not have to like everything about another person or group. Other people may not

HEALTH IN A DIVERSE WORLD

Racism: An Emerging Threat on Campus?

Is racial unrest a growing threat on American campuses or a byproduct of media sensationalism? In a 1998 report of hate crime data from 487 U.S. colleges and universities with enrollments over 5,000, the *Chronicle of Higher Education* concluded that only a handful of hate crimes had occurred. The report left many to wonder if it was possible that so many schools had so little "hateful intolerance" going on in the last couple of years. An accompanying article commented on the paucity of reported hate crimes, asking, "Are colleges and universities oases of harmony, without any hate crimes, or do they merely 'hate' to report crimes on their campuses?" Apparently, only a handful of reporting schools mentioned any difficulties whatsoever in these areas.

Many people feel, in fact, that intolerance is growing on campuses. As incidents of racial hostility on campuses flare and hostile interracial sentiments become apparent, many campuses have enacted punitive measures to ensure that racial intolerance is squelched. But this, too, has been criticized, as opponents argue that some of the measures erode freedom of speech. They also point out what some feel is uneven punishment, as some groups are punished while others seem to avoid punishment. As a reporter for the *New York Times* noted: "Aside from the inherent problems of defining [verbal] harassment, vilification and intolerance—is the racial hatred preached by such African American leaders as Louis Farrakhan and Angela Davis any worse than that preached by white, skinhead neo Nazis?—The proposed limits on freedom of expression, no matter how well-meaning, should raise caution flags."

Do you think the numbers from the *Chronicle of Higher Education* story are accurate? What factors do you think contributed to these low numbers? What indicators of intolerance are present on your campus? In your community?

Sources: R. Fenske and L. Gordon, "Reducing Racial and Ethnic Hate Crimes on Campus: The Need for Community," in Hoffman, A., *Violence on Campus: Defining the Problems, Strategies for Action* (Gaithersburg, MD: Aspen Publishing, 1998); K. Lively, "Most Colleges Appear Unaware of Requirements that They Track Hate Crimes," *Chronicle of Higher Education,* May 8, 1998, A57; and F. Barringer, "Free Speech and Insults on Campus," *New York Times,* April 15, 1989, A11.

---

like everything about you, either. However, respecting people's right to be different is a part of being a healthy, integrated individual.

- Examine your own values in determining the relative worth of your friends and the others in your life. Are you judgmental? Are you intolerant of others' differences? How do you resolve your own tendencies to be judgmental and bigoted? Do you judge people on appearances? Do you take time to get to know who they are as individuals?

WHAT DO YOU THINK?

Why do you think people are motivated to initiate bias or hate crimes against people they do not know? What can you do to reduce the risk of such crimes in your area? What should be done nationally?

▶ *Gang Violence*   The growing influence of street gangs has had a harmful impact on the health of our country. Drug abuse, gang shootings, beatings, thefts, carjackings, and the possibility of being caught in the middle between gangs at war have led to whole neighborhoods being held hostage by gang members. Once thought to be a phenomenon that occurred only in inner-city areas, gang violence now occurs in both rural and suburban communities, particularly in the southeast, southwest, and western regions of the country.

What causes young people to join gangs? Although these causes are complex, gangs apparently meet the needs of many of today's young people. They provide a sense of belonging to a "family" that gives them self-worth, companionship, security, and excitement. In other cases, they provide a means of attaining economic security through criminal activity, drug sales, or prostitution. Once young people become involved in the gang subculture, it is difficult for them to get out. Threats of violence or fear of not making it on their own dissuade even those people who are most seriously trying to get out.

Gang membership varies considerably from region to region. The age range of gang members is typically 12 to 22 years. Risk factors include low self-esteem, academic problems, low socioeconomic status, alienation from family and society, a history of family violence, and living in gang-controlled neighborhoods.

The best means of preventing a person from joining a gang is trying to keep that person connected to positive influences and programs. From a child's early years, the focus should be on reducing alienation from friends, family, and school. Also, any student who has learning disabilities or other problems that make it hard for him or her to keep up should have alternative activities at which he or she can succeed.

Prevention programs that are community-based and that involve families, social service organizations, and law enforcement, school, and city officials in a coordinated and visible effort have been shown to be most effective. Rather than thinking of such youths only as gang members, community members must begin to think of them as people whose circumstances made them susceptible to the gang lifestyle.

In part because the number of gangs and gang-related crimes grows daily, Congress passed a crime bill in 1994 that included the hiring of 100,000 additional police officers, a ban on assault weapons, reform of the welfare system, the creation of a national network of neighborhood banks to boost communities' economic development, and the establishment of "boot camps" for young nonviolent offenders. These boot camps would keep offenders out of prison yet instill discipline, self-esteem, and respect for the law. Public health professionals have long advocated prevention rather than intervention. Examining the underlying causes of violence should provide evidence for finding system-wide changes in the social environment.

Domestic Violence

During the last decade, the subject of domestic violence grabbed our attention. Televison coverage of the O. J. Simpson case, Phil Hartman's death, and lesser known cases of children being brutally beaten, burned, or sexually assaulted brought ugly visages into our living rooms every evening. We are left to wonder how people can brutalize, both emotionally and physically, their loved ones within the confines of a family. Even as murders and assaults on the street are declining, evidence points to a growing incidence of vicious crimes taking place in the living rooms and bedrooms of America.

▶ *Spousal Abuse* Domestic violence is a widespread social problem affecting all races, ethnic groups, economic classes, and both sexes. By most estimates, it is the most common and least reported crime in the United States today. **Domestic violence** refers to the use of force to control and maintain power over another person in the home environment; it includes both actual harm and the threat of harm.[25] It can involve emotional abuse, verbal abuse, threats of physical abuse, and actual physical violence ranging from slapping and shoving to bone-breaking beatings, rape, and homicide.

▶ *Women as Victims* While young men are more apt to become victims of violent acts perpetrated by strangers, women

"Take Back the Night" vigils and marches have done a lot to increase awareness on college campuses about the issue of violence against women.

are much more likely to become victims of violent acts perpetrated by spouses, lovers, ex-spouses, and ex-lovers. In 1997, more than 6 million women were victims of assault. In fact, 6 of every 10 women in the United States will be assaulted at some time in their lives by someone they know.[26–28] Every year, approximately 12 percent of married women are the victims of physical aggression perpetrated by their husbands, according to a national survey.[29] These acts of aggression often include pushing, slapping, and shoving.

Some women experience much more severe acts of aggression. About 4 percent of married women each year are the victims of violence that takes the form of beating and/or threats of or actual harm caused by use of a knife or a gun.[30] In fact, acts of aggression by a husband or boyfriend are one of the most common causes of death for young women, and roughly 2,200 women in the United States are killed each year by their partners or ex-partners.[31] Over a recent 10-year period, according to the National Crime Survey, on average, more than 2 million assaults on women occurred each year. More than two-thirds of these assaults were committed by someone the woman knew.[32]

The following United States statistics indicate the seriousness of this long-hidden problem:[33,34]

* The most vulnerable female victims are African American and Hispanic, live in large cities, are young and unmarried, and are far from their families.
* Every 15 seconds, someone batters a woman.
* Only 1 in every 250 such assaults is reported to the police.
* More than a third of women victims of domestic violence are severely abused on a regular basis.
* About five women are killed every day in domestic violence incidents.
* Three of every four women murdered are killed by their husbands.

Domestic violence The use of force to control and maintain power over another person in the home environment; it includes both actual harm and the threat of harm.

- Domestic violence is the single greatest cause of injury to women, surpassing rape, mugging, and auto accidents combined.
- About 25 to 45 percent of all women who are battered are battered during pregnancy.
- One-quarter of suicide attempts by women occur as a result of domestic violence.

How many times have you heard of a woman who is repeatedly beaten by her partner or spouse and asked, "Why doesn't she just leave him?" There are many reasons. Many women, particularly those with small children, are financially dependent on their partners. Others fear retaliation against themselves or their children. Some women hope that the situation will change with time (it rarely does); others stay because their cultural or religious beliefs forbid divorce. Finally, there are women who still love the abusive partner and are concerned about what will happen to him if they leave.[35]

Psychologist Lenore Walker developed a theory known as the "cycle of violence" to explain how women can get caught in a downward spiral without knowing what is happening to them.[36] The cycle has several phases:

- *Phase One: Tension Building.* In this phase, minor battering occurs, and the woman may become more nurturant, more pleasing, and more intent on anticipating the spouse's needs in order to forestall another violent scene. She assumes guilt for doing something to provoke him and tries hard to avoid doing it again.
- *Phase Two: Acute Battering.* At this stage, pleasing her man doesn't help and she can no longer control or predict the abuse. Usually, the spouse is trying to "teach her a lesson," and when he feels he has inflicted enough pain, he'll stop. When the acute attack is over, he may respond with shock and denial about his own behavior. Both batterer and victim may soft-peddle the seriousness of the attacks.
- *Phase Three: Remorse/Reconciliation.* During this "honeymoon" period, the batterer may be kind, loving, and apologetic, swearing he will never act violently toward the woman again. He may "behave" for several weeks or months, and the woman may come to question whether she overrated the seriousness of past abuse. Then the kind of tension that precipitated abusive incidents in the past resurfaces, he loses control again, and he once more beats the woman. Unless some form of intervention breaks this downward cycle of abuse, contrition, further abuse, denial, and contrition, it will repeat again and again—perhaps ending only in the woman's, or rarely, the man's death.

It is very hard for most women who get caught in this cycle of violence (which may include forced sexual relations and psychological and economic abuse as well as beatings) to summon up the courage and resolution to extricate themselves. Most need effective outside intervention.

▶ *Men as Victims*   Men also are victims of domestic violence. Approximately 12 percent of men reported that their wives engaged in physically aggressive behaviors against them in the past year—nearly the same percentage as women. The difference between male and female batterers is twofold. First, although the frequency of physical aggression may be the same, the impact of physical aggression by men against women is drastically different: women are typically injured in such incidents two to three times more often than are men.[37] These injuries tend to be more severe and have resulted in significantly more deaths. Women engage in moderate aggression, such as pushing and shoving, at rates almost equal to men. But the severe form of aggression that is likely to land the victim in the hospital is almost always a male-against-female form of aggression. Consequently, men generally report that they do not live in fear of their wives.

▶ *Causes of Domestic Violence*   There is no single explanation for why people tend to be abusive in relationships. Although alcohol abuse is often associated with such violence, marital dissatisfaction seems to also be a predictor of physical abuse.[38] Numerous studies also point to differences in the communication patterns between abusive relationships and nonabusive relationships.[39] While some argue that the hormone testosterone is the cause of male aggression, studies have failed to show a strong association between physical abuse in relationships and this hormone.[40] Many experts believe that men who engage in severe violence are more likely than other men to suffer from personality disorders.[41]

It is important to remember that it is the dynamics that both people bring to a relationship that result in violence and allow it to continue. Obtaining help from community support and counseling services may help determine the underlying basis of the problem and may help the victim and the batterer come to a better understanding of the actions necessary to stop the cycle of abuse.

▶ *Child Abuse*   Children raised in families in which domestic violence and/or sexual abuse occur are at great risk for damage to their personal health and well-being. The effects of such violent acts are powerful and can be very long-lasting. **Child abuse** refers to the systematic harm of a child by a caregiver, generally a parent.[42] The abuse may be sexual, psychological, physical, or any combination of these. Although exact figures are lacking, many experts believe that there are over 2 million cases of child abuse every year in the United States involving severe injury, permanent disability, and/or death.

Child abusers exist in all gender, social, ethnic, religious, and racial groups.

Certain personal characteristics tend to be common among child abusers: the experience of being abused as a child, poor self-image, feelings of isolation, extreme frustration with life, higher stress or anxiety levels than normal, a tendency to abuse drugs and/or alcohol, and unrealistic expectations of the child. It is also estimated that half to three-quarters of men who batter their female partners also batter children. In fact, spouse abuse is the single most identifiable risk factor for predicting child abuse. Finally, children with handicaps or other "differences" are more likely to be abused.

▶ *Child Sexual Abuse* **Sexual abuse of children** by adults or older children includes sexually suggestive conversations; inappropriate kissing; touching; petting; oral, anal, or vaginal intercourse; and other kinds of sexual interaction. The most frequent abusers are a child's parents or companions or spouses of the child's parents. Next most frequent are grandfathers and siblings. Girls are more commonly abused than boys, although young boys are also frequent victims, usually of male family members. Between 20 and 30 percent of all adult women report having had an unwanted childhood sexual encounter with an adult male, usually a father, uncle, brother, or grandfather. It is a myth that male deviance or mental illness accounts for most incidents of sexual abuse of children: "Stories of retrospective incest patients typically involved perpetrators who are 'Everyman'—attorneys, mental health practitioners, businessmen, farmers, teachers, doctors, and clergy."[43]

Most sexual abuse occurs in the child's home. Risky situations include:[44]

1. When the child lives without one of his or her biological parents.
2. When the mother is unavailable to the child either because she is working outside the home or because she is disabled or ill.
3. When the parents' marriage is unhappy or rife with conflict.
4. When the child has a poor relationship with his or her parents or is subjected to extremely punitive discipline.
5. When the child lives with a stepfather.

Child abuse The systematic harming of a child by a caregiver, generally a parent.

Sexual abuse of children Sexually suggestive conversations; inappropriate kissing; touching; petting; oral, anal, or vaginal intercourse; and/or other kinds of sexual interaction between a child and an adult or an older child.

Sexual assault Any act in which one person is sexually intimate with another person without that other person's consent.

Rape Sexual penetration without the victim's consent.

Child sexual abuse has serious ramifications in later life. For example, 99 percent of the inmates in the maximum security prison at San Quentin were either abused or raised in abusive households; and 300,000 children between the ages of 8 and 15 are living on the nation's streets, willing to prostitute themselves to survive rather than to return to abusive households they ran away from.[45]

Most people who were abused as children do not end up as convicts or prostitutes, but most do bear spiritual, psychological, and/or physical scars. Clinical psychologist Marjorie Whittaker has found that "of all forms of violence, incest and childhood sexual abuse are considered among the most 'toxic' because of their violations of trust, the confusion of affection and coercion, the splitting of family alignments, and serious psychological and physical consequences."[46]

Not all child violence is physical. Psychological violence—assaults on your personality, character, competence, independence, or general dignity as a human being—is also detrimental. The negative consequences of this kind of victimization in close relationships can be harder to discern and therefore harder to combat. They include depression, lowered self-esteem, and a pervasive fear of doing something that will offend the abuser.

> ·········· **WHAT DO YOU THINK?**
>
> What factors in society lead to child abuse and neglect? What are common characteristics of children's abusers? Why are family members often the perpetrators of child abuse and child sexual abuse? What actions can be taken to prevent such behaviors?

Sexual Victimization

As with all forms of violence, men and women alike are susceptible to sexual victimization. However, sexual violence against women is of epidemic proportions in this country. In fact, sexual battering is the single greatest cause of injury to women in the United States, occurring more frequently than car accidents, muggings, and rapes combined.[47] One-quarter to one-third of high school and college students report involvement in dating violence, as perpetrators, victims, or both.[48]

▶ *Sexual Assault and Rape* **Sexual assault** is any act in which one person is sexually intimate with another person without that person's consent. This may range from simple touching to forceful penetration and may include such things as ignoring indications that intimacy is not wanted, threatening force or other negative consequences, and actually using force.

Rape is the most extreme form of sexual assault and is defined as "penetration without the victim's consent."[49] Whether committed by an acquaintance, a date, or a stranger, rape is a criminal activity that usually has serious emotional,

psychological, social, and physical consequences for the victim. Most victims are young females, with 29 percent under 11 years of age, 32 percent between the ages of 11 and 17, and 22 percent between ages of 18 and 24.[50] Neft and Levine report that rape is thought to be the most underreported of all violent crimes in the United States, with estimates ranging from 310,000 to 700,000 rapes and other sexual assaults on women every year.[51]

Incidents of rape generally fall into one of two types—aggravated rape and simple rape. An **aggravated rape** involves multiple attackers, strangers, weapons, or physical beatings. A **simple rape** is perpetrated by one person, whom the victim knows, and does not involve a physical beating or the use of a weapon. Most incidents of rape are classified as simple rapes, with one report suggesting that 82 percent of female rape victims have been victimized by acquaintances (53%), current or former boyfriends (16%), current or former spouses (10%), or other relatives (3%). With almost half of all rape charges dismissed before the cases reach trial and a perceived lack of male understanding of the effects of rape on women, it's easy to understand why experts feel that "simple" rape is seriously underreported and ignored.[52]

▶ *Acquaintance or Date Rape*   Although the terms *date rape*, or *friendship rape,* and *acquaintance rape* have become standard terminology and often seem interchangeable, they are typically misused. Not all rapes occur on dates, not all of the relationships are friendships, and sometimes the term *acquaintance* is used all too loosely. Many acquaintance rapes occur as the result of incidental contact at a party or when groups of people congregate at one person's house. These are crimes of opportunity, not necessarily a prearranged date. This is an important distinction in that the use of the term *date* may suggest that there is always some type of reciprocal interaction that has been arranged in advance. While most date or acquaintance rapes happen to women aged 15 to 21 years, the 18-year-old new college student is the most likely victim.[53]

Date rape is not simply miscommunication; it is an act of violence. Susan Jacoby puts it this way:

> Some women (especially the young) initially resist sex not out of real conviction but as part of the elaborate persuasion and seduction rituals accompanying what was once called courtship. And it is true that many men (again, especially the young) take pride in the ability to coax a woman a step further than she intended to go. But these mating rituals do not justify or even explain date rape. Even the most callow youth is capable of understanding the difference between resistance and genuine fear; between a halfhearted "no, we shouldn't" and tears or screams.[54]

▶ *Sexual Harassment*   If we think of violence as including verbal abuse and the threat of coercion, then sexual harassment is a form of violence. **Sexual harassment** is defined as any form of unwanted sexual attention. Under Title VII of the Civil Rights Act, sexual harassment is "unwelcomed sexual advances, requests for sexual favors, and other verbal or physical contact of a sexual nature." Despite what might appear to be clear definitions, sexual harassment is very difficult for most people to identify and almost impossible to agree on. While many people would say that sexual harassment is anything that the offended person *believes* is harassment, others will say that this explanation is too nebulous.

The issue of sexual harassment was brought to the collective conscious of society in the early 1990s when Anita Hill charged Supreme Court justice nominee Clarence Thomas with sexual harassment in a previous employment environment. The alleged harassment was partly in the form of sexually offensive humor, not all directed at the victim. What had long been dismissed as harmless behavior became a cause for concern in business, academia, and government. In all areas, leaders established policies to protect victims and to punish offenders. Some colleges and universities offered courses designed to sensitize students to the harmful effects of racial and sexual verbal assaults, and most schools began offering workshops on identifying and preventing sexual harassment.

Aggravated rape   Rape that involves multiple attackers, strangers, weapons, or a physical beating.

Simple rape   Rape by one person known to the victim and that does not involve a physical beating or use of a weapon.

Sexual harassment   Any form of unwanted sexual attention.

It's always important to watch what you say and how you say it, but nowhere is this more true than at your job. Learning what constitutes sexual harassment may save you embarrassment in the future. A simple compliment on a colleague's appearance can be offensive if stated without sensitivity, regardless of the intent. "You look very nice today" can become offensive if stated as, "That dress looks great on your body." Even if the person enjoys your comment, you have to remember that others may overhear your remarks. If you are known as someone who makes such comments, you may be considered a risk the next time a possible promotion comes up. Such comments, however, only touch the tip of the iceberg on most sexual harassment issues. The recent Paula Jones and Monica Lewinsky scandals have helped keep sexual harassment issues in the forefront and have brought attention to other aspects of sexual harassment, issues such as improper touching, improper suggestions, and inappropriate uses of power.

Most companies now have sexual harassment policies in place, as well as procedures for dealing with it. If you feel you are being harassed, there are several actions you can take. The most important thing you can do immediately after an incident occurs is to be assertive to ensure that it will not be repeated. In addition:

- *Ask the harasser to stop.* Be clear and direct about what is bothering you and why you are upset: "I don't like this joke/touch/remark/look. It makes me feel uncomfortable and it is hard for me to work/participate/be your friend, etc." This may be the first indication the person has ever had that such behavior is inappropriate. This will usually stop the harassment.
- *Document the harassment.* Make a record of the incident. If the harassment becomes intolerable, having a record of exactly what occurred (and when and where) will be helpful in making your case.
- *Complain to a higher authority.* Talk to your manager about what happened. If the manager or supervisor doesn't take you seriously, find out what the internal grievance procedures are for your organization.
- *Remember that you have not done anything wrong.* You will likely feel awful after being harassed (and especially so if you have to complain to superiors). However, you should feel proud that you are not keeping silent. The person harassing you is wrong, not you. If the situation becomes so uncomfortable that you feel you can't work in the same place as the harasser, why should you be the one to have to leave?

WHAT DO YOU THINK?

Why do you think women are often reluctant to report sexual harassment cases? Why do you think so many men report that they were unaware of their own sexually harassing behaviors? What can be done to increase awareness in this area?

▶ *Social Contributors to Sexual Assault* According to many experts, certain common assumptions in our society prevent the recognition by both the perpetrator and the wider public of the true nature of sexual assault.[55] The most important of these assumptions are the following.[56]

- *Minimization:* It is often assumed that sexual assault of women is rare because official crime statistics, including the Uniform Crime Reports of the FBI, show very few rapes per thousand population; however, this is the most underreported of all serious crimes. Researchers in this area have found that nearly 25 percent of women in the United States have been raped.
- *Trivialization:* Incredibly enough, sexual assault of women is still often viewed as a jocular matter. During a gubernatorial election in Texas a few years back, one of the candidates reportedly compared a bad patch of weather to rape: "If there's nothing you can do about it, just lie back and enjoy it." (He lost the election—to a woman.)
- *Blaming the victim:* Many discussions of sexual violence against women display a sometimes unconscious assumption that the woman did something to provoke the attack—that she dressed too revealingly or flirted too outrageously.
- *"Boys will be boys":* This is the assumption that men just can't control themselves once they become aroused.

Over the years, psychologists and others have proposed many theories to explain why many males sexually victimize women. In one study, almost two-thirds of the male respondents had engaged in intercourse unwanted by the woman, primarily because of male peer pressure.[57] Peer pressure is certainly a strong factor in such behavior, but a growing body of research suggests that sexual assault is encouraged by the normal socialization processes that males experience daily.[58]

- *Male socialization.* Throughout our lives, we are exposed to social norms that "objectify" women. Media portrayals of half-dressed and undressed women in seductive poses promoting products, for instance, contribute to sex-role stereotyping. These portrayals often show males as aggressors and females as targets of aggression. In addition, men are exposed from an early age to anti-female jokes and vulgar and obscene terms for women. These reinforce the idea that females are lesser beings who may be pushed around with impunity.[59] Males are also discouraged from acting in ways that society views as feminine. They are told to strive for power, status, and control; are encouraged to act tough and unemotional; and are expected to be aggressive and to take risks.
- *Male attitudes.* Several studies have confirmed a greater tolerance of rape in men who accept the myth that rape is something women secretly desire, who believe in adversarial relationships between men and women,

Guns are a common part of life in many households in this country. What kind of effect might this have on the children in these homes?

········· ▶ WHAT DO YOU THINK?

What factors make men likely to commit sexual assault and/or rape? What might be effective in preventing such behaviors?

Campus Crime

In the early 1970s, campus "crime" consisted mainly of plagiarism, cheating on an exam, and occasional "streaking." Today there are murders, rapes, vicious assaults, and robberies on campus. While the majority of crimes on campus are larceny, vandalism, and setting off fire alarms illegally, it's clear that students' "home away from home" has undergone a shocking change. Much of the violent crime on campus seems to be fueled by alcohol abuse and other personal problems.

Traditionally, most campus crimes were handled internally. This has changed as more states have passed legislation requiring that colleges and universities warn their students about crime and danger both on campus property and in off-campus housing that they recommend.[63]

In July 1992, Congress passed the Campus Sexual Assault Victim's Bill of Rights, known as the Ramstad Act. Among other things, the act gives victims the right to call in off-campus authorities to investigate serious campus crimes. In addition, universities must set up educational programs and notify students of available counseling. Even with these and many more resources available to them, college safety officials believe that the number of crimes reported are probably significantly less than those actually committed.

▶ **Sexual Assault on Campus**   Most studies of the frequency of sexual assault among college students indicate that from 25 percent to 60 percent of college men have engaged in some form of sexually coercive behavior.[64] This is consistent with the 27.5 percent of college women who have reported experiencing rape or attempted rape since they were 14 years old, and the 54 percent who claim to have been sexually victimized (forced to endure unwanted petting, kisses, and other advances).[65] In one survey, only 39 percent of the men sampled denied coercive involvement, 28 percent admitted to having used a coercive method at least once, and 15 percent admitted that they had forced a woman to have intercourse at least once.[66]

The fact is that coercive sex or date rape is seldom reported to campus police, and when a rape victim seeks help at the campus health center, the center is not compelled to report the rape in the crime report. In one study, 20 percent of female respondents at a midwestern university reported that they had been raped by someone they knew, but only 8 percent of them reported it to the police. Similar findings were reported at another midwestern university, where 20 percent of 247 women interviewed said they had experienced date rape, but few had reported it.[67] Needless to say,

who condone violence against women, or who hold traditional attitudes toward sex roles. Such men are more apt to blame the victim and are more likely to commit rape themselves if they think they will get away with it.[60]

- *Male sexual history and hostility.* Most rapists are not abnormal or psychologically disturbed. Rather, they tend to be people whose childhoods involved early, multiple sexual experiences (both forced and voluntary) and who feel hostility toward women.[61]
- *Male misperceptions.* Men who are convinced that women really want sex even if they say they don't are more likely than other men to perpetrate sexual assaults. They more readily misinterpret women's words and behavior and act on their misinterpretations—only to be surprised later when women claim that they have been assaulted.[62]
- *Situational factors.* Several situations increase the likelihood that men will engage in coercive or aggressive sexual behaviors. Dates in which the male makes all the decisions, pays, drives, and in general controls what happens are more likely to end in sexual aggression. Alcohol and drug use increases the likelihood and severity of sexual assault. Length of relationship is another important situational factor: the more long-standing the relationship, the greater the chance of an assault. Finally, males who belong to a close-knit social group involving intense interaction are more prone to engage in a peer-pleasing assault.

other related sexual violations, such as obscene phone calls, stalking, sexual molestation that does not result in penetration, exhibitionism, voyeurism, and attempted rape, go equally unreported.[68]

▶ *Sexual Harassment on Campus*   How pervasive is sexual harassment in U.S. schools and universities? According to a major national study by the American Association of University Women (AAUW), entitled *Hostile Hallways*, four out of five students attending public schools have been sexually harassed by other students. Over one-third of these incidents are reported to occur before the seventh grade. Another study indicates that 90 percent of undergraduate women and 52 percent of graduate women report at least one negative experience from male students, and that the students most likely to harass these women are members of fraternities, athletic teams, and all-male groups and cliques; men who are defiant or angry at women; and those who have been abused themselves.[69,70]

While peers pose the threat of harassment, a study by the Institute of Social and Economic Research at Cornell University reported that 61 percent of upperclass and graduate students experienced, "unwanted sexual attention from someone of authority within the University."[71] Typically, these attentions come from male professors and range from affairs of male faculty with married and unmarried female students; to demands for sex, with threats of lower grades for noncompliance; to sexually offensive and hostile environments in the classroom.[72] Because of many reported offenses by faculty members, many universities have strict codes of conduct relating to faculty–student consensual as well as nonconsensual relationships. Many of these policies stem from reported difficulties with power and control between faculty and students and the potential for adverse consequences that might evolve.

········ **WHAT DO YOU THINK?**

What policies does your college or university have with respect to consensual relationships between faculty members and students? Do you think that consenting adults should have the right to interact, regardless of their positions within a system or workplace? What are the potential dangers of such interactions?

REDUCING RISKS

After a violent act is committed against someone we know, we acknowledge the horror of the event, express sympathy for the victim, and then go on with our lives. But the person who has been brutalized often takes a long time to recover—and sometimes complete recovery from the assault is not possible. In this section we discuss prevention of violence

and abuse rather extensively because it is far better to stop a violent act than to recover from it.

Self-Defense against Rape

Rape can occur no matter what preventive actions you take, but there are some commonsense self-defense tactics that should lower your risk. Self-defense is a process that includes increased awareness, learning self-defense techniques, taking reasonable precautions, and developing the self-confidence and judgment needed to determine appropriate responses to different situations.[73] Figure 4.1 identifies some practical tips for preventing personal assaults.

In Your Car

- Always keep your doors and windows locked
- Purchase cars with an alarm system and remote entry
- Don't stop for vehicles in distress; call for help
- If your car breaks down, lock the doors and wait for help from the police
- If you think someone is following you, do not drive to your home; drive to a busy place and attract attention
- Stick to well-traveled routes
- Keep your car in good running order and always fully gassed
- On long trips, don't make it obvious you're traveling alone
- Do not sleep in your car along the interstate highways
- Carry a cell phone with programmed emergency numbers

On the Street

- Walk/jog at a steady pace
- Walk/jog with others
- At night, avoid dark parking lots, wooded areas, and any place that offers an assailant good cover
- Listen for footsteps and voices
- Be aware of cars that keep driving around in your area
- Vary your running/walking routes
- Carry pepper spray or other deterrents, or walk/jog with a dog... the bigger the better!
- Carry change to make a phone call
- Tell others where you are going, your route, and when you'll return

Figure 4.1
Preventing Personal Assaults

Gun Control: Issues and Choices

Nearly 30 years ago, *Time* magazine ran a feature entitled "The Gun in America," which summarized the feelings of a nation reeling from the deaths of John F. Kennedy, Robert Kennedy, and Martin Luther King, Jr. The bloodshed of those years emerged out of many causes, one of them the long-standing American romance with guns—the mystique and abundance of firearms and the ease with which they moved from one hand to another until they fell into the wrong one. The national disgust that followed led to passage of the Gun Control Act of 1968, a milestone law that banned most interstate sales, licensed most gun dealers, and barred felons, minors, and the mentally ill from owning guns.

Today, the battlegrounds of gun violence have surfaced on our nation's playgrounds and in our nation's schools. No place is safe, and protection seems impossible. Recent statistics suggest that one in two high schoolers is threatened or injured with a weapon each year. And while juvenile crime as a whole is down—even more dramatically than the already precipitous drop in adult crime—the number of youths murdered by firearms went up 153 percent from 1985 to 1995! In some ways, the recent school killings across the country are aberrations. The percentage of households that own guns is actually declining, from a decades-long average of about 45 percent to something closer to 40 percent. All the same, there are still nearly as many firearms in the United States as people, more than 235 million by some estimates. At a time when crime rates are dropping, gun crime is dropping, too. But gun murders in the United States are still far more common than they were 30 years ago, and much more common than they are in other Western industrial nations. We've plateaued into a bad situation.

Since 1968's gun control legislation, the only major gun legislation to date has been passage of the Brady Bill, which requires background checks of purchasers, and the assault-gun ban. Although there is talk about passage of a gun safety-lock law and special "owner-use only" imprinting on guns, Congress is unlikely to pass any major gun control in the near future. In fact, the trend is moving toward more deregulation of guns and laws that permit concealed weapons in many of our states. The number of states that permit concealed weapons has gone from eight to 31 since 1985. A recent book, *More Guns, Less Crime: Understanding Crime and Gun Laws,* has analyzed crime rates in the 10 states that passed right-to-carry laws between 1977 and 1992. The author contends that after concealed-weapons laws were enacted, murders fell an average of 8 pecent, rapes 5 percent, and aggravated assaults by 7 percent at a time when murders, rapes, and assaults were increasing in states without such laws. Criminologists, researchers, and gun control lobbyists say that the book's research has been poorly conducted, its statistics suspect, and its conclusions, dangerous. Who are we to believe?

While millions believe passionately that their right to bear arms, their personal safety against tyranny, and their hunting rights could be severely curtailed, others believe that we have gone too far in "protecting" our rights, that outgunned police forces and the typical citizen on the street face undue risks as others maintain their right to own assault weapons. In fact, some even argue that events such as the school shootings could have been prevented if teachers had had the right to carry guns for protection! Imagine thinking of your elementary school teacher toting a .38-caliber pistol in his or her purse. On the other hand, many of us have wondered about buying guns for "protection" as violence seems to escalate. Concealed weapons appeal to those who fear for their own safety and want a means to fight back. But what's to say that people won't overreact to perceived threats or to the slightest provocation?

Recent lawsuits against gun manufacturers raise yet another controversial issue. Are gun manufacturers liable for the violent homicides that occur in much the same way that the tobacco industry is being held liable for deaths from cigarette smoking? The attorneys general of several states feel they are and are taking these suits to court as of this writing. They argue that many deaths are preventable through better monitoring of sales and curtailing production of armor-piercing bullets and repeat-style assault weapons. They argue that producing guns that fire only if the original owner is shooting them is possible, but that gun manufacturers refuse to produce them.

In the future, average citizens will be forced to make choices that may affect the lives of their families, their coworkers, and their friends. What can you do?

- Investigate the facts about gun-related violence. Your best data sources are federal or state crime statistics, rather than political or special interest groups, which might have a vested interest in proving their points.
- Review the points made by the National Rifle Association and compare their data with federal or state crime data and data from groups lobbying for antigun protection. Consider the pros and cons of each argument.
- Consider what the antigun movement is really advocating. Would their actions really keep hunters from buying hunting rifles, or homeowners from having handguns in their homes if they wanted to protect themselves? Would user IDs on guns, which would not allow anyone but the original purchaser to operate the weapon, be acceptable to the NRA? Why or why not?
- Carefully analyze the opinions and voting records of your state and national political representatives regarding gun control. Are they voting in ways that support your own beliefs? If not, are there others who might?

Source: Richard Lacayo, "Still Under the Gun," *Time,* July 6, 1998, 32–56.

What to Do When a Rape Occurs

If you are a rape victim, you should be the one to report the attack. This gives you a sense of control. You should also follow these instructions:

✓ Call 911 (if available).
✓ Do not bathe, shower, douche, clean up, or touch anything that the attacker may have touched.

✓ Do not throw away or launder the clothes you were wearing, as they will be needed as evidence.
✓ Bring a clean change of clothes to the clinic or hospital.
✓ Contact the Rape Assistance Hotline in your area and ask for advice on therapists or counseling if you need additional help or advice.

If it is a friend who is raped, here's how you can help:

✓ Believe her and don't ask questions that may appear to implicate her in the assault.

✓ Recognize that rape is a violent act and that the victim was not looking for this to happen.
✓ Encourage her to see a doctor immediately, as she may have medical needs but be too embarrassed to seek help on her own.
✓ Encourage her to report the crime.
✓ Be understanding and let her know that you will be there for her.
✓ Recognize that this is an emotional recovery and it may take 6 months to a year for her to bounce back.
✓ Encourage her to seek counseling.

▶ *Taking Control* Most rapes by assailants unknown to the victim are planned in advance. They are frequently preceded by a casual, friendly conversation. Although many women have said that they started to feel uneasy during such a conversation, they denied the possibility of an attack to themselves until it was too late. Listen to your feelings and trust your intuition. Be assertive and direct to someone who is getting out of line or threatening—this may convince the would-be rapist to back off. Stifle your tendency to be "nice" and don't fear making a scene. Let him know that you mean what you say and are prepared to defend yourself:

- *Speak in a strong voice and use statements like "Leave me alone" rather than questions like "Will you please leave me alone?"* Avoid apologies and excuses.
- *Maintain eye contact with the would-be attacker.*
- *Sound as if you mean what you say.*
- *Stand up straight, act confident, and remain alert.* Walk as if you own the sidewalk.[74]

Many rapists use certain ploys to initiate their attacks. Among the most common are:

- *Request for help.* This allows him to get close—to enter your house to use the phone, for instance.
- *Offer of help.* This can also help him gain entrance to your home: "Let me help you carry that package."
- *Guilt trip.* "Gee, no one is friendly nowadays. . . . I can't believe you won't talk with me for just a little while."
- *Purposeful accident.* He may bump into the back of your car, and then assault you when you get out to see the extent of the damage. Don't stop unless you have to in these situations, and if you do stop, stay in your car with the doors locked.

- *Authority.* Many women fall for the old "policeman at the door" ruse. If anyone comes to your door dressed in policemen's garb, ask him to show you his ID before you unlock the door. You can also call the police department to get a confirmation on his ID.

If you are attacked, act immediately:

- *Don't worry about causing a scene.* Draw attention to yourself and your assailant. If attacked, scream "Fire" loudly. Research has shown that passersby are much more likely to assist or help if they hear the word *fire* than just a scream. Your attacker may also be caught off balance by the action.
- *Report the attack* to the appropriate authorities at once.

To prevent an attack from occurring:

- *Always be vigilant.* Even the safest cities and towns have rapes. Don't be fooled by a sleepy-little-town atmosphere.
- *Use campus escort services whenever possible.*
- *Be assertive in demanding a well-lit campus.*
- *Don't use the same routes all the time.* Think about your movement patterns and vary them accordingly.
- *Don't leave a bar alone with a friendly stranger.* Stay with your friends, and let the friendly stranger come along. Don't give your address to anyone you don't know.
- *Let friends/family know where you are going, what route you'll take, and when to expect your return.*
- *Stay close to others.* Avoid shortcuts through dark or unlit paths. Don't be the last one to leave the lab or library late at night.
- *Keep your windows and doors locked.* Don't answer the door to strangers.

Dealing with Campus Violence

Increasingly, college campuses have become microcosms of the greater society, complete with all of the risks, hazards, and dangers people face in the world. Because of a recognition of the seriousness of the threats, the liability issues, and the damage to the reputations of revered institutions, many college administrators have been very proactive in establishing violence-prevention policies, programs, and services. They have begun to reach out to members of the campus community, the local community, and members of law enforcement and social services to protect students and the communities in which college students live. They have made greater efforts to partner with the local communities in joint efforts to reduce violence. Changes have been in the form of a number of strategies.[75]

▶ *Changing Roles*   In an effort to increase student protection, campus law enforcement has changed over the years in both numbers and its authority to prosecute student offenders. Campus police have the responsibility for emergency responses to threats to college and departmental safety, threats to human resources, threats to the general campus environment, threats from substance abuse and drunk driving, traffic and bicycle safety, vandalism, and other student acts that threaten the safety of a campus population. They have the power to enforce laws with students in the same way they are handled in the general community. In fact, many campuses now hire state troopers or local law enforcement staff to deal with campus issues rather than having a separate law enforcement office run through the university.

Many of these law enforcement groups follow a *community policing* model in which officers have specific responsibilities for certain areas of campus, departments, or events. By narrowing the scope of each officer's territory, officers get to know people in the area and are better able to anticipate and prevent risks, thereby improving the safety of an area. This is different from the old policy of security swooping only in times of trouble.

▶ *Prevention Efforts*   In response to an epidemic of violence on campuses, many colleges and universities now have crime prevention/safety specialists working in their law enforcement agencies. These specialists work to improve university policies and procedures to reduce student risk. The following are among the activities that are commonly recommended:

- A rape awareness and education program for members of the campus community
- A crime prevention orientation program for new faculty and staff as well as students
- Specialized safety workshops for unique groups, such as commuters, international students, athletes, and disabled students
- The use of printed and electronic educational messages about personal safety
- A student notification process for information about special hazards

- Alcohol and drug programs dealing with policy, awareness, education, and enforcement
- A "grounds safety" program, which includes measures such as making sure that shrubs are removed from dark areas and that the campus is well lit
- A system of emergency call boxes or telephones across campus
- Escort services for students who must be out after dark
- Motorist assistance programs for persons with car trouble
- Antitheft programs, including regular patrols of parking lots and other areas of a campus
- Victim advocacy programs, such as rape or abuse counseling

▶ *The Role of Student Affairs*   Although there may be some overlap between law enforcement activities, student affairs offices need to play a vital role in any procedures enacted on campus, both for preventing problems from arising and in resolving problems once they occur. They should monitor progress, identify potential threats, and advocate for improvements in any areas found to be deficient. A student affairs office can play a key role in making sure that mental health services, student assistance programs, and other services on campus are of the highest quality, are easily accessible, and meet student needs. A human services or student affairs office on campus should be connected to students; and students should be acutely aware of their presence and the services and supports that they offer. If these services are not visible or proactive in ensuring campus safety, a careful assessment of their roles and responsibilities should be made. Student leadership can play a major role in shaping the vision of these offices and ensuring that they are advocating fully for the campus population.

Community Strategies for Preventing Violence

Since the causes of homicide and assaultive violence are complex, community strategies for prevention must be multidimensional. Typical strategies for individual prevention include:[76]

- Developing and implementing educational programs to teach people communication, conflict-resolution, and coping skills.
- Working with individuals to help them develop a sense of personal self-esteem and respect for others.
- Rewarding youngsters for good behavior. Never spanking a child when angry. Children need to know that anger is sometimes acceptable, but violence never is. Use family meetings to resolve conflicts.
- Establishing and enforcing policies that forbid discrimination on the basis of gender, religious affiliation, race, sexual orientation, marital status, and age.
- Increasing and enriching educational programs for family planning.

Recognizing and Preventing Violence in American Schools

Pearl, Mississippi . . . Paducah, Kentucky . . . Jonesboro, Arkansas . . . Springfield, Oregon . . . Littleton, Colorado . . .

Normally, a list of these towns would mean nothing to the average American. Today, however, it serves as a roll call of a trend in recent years that has sent shudders throughout the country. Each represents the scene of a school shooting, incidents in which one or more students fired upon classmates and teachers, and in at least one case, upon themselves, killing many and injuring even more. Each has left everyone—parents, school and city officials, legislators, and students—searching for explanations. What led the students to do this? What could have been done to prevent it?

These incidents have left us with a distorted, yet troubling view of America's schools and have provided a clear indication that attention needs to be paid to reduce the risk of additional violence. Officials at all levels have responded with efforts to find answers, to put preventive measures into place, and to identify warning signs. After the Oregon shootings in 1998, President Clinton even directed the departments of Education and Justice to examine the issues and develop a National "Early Warning Guide" to help adults reach out to troubled children quickly and effectively.

Although it isn't possible to predict all violence, often there are early warning signs. For example, we know from research that most children who become violent toward self or others feel rejected and psychologically victimized and may have exhibited aggressive behavior in early life, often toward pets or smaller children. Below is a list of behaviors considered to be common denominators in past incidents. Remember, however, that such profiles are not always accurate, and there is a danger in stigmatizing students who demonstrate one or more of these warning signs. As such, they should be used only as indicators and as aids in identifying and referring at-risk kids.

- Social withdrawal
- Excessive feelings of rejection and isolation
- Feelings of being persecuted
- Poor academic performance and little interest in school
- Expression of violence in writing or drawing
- Uncontrolled anger
- Impulsive and chronic bullying and harassment of others
- History of discipline problems
- History of violent and aggressive behavior
- Affiliation with gangs
- Fascination with and access to weapons, particularly guns
- Background of drug or alcohol use

While socioeconomic status has historically been a harbinger of violence, what sets the recent incidence of school shootings apart is that the shooters have tended to come from middle to upper class, well-educated families and have what appear to be many of the positive assets once thought necessary to protect them from violence. In each case, the communities were rocked to learn that "it *can* happen here."

Is it safe to send our children to school anymore? While it is understandable for people, parents in particular, to be shaken by these incidents, the answer to the preceding question is "yes." Statistically, America's schools continue to be among the safest places for children; in fact, they are far safer than on our nation's streets or even in their homes.

While it is important to note the early warnings of such violence, it is also important to note that the schools and communities that provide the safest environments for recognizing and avoiding risks:

- Focus on academic achievements
- Involve families in meaningful ways
- Develop links to community
- Emphasize positive relationships between students and staff
- Discuss safety issues openly
- Treat students with equal respect
- Provide outlets for students to share their concerns
- Help children feel safe expressing their feelings
- Have in place a system for referring children who are suspected of being abused or neglected
- Offer extended day programs for children
- Promote good citizenship and character
- Identify problems and assess progress toward solutions
- Support students in making the transition to adult life and the workplace

For more information and a complete narrative on what communities, schools, parents, and individuals can do to make schools safer for all, visit the National Resource Center for Safe Schools online at http://www.safetyzone.org

STUDENTS SPEAK UP:

What is happening with young people that makes them turn on their classmates and teachers with such extreme violence? What do you think is the best way to prevent or stop school shootings?

Sources: "Early Warning, Timely Response: A Guide to Safe Schools," National Resource Center for Safe Schools, http://www .safetyzone.org; "Warning Signs," American Psychological Association, http://www.uncg .edu/edu/ericcass/violence/docs/warning.htm

- Increasing identification by health-care and social service programs of violence victims.
- Improving treatment and support for victims.
- Treating the psychological as well as the physical consequences of violence.

UNINTENTIONAL INJURIES

As stated previously, unintentional injuries are those that occur without anyone planning or intending that harm occur. For whatever reason, people are in the absolute wrong place at the wrong time, and the setting and circumstances as well as human judgment errors combine to injure or harm another person. Examples of unintentional injuries are those that result from car accidents, falls, water accidents/drowning, accidental gunshots, recreational accidents, and workplace injuries. Hunters die from stray bullets while hunting, swimmers drown when they underestimate currents or water conditions, people slip and fall over things left on the floor, and lapses in attention lead to auto mishaps. These events result in unintended pain, suffering, and possibly even death. Most efforts to prevent unintentional injuries focus on changing something about the *person*, the *environment*, or the *circumstances* (policies, procedures) that put people in harm's way.

Residential Safety

Injuries within the home typically occur in the form of falls, burns, or intrusions by others. Some populations, such as the elderly, are particularly vulnerable to household injuries; however, the elderly are not the only likely victims. Each year, hundreds of children suffer severe burns or die from accidental fires, falls, and other home-based injuries. To reduce your risk of injuries, consider the following:

▶ Fall-Proofing Your Home
- Eliminate clutter, particularly things that you may stumble over in the dark. Leave nothing lying around on the floor.
- Make sure all rugs are securely fastened to the floor and don't slide when stepped on. Inexpensive rubberized mats or strip will hold rugs in place on even the most slippery of floors.
- Train your pets to stay out from under your feet. Many an unsuspecting person has ended up on the floor while trying to avoid a pet.
- Make sure handrails are secure and within easy reach. All stairs should have slip-proof tread.
- Install slip-proof mats or decals in showers and tubs. Handrails and places to grab for stability in tubs and showers are always good ideas.

▶ Avoiding Burns
- Make sure that all cigarettes are carefully extinguished in ash trays before going to bed. Don't smoke and drink before bed. Don't smoke in bed at any time! Don't throw spent matches in the trash where paper and other combustibles might lead to fire. Set them in a container of water until completely soaked.
- Keep all lamps away from drapes, linens, and paper on your desk, particularly halogen lights or specialty lamps that can get extremely hot.
- Keep all hotpads and kitchen cloths away from stove burners at all times. When you finish using one, set it far from the stove on a counter until the next use.
- Keep candles under control and away from other combustible areas. While it may seem romantic to go to sleep by candlelight, it is highly risky and should never be done.
- Whenever possible, purchase stoves and ovens with controls on the front panel so that you can avoid reaching over hot foods to change burner temperature.
- Use caution when lighting barbecue grills and other home-based fires. Never spray combustible fluids directly onto the fire.
- Have chimneys and fireplaces checked regularly for build-up of flammable soot and byproducts of burning.
- Have furnaces serviced annually, and be sure the filters are changed.
- Avoid overloading electrical circuits with appliances and cords. Older buildings are at particular risk.
- Program phones with emergency numbers for speed dialing, and keep these numbers in clear sight near phones as well.
- Replace batteries in fire alarms regularly, and test them regularly to make sure the batteries are working.
- Have the proper fire extinguishers ready in case of fires (see Figure 4.2).

Fire extinguishers are labeled A, B, and C, depending on the kind of fire they are designed to extinguish. They also are numbered according to the size of the fire they can put out. The higher the number, the greater the capacity.

TYPE	USES
A	Ordinary combustibles (paper, wood, cloth)
B	Flammable liquids (grease, gas, paints, solvents)
C	Electrical equipment (TVs, fuse boxes, wiring)

Figure 4.2
Do You Have an Appropriate Fire Extinguisher?

▶ Preventing Unwanted Intruders

- Close blinds and drapes whenever you are away and in the evening when you are in your home. Remove large bushes and obstructions from around your windows and doors so that anyone lurking outside will be seen by others.
- Install dead-bolt locks on all doors and locks on windows. Put a peephole in the main entryways to your home, and do not let anyone in without checking.
- If you have a screen door, lock it. If someone comes to the door, this door serves as a barrier between you and any unknown visitors.
- Check out low-cost alarm systems for your home. If possible, have one installed.
- If possible, rent apartments that require a security code or clearance before entry can be gained.
- Avoid apartments that are easily accessible, such as first-floor units with large patio doors that are hidden from view by passers-by.
- Don't give information about your home or schedule to telephone solicitors. Try to vary the times of day that you come home for lunch or quick stops to check on things.
- Don't let repairmen in without identification. Preferably, your landlord should give you information about such visits well in advance. Have someone else in the house when repairmen are there working. Remember that just because someone is licensed to fix your refrigerator does not mean the person can be trusted.
- Avoid dark parking structures, laundry rooms, and the like. Try to use these areas only when others are around, and when they are well lit.
- Tell friends where you are going and when you should be returning.
- Use initials for first names on your mailbox and phone listing. Keep your address out of phone books.
- Know the numbers for emergency assistance, such as 911. Remember that many intruders do not actually cut your phone line, as seen on TV. It is much more common for them to simply pick up the receiver in another room as they walk through, thereby disabling a bedroom phone. Keep a cell phone near your bed and have it programmed to 911.
- Get to know your neighbors. Organize a neighborhood watch.
- Be careful of "doggy doors." Some thieves will have their smallest associate crawl through and open up the house for entry.
- Be careful of skylights and other areas that open up from the outside. Keep them locked and bolted.
- If away, set the lights in different rooms on timers set to come on and go off at different times. Stop your mail and newspaper.

Although no amount of security will prevent all threats of intrusion, following these precautions, as well as actively searching for low-crime, well-maintained housing, are good steps toward preventing unwanted invasions. Usually intruders are searching for items to sell and enter with theft in mind. If you encounter an intruder it is far better to give them your money than to actively engage them in battle.

······ WHAT DO YOU THINK?

Do a "spot check" of your home. What areas might pose a risk for home accidents or forced entry? Do you have a fire extinguisher in your house? Do you know the number of the local fire department or police department? What would you do if the house caught on fire and you needed to escape immediately?

Workplace Safety

During an average week in America, adults spend most of their waking hours on the job. While some of these hours are pleasant and productive, many pose very real physical and emotional hazards for unsuspecting individuals. Job stress, job burnout, hostile or abusive interactions with others, discrimination, power struggles, sexual harassment, and a host of other threats are possible whenever you have people cloistered together for prolonged periods of time. The nature of the job itself, the corporate culture, and the policies and procedures that characterize certain jobs can add to stressful workplace problems.

▶ **Fatal Injuries** Certain industries are inherently more hazardous and present far greater risks for injuries and fatalities than others. Jobs with the highest fatality rates and injury rates are found in outdoor occupations, in which workers are not in an office or factory. While workplaces have begun serious programming, policies, and services designed to reduce risks, the following statistics continue to provide indicators of a serious problem:[77]

- In 1997, job-related fatalities reached their highest levels since record-keeping began.
- Highway crashes were the leading cause of on-the-job fatalities and accounted for 22 percent of 1997 fatal work injury totals. Most involved truck drivers.
- Twenty percent of worker fatalities resulted from other types of transportation-related incidents, such as tractors and forklifts overturning in fields or warehouses, workers being struck by vehicles, aircraft and railway crashes, and water vessels capsizing.
- Workplace homicides declined in the past 6 years, but continued as the second leading cause of death. Co-worker disputes, former co-worker disputes, and shootings during the course of robbery led the list of potential worker threats.
- Falls and being struck by objects were the next leading causes of worker fatality, as well as electrocutions.

- Commercial fishing was among the most dangerous occupations.
- On average, about 17 workers were fatally injured each day in 1997. Hundreds more were permanently and/or temporarily disabled.
- Most fatally injured workers under 16 years of age were killed while doing farm work.

▶ *Nonfatal Work Injuries*   Although deaths capture media attention, many workers are seriously injured or disabled and are forced to suffer silently. Chronic, debilitating pain and other injuries to workers can cause great economic strain on organizations due to worker's compensation claims and numbers of days lost from work. Injuries that cause the greatest number of lost-work days include carpal tunnel syndrome, hernia, amputation of a limb, fractures, sprains and strains (often of the back), cuts or lacerations, and chemical burns.[78] While each has the potential to be life-threatening, they more

commonly cause workers to stay home from the job. In fact, nearly half of all workers afflicted with carpal tunnel syndrome missed 30 days or more of work in 1997. Because so many of these worker injuries are due to repetitive motion, overexertion, or inappropriate motion, they are largely preventable through worker training and other employee techniques designed to reduce employees' risks.

WHAT DO YOU THINK?

What can be done to prevent fatal injuries? Nonfatal injuries? Are students on your campus at risk of injury from any of the problems discussed? Are there safety prevention strategies in place on your campus? Who is in charge of student safety?

Taking Charge
Managing Campus Safety

College campuses today may be healthy places for student interactions, but they can also be settings for violent and aggressive interactions between students. Most campuses have initiated programs, services, and policies designed to protect students from potential threats against their personal health and safety. Setting limits on

where you go, at what time, and with whom you hang around are themes of this chapter. What types of limits do you set yourself when you're out with friends, either casual or intimate? Answering the following questions may help you determine your college administrators' degree of interest in and commitment to a violence-free setting.

CHOICES FOR CHANGE

MAKING PERSONAL CHOICES

✓ Do you decide before going on a date to limit your sexual behavior?

✓ Do you travel in groups whenever possible?

✓ Do you avoid being out alone at night?

✓ Do you avoid high-crime areas?

✓ Do you take the precautions necessary to reduce your risk of injury from violence?

MAKING COMMUNITY CHOICES

✓ Does your health center offer workshops on rape prevention and the prevention of other sexual offenses?

✓ Does your campus offer courses focusing on understanding human diversity?

✓ Does your campus offer workshops/information for students to help them avoid situations that put them at risk for violent sexual or other interactions?

✓ Does your campus offer confidential counseling and/or assistance to victims of sexual assault?

✓ Does your campus offer workshops/educational sessions dealing with suicide?

✓ Does your campus offer information/workshops/services dealing with partner/domestic violence?

✓ Does your campus have strict substance abuse policies?

✓ Are services such as rides and escort services available to students after hours to prevent rapes/assaults? Has your university increased the role of campus security to improve student safety?

✓ Is your campus well-lighted and open in the evenings?

✓ Are campus health educators, counselors, and other professionals trained to spot victimization in clients and recommend appropriate services?

✓ Does your campus have a code of conduct that mandates swift and prudent punishment for alcohol and other drug abuse and acts of campus violence?

SUMMARY

- Intentional injuries are those incurred as a result of actions committed with intent to harm. Unintentional injuries are the result of actions with no intent to harm. Violence is at epidemic levels in the United States. There are many factors that lead people to be violent. Among them are anger and substance abuse.

- Violence affects everyone in society—from the direct victims, to those who live in fear, to those who pay higher taxes and insurance premiums. Over half of homicides are committed by people who knew their victims. Bias and hate crimes divide people, but teaching tolerance can reduce risks. Gang violence continues to grow but can be combated by programs aimed at reducing the problems

that lead to gang membership. Violence on campus may be increasing, but the victims' rights have also increased as a result of several major pieces of legislation.

- Many crimes of general society are now commonplace at universities and colleges, including personal assaults, harassment, hate crimes, and even murder.

- Prevention of violent acts begins with keeping yourself out of situations in which harm may occur. There are several avenues available for reducing risks, including community, school, workplace, and individual strategies.

- Unintentional injuries frequently occur in our own homes and worksites and can exact a heavy toll on Americans.

DISCUSSION QUESTIONS

1. What are the major types of crimes in the United States? What is the difference between primary and reactive aggression?
2. What are the major factors that lead to violent acts?
3. Who tends to be susceptible to the appeal of gang membership? What actions can we take to keep young kids out of gangs?
4. Compare spousal abuse against men and against women: What are the differences? What are the similarities? What are the causes of domestic violence?

5. What puts a child at risk for abuse? Is there anything that can be done to prevent or to decrease the amount of child abuse?
6. What is sexual harassment and what factors contribute to it in the workplace?
7. What factors increase your risk for sexual assault?
8. What do you think are the most effective violence prevention strategies on your campus?
9. What steps can you take to lower your risk of injury from unintentional violence?

APPLICATION EXERCISE

Reread the *What Do You Think?* scenario at the beginning of the chapter and answer the following questions:

1. Think about the violent incidents listed. What do you think are the major reasons that these situations occur? What actions could we take as a society to reduce violence? What actions could be taken on your campus?

2. Do you think that your campus is immune to situations such as what happened to Matthew Shepard? What is being done to encourage tolerance?
3. How safe is your campus? What policies, procedures, or safeguards are in place to protect you?

OBJECTIVES

▶ Explain the characteristics of intimate relationships, the purposes they serve, and the types of intimacy that each of us may be able to have.

▶ Explain how relationships develop, and describe the factors that influence their formation and maintenance.

▶ Discuss the difference between men and women in relationships.

▶ Discuss what remaining single means for many Americans.

▶ Examine child-rearing practices in the United States and the importance of a healthy family environment.

▶ Discuss the warning signs of relationship decline, where you can go to get help with a relationship crisis, and factors that ultimately lead to relationship problems.

▶ Define sexual identity, and discuss the role of gender identity.

▶ Identify the components of male and female reproductive anatomy and physiology and their functions.

▶ Discuss the options available for the expression of one's sexuality.

▶ Classify sexual dysfunctions and describe each disorder.

5

Healthy Relationships and Sexuality

Making Commitments

WE NEED RELATIONSHIPS WITH OTHERS to know that we are truly alive. While we strive for positive relationships with our friends, family, and significant others, we sometimes find ourselves in relationships that result in an emotional roller coaster. While negative relationships may cause us distress, intimate relationships that have gone bad can send us in a downward spiral emotionally and physically. How can we ensure that the relationship in which we are investing our time, energy, and emotion is a healthy one? What are the characteristics of a healthy relationship? How do our relationships contribute to our overall health and well-being?

All relationships involve a degree of risk. However, without the risk of friendships, intimacy, and shared experiences, most of us would not grow, would not be sufficiently stimulated, and life would hold no excitement. Those of us who choose to take risks—who let ourselves feel, love, and express our deepest emotions—are vulnerable to great love as well as great unhappiness. Taking a look at our intimate and non-intimate relationships, components of our sexual identity, our gender roles, and our sexual orientation may help us better understand who we are in our life and our relationships. Ultimately, this understanding will prepare us to make healthful, responsible, and satisfying decisions about our relationships and sexuality.

CHARACTERISTICS OF INTIMATE RELATIONSHIPS

There are many possible definitions of **intimate relationships.** One classic definition calls these relationships "close relationships with another person in which you offer, and

are offered, validation, understanding, and a sense of being valued intellectually, emotionally, and physically."[1] In this context, friends, family, lovers, partners, and even people you work with or interact with at the grocery store may be included in the sphere of intimate interactions. However, most experts today tend to focus more on family, close friendships, and romantic relationships when they discuss intimate relationships.

For the purposes of this chapter, we define intimate relationships in terms of three characteristics: *behavioral interdependence, need fulfillment,* and *emotional attachment.* Each of these three characteristics may be related to interactions with family, close friends, and romantic relationships.[2]

Behavioral interdependence refers to the mutual impact that people have on each other as their lives and daily activities become intertwined. What one person does may influence what the other person may want to do and can do. Such interdependence may become stronger over time to the point that each person would find a great void in his or her life if the other person was gone.

Another characteristic of intimate relationships is that they serve to fulfill psychological needs and so are a means of *need fulfillment.* These needs may often be met only through relationships with others:

- The need for approval and for a sense of purpose in life—requiring the sense that what we say and do counts.
- The need for intimacy—requiring someone with whom we can share our feelings freely.
- The need for social integration—requiring someone with whom we can share our worries and concerns.
- The need for being nurturant—requiring someone whom we can take care of.
- The need for assistance—requiring someone to help us in times of need.

The emotional bonds that characterize intimate relationships know no boundaries.

- The need for reassurance or affirmation of our own worth—requiring someone who will tell us that we matter.

In close, rewarding, intimate relationships, partners or friends meet each other's needs. They disclose feelings, share confidences, and discuss practical concerns, helping each other and providing reassurance. They serve as major sources of social support and reinforce our feelings that we are important and serve a purpose in life.

Emotional availability, the ability to give to and receive from others emotionally without fear of being hurt or rejected, is another characteristic of intimate relationships. At times, all of us may need to protect ourselves psychologically by making ourselves unavailable emotionally. For example, after the end of a painful relationship, it may be wise to avoid jumping into another relationship. By holding back, a person may take time for introspection and healing as well as considering the "lessons learned." Because of intense trauma, some

---

Intimate relationships   "[C]lose relationships with another person in which you offer, and are offered, validation, understanding, and a sense of being valued intellectually, emotionally, and physically."

Emotional availability   The ability to give to and receive from other people emotionally without being inhibited by fears of being hurt.

---

people find it too difficult to be fully available in relationships. This may cause difficulty for those trying to break down barriers.

In addition to behavioral interdependence and need fulfillment, intimate relationships involve strong bonds of *emotional attachment,* or feelings of love and attachment. The intimacy level experienced by any two people cannot easily be judged by those outside the relationship. Individuals share their inner selves so differently that it is impossible to assign a clear meaning to any given action. Friendship relationships can be very intimate and contribute essential elements to a person's sense of inclusion and well-being. Love relationships may be very intimate and include many aspects of intimacy in addition to sexual sharing. Often, when we hear the word *intimacy* we immediately think about a sexual relationship. A relationship may be very intimate and not be sexual, although sex may be an important part of an intimate relationship. Important relationships having high levels of intimacy may be either sexual or nonsexual. Two people can be emotionally intimate (share feelings) or spiritually intimate (share spiritual beliefs and meanings), or be intimate friends. In each of these intimate interactions, sex is not the defining behavior.

············ **WHAT DO YOU THINK?**

Consider the "needs" discussed in the last section. Who would you go to, or who currently helps meet your psychological needs, in each of these areas? Who, if anyone, do you help meet these needs?

FORMING INTIMATE RELATIONSHIPS

Throughout our lives, we go through predictable patterns of relationships. In our early years, our families are our most significant relationships. Gradually, our relationships widen to include circles of friends, co-workers, and acquaintances. Ultimately, most of us develop romantic or sexual relationships with significant others. Each of these relationships plays a significant role in psychological, social, spiritual, and physical health. Each has the potential either to serve as a growth experience or to "bring us down" as a result of unhealthy interactions.

Families: The Ties that Bind

Although many people consider the family the foundation of American society and talk about a return to "family values" as a desirable objective, it is clear that the modern American family may look quite different from families of previous generations. The *Leave It to Beaver* family type encouraged during the 1950s, composed of Mom with her apron, staying at home and content with her role as mother and spouse; Dad with his briefcase, trying to move up the corporate ladder; and two or three happy, well-adjusted children, is often not the norm. Over half of today's moms work outside the home and large numbers of children are raised by single parents, grandparents, relatives, stepparents, nannies, day-care centers, and other "parents."

Regardless of the form or structure of each family, all families have in common one unique characteristic: the special caring, regard, and bonding that a group of people having shared interests have for each other. Whether the family is related by birth, a high level of love and regard, living arrangement, or some other factor, the family network often provides the sense of security that humans need to develop into healthy adults. In fact, because the definition of *family* changes dramatically from culture to culture and from place to place over time, no clear definition of *family* exists. Families are not inherently good or bad based on the structure or roles that people bring to the family setting. Those that result in the most positive health outcomes for all members appear to be those that offer a sense of security, safety, and love, and that provide the opportunity for members to grow as a result of positive interactions.

Today's Family Unit

The United Nations defines seven basic types of families, including single-parent families, communal families (unrelated people living together for ideological, economic, or other reasons), extended families, and others. But most Americans think of family in terms of the "family of origin" or the "nuclear family." The *family of origin* includes the people present in the household during a child's first years of life—usually parents and siblings. However, the family of origin may also include a stepparent, parents' lovers, or significant others such as grandparents, aunts, or uncles. The family of origin has a tremendous impact on the child's psychological and social development. The *nuclear family* consists of parents (usually married, but not necessarily) and their offspring.

If parents are not afraid to share feelings, affection, or love with each other and their offspring, their children are more likely to become emotionally connected adults. If the home environment provides stability and seems a safe place to be, it is likely that the children will learn to express feelings and develop intimacy skills. Sibling interactions provide a way to learn and practice interpersonal skills. The family of origin and the nuclear family have the potential for encouraging significant positive interactions and growth. People can practice positive behaviors and learn the rights and wrongs of negative behaviors in a safe and nonjudgmental environment when the family itself is healthy. However, if the family is psychologically or physically unhealthy, it may pose significant

barriers to later relationships, as we discuss later, in the section on dysfunctional families.

Establishing Friendships

A Friend is one who knows you as you are
understands where you've been
accepts who you've become, and
still gently invites you to grow.
                              —Author Unknown

Good friends—they can make a boring day fun, a cold day warm, or a gut-wrenching worry disappear. They can make us feel like we belong, that we matter, and that we have the strength to get through just about anything. They can also make us angry, disappoint us, or seriously jolt our own comfortable ideas about being right or wrong. No friendship is perfect, few are fault-free, and most need careful attention if they are to remain stable over time. Psychologists discuss friendships in terms of sharing of common ideals, attitudes, and beliefs.[3] While we all know that friends enrich our lives, most people don't realize that there are real health benefits to strong social bonds like friendship. Social support has been shown to boost the immune system, improve the quality and possibly the length of life, and even reduce the risks for heart disease.[4]

Although most of us have a fairly clear idea of the distinction between a friend and a lover, this difference is not always easy to verbalize. Some people believe that the major difference is that there is no intimate physical involvement between friends. Others have suggested that intimacy levels are much lower between friends than between lovers. Confused? You are probably not alone. Surprisingly, there has not been a great deal of research to clarify these terms. Psychologists Jeffrey Turner and Laurna Rubinson provide a basic overview of what friendship actually entails:[5]

- *Enjoyment.* Friends enjoy each other's company most of the time, although there may be temporary states of anger, disappointment, or mutual annoyance.
- *Acceptance.* Friends accept each other as they are, without trying to change or make the other into a different person.
- *Trust.* Friends have mutual trust; each assumes that the other will act in his or her friend's best interests.
- *Respect.* Friends respect each other; each assumes that the other exercises good judgment in making life choices.
- *Mutual assistance.* Friends are inclined to assist and support one another. Specifically, they can count on each other in times of need, trouble, or personal distress.
- *Confiding.* Friends share experiences and feelings with each other that they don't share with other people.
- *Understanding.* Friends have a sense of what is important to each and why each behaves as he or she does.
- *Spontaneity.* Friends feel free to be themselves in the relationship rather than required to play a role, wear a mask, or inhibit revealing personal traits.

According to psychologist Dan McAdams, most of us are fortunate to develop one or two lasting friendships in a lifetime.[6]

Significant Others, Partners, Couples

Although family and friends are necessary intimate relationships, most people choose at some point whether or not to enter into an intimate sexual relationship with another person. Numerous studies have analyzed the ways in which couples form significant partnering relationships. Most couples fit into one of four categories of significant sexual or committed relationships: married heterosexual couples, cohabiting heterosexual couples, lesbian couples, and gay male couples. These groups are discussed in greater detail later in this chapter.

Love relationships in each of these four groups typically include all the characteristics of friendship as well as other characteristics related to passion and caring:[7]

- *Fascination.* Lovers tend to pay attention to the other person even when they should be involved in other activities. They are preoccupied with the other and want to think about, look at, talk to, or merely be with the other.
- *Exclusiveness.* Lovers have a special relationship that usually precludes having the same relationship with a third party. The love relationship takes priority over all others.
- *Sexual desire.* Lovers want physical intimacy with the partner, desiring to touch, hold, and engage in sexual activities with the other. They may choose not to act on these feelings because of religious, moral, or practical considerations.
- *Giving the utmost.* Lovers care enough to give the utmost when the other is in need, sometimes to the point of extreme sacrifice.
- *Being a champion/advocate.* The depth of lovers' caring may show up as an active, unselfish championing of each other's interests and a positive attempt to ensure that the other succeeds.

For obvious reasons, the best love relationships share friendships, and the best friendships include several love components. Both relationships share common bonds of nurturance, enhancement of personal well-being, and a genuine sense of mutual regard, trust, and security. Healthy friendships and love relationships can greatly enhance overall health and lead to sustained personal growth throughout one's life.

WHAT DO YOU THINK?

What is the difference between a friend and someone you'd select as a partner? Only sex? Can you have a good relationship with a partner and *not* have sex? Can you have sex with a friend and be just friends? What are the key issues in both instances?

This Thing Called Love

What is love? Finding a definition of love may be more difficult than listing characteristics of a loving relationship. The term *love* has more entries in *Bartlett's Familiar Quotations* than does any other word except *man*.[8] This four-letter word has been written about and engraved on walls; it has been the theme of countless novels, movies, and plays. There is no one definition of *love,* and the word may mean different things to people depending on cultural values, age, gender, and situation.

Many social scientists maintain that love may be of two kinds: *companionate* and *passionate*. Companionate love is a secure, trusting attachment, similar to what we may feel for family members or close friends. In companionate love, two people are attracted, have much in common, care about each other's well-being, and express reciprocal liking and respect. Passionate love is, in contrast, a state of high arousal, filled with the ecstasy of being loved by the partner and the agony of being rejected.[9] The person experiencing passionate love tends to be preoccupied with his or her partner and to perceive the love object as being perfect.[10] According to Hatfield and Walster, passionate love will not occur unless three conditions are met.[11] First, the person must live in a culture in which the concept of "falling in love" is idealized. Second, a "suitable" love object must be present. If the person has been taught by parents, movies, books, and peers to seek partners having certain levels of attractiveness or belonging to certain racial groups or having certain socioeconomic status and none is available, the person may find it difficult to allow him- or herself to become involved. Finally, for passionate love to occur, there must be some type of physiological arousal that occurs when a person is in the presence of the object of desire. Sexual excitement is often the way in which such arousal is expressed.

In his article "The Triangular Theory of Love," researcher Robert Sternberg attempts to clarify further what love is by isolating three key ingredients:

- *Intimacy.* The emotional component, which involves feelings of closeness.
- *Passion.* The motivational component, which reflects romantic, sexual attraction.
- *Decision/commitment.* The cognitive component, which includes the decisions you make about being in love and the degree of commitment to your partner.

According to Sternberg's model, the higher the levels of intimacy, passion, and commitment, the more likely a person is to be involved in a healthy, positive love relationship.

Anthropologist Helen Fisher, a research associate at the American Museum of Natural History and author of *Anatomy of Love: The Natural History of Monogamy, Adultery, and Divorce,* has attempted to shed light on the process of falling in love.[12] According to Fisher (and others), attraction and falling in love follow a fairly predictable pattern based on (1) *imprinting,* in which our evolutionary patterns, genetic predispositions, and past experiences trigger romantic reaction; (2) *attraction,* in which neurochemicals produce feelings of euphoria and elation;

(3) *attachment,* in which endorphins—natural opiates—cause lovers to feel peaceful, secure, and calm; and (4) *production of a cuddle chemical,* in which the brain secretes the chemical *oxytocin,* thereby stimulating sensations during lovemaking and eliciting feelings of satisfaction and attachment.[13]

Lovers who claim that they are swept away by passion may not, therefore, be far from the truth.

> A meeting of the eyes, a touch of the hands or a whiff of scent may set off a flood that starts in the brain and races along the nerves and through the blood. The familiar results—flushed skin, sweaty palms, heavy breathing—are identical to those experienced when under stress. Why? Because the love-smitten person is secreting chemical substances such as dopamine, nor-epinephrine, and phenylethylamine (PEA) that are chemical cousins of amphetamines.[14]

Although attraction may in fact be a "natural high," with PEA levels soaring, this hit of passion loses effectiveness over time as the body builds up a tolerance. Needing a continual fix of passion, many people may become attraction junkies, seeking the intoxication of love much as the drug user seeks a chemical high.[15]

Fisher speculates that PEA levels drop significantly over a three-to-four-year period, leading to the "four-year itch" that shows up in the peaking fourth-year divorce rates present in over 60 cultures. Those romances that last beyond the four-year decline of PEA are influenced by another set of chemicals, known as endorphins, soothing substances that give lovers a sense of security, peace, and calm.[16]

Oxytocin is also being studied for its role in the love formula. Produced by the brain, it sensitizes nerves and stimulates muscle contractions, the production of breast milk, and the desire for physical closeness between mother and infant. Scientists speculate that oxytocin may encourage similar cuddling between men and women. Oxytocin levels have also been shown to increase dramatically during orgasm for both men and women.[17]

In addition to such possible chemical influences, our past experiences may significantly affect our attractions for others. Our parents' modeling of traits we believe are desirable or undesirable may play a role in drawing us to people with similar traits. Many researchers have investigated the possible link between males seeking their own mothers in partners and females seeking their fathers in partners. To date, research on chemical attractions and parent-seeking tendencies is inconclusive and should be viewed only as preliminary findings. Much more research is needed to confirm these provocative new attraction theories.

GENDER ISSUES

In any relationship, understanding and communication are important ingredients for success. Sometimes it may seem that the relating styles of men and women are so different that obtaining true understanding and open communication may

Most people have romanticized views of what it means to "fall in love," but while such times can be a period of elation and head-spinning days, lasting relationships require equal commitment and effort on the part of both people.

be next to impossible. Deborah Tannen summarized the frustration often felt between men and women who are trying to relate to one another in her best-selling book *You Just Don't Understand: Women and Men in Conversation.*[18] According to Tannen, men's and women's social conditioning is so different that it is almost as if they are raised in two different cultures. Women are brought up to feel comfortable and to share freely in their intimate relationships. They tend to be more nurturing and less afraid to share their fears, anxieties, and emotions. It's okay if they cry, scream, or express wide emotional swings. Big boys, however, are not supposed to cry—at least according to popular beliefs. Unlike their female counterparts, they are not supposed to show emotions, and they are brought up to believe that being strong is often more important than having close friendships. As a result, according to research, only 1 male in 10 has a close male friend to whom he divulges his innermost thoughts.[19]

Why the Differences?

Although there are various theories about why males and females relate in the way they do, Lillian Rubin's historic work has received the most widespread acceptance. Rubin sees a serious barrier to intimacy in what she considers a basic difference in the development patterns of men and women.[20] In her view, men are less able to express emotions and achieve intimacy than are women owing to the process of identity development in infancy, which she sees as more difficult for males than for females. Males initially achieve intimacy with a female caregiver, usually a mother, at a preverbal stage. By the time

Like Parents, Like Children? Patterns of Relationship Attachment Styles

Have you read just one too many articles or heard yet another talk show in which parents get the rap for your current inability to relate to others? Can't buy yourself love because of all of that damage done to you in your formative years? While there are some glimmers of truth in all of the hype, it is important to note that most previous research on relationships and attachment styles has focused exclusively on college students and distressed individuals, such as incest survivors. So, what should you believe?

Recently, Kristin D. Mickelson and Ronald Kessler, both of Harvard Medical School, and Phillip Shaver of the University of California at Davis have examined for the first time the forms of interpersonal attachment in a representative sample of U.S. adults. In their research, three distinct patterns of adult attachment styles surfaced:

Secure attachment styles: Foster lasting relationships marked by trust and compromise

Avoidant attachment styles: Result in dread or disdain for emotional intimacy in relationships

Anxious (or ambivalent) attachment styles: Lead to insecurity about close relationships and manipulative attempts to control romantic patterns

According to their research nearly 20 percent of 18- to 24-year-olds display anxious attachment, compared with only 8 percent of 45- to 54-year-olds. The national results also suggest that neither of the insecure attachment styles stem simply from having had poor relations with one's parents. Rather, the styles exhibit strong links to early traumas such as physical abuse or serious neglect. Parental substance abuse, divorce, and financial adversity also frequently characterize the childhoods of participants reporting insecure adult attachments. Insecure attachment seems to be about the absence of emotional trust in others. Fortunately, the majority of subjects exhibited secure attachment styles, indicating a greater likelihood of successful attachment forming and more stable relationships.

While it is impossible to know who will tend to fit into the foregoing categories, the likelihood of a dysfunctional family leading to dysfunctional relationships seems to be supported. The bottom line: when checking sexual histories with potential partners, a brief check of family history and interactions may do much to reduce your risks of problem relationships in the future.

Source: K. Mickelson, R. Kessler, and R. Shaver. "U.S. Survey Explores Relationship Styles," *Science News.* November 15, 1997, 309.

---

they have developed verbal skills, boys have physically separated from the caregiver. Thus, for males, intimacy may consist of physical proximity rather than verbal sharing. Because females do not need to separate themselves from a female caregiver, they do not separate their feelings of intimacy from their verbal constructs. Consequently, women are more likely to be able to express intimacy verbally than are men. This male/female disparity in the ability to express emotions is both the single greatest difference between the sexes and the greatest threat to intimacy in many relationships. Rubin's theories have received widespread acceptance among sociologists and psychologists today. The disparity in the ability to express emotions may account for common female complaints about male attitudes toward sex. Rubin feels that emotion generates sexual feelings in women, whereas sexual feelings generate emotion in men. Sex, it seems, is one area in which men are allowed to contact deeper emotional states.

WHAT DO YOU THINK?

Who are the people with whom you feel most comfortable talking about very personal issues? Do you talk with both males and females about these issues, or do you tend to gravitate toward just one sex? Why do you think you do this?

Picking Partners

Just as males and females may find different ways to express themselves, the process of partner selection also shows distinctly different patterns. In both males and females, more than just chemical and psychological processes influence the choice of partners. One of these factors is *proximity,* or being in the same place at the same time. The more you see a person in your hometown, at social gatherings, or at work, the more likely that an interaction will occur. Thus, if you live in New York, you'll probably end up with another New Yorker.

You also pick a partner based on *similarities* (attitudes, values, intellect, interests); the old adage that "opposites attract" usually isn't true.

If your potential partner expresses interest or liking, you may react with mutual regard known as *reciprocity.* The more you express interest, the safer it is for someone else to return the regard, and the cycle spirals onward.

Another factor that apparently plays a significant role in selecting a partner is *physical attraction.* Whether such attraction is caused by a chemical reaction or a socially learned behavior, males and females appear to have different attraction criteria. Men tend to select their mates primarily on the basis of youth and physical attractiveness. Although physical attractiveness is an important criterion for women in mate selection, they tend to place higher emphasis on partners who are somewhat older, have good financial prospects, and are dependable and industrious.

BARRIERS TO INTIMACY

Obstacles to intimacy include lack of personal identity, emotional immaturity, and a poorly developed sense of responsibility. The fear of being hurt, low self-esteem, mishandled hostility, chronic "busyness" (and its attendant lack of emotional presence), a tendency to "parentify" loved ones, and a conflict of role expectations may be equally detrimental. In addition, individual insecurities and difficulties in recognizing and expressing emotional needs can lead to an intimacy barrier. These barriers to intimacy may have many causes, including the different emotional development of men and women or an upbringing in a dysfunctional family.

Dysfunctional Families

As noted earlier, the ability to sustain genuine intimacy is largely developed in the family of origin. Unfortunately, sharing, trust, and openness do not always occur in the family. In fact, the assumption that such intimacy existed in the family of origin may actually be unrealistic. As adults, we may discover that although we thought our family encouraged emotional intimacy, it was actually judgmental, full of expectations, and, in many ways, dysfunctional. A **dysfunctional family** is one in which the interaction between family members inhibits psychological growth rather than encourages self-love, emotional expression, and individual growth. If you were to examine even the most pristine family under a microscope, you would likely find some type of dysfunction. No group of people who live together day in and day out can interact perfectly all the time. However, many people have begun to overuse the term *dysfunctional* to refer to even the smallest problems in the family unit. As such, the term becomes relatively meaningless. True dysfunctionality refers to settings where negative interactions are the norm rather than the exception. Children raised in these settings tend to face tremendous obstacles to growing up healthy. Coming to terms with past hurts may take years. However, with careful planning and introspection, support from loved ones, and counseling when needed, children from even the worst homes have proved to be remarkably resilient. Many are able to forget the past and to focus on the future, developing into healthy, well-adjusted adults. But some have problems throughout their lives.[21] For example, adults who grew up with alcoholic parents may have serious problems creating and maintaining intimate relationships. The family messages that these children receive are typically very contradictory, as the family usually tries to hide the presence of alcohol abuse in the home. It is important to note that dysfunctional families are found in every social, ethnic, religious, economic, and racial group.

Recently, social scientists have been studying the impact of the alcoholic home environment on the sexual and intimate behavior of adult children of alcoholics (ACOAs). Therapist Mary Ann Klausner was one of the first to identify a number of intimacy problems as typical of ACOAs. Many ACOAs claim that they become involved in unhealthy relationships, have difficulty trusting others, have problems in communicating with partners, and have difficulty defining a healthy relationship.[22] Research supporting this theory is conflicted, with many questions about the ACOA role in subsequent relationships.

Another tragically large group of people struggling with intimacy problems originating in the family of origin are survivors of childhood emotional, physical, and sexual abuse (see Chapter 4).

Jealousy in Relationships

"Jealousy is like a San Andreas fault running beneath the smooth surface of an intimate relationship. Most of the time, its eruptive potential lies hidden. But when it begins to rumble, the destruction can be enormous."[23] **Jealousy** has been described as an aversive reaction evoked by a real or imagined relationship involving your partner and a third person.

Contrary to what many of us may believe, jealousy is not a sign of intense devotion or of passionate love for the person who is the target of it. Instead, jealousy is often a sign of underlying problems that may prove to be a significant barrier to a healthy intimate relationship. The roots of jealous feelings and behaviors may run deep. Causes of jealousy typically include the following:

- *Overdependence on the relationship.* People who have few social ties and who rely exclusively on their significant others tend to be fearful of losing them.
- *High value on sexual exclusivity.* People who believe that sexual exclusiveness is a crucial indicator of a love relationship are more likely to become jealous.
- *Severity of the threat.* People may feel uneasy if a person with a fantastic body, stunning good looks, and a great personality appears interested in their partners. But they may brush off the threat if they appraise the person as "unworthy" in terms of appearance or other characteristics.
- *Low self-esteem.* People who feel good about themselves are less likely to feel unworthy and to fear that someone else is going to snatch their partners away from them. The underlying question that torments people with low self-esteem is, "Why would anyone want me?"
- *Fear of losing control.* Some people need to feel in control of the situation. Feeling that they may be losing the attachment of or control over a partner can cause jealousy.

Although men and women react differently to jealousy, in both sexes it appears to be related to the expectation that it would be difficult to find another relationship if the current one should end. For men, jealousy is positively correlated with self-evaluative dependency, the degree to which the man's self-esteem is affected by his partner's judgments.

COMMITTED RELATIONSHIPS

Feelings of love or sexual attraction are not always equated with commitment in a relationship. There can be love without commitment and there can be sex without commitment. Commitment in a relationship with another person means that there is an intent to act over time in a way that perpetuates the well-being of the other person, yourself, and the relationship. A committed relationship involves tremendous diligence on the part of both partners. Over the years, partners learn about one another and constantly adjust the direction of their relationship. What separates committed from uncommitted relationships is the willingness of committed partners to dedicate themselves toward acquiring and using the skills that will ensure a lasting relationship.

Marriage

Marriage is the traditional committed relationship in many societies around the world. For many people, marriage is the ultimate expression of a committed relationship. When two people marry in the United States, they enter into a legal agreement that includes shared financial plans, property, and responsibility in raising children. For religious people, marriage is also a sacrament that stresses the spirituality, rights, and obligations of each person. Close to 90 percent of all Americans marry at least once, compared to 95 percent in the 1970s. However, the United States Census Bureau reports that in recent years Americans have become more particular about commitment and more reluctant to marry young. In 1996, the median age for first marriage was higher than ever before: 26.3 years for men and 24.0 years for women, compared with 22.5 and 20.6, respectively, in 1970.[24] These numbers have continued to increase. Nearly 80 percent of people who divorce will remarry, indicating that most married couples find marriage desirable.

Most Americans believe that marriage involves **monogamy,** or exclusive sexual involvement with one partner. The lifetime pattern for many Americans appears to be **serial monogamy,** which means that a person has a monogamous sexual relationship with one partner for the duration of a relationship before moving on to another monogamous relationship. Some people prefer to have an **open relationship,** or open marriage, in which the partners agree that there may be sexual involvement for each person outside their relationship.

Humans are not naturally monogamous; that is, most of us are capable of being sexually and/or emotionally involved with more than one person at a time. Yet, American society frowns on involvement with an outsider when we are involved in a relationship and profess to be committed. Many people find themselves being attracted to others while in a relationship and consciously try to stop any subsequent interactions. Others find themselves involved unintentionally. Still others actively seek out extra-relationship affairs. Whether by choice or chance, sexual infidelity is an extremely common factor in divorces and breakups.

As with all relationships, there are marriages that work well and bring much satisfaction to the partners, and there are marriages that are unhealthy for the people involved. A good marriage can yield much support and stability, not only for the couple, but also for those involved in the couple's life. Considerable research also indicates that married people live longer, are happier, remain mentally alert longer, and suffer fewer bouts with physical and mental ailments. Some research suggests that today's women who choose marriage may not be as happy as their parents were and that the happiness of never-married men had increased. Whether due to the increasing pressures on women to work, take care of the family, and perform multiple roles, or to some other expectations, these figures may provide an indication of future problems. Because marriage is socially sanctioned and highly celebrated in our culture, there are numerous incentives for couples to stay together and to improve their relationships. Behavioral scientists agree that couples who make some type of formal commitment are more likely to stay together and develop the fulfilling relationship they initially sought than are those who do not commit.

Dysfunctional family   A family in which the interaction between family members inhibits rather than enhances psychological growth.

Jealousy   An aversive reaction evoked by a real or imagined relationship involving a person's partner and a third person.

Monogamy   Exclusive sexual involvement with one partner.

Serial monogamy   Monogamous sexual relationship with one partner before moving on to another.

Open relationship   A relationship in which partners agree that there can be sexual involvement outside the relationship.

Cohabitation

For various reasons, many people prefer to live together without the bonds of matrimony. Commonly called **cohabitation,** this type of relationship is defined as two people who have an intimate connection with each other who live together in the same household. The relationship can be very stable with a high level of commitment between the partners. Cohabitation that lasts a designated number of years (usually seven) constitutes a **common-law marriage** for purposes of real estate and other financial obligations in some states.

Although cohabitation is a viable alternative for some, many cohabitors eventually marry because of pressures from parents and friends, difficulties in obtaining insurance and tax benefits, legal issues over property, and a host of other reasons. In addition, many cohabitors simply decide they want to solidify their relationships.

The disadvantage of cohabitation lies in the lack of societal validation for the relationship and, in some cases, in the societal disapproval of living together without being married. Cohabiting partners do not usually experience the social incentives to stay together that they would if they were married. If they decide to separate, however, they do not experience the legal problems involved in going through a divorce. In 1996 Congress reaffirmed the tax advantages due married couples, and effectively blocked cohabiting heterosexual and homosexual couples from these benefits through the "Defense of Marriage Bill." Today, controversy over the validation of marriage as the only means of eligibility for tax deductions, health insurance, and other benefits continues, particularly in Hawaii, where same-sex marriages have been legalized.

:········· **WHAT DO YOU THINK?**

Although there are advantages and disadvantages in marriage, most people feel that marriage is a desirable option. Are there any advantages in remaining single? What are potential disadvantages? Are there any societal or organizational supports for the single lifestyle?

Gay and Lesbian Partnerships

Most people seek intimate, committed relationships during their adult years. This is no different for gay and lesbian (homosexual) couples. Lesbians and gay men are socialized like other people in our culture and tend to place a high value on relationships. They seek the same things in their primary relationships as do heterosexual partners: friendship, communication, validation, companionship, and a sense of stability. Studies of lesbian couples indicate high levels of attachment and satisfaction and a tendency toward monogamous, long-term relationships. Gay men, too, tend to form committed, long-term relationships, especially as they age.

Challenges to successful lesbian and gay male relationships often stem from the discrimination they face as homosexuals and to difficulties dealing with social, legal, and religious doctrines. For lesbian and gay couples, cohabiting is usually the only available option, although recognition of same-sex marriages has been the focus of heated debate in some states, including Hawaii, Vermont, and California.

SUCCESS IN COMMITTED RELATIONSHIPS

Because the traditional marriage ceremony includes the vow "till death do us part," the definition of success in a relationship tends to be based on whether a couple stays together over the years. Many have questioned the validity of loveless marriages, in which two people stay together for the sake of the kids, for fear of societal condemnation, for financial security, or because they are afraid to be alone. Such relationships lead to emotional and physical abuse, depression, and a host of other difficulties. Selecting the "right" partner is only half of the battle. Learning to communicate, respecting one another, and having a genuine fondness for one another are more important to relationship success than a marriage certificate. Many social scientists agree that the ideal in relating to another person is to develop a committed bond, the boundaries and form of which can change to allow the maximum degree of growth over time.

Partnering Scripts

Most parents love their children and want them to be happy. They often believe that their children will achieve happiness by living much as they have. They chose to marry and raise a family, and they expect their children to follow a similar pattern. Accordingly, children are reared with a very strong script for what is expected of them as adults. This "scripting" is part of what maintains stability within a society. By individuals partnering with someone similar to their families of origin, groups within society remain discernible; children of upper-class parents usually remain in the upper class, children of white partners usually marry a white partner, and so forth. Each group in society has its own partnering script that includes similarities of sex, age, social class, race, religion, physical attributes, and personality types of the prospective partner. By adolescence, people generally know exactly what type of person they are expected to befriend or to date. If you are unsure of the partnering scripts by which you were raised, just picture whom you could or couldn't bring home to meet your family.

For people who select a potential mate based on the script with which they were raised, an elaboration of the concept may seem unnecessary. Yet there are two reasons why it is important to consider the concept of partnering scripts:

(1) you may be among the group that has not chosen an "appropriate" partner, or (2) social approval of your mate selection may bring with it other subtle expectations of your behavior as a couple.

People who have not chosen an "appropriate" partner are subject to a great deal of external stress. Recognizing that this stress is external to the relationship can help alleviate criticism and distancing between the partners. Society provides constant reinforcement for traditional couples, but it withholds this reinforcement from couples of the same sex, mixed race, mixed religion, and mixed age. Social reinforcement includes invitations to events, inquiries about a partner who is not present, and introductions to friends and family. In addition to denying reinforcement to such a couple, friends and family often blame the "inappropriateness" of the couple if the relationship fails.

Yet, despite these obstacles, many nontraditional relationships survive and flourish. For example, the number of interracial marriages has quadrupled since the late 1960s.

People who choose an "appropriate" partner usually have plenty of validation for the relationship. The love and support they feel from friends and family is genuine. It also comes with expectations of what will occur within the relationship. Decisions that the couple feel should be exclusively theirs may provoke unsolicited advice from friends and family.

ACCESSING YOUR HEALTH ON THE INTERNET

Check out the following Internet sites related to relationships, intimacy, family, and sexuality.

1. *Couples National Network.* Link into a network for same-gender couples and singles, with resources for dealing with issues that generally arise.

   http://www.couples-national.org

2. *Sexuality Information and Education Council of the United States (SIECUS).* Information, guidelines, and materials for advancement of healthy and proper sex education.

   http://www.siecus.org

3. *Go Ask Alice.* An interactive question and answer line out of the Columbia University Health Services. "Alice" is available to answer questions each week about any health-related issues, including relationships, nutrition and diet, exercise, drugs, sex, alcohol, and stress.

   http://www.goaskalice.columbia.edu

WHAT DO YOU THINK?

What characteristics are most important to you in a potential partner? Which of these would be important to your parents or friends? If your parents or friends didn't like a potential partner, how important would their opinion be? What would you do in this situation?

Being Self-Nurturant

Learning how you function emotionally and how to nurture yourself through all life's situations is a lifelong task. You should certainly not postpone intimate connections with others until you have achieved this state. There does, however, seem to be a certain level of individual maturity that needs to be reached before a successful intimate relationship becomes possible.

Two concepts that are especially important to knowing yourself and maintaining a good relationship are "accountabil-

Cohabitation Living together without being married.

Common-law marriage Cohabitation lasting a designated period of time (usually seven years) that is considered legally binding in some states.

Accountability Accepting responsibility for personal decisions, choices, and actions.

Self-nurturance Developing individual potential through a balanced and realistic appreciation of self-worth and ability.

ity" and "self-nurturance." **Accountability** means that both partners see themselves as responsible for their own decisions and actions. The other person is not held responsible for the positive or negative experiences in life. This eliminates the very common feeling of being "used" in a relationship. Each and every choice is one's own responsibility. A partner can no longer leave a relationship saying, "She ruined my life," or, "He made me do it!" When two people are accountable for their own emotional states, partners can be angry, sad, or frustrated without the other person taking it personally. Accountable people may even say something like, "This has nothing to do with you; I just happen to be angry right now."

Self-nurturance goes hand-in-hand with accountability. In order to make good choices in life, a person needs to maintain a balance of sleeping, eating, exercising, working, relaxing, and socializing. When the balance is disrupted, as it will inevitably be, self-nurturing people are patient with themselves and try to put things back on course. When they make bad choices, as all people do, self-nurturing people learn from the experience. Two people who are on a path of accountability and self-nurturance together have a much better chance of maintaining satisfying relationships.

Elements of Good Relationships

Relationships that are satisfying and stable share certain elements. Some of these are achieved through conscious efforts and communication; others evolve over time. People in healthy committed relationships trust one another. Without trust, intimacy will not develop and the relationship will experience trouble and possible failure. **Trust** can be defined as the degree of confidence felt in a relationship. Trust includes three fundamental elements: predictability, dependability, and faith.

- *Predictability* means that you can predict your partner's behavior. This sense of predictability is based on the knowledge that your partner acts in consistently positive ways.
- *Dependability* means that you can rely on your partner to give support in all situations, particularly in those in which you feel threatened with hurt or rejection.
- *Faith* means that you feel absolutely certain about your partner's intentions and behavior.

Trust can be developed even in relationships in which it is initially lacking. The key is learning to interpret a partner's behavior. Although changing a partner's behavior may not be possible, changing the interpretation and reaction to it is. In good relationships, people interpret each other's behavior in the context of the current relationship. They acknowledge each other's positive qualities and allow room for mistakes. They do not overreact to behaviors that remind them of previous sensitive events that trigger emotional insecurities. For example, if a partner in an earlier relationship was continually flirting with other people and cheating on you, a current partner dancing with someone else at a party could unknowingly trigger the unpleasant memories of infidelity. Trusting people never assume that a current partner will behave as an earlier partner did.

Trust and intimacy are the foundation of healthy committed relationships. Spouses who like and enjoy one another as people and find each other interesting frequently are happier than those who don't. Many spouses describe their partners as their best friends. Although most marriages have their share of ups and downs, members of successful couples are able to talk to, listen to, and touch one another in an atmosphere of caring. They value a good sense of humor and exhibit communication, cooperation, and the ability to resolve conflicts constructively.

Sexual intimacy is also a major part of healthy relationships, but sex is not a major reason for the existence of the relationship. Some couples admit to sexual dissatisfaction within their relationships but feel the relationship is more important than sexual satisfaction. Rather than seek an outlet in an extramarital affair, those who are dissatisfied with their sex lives adjust and spend little energy worrying about it because the relationship is satisfying in other, more important ways. Many couples report that as communication and trust increase in a long-term, committed relationship, the entire sexual relationship also improves.

One important quality of successful relationships is a shared and cherished history, including private jokes, code words and nicknames, rituals, emotions, and significant shared time and activities. Equally important is luck. Luck in choosing a partner was first, followed by luck in life events. Certain events, such as major illnesses, unemployment, career failures, family feuds, or the death of a child, can derail an otherwise good marriage. Determination to succeed as a couple can help offset these occurrences, but some couples seem destined to endure more tragedy than others and the tragedies can undermine the relationship.

STAYING SINGLE

While many people choose to marry, have children, and follow in the footsteps of their ancestors, increasing numbers of young and older adults elect to remain single. In 1970, 18.9 percent of adult men and 13.7 percent of adult women had decided that marriage wasn't for them. By the early 1990s, the proportion of adult Americans who were single by choice or by chance (often after failed marriages) had increased to slightly over 37 percent of adult men and over 41 percent of adult women. These statistics indicate that:

- Americans who choose marriage now choose it much later in life
- it is estimated that by the year 2000, over 10 percent of all people will never marry
- people marrying today have more than a 50 percent chance of divorcing
- increasing numbers of widows and widowers are opting not to remarry

Today, large numbers of people choose to or are forced by circumstances to remain single. While many of these people seek or have sought committed relationships, in the absence of a suitable partner, they find singlehood preferable. As more women earn financial independence, they are less likely to remarry after divorce. Singles clubs, social outings arranged by communities and churches, extended family environments, and a large number of social services support the single lifestyle. Although some research indicates that single people live shorter lives, are more unhappy, are more likely to be financially distressed, and are more prone to illnesses than their married counterparts, other studies refute these conclusions. Many single people live rich, rewarding lives and maintain a large network of close friends and families. Although sexual intimacy may or may not be present, the intimacy achieved through other interactions with loved ones is a key aspect of the single person's lifestyle.

HAVING CHILDREN . . . OR NOT?

When a couple decides to raise children, their relationship changes. Resources of time, energy, and money are split many ways, and the partners no longer have each other's undivided attention. Babies and young children do not time their requests for food, sleep, and care to the convenience of adults. Therefore, individuals or couples whose own basic needs for security, love, and purpose are already met make better parents. Any stresses that already exist in a relationship are further accentuated when parenting is added to the list of responsibilities. Having a child does not save a bad relationship and, in fact, only seems to compound the problems that already exist. A child cannot and should not be expected to provide the parents with self-esteem and security.

Changing patterns in family life affect the way children are raised. In modern society, it is not always clear which partner will adjust his or her work schedule to provide the primary care of children. Nearly half a million children per year become part of a blended family when their parents remarry; remarriage creates a new family of stepparents and stepsiblings. In addition, an increasing number of individuals are choosing to have children in a family structure other than a heterosexual marriage. Single women can choose adoption or alternative (formerly "artificial") insemination as a way to create a family. Single men can choose to adopt or can obtain the services of a surrogate mother. Regardless of the structure of the family, certain factors remain important to the well-being of the unit: consistency, communication, affection, and mutual respect.

Some people become parents without a lot of forethought. Some children are born into a relationship that was supposed to last and didn't. This does not mean it is too late to do a good job of parenting. Attention, consistency, and caring can be provided by other adults if a parent cannot be physically or emotionally present for a period of time. Children are amazingly resilient and forgiving if parents show respect to them and communicate about household activities that affect their lives. Even children who grew up in a household of conflict can feel loved and respected if the parents treat them fairly. This means that parents take responsibility for any of their own conflicts and make it clear to the children that they are not the reason for the conflict.

Today, families that want their dream of a nice home in suburbia may have two working partners to achieve that dream. That's why more than 80 percent of all mothers with children under the age of 5 go to work outside of the home. Day care, extended family and friends, grandparents, neighbors, and nannies "mind the kids."

With the demise of the "Cleaver family," society must adjust and adapt. In 1997, extended family leave arrangements allowed parents more latitude in taking time from work to raise their kids, attend school events, take the kids to the doctor, and other tasks.

Trust The degree of confidence felt in a relationship.

Autonomy The ability to care for oneself emotionally, socially, and physically.

⋯⋯ **WHAT DO YOU THINK?**

What are the essential characteristics of a healthy "family" environment? Why is having such an environment so important to the future development of our children?

WHEN RELATIONSHIPS FALTER

The Warning Signs

The symptoms of a troubled relationship are relatively easy to recognize. Many couples choose to ignore them, however, until the situation erupts into some type of emotional confrontation. By then, the relationship may be beyond salvaging.

Breakdowns in relationships usually begin with a change in communication, however subtle. Either partner may stop listening, ceasing to be emotionally present for the other. In turn, the other feels ignored, unappreciated, or unwanted. Unresolved conflicts may increase, and unresolved anger can cause problems in sexual relations, with one partner not wanting sex and perhaps giving in and subsequently feeling used.

When a couple who previously enjoyed spending time alone together find themselves continually in the company of others, spending time apart, or preferring to stay home alone, it may be a sign that the relationship is in trouble. Of course, individual privacy and **autonomy** (the ability to care for oneself emotionally, socially, and physically) are important. If, however, a partner decides to make a change in the amount and quality of time spent together without the input or understanding of the other, it may be a sign of hidden problems.

People with a good sense of their own identity and the ability to nurture themselves will not allow themselves to be treated poorly in a relationship. However, college students, particularly those who have remained socially isolated and who are far from family and hometown friends, may be particularly vulnerable. You may find yourself dependent on unhealthy relationships for shared rental arrangements, transportation, child care, and other obligations. In these situations, emotional abuse is often unidentified yet can have devastating effects on the self-esteem of both the abused and the abuser. You may mistake unwanted sexual advances for physical attraction or love and find yourself in situations that are far from the idyllic love scenes you may watch on television. Without a network of friends and supporters to talk with, to obtain validation for your feelings, and/or to share your concerns, you may find yourself in a relationship that is headed nowhere. Breaking up may be difficult and support for your breakup may not be there when you need it. Knowing how to access the services of trained counselors through your student health services or other community and campus groups is critical in these situations.

Why Relationships End

Each year, more than a million couples in the United States end their marriages. Many others end relationships of all types. The reasons for relationship breakdown are numerous. Tragedies such as the death of a loved one, serious illness of one partner, severe financial reverses, and career failures certainly contribute to divorces and relationship endings. Somehow, communication and cooperation between partners break down under the additional stress of these burdens.

What about breakups between people who have never experienced these tragedies? These breakups arise from unmet expectations regarding marriage or relationships in general or personal roles within the relationship. Many people enter marriage with expectations about what marriage will be like and how they and their partner will behave. Many people enter relationships looking for someone to fill the empty spots in their lives. Still others are looking for beautiful ornaments to be associated with rather than meaningful relationships. Failure to communicate such expectations to your partner can lead to resentment and disappointment. Because many premarital expectations may be unreasonable, early exploration of these expectations is important. This exploration may take place together or within a support program.

Differences in sexual needs may also contribute to the demise of a relationship. Many partners find that their spouses desire sex at different times or in different styles and frequencies than they do. Unless sexual differences are resolved, one or both partners may begin to feel used and resent sexual activity. In other cases, the deterioration of a relationship cannot be attributed to any one event or action. Sometimes, because people fall in love so quickly, once they really get to know the other person the initial "click" that seemed so important begins to fade. Sometimes the man or woman of your dreams may become your worst nightmare. It is often interesting to think back on the past loves of your life and to wonder how you ever could have thought that a particular person was so wonderful. Is it because you've changed? Or is it because the other person never made any changes? The bottom line is that if couples do not grow together, they often grow apart. Without a commitment to working on their differences, many find it easier to move on, and this decision may be best for all concerned.

Coping with Loneliness

Some people find establishing and maintaining relationships difficult. Others find that through death, illness, or distance, their relationships disappear or grow dim with time. Loneliness, or the unfulfilled desire to engage in a close personal relationship, is difficult.

Newly single people may experience great loneliness and an intense desire for new relationships. They may deal with their loneliness through such destructive behaviors as sexual affairs, workaholism, or abuse of drugs, alcohol, or food. When their situation appears hopeless, some people may opt for suicide.

People who acknowledge the difficulty of what they are going through and share their feelings with others heal faster and more completely than those who are isolated.

Reflecting on the beginning, the course, and the ending of the relationship can help you avoid the same mistakes in the future. Concentrating on the negative aspects of past behavior of an ex-partner is a natural tendency but is only helpful in getting in touch with emotions or in learning from the situation. It is equally important to spend time remembering what was loved in the other person and what is lovable about oneself.

BUILDING BETTER RELATIONSHIPS

Fighting between couples can become just as habitual as making the bed. The same fight, the same discussion rears its nasty little head over and over again until it begins to take on a life of its own. Over the past 20 years, psychologists have made a science of the joys and devastations of couples' relationships. They've come to understand, at least in part, why some relationships happily endure and what contributes to the hell-hole interactions that claim over half of all first marriages, usually within the first 7 years.[25] Although these same psychologists note that most marriages start with great optimism and true love, they get into trouble for a very humbling reason. "We just don't know how to handle the negative feelings that are the unavoidable by-product of the differences between two people, the very differences that attract them to each other in the first place. Think of it as the friction any two bodies would generate rubbing against each other countless times each day," says Howard Markman, Ph.D., professor of psychology at the University of Denver.[26] According to Markman, most unhappy couples don't need therapy; they need education in how relationships work and the special skills that make them work well. Markman and others subscribe to a way of thinking that represents a change in mental health counseling. Rather than treating relationship problems as part of a disease, these forward-thinking psychologists promote **psychoeducation,** the teaching of crucial psychological skills—giving people knowledge so they can help themselves. Examples of some of these psychoeducation courses include the options shown in the Consumer Health box.

Regardless of what form of therapy you select, you must make sure that you are getting help from a reputable, board-certified or licensed couples therapist. Remember that you aren't going into therapy to be told what to do, to become dependent

Psychoeducation The teaching of crucial psychological skills, giving people knowledge so they can help themselves.

CONSUMER HEALTH

Seeking Help for Troubled Relationships

Often, people seek help for relationships only when they are in a desperate attempt to save a failing one. Instead of trying to *fix* a broken relationship, there are many options available to couples that will help them develop the skills necessary to prevent problems, or, at the very least, to reduce the negative consequences when problems do appear. Every community has programs that are similar to these. Check around and ask questions at your local student counseling center or community center. Try to find reputable, licensed professionals who are endorsed by members of your clergy or university or college student service group, or go through your county or city mental health service department. You may even phone some of these sources to determine if there is a similar group near to you.

The following skills-training classes are built on both clinical experience and research. All have mutually influenced each other. Most teach similar core skills but differ on theory. Most employ a variety of trained instructors, including therapists, nontherapist couples, and often, clergy.

Premarital Enhancement Program (PEP): Its aim is to teach partners how to fight appropriately. Ground rules are established via The Floor, where one partner becomes the speaker and the other the listener, and then they switch. It forces couples to stay engaged and communi-

cate openly without withdrawing or attacking one another.

Couple Communication: The Smart Love Course Source: This class is based on the assumption that everything is negotiable in a relationship and that people have many choices. Its emphasis is on shifting reliance on the external—extended family, church, and so on—to an internal support system, in which couples learn to talk about issues and work out solutions. The focus is on self-awareness, self-caring, self-honesty, knowing what one wants, and learning to ask for it. Couples use an "awareness wheel" to prompt awareness of thoughts, feelings, wants, actions and sensory data that may be influencing them and to prompt conversation. The course consists of four 2-hour classes that cost from $230 to $320, depending on location. Contact Interpersonal Communications Programs at 303-794-1764.

Relationship Enhancement (RE): This course starts with the concept of empathy or compassion training—learning to see things from the partner's perspective. Couples work on empathetic listening and responding in honest ways. Using the X-ray as a guiding metaphor, this program encourages couples to look for feelings and motives their partners haven't expressed—probably out of fear of rejection or anger. Trained coaches work with couples to help them make choices that fit their relationship. Couples can choose from group marathons of four 4-hour Saturday afternoons, weekend courses (all day Saturday and Sunday), and day and half-day individual instruction. The course costs $285. Contact the National Institute

for Relationship Enhancement at 800-432-6454.

Prevention and Relationship Enhancement Program (PREP): Rather than focusing on shared meaning between partners, PREP focuses on their differences. It tries to foster egalitarian fighting, in which there are ground rules for handling conflict that protect relationships from the ravages of poorly handled emotion. Emphasis is placed on containment of negative emotions and working toward positive resolution of issues. [Taught in two-week version—one weekend day and two weekday evenings.] This program also is available on video tape and in book form. Contact PREP at 303-759-9931.

Marriage Survival Kit: It teaches five basic skills for conflict resolution: (1) using a softened startup. (2) accepting influence, (3) repairing or putting the brakes on conflict, (4) making use of physiologic soothing when conflicts get out of control, and (5) de-escalating discord. Available in the Seattle area ($300 per couple). A 40-minute video is available for $29.95. Contact Seattle Marital and Family Institute at 206-523-9042.

We Can Work It Out: This course helps couples hear each other and give and get necessary feedback. It bolsters the sense of relationship efficacy—couples' beliefs that they can get through this—and highlights the importance of expecting success. Taught in the Washington, D.C. area over a weekend (for $1,100). Contact the Center for Family Psychology at 202-319-4474.

Source: Hara Estroff Marano, "Love Lessons: 6 New Moves to Improve Your Relationship," *Psychology Today,* March/April 1997, 86.

on it to make your relationship work. You should be coming away from therapy with ideas on how to work through the difficulties that you and your partner are experiencing—ways to better understand the dynamics between you. After you

have worked on your relationship, utilizing the skills that are inherent in this type of training, you will be better able to determine whether your current relationship is something you really want to continue to work on.

Working to develop skills that will help protect you in a relationship and also help your relationship grow and flourish is an important step in achieving relationship help. Learning to be empathetic to others' needs, strengths, and weaknesses, and having the compassion to take the time to help them work with you to improve your interactions are key to relationship stability. In addition, learning to not take yourself quite so seriously, learning to forgive others' slips or slights, and working to overcome your own fears, angry reactions, and overreactions will help keep the blowups to a minimum.

YOUR SEXUAL IDENTITY

Your **sexual identity** is determined by a complex interaction of genetic, physiological, and environmental factors. The beginning of your sexual identity occurs at conception with the combining of chromosomes that determine your sex. Actually, it is your biological father who determines whether you will be a boy or a girl. Here's how it works. All eggs (ova) carry an X sex chromosome; sperm may carry either an X or a Y chromosome. If a sperm carrying an X chromosome fertilizes an egg, the resulting combination of sex chromosomes (XX) provides the blueprint to produce a female. If a sperm carrying a Y chromosome fertilizes an egg, the XY combination produces a male (see Figure 5.1).

The genetic instructions included in the sex chromosomes lead to the differential development of male and female

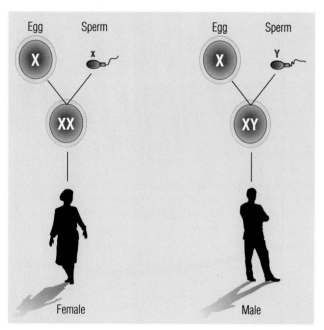

Figure 5.1
How Sex Is Determined

gonads at about the eighth week of fetal life. Once the male gonads (testes) and the female gonads (ovaries) are developed, they play a key role in all future sexual development because the gonads are responsible for the production of sex hormones. The primary sex hormones produced by females are estrogen and progesterone. In males, the hormone of primary importance is testosterone. The release of testosterone in a maturing fetus signals the development of a penis and other male genitals. If no testosterone is produced, female genitals form.

At the time of **puberty,** sex hormones again play major roles in development. Hormones released by the **pituitary gland,** called gonadotropins, stimulate the gonads (testes and ovaries) to make appropriate sex hormones. The increase of estrogen production in females and testosterone production in males leads to the development of **secondary sex characteristics.** The development of secondary sex characteristics in males includes deepening of the voice, development of facial and body hair, and growth of the skeleton and musculature. In females, the development of secondary sex characteristics includes growth of the breasts, widening of the hips, and the development of pubic and underarm hair.

Gender Identity and Roles

Thus far, we have described sexual identity only in terms of a person's sex. Sex simply refers to the biological condition of being male or female based on physiological and hormonal differences. **Gender,** on the other hand, refers to your sense of masculinity or femininity as defined by the society in which you live. Each of us expresses our maleness or femaleness to others on a daily basis by the **gender roles** we play. **Gender identity** refers to your personal sense or awareness of being masculine or feminine, a male or a female. It may sometimes be difficult for you to express your true sexual identity because you feel bound by existing gender-role stereotypes. **Gender-role stereotypes** are generalizations about how males and females should express themselves and the characteristics each possesses. Our traditional sex roles are an example of gender-role stereotyping. Men are thought to be independent, aggressive, better in math and science, logical, and always in control of their emotions. Women, on the other hand, are traditionally expected to be passive, nurturing, intuitive, sensitive, and emotional. **Androgyny** is the combination of traditional masculine and feminine traits in a single person. Androgynous people do not always follow traditional sex roles but, rather, try to act appropriately based on the given situation. The process by which a society transmits behavioral expectations to its individual members is called **socialization.** Gender roles are shaped or socialized by our parents, peers, schools, textbooks, advertisements, and many forms of media including television, music, and movies. Think about the current television shows you watch. Do the characters play out traditional gender roles?

By now you can see that defining your sexual identity is not a simple matter. It is a lifelong process of growing and learning. Your sexual identity is made up of the unique combination of your sex, gender identity, chosen gender roles, sexual orientation, and personal experiences. No other person on this earth is exactly like you, and it is up to you to take every opportunity to get to know and like yourself so that you may enjoy your life to the fullest.

········ **WHAT DO YOU THINK?**

Have you ever challenged existing gender-role stereotypes? What was the outcome? Do you think men and women have the same degree of freedom in gender role expression?

REPRODUCTIVE ANATOMY AND PHYSIOLOGY

Sexual activity is physical in nature and depends on anatomical and physiological characteristics and conditions. An understanding of the functions of the male and female reproductive systems will help you derive pleasure and satisfaction from your sexual relationships, be sensitive to your partner's wants and needs, and be more responsible in your choices regarding your own sexual health.

Female Reproductive Anatomy and Physiology

The female reproductive system includes two major groups of structures, the external genitals and the internal genitals (see Figure 5.2 on page 113). The **external female genitals** include all structures that are outwardly visible and are often referred to as the vulva. Specifically, the **vulva,** or external genitalia, includes the mons pubis, the labia minora and majora, the clitoris, the urethral and vaginal openings, and the vestibule of the vagina. The **mons pubis** is a pad of fatty tissue covering the pubic bone. The mons serves to protect the pubic bone, and after puberty it becomes covered with coarse hair. The **labia minora** are folds of mucous membrane and the **labia majora** are folds of skin and erectile tissue that enclose the urethral and vaginal openings. The labia minora are found just inside the labia majora.

The female sexual organ whose only known function is sexual pleasure is called the **clitoris.** It is located at the upper end of the labia minora and beneath the mons pubis. Directly below the clitoris is the **urethral opening** through which urine leaves the body. Below the urethral opening is the vaginal opening, or opening to the **vagina.** In some women, the vaginal opening is covered by a thin membrane called the **hymen.** It is a myth that an intact hymen is proof of virginity. The **perineum** is the area between the vulva and the anus. Although not technically part of the external genitalia, the tissue is this area has many nerve endings and is sensitive to touch; it can play a part in sexual excitement.

Sexual identity   Recognition of ourselves as sexual beings; a composite of biological sex, gender identity, gender roles, and sexual orientation.

Gonads   The reproductive organs in a male (testes) or female (ovaries).

Puberty   The period of sexual maturation.

Pituitary gland   The endocrine gland controlling the release of hormones from the gonads.

Secondary sex characteristics   Characteristics associated with gender but not directly related to reproduction, such as vocal pitch, degree of body hair, and location of fat deposits.

Gender   Your sense of masculinity or femininity as defined by the society in which you live.

Gender roles   Expression of maleness or femaleness exhibited on a daily basis.

Gender identity   Your personal sense or awareness of being masculine or feminine, a male or female.

Gender-role stereotypes   Generalizations concerning how males and females should express themselves and the characteristics each possesses.

Androgyny   Combination of traditional masculine and feminine traits in a single person.

Socialization   Process by which a society identifies behavioral expectations to its individual members.

External female genitals   The mons pubis, labia majora and minora, clitoris, urethral and vaginal openings, and the vestibule of the vagina and its glands.

Vulva   The female's external genitalia.

Mons pubis   Fatty tissue covering the pubic bone in females; in physically mature women, the mons is covered with coarse hair.

Labia minora   "Inner lips" or folds of tissue just inside the labia majora.

Labia majora   "Outer lips" or folds of tissue covering the female sexual organs.

Clitoris   A pea-sized nodule of tissue located at the top of the labia minora.

Urethral opening   The opening through which urine is expelled.

Vagina   The passage in females leading from the vulva to the uterus.

Hymen   Thin tissue covering the vaginal opening.

Perineum   Tissue extending from the vulva to the anus.

Ritual Genital Mutilation

Cultures in some parts of Africa and the Middle East ritually mutilate or remove the entire clitoris, not just the clitoral hood. Removal of the clitoris, or clitoridectomy, is a rite of initiation into womanhood in many of these predominantly Islamic cultures. It is often performed as a puberty ritual in late childhood or early adolescence (not at birth, like male circumcision).

The clitoris gives rise to feelings of sexual pleasure in women. Its removal or mutilation represents an attempt to ensure the girl's chastity since it is assumed that uncircumcised girls are consumed with sexual desires (Ahmed, 1991). Cairo physician Said M. Thabit says, "With circumcision we remove the external parts, so when a girl wears tight nylon underclothes she will not have any stimulation" (cited in Mac-Farquhar, 1996, p. A3). Some groups in rural Egypt and in the northern Sudan, however, perform clitoridectomies primarily because it is a social custom that has been passed down from ancient times (Toubia, 1994). Some perceive it as part of their faith in Islam. However, neither Islam nor any other religion requires it (MacFarquhar, 1996). Ironically, many young women do not grasp that they are victims. They assume that clitoridectomy is part of being female (Rosenthal, 1994).

Clitoridectomies are performed under unsanitary conditions without benefit of anesthesia (Rosenthal, 1993). Medical complications are common, including infections, bleeding, tissue scarring, painful menstruation, and obstructed labor (Toubia, 1994). The procedure is psychologically traumatizing (Toubia, 1994). An even more radical form of clitoridectomy, called *infibulation* or pharaonic circumcision, is practiced widely in the Sudan. Pharaonic circumcision involves complete removal of the clitoris along with the labia minora and the inner layers of the labia majora. After removal of the skin tissue, the raw edges of the labia majora are sewn together. Only a tiny opening is left to allow passage of urine and menstrual discharge. The sewing together of the vulva may be intended to ensure the girls' chastity until marriage. Medical complications are common, including menstrual and urinary problems, and even death. After marriage, the opening is enlarged to permit intercourse. Enlargement is a gradual process that is often made difficult by scar tissue from the circumcision. Hemorrhaging and tearing of surrounding tissues are common consequences. It may take three months or longer before the opening is large enough to allow penile penetration. Mutilation of the labia is now illegal in the Sudan, although the law continues to allow removal of the clitoris. Some African countries have outlawed clitoridectomies, although such laws are rarely enforced (Rosenthal, 1993).

Millions of women in Africa and the Middle East—85 to 114 million by some estimates (Kaplan, 1993)—have undergone removal of the clitoris and the labia minora. Clitoridectomies remain common or even universal in nearly 30 coun-

tries in Africa, in many countries in the Middle East, and in parts of Malaysia, Yemen, Oman, Indonesia, and the India-Pakistan subcontinent (Rosenthal, 1995). Thousands of African immigrant girls living in European countries and the United States have also been mutilated (Dugger, 1996b).

Do not confuse male circumcision with the maiming inflicted on girls. Former representative Patricia Schroeder of Colorado depicts the male equivalent of female genital mutilation as cutting off the penis (Dugger, 1996b). The *New York Times* columnist A. M. Rosenthal (1995) calls female genital mutilation the most widespread existing violation of human rights in the world. The Pulitzer Prize–winning, African American novelist Alice Walker has condemned it in her novel *Possessing the Secret of Joy* (1992). She called for its abolition in her book and movie *Warrior Marks.*

In 1996, the United States outlawed ritual genital mutilation within its borders. The government also directed U.S. representatives to world financial institutions to deny aid to countries that have not established educational programs to bring an end to the practice (Dugger, 1996b). Yet calls from Westerners to ban the practice in parts of Africa and the Middle East have sparked controversy on grounds of "cultural condescension"— that people in one culture cannot dictate the cultural traditions of another. Yet for Alice Walker, "torture is not culture." As the debate continues, some 2 million African girls continue to undergo ritual genital mutilations each year.

Source: Adapted from A. R. Rathus, J. S. Nevid, and L. Fichner-Rathus, *Essentials of Human Sexuality* (Boston: Allyn and Bacon, 1998), 30–31.

The **internal female genitals** of the reproductive system include the vagina, uterus, fallopian tubes, and ovaries. The vagina is a tubular organ that serves as a passageway from the uterus to the outside of a female's body. This passageway allows menstrual flow to exit from the uterus during a female's monthly cycle and serves as the birth canal during childbirth. The vagina also receives the penis during intercourse. The **uterus,** also known as the womb, is a hollow, muscular, pear-shaped organ. Hormones acting on the inner lining of the uterus, called the **endometrium,** either prepare the uterus for implantation and development of a fertilized egg or signal that no fertilization has taken place, in which case the endometrium deteriorates and becomes menstrual flow.

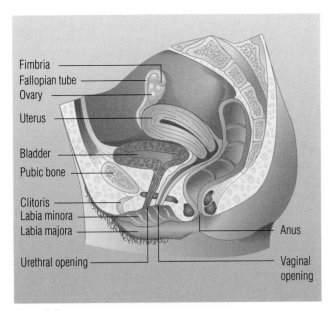

Fimbria
Fallopian tube
Ovary
Uterus
Bladder
Pubic bone
Clitoris
Labia minora
Labia majora
Urethral opening
Anus
Vaginal opening

Figure 5.2

Side View of the Female Reproductive Organs

Source: From Jeffrey S. Turner and Laurna Rubinson, *Contemporary Human Sexuality,* ©1993, 64. Reprinted by permission of Prentice-Hall, Englewood Cliffs, NJ.

The lower end of the uterus is called the **cervix** and extends down into the vagina. The **ovaries** are almond-sized structures suspended on either side of the uterus. The ovaries produce the hormones estrogen and progesterone and are also the reservoir for immature eggs. All the eggs a female will ever have are present in the ovaries at birth. Eggs mature and are released from the ovaries in response to hormone levels. Extending from the upper end of the uterus are two thin, flex-ible tubes called the **fallopian tubes.** The fallopian tubes are where sperm and egg meet and fertilization takes place. Following fertilization, the fallopian tubes serve as the passageway to the uterus, where the fertilized egg implants and development continues.

▶ *The Onset of Puberty and the Menstrual Cycle* With the onset of **puberty,** the female reproductive system matures, and the development of secondary sex characteristics transforms young girls into young women. Under the direction of the endocrine system, the **pituitary gland,** the **hypothalamus,** and the ovaries all secrete hormones that act as the chemical messengers among them. Working in a feedback system, hormonal levels in the bloodstream act as the trigger mechanism for release of more or different hormones (see Figure 5.3 on page 114).

At around the age of 11 or 12 in females, the hypothalamus receives the message to begin secreting **gonadotropin-releasing hormone (GnRH).** The release of GnRH in turn signals the pituitary gland to release hormones called gonadotropins. **Follicle-stimulating hormone (FSH)** and **luteinizing hormone (LH)** are two gonadotropins, and their role is to signal the gonads, in this case the ovaries, to start producing **estrogens** and **progesterone.** Increased estrogen levels assist in the development of female secondary sex characteristics. In addition, estrogens are responsible for regulating the reproductive cycle. The normal age range for the onset of the first menstrual period, termed the **menarche,** is 10 to 16 years, with the average age being 13 or 14 years.

The average menstrual cycle is 28 days long and divided into three phases: the proliferatory phase, the secretory phase, and the menstrual phase. During the proliferatory phase, the pituitary gland releases FSH and LH. The FSH acts on the ovaries to stimulate the maturation process of several **ovarian follicles (egg sacs).** These follicles secrete estrogens and, in

Internal female genitals The vagina, uterus, fallopian tubes, and ovaries.

Uterus (womb) Hollow, pear-shaped muscular organ whose function is to contain the developing fetus.

Endometrium Soft, spongy matter that makes up the uterine lining.

Cervix Lower end of the uterus that opens into the vagina.

Ovaries Almond-sized organs that house developing eggs and produce hormones.

Fallopian tubes Tubes that extend from the ovaries to the uterus.

Puberty The maturation of the female or male reproduction system.

Pituitary gland A gland located deep within the brain; controls reproductive functions.

Hypothalamus An area of the brain located near the pituitary gland. The hypothalamus works in con-junction with the pituitary gland to control reproductive functions.

Gonadotropin-releasing hormone (GnRH) Hormone that signals the pituitary gland to release gonadotropins.

Follicle-stimulating hormone (FSH) Hormone that signals the ovaries to prepare to release eggs and to begin producing estrogens.

Luteinizing hormone (LH) Hormone that signals the ovaries to release an egg and to begin producing progesterone.

Estrogens Hormones that control the menstrual cycle.

Progesterone Hormone secreted by the ovaries; helps keep the endometrium developing in order to nourish a fertilized egg; also helps maintain pregnancy.

Menarche The first menstrual period.

Ovarian follicles (egg sacs) Areas within the ovary in which individual eggs develop.

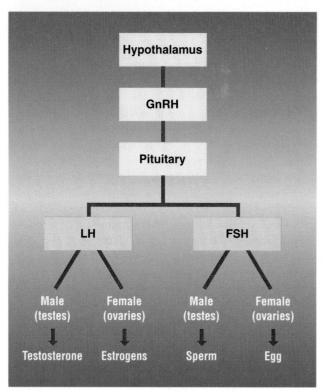

Figure 5.3
Hormonal Direction of the Human Reproductive System

response to this estrogen stimulation, the lining of the uterus, the endometrium, begins to grow and develop. The inner walls of the uterus become coated with a thick, spongy lining composed of blood and mucus. In the event of fertilization, the endometrial tissue will become a nesting place for the developing embryo. The increased estrogen level also signals the pituitary to slow down FSH production but to increase LH secretion. Of the several follicles developing in the ovaries, only one each month normally reaches complete maturity. Under the influence of LH, this one ovarian follicle rapidly matures, and on or about the fourteenth day of the proliferatory phase, it releases an ovum into the fallopian tube—a process referred to as **ovulation.** Just prior to ovulation, the mature egg's follicle begins to increase secretion of progesterone, the first function of which is to spur the addition of further nutrients to the developing endometrium.

After ovulation, the ovarian follicle is converted into the *corpus luteum,* or yellow body, which continues to secrete estrogen and progesterone but in decreasing amounts. In addition, FSH also falls back to its preproliferatory levels. Essentially, the woman's body is "waiting" to see whether fertilization will occur. During this time after ovulation, LH declines, and progesterone levels begin to rise, causing additional tissue growth in the endometrium. This phase of the cycle is called the secretory phase.

If fertilization takes place, cells surrounding the developing embryo release a hormone called **human chorionic**

gonadotropin (HCG). This hormone leads to increased levels of estrogen and progesterone secretion, which maintains the endometrium while signaling the pituitary gland not to start a new menstrual cycle.

When fertilization does not occur, the egg gradually disintegrates within approximately 72 hours. The corpus luteum gradually becomes nonfunctional, causing levels of progesterone and estrogen to decline. As hormonal levels decline, the endometrial lining of the uterus loses its nourishment, dies, and is sloughed off as menstrual flow. Menstruation is the third phase of the menstrual cycle.

Some issues associated with menstruation that you may be interested in reading about are premenstrual syndrome (PMS), toxic shock syndrome (TSS), and dysmenorrhea, or painful menstruation.

▶ *Menopause* Just as menarche signals the beginning of a female's potential reproductive years, **menopause**—the permanent cessation of menstruation—signals the end. Generally occurring between the ages of 50 and 55, menopause results in decreased estrogen levels, which may produce troublesome symptoms in some women. Decrease in vaginal lubrication, hot flashes, headaches, dizziness, and joint pains have all been associated with the onset of menopause. Since estrogen plays a protective role in women by guarding against heart disease and osteoporosis (loss of bone mineral density), postmenopausal women may not only reduce some of the symptoms associated with menopause but also regain some protection against heart disease and osteoporosis by going on hormone-replacement therapy (HRT), or estrogen-replacement therapy (ERT). Unfortunately, HRT is not without potential risk. Increased risk of endometrial cancer (the lining of the uterus), gallstones, and breast cancer has been reported in some women.[27] All women need to discuss the risks and benefits of HRT with their health-care provider and come to an informed decision. Certainly lifestyle changes, such as regular exercise and a diet low in fat and adequate in calcium, can also help protect postmenopausal women from heart disease and osteoporosis.

> ············ **WHAT DO YOU THINK?**
>
> Why is it so important that we understand the function of our sexual anatomy? Do men need to understand how the menstrual cycle works? Why? Some people are not comfortable using the medical terms for parts of the sexual anatomy. Why do you think this is so?

Male Reproductive Anatomy and Physiology

The structures of the male reproductive system may be divided into external and internal genitals (see Figure 5.4). The penis and the scrotum make up the **external male**

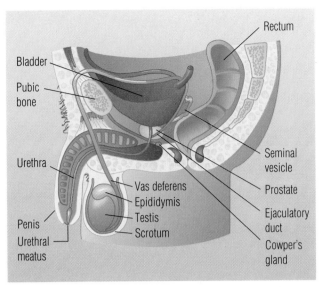

Figure 5.4

Side View of the Male Reproductive Organs

Source: From Jeffrey S. Turner and Laurna Rubinson, *Contemporary Human Sexuality,* ©1993, 64. Reprinted by permission of Prentice-Hall, Englewood Cliffs, NJ.

genitals. The **internal male genitals** include the testes, epididymides, vasa deferentia, and urethra, and three other structures—the seminal vesicles, the prostate gland, and the Cowper's glands—that secrete components that, with sperm, make up semen. These three structures are sometimes referred to as the **accessory glands.**

The **penis** serves as the organ that deposits sperm in the vagina during intercourse. The urethra, which passes through the center of the penis, acts as the passageway for both semen and urine to exit the body. During sexual arousal, the spongy tissue in the penis becomes filled with blood, making the organ stiff, or erect. Further sexual excitement leads to **ejaculation,** a series of rapid spasmodic contractions that propel semen out of the penis.

Situated behind the penis and also outside the body is a sac called the **scrotum.** The scrotum serves to protect the testes and also helps control the temperature within the testes, which is vital to proper sperm production. The **testes** (singular: *testis*) are egg-shaped structures in which sperm are manufactured. The testes also contain cells that manufacture **testosterone,** the hormone responsible for the development of male secondary sex characteristics.

Spermatogenesis is the term used to describe the development of sperm. Like the maturation of eggs in the female, this process is governed by the pituitary gland. Follicle-stimulating hormone (FSH) is secreted into the bloodstream to stimulate the testes to manufacture sperm. Immature sperm are released into a comma-shaped structure on the back of the testis called the **epididymis** (plural: *epididymides*), where they ripen and reach full maturity.

The epididymis contains coiled tubules that gradually "unwind" and straighten out to become the **vas deferens.** The two vasa deferentia, as they are called in the plural, make up the tubular transportation system whose sole function is to store and move sperm. Along the way, the **seminal vesicles** provide sperm with nutrients and other fluids that compose **semen.**

The vasa deferentia eventually connect each epididymis to the ejaculatory ducts, which pass through the prostate gland and empty into the urethra. The **prostate gland** contributes more fluids to the semen, including chemicals to aid the sperm in fertilization of an ovum, and, more importantly, a chemical that neutralizes the acid in the vagina to make its environment more conducive to sperm motility (ability to move) and potency (potential for fertilizing an ovum).

Just below the prostate gland are two pea-shaped nodules called the Cowper's glands. Their primary function is to

Ovulation The point of the menstrual cycle at which a mature egg ruptures through the ovarian wall.

Human chorionic gonadotropin (HCG) Hormone that calls for increased levels of estrogen and progesterone secretion if fertilization has taken place.

Menopause The permanent cessation of menstruation.

External male genitals The penis and scrotum.

Internal male genitals The testes, epididymides, vasa deferentia, ejaculatory ducts, urethra, and accessory glands.

Accessory glands The seminal vesicles, prostate gland, and Cowper's glands.

Penis Male sexual organ designed for releasing sperm into the vagina.

Ejaculation The propulsion of semen from the penis.

Scrotum Sac of tissue that encloses the testes.

Testes Two organs, located in the scrotum, that manufacture sperm and produce hormones.

Testosterone The male sex hormone manufactured in the testes.

Spermatogenesis The development of sperm.

Epididymis A comma-shaped structure atop the testis where sperm mature.

Vas deferens A tube that transports sperm toward the penis.

Seminal vesicles Storage areas for sperm where nutrient fluids are added to them.

Semen Fluid containing sperm and nutrient fluids that increase sperm viability and neutralize vaginal acid.

Prostate gland Gland that secretes nutrients and neutralizing fluids into the semen.

Circumcision: Take It or Leave It?

One decision facing parents of a newborn boy is whether to have him circumcised. Circumcision involves the surgical removal of the foreskin, a flap of skin covering the tip of the penis. As a procedure, circumcision has been around for millennia, dating as far back as Egyptian times, more than 4,500 years ago, when priests performed circumcision on their newborn boys as a form of purification rite. To this day, it is an important religious ritual in Islamic and Jewish communities worldwide. It became popularized in the United States in the early 1900s in the belief that it promoted good hygiene and discouraged masturbation. During World War II, its benefits were extolled when it was discovered that, in the unsanitary conditions of the battlefield, circumcised male soldiers had far fewer infections than did their uncircumcised counterparts. Today, the American Academy of Pediatrics (AAP) estimates that nearly 1.2 million infant males, or about 70 percent of all newborn males, born in this country are circumcised each year. Outside of the United States, the practice is far less common.

For decades, the decision was relatively automatic for most parents in the United States, as the majority of circumcisions have been performed out of religious or cultural tradition or because of concerns over hygiene. In recent years, however, questions and issues over the procedure have surfaced. Some advocacy groups consider it to be cruel, barbaric, and unnecessary, citing studies that have questioned the potential harm of the loss of erogenous tissue and the possibility of long-lasting trauma to the child. Propo-

nents of circumcision have pointed to studies that have suggested a slightly greater risk for penile cancer and some sexually transmitted infections among uncircumcised males. Who is right? Who is wrong? Probably nobody, as little conclusive evidence supports or refutes either side.

In an effort to draw closure to the issue, a special task force convened by the AAP recently concluded that although evidence indicates certain medical benefits of circumcision, they are not essential to the future health of the child. However, the AAP does not consider the findings compelling enough to recommend routine circumcision. What they do consider essential is that parents make an informed decision based on the known benefits and risks.

Possible Benefits of Circumcision:

- *Fewer urinary tract infections:* Boys who are not circumcised are at least four times more likely to develop a UTI in their first year of life. A history of chronic UTIs is speculated by some to lead to damaged kidneys in later life.
- *Reduced risk of penile cancer:* Although the rate of penile cancer is relatively low, uncircumcised males tend to be more susceptible.
- *Reduced risk of HIV and other STIs:* Uncircumcised men face a slightly greater risk of infection after exposure to HIV or other STIs. However, personal behavioral practices, notably attitudes toward safer sex and the use of a condom during all intercourse, still serve as the greatest risk indicator to all men.
- *Smaller risk of transmitting infectious pathogens to sex partners:* Uncircumcised males face a greater risk of bacterial and fungal growth development under the foreskin. However, men who clean this area fastidiously reduce the risk considerably, as well as the likelihood of transmitting any organisms to sex partners.

Potential Risks of Circumcision:

- *Pain:* Surprisingly, about 45 percent of circumcisions are performed without pain relief. Critics note the painful cries of infants and question whether such trauma may leave permanent psychological damage. The AAP now recommends the use of an analgesic to reduce potential pain during the procedure.
- *Potential complications:* Although actual procedural risks of circumcisions are minor, complications can result, including mild bleeding and localized infection. Without a clear and essential benefit to a boy's well-being, either medically or emotionally, the risk is seen as unnecessary.
- *Loss of sensation at the tip of the penis:* Although some have reported this, it usually is only a very mild loss of sensation and may go away with time.

Ultimately, circumcision is more of a personal choice than a dramatic and inhumane event or a medical necessity. In summary, the trauma of thinking about circumcision may be worse than the actual event, both from the perspective of the infant and the man he will grow to be.

STUDENTS SPEAK UP:

What decision do you think you would choose for your son? On what is your decision based?

Sources: "Circumcision Policy Statement," *Pediatrics* 103 (1999): 686–693; Christine Gorman, "Unkindest Cut? Summary of the American Academy of Pediatrics Report," *Time,* March 15, 1999; J. Taylor, "The Prepuce: Specialized Mucosa of the Penis and Its Loss to Circumcision," *British Journal of Urology* 77 (1996): 291–295; A. Taddio, "Effect of Neonatal Circumcision on Pain Response during Subsequent Routine Vaccination," *The Lancet* 349 (1997): 599–603.

secrete a fluid that lubricates the urethra and neutralizes any acid that may remain in the urethra after urination. Urine and semen do not come into contact with each other. During ejaculation of semen, the tube to the urinary bladder is closed off by a small valve.

EXPRESSING YOUR SEXUALITY

Finding healthy ways to express your sexuality is an important part of developing sexual maturity. The Assess Yourself box identifies the characteristics of a sexually healthy adult. With the many avenues of sexual expression open to you, discovering one that will bring you satisfaction can be very difficult.

Human Sexual Response

Sexual response is a physiological process that involves different stages. The biological goal of the response process is the reproduction of the species. Human psychological traits greatly influence sexual response and sexual desire. Thus, we may find relationships with one partner vastly different from those we might experience with other partners.

Sexual response generally follows a pattern. Laboratory research has delineated four stages within the response cycle, and researchers agree that each individual has a personal response pattern that may or may not conform to the stages observed in experimental research. Both males and females exhibit four common stages: excitement/arousal, plateau, orgasm, and resolution. Identification of these stages was achieved in laboratory situations in which genital response was carefully measured using specially designed instruments. Regardless of the type of sexual activity (stimulation by a partner or self-stimulation), the response stages are the same.

During the first stage, *excitement/arousal,* male and female genital responses are caused by **vasocongestion,** or increased blood flow in the genital region. Increased blood flow to these organs causes them to swell. The vagina begins to lubricate in preparation for penile penetration and the penis becomes partially erect. Both sexes may exhibit a "sex flush," or light blush all over their bodies. Excitement/arousal can be generated by touching other parts of the body, by kissing, through fantasy, by viewing films or videos, or by reading erotic literature.

The *plateau phase* is characterized by an intensification of the initial responses. Voluntary and involuntary muscle tensions increase. The female's nipples and the male's penis become erect. A few drops of fluid, which may contain sperm, are secreted from the penis at this time. This fluid is termed *pre-ejaculatory fluid.*

During the *orgasmic phase,* vasocongestion and muscle tensions reach their peak, and rhythmic contractions occur through the genital regions. In females, these contractions are centered in the uterus, the outer vagina, and the anal sphincter. In males, the contractions occur in two stages. First, contractions within the prostate gland begin propelling semen through the urethra. In the second stage, the muscles of the pelvic floor, the urethra, and the anal sphincter contract. Semen usually, but not always, is ejaculated from the penis. In both sexes, spasms in other major muscle groups also occur, particularly in the buttocks and abdomen. Feet and hands may also contract, and facial features often contort.

Muscle tension and congested blood subside in the *resolution phase,* as the genital organs return to their prearousal states. Both sexes usually experience deep feelings of well-being and profound relaxation. In some males, a *refractory period* occurs. Males experience a period of time in which their systems are incapable of subsequent arousal. This refractory period may last from a few minutes to several hours. The length of the refractory period increases with age.

Following orgasm and resolution, many females are capable of being aroused and brought to orgasm again. Males and females experience the same stages in the sexual response cycle; however, the length of time spent in any one stage is variable. Thus, one partner may be in the plateau phase while the other is in the excitement or orgasmic phase. Such variations in response rates are entirely normal. Some couples believe that simultaneous orgasm is desirable for sexual satisfaction. Although simultaneous orgasm is pleasant, so are orgasms achieved at different times.

Sexual pleasure and satisfaction are possible without orgasm or intercourse. Achieving sexual maturity includes learning that sex is not a contest with a real or imaginary opponent. The sexually mature person enjoys sexual activity whether or not orgasm occurs. Expressing love and sexual feelings for another person involves many pleasurable activities, of which intercourse and orgasm may only be a part.

···· WHAT DO YOU THINK?

Why do we place so much importance on orgasm? Can sexual pleasure and satisfaction be achieved without orgasm? What is the role of desire in sexual response?

Sexual Orientation

An essential part of your sexual identity is your sexual orientation. **Sexual orientation** refers to a person's enduring emotional, romantic, sexual, or affectionate attraction to other persons. You may be primarily attracted to members of the

Vasocongestion The engorgement of the genital organs with blood.

Sexual orientation A person's enduring emotional, romantic, sexual, or affectionate attraction to other persons.

other sex (**heterosexual**), your same sex (**homosexual**), or both sexes (**bisexual**).

Homosexuality refers to emotional and sexual attachment to persons of your same sex. Many homosexuals prefer the use of the terms *gay* and *lesbian* to describe their sexual orientations, as these terms go beyond the exclusively sexual connotation of the term *homosexual*. The term *gay* can be applied to both men and women, but the term *lesbian* is applied only to women.

Bisexuality refers to emotional attachment and sexual attraction to members of both sexes. Bisexuals may face great social stigma, as they are often ostracized by homosexuals as well as by heterosexuals. Little research has been done on this segment of the population, and many bisexuals remain hidden or closeted.

Throughout history, the mental health status of gays and lesbians has been debated by scientists and laypersons alike. Recently, the issue of homosexuality as a treatable "disease" has been resurrected. Therapies labeled as conversion or reparative therapies are being promoted in a series of full-page print ads in national newspapers and in television ads. Mental health professionals have found these ads so troubling that a special resolution was passed by the American Psychological Association reaffirming that homosexuality is *not* a disease or disorder in need of treatment or a "cure."[28]

Most researchers today agree that sexual orientation is best understood using a multifactorial model, which incorporates biological, psychological, and socioenvironmental factors.[29–32] Biological explanations focus on research into genetics, hormones (perinatal and postpubertal), and differences in brain anatomy, while psychological and socioenvironmental explanations examine parent–child interactions, sex roles, and early sexual interactions. Collectively, this growing body of research suggests that the origins of homosexuality, like heterosexuality, are complex. To diminish the complexity of sexual orientation to "a choice" is a clear misrepresentation of current research.

Much of people's need for "explaining" homosexual needs, feelings, and behaviors arise from a fear of the unknown. In many instances, those fears are irrational. Irrational fear or hatred of homosexuality creates antigay prejudice and is expressed as **homophobia.** Homophobia in our society is expressed in many ways, subtle and not so subtle. Homophobic behaviors range from avoiding hugging same-sex friends to name-calling and physical attacks. Herek surveyed 2,000 gay and lesbian people and found that one in eight women and one in six men had been victimized in the preceding 5 years because of their sexual orientation.[33] The recent attack and murder of Matthew Shepard, a University of Wyoming gay student, illustrates the potential outcome of hate fueled by antigay prejudice. Legislation to expand federal jurisdiction over hate crimes and expand categories of hate crimes to include gender, sexual orientation, and disability, known as The Hate Crimes Prevention Act of 1998, is currently pending in the United States Congress.

WHAT DO YOU THINK?

Why is sexual orientation the subject of so much controversy in our society? Do you think homophobic behavior is on the decline in this country? What can you do to help prevent hate crimes?

Normalcy and Sexual Behavior

Every society sets standards and attempts to regulate sexual behavior. Boundaries arise that distinguish good from bad or acceptable from unacceptable and result in criteria used to establish what is viewed as normal or abnormal. Common sociocultural standards for sexual arousal and behavior in Western culture today include:

- *The Heterosexual Standard:* Sexual attraction should be to members of the other sex.
- *The Coital Standard:* Penile/vaginal intercourse (coitus) is viewed as the ultimate sex act.
- *The Orgasmic Standard:* All sexual interaction should lead to orgasm.
- *The Two-Person Standard:* Sex is an activity to be experienced by two.
- *The Romantic Standard:* Sex should be related to love.
- *The Safer Sex Standard:* If we choose to be sexually active, we should act to prevent unintended pregnancy or disease transmission.[34]

It is important to remember that these are not laws or rules, but rather social scripts that have been adopted over time. Rather than making blanket judgments about what is normal or abnormal, Kelly suggests we view sexual attraction and sexual actions in relative terms by asking the following questions:[34]

- Is a behavior healthy and fulfilling for a particular person?
- Is it safe?
- Does it lead to the exploitation of others?
- Does it take place between responsible, consenting adults?

In this way, behavior can be viewed along a continuum that takes into account many individual factors. As you read about the options for sexual expression in the pages ahead, use these questions to help explore your feelings about what is normal for you.

Options for Sexual Expression

The range of human sexual expression is virtually infinite. What you find personally satisfying and enjoyable may not be an option for someone else. The ways you choose to meet your sexual needs today may be very different two weeks or two years from now. Knowing and accepting yourself as a sexual person with individual desires and preferences is the first step in achieving sexual satisfaction.

Celibacy   Celibacy is avoidance of or abstention from sexual activities with others. A completely celibate person also does not engage in masturbation (self-stimulation), whereas a partially celibate person avoids sexual activities with others but may enjoy autoerotic behaviors such as masturbation. Some individuals choose to be celibate for religious or moral reasons. Others may be celibate for a period of time due to illness, the breakup of a long-term relationship, or lack of an acceptable partner. For some, celibacy is a lonely, agonizing state, but others find that it can be a time for introspection, value assessment, and personal growth.

Autoerotic Behaviors   The goal of **autoerotic behaviors** is sexual self-stimulation. Sexual fantasy and masturbation are the two most common autoerotic behaviors. **Sexual fantasies** are sexually arousing thoughts and dreams. Fantasies may reflect real-life experiences or forbidden desires or may provide the opportunity for practice of new or anticipated sexual experiences. The fact that you may fantasize about a particular sexual experience does not mean that you want to, or have to, act that experience out. Sexual fantasies are just that—fantasy. Another common autoerotic behavior is **masturbation.** Masturbation is self-stimulation of the genitals. Although many people feel uncomfortable discussing masturbation, it is a common sexual practice across the life span. Masturbation is a natural, pleasure-seeking behavior in infants and children. It is a valuable and important means for adolescent males and females, as well as adults, to explore their sexual feelings and responsiveness. In addition, masturbation is an important

means of sexual expression for older adults who have lost a lifelong companion or whose companion has a prolonged illness.

Kissing and Erotic Touching   Kissing and erotic touching are two very common forms of nonverbal sexual communication or expression. Both males and females have **erogenous zones,** or areas of the body that when touched lead to sexual arousal. Erogenous zones may include genital as well as nongenital areas, such as the earlobes, mouth, breasts, and inner thighs. Almost any area of the body can be conditioned to respond erotically to touch. Spending time with your partner exploring and learning about his or her erogenous areas is another pleasurable, safe, and satisfying means of sexual expression.

Oral-Genital Stimulation   **Cunnilingus** is the term used for oral stimulation of a female's genitals, and **fellatio** is the term used for oral stimulation of a male's genitals. Many partners find oral-genital stimulation an intensely pleasurable means of sexual expression. It is estimated that by the age of 35, 90 percent of Americans have experienced oral-genital stimulation at least once.[35] For some people, oral sex is not an option because of moral or religious beliefs. It is necessary to remember that HIV and other sexually transmitted diseases (STDs) can be transmitted via unprotected oral-genital sex. Use of an appropriate barrier device is strongly recommended if either partner's disease status is in question or unknown.

Vaginal Intercourse   The term *intercourse* is generally used to refer to **vaginal intercourse,** or insertion of the penis into the vagina. *Coitus* is another term for vaginal intercourse, which is the most often practiced form of sexual expression for most couples. A great variety of positions can be used during coitus. Examples include the missionary position (man on top facing the woman), woman on top, side by side, or man behind (rear entry). Many partners enjoy changing and experimenting with different positions. Sexual intercourse can take on different meanings under different circumstances. It can be a hurried, unplanned event involving little communication in the back seat of a car or an erotic, sensual experience including the exchange of love and mutual emotions in a private setting. Knowledge of yourself and your body, along with your ability to communicate effectively with others, will play a large part in determining the enjoyment or meaning of intercourse for you and your partner. Whatever your circumstance, you should practice safe sex to avoid disease transmission or unwanted pregnancy.

Anal Intercourse   The anal area is highly sensitive to touch, and some couples find pleasure in the stimulation of this area. **Anal intercourse** is insertion of the penis into the anus. Stimulation of the anus by mouth or with the fingers is also practiced. As with all forms of sexual expression, anal

---

Heterosexual   Refers to attraction to and preference for sexual activity with people of the opposite sex.

Homosexual   Refers to attraction to and preference for sexual activity with people of the same sex.

Bisexual   Refers to attraction to and preference for sexual activity with people of both sexes.

Homophobia   Irrational hatred or fear of homosexuals or homosexuality.

Celibacy   State of not being involved in a sexual relationship.

Autoerotic behaviors   Sexual self-stimulation.

Sexual fantasies   Sexually arousing thoughts and dreams.

Masturbation   Self-stimulation of genitals.

Erogenous zones   Areas in the body of both males and females that, when touched, lead to sexual arousal.

Cunnilingus   Oral stimulation of a female's genitals.

Fellatio   Oral stimulation of a male's genitals.

Vaginal intercourse   The insertion of the penis into the vagina.

Anal intercourse   The insertion of the penis into the anus.

SKILLS FOR BEHAVIOR CHANGE

How Do You Classify Sexual Behaviors?

When discussing sexual behaviors, we often hear or use the words, *natural, normal, moral, unnatural, abnormal,* or *immoral* to describe those behaviors. Review the sexual behaviors listed in the table and check whether you believe the behavior is natural or unnatural, normal or abnormal, and moral or immoral.

- What criteria did you use for identifying a behavior as natural or unnatural?

- What criteria did you use for identifying a behavior as normal or abnormal?
- What criteria did you use for identifying a behavior as moral or immoral?
- Do you use similar or different criteria for defining *natural, normal,* and *moral*? Why or why not?

Source: Adapted from B. Strong, *The Resource Book: A Teacher's Tool Kit,* Mountain View, CA: Mayfield Publishing Company (Worksheet #3, Classifying Sexual Behavior).

	Natural/Unnatural	Normal/Abnormal	Moral/Immoral
Sexual intercourse			
Oral sex			
Gay/lesbian sex			
Masturbation			
Extramarital sex			
Premarital sex			
Anal intercourse			

stimulation or intercourse is not for everyone. If you do enjoy this form of sexual expression, remember to use condoms to prevent disease transmission. Also, anything inserted into the anus should not be directly inserted into the vagina, as bacteria commonly found in the anus can cause infections when introduced into the vagina.

Variant Sexual Behavior

Although attitudes toward sexuality have changed radically since the Victorian era, some people believe that any sexual behavior other than heterosexual intercourse is abnormal, deviant, or perverted. Rather than using these value-laden terms, people who study sexuality prefer to use the term **variant sexual behavior** to describe sexual behaviors that are not engaged in by most people. The following list of variant sexual behaviors includes behaviors that are illegal in some states and some behaviors that could be harmful to others:

- *Group sex.* Sexual activity involving more than two people. Participants in group sex run a high risk of exposure to AIDS and other sexually transmitted diseases.

- *Transvestitism.* The wearing of clothing of the opposite sex. Most transvestites are male, heterosexual, and married.
- *Transsexualism.* Strong identification with the opposite sex in which men or women feel that they are "trapped in the wrong body." In some cases, transsexuals undergo sex-change operations. Since the 1960s, 4,000 of these operations have been performed in the United States.
- *Fetishism.* Describes sexual arousal achieved by looking at or touching inanimate objects, such as underclothing or shoes.
- *Exhibitionism.* The exposure of one's genitals to strangers in public places. Most exhibitionists are seeking a reaction of shock or fear from their victims. Exhibitionism is a minor felony in most states.
- *Voyeurism.* Observing other people for sexual gratification. Most voyeurs are men who attempt to watch women undressing or bathing. Voyeurism is an invasion of privacy and is illegal in most states.
- *Sadomasochism.* Sexual activities in which gratification is received by inflicting pain (verbal or physical abuse) on a partner or by being the object of such infliction. A sadist is a person who receives gratification from inflicting pain,

and a masochist is a person who receives gratification from experiencing pain.

- *Pedophilia.* Sexual activity or attraction between an adult and a child. Any sexual activity involving a minor, including possession of child pornography, is illegal.

········ **WHAT DO YOU THINK?**

What criteria are used in our society to identify normal sexual behaviors? What criteria do you use? Why are some individuals more open to trying a variety of sexual behaviors than are others?

DIFFICULTIES THAT CAN HINDER SEXUAL FUNCTIONING

Research indicates that problems that can hinder sexual functioning are quite common in this country. The label given to the various problems that can interfere with sexual pleasure is **sexual dysfunction.** You should not be embarrassed if you experience a sexual dysfunction at some point in your life. You can have breakdowns involving your sexual function just as you can have breakdowns in any of your other body systems. Sexual dysfunctions can be divided into four major classes: sexual desire disorders, sexual arousal disorders, orgasm disorders, and sexual pain disorders. We will look briefly at each of these categories. In most cases, sexual dysfunctions can be treated successfully if both partners are willing to work together to solve the problem.

Variant sexual behavior A sexual behavior that is not engaged in by most people.

Sexual dysfunction Problems associated with achieving sexual satisfaction.

Inhibited sexual desire (ISD) Lack of sexual appetite or simply a lack of interest and pleasure in sexual activity.

Sexual aversion disorder Type of desire dysfunction characterized by sexual phobias and anxiety about sexual contact.

Erectile dysfunction (impotence) Also known as impotence; difficulty in achieving or maintaining a penile erection sufficient for intercourse.

Premature ejaculation Ejaculation that occurs prior to or almost immediately following penile penetration of the vagina.

Sexual Desire Disorders

The most frequent problem that causes people to seek out a sex therapist is **ISD,** or **inhibited sexual desire.**[36] ISD is the lack of a sexual appetite or simply a lack of interest and pleasure in sexual activity. In some instances, it can result from stress or boredom with sex. **Sexual aversion disorder** is another type of desire dysfunction, characterized by sexual phobias (unreasonable fears) and anxiety about sexual contact. The psychological stress of a punitive upbringing, rigid religious background, or a history of physical or sexual abuse may be one source of these desire disorders.

Sexual Arousal Disorders

The most common disorder in this category is erectile dysfunction. **Erectile dysfunction,** or **impotence,** is difficulty in achieving or maintaining a penile erection sufficient for intercourse. At some time in his life, every man experiences impotence. Causes are varied and include underlying diseases, such as diabetes or prostate problems; reactions to some medications (for example, medication for high blood pressure); depression; fatigue; stress; alcohol; performance anxiety; and guilt over real or imaginary problems (such as when a man compares himself to his partner's past lovers).

Some 30 million men in this country, half of whom are under the age of 65, suffer from impotence. Impotence generally becomes more of a problem as men age, affecting one in four men over the age of 65. Recently the FDA approved the drug Viagra (sildenafil citrate) for the treatment of impotence. Response to the drug's release was record breaking. Taken by mouth one hour before sexual activity, Viagra was reported to successfully manage erectile dysfunction in 60 to 80 percent of cases during clinical trials.[37] The medication is not, however, without side effects or risk. The most commonly reported side effects include headache, flushing, stomach ache, urinary tract infection, diarrhea, dizziness, rash, and mild and temporary visual changes. In addition, since its release, there have been 69 reported deaths in the United States among Viagra users, prompting more caution in prescribing it to patients with known cardiovascular disease and those taking commonly prescribed short- and long-acting nitrates such as nitroglycerin.[38]

Orgasm Disorders

Up to 50 percent of the male population is affected by premature ejaculation at some time in their lives. **Premature ejaculation** is ejaculation that occurs prior to or very soon after the insertion of the penis into the vagina. Treatment for premature ejaculation involves a physical examination to rule out organic causes. If the cause of the problem is not physiological, therapy is available to help a man learn how

Recent studies indicate that some degree of sexual dysfunction is much more common than once thought. New treatments, such as Viagra, have helped many couples regain satisfying sexual relationships.

to control the timing of his ejaculation. Fatigue, stress, performance pressure, and alcohol use can all be contributing factors to orgasmic disorders in men.

When a woman is unable to achieve orgasm, termed **female orgasmic disorder,** she often blames herself and learns to fake orgasm in order to avoid embarrassment or preserve her partner's ego. Contributing to this response are the messages women have historically been given about sex as marital duty rather than as a pleasurable act for both parties. Like men who experience orgasmic disorders, the first step in treatment is a physical exam to rule out organic causes.

Masturbation is usually a primary focus in teaching a woman to become orgasmic. Through masturbation, a woman can learn how her body responds sexually to various types of touch. Once a woman has become orgasmic through masturbation, she learns to communicate her needs to her partner.

Sexual Pain Disorders

Two common disorders in this category are dyspareunia and vaginismus. **Dyspareunia** is pain experienced by a female during intercourse. This pain may be caused by diseases such as endometriosis, uterine tumors, chlamydia, gonorrhea, or urinary-tract infections. Damage to tissues during childbirth and insufficient lubrication during intercourse may also cause pain or discomfort. Dyspareunia can also be psychological in origin. As with other problems, dyspareunia can be treated with good results.

Vaginismus is the involuntary contraction of vaginal muscles, making penile insertion painful or impossible. Most

cases of vaginismus are related to fear of intercourse or to unresolved sexual conflicts. Treatment of vaginismus involves teaching a woman to achieve orgasm through nonvaginal stimulation.

Seeking Help

Many theories and treatment models exist for those seeking help for sexual dysfunction. A first important step is choosing a qualified sex therapist or counselor. A national organization, the American Association of Sex Educators, Counselors, and Therapists, or AASECT, has been in the forefront of establishing criteria for certifying sex therapists. These criteria include appropriate degree(s) in one of the helping professions, specialized coursework in human sexuality, and sufficient hours of practical therapy work under the direct supervision of an already certified sex therapist. Lists of certified counselors and sex therapists, as well as clinics that treat sexual dysfunctions, can be obtained by contacting AASECT or the Sexuality Information and Education Council of the United States (SIECUS).

Drugs and Sex

Because psychoactive drugs affect our entire physiology, it is only logical that they affect our sexual behavior. Promises of increased pleasure make drugs very tempting to those seeking greater sexual satisfaction. Too often, however, drugs become central to sexual activities and damage the relationship.

Alcohol is notorious for reducing inhibitions and giving increased feelings of well-being and desirability. At the same time, alcohol inhibits sexual response; thus, the mind may be willing, but not the body.

Perhaps the greatest danger associated with use of drugs during sex is the tendency to blame the drug for negative behavior. A sexually mature person carefully examines risks and benefits and makes decisions accordingly. If drugs are necessary to increase erotic feelings, it is likely that the partners are being dishonest about their feelings for each other.

Of growing concern in recent years is the increased use of "date-rape drugs." These have become popular among college students and are often used in combination with alcohol.[39] Both Rohypnol and GHB, or gammahydroxybutyrate, have

---

Female orgasmic disorder   The inability to achieve orgasm.

Dyspareunia   Pain experienced by women during intercourse.

Vaginismus   A state in which the vaginal muscles contract so forcefully that penetration cannot be accomplished.

been used to facilitate rape. The drugs are often slipped into the drinks of unsuspecting women at bars or parties, resulting in initial disinhibition and a state of induced amnesia. In response to this growing problem, Congress passed a bill outlawing use of Rohypnol and other date-rape drugs and increasing penalties for the manufacture, distribution, or possession of Rohypnol. To prevent exposure to date-rape drugs, do not allow strangers to buy you a drink, never leave a drink unattended, and never drink a substance from an unknown source (e.g., "punch drinks").

.... **WHAT DO YOU THINK?**

Why do we find it so difficult to discuss sexual dysfunction in our society? Do you think it is more difficult for men than for women to talk about dysfunction?

$Taking\ Charge$ ....

Managing Your Relationships and Sexual Behavior

Think about the relationships in your life. Are you satisfied with the number of friends you have and with the quality of your friendships? Are you involved in a sexual relationship? Is the relationship where you want it to be? Do you feel that you are a sexually healthy person? Use the information in this chapter to answer the following questions and to assess your attitudes about your relationships and your sexuality.

CHECKLIST FOR CHANGE

MAKING PERSONAL CHOICES

✓ What relationships are most important to you? How have these relationships affected your relationships with others?

✓ What do you expect in a long-term, committed relationship? What would you be willing to accept in terms of behaviors from your committed partner?

✓ What do you think are the three most important attributes of a friend? Have you displayed these attributes when dealing with your friends?

✓ Do you feel comfortable with yourself sexually? Do you know the function and location of the structures that make up the male and female sexual anatomy?

✓ Do you know what your options are for expressing your sexuality? Have you reviewed the options and identified those you may be willing to try?

✓ Do you need to work on developing any new skills that will help you reach your goals regarding your sexual self?

MAKING COMMUNITY CHOICES

✓ Do you reach out to friends who are having problems in their relationships?

✓ Do you try to work through your problems with others, or do you run from, avoid, or get angry about your difficulties?

✓ Do you know what community resources are available to help people with questions about sexuality-related issues?

✓ Have you taken the time to become informed about sexual issues and concerns in your community?

SUMMARY

• Intimate relationships have several different characteristics, including behavioral interdependence, need fulfill-ment, and emotional attachment. Each of these characteristics plays a significant role in determining how happy, healthy, and well adjusted you are as you interact with others.

- Family, friends, and partners or lovers provide the most common opportunities for intimacy. Each of these relationships may have healthy and/or unhealthy characteristics that may serve to influence our daily level of functioning.

- Men and women often relate very differently in intimate relationships. Understanding these differences and learning how to deal with them are important aspects of healthy relationships.

- Remaining single is more common than ever before. Most single people lead healthy, happy, and well-adjusted lives.

- The decision to have children should involve careful thought and planning, and parents should have the emotional maturity necessary to provide a healthy environment for their children.

- Before relationships fail, there are often many warning signs. By recognizing these signs and taking action to change behaviors, partners may save and/or enhance their relationships. In fact, there are many strategies

for building better relationships. Look at your own behaviors—those things you may need to change and those things that you are willing to do to help develop a relationship.

- Sexual identity is determined by a complex interaction of genetic, physiological, and environmental factors. Biological sex, gender identity, gender roles, and sexual orientation are all part of our sexual identity.

- Sexuality can be expressed in many ways. Physiologically, males and females, while different, both experience four phases of sexual response: excitement/arousal, plateau, orgasm, and resolution.

- Sexual orientation refers to a person's enduring emotional, romantic, sexual, or affectionate attraction to other persons. Irrational hatred or fear of homosexuality is termed *homophobia*.

- Sexual dysfunctions can be classified into sexual desire disorders, sexual arousal disorders, orgasm disorders, and sexual pain disorders. Use of various drugs can also lead to sexual dysfunction.

DISCUSSION QUESTIONS

1. What are the characteristics of intimate relationships? What is behavioral interdependence, need fulfillment, and emotional attachment, and why are each of these important in subsequent relationship development?

2. What are the common types of intimate relationships? Think about your own intimate relationships. Why would you characterize them as intimate?

3. Why are your relationships with your family important? Explain how your family unit was similar to or different from the traditional family unit in early America? Who made up your family of origin? Your nuclear family?

4. List and describe the characteristics that are important in a good friend. Who is your best friend right now? What things can you do to improve your current relationships

with friends? Based on this discussion, what do you value most in a friend?

5. In what ways may men and women differ in their interpersonal relationships?

6. Discuss the cycle of changes that occurs in our bodies in response to various hormones (e.g., sexual differentiation while in the womb, secondary sex characteristics at puberty, menopause).

7. How can we remove the stigma that surrounds sexual dysfunction so that individuals feel more open to seeking help? Are men and women impacted differently by sexual dysfunction?

8. How has the campus bar scene changed in response to the increased incidence of date-rape drug use?

APPLICATION EXERCISE

Reread the *What Do You Think?* scenario at the beginning of the chapter and answer the following questions:

1. From what sources might Erica and Chris be getting information that would lead them to question the normalcy of their sexual behaviors?

2. Is there a "golden" standard for sexual behavior that fits all people and all circumstances?

3. If Erica and Chris are comfortable and satisfied with their current sexual behaviors, are they therefore normal?

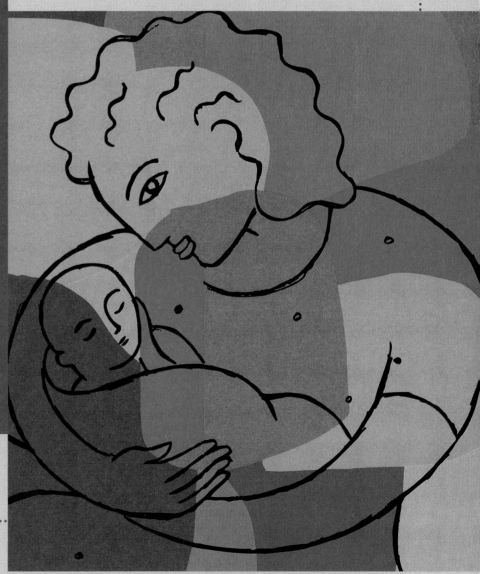

6

Birth Control, Pregnancy, and Childbirth

Managing Your Fertility

OBJECTIVES

▶ List permanent and reversible contraceptive methods, discuss their effectiveness in preventing pregnancy and sexually transmitted diseases, and describe how these methods are used.

▶ Summarize the legal decisions surrounding abortion and the various types of abortion procedures used today.

▶ Discuss emotional health, maternal health, financial evaluation, and contingency planning in terms of your own life's goals as aspects that you should consider before becoming parents.

▶ Explain the importance of prenatal care and the process of pregnancy.

▶ Describe the basic stages of childbirth as well as some of the complications that can arise during labor and delivery.

▶ Review some of the primary causes of and possible solutions to infertility.

FERTILITY IS A MIXED BLESSING for some women. The ability to participate in the miracle of birth is an overwhelming experience for many. Yet the responsibility to control one's fertility can also seem overwhelming. Today, we not only understand the intimate details of reproduction but also possess technologies designed to control or enhance our fertility. Along with information and technological advance comes choice, and choice goes hand in hand with responsibility. Choosing if and when to have children is one of our greatest responsibilities. A woman and her partner have much to consider before planning or risking a pregnancy. Children, whether planned or unplanned, change people's lives. They require a lifelong personal commitment of love and nurturing.

Before you plan or risk a pregnancy, you have the responsibility to make certain you are physically, emotionally, and financially prepared to care for another human being. One measure of maturity is the ability to discuss reproduction and birth control with one's sexual partner before succumbing to sexual urges. Men often assume that their partners are taking care of birth control. Women often feel that if they bring up the subject, it implies that they are "easy" or "loose." You will find embarrassment-free discussion a lot easier if you understand human reproduction and contraception and honestly consider your attitudes toward these matters before you get into compromising situations.

METHODS OF FERTILITY MANAGEMENT

Conception refers to the fertilization of an ovum by a sperm. The sperm enters the ovum. Its tail breaks off, and a protective chemical barrier secreted by the ovum surrounds the sperm and prevents other sperm from entering. The following conditions are necessary for conception:

1. A viable egg.
2. A viable sperm.
3. Possible access to the egg by the sperm.

The term **contraception** refers to methods of preventing conception. Sometimes the term *birth control* is used interchangeably with contraception, but it implies that a couple or individual is using methods to limit the number of children who are birthed. Thus, birth control is more equivalent to family planning. All of these methods offer control over when and whether pregnancies occur. However, since people first associated sexual activity with pregnancy, society has searched for a simple, infallible, and risk-free method of preventing pregnancy. We have not yet found one.

Another important concept allows us to evaluate the effectiveness of a particular contraceptive method. For every contraceptive method discussed in this chapter (see Table 6.1) the *perfect failure rate* and *typical use failure rate* can be found. Perfect failure rate refers to the number of pregnancies that are likely to occur in a year (per 100 uses of method during sexual intercourse) if the method is used absolutely perfectly, that is, without any error. More practical is the typical use failure rate. This refers to the number of pregnancies that are likely to occur with typical use, that is, with the normal number of errors, memory lapses, and incorrect or incomplete use. This information is much more practical for people in helping them make informed decisions about contraceptive methods.

Our present methods of contraception fall into two categories: *reversible methods,* such as the pill, condoms, and abstinence; and *permanent methods,* such as vasectomy (for men) and tubal ligation (for women). Let's discuss some of the methods in each category in detail so you will have the information you need to make an informed choice.

Reversible Contraception

▶ **Abstinence and "Outercourse"** Strictly defined, abstinence means deliberately shunning intercourse. This strict definition would allow one to engage in such forms of sexual intimacy

Fertility A person's ability to reproduce.

Conception The fertilization of an ovum by a sperm.

Contraception Methods of preventing conception.

TABLE 6.1

Percentage of Women Experiencing an Unintended Pregnancy during the First Year of Typical Use and the First Year of Perfect Use of Contraception and the Percentage Continuing Use at the End of the First Year: United States

METHOD[1]	% of Women Experiencing an Unintended Pregnancy within the First Year of Use		% OF WOMEN CONTINUING USE AT ONE YEAR[4]
	TYPICAL USE[2]	PERFECT USE[3]	
Chance[4]	85	85	40
Spermicides[5]	26	6	63
Periodic abstinence	25		
Calendar		9	
Ovulation method		3	
Symptothermal[6]		2	
Post-ovulation		1	
Cap[7]			
Parous women	40	26	42
Nulliparous women	20	9	56
Sponge			
Parous women	40	20	42
Nulliparous women	20	9	56
Diaphragm[7]	20	6	56
Withdrawal	19	4	
Condom[8]			
Female (reality)	21	5	56
Male	14	3	61
Pill	5		71
Progestin only		0.5	
Combined		0.1	
IUD			
Progesterone T	2.0	1.5	81
Copper T 380A	0.8	0.6	78
LNg 20	0.1	0.1	81
Depo-Provera	0.3	0.3	70
Norplant and Norplant-2	0.05	0.05	88
Female sterilization	0.5	0.5	100
Male sterilization	0.15	0.10	100

Emergency Contraceptive Pills: Treatment initiated within 72 hours after unprotected intercourse reduces the risk of pregnancy by at least 75%.[9]

Lactational Amenorrhea Method: LAM is a highly effective, *temporary* method of contraception.[10]

....

[1]Among typical couples who initiate use of a method (not necessarily for the first time), the percentage who experience an accidental pregnancy during the first year if they do not stop use for any other reason.

[2]Among couples who initiate use of a method (not necessarily for the first time) and who use it perfectly (both consistently and correctly), the percentage who experience an accidental pregnancy during the first year if they do not stop use for any other reason.

[3]Among couples attempting to avoid pregnancy, the percentage who continue to use a method for 1 year.

[4]The percentages becoming pregnant in columns (2) and (3) are based on data from populations where contraception is not used and from women who cease using contraception in order to become pregnant. Among such populations, about 89% become pregnant within 1 year. This estimate was lowered slightly (to 85%) to represent the percentages who would become pregnant within 1 year among women now relying on reversible methods of contraception if they abandoned contraception altogether.

[5]Foams, creams, gels, vaginal suppositories, and vaginal film.

[6]Cervical mucus (ovulation) method supplemented by calendar in the pre-ovulatory and basal body temperature in the post-ovulatory phases.

[7]With spermicidal cream or jelly.

[8]Without spermicides.

[9]The treatment schedule is one dose within 72 hours after unprotected intercourse, and a second dose 12 hours after the first dose. The Food and Drug Administration has declared the following brands of oral contraceptives to be safe and effective for emergency contraception: Ovral (1 dose is 2 white pills), Alesse (1 dose is 5 pink pills), Nordette or Levlen (1 dose is 4 light-orange pills), Lo/Ovral (1 dose is 4 white pills), Triphasil or Tri-Levlen (1 dose is 4 yellow pills).

[10]However, to maintain effective protection against pregnancy, another method of contraception must be used as soon as menstruation resumes, the frequency or duration of breastfeeds is reduced, bottle feeds are introduced, or the baby reaches 6 months of age.

Source: R. Hatcher et al., Contraceptive Technology, 17th ed. (New York: Ardent Media, Inc., 1998), 216, citing update of Trussell and Kost (1987) and Trussell et al. (1990c). See Chapter 31.

as massage, kissing, and solitary masturbation. But many people today have broadened the definition of abstinence to include all forms of sexual contact, even those that do not culminate in sexual intercourse.

Couples who go a step farther than massage and kissing and engage in such activities as oral-genital sex and mutual masturbation are sometimes said to be engaging in "outercourse." Like abstinence, outercourse can be 100 percent effective for birth control as long as the male does not ejaculate near the vaginal opening. Unlike abstinence, however, outercourse is not 100 percent effective against sexually transmitted diseases (STDs). Oral-genital contact can result in transmission of an STD, although the practice can be made safer by using a condom on the penis or a dental dam on the vaginal opening.

▶ *The Condom* The **condom** is a strong sheath of latex rubber or other material designed to fit over an erect penis. The condom catches the ejaculate, thereby preventing sperm migration toward the egg. The condom is the only temporary means of birth control available for men and the only barrier that effectively prevents the spread of STDs and AIDS. They may also slow or reduce the development of cervical abnormalities in women that can lead to cancer. Regardless of your preferred method of birth control, you should always use a condom. Condoms come in a wide variety of styles: colored, ribbed for "extra sensation," lubricated, nonlubricated, and with or without reservoirs at the tip. All may be purchased with or without spermicide in pharmacies, in some supermarkets, in some public bathrooms, and in many health clinics. A new condom must be used for each act of intercourse or oral sex.

Condoms must be rolled on the penis before the penis touches the vagina, and held in place when the penis is removed from the vagina after ejaculation. For greatest efficacy, they should be used with a spermicide containing nonoxynol-9, the same agent found in many of the contraceptive foams and creams that women use. If necessary or desired, users can lubricate their own condoms with contraceptive foams, creams, and jellies or other water-based lubricants, such as K-Y jelly, ForPlay Lubricants, Astroglide, Wet or Aqua Lube, to name just a few. However, products such as baby oil, cold creams, petroleum jelly, vaginal yeast infection medications, or hand and body lotions should never be used. These products contain mineral oil and will begin to disintegate the latex condom within 60 seconds.

The efficacy of condoms can be compromised and the likelihood of their breaking during intercourse is increased when they are old or poorly stored. To maintain effectiveness, condoms should be stored in a cool place (not wallet or hip pocket) and they should be inspected for small tears before use.

For some people, a condom ruins the spontaneity of sex. Stopping to put it on breaks the mood for them. Others report that the condom decreases sensation. These inconveniences contribute to improper use of the device. Couples

who learn to put the condom on together as part of foreplay are generally more successful with this form of birth control.[1]

▶ *Oral Contraceptives* **Oral contraceptive** pills were first marketed in the United States in 1960. Their convenience quickly made them the most widely used reversible method of fertility control.

Most oral contraceptives work through the combined effects of synthetic estrogen and progesterone. Because the levels of estrogen in the pill are higher than those produced by the body, the pituitary gland is never signaled to produce follicle-stimulating hormone (FSH), without which ova will not develop in the ovaries. Progesterone in the pill prevents proper growth of the uterine lining and thickens the cervical mucus, forming a barrier against sperm.

Pills are meant to be taken in a cycle. At the end of each three-week cycle, the user discontinues the drug or takes a placebo pill for one week. The resultant drop in hormones causes the uterine lining to disintegrate, and the user will have a menstrual period, usually within one to three days. The same cycle is repeated every 28 days. Menstrual flow is generally lighter than in a non-pill user because the hormones in the pill prevent thick endometrial buildup.

Today's pill is different from the one introduced more than three decades ago. The original pill contained large amounts of estrogen, which caused certain risks for the user, whereas the current pill contains the minimal amount of estrogen necessary to prevent pregnancy.

Because the chemicals in oral contraceptives change the way the body metabolizes certain nutrients, all women using the pill should check with their prescribing practitioners regarding dietary supplements. The nutrients of concern include vitamin C and the B-complex vitamins—B_2, B_6, and B_{12}. A nutritious diet that includes whole grains, fresh fruits and vegetables, lean meats, fish and poultry, and nonfat dairy products is advised.

Oral contraceptives can interact negatively with other drugs. For example, some antibiotics diminish the pill's effectiveness and may require an adjustment in dosage to maintain the desired effectiveness. Women in doubt should check with their prescribing practitioners, their pharmacists, or other knowledgeable health professionals.

Return of fertility may be delayed after discontinuing the pill, but the pill is not known to cause infertility. Women who had irregular menstrual cycles before going on the pill are more likely to have problems conceiving, regardless of pill use.

Use of the pill is convenient and does not interfere with lovemaking. It may lessen menstrual difficulties, such as cramps and premenstrual syndrome (PMS). Women using oral contraceptives have lower risks for developing endometrial and ovarian cancers. They are also less likely than nonusers to develop fibrocystic breast disease. In addition, pill users have lower incidences of ectopic pregnancies, ovarian cysts, pelvic inflammatory disease, and iron deficiency anemia.[2] But possible serious health problems associated with the pill include the tendency for pill users' blood to form clots and an increased risk for high blood pressure in a few women. Clotting can lead to strokes or heart attacks. The risk is low for most healthy women under 35 who do not smoke; it increases with age and, especially, with cigarette smoking.

One of its greatest disadvantages is that it must be taken every day. If a woman misses taking one pill, she is advised to use an alternative form of contraception for the remainder of that cycle. Another disadvantage is that the pill does not protect against sexually transmitted infections (STIs). The cost of the pill may also be a problem for some women. Finally, some teenagers report that the requirement to have a complete gynecological examination in order to get a prescription for the pill is a huge obstacle. Fully 69 percent of female teenagers think that this requirement frightens their peers away from use of the pill.[3] Educating young women about what goes on in a gynecological exam would certainly help ease their anxiety.

▶ *Progestin-Only Pills* Progestin-only pills (or minipills) contain small doses of progesterone. Women who feel uncertain about using estrogen pills, who suffer from side effects related to estrogen, or who are nursing may want to take these pills rather than combination pills. There is still some question about the specific ways progestin-only pills work. Current thought is that they change the composition of the cervical mucus, thus impeding sperm travel. They may also inhibit ovulation in some women. The effectiveness rate of progestin-only pills is 96 percent, which is slightly lower than that of estrogen-containing pills. Also, their use usually leads to irregular menstrual bleeding. As with all oral contraceptives, the user has no protection against STDs.

▶ *Emergency Contraceptive Pills* There are more than 2.7 million unintended pregnancies per year in the United States and nearly half are due to contraceptive failure. According to the Centers for Disease Control and Prevention, more than 11 million American women report using contraceptive methods associated with high failure rates, including condoms, withdrawal, periodic abstinence, and diaphragms. These facts led

the Food and Drug Administration (FDA) to approve the "Preven Emergency Contraceptive Kit."[4]

Emergency contraception can be used when a condom breaks, after a sexual assault, or any time unprotected sexual intercourse occurs. **Emergency contraceptive pills (ECPs)** are ordinary birth control pills containing the hormones estrogen and progestin. Although the therapy is commonly known as the morning-after pill, the term is misleading; ECPs can be used up to 72 hours beyond. The use of ECPs can reduce the risk of pregnancy by 75 percent.

Emergency contraceptives require a prescription. After a woman determines she is not pregnant, by using the pregnancy test included in the kit, the first dose of two light blue emergency pills is taken as soon as possible, within 72 hours after sex with a known or suspected birth control failure or sex without birth control. The second dose is taken 12 hours later.[5] The most common side effects related to emergency use are nausea, vomiting, menstrual irregularities, breast tenderness, headache, abdominal pain and cramps, and dizziness.

Emergency minipills contain progestin only. Like ECPs, minipills can be used immediately after unprotected intercourse and up to 72 hours beyond. Emergency minipills are equally as effective as ECPs, but nausea and vomiting are far less common. Emergency minipills are an excellent alternative for most women who cannot use ECPs that contain estrogen.

▶ *Foams, Suppositories, Jellies, and Creams* Like condoms, jellies, creams, suppositories, and foam do not require a prescription. Chemically, they are referred to as **spermicides**— substances designed to kill sperm. Foams, suppositories, jellies, and creams usually contain nonoxynol-9, a detergent believed to be effective in also killing viruses, bacteria, and other organisms. Although they are not recommended as the primary form of contraception, spermicides are often recommended for use with other forms of contraception. While they help prevent the spread of certain STDs, they are most effective when used in conjunction with a condom.

Jellies and creams are packaged in tubes, and foams are available in aerosol cans. All have tubes designed for insertion into the vagina. They must be inserted far enough to cover the cervix, providing both a chemical barrier that kills sperm and a physical barrier that stops sperm from continuing toward an egg.

Suppositories are waxy capsules that are placed deep in the vagina and melt once they are inside. They must be inserted 10 to 20 minutes before intercourse to have time to melt but no longer than one hour prior to intercourse or they lose their effectiveness. Additional contraceptive chemicals must be applied for each subsequent act of intercourse (see Figure 6.1 on page 130).

▶ *The Female Condom* This new contraceptive device for internal use by women has now been approved by the FDA. The **female condom** is a single-use, soft, loose-fitting polyurethane sheath. It is designed as one unit with two diaphragm-like rings. One ring, which lies inside the sheath,

---

Condom   A sheath of thin latex or other material designed to fit over an erect penis and to catch semen upon ejaculation.

Oral contraceptives   Pills taken daily for three weeks of the menstrual cycle which prevent ovulation by regulating hormones.

Emergency contraceptive pills (ECPs)   Drugs taken within three days after intercourse to prevent fertilization or implantation.

Spermicides   Substances designed to kill sperm.

Female condom   A single-use polyurethane sheath for internal use by women.

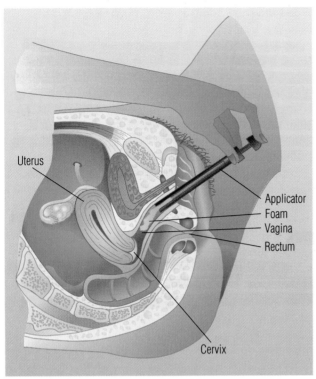

Uterus

Applicator
Foam
Vagina
Rectum

Cervix

Figure 6.1
The Proper Method of Applying Spermicide within the Vagina

serves as an insertion mechanism and internal anchor. The other ring, which remains outside the vagina once the device is inserted, protects the labia and the base of the penis from infection.

▶ *The Diaphragm with Spermicidal Jelly or Cream*   The **diaphragm** is a soft, shallow cup made of thin latex rubber. Its flexible, rubber-coated ring is designed to fit snugly behind the pubic bone in front of the cervix and over the back of the cervix on the other side. Diaphragms are manufactured in different sizes and must be fitted to the woman by a trained practitioner. The practitioner should also be certain that the user knows how to insert her diaphragm correctly before she leaves the practitioner's office.

Diaphragms must be used with spermicidal cream or jelly. The spermicide is applied to the inside of the diaphragm before insertion. The jelly or cream is held in place by the diaphragm, creating a physical and chemical barrier against sperm. Additional spermicide must be applied before each subsequent act of intercourse, and the diaphragm must be left in place for six to eight hours after intercourse to allow the chemical to kill any sperm remaining in the vagina (see Figure 6.2). *Taken out in 24 hrs.*
Using the diaphragm during the menstrual period or leaving the diaphragm in place beyond the recommended time slightly increases the user's risk of developing **toxic shock syndrome (TSS).** This condition results from a type of

fitted by physician

bacteria that multiplies and spreads to the bloodstream and causes sudden high fever, rash, nausea, vomiting, diarrhea, and a sudden drop in blood pressure. If not treated, TSS can be fatal. The diaphragm (as well as tampons left too long in place) creates conditions conducive to the growth of these bacteria. To reduce the risk of TSS, women should wash their hands carefully with soap and water before inserting or removing the diaphragm.

Another problem with the diaphragm is that it can put undue pressure on the urethra, blocking urinary flow and predisposing the user to bladder infections. A further disadvantage is that inserting the device can be awkward, especially if the woman is rushed. When inserted incorrectly, the effectiveness rate of the diaphragm decreases.

▶ *Cervical Cap*   The **cervical cap** is a small cup made of latex that is designed to fit snugly over the entire cervix. It must be fitted by a practitioner and is designed for use with contraceptive jelly or cream. It is somewhat more difficult to insert than a diaphragm because of its smaller size.

The cap keeps sperm out of the uterus. It is held in place by suction created during application. Insertion may take place anywhere up to two days prior to intercourse, and the device must be left in place for six to eight hours after intercourse. The maximum length of time the cap can be left on the cervix is 48 hours. If removed and cleaned, it can be reinserted immediately.

Some women report unpleasant vaginal odors after use. Because the device can become dislodged during intercourse, placement must be checked frequently. It cannot be used during the menstrual period or for longer than 48 hours because of the risk of toxic shock syndrome.

▶ *Intrauterine Devices*   Widespread use of **intrauterine devices (IUDs)** for contraception began in the mid-1960s, when these devices were advertised as less risky and more convenient than the pill. However, the devices began to fall

Diaphragm   A latex, saucer-shaped device designed to cover the cervix and block access to the uterus; should always be used with spermicide.

Toxic shock syndrome (TSS)   A potentially life-threatening disease that occurs when specific bacterial toxins are allowed to multiply unchecked in wounds or through improper use of tampons or diaphragms.

Cervical cap   A small cup made of latex that is designed to fit snugly over the entire cervix.

Intrauterine device (IUD)   A T-shaped device that is implanted in the uterus to prevent pregnancy.

Withdrawal   A method of contraception that involves withdrawing the penis from the vagina before ejaculation. Also called "coitus interruptus."

Depo-Provera   An injectable method of birth control that lasts for three months.

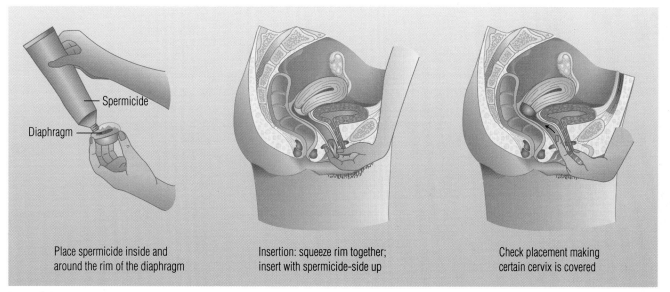

Place spermicide inside and around the rim of the diaphragm

Insertion: squeeze rim together; insert with spermicide-side up

Check placement making certain cervix is covered

Figure 6.2
The Proper Use and Placement of a Diaphragm

out of favor in the mid-1970s following negative publicity about the Dalkon shield, a device associated with pelvic inflammatory disease and sterility. The manufacturer stopped making Dalkon shields in 1975.

We are not certain how IUDs work despite the fact that women have been using them since 1909. Although it was once thought that IUDs act by preventing implantation of a fertilized egg, most experts now believe that they interfere with the sperm's fertilization of the egg.

Two IUDs are currently available. The first, the Progestasert, is a T-shaped plastic device that contains synthetic progesterone. It slowly releases the progesterone. The practitioner must remove this IUD and insert a new one every year. The second, the ParaGuard, is also T-shaped, but it has copper wrapped around the shaft and does not contain any hormones. It can be left in place for four years before replacement.

A physician must fit and insert the IUD. For insertion, the device is folded and placed into a long, thin plastic applicator. The practitioner measures the depth of the uterus with a special instrument and then uses these measurements to place the IUD accurately. When in place, the arms of the T open out across the top of the uterus. One or two strings extend from the IUD into the vagina so the user can check to make sure that her IUD is in place. The device is removed by a practitioner when desired.

The discomfort and cost of insertion of IUDs may be a disadvantage for some. When in place, the device can cause heavy menstrual flow and severe cramps. There is a risk of uterine perforation. Women using IUDs have a higher risk of ectopic pregnancy, pelvic inflammatory disease, infertility, and tubal infections. If a pregnancy occurs while the IUD is in place, the chance of miscarriage is 25 to 50 percent. Removal of the device as soon as the pregnancy is known is advised.

Doctors often offer therapeutic abortion to women who become pregnant while using an IUD because of the serious risks (including premature delivery, infection, and congenital abnormalities) associated with continuing the pregnancy.

▶ *Withdrawal* This often ineffective method of birth control is most commonly used by people who have not taken the time to consider alternatives. The withdrawal method involves withdrawing the penis from the vagina just prior to ejaculation. Because there can be up to half a million sperm in the drop of fluid at the tip of the penis before ejaculation, this method is unreliable. Timing withdrawal is also difficult; males concentrating on accurate timing may not be able to relax and enjoy intercourse.

New Methods of Birth Control

Hormone types

▶ *Depo-Provera* **Depo-Provera** is a long-acting synthetic progesterone that is injected intramuscularly every three months. Although used in other countries for years, the FDA did not approve it for use in the United States until 1992. Researchers believe that the drug prevents ovulation.

Depo-Provera encourages sexual spontaneity because the user does not have to remember to take a pill or to insert a device. Those who want to start a family can easily decide to do so without much of a waiting period. There are fewer health problems associated with Depo-Provera than with estrogen-containing pills. The main disadvantage is irregular bleeding, which can be troublesome at first, but within a year, most women are amenorrheic (have no menstrual periods). Weight gain (an average of five pounds in the first year) is common. Other possible side effects include dizziness, nervousness, and

CONSUMER HEALTH

Today's *Sponge* Makes a Comeback

In 1995, many women were crestfallen when a popular over-the-counter contraceptive choice and an FDA-approved product, *Today's* sponge, was taken off the market. After an FDA inspection raised concern over the air and water quality in the plant that manufactured the sponge, there were some questions over the potential for an abundance of bacteria, an exposure the FDA felt could have compromised the safety of the product and women who used it. As a result, despite the fact that the product itself still met all FDA standards, the manufacturer halted production due to the prohibitive cost of upgrading the plant in order to pass inspection.

Now under different ownership, Allendale pharmaceutical company has addressed the environmental issues of the plant and plans once again to stock the shelves with *Today's* sponge. The product will be no different than its last configuration. It has retained its donut-shape and continues to be coated in nonoxynol-9 spermicide. Its ease of use requires simply inserting it into the vagina and pushing it up to cover the cervix. Removal is equally simple; just pull on the loop. This device can be inserted up to 24 hours before intercourse and does not require repeat applications for repeated intercourse.

The demise of the sponge in 1995 became part of contemporary folklore when it was parodied on the popular television comedy, *Seinfeld*. When one of the characters, "Elaine," found herself hoarding the limited supply of sponges still on the shelves, she also began to use it as a basis for rating the romantic potential of men she met. A relationship that had potential was considered to be *spongeworthy*, which meant Elaine might be willing to dip into her precious supply of sponges at some point. As in many cases, pop culture served as a fair barometer of contemporary society as the show reflected the feelings of many women around the country who felt a real loss when the sponge was no longer produced. Soon there will be no need for anymore hoarding.

---

headache. Unlike other methods of contraception, this method cannot be stopped immediately if problems arise.

▶ *Norplant* Approved for use by the FDA in 1990 and marketed since February 1991 for use in the United States, Norplant is one the newest forms of hormonal contraception. It has been tested by more than 1 million women in 45 countries and is now approved for use in 14 countries. Increasing numbers of women in the United States are considering this option because of its convenience, effectiveness, and safety. Six silicon capsules that contain progestin are surgically inserted under the skin of a woman's upper arm. For five years, small amounts of progestin are continuously released. The progestin in Norplant works the same way as oral contraceptives do; it suppresses ovulation, prevents growth of uterine lining, and thickens the cervical mucus.

Norplant is one of the most effective methods of birth control ever developed. A serious disadvantage to Norplant use, however, is its lack of protection against STDs.

Norplant can be inserted by a specially trained doctor, nurse, or nurse practitioner in 10 to 15 minutes. A local anesthetic is administered to the upper arm, a small injection is made, and, with a special needle, the six capsules are placed just under the skin in a fan shape. The capsules are similarly removed after five years or, if necessary, at any point after their insertion.

The capsules usually cannot be seen, nor does insertion leave a scar in most women. At this time, no serious side effects are known. Less serious side effects include irregular bleeding and irregular menstrual periods, acne, weight gain, breast tenderness, headaches, nervousness, depression, and nausea.

Norplant is one of the most effective reversible methods of fertility control. In addition to being very convenient, the implant is easy for a trained practitioner to do, so there is little chance of error. It costs less than the pill—$550 compared to $1,180 over five years.[6] Medical assistance programs in many states will pay this cost for poor women.

▶ *Vaginal Ring* A method that is not yet approved by the FDA but that appears promising is the vaginal ring. Rings that are 2 to 3 inches in diameter and contain estrogen and progesterone or progesterone alone are placed by a woman in her vagina. They may be left in place continuously or removed every three weeks for one week to allow regular bleeding. The rate of effectiveness is similar to that of the pill.

Contraceptives for Men?

The development of a new method of birth control for men has been slow. There has not been a new method of birth control for men since the mass production of condoms became possible. However, researchers have been searching for a safe, effective, reliable form of contraceptives for men. Among the possibilities are weekly injections or implants of

Contraception around the World

Nearly 50 percent of all the world's couples of reproductive age currently use some form of contraception. Sterilization is the most commonly used method of birth control worldwide, followed by IUDs, oral contraceptives, condoms, and natural family-planning methods. The differences among countries and contraceptive use can be quite dramatic and are influenced by a variety of factors, such as access to services, availability, cost, and political, cultural, and religious factors. Examples of such differences can be seen by examining the following countries:

BRAZIL

- The most popular methods of contraception are female sterilization (44%), the pill (41%), vasectomy (9%), abstinence and withdrawal (6.2%), condoms (2.5%), IUDs (1.5%), other (3.5%).
- Sterilization, the most common form of birth control, is illegal.
- The government in Brazil provides no public system for delivery of contraceptives or the funding of contraceptives.

GERMANY

- Oral contraceptive pills, IUDs, barrier methods, and sterilization are available and are covered by insurance.
- The most popular methods of contraception are birth control pills (55%), some sort of barrier method (10%), or IUD (13%), sterilization (5%), and natural methods of contraception (8%).
- In Germany's eastern states, women under 20 years of age can legally obtain contraceptives free of charge.

KENYA

- Cultural and religious beliefs prohibit the use of contraceptives.
- Pills, IUDs, injectables, and "natural planning" are methods currently used, with injectables being the preferred method because they can easily be hidden from the men.
- Only 12 percent of Kenyan men currently use condoms.

CHINA

- In 1979 China developed a one-child family policy.
- Contraceptives are provided free of charge.
- Contraception is still seen only as family planning and not as prevention of sexually transmitted infections.
- IUDs, tubectomies, vasectomies, and induced abortions are considered birth control.

Source: S. L. Caron, *Cross Cultural Perspectives on Human Sexuality* (Boston: Allyn and Bacon, 1998).

---

testosterone enathate, a synthetic version of the male sex hormone, to lower and eventually stop sperm production; vaccines that impair sperm production; and progestin-related drugs to reduce sperm counts.

A number of hormones are currently under study. One testosterone derivative suppresses sperm production enough to provide reliable protection. However, weekly injections of testosterone are required, and it is suggested that many men would find this an impractical solution. To complicate matters further, the time from the beginning of the injections until the sperm count is suppressed satisfactorily can be fairly lengthy, requiring the use of another birth control method during the same period.[7]

Vaccines that show the greatest promise appear to be the those that use either the follicle stimulating hormone (FSH) or luteinizing hormone releasing factor (LHRH). The FSH vaccine eliminates sperm while maintaining normal testosterone levels. In contrast, the vaccine using LHRH shuts down testosterone and sperm production. A side effect of this vaccine is the potential for diminished sex drive due to reduced levels of testosterone. This side effect could be reduced, however, by taking a testosterone supplement.[8]

Fertility Awareness Methods

Methods of fertility control that rely upon the alteration of sexual behavior are called **fertility awareness methods (FAM).** These methods include observing female "fertile periods" by examining cervical mucus and/or keeping track of internal temperature and then abstaining from sexual intercourse (penis-vagina contact) during these fertile times.

Two decades ago, the "rhythm method" was the object of much ridicule because of its low effectiveness rates. However, it was the only method of birth control available to women belonging to religious denominations that forbid the use of oral contraceptives, barrier methods, and sterilization. Our

Norplant A long-lasting contraceptive that consists of six silicon capsules surgically inserted under the skin in a woman's upper arm.

Fertility awareness methods (FAM) Include several types of birth control that require alteration of sexual behavior rather than chemical or physical intervention into the reproductive process.

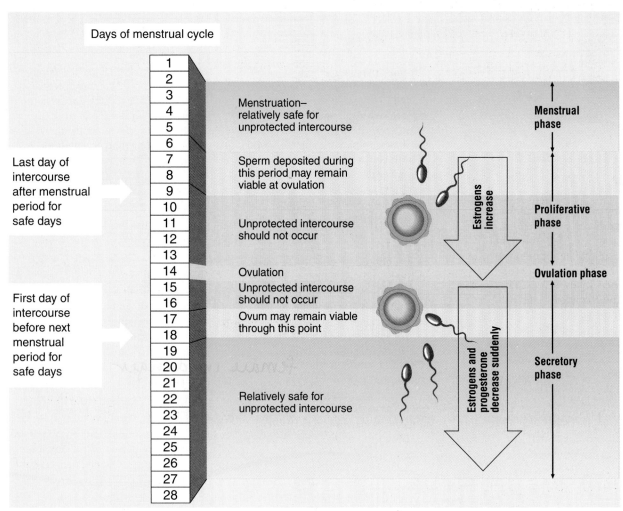

Days of menstrual cycle

Last day of intercourse after menstrual period for safe days

First day of intercourse before next menstrual period for safe days

Menstruation–relatively safe for unprotected intercourse

Sperm deposited during this period may remain viable at ovulation

Unprotected intercourse should not occur

Ovulation
Unprotected intercourse should not occur

Ovum may remain viable through this point

Relatively safe for unprotected intercourse

Menstrual phase

Estrogens increase

Proliferative phase

Ovulation phase

Estrogens and progesterone decrease suddenly

Secretory phase

Figure 6.3
The Fertility Cycle

present reproductive knowledge enables women and their partners to use natural methods of birth control with fewer risks of pregnancy, although these methods remain far less effective than others.

Fertility awareness methods of birth control rely upon basic physiology (see Figure 6.3). A released ovum can survive for up to 48 hours after ovulation. Sperm can live for as long as five days in the vagina. Natural methods of birth control teach women to recognize their fertile times. Changes in cervical mucus prior to and during ovulation and a rise in basal body temperature are two indicators frequently used in natural contraceptive techniques. Another method involves charting a woman's menstrual cycle and ovulation times on a calendar. Any combination of these methods may be used to determine fertile times more accurately.

▶ *Cervical Mucus Method* The **cervical mucus method** requires women to examine the consistency and color of their normal vaginal secretions. Prior to ovulation, vaginal mucus becomes gelatinous and stringy in consistency, and normal

vaginal secretions may increase. Sexual activity involving penis-vagina contact must be avoided while this "fertile mucus" is present and for several days following the mucus changes.

▶ *Body Temperature Method* The **body temperature method** relies on the fact that the female's basal body temperature rises between 0.4 and 0.8 degrees after ovulation has occurred. For this method to be effective, the woman must chart her temperature for several months to learn to recognize her body's temperature fluctuations. Abstinence from penis-vagina contact must be observed preceding the temperature rise until several days after the temperature rise was first noted.

▶ *The Calendar Method* The **calendar method** requires the woman to record the exact number of days in her menstrual cycle. Since few women menstruate with complete regularity, a record of the menstrual cycle must be kept for 12 months, during which time some other method of birth control must be used. The first day of a woman's period is counted as day 1. To determine the first fertile unsafe day of the cycle, she subtracts

18 from the number of days in the shortest cycle. To determine the last unsafe day of the cycle, she subtracts 11 from the number of days in the longest cycle. This method assumes that ovulation occurs during the midpoint of the cycle. The couple must abstain from penis-vagina contact during the fertile time.

Women interested in fertility awareness methods of birth control are advised to take supervised classes in their use. The risks of an unwanted pregnancy are great for the untrained woman. Reading a book or watching a film on the subject or talking to the proprietor of the local health food store will not provide the necessary training to ensure maximum effectiveness. Incidentally, information on these methods can be helpful to couples who are trying to conceive.

Permanent Contraception

Sterilization has become the leading method of contraception for women (10.7 million women), closely followed by the oral contraceptive pill (10.4 million women).[9] Since the 1970s, perfection of sterilization procedures has made this method popular. Although some of the newer surgical techniques make reversal of sterilization theoretically possible, anyone considering sterilization should assume that the operation is *not reversible*. Before becoming sterilized, people should think through such possibilities as divorce and remarriage or a future improvement in their financial status that may make them want a larger family.

▶ *Female Sterilization*   One method of sterilization in females is called tubal ligation. It is achieved through a surgical procedure that involves tying the fallopian tubes closed or cutting them and cauterizing (burning) the edges to seal the tubes so that access by sperm to released eggs is blocked. The opera-

tion is usually done in a hospital on an outpatient basis. First, the abdomen is inflated with carbon dioxide gas through a small incision in the navel. The surgeon then inserts a *laparoscope* into another incision just above the pubic bone. This specially designed instrument has a fiber-optic light source that enables the physician to see the fallopian tubes clearly. Once located, the tubes are cut and tied or cauterized.

Ovarian and uterine functions are not affected by a tubal ligation. The woman's menstrual cycle continues, and released eggs simply disintegrate and are absorbed by the lymphatic system. As soon as her incision is healed, the woman may resume sexual intercourse with no fear of pregnancy.

As with any kind of surgery, there are risks. Some patients are given general anesthesia, which presents a small risk; others receive local anesthesia. The procedure itself usually takes less than an hour, and the patient is generally allowed to return home within a short time after waking up. Women considering a tubal ligation should thoroughly discuss all the risks with their physician before the operation.

The hysterectomy, or removal of the uterus, is a method of sterilization requiring major surgery. It is usually done only when the patient has a disease of or damage to the uterus.

female in danger

▶ *Male Sterilization*   Sterilization in men is less complicated than in women. The procedure, called a vasectomy, is usually done on an outpatient basis using a local anesthetic. The surgeon (generally a urologist) makes an incision on each side of the scrotum. The vas deferens on each side is then located, and a piece is removed from each. The ends are usually tied or sewn shut (see Figure 6.4).

Cervical mucus method   A birth control method that relies upon observation of changes in cervical mucus to determine when the woman is fertile so the couple can abstain from intercourse during those times.

Body temperature method   A birth control method that requires a woman to monitor her body temperature for the rise that signals ovulation and to abstain from intercourse around this time.

Calendar method   A birth control method that requires mapping the woman's menstrual cycle on a calendar to determine presumed fertile times and abstaining from penis-vagina contact during those times.

Sterilization   Permanent fertility control achieved through surgical procedures.

Tubal ligation   Sterilization of the female that involves the cutting and tying off of the fallopian tubes.

Hysterectomy   The removal of the uterus.

Vasectomy   Sterilization of the male that involves the cutting and tying of both vasa deferentia.

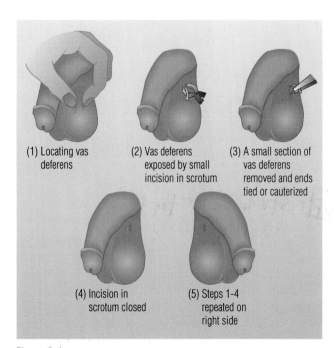

(1) Locating vas deferens

(2) Vas deferens exposed by small incision in scrotum

(3) A small section of vas deferens removed and ends tied or cauterized

(4) Incision in scrotum closed

(5) Steps 1-4 repeated on right side

Figure 6.4
Vasectomy

The man usually experiences some discomfort, local pain, swelling, and discoloration for about a week. In a small percentage of cases, more serious complications occur: formation of a blood clot in the scrotum (which usually disappears without medical treatment), infection, and inflammatory reactions. Because sperm are stored in other areas of the reproductive system besides the vasa deferentia, couples must use alternative methods of birth control for at least one month after the vasectomy. The man must check with his physician (who will do a semen analysis) to determine when unprotected intercourse can take place. The pregnancy rate in women whose partners have had vasectomies is about 15 in 10,000.

Many men are reluctant to consider sterilization because they fear the operation will affect their sexual performance. Such fears are unfounded (although not abnormal) and can be alleviated by talking to men who have already been vasectomized.

A vasectomy in no way affects sexual response. Because sperm constitute only a small percentage of the semen, the amount of ejaculate is not changed significantly. The testes continue to produce sperm, but the sperm are prevented from entering the ejaculatory duct because of the surgery. After a time, sperm production may diminish. Any sperm that are manufactured disintegrate and are absorbed into the lymphatic system.

Although a vasectomy should be considered a permanent procedure, surgical reversal is sometimes successful in restoring fertility. Recent improvements in microsurgery techniques have resulted in annual pregnancy rates of between 40 and 60 percent for women whose partners have had reversals. The two major factors influencing the success rate of reversal are the doctor's expertise and the time elapsed since the vasectomy.

········· **WHAT DO YOU THINK?**

Who do you think is responsible for deciding which method of contraception should be used in a sexual relationship? What are some examples of good opportunities for you and your partner to have a discussion about contraceptives? What do you think are the biggest barriers in our society to the use of condoms?

STOP : study above for final
ABORTION

In 1973, the landmark Supreme Court decision in *Roe v. Wade* stated that the "right to privacy . . . founded on the Fourteenth Amendment's concept of personal liberty . . . is broad enough to encompass a woman's decision whether or not to terminate her pregnancy."[10] The decision maintained that during the first trimester of pregnancy, a woman and her practitioner have the right to terminate the pregnancy through **abortion** without legal restrictions. It allowed individual

states to set conditions for second-trimester abortions. Third-trimester abortions were ruled illegal unless the mother's life or health was in danger.

In July 1989, in *Webster v. Reproductive Health Services*, the Supreme Court, by a vote of five to four, gave states the right to impose certain new restrictions on abortions. This decision, along with three subsequent rulings, paved the way for individual state interpretations of abortion acceptability. In recent years, strict abortion laws have been proposed in many states. There is intense political debate as abortion opponents put pressure on state and local governments to pass laws prohibiting the use of public funds for abortion as well as for abortion counseling. Abortions cannot be performed in publicly funded clinics in some states, and other states have laws requiring parental notification before a teenager can obtain an abortion. Although *Roe v. Wade* has not been overturned, it faces many future challenges.

Prior to the legalization of first- and second-trimester abortions, women wishing to terminate a pregnancy had to travel to a country where the procedure was legal, consult an illegal abortionist, or perform their own abortions. The last two methods led to death from hemorrhage or infection in some cases and to infertility from internal scarring in others.

Before the 1973 Supreme Court ruling, approximately 480,000 illegal abortions were performed in the United States each year, one-third of them on married women. Since the 1973 decision, the law has been continually challenged by groups that are convinced that the termination of a pregnancy is murder. Those who oppose abortion believe that the embryo or fetus is a human being with rights that must be protected. Although many opponents work through the courts and the political process, attacks on abortion clinics and on doctors who perform abortions are increasingly common. Nearly all clinics have faced some form of violent threats or acts of violence. Recent legal changes, such as the Freedom of Access to Clinic Entrance Act (FACE), offer some relief to the harassment and violence directed at abortion clinics. However, because of such acts, the biggest threat to a woman's access to an abortion now is the clinical supply rather than legal restrictions.[11]

More than 1.5 million abortions are performed in the United States every year, representing almost a fourth of all pregnancies.[12] It is estimated that 3 of every 100 American women will have had one abortion by the age of 44. About one-half of all abortions are performed because of failed contraception; the others occur in the 9 percent of sexually active women who do not use birth control. The majority of abortions, 90 percent, are performed within 12 weeks of fertilization; only 2 of every 1,000 are performed more than 20 weeks after fertilization.[13]

The best birth control methods can fail. Women may be raped. Pregnancies can occur despite every possible precaution. When an unwanted pregnancy does occur, the decision whether to terminate, to carry to term and keep the baby, or to carry to term and give the baby away must be made. This is a personal decision to be made by each woman based on her personal beliefs, values, and resources after careful consideration of all alternatives.

Methods of Abortion

The type of abortion procedure used is determined by how many weeks pregnant the woman is. Pregnancy length is calculated from the first day of a woman's last menstrual period.

If performed during the first trimester of pregnancy, abortion presents a relatively low risk to the mother. The most commonly used method of first-trimester abortion is **vacuum aspiration.** The procedure is usually performed with local anesthetic. The cervix is dilated with instruments or by placing *laminaria,* a sterile seaweed product, in the cervical canal. The laminaria is left in place for a few hours or overnight and slowly dilates the cervix. After it is removed, a long tube is inserted into the uterus through the cervix. Gentle suction is then used to remove the fetal tissue from the uterine walls.

Pregnancies that progress into the second trimester can be terminated through **dilation and evacuation (D&E),** a procedure that combines vacuum aspiration with a technique called **dilation and curettage (D&C).** For this procedure, the cervix is dilated with laminaria for one to two days and a combination of instruments and vacuum aspiration is used to empty the uterus (see Figure 6.5). Second-trimester abortions are frequently done under general anesthetic. Both procedures can be performed on an outpatient basis (usually in the physician's office) with or without pain medication. Generally, however, the woman is given a mild tranquilizer to help her relax. Both procedures may cause moderate to severe uterine cramping and blood loss.

The **hysterotomy,** or surgical removal of the fetus from the uterus, may be used during emergencies or when the mother's life may be in danger and when other types of abortions are deemed too dangerous.

The risks associated with abortions include infection, incomplete abortion (when parts of the placenta remain in the uterus), missed abortion (when the fetus is not actually removed), excessive bleeding, and cervical and uterine trauma.

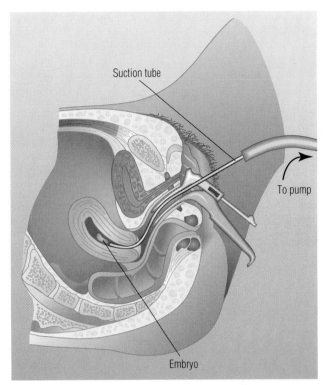

Figure 6.5
Vacuum Aspiration Abortion

Follow-up and attention to dangerous signs decrease the chances of any long-term problems.

The mortality rate for first-trimester abortions averages out to 0.8 per 100,000. The rate for second-trimester abortions is higher, 4.3 per 100,000. This higher rate is due to the increased risk of uterine perforation, bleeding, infection, and incomplete abortion due to the fact that the uterine wall becomes thinner as the pregnancy progresses.

Two other methods used in second-trimester abortions, though less commonly than the D&E method, are prostaglandin or saline **induction abortions.** In these methods, prostaglandin hormones or a saline solution is injected into the uterus. The injected solution kills the fetus and causes labor contractions to begin. After 24 to 48 hours the fetus and placenta are expelled from the uterus.

In 1996, controversy arose over a rarely performed type of abortion known as late-term abortion. Performed during the third trimester, the procedure involves partial delivery of the fetus through the birth canal, allowing the doctor the access to aspirate the brain tissue. This issue was hotly contested on Capitol Hill before being overruled. Proponents of the bill cited concern over the possible use of the procedure for non-emergency reasons. Opponents argued that the procedure is used only when the life of the mother is threatened. The Centers for Disease Control and Prevention (CDC) estimates that of the total number of abortions performed in a given year, 1.3 percent are late-term abortions.

Abortion The medical means of terminating a pregnancy.

Vacuum aspiration The use of gentle suction to remove fetal tissue from the uterus.

Dilation and evacuation (D&E) An abortion technique that combines vacuum aspiration with dilation and curettage; fetal tissue is both sucked and scraped out of the uterus.

Dilation and curettage (D&C) An abortion technique in which the cervix is dilated with laminaria for one to two days and the uterine walls are scraped clean.

Hysterotomy The surgical removal of the fetus from the uterus.

Induction abortion A type of abortion in which chemicals are injected into the uterus through the uterine wall; labor begins and the woman delivers a dead fetus.

RU-486

Several years ago it appeared that the drug **RU-486** would be approved by the FDA for use in the United States. Heavy opposition from various groups, however, delayed such approval, except for use in clinical trials. Although full approval is expected in 2000, opposition continues to be strong. RU-486 (Mifepristone) is a steroid hormone that induces abortion by blocking the action of progesterone, a hormone produced by the ovaries and placenta that maintains the lining of the uterus. Similar in structure to progesterone, RU-486 binds to cell receptor sites normally occupied by progesterone, causing the breakdown of the uterine lining. As a result, the uterine lining and the embryo are expelled from the uterus and the pregnancy is terminated.

Treatment consists of the ingestion of three pills of RU-486. A dose of prostaglandins must be administered 48 hours later to encourage contractions of the uterus. Ninety-six percent of women who take these two drugs during the first nine weeks of pregnancy will experience a complete abortion. The side effects of this treatment are similar to those reported during heavy menstruation and include cramping, minor pain, and nausea. Approximately 1 in 1,000 women requires a blood transfusion because of severe bleeding. The procedure does not require hospitalization; women may be treated on an outpatient basis.

While RU-486's nickname, "the abortion pill," may imply an easy process, treatment does involve more steps for the woman than does a traditional abortion. A traditional abortion takes about 15 minutes followed by a physical recovery of about one day. A first visit to the clinic involves a physical exam and taking three mifepristone tablets, which may cause minor side effects such as nausea, headaches, weakness, and fatigue. The patient returns two days later for a dose of prostaglandins (trade name: misoprostal), which cause contractions of the uterus, which expel the fertilized egg. Women are required to stay under observation at the clinic for four hours. A return visit is required 12 days later because the pills fail to expel the fetus completely in 4 percent of cases, and a clinical abortion is then necessary.[14]

WHAT DO YOU THINK?

If you or your partner unexpectedly became pregnant, would you choose to terminate the pregnancy? How might an abortion affect your relationship? If you were married, would your decision be different? Why?

PLANNING A PREGNANCY

The technological ability to control your fertility gives you choices not available when your parents were born. The loosening of social restrictions in the areas of marriage and parenting also affords single men and women the opportunity to become parents. Regardless of whether you are married or single, the preparation to become a parent involves similar considerations and decisions. If you are in the process of deciding whether to have children, you need to take the time to evaluate your emotions, finances, and health.

Emotional Health

The first and foremost evaluation you should make is why you want to have a child: To fulfill an inner need to carry on the family? Out of loneliness? Can you care for this new human being in a loving and nurturing manner? Are you ready to make all the sacrifices necessary to bear and raise a child? You can prepare yourself for this change in your life in several ways. Reading about parenthood, taking classes, talking to parents of children of all ages, and joining a support group are all helpful forms of preparation. If you choose to adopt, you will find many support groups available to you as well.

Maternal Health

Before becoming pregnant, a woman should have a thorough medical examination. **Preconception care** should include assessment of possible pregnancy complications. Medical problems such as diabetes and high blood pressure should be discussed as should any genetic disorders that run in either family.

Paternal Health

It is common wisdom that mothers-to-be should steer clear of toxic chemicals that can cause birth defects. Even women who are trying to conceive are cautioned to avoid toxic environments and to eat a nourishing diet, to stop smoking and drinking alcohol, and to avoid most medications.

Now similar precautions are being urged for fathers-to-be. New research suggests that a man's exposure to chemicals influences not only his ability to father a child but also the future health of his child. Fathers-to-be have been overlooked in the past for several reasons. Researchers assumed that the genetic damage leading to birth defects and other health problems always occurred while a child was in the mother's womb. After all, they reasoned, that's where embryonic and fetal development take place. Conventional medical wisdom also held that defective-looking sperm (those with misshapen heads, crooked tails, or retarded swimming ability) were incapable of fertilizing an egg.

Scientists have recently discovered that how sperm look has little to do with how they act. Misshapen sperm can penetrate an egg, and they do not necessarily carry defective genetic goods. Moreover, sperm that look healthy and swim well can be the true genetic culprits. DNA fluorescent markers have identified normal-looking, yet genetically flawed, sperm that carry too many or too few chromosomes. Fathers contribute the extra chromosome 21 in about 6 percent of children with Down syndrome, which causes mental retardation; the extra X chromosome in 50 percent of boys with Klinefelter's syndrome, which causes abnormal sexual development; and the shortened chromosome 15 in about 85 percent of children with Prader-Willi syndrome, a disorder characterized by retardation and obesity.

Although some birth defects are caused by the random errors of nature, it now appears that some disorders can be traced to sperm damaged by chemicals. Sperm are naturally vulnerable to toxic assault and genetic damage. Many drugs and ingested chemicals can readily invade the testes from the bloodstream; others ambush sperm after they leave the testes and pass through the epididymides, where they mature and are stored. By one route or another, half of 100 chemicals studied so far (including by-products of cigarette smoke) apparently harm sperm.

Some researchers believe that Vitamin C is nature's way of protecting sex cells from damage. Bad diets, exposure to toxic chemicals, cigarette smoking, and not enough foods rich in Vitamin C are probably the biggest culprits in sperm damage.[15]

Financial Evaluation

You also need to evaluate your finances. First check your medical insurance: Does it provide pregnancy benefits? If not, you can expect to pay between $1,500 and $5,000 for medical care during pregnancy and birth—and substantially more if complications arise. Both partners should find out about their employers' policies concerning parental leave including length of leave available and conditions for returning to work.

Raising a child exacts a tremendous strain on most family's finances. Expenses during the first year of life averaged $5,774 in 1990. The expense of raising a child from birth to 21 years of age is presently estimated to be over $250,000—not including the cost of a college education!

The cost and availability of quality child care should also be considered. Prospective parents should realistically assess how much family assistance they can expect with a new baby as well as the availability of nonfamily child care. While you may be aware of the federal tax credit available for child care, you may not be aware of how little assistance it provides: between a maximum of $480 for one child in a family having income of over $28,000 to a maximum of $720 for one child

in a family having income of under $10,000. A second child doubles the credit; but no further assistance is provided for a third child or more children. How much does full-time child care cost? It averages between $5,000 and $10,000 a year, depending on your location (urban areas tend to cost more).

Contingency Planning

A final consideration is how to provide for the child should something happen to you and your partner. If both of you were to die while the child is young, do you have relatives or close friends who would raise the child? If you have more than one child, would they have to be split up or could they be kept together? Unpleasant though it may be to think about, this sort of contingency planning is highly important. Children who lose their parents are usually heartbroken and confused. A prearranged plan of action may help smooth their transition into new families.

.... **WHAT DO YOU THINK?**

Do you think most parents plan when they will have their children? At what point in your life do you think you will be ready to take on the responsibilities of becoming a parent? What are your biggest concerns about parenthood?

PREGNANCY

Prenatal Care

A successful pregnancy requires the mother's ability to take good care of herself and her unborn child. It is essential to have regular medical checkups, beginning as soon as possible (certainly within the first three months). Early detection of fetal abnormalities and identification of high-risk mothers and infants are the major purposes of prenatal care. On the first visit, the practitioner should obtain a complete medical history of the mother and her family and note any hereditary conditions that could put a woman or her fetus at risk.

Regular checkups to measure weight gain and blood pressure and monitor the size and position of the fetus should continue throughout the pregnancy. This early care reduces infant mortality and low birthweight. A study group for the American College of Obstetricians and Gynecologists recommends seven or eight prenatal visits for women with low-risk pregnancies. Unfortunately, prenatal care is not equally available to all pregnant women. Approximately 30 percent of pregnant teenagers and unmarried women do not have adequate access to prenatal care. Babies of mothers who received no prenatal care are about 10 times more likely to die in the first month of life than are babies of mothers who did get prenatal care.

RU-486 A steroid hormone that induces abortion by blocking the action of progesterone. Testing in the United States began in late 1994.

Preconception care Medical care received prior to becoming pregnant that helps a woman assess and address potential maternal health.

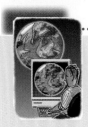

ACCESSING
YOUR HEALTH
ON THE INTERNET

Check out the following Internet sites related to birth control, pregnancy, and childbirth.

1. *The National Parenting Center.* This site invites parents to expand their parenting skills and strengths by sharing information in chat rooms and in an online newletter.

   http://www.tnpc.com/

2. *Safer Sex.* Provides information on safer sex issues. Discusses such issues as what is safer sex, is oral sex safe, women and safer sex and links to other web sites.

   http://www.safersex.org/safer.sex/

3. *Childbirth.Org.* Information to encourage parents to be good consumers, knowing their options and how to provide themselves with the best possible care essential to a healthy pregnancy.

   http://childbirth.org

4. *Loma Linda University Medical Center, Center for Fertility and InVitro Fertilization.* Complete information about all fertility options.

   http://www.llu.edu/llmuc/fertility/ivf.html

Additional concerns include the mother's physical condition, her level of nutrition, her confidence in her ability to give birth, her use of drugs and medications, and the availability of a skilled practitioner who can oversee the pregnancy and delivery. A woman planning a pregnancy also needs a support system (spouse or partner, family, friends, community groups) willing to give her and her child the love and emotional support needed during and after her pregnancy.

▶ *Choosing a Practitioner* A woman should carefully choose a practitioner to attend her pregnancy and delivery. If possible, this choice should be made before she becomes pregnant. Recommendations from friends who were satisfied with the care they received during pregnancy may be a good starting point. The woman's family physician may also be able to recommend a specialist. The pregnant woman needs to find a practitioner she can trust with both her own life and that of the baby and with whom she can communicate freely.

When choosing a practitioner, parents should ask a number of questions concerning credentials and professional qualifications. Besides this information, a pregnant woman must ask questions specific to her condition. Prospective parents should also inquire about the practitioner's experience in handling various complications, commitment to being at the mother's side during delivery, and beliefs and practices con-

cerning the use of anesthesia, fetal monitoring, induced labor, and forceps delivery. What are the practitioner's attitudes toward birth control, abortion, and alternative birthing procedures? The practitioner's approach to nutrition and medication during pregnancy should be similar to the woman's own. Finally, the parents must learn under what circumstances the practitioner would perform a cesarean section.

Two types of physicians can attend pregnancies and deliveries. The *obstetrician-gynecologist* (ob-gyn) is an M.D. who specializes in obstetrics (pregnancy and birth) and gynecology (care of women's reproductive organs). These practitioners are trained to handle all types of pregnancy and delivery-related emergencies.

A *family practitioner* is a licensed M.D. who provides comprehensive care for people of all ages. The majority of family practitioners have obstetrical experience but will refer a patient to a specialist if necessary. Unlike the ob-gyn, the family practitioner can serve as the baby's physician after attending the birth.

Midwives are also experienced practitioners who can attend both pregnancies and deliveries. *Certified nurse-midwives* are registered nurses having specialized training in pregnancy and delivery. Most midwives work in private practice or in conjunction with physicians. Those who work with physicians have access to traditional medical facilities to which they can turn in an emergency. *Lay midwives* may or may not have extensive training in handling an emergency. They may be self-taught rather than trained through formal certification procedures.

▶ *Alcohol and Drugs* A woman should avoid all types of drugs during pregnancy. Even common over-the-counter medications such as aspirin and beverages such as coffee and tea can damage a developing fetus.

During the first three months of pregnancy, the fetus is especially subject to the **teratogenic** (birth defect-causing) effects of some chemical substances. The fetus can also develop an addiction to or tolerance for drugs that the mother is using.

Of particular concern to medical professionals is the use of tobacco and alcohol during pregnancy. Women who are heavy drinkers may have normal first babies but subsequently deliver children having fetal alcohol syndrome. The symptoms of **fetal alcohol syndrome (FAS)** include mental retardation, slowed nerve reflexes, and small head size. The exact amount of alcohol necessary to cause FAS is not known, but researchers doubt that any level of alcohol consumption is safe. Therefore, total abstinence from alcohol during pregnancy is recommended.

Cigarette smoking during pregnancy has more predictable effects than does alcohol. Studies have shown a 25 to 50 percent higher rate of fetal and infant deaths among women who smoke during pregnancy compared with those who do not.[16] Women who smoke more than 10 to 15 cigarettes a day during pregnancy have higher rates of miscarriage, stillbirth, premature births, and low-birthweight babies than do nonsmokers. Smoking restricts the blood supply to the developing fetus and thus limits oxygen and nutrition delivery and waste removal. It appears to be a significant factor in the development of cleft lip and palate, and a significant relationship has been shown between both smoking and "secondhand" smoke and sudden infant death syndrome.[17] Fetal research on the effects of "second-hand" or sidestream smoke (inhaling smoke produced by others) is inconclusive, but babies whose parents smoke can be twice as susceptible to pneumonia, bronchitis, and related illnesses as other babies. Recent statistics for the United States show that tobacco use in pregnant women has steadily fallen since 1989.

▶ *X-rays*   X-rays present a clear danger to the fetus. Although most diagnostic tests produce minimal amounts of radiation, even low levels may cause birth defects or other problems, particularly if several low-dose X-rays are taken over a short time period. Pregnant women are advised to avoid X-rays unless absolutely necessary.

▶ *Nutrition and Exercise*   Pregnant women have additional needs for protein, calories, and certain vitamins and minerals, so their diets should be carefully monitored by a qualified practitioner. Special attention should be paid to getting enough folic acid (found in dark leafy greens), iron (dried fruits, meats, legumes, liver, egg yolks), calcium (nonfat or lowfat dairy products, some canned fish), and fluids. Vitamin supplements can correct some deficiencies, but there is no true substitute for a well-balanced diet. Starting January 1, 1998, manufacturers of breads, pastas, rice, and other grain products were required to add folic acid to their products in a move to help reduce neural tube defects in newborns. Folic acid, when consumed before and during early pregnancy, reduces the risk of spina bifida, a common disabling birth condition resulting from failure of the spinal column to close. Babies born to mothers whose nutrition has been poor run high risks of substandard mental and physical development.

Weight gain during pregnancy helps nourish a growing baby. For a woman of normal weight before pregnancy, the acceptable weight gain during pregnancy ranges from 25–35 pounds; a woman carrying twins needs to gain about 35–45 pounds. Usually the mother can expect to gain about 10 pounds during the first 20 weeks and about 1 pound per week during the rest of the pregnancy.

Of the total number of pounds gained during pregnancy, about 6–8 are the baby's weight. The baby's birthweight is important, since low weight can mean health problems during labor and the baby's first few months. Eating right and gaining enough weight helps reduce the chances of having a low-birthweight baby. If a woman gains an appropriate amount of weight while pregnant, chances are that her baby will gain

A doctor-approved exercise program during pregnancy not only helps the mother control her weight, but also contributes to easier deliveries and healthier babies.

weight properly, too. Pregnancy is not a time to think about losing weight—doing so may endanger the baby.[18]

As in all other stages of life, exercise is an important factor in weight control during pregnancy as well as in overall maternal health. A balanced 45-minute exercise session three days per week has been associated in one study with heavier-birthweight babies, fewer surgical births, and shorter hospital stays after birth. Pregnant women should consult with their physicians before starting any exercise program.

▶ *Other Factors*   A pregnant woman should avoid exposure to toxic chemicals, heavy metals, pesticides, gases, and other hazardous compounds. She should not clean cat-litter boxes because cat feces can contain organisms that cause a disease called toxoplasmosis. If a pregnant woman contracts this disease, her baby may be stillborn or suffer mental retardation or other birth defects.

Before becoming pregnant, a woman should be tested to determine if she has had rubella (German measles). If she has not had the disease, she should get an immunization for it and wait the recommended length of time before becoming pregnant. A rubella infection can kill the fetus or cause blindness or hearing disorders in the infant. If the woman has ever had genital herpes, she should inform her physician. The physician may want to deliver the baby by cesarean section, especially if the woman has active lesions.

Teratogenic   Causing birth defects; may refer to drugs, environmental chemicals, X-rays, or diseases.

Fetal alcohol syndrome (FAS)   A collection of symptoms, including mental retardation, that can appear in infants of women who drink too much alcohol during pregnancy.

Contact with an active herpes infection during birth can be fatal to the infant.

A Woman's Reproductive Years

More than half of the average American woman's expected life span is spent between menarche (first menses) and menopause (last menses), a period of approximately 40 years. During this 40-year period, she must make many decisions regarding her reproductive health. Deciding if and when to have children, as well as how to prevent pregnancy when necessary, are long-term concerns.

Today, a woman over 35 who is pregnant has plenty of company. While births to women in their 20s are declining, the rate of first births to women between the ages of 30 and 39 has doubled in the past decade, and births to women over 39 have increased by more than 50 percent. Many women who wait until their 30s to consider having a child find themselves wondering, "Am I too old to have a baby?" Researchers believe that there is a decline in both the quality and viability of eggs produced after age 35. Statistically, the chances of having a baby with birth defects do rise after the age of 35. **Down syndrome,** a condition characterized by mild to severe mental retardation and a variety of physical abnormalities, is the most commonly occurring genetic condition. One in every 800 to 1,000 live births a year is a child with Down syndrome, representing approximately 5,000 births per year in the United States alone. A common myth is that most children with Down syndrome are born to older parents. The truth is that 80 percent of children born with Down syndrome are born to women younger than 35 years of age. However, the incidence of births of children with Down syndrome increases with age. The incidence of Down syndrome in babies born to a mother aged 20 is 1 in 10,000 births; it rises to 1 in 400 by age 35, to 1 in 110 by age 40, and to 1 in 35 when she is 45.[19]

Women who choose to delay motherhood until their late 30s also worry about their physical ability to carry and deliver their babies. For these women, a comprehensive exercise program will assist in maintaining good posture and promoting a successful delivery.

There are some advantages to having a baby later in life. In fact, many doctors are encouraging older women to become pregnant because they find that these women tend to be more conscientious about following medical advice during pregnancy and more psychologically mature and ready to include an infant in their family than are some younger women.

Pregnancy Testing

A woman may suspect she is pregnant before she has any type of pregnancy tests. A typical sign is a missed menstrual period, yet this is not always an accurate indicator. A woman can miss her period for a variety of reasons: stress, exercise, emotional upset. Confirmation of a pregnancy can be obtained from a pregnancy test scheduled in a medical office or birth control clinic.

Women who wish to know immediately whether or not they are pregnant can purchase home pregnancy test kits. These kits, sold over the counter in drugstores, are about 85 to 95 percent reliable. A positive test is based on the secretion of **human chorionic gonadotropin (HCG)** found in the woman's urine. Home test kits come equipped with a small sample of red blood cells coated with HCG antibodies to which the user adds a small amount of urine. If the concentration of HCG is great enough, it will clump together with the HCG antibodies, indicating that the user is pregnant.

There are some problems with the accuracy of these home tests. If taken too early in the pregnancy, they may show a false negative. Other causes of false negatives are unclean test tubes, ingestion of certain drugs, and vaginal or urinary infections. Accuracy also depends on the quality of the test itself and the user's ability to perform it and interpret the results. Blood tests administered and analyzed by a medical laboratory give more accurate results.

The Process of Pregnancy

Pregnancy begins the moment a sperm fertilizes an ovum in the fallopian tubes (see Figure 6.6). From there, the single cell multiplies, becoming a sphere-shaped cluster of cells as it travels toward the uterus, a journey that may last three to four days. Upon arrival, the embryo burrows into the thick, spongy endometrium and is nourished from this carefully prepared lining.

Down syndrome   A condition characterized by mental retardation and a variety of physical abnormalities.

Human chorionic gonadotropin (HCG)   Hormone detectable in blood or urine samples of a mother within the first few weeks of pregnancy.

Trimester   A three-month segment of pregnancy; used to describe specific developmental changes that occur in the embryo or fetus.

Embryo   The fertilized egg from conception until the end of two months' development.

Fetus   The name given the developing baby from the third month of pregnancy until birth.

Placenta   The network of blood vessels that carries nutrients to the developing infant and carries wastes away; it connects to the umbilical cord.

Amniocentesis   A medical test in which a small amount of fluid is drawn from the amniotic sac; it tests for Down syndrome and genetic diseases.

Amniotic sac   The protective pouch surrounding the baby.

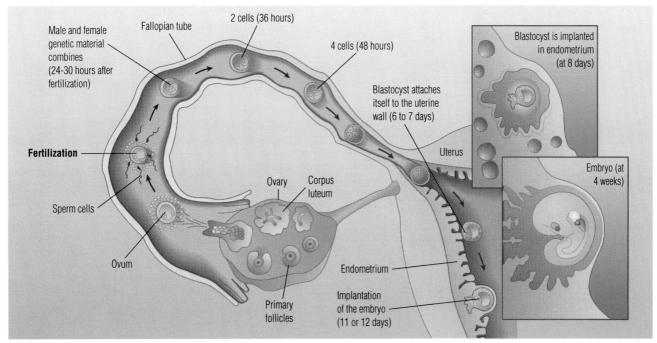

Figure 6.6
Fertilization

Early Signs of Pregnancy The first sign of pregnancy is usually a missed menstrual period (although some women "spot" in early pregnancy, and such spotting may be mistaken for a period). Other signs of pregnancy include:

- Breast tenderness
- Emotional upset
- Extreme fatigue
- Nausea
- Sleeplessness
- Vomiting (especially in the morning)

Pregnancy typically lasts 40 weeks. The due date is calculated from the expectant mother's last menstrual period. Pregnancy is typically divided into three phases, or **trimesters,** of approximately three months each.

The First Trimester During the first trimester, there are few noticeable changes in the maternal body. The expectant mother may urinate more frequently and experience morning sickness, swollen breasts, or undue fatigue. But these symptoms may not be frequent or severe, so she may not realize she is pregnant at this time unless she has a pregnancy test.

During the first two months after conception, the **embryo** differentiates and develops its various organ systems, beginning with the nervous and circulatory systems. At the start of the third month, the embryo is called a **fetus,** indicating that all organ systems are in place. For the rest of the pregnancy, growth and refinement occur in each major body system so that they can function independently, yet in coordination, at birth.

The Second Trimester At the beginning of the second trimester, physical changes in the mother become more visible. Her breasts swell and her waistline thickens. During this time, the fetus makes greater demands upon the mother's body. In particular, the **placenta,** the network of blood vessels that carry nutrients and oxygen to the fetus and fetal waste products to the mother, becomes well established.

The Third Trimester From the end of the sixth month through the ninth is considered the third trimester. This is the period of greatest fetal growth. The fetus gains most of its weight during these last three months. During the third trimester, the fetus must get large amounts of calcium, iron, and nitrogen from the food the mother eats. Approximately 85 percent of the calcium and iron the mother digests goes into the fetal bloodstream.

Although the fetus may live if it is born during the seventh month, it needs the layer of fat it acquires during the eighth month and time for the organs (especially the respiratory and digestive organs) to develop to their full potential. Babies born prematurely thus usually require intensive medical care.

Prenatal Testing and Screening

Modern technology has enabled medical practitioners to detect health defects in a fetus as early as the 14th to 18th weeks of pregnancy. One common testing procedure, **amniocentesis,** which is strongly recommended for women over the age of 35, involves inserting a long needle through the mother's abdominal and uterine walls into the **amniotic sac,** the protective pouch surrounding the baby (see Figure 6.7 on page 144). The needle draws out 3 to 4 teaspoons of

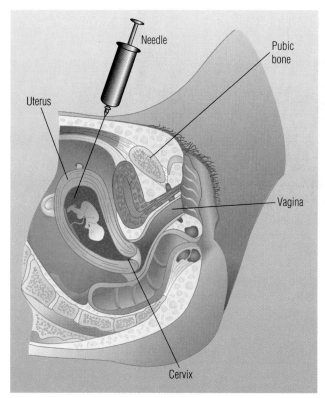

Figure 6.7
The process of amniocentesis can detect certain congenital problems as well as the sex of the fetus.

fluid, which is analyzed for genetic information about the baby. This test can reveal the presence of 40 genetic abnormalities, including Down syndrome, Tay-Sachs disease (a fatal disorder of the nervous system common among Jewish people of Eastern European descent), and sickle-cell anemia (a debilitating blood disorder found primarily among blacks). Amniocentesis can also reveal the sex of the child, a fact many parents choose not to know until the birth. Although widely used, amniocentesis is not without risk. Chances of fetal damage and miscarriage as a result of testing are 1 in 400.

Another procedure, *ultrasound* or *sonography,* uses high-frequency sound waves to determine the size and position of the fetus. Ultrasound can also detect defects in the central nervous system and digestive system of the fetus. Knowing the position of the fetus assists practitioners in performing amniocentesis and in delivering the child. In 1999, a new three-dimensional ultrasound technique clarified the images and improved doctors' efforts at detecting and treating defects prenatally.

A third procedure, *fetoscopy,* involves making a small incision in the abdominal and uterine walls and then inserting an optical viewer into the uterus to view the fetus directly. This method is still experimental and involves some risk. It causes miscarriage in approximately 5 percent of cases.

A fourth procedure, *chorionic villus sampling (CVS),* involves snipping tissue from the developing fetal sac. CVS

can be used at 10 to 12 weeks of pregnancy, and the test results are available in 12 to 48 hours. This test is an attractive option for couples who are at high risk for having a baby with Down syndrome or a debilitating hereditary disease.

If any of these tests reveals a serious birth defect, parents are advised to undergo genetic counseling. In the case of a chromosomal abnormality such as Down syndrome, the parents are usually offered the option of a therapeutic abortion. Some parents choose this option; others research their unborn child's disability and decide to go ahead with the birth and offer the baby the love and support all children deserve.

········ WHAT DO YOU THINK?

What are your most important concerns when considering a health-care practitioner for your or your partner's pregnancy? What behaviors might you or your partner need to change if you found out that you or your partner were pregnant? Are there any behaviors that you would consider integrating into your lifestyle now that would be of benefit to you or your partner, if you were planning a pregnancy? How much emphasis should be placed on male preconception planning, if any?

CHILDBIRTH

Choosing Where to Have Your Baby

Today's prospective mothers have many delivery options. These range from the traditional hospital birth to home birth. When considering birthing alternatives, parental values are important. (See Skills for Behavior Change box on page 146.) Many couples, for instance, feel that the modern medical establishment has dehumanized the birth process; thus they choose to deliver at home or at a *birthing center,* a homelike setting outside a hospital where women can give birth and receive postdelivery care by a team of professional practitioners, including physicians and registered nurses. Financial considerations are also important, and a couple's income and insurance coverage will often dictate its choice.

Transition   The process during which the cervix becomes nearly fully dilated and the head of the fetus begins to move into the birth canal.

Episiotomy   A straight incision in the mother's perineum.

Perineum   The area between the vulva and the anus.

Afterbirth   The expelled placenta.

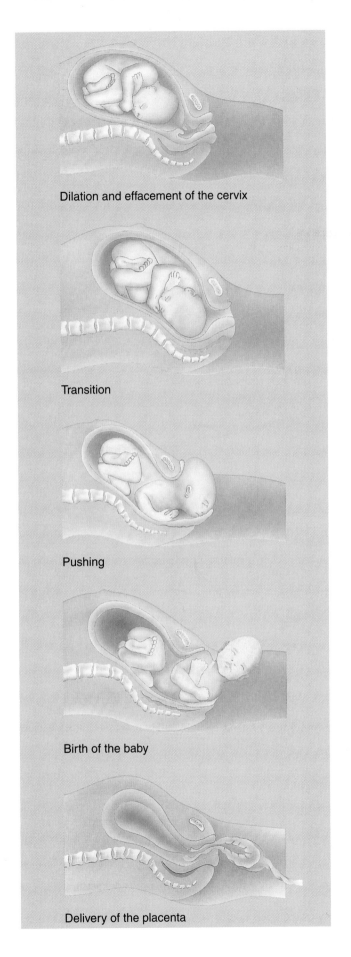

Dilation and effacement of the cervix

Transition

Pushing

Birth of the baby

Delivery of the placenta

Labor and Delivery

The birth process has three stages. The exact mechanisms that signal the mother's body that the baby is ready to be born are unknown. During the few weeks preceding delivery, the baby normally shifts and turns to a head-down position, and the cervix begins to dilate (open up). The junction of the pubic bones also loosens to permit expansion of the pelvic girdle during birth.

In the first stage of labor, the amniotic sac breaks, causing a rush of fluid from the vagina (commonly referred to as "breaking of the waters"). Contractions in the abdomen and lower back also signal the beginning of labor. Early contractions push the baby downward, putting pressure on the cervix and thereby causing it to dilate further. The first stage of labor may last from a couple of hours to more than a day for a first birth, but is usually much shorter during subsequent births.

The end of the first stage of labor, called **transition,** is the process when the cervix becomes fully dilated and the baby's head begins to move into the vagina, or the birth canal. Contractions usually come quickly during transition. Transition usually lasts 30 minutes or less.

The second stage of labor follows transition when the cervix has become fully dilated. Contractions become rhythmic, stronger, and more painful as the uterus works to push the baby through the birth canal. The second stage of labor (called the *expulsion stage*) may last between one and four hours and concludes when the infant is finally pushed out of the mother's body. In some cases, the attending practitioner will do an **episiotomy,** a straight incision in the mother's **perineum,** to prevent the baby's head from causing tearing of vaginal tissues and to speed the baby's exit from the vagina. Sometimes women can avoid the need for an episiotomy by exercising and getting good nutrition throughout pregnancy, by trying different birth positions, or by having an attendant massage the perineal tissue. However, the skin's natural elasticity and the baby's size are limiting factors.

After delivery, the attending practitioner cleans the baby's mucus-filled breathing passages, and the baby takes its first breath, generally accompanied by a loud wail.

In the meantime, the mother continues into the third stage of labor, during which the placenta, or **afterbirth,** is expelled from the womb. This stage is usually completed within 30 minutes after delivery. The umbilical cord is then tied and severed. The stump of cord attached to the baby's navel dries up and drops off within a few days.

Most mothers prefer to have their new infants placed next to them following the birth. Together with their spouse or partner, they feel a need to share this time of bonding with their infant.

Figure 6.8
The Birth Process

SKILLS
FOR
BEHAVIOR
CHANGE

Developing a Birth Plan

Birth plans are ideas and expectations that you have about the birth of your baby. They are used to help people with whom you come into contact during your labor and birth to know a bit more about you, how you have prepared for this baby, and what you want from the birth. A lot of people misunderstand and assume that you are writing orders for people to follow. (If only labor would allow us to do this!) But the birth plan simply serves as a guideline so that those assisting you know your wishes and desires. A birth plan might address some of the following issues:

- Do you want mobility or do you wish to be confined to a bed?
- Do you want a routine IV, a heparin lock, or nothing at all?
- Do you want to wear your own clothing?
- Do you want to listen to music during the birthing process?
- Do you prefer to use the tub or the shower?
- Do you want pain medications or do you want to avoid them?
- Do you have preferences for which pain medications you want?
- Would you prefer a certain position in which to give birth?
- Would you like an episiotomy? Or, are there certain measures you want used to avoid one?

- If you need a cesarean, do you have any special requests?
- For home and birth center births, what are your plans in case of transport?
- What will be the role of the father during delivery?

As you can see there are many topics that may be addressed in a birth plan. All should be discussed prenatally with your care provider. It is preferred that they be written down and even signed by your care provider if you are going to a birth center or hospital.

There are many types of birth plans in written format. Some are many pages long, and some are just a single paragraph that simply "sets the tone" for the birth. There is always a happy medium, and only you will know what works for you.

Birth Alternatives

Expectant parents have several options for their infant's birth and their participation in it. Although several of these methods have decreased in popularity, all continue to be used.

▶ **Lamaze Method** This birth alternative is the most popular one in the United States. Pre-labor education classes teach the mother to control her pain through special breathing patterns, focusing exercises, and relaxation. Lamaze births usually take place in a hospital or birthing center with a physician or midwife in attendance. The husband (or labor coach) assists by giving emotional support, physical comfort (massage and ice chips), and coaching for proper breath control during contractions. Lamaze proponents discourage the use of drugs.

▶ **Harris Method** Parents using this alternative are taught by registered nurses. Gentle touching and controlled breathing are stressed. Husbands (or other partners) provide emotional support while a physician-nurse team essentially controls the labor and delivery. Drugs are not prohibited.

▶ **Childbirth without Fear** Sometimes called the Read Method, this method advocates education for understanding of the birth process. Mothers are taught to recognize that anticipation of pain creates more pain. Relaxation is stressed.

The husband or other partner provides emotional support. Drugs are not prohibited.

▶ **Leboyer Method** Leboyer proponents believe that birth in the standard delivery room is a traumatic experience for the baby. The Leboyer method allows the mother to deliver in a dark and quiet setting. Immediately after delivery, the infant is placed in a warm bath to ease its transition to life outside the womb. Drug use is discouraged.

Drugs in the Delivery Room

Because painkilling drugs given to the mother during labor can cause sluggish responses in the newborn, many women choose drug-free labors and deliveries. Drug-free labor involves the use of exercise, massage, and controlled rhythmic breathing to control pain. Many women who choose "natural" childbirth mistakenly believe that the exercises they are taught in their classes will make their labor and delivery painless. When their time comes to give birth, they may feel inadequate because they experience the normal pain associated with childbirth. Pain is to be expected, and if it becomes too intense, the mother can be given painkilling medication.

A discussion with the attending physician before the birth of the baby will alert the mother to the practitioner's feelings about the use of painkilling drugs during delivery. Many experts believe that women should be offered the option

146   *Part Two   Creating Healthy and Caring Relationships*

of drugs during delivery both before and during the event. To refuse to give a mother medicine to take the edge off the pain is considered poor medical practice by some authorities.

Breast-Feeding and the Postpartum Period

Although the new mother's milk will not begin to flow for two or more days, her breasts secrete a thick yellow substance called *colostrum*. Because this fluid contains vital antibodies to help fight infection, the newborn baby should be allowed to suckle.

As a result of recent scientific findings, the American Academy of Pediatrics has strongly recommended that full-term newborns be breast-fed. This recommendation does not mean that breast milk is the only adequate method of nourishing a baby. Prepared formulas can provide nourishment that allows a baby to grow and thrive.

Still, there are many advantages to breast-feeding. Breast milk is perfectly suited to a baby's nutritional needs. Breast-fed babies have fewer illnesses and a much lower hospitalization rate because breast milk contains maternal antibodies and immunological cells that stimulate the infant's immune system. When breast-fed babies do get sick, they recover more quickly. They are also less likely to be obese than babies fed on formulas, and they have fewer allergies.

When deciding whether to breast- or bottle-feed, mothers need to consider their own desires and preferences. Both feeding methods can supply the physical and emotional closeness so essential to the parent-child relationship.

The *postpartum period* lasts from four to six weeks after delivery. During this time, the mother's reproductive organs revert to a nonpregnant state. Many women experience energy depletion, anxiety, mood swings, and depression during this period. This experience, known as **postpartum depression,** appears to be a normal end-product of the birth process. For most women, the symptoms gradually disappear as their bodies return to normal. For others, the symptoms, coupled with the stresses of managing a new family, can cause more severe depression that lasts for several months.

Complications

Problems and complications can occur during labor and delivery even following a successful pregnancy. Such possibilities should be discussed with the practitioner prior to labor so the mother understands what medical procedures may be

Breast-feeding is one way to enhance the development of intimate bonds between mother and child.

necessary for her safety and for that of her child. Although pregnancy still involves a certain amount of risk, the risk is lower than for many other common activities.

▶ *Cesarean Section (C-section)* If labor lasts too long or if a baby is presenting wrong (about to exit the uterus anything but head first), a **cesarean section (C-section)** may be necessary. This surgical procedure involves making an incision across the mother's abdomen and through the uterus to remove the baby. This operation is also performed in cases in which labor is extremely difficult, maternal blood pressure falls rapidly, the placenta separates from the uterus too soon, the mother has diabetes, or other problems occur.

A cesarean section can be traumatic for the mother if she is not prepared for it. The rate of delivery by cesarean section in the United States increased from 5 percent in the mid-1960s to more than 25 percent by 1988, but leveled off to approximately 20 percent in 1995.[20] Risks to the mother are the same as for any major abdominal surgery, and recovery from birth takes considerably longer after a C-section. Although a cesarean section may be necessary in certain cases, some physicians and critics feel that the option has been used too frequently in this country. The federal government's Centers for Disease Control and Prevention (CDC) believes that about one in three of the cesarean

---

Postpartum depression The experience of energy depletion, anxiety, mood swings, and depression that women may feel during the postpartum period.

Cesarean section (C-section) A surgical procedure in which a baby is removed through an incision made in the mother's abdominal and uterine walls.

deliveries performed in 1991 were unnecessary. The CDC hopes to lower the rate of cesareans in the United States to 15 per 100 births by the year 2000, a level the agency considers to be medically appropriate.

The old adage was "once a cesarean, always a cesarean." Now, however, surgical techniques allow some women who have had a cesarean section to deliver later children vaginally. Guidelines published by the American College of Obstetricians and Gynecologists give an estimated 50 to 80 percent of women the option of a vaginal birth after cesarean (VBAC). Cesarean sections are still necessary if the original incision runs from the top to the bottom of the uterus (as opposed to across); if the baby is over 9 pounds; if the birth is multiple; or if the mother has a medical condition that would make vaginal delivery difficult or dangerous, such as a very small pelvis, chronic high blood pressure, or diabetes.

▶ *Miscarriage*   One in 10 pregnancies does not end in delivery. Loss of the fetus before it is viable is called a **miscarriage** (also referred to as spontaneous abortion). An estimated 70 to 90 percent of women who miscarry eventually become pregnant again.

Reasons for miscarriage vary. In some cases, the fertilized egg has failed to divide correctly. In others, genetic abnormalities, maternal illness, or infections are responsible. Maternal hormonal imbalance may also cause a miscarriage, as may a weak cervix or toxic chemicals in the environment. In most cases, the cause is not known.

A blood incompatibility between mother and father can cause **Rh factor** problems, and sometimes miscarriage. Rh is a blood protein. Rh problems occur when the mother is Rh-negative and the fetus is Rh-positive. During a first birth, some of the baby's blood passes into the mother's bloodstream. An Rh-negative mother may manufacture antibodies to destroy the Rh-positive blood introduced into her bloodstream at the time of birth. Her first baby will be unaffected, but subsequent babies with positive Rh factor will be at risk for a severe anemia called *hemolytic disease* because the mother's Rh antibodies will attack the fetus's red blood cells.

Medical advances now offer both prevention and treatment for this condition. The mother and fetus can be tested, and if Rh incompatibility is found, intrauterine transfusions can be given or an early delivery by cesarean section can be done, depending upon the individual case. Prevention of the problem is preferable to treatment. All women with Rh-negative blood should be injected with a medication called RhoGAM within 72 hours of any birth, miscarriage, or abortion. This injection will prevent them from developing the Rh antibodies.

Another cause of miscarriage is **ectopic pregnancy,** or implantation of a fertilized egg outside the uterus. A fertilized egg may implant itself in the fallopian tube or, occasionally, in the pelvic cavity. Because these structures are not capable of expanding and nourishing a developing fetus, the pregnancy cannot continue. Such pregnancies are surgically terminated. Most often, the affected fallopian tube is also removed.

Ectopic pregnancy is generally accompanied by pain in the lower abdomen or an aching feeling in the shoulders as the blood flows up toward the diaphragm. If bleeding is significant, blood pressure drops and the woman can go into shock. If an ectopic pregnancy goes undiagnosed and untreated, the fallopian tube ruptures, and the woman is then at great risk of hemorrhage, peritonitis (infection in the abdomen), and even death.

Over the past 12 years, the incidence of ectopic pregnancy has tripled, and no one really understands why. We do know that ectopic pregnancy is a potential side effect of pelvic inflammatory disease (PID), which has become increasingly common in recent years, because the scarring or blockage of the fallopian tubes characteristic of this disease prevents the fertilized egg from passing to the uterus. About 50 percent of women who have had an ectopic pregnancy conceive again. But women who have had one ectopic pregnancy run a higher risk of having another.

Stillbirth is one of the most traumatic events a couple can face. A stillborn baby is one that is born dead, often for no apparent reason. The grief experienced following a stillbirth is usually devastating. Nine months of happy anticipation have been thwarted. Family, friends, and other children may be in a state of shock, needing comfort and not knowing where to turn. The mother's breasts produce milk, and there is no infant to be fed. A room with a crib and toys is left empty.

The grief can last for years, and both partners may blame themselves or each other at some time. Some communities have groups called the Compassionate Friends to help parents and other family members through this grieving process. This

Miscarriage   Loss of the fetus before it is viable; also called spontaneous abortion.

Rh factor   A blood protein related to the production of antibodies. If an Rh-negative mother is pregnant with an Rh-positive fetus, the mother will manufacture antibodies that can kill the fetus, causing miscarriage.

Ectopic pregnancy   Implantation of a fertilized egg outside the uterus, usually in a fallopian tube; a medical emergency that can end in death from hemorrhage for the mother.

Stillbirth   The birth of a dead baby.

Infertility   Difficulties in conceiving.

Pelvic inflammatory disease (PID)   An infection that scars the fallopian tubes and consequently blocks sperm migration, causing infertility.

Endometriosis   A disorder in which uterine lining tissue establishes itself outside the uterus; it is the leading cause of infertility in the United States.

Low sperm count   A sperm count below 60 million sperm per milliliter of semen; it is the leading cause of infertility in men.

nonprofit organization is for parents who have lost a child of any age for any reason.

▶ *Sudden Infant Death Syndrome* The sudden death of an infant under one year of age, for no apparent reason, is called sudden infant death syndrome (SIDS). While SIDS is the leading cause of death for children aged 1 month to 1 year, affecting about 1 in 1,000 infants in the United States each year, it is not a disease. Rather, it is ruled the cause of death after all other possibilities are ruled out. A SIDS death is sudden and silent; the death occurs quickly, often associated with sleep and no signs of suffering.

Because SIDS is a diagnosis of exclusion, doctors do not know what causes SIDS. However, research done in countries including England, New Zealand, Australia, and Norway has shown that by placing children on their backs or sides to sleep, the rate of SIDS was cut by as much as half. In 1994, the American Academy of Pediatrics began a campaign called "Back to Sleep," urging American parents to lay their infants on their backs when they put them to sleep. Additional precautions against SIDS include having a firm surface for the infant's bed, not allowing the infant to become too warm, maintaining a smoke-free environment, having regular pediatric visits, breast-feeding, and seeking prenatal care.

Any sudden, unexpected death threatens one's sense of safety and security. This is especially true in a sudden infant death. The lack of a discernible cause, the suddenness of the tragedy, and the involvement of the legal system makes a SIDS death especially difficult, leaving a great sense of loss and a need for understanding.

WHAT DO YOU THINK?

Have you talked to your health-care provider about a birth plan and arranged for it to be in your chart? What do you think would be the advantages and disadvantages of breast-feeding?

INFERTILITY

An estimated one in six American couples experiences **infertility,** or difficulties in conceiving. The reasons for this phenomenon include the trend toward delaying childbirth (as a woman gets older, she is less likely to conceive), and the rise in the incidence of pelvic inflammatory disease.

Causes in Women

One cause of infertility in women is **pelvic inflammatory disease (PID),** a serious infection that scars the fallopian tubes and blocks sperm migration. PID is a collective name for any extensive bacterial infection of the female pelvic organs, particularly the uterus, cervix, fallopian tubes, and ovaries. Symptoms of PID include severe pain, fever, and sometimes vaginal discharge.

The past 25 years have brought a tremendous increase in the number of PID cases. Although in 1970 there were only 17,800 cases of PID, there are now about one million per year. During their reproductive years, 1 in 7 women report having been treated for PID.[21] Tens of thousands of women have been rendered sterile by PID in recent years. One case of PID causes sterility in 10 to 15 percent of women, and 50 to 75 percent become sterile after three or four infections.[22] If PID is treated early, serious illness can be avoided. An array of antibiotics can be used to prevent PID-related complications. In some cases, follow-up exams at 7 to 10 days, and then at 4 to 6 weeks, are recommended.

Endometriosis is the leading cause of infertility in women in the United States. In this disorder, parts of the endometrial lining of the uterus implant themselves outside the uterus—in the fallopian tubes, lungs, intestines, outer uterine walls, ovarian walls, and/or on the ligaments that support the uterus. The disorder can be treated surgically or with hormonal preparations. Success rates vary.

Causes in Men

Among men, the single largest fertility problem is **low sperm count.** Although only one viable sperm is needed for fertilization, research has shown that all the other sperm in the ejaculate aid in the fertilization process. There are normally 60 to 80 million sperm per milliliter of semen. When the count drops below 20 million, fertility begins to decline.

Low sperm count may be attributable to environmental factors such as exposure of the scrotum to intense heat or cold, radiation, or altitude, or even to wearing excessively tight underwear or outerwear. The mumps virus damages the cells that make sperm. Varicose veins above one or both testicles can also render men infertile. Male infertility problems account for around 40 percent of infertility cases.

Treatment

For the couple desperately wishing to conceive, the road to parenthood may be frustrating. Fortunately, medical treatment can identify the cause of infertility in about 90 percent of affected couples. The chances of becoming pregnant range from 30 to 70 percent, depending on the specific cause of the infertility. The countless tests and the invasion of privacy that characterize some couples' efforts to conceive can put stress on an otherwise strong, healthy relationship. Before starting fertility tests, the wise couple will reassess their priorities. Some will choose to undergo counseling to help them clarify their feelings about the fertility process. A good physician or fertility team will take the time to ascertain the couple's level of motivation.

Fertility work-ups can be very expensive, and the costs are not usually covered by insurance companies. Fertility work-ups for men include a sperm count, a test for sperm motility, and analysis of any disease processes present. Such procedures should only be undertaken by a qualified urologist. Women are thoroughly examined by an obstetrician/gynecologist for the composition of cervical mucus, extent of tubal scarring, and evidence of endometriosis.

Complete fertility work-ups may take four to five months and can be unsettling. The couple may be instructed to have sex "by the calendar" to increase their chances of conceiving. In some cases, surgery can correct structural problems such as tubal scarring. In others, administering hormones can improve the health of ova and sperm. Sometimes pregnancy can be achieved by collecting the husband's sperm from several ejaculations and inseminating the wife at a later time.

When all surgical and hormonal methods fail, the couple still has some options. These, too, can be very expensive. **Fertility drugs** such as Clomid and Pergonal stimulate ovulation in women who are not ovulating. Ninety percent of women who use these drugs will begin to ovulate, and half will conceive.

Fertility drugs are associated with a great number of side effects, including headaches, irritability, restlessness, depression, fatigue, edema (fluid retention), abnormal uterine bleeding, breast tenderness, vasomotor flushes (hot flashes), and visual difficulties. Women using fertility drugs are also at increased risk of multiple ovarian cysts (fluid-filled growths) and liver damage. The drugs sometimes trigger the release of more than one egg. Thus a woman treated with one of these drugs has a 1 in 10 chance of having multiple births. Most such births are twins, but triplets and even quadruplets are not uncommon.

Alternative insemination of a woman with her partner's sperm is another treatment option. This technique has led to an estimated 250,000 births in the United States, primarily for couples in which the man is infertile. If this procedure fails, the couple may choose insemination by an anonymous donor through a "sperm bank." Many men sell their sperm to such banks. The sperm are classified according to the physical characteristics of the donor (for example, blonde hair, blue eyes), and then frozen for future use. Sperm can survive in this frozen state for up to five years. The woman being inseminated usually chooses sperm from a man whose physical characteristics resemble those of her partner or match her own personal preferences.

In the last few years, concern has been expressed about the possibility of transmitting the AIDS virus through alternative insemination. As a result, donors are routinely screened for the disease before they donate.

In vitro fertilization, often referred to as "test tube" fertilization, involves collecting a viable ovum from the prospective mother and transferring it to a nutrient medium in a laboratory, where it is fertilized with sperm from the woman's part-

ner or a donor. After a few days, the embryo is transplanted into the mother's uterus, where, it is hoped, it will develop normally. Until 1984, in vitro fertilization was classified as "experimental." Since then, it has moved into the mainstream of standard infertility treatments. Since 1984, the in vitro process has been responsible for 26,000 births in the United States alone.

In **gamete intrafallopian transfer (GIFT),** the egg is "harvested" from the wife's ovary and placed in the fallopian tube with her husband's sperm. Less expensive and time-consuming than in vitro fertilization, GIFT mimics nature by allowing the egg to be fertilized in the fallopian tube and to migrate to the uterus according to the normal timetable.

Intracytoplasmic sperm injection (ICSI) was first performed successfully in 1992. Basically, a sperm cell is injected into an egg. This complex procedure required researchers to learn how to manipulate both the egg and the sperm without damaging them. This technique can help men with low sperm counts or motility, and even those who cannot ejaculate or have no live sperm in their semen as a result of vasectomy, chemotherapy, or a medical disorder. Scientists have examined a thousand babies born using this technique and have found no higher rate of birth defects than in the general population. Nonetheless, this procedure is still considered experimental.

In **nonsurgical embryo transfer,** a donor egg is fertilized by the husband's sperm and then implanted in the wife's uterus. This procedure may also be used in cases involving the transfer of an already-fertilized ovum into the uterus of another woman.

Fertility drugs Hormones that stimulate ovulation in women who are not ovulating; often responsible for multiple births.

Alternative insemination Fertilization accomplished by depositing a partner's or a donor's semen into a woman's vagina via a thin tube; almost always done in a doctor's office.

In vitro fertilization Fertilization of an egg in a nutrient medium and subsequent transfer back to the mother's body.

Gamete intrafallopian transfer (GIFT) An egg is harvested from the female partner's ovary and placed with the male partner's sperm in her fallopian tube, where it is fertilized and then migrates to the uterus for implantation.

Intracytoplasmic sperm injection (ICSI) Fertilization is accomplished by injecting a sperm cell directly into an egg.

Nonsurgical embryo transfer In vitro fertilization of a donor egg by the male partner's (or donor's) sperm and subsequent transfer to the female partner's or another woman's uterus.

Eggs for Sale: Ethical Considerations

Not all that long ago, a couple wanting to have a child and experiencing difficulty conceiving had few options available to them. Normally, the circumstances meant a choice between continuing to try (and hoping fate would be on their side) and adoption. But as medical research and technology advanced and our knowledge of the human body and its workings grew, along came in vitro fertilization and fertility drugs. Eventually, this research spawned a number of other additional options, each as or more remarkable than the previous.

Initially, the options centered solely around the viability of the couple, but in the past twenty years we've seen an equally remarkable growth in the involvement of third parties, also called "assisted reproduction." This has ranged from the use of the sperm or egg of a known person or a stranger to surrogacy, wherein another woman is implanted with the fertilized egg from the couple and carries the embryo and fetus to full term. In exchange, the third party often receives some compensation for involvement.

All of these advances answered the prayers of many, but it also left some people questioning whether science and technology had removed the "miracle" from conception. Many of the options were not without opposition, but most people accepted the advances because of the benefit they provided the couple "fulfilling a lifelong dream." Questions arose immediately, however, about the role money played in determining for whom these options were available. Whether undergoing medical fertilization procedures, exploring various domestic and international adoption possibilities, or arranging for a third-party option, extra expenses are incurred—expenses that can be prohibitive to a large portion of the U.S. population. Many felt it was only a matter of time before some of these options were abused.

Nowhere is abuse of the system more possible or the controversy more heated than in third-party arrangements. The ethical and moral considerations of surrogacy have been questioned from the beginning. What are the surrogates' rights? Does the surrogate have a right to maintain a relationship with the child? What are the couple's rights? Such questions have led to a number of bitter, drawn-out court battles, which have caused some to avoid consideration of the surrogacy option altogether. Sperm and egg donorship, however, has been considerably less controversial . . . until recently.

In 1999, a couple of incidents occurred that sent egg and sperm donation into a new direction, one that has rocked ethicists across the United States. The first occurred in the spring of 1999, when a California couple, through their attorney, placed ads in university student newspapers across the country, offering $50,000 for a viable egg from a female college student who met very specific biological and intellectual criteria, such as age, height, athleticism, and scholastic aptitude. The universities were not just *any* universities, however; rather, they were the top academic universities in the country, such as Harvard, Yale, Princeton, and Stanford. Prior to this offer, the standard payment for egg donation ranged between $3,000 and $5,000, usually enough to cover the donor's expenses. The offer of the California couple, however, raised the standards and began a movement toward what fertility specialists refer to as "commodification." Sperm and egg donation, in general, carries the responsibility of accepting that, in time, a child may exist that was produced from the donor's sperm or egg, a child that carries his or her genetic map. But for a student squeezing by on a limited budget, $50,000 became a very tempting offer, and left more than a few college women conflicted over it.

The second incident that took commodification of egg donation to an even higher level was the creation of a website in the fall of 1999 dedicated to the auctioning of donated eggs of beautiful models for fees as high as $150,000. Photographer Ron Harris created his new "business" on the premise that beauty is a valuable commodity in our culture, one that gains one certain advantages; therefore, "If you could increase the chance of reproducing beautiful children, and thus giving them an advantage in society, would you?" Although many people have questioned whether the site is legitimate or just a hoax, its premise has stirred controversy.

In both cases, the practice is, or would be, entirely legal. The controversy involves the ethical considerations. The option of "selecting" your child's possible characteristics based on the known characteristics of the donor has existed for years, although not without opposition. Such information can even be viewed over the Internet by visiting the sites of various fertility centers. This latest twist, however, turns sperm and eggs into commodities. Ethicists argue that such practices "devalue respect for human life" and "promote disrespect for what gives individuals their worth, which is not appearance, but character."

STUDENTS SPEAK UP:

What do you think about the "commodification" of sperm and eggs? Would you have taken the offer of $50,000 for your sperm or egg? What are additional ethical issues that could arise as a result of the commodification of egg and sperm donorship?

Sources: "Ethical Issues," Centre for Reproductive Medicine: www.repromed.co.uk/Fertility/EggRecipient/ethical_issues.htm (1999); Jonathan D. Moreno, Ph.D., "Bidding on Beauty: Models' Eggs Go on the Auction Block," *ABCNEWS.com* www.abcnews.go.com/sections/living/Bioethics/bioethics_14.html; Carey Goldberg, "Selling Fashion Models' Egg Online Raises Ethics Issues," *New York Times*, October 23, 1999. Also see web site www.nytimes.com/library/tech/99/10/biztech/articles; "Come up to beauty," web site www.ronharris.com Ron Harris, Inc. (1999).

Embryo transfer is another treatment for infertility. In this procedure, an ovum from a donor's body is artificially inseminated by the husband's sperm, allowed to stay in the donor's body for a time, and then transplanted into the wife's body.

Some laboratories are experimenting with **embryo freezing,** in which a fertilized embryo is suspended in a solution of liquid nitrogen. When desired, it is gradually thawed and implanted into the prospective mother. The first United States birth of a frozen embryo was reported in June 1986. In the future, this technique may make it possible for young couples to produce an embryo and save it for later implantation when they are ready to have a child, thus reducing the risks of fertilization of older eggs.

Embryo adoption programs are now available. Infertile couples, whose only prior hope for children was adoption, have a new alternative—embryo adoption. The embryos are originally collected from couples who want children via in vitro fertilization. These couples often donate and freeze extra embryos in case the procedure fails, or if they later want to have more children. These couples can now donate their unneeded embryos to infertile couples. The adopting couple would have the experience of pregnancy and could control prenatal care. The cost is approximately four thousand dollars for the embryos to be thawed and transferred to an infertile woman's uterus or fallopian tubes.

The ethical and moral questions surrounding experimental methods of infertility treatments are staggering. Before moving forward with any of the infertility treatments, individuals need to ask themselves a few important questions. Has infertility been absolutely confirmed? Are reputable infertility counseling services accessible? Have all possible alternatives been explored? Have all the potential risks and side effects associated with infertility treatment been considered? Have all affected parties examined their attitudes, values, and beliefs about conceiving a child using an infertility treatment? Finally, individuals considering alternative methods of conception need to consider what and how they will tell the child about their method of conception.

Surrogate Motherhood

Between 60 and 70 percent of infertile couples are able to conceive after treatment. The rest decide to live without children, to adopt, or to attempt surrogate motherhood. In this option, the couple hires a woman to be alternatively inseminated by the husband. The surrogate then carries the baby to term and surrenders it upon birth to the couple. Surrogate mothers are reportedly paid about $10,000 for their services and are reimbursed for medical expenses. Legal and medical expenses can run as high as $30,000 for the infertile couple. Couples considering surrogate motherhood are advised to consult a lawyer regarding contracts.

Most legal documents drawn up for childless couples and surrogate mothers stipulate that the surrogate must undergo amniocentesis and that if the fetus is defective, she must con-

sent to an abortion. In that case, or if the surrogate miscarries, she is reimbursed for her time and expenses. The prospective parents must also agree to take the baby if it is carried to term, even if it is unhealthy or deformed.

Adoption

For couples that have decided that biological child birth is not an option for them, adoption provides an alternative to bearing a child. Currently, about 50,000 children are available for adoption in the United States every year. This is far fewer than the number of couples seeking adoptions. By some estimates, only 1 in 30 couples receive the children they want. On average, couples spend 2 years and $100,000 on the adoption process.

Because the number of children available for adoption is limited, young women considering placing their child for adoption have gained new leverage. Increasingly, couples wishing to adopt have turned to independent adoptions arranged by a lawyer, or they may directly negotiate with the birth mother. Independent adoptions now surpass those arranged by social service agencies.

·········· **WHAT DO YOU THINK?**

How much time and money would you be willing to invest in infertility treatments if you were to find that you and your partner had infertility problems? Do you think that single women and lesbians should have equal access to alternative methods of insemination? Why or why not? Do you think single women or men and gay males or lesbians should have equal opportunities at adoption? How do you think society views these types of adoptions? Why?

Embryo transfer   Artificial insemination of a donor with male partner's sperm; after a time, the embryo is transferred from the donor to the female partner's body.

Embryo freezing   The freezing of an embryo for later implantation.

Embryo adoption programs   A procedure whereby an infertile couple is able to purchase frozen embryos donated by another couple.

Taking Charge
Managing Your Fertility

After reading this chapter, you should realize that pregnancy, childbirth, and reproductive issues are not to be taken lightly. The choices between different types of birth control and the ethical issues surrounding fertility are complex. It's important to take control of your own fertility and to share this responsibility in your relationships. Is birth control an option for you? Have you considered birth control options and which would be most appropriate for you? Be sure to examine all potential side effects and drug interactions. The following questions can help you determine your level of readiness regarding reproduction and sexual health.

CHECKLIST FOR CHANGE

MAKING PERSONAL CHOICES

✓ If you are in a stable relationship and are considering having a child, is it something both you and your partner want?

✓ Do you know and feel comfortable with your philosophical beliefs about children?

✓ Do you feel comfortable discussing birth control with your partner?

✓ Do you feel comfortable choosing a method of birth control that meets the needs of both yourself and your partner?

✓ Are you familiar with the resources available if you have trouble conceiving?

✓ Have you discussed alternatives should you become or get someone pregnant?

MAKING COMMUNITY CHOICES

✓ Have you taken the time to become educated about the issues and concerns related to parenting?

✓ Do you listen with an open mind to issues involving reproduction and sexual health and then make informed decisions?

✓ When you think about having children, do you think of it in terms of long-range planning?

✓ Are you an advocate for people making choices that are in their best interest, regardless of your own personal philosophy or opinions?

✓ Do you believe in providing support for community agencies and social services that assist in meeting the sexual and reproductive health needs of your community?

✓ Do you try to volunteer your time to other people or agencies that may need your assistance?

SUMMARY

- Only latex condoms, when used correctly for oral sex or intercourse, are effective in preventing sexually transmitted diseases. Other contraceptive methods include abstinence, outercourse, oral contraceptives, foams, jellies, suppositories, creams, the female condom, the diaphragm, the cervical cap, intrauterine devices, withdrawal, Norplant, Depo-Provera, and the vaginal ring. Fertility awareness methods rely on altering sexual practices to avoid pregnancy. Sterilization is permanent contraception.

- Abortion is currently legal in the United States through the second trimester. Abortion methods include vacuum aspiration, dilation and evacuation (D&E), dilation and curettage (D&C), hysterotomy, induction abortion, and RU-486 "abortion pills."

- Parenting is a demanding job requiring careful planning. Emotional health, maternal health, financial evaluation, and contingency planning all need to be taken into account.

- Prenatal care includes a complete physical exam within the first trimester, avoidance of alcohol and drugs, cigarettes, X-rays, and chemicals having teratogenic effects. Full-term pregnancy covers three trimesters.

- Childbirth occurs in three stages. Birth alternatives include the Lamaze, Harris, "childbirth without fear," and Leboyer methods. Parents should jointly make decisions about labor early in the pregnancy to be better prepared for labor when it occurs. Complications of pregnancy and childbirth include miscarriage, ectopic pregnancy, stillbirth, and cesarean section.

- Infertility in women may be caused by pelvic inflammatory disease or endometriosis. In men, it may be caused by low sperm count. Treatment may include alternative insemination, in vitro fertilization, gamete intrafallopian transfer, nonsurgical embryo transfer, and embryo transfer. Surrogate motherhood involves hiring a fertile woman to be alternatively inseminated by the male partner.

DISCUSSION QUESTIONS

1. Draw up a list of the most effective contraceptive methods. What are the drawbacks that prevent their use? What medical conditions would keep you from using them? What are the characteristics of the methods you think would be most effective for you and why?

2. What are the most important considerations for you in deciding whether you are ready to become a parent? What factors will you take into consideration regarding the number of children you will have?

3. Discuss the growth of the fetus through the three trimesters. What medical checkups or tests should be done during each trimester?

4. List the various types of decisions parents face when thinking about having a child. Consider the varied methods of childbirth, where to deliver the baby, whether to use pain-killing drugs during delivery, whether to have an episiotomy, or at what point to have a C-section. How does a parent decide what to do?

5. If you and your partner were having difficulty conceiving, what would your options be? If either of you proved infertile, what would your options be then?

APPLICATION EXERCISE

Reread the *What Do You Think?* scenario at the beginning of the chapter and answer the following questions.

1. Based on what you have read, what are the health problems that Paige's child could experience as a result of her use of alcohol and cigarettes? Would Matt's use of alcohol and cigarettes have any possible effect on their child?

2. Should establishments such as bars and restaurants be held liable for serving alcohol to a pregnant woman? Should legislation be passed that would make such practices illegal?

OBJECTIVES

▶ Identify the signs of addiction.

▶ List the six categories of drugs and explain the routes of administration that drugs take into the body.

▶ Discuss proper drug use and explain how hazardous drug interactions occur.

▶ Discuss types of over-the-counter drugs and general precautions to be taken with them.

▶ Discuss the key questions you should ask in order to make intelligent decisions about drug use.

▶ Discuss patterns of illicit drug use, including who uses illicit drugs and why they use them.

▶ Describe the use and abuse of controlled substances, including cocaine, amphetamines, marijuana, opiates, psychedelics, deliriants, designer drugs, and inhalants.

▶ Profile overall illegal drug use in the United States, including frequency, financial impact, arrests for drug offenses, and impact on the workplace.

7

Licit and Illicit Drug Use

Understanding Addictions

During the past several months, Paul has been having problems concentrating on his schoolwork and maintaining the grades he is accustomed to receiving. He's had trouble staying up late to work on papers, can't seem to get to his morning classes, and spends a great deal of time sleeping. He has become concerned about the funk he seems to be in. He's lost interest in spending time with his friends, and doesn't seem to have interest in much of anything lately. Paul has read several brochures about the use of St. John's wort to treat depression and has decided that this is something he might try.

What is one of the first steps Paul should take if he thinks he is possibly depressed? What type of information would be important for Paul to have about St. John's wort? What are the possible dangers associated with self-medicating? What type of regulations does the Food and Drug Administration have in overseeing herbal remedies?

W E LIKE TO FEEL GOOD. Sometimes we like to change our awareness of things in order to optimize that sense of well-being. While there are many healthy ways for us to make ourselves feel good, there are also many ways to fool ourselves into thinking that we are well, when we are in fact using destructive or compulsive behaviors to induce that feeling. Such behaviors may include illicit drug use, abusing legal substances, or any of a number of addictions, which wreak havoc in our lives. In this chapter, we will look at the addiction process as well as healthy and unhealthy ways in which people use substances to enhance or detract from their lives.

DEFINING ADDICTION

Addiction is continued involvement with a substance or activity despite ongoing negative consequences. Addictive behaviors initially provide a sense of pleasure or stability that is beyond the addict's power to achieve otherwise. Eventually, the addictive behavior is necessary to give the addict a sense of normalcy.

Physiological dependence is only one indicator of addiction. **Psychological** dynamics play an important role, which explains why behaviors not related to the use of chemicals—gambling, for example—may also be addictive. In fact, psychological and physiological dependence are so intertwined that it is not really possible to separate the two. For every psychological state, there is a corresponding physiological state. In other words, everything you feel is tied to a chemical process occurring in your body.[1] Thus, addictions once thought to be entirely psychological in nature are now understood to have physiological components.

To be addictive, a behavior must have the potential to produce a positive mood change. Chemicals are responsible for the most profound addictions, not only because they produce dramatic mood changes, but also because they cause cellular changes to which the body adapts so well that it eventually requires the chemical in order to function normally. Yet other behaviors, such as gambling, spending, working, and sex, also create changes at the cellular level along with positive mood changes. Although the mechanism is not well understood, all forms of addiction probably reflect dysfunction of certain biochemical systems in the brain.[2]

Traditionally, diagnosis of an addiction was limited to drug addiction and was based on three criteria: (1) the presence of an abstinence syndrome, or **withdrawal**—a series of temporary physical and psychological symptoms that occurs

painkillers #1 abused legal drug

Addiction Continued involvement with a substance or activity despite ongoing negative consequences.

Withdrawal A series of temporary physical and biopsychosocial symptoms that occurs when the addict abruptly abstains from an addictive chemical or behavior.

Relapse The tendency to return to the addictive behavior after a period of abstinence.

Compulsion Obsessive preoccupation with a behavior and an overwhelming need to perform it.

Obsession Excessive preoccupation with an addictive object or behavior.

Loss of control Inability to predict reliably whether any isolated involvement with the addictive object or behavior will be healthy or damaging.

Negative consequences Physical damage, legal trouble, financial ruin, academic failure, family dissolution, and other severe problems associated with addiction.

Denial Inability to perceive or accurately interpret the effects of the addictive behavior.

Internet Addiction

Are you caught up in "surfin' the web?" How many hours per day do you spend either e-mailing someone or checking out different sites? There's no doubt about it, the Internet has taken commerce and communication to a new level. One look at the happenings on Wall Street with regard to Internet and technology stocks during the last months of 1998 and first months of 1999 tell you that the fever has caught on and is not likely to subside. There is growing evidence that the Internet also poses many risks and that some Internet users are wrestling with a true addiction. The signs of Internet addiction include:

- Daily time spent online
- Skipping meals, including lunch at work, to spend time on the 'Net
- Logging on to the Internet, even when busy at work
- Checking e-mail numerous times daily
- Hiding or lying about the amount of time spent online
- Denial
- Losing track of time online; spending more time than intended

Now consider the potential for a problem:

- There are an estimated 47 million current Internet users.[1]
- There will be more than 116 million Americans online by 2002.[2]
- There could be as many as 15 million computer addicts.[3]
- In a recent study, individuals who met the definition of Internet addiction spent an average of 38 hours per week online.[4]

STUDENTS SPEAK OUT:

Do you think Internet addiction could be a problem among your friends? What might be some potential problems of such an addiction?

Source for Signs of Internet Addiction: Center for Online Addiction, http://netaddiction.com/resources/index.htm

Sources:

1. K. Young, *Internet Addiction: The Emergence of a New Clinical Disorder,* Center for Online Addiction Website. http://netaddiction.com/articles/newdisorder.htm
2. R. W. Greene, *Internet Addiction: Is It Just This Month's Hand-Wringer for Worrywarts, or a Genuine Problem?* (1998), Computer-World Online. http://www.computerworld.com/home/features.nsf/all/980921id
3. D. Seaman, *Hooked Online* (1998), Time Select/Quarterly Business Report. http://cgi.pathfinder.com/time/magazine/1998/dom/981012/time_select.quarterly_b3a.html
4. K. Young, *What Makes the Internet Addictive: Potential Explanations for Pathological Internet Use* (1997). http://netaddiction.com/articles/habitforming.htm

when the addict abruptly stops using the drug; (2) an associated pattern of pathological behavior (deterioration in work performance, relationships, and social interaction); and (3) **relapse,** the tendency to return to the addictive behavior after a period of abstinence. Furthermore, until recently, health professionals were unwilling to diagnose an addiction until medical symptoms appeared in the patient. Now we know that although withdrawal, pathological behavior, relapse, and medical symptoms are valid indicators of addiction, they do not characterize all addictive behavior.

Signs of Addiction

Studies show that all animals share the same basic pleasure and reward circuits in the brain that turn on when they come into contact with addictive substances or engage in something pleasurable, such as eating or orgasm. We all engage in potentially addictive behaviors to some extent because some are essential to our survival and are highly reinforcing, such as eating, drinking, and sex. At some point along the continuum, however, some individuals are not able to engage in these or other behaviors moderately and become addicted to a substance or behavior.

Most experts agree that there are some universal signs of addiction. All addictions are characterized by four common symptoms: (1) **compulsion,** which is characterized by **obsession,** or excessive preoccupation with the behavior and an overwhelming need to perform it; (2) **loss of control,** or the inability to predict reliably whether any isolated occurrence of the behavior will be healthy or damaging; (3) **negative consequences,** such as physical damage, legal trouble, financial problems, academic failure, and family dissolution, which do not occur with healthy involvement in any behavior; and (4) **denial,** or the inability to perceive that the behavior is self-destructive. These four components are present in all addictions, whether chemical or behavioral.

The Addictive Process

Addiction is a process that evolves over time. It begins when a person repeatedly seeks the illusion of relief to avoid unpleasant feelings or situations. This pattern is known as

Addiction Issues Worldwide

In the past decade, the changing economic and political climate around the globe has led to an increasingly "borderless" world. Food, music, fashion, and, unfortunately, drug consumption and addiction have flooded across borders into previously isolated areas. The following are some of the biggest global issues related to addiction, according to the World Health Organization (WHO):

Injecting drug use is increasing: The number of countries reporting drug injection rose from 80 in 1989 to 126 in 1997. As we know, injecting drugs is one risk factor for spreading blood-borne diseases such as HIV and hepatitis B and C. Recent figures indicate that drug injection is responsible for 100,000 to 200,000 deaths yearly worldwide.

Inhalants are a continuing problem: In both developed and developing nations, inhalant use is increasing, especially among marginalized groups such as street children, women, and indigenous peoples.

The death toll from tobacco addiction is rising: Around the world, approximately 47 percent of men and 12 percent of women smoke. More men smoke in both developing and developed countries, although the proportion of women smoking is much higher in developed nations. By the year 2020, tobacco addiction and resulting death will be responsible for 9 percent of deaths globally, more than any other single risk factor or disease.

Alcohol problems in developing nations are increasing rapidly: Only limited treatment programs, educational interventions, and policies are in place. Health professionals in some developing nations have been inadequately trained to discuss alcohol, drug use, and addictions with their patients.

Source: World Health Organization Web Site, Fact Sheets, http://www.who.int/inf-fs/en/

---

nurturing through avoidance and is a maladaptive way of taking care of emotional needs. As a person becomes increasingly dependent on the addictive behavior, there is a corresponding deterioration in relationships with family, friends, and co-workers; in performance at work or school; and in personal life. Eventually, addicts do not find the addictive behavior pleasurable but consider it preferable to the unhappy realities they are seeking to escape.

WHAT DO YOU THINK?

What might you do if you began to see signs of addiction in your friend? How could you be sure that what you were seeing was an addiction and not just the results of normal college experiences?

DRUG DYNAMICS

Drugs work because they physically resemble the chemicals produced naturally within the body (see Figure 7.1). For example, many painkillers resemble the endorphins ("morphine within") that are manufactured in the body. Most bodily processes result from chemical reactions or from changes in electrical charge. Because drugs possess an electrical charge and a chemical structure similar to chemicals that occur naturally in the body, they can affect physical functions in many different ways.

A current explanation of drug actions is the *receptor site theory,* which states that drugs attach themselves to specific **receptor sites** in the body. These sites are specialized cells to which a drug is able to attach because of its size, shape, electrical charge, and chemical properties. Most drugs can attach at multiple receptor sites located throughout the body in such places as the heart and blood system, the lungs, liver, kidneys, brain, and gonads (testicles or ovaries). The physiology of drug activity and its effect on human behavior is very complex.

Types of Drugs

Scientists divide drugs into six categories: prescription drugs, OTC preparations, recreational substances, herbal preparations, illicit drugs, and commercial drugs. These classifications are based primarily on drug action, although some classifications are based on the source of the chemical in question. Each category includes some drugs that stimulate the body, some that depress body functions, and others that produce hallucinations. Each category also includes **psychoactive drugs,** which have the potential to alter a person's mood or behavior.

- **Prescription drugs** are those substances that can be obtained only with the written prescription of a licensed physician. More than 10,000 types of prescription drugs

Short term use

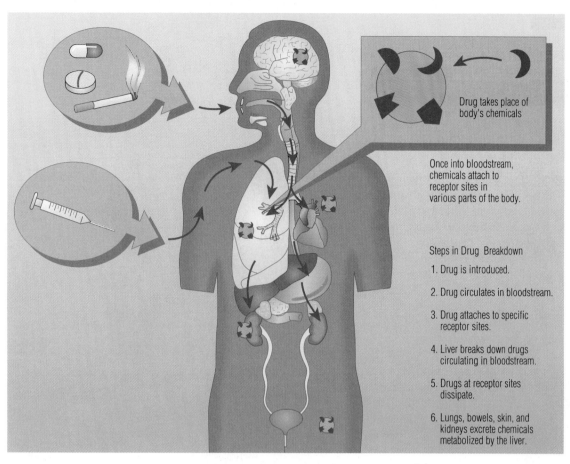

Once into bloodstream, chemicals attach to receptor sites in various parts of the body.

Drug takes place of body's chemicals

Steps in Drug Breakdown

1. Drug is introduced.

2. Drug circulates in bloodstream.

3. Drug attaches to specific receptor sites.

4. Liver breaks down drugs circulating in bloodstream.

5. Drugs at receptor sites dissipate.

6. Lungs, bowels, skin, and kidneys excrete chemicals metabolized by the liver.

Figure 7.1

How the Body Metabolizes Drugs

are sold in the United States, representing 1,500 different types of drugs, with 20 to 50 new medications approved by the FDA each year.[3]

Nurturing through avoidance   Repeatedly seeking the illusion of relief to avoid unpleasant feelings or situations, a maladaptive way of taking care of emotional needs.

Receptor sites   Specialized cells to which drugs can attach themselves.

Psychoactive drugs   Drugs that have the potential to alter mood or behavior.

Prescription drugs   Medications that can be obtained only with the written prescription of a licensed physician.

Over-the-counter (OTC) drugs   Medications that can be purchased in pharmacies or supermarkets without a physician's prescription.

Recreational drugs   Legal drugs that contain chemicals that help people to relax or socialize.

Herbal preparations   Substances that are of plant origin that are believed to have medicinal properties.

Illicit (illegal) drugs   Drugs whose use, possession, cultivation, manufacture, and/or sale are against the law because they are generally recognized as harmful.

Short term use

- **Over-the-counter (OTC) drugs** can be purchased in pharmacies, supermarkets, and discount stores. Each year, Americans spend over $14 billion on OTC products, and the market is increasing at the rate of 20 percent annually. It is projected that the OTC market will reach sales of $28 billion by the year 2010.[4] More than 300,000 OTC products are available in stores and pharmacies. An estimated three out of four people routinely self-medicate with these drug products.

- **Recreational drugs** belong to a somewhat vague category whose boundaries depend upon how people define *recreation*. Generally, drugs in this category contain chemicals used to help people relax or socialize. Most of them are legally sanctioned even though they are psychoactive. Alcohol, tobacco, coffee, tea, and chocolate products are usually included in this category.

- **Herbal preparations** form another vague category. Included among these approximately 750 substances are herbal teas and other products of botanical origin that are believed to have medicinal properties.

- **Illicit (illegal) drugs** are the most notorious substances. Although laws governing their use, possession, cultivation, manufacture, and sale differ from state to state, illicit drugs are generally recognized as harmful. All of these substances are psychoactive.

- **Commercial preparations** are the most universally used yet least commonly recognized chemical substances having drug action. More than 1,000 of these substances exist, including such seemingly benign items as perfumes, cosmetics, household cleansers, paints, glues, inks, dyes, gardening chemicals, pesticides, and industrial by-products.

10-11 yrs. start experimenting w/ inhalents

Routes of Administration of Drugs

Route of administration refers to the way in which a given drug is taken into the body. Common routes are oral ingestion, injection, inhalation, inunction, and suppository.

Oral ingestion is the most common route of administration. Drugs that you swallow include tablets, capsules, and liquids. Oral ingestion of a drug generally results in relatively slow absorption compared to other methods of administration because the drug must pass through the stomach, where it is acted on by digestive juices, and then move on to the small intestine before it enters the bloodstream.

1 hr.

Many oral preparations are coated to keep them from being dissolved by corrosive stomach acids before they reach the intestine as well as to protect the stomach lining from irritating chemicals in the drugs. If your stomach contains food, absorption will be slower than if your stomach is empty. Some drugs must not be taken with certain foods because the food will inhibit the drug's action. Others must be taken with food to prevent stomach irritation.

Depending on the drug and the amount of food in the stomach, drugs taken orally produce their effects within 20 minutes to 1 hour after ingestion. The only exception is alcohol, which takes effect sooner because some of it is absorbed directly into the bloodstream from the stomach.

Injection, another common form of drug administration, involves the use of a hypodermic syringe to introduce a drug into the body. This method can result in rapid absorption, depending on the type of injection. **Intravenous injection, or injection directly into a vein,** puts the chemical in its most concentrated form directly into the bloodstream. Effects will be felt within three minutes, making this route extremely effective, particularly in medical emergencies. But injection of many substances into the bloodstream may cause serious or even fatal reactions. In addition, some serious diseases, such as hepatitis and AIDS, can be transferred in this way. For this reason, intravenous injection can be one of the most dangerous routes of administration.

sec. min.

Intramuscular injection results in much slower absorption than intravenous injection. This type of injection places the hypodermic needle into muscular tissue, usually in the buttocks or the back of the upper arm. Normally used to administer antibiotics and vaccinations, this route of administration ensures a slow and consistent dispersion of the drug into the body tissues.

Subcutaneous injection puts the drug into the layer of fat directly beneath the skin. Its common medical uses are for administration of local anesthetics and for insulin replacement

Diabetics learn to administer daily doses of replacement insulin by subcutaneous injection.

therapy. A drug injected subcutaneously will circulate even more slowly than an intramuscularly injected drug because it takes longer to be absorbed into the bloodstream.

Inhalation refers to administration of drugs through the nostrils. This method transfers the drug rapidly into the bloodstream through the alveoli (air sacs) in the lungs. Some examples of illicit inhalation are cocaine sniffing and the inhalation of aerosol sprays, gases, or fumes from solvents. Effects are frequently noticed immediately after inhalation, but they do not last as long as with the slower routes of administration because only small amounts of a drug can be absorbed and metabolized in the lungs.

Inunction introduces chemicals into the body through the skin. A common example of this method of drug administration is the small adhesive patches that are used to alleviate motion sickness. These patches, which contain a prescription medicine, are applied to the skin behind one ear, where they slowly release their chemicals to provide relief for nauseated travelers. Another example is the nicotine patch.

slow

Suppositories are drugs that are mixed with a waxy medium designed to melt at body temperature. The most common type of suppository is inserted into the anus until it is past the rectal sphincter muscles, which hold it in place. As the wax melts, the drug is released and absorbed through the rectal walls into the bloodstream. Since this area of the anatomy contains many blood vessels, the effects of the drug are usually felt within 15 minutes. Other types of suppositories are for use in the vagina. Vaginal suppositories usually release drugs, such as antifungal agents, that treat problems in the vagina itself as opposed to drugs meant to travel in the bloodstream.

······· **WHAT DO YOU THINK?**

What types of drugs do you most commonly use? Discuss the reasons that you typically use these drugs. How frequently do you read the instructions for taking oral medications? Have there been circumstances when you have not taken the medication as directed, and have the medications been less effective?

DRUG USE, ABUSE, AND INTERACTIONS

Many people fail to take the time needed to make intelligent decisions when considering the use of a drug. Although drug abuse is usually referred to in connection with illicit and recreational psychoactive drugs, many people abuse and misuse prescription and OTC medications. **Drug misuse** is generally considered to be the use of a drug for a purpose for which it was not intended. For example, using a friend's high-powered prescription painkiller for your headache is a misuse of that drug. This is not too far removed from **drug abuse,** or the excessive use of any drug. The misuse and abuse of drugs may lead to *addiction,* the habitual reliance on a substance or behavior to produce a desired mood.

There are risks and benefits to the use of any type of chemical substance. Intelligent decision making requires a clear-headed evaluation of these risks and benefits. In order to compare drug risks to benefits, you may want to create a profile for each drug you use or are considering using. A *drug profile* consists of a set of answers to specific questions about a drug.

Individual Response to Psychoactive Drugs

Individuals differ in how they respond to psychoactive drugs. Two environmental factors that bear on both the main effects and the side effects of psychoactive drugs are set and setting. Set is the total internal environment, or mindset, of a person at the time a drug is taken. Physical, emotional, and social factors work together or against one another to influence the drug's effect on that particular person. Expectations of what the drug will or will not do are also part of the set. For example, a young woman who reads two pages of reported side effects for a particular drug may experience more side effects after taking that drug than someone who was not exposed to this information. In other cases, set may be related to the user's mood. A depressed person using marijuana for a lift may find that the drug actually deepens the depression. Similarly, someone who is already giddy may become even sillier after using the drug.

If set refers to the internal environment, setting is the drug user's total external environment. It encompasses both the physical and social aspects of that environment at the time the person takes the psychoactive drug. If the user is surrounded by wild colors, heavy-metal rock music, and a noisy crowd of people, the drug will generally produce a very different effect than when it is taken in a quiet place with soft music and relaxed company.

Commercial preparations   Commonly used chemical substances including cosmetics, household cleaning products, and industrial by-products.

Route of administration   The manner in which a drug is taken into the body.

Oral ingestion   Intake of drugs through the mouth.

Injection   The introduction of drugs into the body via a hypodermic needle.

Intravenous injection   The introduction of drugs directly into a vein.

Intramuscular injection   The introduction of drugs into muscles.

Subcutaneous injection   The introduction of drugs into the layer of fat directly beneath the skin.

Inhalation   The introduction of drugs through the nostrils.

Inunction   The introduction of drugs through the skin.

Suppositories   Mixtures of drugs and a waxy medium designed to melt at body temperature that are inserted into the anus or vagina.

Drug misuse   The use of a drug for a purpose for which it was not intended.

Drug abuse   The excessive use of a drug.

Set   The total internal environment, or mindset, of a person at the time a drug is taken.

Setting   The total external environment of a person at the time a drug is taken.

Drug Interactions

Sharing medications, using outdated prescriptions, taking higher doses than recommended, or using medications as a substitute for dealing with personal problems may result in serious health consequences. But so may engaging in poly-drug use: taking several medications or illegal drugs simultaneously may result in very dangerous problems associated with drug interactions. The most hazardous interactions are synergism, antagonism, inhibition, and intolerance. Hazardous interactions may also occur between drugs and foods and nutrients.

over the counter **Synergism,** also known as potentiation, is an interaction of two or more drugs in which the effects of the individual drugs are multiplied beyond what would normally be expected if they were taken alone. Synergism can be expressed mathematically as: $2 + 2 = 10$.

A synergistic interaction is most likely to occur when *central nervous system depressants* are combined. Included in this category are alcohol, opiates (morphine, heroin), antihistamines (cold remedies), sedative hypnotics (Quaaludes), minor tranquilizers (Valium, Librium, and Xanax), and barbiturates. The worst possible combination is alcohol and barbiturates (sleeping preparations such as Seconal and phenobarbital) because the combination of these depressants leads to a slow-down of the brain centers that normally control vital functions. Respiration, heart rate, and blood pressure can drop to the point of inducing coma and even death.

Prescription drugs carry special labels warning the user not to combine the drug with certain other drugs or with alcohol. Many OTC preparations carry similar warning labels. Because the dangers associated with synergism are so great, you should always verify any possible drug interactions before using a prescribed or OTC drug. Pharmacists, physicians, drug information centers, or community drug education centers can answer your questions. Even if one of the drugs in question is an illegal substance, you should still attempt to determine the dangers involved in combining it with other drugs. Health-care professionals are legally bound to maintain confidentiality even when they know that a client is using illegal substances.

Antagonism, although not usually as serious as synergism, can produce unwanted and unpleasant effects. In an antagonistic reaction, drugs work at the same receptor site so that one drug blocks the action of the other. The "blocking" drug occupies the receptor site, preventing the other drug from attaching, and this creates alterations in absorption and action. *cuts + colds*

Inhibition is a type of interaction in which the effects of one drug are eliminated or reduced by the presence of another drug at the receptor site. One common inhibitory reaction occurs between antacid tablets and aspirin. The antacid inhibits the absorption of aspirin, making it less effective as a pain reliever. Other inhibitory reactions occur between alcohol and contraceptive pills and between antibiotics and contraceptive pills. Alcohol and antibiotics may diminish the effectiveness of birth control pills in some women.

Intolerance occurs when drugs combine in the body to produce extremely uncomfortable reactions. The drug Antabuse, used to help alcoholics give up alcohol, works by producing this type of interaction. It binds liver enzymes (the chemicals the liver produces to break down alcohol), making it impossible for the body to metabolize alcohol. As a result, the user of Antabuse who drinks alcohol experiences nausea, vomiting, and, occasionally, fever.

Cross-tolerance occurs when a person develops a physiological tolerance to one drug and shows a similar tolerance to selected other drugs as a result. Taking one drug may actually increase the body's tolerance to another drug. For example, cross-tolerance can develop between alcohol and barbiturates, two depressant drugs.

WHAT DO YOU THINK?

What are some situations in which students misuse drugs? Other than alcohol, what are some other drugs that students abuse while they are at college? What are some specific times during the academic school year when a person's set could lead to a greater chance of detrimental effects related to drug use? What drugs tend to be the drugs of choice during these times?

PRESCRIPTION DRUGS

male + female should not share!

Even though prescription drugs are administered under medical supervision, the wise consumer still takes precautions. Hazards and complications arising from the use of prescription drugs are common. Responsible decision making about prescription drug use requires the consumer to acquire basic drug knowledge.

pregnant must be careful

Types of Prescription Drugs

Prescription drugs can be divided into dozens of categories. Those of most interest to college students are discussed later; others are explored in the chapters on birth control, infectious and sexually transmitted diseases, cancer, and cardiovascular disease. Some of the most common are discussed here.

Antibiotics are drugs used to fight bacterial infection. Bacterial infections continue to be the most common serious diseases in the United States and throughout the world. The vast majority of these can be cured with antibiotic treatment. There are currently close to 100 different antibiotic drugs used to kill or stop bacterial growth. They may be dispensed by intramuscular injection or in tablet or capsule form. Some, called broad-spectrum antibiotics, are designed to control disease caused by a number of bacterial species. These medications may also kill off helpful bacteria in the body, thus triggering secondary infections. For example, some types of vaginal infections are related to long-term use of antibiotics.

Analgesics are pain relievers. The earliest pain relievers were made of derivatives manufactured from the opium poppy. Most pain relievers work at receptor sites by interrupting pain signals. Some analgesics are available as OTC drugs.

aspirin

Some analgesics are called NSAID (nonsteroidal antiinflammatory drug) types. The pharmacological action of these drugs is such that they are sometimes called **prostaglandin inhibitors.** Prostaglandins are chemicals that resemble hormones and are released by the body in response to pain. When a painful stimulus, such as a cut or scrape, occurs, nerve cells near the site of the pain release prostaglandins. (Scientists believe that the additional pain caused by the release of prostaglandins signals the body to begin the healing process.) Prostaglandin inhibitors restrain the release of prostaglandins, thereby reducing the pain. The most common NSAIDs are ibuprofen (Motrin) and naproxen sodium (Anaprox). Both are used in prescription strength to relieve inflammatory conditions (such as arthritis) and are effective in relieving minor to moderate joint and muscle pain. The principal adverse side effects include stomach irritation, kidney damage, tinnitus (ringing in the ears), dizziness, and swelling from fluid retention. Most prescription NSAIDs have similar side effects and pharmacological action.

Most analgesics have side effects, the most common of which is drowsiness due to the depression of the central nervous system. Some labels caution specifically against driving or operating heavy machinery when using analgesics, and most state that they should not be taken with alcohol.

Sedatives are central nervous system depressants that induce sleep and relieve anxiety. Because of the high incidence of anxiety and sleep disorders in the United States, drugs that encourage relaxation and drowsiness are frequently prescribed and are usually included on the list of top-selling prescription drugs.[5] The potential for addiction is high. Detoxification can be life-threatening and must be medically supervised.

Tranquilizers are another form of central nervous system depressant. They are classified as major tranquilizers and

Sleep!

minor tranquilizers. The most powerful tranquilizers are used in the treatment of major psychiatric illnesses. When used appropriately, these strong sedatives are capable of reducing violent aggressiveness and self-destructive impulses.

The so-called minor tranquilizers gained much notoriety in the late 1960s and early 1970s when consumer groups discovered that these drugs—known by their trade names Valium, Librium, and Miltown—were the most commonly prescribed medication in the United States. They were often prescribed for women who suffered from anxiety. These drugs have a high potential for addiction, and many people became physically and psychologically dependent on them. When the media reported on the widespread and casual prescribing of these drugs, physicians were forced to reevaluate the practice. Today a doctor is more likely to suggest psychotherapy or counseling for patients suffering from anxiety.

Antidepressants are medications typically used to treat endogenous major depression, although occasionally they are used to treat other forms of depression that may be resistant to conventional therapy. There are several groups of antidepressant medications approved for use in the United States. The first to be used to treat depression were monoamine oxidase (MAO) inhibitors, which were discovered in the 1960s by scientists searching for drugs to treat tuberculosis. The most commonly used antidepressants are the tricyclic medications, but perhaps the best known are the SSRIs, or selective serotonin reuptake inhibitors, which include the drugs Prozac and Zoloft. Although, as a group, tricyclic medications are most commonly prescribed, Prozac is the most frequently prescribed antidepressant.

Amphetamines are stimulants that are prescribed less commonly now than in the past. Like many psychoactive drugs, they are purchased both legally and illegally. Amphetamines suppress appetite and elevate respiration, blood pressure, and pulse rate. Ritalin and Cylert are prescription amphetamines that are used in the treatment of attention-deficit/hyperactivity disorder in children. A newer prescription drug used in the treatment of obesity is Pondimin.

most commonly used illegal drugs!

Polydrug use   The use of multiple medications or illicit drugs simultaneously.

Synergism   An interaction of two or more drugs that produces more profound effects than would be expected if the drugs were taken separately.

Antagonism   A type of interaction in which two or more drugs work at the same receptor site.

Inhibition   A type of interaction in which the effects of one drug are eliminated or reduced by the presence of another drug at the receptor site.

Intolerance   A type of interaction in which two or more drugs produce extremely uncomfortable symptoms.

Cross-tolerance   The development of a tolerance to one drug that reduces the effects of another, similar drug.

Antibiotics   Prescription drugs designed to fight bacterial infection.

Analgesics   Pain relievers.

Prostaglandin inhibitors   Drugs that inhibit the production and release of prostaglandins associated with arthritis or menstrual pain.

Sedatives   Central nervous system depressants that induce sleep and relieve anxiety.

Tranquilizers   Central nervous system depressants that relax the body and calm anxiety.

Antidepressants   Prescription drugs used to treat clinically diagnosed depression.

Amphetamines   Prescription stimulants not commonly used today because of the dangers associated with them.

Tolerance to these powerful stimulants develops rapidly, and the user trying to cut down or quit may experience unpleasant **rebound effects.** These severe withdrawal symptoms, peculiar to stimulants, include depression, irritability, violent behavior, headaches, nausea, and deep fatigue.

Use of Generic Drugs

Generic drugs, medications sold under a chemical name rather than under a brand name, have gained popularity in recent years. These alternatives to more expensive brand-name drugs contain the same active ingredients as their brand-name counterparts.

There is some controversy about the effectiveness of some generic drugs because substitutions are often made in minor ingredients and these can affect the way the drug is absorbed, causing discomfort or even an allergic reaction in some users. Therefore, you must note any allergic reactions you have to medications and tell your doctor, who can prescribe an alternative drug. A list of medicines that can be interchanged has been approved in some states.

Generic drugs can help to reduce health-care costs because their price is often less than half that of the brand-name drugs they are substitutes for. But not all drugs are available as generics, and generic equivalents are not always recommended.

OVER-THE-COUNTER DRUGS

Over-the-counter (OTC) drugs are nonprescription substances we use in the course of self-diagnosis and self-medication. More than one-third of the time people treat their routine health problems with OTC medications to receive symptomatic relief from their ailments. In an effort to cure themselves, American consumers spend in excess of $14 billion yearly on OTC preparations for relief of everything from runny noses to ingrown toenails. There are 40,000 OTC drugs and more than 300,000 brand names for those drugs. Most OTC drugs are manufactured from a basic group of 1,000 chemicals. The many different OTC drugs available to us are produced by combining as few as 2 and as many as 10 substances.

40 bil → OTC 60-65%

How Prescription Drugs Become OTC Drugs

Americans have become more aware of and vocal about the need for better drugs to self-medicate in recent years. In response to consumer pressures, the Food and Drug Administration (FDA) has adopted a switching policy whereby it regularly reviews prescription drugs to evaluate how suitable they would be as OTC products. For a drug to be switched from prescription to OTC status, it must meet the following criteria:

1. The drug has been marketed as a prescription drug for at least three years.
2. The use of the drug has been relatively high during the time it was available as a prescription drug.
3. Adverse drug reactions are not alarming, and the frequency of side effects has not increased during the time the drug was available to the public.

Since this policy has been in effect, the FDA has switched approximately 50 drugs from prescription to OTC status. Some examples are ibuprofen (Advil, Nuprin), the analgesic/anti-inflammatory medicine naproxen sodium (Aleve), and the antihistamine Benadryl. Many more prescription drugs are currently being considered for OTC status.

Types of OTC Drugs

The FDA has categorized 26 types of OTC preparations. Those most commonly used are analgesics, cold/cough/allergy and asthma relievers, stimulants, sleeping aids and relaxants, and dieting aids.

▶ Analgesics We spend more than $2 billion annually on internal (taken by mouth) analgesics, the largest sales category of OTC drugs in the United States. Although these pain relievers come in several forms, aspirin, acetaminophin (Tylenol, Pamprin, Panadol), and ibuprofen-like drugs such as naproxen (Aleve) and ketoprofen (Orudis) are the most common.

Aspirin relieves pain by inhibiting the body's production of prostaglandins. It brings down fever by increasing the flow of blood to the skin surface, which causes sweating and therefore cooling of the body. Aspirin has also long been used to reduce the inflammation and swelling of arthritis. Recently it has been discovered that aspirin's anticoagulant (interference with blood clotting) effects make it a useful medication for reducing the chances of repeat heart attacks in people who have already had one heart attack.

Despite the fact that aspirin has been commonly used as a medication for nearly a century, it is not as harmless as many people think. Possible side effects include allergic reactions, ringing in the ears, stomach bleeding, and ulcers. Combining aspirin with alcohol can compound aspirin's gastric irritant properties.

In addition, research has linked aspirin to a potentially fatal condition called Reye's syndrome. Children, teenagers, and young adults (up to age 25) who are treated with aspirin while recovering from the flu or chicken pox are at risk for developing the syndrome. Aspirin substitutes are recommended for people in these age groups.

Acetaminophen is an aspirin substitute found in Tylenol and related medications. Like aspirin, acetaminophen is an effective analgesic and antipyretic (fever-reducing drug). It does not, however, provide relief from inflamed or swollen joints. The side effects associated with acetaminophen are generally minimal, though overdose can cause liver damage.

In 1985, certain drugs containing ibuprofen (prostaglandin inhibitors) were switched from prescription to OTC status. Generally marketed as arthritis or menstrual cramp relievers, these drugs are milder versions of the prescription varieties. Examples are Nuprin and Advil.

In 1994, Aleve, the first new type of nonprescription analgesic to become available in a decade, was introduced onto the market. Aleve is a version of the prescription drug Anaprox, a fast-acting, slightly less strong form of the analgesic naproxen. Compared with the other OTC analgesics, Aleve's main distinction is its lasting effect: while the others need to be taken every 4 to 6 hours, once every 8 to 12 hours is sufficient for Aleve.

most used: abused

▶ **Cold, Cough, Allergy, and Asthma Relievers**   These substances are popular OTC remedies for the symptoms that affect millions of sufferers. The operative word in their titles is *reliever.* Most of these medications are designed to alleviate some or all of the discomforting symptoms associated with these upper-respiratory-tract maladies. Unfortunately, no drugs exist to cure the actual diseases. The drugs available provide only temporary relief until the sufferer's immune system prevails over the disease. Aspirin or acetaminophen is used in some cold preparations, as are several other ingredients. Both aspirin and acetaminophen are on the government's lists of Generally Recognized as Safe **(GRAS)** and Generally Recognized as Effective **(GRAE).**

The basic types of OTC cold, cough, and allergy relievers are:

- **Expectorants.** These drugs are formulated to loosen phlegm, allowing the user to cough it up and clear congested respiratory passages. GRAS and GRAE reviewers found no expectorants to be both safe and effective.
- **Antitussives.** These OTC drugs are used to calm or curtail the cough reflex. They are most effective when the cough is "dry," or does not produce phlegm. Oral codeine, dextro-

methorphan, and diphenhydramine are the most common antitussives that are on both the GRAE and GRAS lists.

- **Antihistamines.** These are central nervous system depressants that dry runny noses, clear postnasal drip, clear sinus congestion, and reduce tears.
- **Decongestants.** These remedies are designed to reduce nasal stuffiness due to colds.
- **Anticholinergics.** These substances are often added to cold preparations to reduce nasal secretions and tears. None of the preparations tested was found to be GRAE/GRAS. Some cold compounds contain alcohol in concentrations that may exceed 40 percent.

▶ **Stimulants**   Nonprescription stimulants are sometimes used by college students who have neglected assignments and other obligations until the last minute. The active ingredient in OTC stimulants is caffeine (see Chapter 8). It acts to heighten wakefulness, increase alertness, and relieve fatigue. None of the OTC stimulants has been judged GRAS or GRAE.

Caffiene - no doze

▶ **Sleeping Aids**   In 1995, an estimated 49 percent of the U.S. population experienced insomnia at least 5 nights each month. About 1 percent of the adult population routinely self-medicate their insomnia with OTC sleep aids (such as Nytol, Sleep-eze, and Sominex) that are advertised as providing a "safe and restful" sleep.[6] These drugs are often used to induce the drowsy feelings that precede sleep. The principal ingredient in OTC sleeping aids is an antihistamine called pyrilamine maleate. Chronic reliance on sleeping aids may lead to addiction; people accustomed to using these products may find it impossible to sleep without them.

▶ **Dieting Aids**   Many drugs designed to help people lose weight are available over the counter. Some of these drugs are advertised as "appetite suppressants." Their active chemical is phenylpropanolamine. Its stimulant effects can cause dangerous reactions in people suffering from diabetes or heart or thyroid ailments.

The most potent and frequently used OTC diet aid ingredient is the **sympathomimetic** phenylpropanolamine (Acutrim, Dexatrim). This drug affects the central nervous system, causing reactions similar to those we experience when we are angry or excited. These reactions include a dry mouth and lack of appetite. Estimates show that, when taken as recommended, even the best of these OTC products significantly reduce appetite in less than 30 percent of the users and tolerance occurs in one to three days of use. Clearly, these products have no value in the treatment of obesity. However, there is a $200 million market for these diet aids in the United States.

Most manufacturers of appetite suppressants include a written diet to complement their drug. The majority of these diets contain 1,200 calories. On this number of calories, most people will lose weight without appetite suppressants.

Some people rely on **laxatives** and **diuretics** ("water pills") to aid weight reduction. Frequent use of laxatives to aid

---

Rebound effects   Severe withdrawal effects experienced by users of stimulants, including depression, nausea, and violent behavior.

Generic drugs   Drugs marketed by their chemical name rather than by a brand name.

GRAS list   A list of drugs generally recognized as safe; they seldom cause side effects when used properly.

GRAE list   A list of drugs generally recognized as effective; they work for their intended purpose when used properly.

Sympathomimetics   Drugs found in appetite suppressants that affect the sympathetic nervous system.

Laxative   Medications used to soften stool and relieve constipation.

Diuretic   Drugs that increase the excretion of urine from the body.

weight loss disrupts the body's natural elimination patterns and may cause constipation or even obstipation (inability to have a bowel movement). The use of laxatives to produce weight loss has generally unspectacular results and can rob the body of needed fluids, salts, and minerals.

Use of diuretics as part of a weight-loss plan is also dangerous. Not only will the user gain the weight back upon drinking fluids, but diuretic use may contribute to dangerous chemical imbalances. The potassium and sodium eliminated by diuretics play important roles in maintaining electrolyte balance. Depletion of these vital minerals may cause weakness, dizziness, fatigue, and sometimes death. (See Table 7.1 for a description of possible side effects of OTC drugs.)

Rules for Proper OTC Drug Use

Despite a common belief that OTC products are both safe and effective, indiscriminate use and abuse can occur with these drugs as with all others. For example, excessive or inappropriate use of some nonprescription drugs can cause drug dependence; consequently, people who frequently drop

---

TABLE 7.1
Some Side Effects of OTC Drugs

DRUG	POSSIBLE HAZARDS
Acetaminophen	• Bloody urine, painful urination, skin rash, bleeding and bruising, yellowing of the eyes or skin (even for normal doses) • Difficulty in diagnosing overdose because reaction may be delayed up to a week • Severe liver damage and death (for dose of about 50 tablets) • Liver damage from chronic low-level use
Antacids	• Reduced mineral absorption from food • Possible concealment of ulcer • Reduction of effectiveness for anticlotting medications • Prevention of certain antibiotics' functioning (for antacids that contain aluminum) • Worsening of high blood pressure (for antacids that contain sodium) • Aggravation of kidney problems
Aspirin	• Stomach upset and vomiting, stomach bleeding, worsening of ulcers • Enhancement of the action of anticlotting medications • Potentiation of hearing damage from loud noise • Severe allergic reaction • Association with Reye's syndrome in children and teenagers • Prolonged bleeding time (when combined with alcohol)
Cold medications	• Loss of consciousness (if taken with prescription tranquilizers)
Diet pills, caffeine, decongestants	• Organ damage or death from cerebral hemorrhage
Ibuprofen	• Allergic reaction in some people with aspirin allergy • Fluid retention or edema • Liver damage similar to that from acetaminophen • Enhancement of action of anticlotting medications • Digestive disturbances (half as often as with aspirin)
Laxatives	• Reduced absorption of minerals from food • Creation of dependency
Naproxen sodium	• Potential digestive tract bleeding • Possible stomach cramps • May cause ulcers • Avoid if allergic to aspirin or have heart or kidney problems
Toothache medications	• Destruction of the still-healthy part of a damaged tooth (for medications that contain clove oil)

---

medication into their eyes to "get the red out" or pop antacids after every meal are likely to be addicted.

OTC medications are far more powerful than ever before, and the science behind them is stronger as well. Most of us can use OTC products safely with adequate precautions, but for some people, OTCs can be as toxic as the most dangerous chemicals. Therefore, it is best to do your homework when you use any type of medication. To reduce the incidence of problems, use the following rules to help guide you when using nonprescription drugs:

1. Always know what you are taking. Identify the active ingredients in the product.
2. Know the effects. Be sure you know both the desired and potentially undesired effects of each active ingredient.
3. Read the warnings and cautions.
4. Don't use anything more than one or two weeks.
5. Be particularly cautious if you are also taking prescription drugs.
6. If you have questions, ask your pharmacist.
7. *If you don't need it, don't take it!*

OTC Herbal Products

The World Health Organization estimates that up to 80 percent of the world population relies on traditional medicinal systems—not Western medicine. In the United States, the rising popularity of herbal medicines has been ascribed to a broad search for a more "natural" health system.

Herbal products present a unique category of OTC remedies and are part of a multibillion-dollar industry.[7] They are unique because, despite the presence of active ingredients, there is little or no federal regulation due to a 1994 law supported by the dietary supplement industry, called the Dietary Supplement Health and Education Act (DSHEA).[8] This law requires the government to demonstrate that substances in the herbal products are harmful before they can be removed from the market. This lack of government involvement has led to unproven claims for remedies, such as a natural high, or a natural boost in energy, or weight reduction. Instead, herbal remedies rely on the scruples of their manufacturers for the accuracy of information on the labels. These products are typically purchased through mail orders, health food stores, and alternative health food stores and have brand names such as Cloud 9 and Herbal Ecstacy, in addition to other remedies with conflicting medical claims, such as St. John's wort and Kava.

While most herbal products are probably relatively safe,[9] the lack of understanding by users that some of these products contain very active drugs has led to fatal consequences. For example, a popular Chinese herb, Ma Huang, also called *ephedra,* has been the focus of a great deal of recent attention because one of its primary active ingredients is ephedrine, a stimulant thought to be included in dozens of popular herbal remedies. Ephedrine and other chemically related stimulants have been linked to more than 15 deaths and 400 serious adverse events and likely many more unreported incidents. These drugs, like other stimulants, can produce insomnia, heart attacks, strokes, tremors, and seizures. Consequently, even though the federal government is limited in its ability to regulate these substances, some states have taken action by banning ephedrine-containing stimulants.[10]

Some of the uncertainty that surrounds herbal remedies should soon be clearer. A group known as the German Commission E, a panel of experts, began an investigation into herbal remedies in the late 1970s. Because most European countries, including Germany, classify drugs differently than does the FDA, Germany saw a more urgent need to investigate the efficacy and safety of herbal remedies. The commission evaluated more than 380 herbal remedies and approved more than 250 for use, publishing their findings in *The Complete German Commission E Monographs.* The findings of the German Commission E are expected to open the door for greater understanding of herbal remedies and may in fact provide the impetus for the FDA to become involved. The special insert on Complementary and Alternative Medicines discusses this further.

ILLICIT DRUGS

While some people become addicted to prescription drugs and painkillers, we focus our attention here on illicit drugs—those drugs that are illegal to possess, produce, or sell. We may choose to use illicit drugs ourselves, be forced to watch someone we love struggle with drug abuse, or become the victim of a drug-related crime. At the very least, we are forced to pay increasing taxes for law enforcement and drug rehabilitation. An estimated 9.2 percent of full-time employees of the U.S. workforce is under the influence of illicit drugs or alcohol on any given day.[11]

The good news is that there has been a significant decline in the use of illicit drugs in recent years. Use of most drugs increased from the early 1970s to the late 1970s, peaked between 1979 and 1986, and declined until 1992, from which point the level of illicit drug use has not changed. In 1997, an estimated 13.9 million Americans were illicit drug users, about half the 1979 peak level of 25 million users. Among youth, however, illicit drug use, notably marijuana, has been increasing in recent years.[12]

Illicit drug users come from all walks of life. Not all illicit drug use occurs in dilapidated crack houses and not all users fit the stereotype of the crazed junkie. A 1997 survey conducted by the National Institute on Drug Abuse (NIDA) noted that 6.4 percent of the population age 12 and older reported using an illicit drug during the past year.[13] The reasons for

Illicit drugs   Drugs that are illegal to possess, produce, or sell.

using drugs vary from one situation to another and from one person to another. A person's age, gender, genetic background, physiology, personality, experiences, and expectations are all factors.

Patterns of drug use vary considerably by age. For example, a nationwide study of college campuses reported that approximately 31.2 percent of students had tried marijuana during the previous year.[14] In contrast, only 9 percent of all Americans used marijuana during that time. Approximately 3.6 percent of college students surveyed reported using cocaine in the past year, while only 2.2 percent of all Americans said they had used cocaine during the previous year.

Antidrug programs have been developed to deal with illegal drug use. The major drawback of most of these programs is their failure to take a multidimensional approach. The tendency has been to focus on only one aspect of drug abuse rather than to examine all factors that contribute to the problem. The pressures to take drugs are often tremendous, and the reasons for using them are complex.

People who develop drug problems generally begin with the belief that they can control their drug use. Initially, they often view drug taking as a fun and controllable pastime. Peer influence is a strong motivator, especially among adolescents, who greatly fear not being accepted as part of the group. Other people use drugs to cope with feelings of worthlessness and despair or to battle depression and anxiety. Drugs are seen as the quick answer to life's difficulties in our society. Since the majority of illegal drugs produces physical and psychological dependence, the idea that a person can use these substances regularly without becoming addicted is unrealistic. *up to 6 months can become addicted*

> .... **WHAT DO YOU THINK?**
>
> Do you think we should change or eliminate any of our current laws governing drugs? What characteristics or criteria do we use to determine if a drug's use is legitimate or illegitimate?

CONTROLLED SUBSTANCES

In order to counteract the increased use of illegal drugs and the overuse of certain prescription drugs, Congress passed the Controlled Substances Act of 1970 (Public Law 91-513). This law created categories for both prescription and illegal substances that the federal government felt required strict regulation. The Drug Enforcement Agency (DEA) was founded within the Department of Justice to administer the law.

The law established these control measures for drugs defined as "controlled substances": registration of handlers; record-keeping requirements; quotas on manufacturing;

restrictions on distribution and dispensation; limitation of imports and exports; conditions for storage of drugs; requirements for reporting drug transactions to the government; and criminal, civil, and administrative directives for actions involving illegal drugs or the illegal use of prescription drugs.

The law divided drugs into five "schedules," or categories, based on their potential for abuse, their medical uses, and accepted standards for their safe use (see Table 7.2). Schedule I drugs were those with the highest potential for abuse; they are considered to have no valid medical uses. Although Schedule II, III, IV, and V drugs have known and accepted medical applications, many of them present serious threats to health when abused or misused. Penalties for illegal use were also tied to the schedule level of various drugs. Despite the 1970 law, however, trafficking and manufacturing of illegal drugs in the United States have not diminished.

In 1986, the Drug Free America Act superseded the Controlled Substances Act and expanded penalties for the sale, manufacture, possession, and trafficking of illicit drugs. The goal of the new act was to eliminate drug abuse in schools and communities and to focus efforts on drug rehabilitation, medical treatment, and education.

Hundreds of illegal drugs exist. For general purposes, they can be divided into five representative categories: stimulants, like cocaine; marijuana and its derivatives; depressants, like the opiates; psychedelics and deliriants; and so-called designer drugs. All are Schedule I or Schedule II drugs. These categories include the drugs that are illegal to grow, manufacture, sell, or distribute in any form in the United States.

Cocaine

The rise of **cocaine,** or "coke," as the drug of choice among upper- and middle-class Americans in the 1980s was well chronicled in the media. Professional athletes were frequently banned from competition for cocaine use. National toll-free cocaine hotlines were established. The country became more aware of cocaine abuse with the spread of the relatively inexpensive and smokeable cocaine derivative called crack. Crack use turned into a national epidemic in the mid-1980s.

Between 1987 and 1996, there was a dramatic reversal in patterns of cocaine use. The number of people actively using cocaine fell from 2.9 million to 1.8 million.[15] Nevertheless, an estimated 730,000 Americans used cocaine for the first time in 1997.[16] Some studies have revealed that, in general, cocaine is not as acceptable among high school and college students as it was previously, which undoubtedly has contributed to the decline in its use. Cocaine is no longer viewed as a glamorous drug of the rich and famous but rather as a potentially dangerous substance.

NIDA describes cocaine as "the most powerful naturally occurring stimulant."[17] Despite a few chemical similarities to less potent stimulants, such as those found in coffee and tea, cocaine is very dangerous and cannot be compared with these substances.

TABLE 7.2
How Drugs Are Scheduled

SCHEDULE	CHARACTERISTICS	EXAMPLES
Schedule I	High potential for abuse and addiction; no accepted medical use.	Amphetamine (DMA, STP) Heroin Phencyclidine (PCP) LSD Marijuana Methaqualone
Schedule II	High potential for abuse and addiction; restricted medical use.	Cocaine Codeine* Methadone Morphine Opium Secobarbital (Seconal) Pentobarbital (Nembutal)
Schedule III	Some potential for abuse and addiction; currently accepted medical use.	Butalbital combinations (Fiorinal) Nalorphine Noludar
Schedule IV	Low potential for abuse and addiction; currently accepted medical use.	Chlorpromazine (Thorazine) Phenobarbital Minor tranquilizers
Schedule V	Lowest potential for abuse; accepted medical use.	Robitussin A-C OTC preparations

[handwritten annotations: "illegal drugs" with arrows pointing to Schedule I; "pain killers Vicadin codene"; "precription"]

*Can also be Schedule III or Schedule IV, depending on use.

Source: Information from Drug Enforcement, July 1979; National Institute on Drug Abuse, Statistical Series, Annual Data Report, 1989 (Rockville, MD: U.S. OHHS, 1989), 228–236.

Cocaine is a crystalline white alkaloid powder derived from the leaves of the South American coca shrub (not related to cocoa plants). Coca grows only in the Andes Mountains at elevations between 1,500 and 5,000 feet. Coca leaves have been chewed for their stimulant effects for thousands of years by the Incas and their descendants. Then, in 1860, a German pharmacology graduate student named Albert Niemann "invented" cocaine. He was the first person to extract cocaine from the coca leaf, making possible a pure, stable substance hailed for its curative properties.

With the discovery that cocaine was a potent local anesthetic, the drug's popularity skyrocketed in the late nineteenth and early twentieth centuries. Manufacturers began producing it in larger quantities to answer demand. Patent-medicine men sold bottles of tonic that contained high concentrations of cocaine.

Cocaine A powerful stimulant drug made from the leaves of the South American coca shrub.

The medical establishment grew concerned about the drug when it became apparent that many users suffered from both dependence and unpleasant side effects. In 1914, the Harrison Act outlawed the use of cocaine in the United States.

Methods of Cocaine Use

Cocaine can be taken in several ways. The powdered form of the drug is "snorted" through the nose. Smoking (freebasing) and intravenous injections are more dangerous means of ingesting cocaine.

When cocaine is snorted, it can cause both damage to the mucous membranes in the nose and sinusitis. It can destroy the user's sense of smell, and occasionally it even creates a hole in the septum. Smoking cocaine can cause lung and liver damage. Freebasing has become more popular than injecting in recent years because people fear contracting diseases such as AIDS and hepatitis by sharing contaminated needles. But freebasing involves other dangers. Because the volatile mixes it requires are very explosive, some people have been killed or seriously burned.

Many cocaine users still occasionally "shoot up." Injecting allows the user to introduce large amounts of cocaine into the body rapidly. Within seconds, there is an incredible sense of euphoria. This intense high lasts only 15 to 20 minutes, and then the user heads into a "crash." To prevent the unpleasant effects of the crash, users must shoot up frequently, which can severely damage their veins. Besides AIDS and hepatitis, injecting users place themselves at risk for skin infections, inflammation of the arteries, and infection of the lining of the heart.

Physical Effects of Cocaine

The effects of cocaine are felt rapidly. Snorted cocaine enters the bloodstream through the lungs in less than one minute and reaches the brain in less than three minutes. When cocaine binds at its receptor sites in the central nervous system, it produces intense pleasure. The euphoria quickly abates, however, and the desire to regain the pleasurable feelings makes the user want more cocaine.

Cocaine is both an anesthetic and a central nervous system stimulant. In tiny doses, it can slow heart rate. In larger doses, the physical effects are dramatic: increased heart rate and blood pressure, loss of appetite that can lead to dramatic weight loss, convulsions, muscle twitching, irregular heartbeat, even eventual death due to overdose. Other effects of cocaine include temporary relief of depression, decreased fatigue, talkativeness, increased alertness, and heightened self-confidence. Again, however, as the dose increases, users become irritable and apprehensive and their behavior may turn paranoid or violent.

withdrawl: depression; moody; no joy

▶ **Cocaine-Affected Babies** In the mid-1980s, a problem began to emerge that may have devastating long-term effects on society: the use of cocaine by pregnant women. Because cocaine rapidly crosses the placenta (as virtually all drugs do), the fetus is vulnerable when a pregnant woman snorts or shoots up. It is estimated that between 2.4 and 3.5 percent of pregnant women between the ages of 12 and 34 abuse cocaine. It is difficult to gauge how many newborns have been exposed to cocaine because pregnant women who are users are often reluctant to discuss their drug habit with their health-care providers for fear of prosecution. The most threatening problem during pregnancy is the increased risk of a miscarriage.

Babies exposed to cocaine or crack during pregnancy are more likely to suffer a small head, premature delivery, reduced birthweight, increased irritability, and subtle learning and cognitive deficits. It was once thought that babies who had been exposed to crack or cocaine as fetuses could suffer a number of physical and emotional problems, including permanent malformation of the brain, strokes, sudden infant death syndrome (SIDS), permanent learning disabilities, and behavioral disorders. However, recent research has refuted some of these findings and suggests that a significant number of these children develop problems with learning and language skills that require remedial attention.[18] It is critical that these children are identified early and receive immediate intervention. The cost for special education programs to prevent these children from failing in school is more than $350 million per year nationwide.[19] For both financial and humane reasons, developing prenatal care and education programs for mothers at risk should be a state and local government priority.

withdrawl @ birth

▶ **Freebase Cocaine** Freebase is a form of cocaine that is more powerful and costly than the powder or chip (crack) form. Street cocaine (cocaine hydrochloride) is converted to pure base by removing the hydrochloride salt and many of the "cutting agents." The end product, freebase, is smoked through a water pipe.

Because freebase cocaine reaches the brain within seconds, it is more dangerous than cocaine that is snorted. It produces a quick, intense high that disappears quickly, leaving an intense craving for more. Freebasers typically increase the amount and frequency of the dose. They often become severely addicted and experience serious health problems.

Side effects of freebasing cocaine include weight loss, increased heart rate and blood pressure, depression, paranoia, and hallucinations. Freebase is an extremely dangerous drug

and is responsible for a large number of cocaine-related hospital emergency-room visits and deaths.

▶ **Crack** Crack is the street name given to freebase cocaine that has been processed from cocaine hydrochloride using ammonia or sodium bicarbonate (baking soda) and water and heating the substance to remove the hydrochloride. Crack can also be processed with ether, but this is much riskier because ether is a flammable solvent.

The mixture (90 percent pure cocaine) is then dried. The soapy-looking substance that results can be broken up into "rocks" and smoked. These rocks are approximately five times as strong as cocaine. Because crack is such a pure drug, it takes much less time to achieve the desired high. One puff of a pebble-sized rock produces an intense high that lasts for approximately 20 minutes. The user can usually get three or four hits off a rock before it is used up. Crack is typically sold in small vials, folding papers, or heavy tinfoil containing two or three rocks, and costing between $10 and $20.

A crack user may quickly become addicted to the drug. Addiction is accelerated by the speed at which crack is absorbed through the lungs (it hits the brain within seconds after use) and by the intensity of the high. It is not uncommon for crack addicts to spend over $1,000 a day on their habits.

According to NIDA estimates, in 1996, 4.6 million people had used crack cocaine at least once in their lives and about 1.3 million people had used crack in the previous year.[20] Media attention to the large numbers of crack houses, crack-addicted babies, crack-related crimes, and other problems has drawn national attention to the enormity of the crack problem since the drug first gained notice around 1986.

5 xs more powerful → more intense

▶ **Cocaine Addiction and Society** It is estimated that the annual cost of cocaine addiction in the United States exceeds $100 million. However, there is no way to measure the cost in wasted lives. An estimated 5 million Americans from all socioeconomic groups are addicted to cocaine. Today 5,000 new users try cocaine or crack every day. Federal agencies estimate that 3 to 4 million people had used the drug at least once in the past year. Experts suggest that 10 percent of recreational users will go on to heavy use.[21]

The DEA has to date found no successful method to fight the cocaine and crack epidemic in the United States. Because cocaine is illegal, a complex network has developed to manufacture and sell the drug. Buyers may not always get the product they think they are purchasing. Cocaine marketed for snorting may be only 60 percent pure. Usually, it is mixed, or

---

Freebase The most powerful distillate of cocaine.

Crack A distillate of powdered cocaine that comes in small, hard "chips" or "rocks."

Ice A potent, inexpensive stimulant that has long-lasting effects.

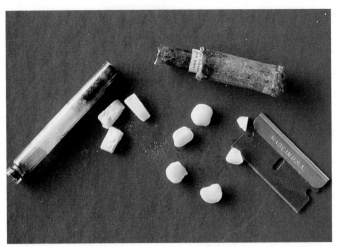

Although new "drugs of choice" make the news frequently, the availability of crack cocaine continues to be a major problem facing drug enforcement officials.

Newer-Generation Stimulants

Methamphetamine is a powerfully addictive drug that strongly activates certain areas of the brain and affects the central nervous system in general. Methamphetamine is closely related chemically to amphetamine, but the central nervous system effects of methamphetamine are greater. A surge in the abuse of high doses of methamphetamine and its frightening social impact caused U.S. Attorney General Janet Reno to propose a "National Methamphetamine Strategy" in 1996; it included plans to deal with criminal activity, violence, and law enforcement problems related to methamphetamine abuse.[22]

Methamphetamine is relatively easy to make, even by individuals without expertise in chemistry. Such people, referred to as "cookers," produce methamphetamine batches using cookbook-style recipes that often include common over-the-counter ingredients such as ephedrine, pseudoephedrine, and phenylpropanolamine. Since 1996, laws have increased the penalties associated with manufacturing methamphetamine.

Methamphetamine effects last considerably longer than those produced by crack and cocaine, and the high lasts anywhere from 6 to 8 hours. The immediate effects of methamphetamine can include irritability and anxiety; increased body temperature, heart rate, and blood pressure; and possible death. The high state of irritability and agitation has been associated with violent behavior in some users.

Ice is a potent methamphetamine that is imported primarily from Asia, particularly from South Korea and Taiwan. It is purer and more crystalline than the version manufactured in many large U.S. cities. Because it is odorless, public use of ice often goes unnoticed.

Typically, ice quickly becomes addictive. Some users have reported severe cravings after using the drug only once. The effects of ice are long-lasting. They include wakefulness, mood elevation, and excitability, all of which appeal to work-addicted young adults, particularly those who must put in long hours in high-stress jobs. Because the drug is very inexpensive and produces such an intense high (lasting from 4 to 14 hours), it has become popular among young people looking for a quick high. A penny-sized plastic bag, called a "paper," may cost $50, but when smoked, it can keep a person high for a few days or for as long as a week. In contrast, an ounce of cocaine causes a high that lasts only about 20 minutes.

Addicts call the sensation from smoking ice *amping,* for the amplified euphoria it gives them. However, as is true of other methamphetamines, the "down" side of this drug can be devastating. Prolonged use can cause fatal lung and kidney damage as well as long-lasting psychological damage. In some instances, major psychological dysfunction has lasted as long as two and a half years after last use. Aggressive behavior is also associated with the drug's use, as evidenced by the dramatic increase in the number of ice-related violent

"cut," with other white powdery substances such as mannitol or sugar, though occasionally, it is cut with arsenic or other cocaine-like powders that may themselves be highly dangerous.

> ········· **WHAT DO YOU THINK?**
>
> How has the crack epidemic affected U.S. society? Have all segments of society been equally affected by crack use? How well do you think our current system of scheduling drugs works?

Amphetamines → physical addiction

The amphetamines include a large and varied group of synthetic agents that stimulate the central nervous system. Small doses of amphetamines improve alertness, lessen fatigue, and generally elevate mood. With repeated use, however, physical and psychological dependence develops. Sleep patterns are affected (insomnia); heart rate, breathing rate, and blood pressure increase; restlessness, anxiety, appetite suppression, and vision problems are common. High doses over long time periods can produce hallucinations, delusions, and disorganized behavior. Abusers become paranoid, fearing everything and everyone. Some become very aggressive or antisocial.

Amphetamines for recreational use are sold under a variety of names. "Bennies" (amphetamine/Benzedrine), "dex" (dextroamphetamine/Dexedrine), and "meth" or "speed" (methamphetamine/Methedrine) are some of the most common. Other street terms for amphetamines are "cross tops," "uppers," "wake-ups," "lid poppers," "cartwheels," and "blackies." Amphetamines do have therapeutic uses in the treatment of attention deficit-hyperactivity disorder in children (Ritalin, Cylert) and of obesity (Pondimin).

prolonged use → kidney : liver damage

crimes.[23] The number of babies born severely addicted to the drug is also increasing at an alarming rate.

Marijuana

Although archaeological evidence documents **marijuana** ("grass," "weed," "pot") use as far back as 6,000 years ago, the drug did not become popular in the United States until the 1960s. Marijuana receives less media attention today than it did then, but it is still the most extensively used illicit drug by far. The National Household Survey on Drug Abuse reports that more than 68.5 million Americans over the age of 12—about 1 in 3—have tried marijuana at least once. About 18 million used the drug during 1996, and 1 million cannot control their use, according to the National Institute on Drug Abuse. An estimated 2.1 million Americans started using marijuana in 1997.[24] Among college students, marijuana is still the most popular illicit drug, as about half of all students report at least having tried marijuana at some time in their lives and 31.2 percent report having used it sometime during the previous year.[25] Marijuana use among youths aged 12 to 17 has increased from 6.0 percent to 8.2 percent, continuing a trend that began in 1992–1993. Since then, the rate of use among America's youth has more than doubled.

▶ *Physical Effects of Marijuana*   Marijuana is derived from either the cannabis sativa or cannabis indica (hemp) plants. The American-grown marijuana of the 1990s is a turbo-charged version of the hippie weed of the late 1960s. Developed using crossbreeding, genetic engineering, and American farming ingenuity, today's top-grade cannabis packs a punch very similar to that of hashish. **Tetrahydrocannabinol (THC)** is the psychoactive substance in marijuana, and the key to determining how powerful a high the marijuana will produce. Whereas marijuana from two decades ago ranged in potency from 1 to 2 percent THC, today's crop averages between 4 and 6 percent. The more refined varieties, usually grown without seeds (such as sinsemilla and Northern Lights), vary between 6 and 8 percent.[26]

Hashish, a potent cannabis preparation derived mainly from the thick, sticky resin of the plant, contains high concentrations of THC. Hash oil, a substance produced by percolating a solvent such as ether through dried marijuana to extract the THC, is a tarry liquid that may contain up to 70 percent THC.

Marijuana can be brewed and drunk in tea. It may also be baked into quick breads or brownies. THC concentrations in such products are impossible to estimate. Most of the time, however, marijuana is rolled into cigarettes (joints) or packed firmly into a pipe. Some people smoke marijuana through water pipes called bongs. Effects are generally felt within 10 to 30 minutes and usually wear off within three hours.

The most noticeable effect of THC is the dilation of the eyes' blood vessels, which produces the characteristic bloodshot eyes. Smokers of the drug also exhibit coughing, dry mouth and throat ("cotton mouth"), increased thirst and appetite, lowered blood pressure, and mild muscular weakness, primarily exhibited in drooping eyelids. Those users who take a high dose in an unfamiliar or uncomfortable setting are more likely to experience anxiety and the paranoid belief that their companions are ridiculing or threatening them.

Users may experience intensified reactions to various stimuli. For example, normal laugh responses may stretch into prolonged giggling and silliness. Colors and sounds, as well as the speed at which things move, may be magnified greatly. High doses of hashish may produce vivid visual hallucinations.

▶ *Effects of Chronic Marijuana Use*   Because the use of marijuana is illegal in most parts of the United States, and because the drug has only been widely used since the 1960s, long-term studies of its effects are difficult to conduct. Also, studies conducted in the 1960s involved marijuana with THC levels that were only a fraction of the levels found in plants today. Thus the results of these studies may not be relevant to the more toxic forms of the drug presently in use. Most of the current information gathered about chronic marijuana use has been obtained from countries such as Jamaica and Costa Rica, where the drug is not illegal. These studies of chronic users (people who have used the drug for 10 or more years) indicate that long-term use of marijuana causes lung damage comparable to that caused by tobacco smoking. Smoking a single joint may be as damaging to the lungs as smoking five tobacco cigarettes. The chemicals do not damage the heart, but the effects of inhaling burning material do. Inhalation of marijuana transfers carbon monoxide to the bloodstream. Because the blood has a greater affinity for carbon monoxide than it does for oxygen, the oxygen-carrying capacity of the blood is diminished. The heart must then work harder to pump the vital element to oxygen-starved tissues.

Other suspected risks associated with marijuana include suppression of the immune system, blood pressure changes, and impaired memory function. Recent studies suggest that pregnant women who smoke marijuana are at a higher risk for stillbirth or miscarriage and for delivering low-birthweight babies and babies with abnormalities of the nervous system. Babies born to women who use marijuana during pregnancy are five times more likely to have features similar to those exhibited by children with fetal alcohol syndrome.

Debates concerning the effects of marijuana on the reproductive system have yet to be resolved. Studies conducted in the mid-1970s suggested that marijuana inhibited testosterone (and thus sperm) production in males and caused chromosomal breakage in both ova and sperm. Subsequent research in these areas is inconclusive. The question of whether the high-level THC plants currently available will increase the risks associated with this drug is, as yet, unanswered.

▶ *Marijuana and Medicine*   Although recognized as a dangerous drug by the U.S. government, marijuana has several

Stimulant or depressant depending on mind set of user.

medical purposes. It has been used to help control the side effects (such as severe nausea and vomiting) produced by chemotherapy (chemical treatment for cancer). It improves appetite and forestalls the loss of lean muscle mass associated with AIDS-related wasting syndrome. Marijuana reduces the muscle pain and spasticity caused by diseases such as multiple sclerosis. It also relieves the eye pressure and pain resulting from glaucoma.[27]

For a number of years, marijuana's legal status for use for medicinal purposes has been hotly debated. So far, 26 states and the District of Columbia have existing laws and resolutions establishing therapeutic research programs allowing doctors to prescribe marijuana or asking the federal government to lift the ban on the medicinal use of marijuana. In 10 states, similar laws have either been repealed or have expired, and 15 states have never had medicinal marijuana laws[28] (see Figure 7.2). In 1996, California made news at election time as voters chose to legalize marijuana for medicinal uses, and voters in Washington state, Alaska, Arizona, Oregon, and Nevada have since followed suit. These new state laws, however, conflict with federal laws against the possession of marijuana and have thereby led to new battles in the courts. In February 1999, attorneys general from a number of western states met with federal officials to discuss reclassifying marijuana as a Schedule II drug. Reclassification would allow marijuana to be prescribed by physicians and would clear up some of the conflict over its medicinal uses.

▶ *Marijuana and Driving* Marijuana use presents clear hazards for drivers of motor vehicles as well as others on the road. The drug substantially reduces a driver's ability to react and to make quick decisions. Studies reveal that 60 to 80 percent of marijuana users indicate that they sometimes drive while high.[29] Studies of automobile accident victims show that 6 to 12 percent of nonfatally injured drivers and 4 to 16 percent of fatally injured drivers had THC in their bloodstreams. Perceptual and other performance deficits resulting from marijuana use may persist for some time after the

Figure 7.2

State Laws on Marijuana as Medicine

Source: National Organization for the Reform of Marijuana Laws; downloaded from Join Together website, 11/18/98: http://www.jointogether.org

high subsides, though users who attempt to drive, fly, or operate heavy machinery often fail to recognize their impairment.

Opiates

The opiates are among the oldest analgesics known to humans. These drugs cause drowsiness, relieve pain, and induce euphoria. Also called **narcotics,** they are derived from the parent drug **opium,** a dark, resinous substance made from the milky juice of the opium poppy. Other opiates include *morphine, codeine,* heroin, and *black tar heroin.*

The word *narcotic* comes from the Greek word for "stupor" and is generally used to describe sleep-inducing substances. For many years, opiates were widely used by the medical community to relieve pain, induce sleep, curb nausea and vomiting, stop diarrhea, and sedate psychiatric patients. During the late nineteenth and early twentieth centuries, many patent medicines contained opiates. Suppliers advertised these concoctions as cures for everything from menstrual cramps to teething pains.

Among the opiates once widely used by medical practitioners was **morphine.** First manufactured in the early nineteenth century, morphine was named after Morpheus, the Greek god of sleep. More powerful than opium, morphine was first widely used as a painkiller during the Civil War.

Marijuana Chopped leaves and flowers of the cannabis indica or cannabis sativa plant (hemp); a psychoactive stimulant that intensifies reactions to environmental stimuli.

Tetrahydrocannabinol (THC) The chemical name for the active ingredient in marijuana.

Hashish The sticky resin of the cannabis plant, which is high in THC.

Narcotics Drugs that induce sleep and relieve pain; primarily the opiates.

Opium The parent drug of the opiates; made from the seedpod resin of the opium poppy.

Morphine A derivative of opium; sometimes used by medical practitioners to relieve pain.

Codeine, a less powerful analgesic derived from morphine, also became popular.

Growing concern about addiction led to government controls of narcotic use. The Harrison Act of 1914 prohibited the production, dispensation, and sale of opiate products unless prescribed by a physician. Subsequent legislation required physicians prescribing opiates to keep careful records. Physicians are still subject to audits of their prescriptions of these agents.

Some of the opiates are still used today for medical purposes. Morphine is sometimes prescribed by doctors in hospital settings for relief of severe pain. Codeine is found in prescription cough syrups and in other pain-killers. Several prescription drugs, including Percodan, Demerol, and Dilaudid, contain synthetic opiates. All opiate use is strictly regulated.

▶ *Physical Effects of Opiates*   Opiates are powerful central nervous system depressants. In addition to relieving pain, these drugs lower heart rate, respiration, and blood pressure. Side effects include weakness, dizziness, nausea, vomiting, euphoria, decreased sex drive, visual disturbances, and lack of coordination. Of all the opiates, heroin is the most notorious. Because all opiate addiction follows a similar progression, we will use heroin as a model for narcotic abuse.

w/in 3 weeks → tolerance

▶ *Heroin Addiction*   **Heroin** and **black tar heroin** are illegal opiates. Heroin is a white powder derived from morphine. Black tar heroin is a sticky, dark brown, foul-smelling substance. It is estimated that 600,000 Americans use heroin.[30] Authorities believe that the United States is at the beginning of a new heroin epidemic, which may result in increased crime and further spread of AIDS. There is concern that this epidemic will be worse than previous ones because the drug is now two to three times more available than ever before. The contemporary version of heroin is so potent that users can get high by snorting or smoking the drug rather than by injecting it and putting themselves at risk for AIDS (see Chapter 13). Once primarily an inner-city drug, heroin use is now becoming more widespread among middle-class people who tend to try whatever drug is new and trendy. Many people have switched from cocaine to heroin because the heroin high is not so stimulating and the drug is less expensive than cocaine.

Heroin is a depressant. It produces a dreamy, mentally slow feeling and drowsiness in the user. In addition to its depressant effects, it can cause drastic mood swings in some users, with euphoric highs followed by depressive lows. Heroin also slows respiration and urinary output and constricts the pupils of the eyes. In fact, pupil constriction is a classic sign of narcotic intoxication; hence the image of the stereotypical drug user hiding his eyes behind a pair of dark sunglasses. Symptoms of tolerance and withdrawal can appear within three weeks of the first use of the drug.

The most common route of administration for heroin addicts is "mainlining"—intravenous injection of powdered heroin mixed in a solution—though fear of AIDS has induced some people to change to nonneedle methods. Many users describe the "rush" they feel when injecting themselves as intensely pleasurable, whereas others report unpredictable and unpleasant side effects. The temporary nature of the rush contributes to the drug's high potential for addiction—many addicts shoot up four or five times a day. Mainlining can cause veins to become scarred, and if this practice is frequent enough, the veins collapse. Once a vein has collapsed, it can no longer be used to introduce heroin into the bloodstream. Addicts become expert at locating new veins to use: in the feet, the legs, even the temples. When they do not want their needle tracks (scars) to show, they inject themselves under the tongue or in the groin.

↗ don't work well

▶ *Treatment for Heroin Addiction*   Programs to help heroin addicts kick their habits have not been very successful. The rate of recidivism (tendency to return to previous behaviors) is high. Some addicts resume their drug use even after years of drug-free living because the craving for the injection rush is very strong. It takes a great deal of discipline to seek alternative, nondrug highs.

Heroin addicts experience a distinct pattern of withdrawal. They begin to crave another dose four to six hours after their last dose. Symptoms of withdrawal include intense desire for the drug, yawning, a runny nose, sweating, and crying. About 12 hours after the last dose, addicts experience sleep disturbance, dilated pupils, loss of appetite, irritability, goose bumps, and muscle tremors. The most difficult time in the withdrawal process occurs 24 to 72 hours following last use. All of the preceding symptoms continue, along

Codeine   A drug derived from morphine; used in cough syrups and certain painkillers.

Heroin   An illegally manufactured derivative of morphine, usually injected into the bloodstream.

Black tar heroin   A dark brown, sticky substance made from morphine.

Methadone maintenance   A treatment for people addicted to opiates that substitutes methadone, a synthetic narcotic, for the opiate of addiction.

Psychedelics   Drugs that distort the processing of sensory information in the brain.

Reticular formation   An area in the brain stem that is responsible for relaying messages to other areas in the brain.

Synesthesia   A (usually) drug-created effect in which sensory messages are incorrectly assigned—for example, hearing a taste or smelling a sound.

Hallucination   An image (auditory or visual) that is perceived but is not real.

Lysergic acid diethylamide (LSD)   Psychedelic drug causing sensory disruptions; also called acid.

with nausea, abdominal cramps, restlessness, insomnia, vomiting, diarrhea, extreme anxiety, hot and cold flashes, elevated blood pressure, and rapid heartbeat and respiration. Once the peak of withdrawal has been passed, all these symptoms begin to subside. Still, the recovering addict has many hurdles to jump.

Methadone maintenance is one type of treatment available for people addicted to heroin or other opiates. Methadone is a synthetic narcotic that blocks the effects of opiate withdrawal. It is chemically similar enough to the opiates to control the tremors, chills, vomiting, diarrhea, and severe abdominal pains of withdrawal. Methadone dosage is decreased over a period of time until the addict is weaned off the drug.

Methadone maintenance is controversial because of the drug's own potential for addiction. Critics contend that the program merely substitutes one addiction for another. Proponents argue that people on methadone maintenance are less likely to engage in criminal activities to support their habits than heroin addicts are. For this reason, many methadone maintenance programs are state or federally financed and are available to clients free of charge or at reduced costs.

Psychedelics

The term **psychedelic** was adapted from a Greek phrase meaning "mind manifesting." Psychedelics are a group of drugs whose primary pharmacological effect is to alter feelings, perceptions, and thoughts in the user. The major receptor sites for most of these drugs are in the part of the brain that is responsible for interpreting outside stimuli before allowing these signals to travel to other parts of the brain. This area is called the **reticular formation** and is located in the brain stem at the upper end of the spinal cord (see Figure 7.3). When a psychedelic drug is present at a reticular formation receptor site, messages become scrambled, and the user may see wavy walls instead of straight ones or may smell colors or hear tastes. This mixing of sensory messages is known as **synesthesia.**

In addition to synesthetic effects, users may recall events long buried in the subconscious mind or become less inhibited than they are in a nondrug state. Some psychedelic drugs are erroneously labeled "hallucinogens." Hallucinogens are substances that are capable of creating auditory or visual **hallucinations,** or images that are perceived but are not real. Not all of the psychedelic drugs are capable of producing hallucinations. The most widely recognized psychedelics are LSD, mescaline, psilocybin, and psilocin. All are illegal and carry severe penalties for manufacture, possession, transportation, or sale.

▶ LSD Of all the psychedelics, **lysergic acid diethylamide (LSD)** has achieved the most notoriety. This chemical was first synthesized in the late 1930s by the Swiss chemist Albert Hoffman. It resulted from experiments aimed at deriving

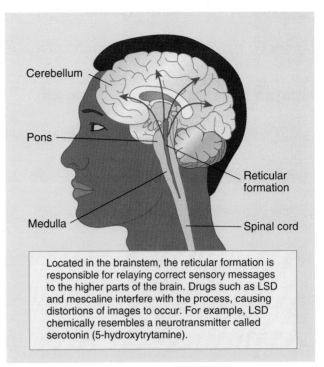

Located in the brainstem, the reticular formation is responsible for relaying correct sensory messages to the higher parts of the brain. Drugs such as LSD and mescaline interfere with the process, causing distortions of images to occur. For example, LSD chemically resembles a neurotransmitter called serotonin (5-hydroxytrytamine).

Figure 7.3
Reticular Formation

medically useful drugs from the ergot fungus found on rye and other cereal grains. Because LSD seemed capable of unlocking the secrets of the mind, psychiatrists initially felt it could be beneficial to patients unable to remember and recognize suppressed traumas. From 1950 through 1968, the drug was used for such purposes.

Media attention was drawn to LSD in the late 1960s. Young people were using the drug to "turn on" and "tune out" the world that gave them the war in Vietnam, race riots, and political assassinations. In 1970, federal authorities, under intense pressure from the public, placed LSD on the list of controlled substances (Schedule I). This ruling did not curtail the use of the drug, however. Its popularity peaked in 1972, then tapered off, primarily because of users' inability to control dosages accurately.

Because of the recent wave of nostalgia for the 1960s, this dangerous psychedelic drug has been making a comeback. Known on the street as "acid," LSD is now available in virtually every state, and its availability is increasing. Over 10 million Americans, most of them under 35 years of age, have tried LSD at least once. LSD especially attracts younger users. In 1995, more than 10 percent of high school seniors reported having tried LSD at least once. Although a national survey of college students showed that 6.8 percent had tried LSD in 1995,[31] it is the fastest-growing illicit drug among the under-20 age group.

An odorless, tasteless, white crystalline powder, LSD is most frequently dissolved in water to make a solution that can then be used to manufacture the street forms of the drug:

ACCESSING YOUR HEALTH ON THE INTERNET

Check out the following Internet sites related to various forms of addiction, drug use, and treatment.

1. *Center for On-Line Addiction.* Information and assistance for those dealing with Internet addiction.

   http://netaddiction.com/

2. *Food and Drug Administration.* News on the latest government-approved drugs and investigations.

   http://www.fda.gov

3. *Healthtouch.* Search for prescription and over-the-counter drug uses and side effects, plus other health-related resources.

   http://www.healthtouch.com

4. *Narcotics Anonymous World Services Office.* This site posts information pertaining to 12-step meetings and provides other support services for drug abusers nationwide.

   http://www.wsoinc.com

5. *National Institute on Drug Abuse.* The home page of this U.S. government agency has information on the latest statistics and findings in drug research.

   http://www.nida.nih.gov/

tablets, blotter acid, and windowpane. What the LSD consumer usually buys is blotter acid—small squares of blotter-like paper that have been impregnated with the liquid. The blotter is swallowed or chewed briefly. LSD also comes in tiny thin squares of gelatin called windowpane and in tablets called microdots, which are less than an eighth of an inch across (it would take 10 or more of these to add up to the size of an aspirin tablet). Microdots and windowpane are just a sideshow; blotter is the medium of choice.

LSD is one of the most powerful drugs known to science and can produce strong effects in doses as low as 20 micrograms. (To give you an idea of how small a dose this is, the average-sized postage stamp weighs approximately 60,000 micrograms.) The potency of the typical dose of LSD currently ranges from 20 to 80 micrograms, compared to 150 to 300 micrograms commonly used in the 1960s.

Despite its reputation for being primarily a psychedelic, LSD produces a large number of physical effects, including slightly increased heart rate, elevated blood pressure and temperature, goose flesh (roughened skin), increased reflex speeds, muscle tremors and twitches, perspiration, increased salivation, chills, headaches, and mild nausea. Since the drug

also stimulates uterine muscle contractions, it can lead to premature labor and miscarriage.

Research into the effects of long-term LSD use has been inconclusive. As with any illegally purchased drug, users run the risk of purchasing an impure product.

The psychological effects of LSD vary from person to person. The set and setting in which the drug is used are very influential factors. Euphoria is the common psychological state produced by the drug, but *dysphoria* (a sense of evil and foreboding) may also be experienced. The drug also shortens attention span, causing the mind to wander. Thoughts may be interposed and juxtaposed as well. The user may thus be able to experience several different thoughts simultaneously. Synesthesia occurs occasionally. Users become introspective, and suppressed memories may surface, often taking on bizarre symbolism. Many more effects are possible, including decreased aggressiveness and enhanced sensory experiences.

Although LSD rarely produces hallucinations, it can create illusions. These distortions of ordinary perceptions may include movement of stationary objects. "Bad trips" are the most publicized risk of LSD. These negative experiences are commonly related to set or setting. The user, for example, may interpret increased heart rate as a heart attack (a "bad body trip"). Often bad trips result when a user confronts a suppressed emotional experience or memory (a "bad head trip") while using the drug.

While there is no evidence that LSD creates a physical dependence, it may well create a psychological dependence. Many LSD users become depressed for one or two days following a trip and turn to the drug to relieve this depression. The result is a cycle of LSD use to relieve post-LSD depression, which often leads to psychological addiction.

WHAT DO YOU THINK?

Are people today using LSD for the same reasons it was used in the 1960s? What are the perceived attractions and what are the dangers of LSD use?

▶ *Mescaline* Mescaline is one of the hundreds of chemicals derived from the **peyote** cactus. The small, buttonlike cactus grows in the southwestern United States and parts of Latin America. Natives of these regions have long used the dried peyote buttons during religious ceremonies.

Users normally swallow 10 to 12 dried peyote buttons. These buttons taste bitter and generally induce immediate nausea or vomiting. Long-time users claim that the nausea becomes less noticeable with frequent use.

Those who are able to keep the drug down begin to feel the effects within 30 to 90 minutes, when mescaline reaches maximum concentration in the brain. (It may persist for up to 9 or 10 hours.) Unlike LSD, mescaline is a powerful hallucinogen. It is also a central nervous system stimulant.

Products sold on the street as mescaline are likely to be synthetic chemical relatives of the true drug. Street names of these products include DOM, STP, TMA, and MMDA. Any of these can be toxic in small quantities.

▶ *Psilocybin* Psilocybin and *psilocin* are the active chemicals in a group of mushrooms sometimes called "magic mushrooms." Psilocybe mushrooms, which grow throughout the world, can be cultivated from spores or can be harvested wild. Because many mushrooms resemble the psilocybe variety, people who use wild mushrooms for any purpose should be certain of what they are doing. Mushroom varieties can easily be misidentified, and mistakes can be fatal. Psilocybin is similar to LSD in physical effects. These effects generally wear off within 4 to 6 hours.

The Deliriants

Delirium is an agitated mental state characterized by confusion and disorientation. Almost all of the psychoactive drugs will produce delirium at high doses, but the **deliriants** produce this condition at relatively low (subtoxic) levels.

▶ *PCP* Phencyclidine, or PCP, is one of the best-known deliriants. It is a synthetic substance that became a black-market drug in the early 1970s. PCP was originally developed as a "disassociative anesthetic," which means that patients administered this drug could keep their eyes open, apparently remain conscious, and feel no pain during a medical procedure. Patients would afterward experience amnesia for the time the drug was in their system. Such a drug had obvious advantages as an anesthetic during surgery, but its unpredictability and drastic effects (postoperative delirium, confusion, and agitation) made doctors abandon it and it was withdrawn from the legal market.

Mescaline A hallucinogenic drug derived from the peyote cactus.

Peyote A cactus with small "buttons" that, when ingested, produce hallucinogenic effects.

Psilocybin The active chemical found in psilocybe mushrooms; it produces hallucinations.

Delirium An agitated mental state characterized by confusion and disorientation that can be produced by psychoactive drugs.

Deliriant Any substance that produces delirium at relatively low doses, including PCP and some herbal substances.

Phencyclidine (PCP) A deliriant commonly called "angel dust."

Designer drug A synthetic analog (a drug that produces similar effects) of an existing illicit drug.

On the illegal market, PCP is a white, crystalline powder that users often sprinkle onto marijuana cigarettes. It is dangerous and unpredictable regardless of the method of administration. Common street names for PCP are "angel dust" for the crystalline powdered form and "peace pill" and "horse tranquilizer" for the tablet form.

The effects of PCP depend on the dosage. A dose as small as 5 mg will produce effects similar to those of strong central nervous system depressants. These effects include slurred speech, impaired coordination, reduced sensitivity to pain, and reduced heart and respiratory rate. Doses between 5 and 10 mg cause fever, salivation, nausea, vomiting, and total loss of sensitivity to pain. Doses greater than 10 mg result in a drastic drop in blood pressure, coma, muscular rigidity, violent outbursts, and possible convulsions and death.

Psychologically, PCP may produce either euphoria or dysphoria. It is also known to produce hallucinations as well as delusions and overall delirium. Some users experience a prolonged state of "nothingness." The long-term effects of PCP use are unknown.

tolerance, abuse, addiction very high

Designer Drugs

Designer drugs are structural analogs (drugs that produce similar effects) of drugs already included under the Controlled Substances Act. These illegal drugs are manufactured by underground chemists to mimic the psychoactive effects of controlled drugs. At present, at least three types of synthetic drugs are available on the illegal drug market: analogs of phencyclidine (PCP), analogs of *fentanyl* and *meperidine* (both synthetic narcotic analgesics), and analogs of amphetamine and methamphetamine, which have hallucinogenic and stimulant properties.[32]

Although PCP analogs have been identified in street samples of drugs, they are less frequently used today than are other forms of designer drugs. Analogs of fentanyl are much more common. The pharmacological properties of most fentanyl analogs are similar to those of heroin or morphine. These analogs are known as synthetic heroin, or "china white." Other fentanyl analogs on the street are often called "Tango and Cash" and "Goodfella." These designer drugs may be addictive and carry the risk for overdose.

Meperidine, commonly known by its trade name Demerol, is a narcotic with several designer analogs. When heroin becomes difficult to obtain, street analogs of meperidine, known as MPPP and PEPAP, often surface. Both of these drugs pose significant risk for overdose. An impure form of MPPP, known as MPTP, has been known to cause an irreversible brain syndrome similar to Parkinson's disease in some users.[33]

Amphetamine and methamphetamine analogs are the most common forms of designer drugs on college campuses today. These analogs often cause hallucinations and euphoria. *Ecstasy* (methylenedioxymethylamphetamine, or MDMA), which was dubbed the "LSD of the 80s," is one such analog that became popular on many college campuses in the 1980s,

CONSUMER HEALTH

Campus Alert!

Every era seems to have its *hot* drug. At one point it was valium, then LSD, and then crack. In the late 1990s, however, college campuses have three of note: Rohypnol (flunitrazepam), also called "Ropies" or "roofies"; GHB (gamma hydroxybutyrate), or as it is known on the street, "Grievous Bodily Harm"; and Special K (Ketamine).

Rohypnol is a very potent tranquilizer similar to valium, but many times stronger. The drug produces a sedative effect, amnesia, muscle relaxation, and a slowing of psychomotor responses. Commonly known as the "date rape" drug, Rohypnol gained notoriety a few years ago when it was reported as a growing problem on college campuses, especially in fraternities. The drug has been added to punch and other drinks at fraternity parties and college social gatherings,

where it is reportedly given to female partiers in hopes of lowering their inhibitions and facilitating potential sexual conquests. To make matters worse, roofies are inexpensive and have been reported to sell for as little as $3 to $5 a pill. While "ropie" fervor has subsided somewhat, it continues to be of concern to campus officials.

No sooner had the immediate threat of Rohypnol died down when it was replaced by the lust for a newer, liquid substance called GHB, or gamma hydroxybutyrate. GHB has a variety of uses, which include being taken as an aphrodisiac to increase one's sense of touch and sexual prowess, as a muscle builder, and as a tranquilizer. Some people also use it as a substitute for alcohol, obtaining the high without the hangover. GHB is an odorless, tasteless fluid that can be made easily at home in a chemistry lab. Like Rohypnol, GHB has been slipped into drinks without being detected, resulting in loss of memory, unconsciousness, amnesia, and even death. Side effects of GHB include nausea, vomiting, seizures, memory loss, hallucinations, coma, and respiratory distress. During the 1980s, GHB was available in U.S. health food stores. Concerns about its

use led the FDA to ban OTC sales in 1990 and push for further controls in 1997.

The Special K we're referring to is not the breakfast cereal, but rather an analog of phencyclidine, and an anesthetic used in many hospital and veterinary clinics around the country. On the street, Special K is most often diverted in liquid form from veterinary offices or medical suppliers. Dealers dry the liquid (usually by cooking it) and grind the residue into powder. Special K causes hallucinations as it inhibits the relay of sensory input; the brain fills the resulting void with visions, dreams, memories, and sensory distortions. The effects of Special K are not as severe as those of Ecstasy, so it has grown in popularity among people who have to go to work or school after a night of partying.

Sources: J. Cloud, "Is Your Kid on K?" *Time,* 20 October 1997, 90–91; D. Rosenberg, "Death of the Party," *Time,* 27 October 1997, 55; S. A. Lyman, C. Hugher-McLain, and G. Thompson, "Date-Rape Drugs: A Growing Concern," *Journal of Health Education* 29: 271–274; Information from Emergencynet NEWS Service, 1996; and Kit Lively, "The 'Date-Rape Drug,'" *Chronicle of Higher Education* 28 June 1996, A29.

and is currently popular among college students and young adults. According to NIDA's 1995 Monitoring the Future study, 4.5 percent of young adults aged 19 to 28 and 3.1 percent of college students have tried MDMA at least once in their lives.[34]

Users claim that Ecstasy provides the rush of cocaine combined with the mind-expanding characteristics of the hallucinogens. Effects begin within 30 minutes and can last 4 to 6 hours. Psychological effects of MDMA include confusion, depression, anxiety, and paranoia. Physical symptoms may include muscle tension, nausea, blurred vision, faintness, chills, and sweating. MDMA also increases heart rate and blood pressure and may destroy neurons that regulate aggression, mood, sexual activity, and sensitivity to pain.[35]

Inhalants

Inhalants are chemicals that produce vapors that, when inhaled, can cause hallucinations as well as create intoxicating and euphoric effects. They are not commonly recognized as drugs. They are legal to purchase and universally available but are potentially dangerous when used incorrectly. These drugs are generally used by young people who can't afford illicit substances.

Some of these agents are organic solvents representing the chemical by-products of the distillation of petroleum products. Rubber cement, model glue, paint thinner, lighter fluid, varnish, wax, spot removers, and gasoline belong to this group. Most of these substances are sniffed by users in search of a quick, cheap high.

Because they are inhaled, the volatile chemicals in these products reach the bloodstream within seconds. An inhaled substance is not diluted or buffered by stomach acids or other body fluids and thus is more potent and dangerous than the same substance would be if swallowed. This characteristic, along with the fact that dosages are extremely difficult to control because everyone has unique lung and breathing capacities, makes inhalants particularly dangerous.

The effects of inhalants usually last for less than 15 minutes. Users may experience dizziness, disorientation, impaired coordination, reduced judgment, and slowed reaction times. Signs of inhalant use include: unjustifiable collection of glues, paints, lacquer thinner, cleaning fluid, and ether; sniffles similar to those produced by a cold; and a smell on the breath similar to the inhalable substance. The effects of inhalants are similar to those of central nervous system depressants. Combining inhalants with alcohol produces a synergistic effect. In addition, these substances in combination can cause severe liver damage that may lead to death.

An overdose of fumes from inhalants can cause unconsciousness. If the user's oxygen intake is reduced during the inhaling process, death can result within five minutes. Whether the user is a first-time or chronic user, sudden sniffing death (SSD) syndrome can be the fatal consequence. This syndrome can occur if a user inhales deeply, then partakes in physical activity or is startled.

tolerance: abuse → low

▶ *Amyl Nitrite* Sometimes called "poppers" or "rush," **amyl nitrite** is often prescribed to alleviate chest pain in heart patients. It is packaged in small, cloth-covered glass capsules that can be crushed to release the active chemical. The drug relieves chest pains because it causes rapid dilation of the small blood vessels and reduces blood pressure. That same dilation of blood vessels in the genital area is thought to enhance sensations or perceptions of orgasm. It also produces fainting, dizziness, warmth, and skin flushing.

▶ *Nitrous Oxide* "Laughing gas" is the popular term for **nitrous oxide.** It is sometimes used as an adjunct to dental anesthesia or minor surgical anesthesia. It is also used as a propellant chemical in aerosol products such as whipped toppings. Users experience a state of euphoria, floating sensations, and illusions. Effects also include pain relief and a "silly" feeling, demonstrated by laughing and giggling (hence the term *laughing gas*). Regulating dosages of this drug can be difficult. Sustained inhalation can lead to unconsciousness, coma, and death.

Slugger Mark McGwire became an American folk hero in 1998 when he broke the Major League record for most home runs in a season, but not without some controversy.

Steroids

Public awareness of **anabolic steroids** has recently been heightened by media stories about their use by amateur and professional athletes, including Arnold Schwarzenegger during his competitive bodybuilding days. Anabolic steroids are artificial forms of the male hormone testosterone that promote muscle growth and strength. These **ergogenic drugs** are used primarily by young men to increase their strength, power, bulk (weight), and speed. These attributes are sought either to enhance athletic performance or to develop the physique that users perceive will make them more attractive and increase their sex appeal.

Most steroids are obtained through black market sources. It is estimated that approximately 17 to 20 percent of college athletes use steroids. Overall, it is estimated that there are 1 million steroid abusers in the United States, many of whom take steroids for noncompetitive bodybuilding.[36] Steroids are available in two forms: injectable solution and pills. Anabolic steroids produce a state of euphoria, diminished fatigue, and increased bulk and power in both sexes. These qualities give steroids an addictive quality. When users stop, they appear to undergo psychological withdrawal, mainly caused by the disappearance of the physique they have become accustomed to.

Several adverse effects occur in both men and women who use steroids. These drugs cause mood swings (aggression and violence), sometimes known as "roid rage"; acne; liver tumors; elevated cholesterol levels; hypertension; kidney disease; and immune system disturbances. There is also a danger of AIDS transmission through shared needles. In women, large doses of anabolic steroids trigger masculine changes,

Inhalants Products that are sniffed or inhaled in order to produce highs.

Amyl nitrite A drug that dilates blood vessels and is properly used to relieve chest pain.

Nitrous oxide The chemical name for "laughing gas," a substance properly used for surgical or dental anesthesia.

Anabolic steroids Artificial forms of the hormone testosterone that promote muscle growth and strength.

Ergogenic drug Substance that enhances athletic performance.

including lowered voice, increased facial and body hair, male pattern baldness, enlarged clitoris, decreased breast size, and changes in or absence of menstruation. When taken by healthy males, anabolic steroids shut down the body's production of testosterone, causing men's breasts to grow and testicles to atrophy.

To combat the growing problem of steroid use, Congress passed the Anabolic Steroids Control Act (ASCA) of 1990. This law makes it a crime to possess, prescribe, or distribute anabolic steroids for any use other than for the treatment of specific diseases. Anabolic steroids are now classified as a Schedule III drug. Penalties for their illegal use include up to five years' imprisonment and a $250,000 fine for the first offense, and up to 10 years' imprisonment and a $500,000 fine for subsequent offenses.

A new and alarming trend is the use of other drugs to achieve the "performance-enhancing" effects of steroids. These steroid alternatives are sought in order to avoid the stiff penalties now in effect against those who possess anabolic steroids without a valid prescription.

The two most common steroid alternatives are gamma hydroxybutyrate (GHB) and clenbuterol. GHB is a deadly, illegal drug that is a primary ingredient in many of these "performance-enhancing" formulas. GHB does not produce a high. It does, however, cause headaches, nausea, vomiting, diarrhea, seizures and other central nervous system disorders, and possibly death. Clenbuterol, another steroid alternative, has become an extremely popular item on the black market. The drug is used in some countries for certain veterinary treatments, but is not approved for any use—in animals or humans—in the United States.

In 1998 new attention was drawn to the issue of steroids and related substances when St. Louis Cardinals slugger Mark McGwire set the sports world on its side with his chase for the home run record. In the course of a locker room interview, McGwire admitted to using a supplement containing androstenedione (andro), an adrenal hormone that is produced naturally in both men and women. Andro raises levels of the male hormone testosterone, which helps build lean muscle mass and promotes quicker recovery after injury. McGwire had done nothing wrong, as the supplement can be purchased over the counter and its use is legal in baseball, although banned by the NFL, NCAA, and the International Olympic Committee. Although few studies have been conducted on andro and no definitive studies have indicated harmful side effects, bans by these organizations are based on certain similarities with illegal steroids, most notably the elevated testosterone levels.

While androstenedione has gained most of the attention, the use of muscle-building supplements goes beyond andro. As noted, androstenedione has been banned by many sports organizations, but visits to the weight rooms and locker rooms of many of these organizations' teams disclose large containers of other supplements intended to help athletes build muscle mass, such as creatine. Although legal, questions remain whether enough research has been on the safety of these supplements. Some people worry that the supplements

may have consequences similar to those of steroids, such as liver damage and heart problems.

> ········· **WHAT DO YOU THINK?**
>
> Do you think androstenedione should be declared illegal? Would you consider using supplements for the sole purpose of increasing your body build and potentially your performance?

ILLEGAL DRUG USE IN THE UNITED STATES

Stories of people who have tried illegal drugs, enjoyed them, and suffered no consequences may tempt you to try them yourself. You may tell yourself it's "just this once," convincing yourself that one-time use is harmless. Given the dangers surrounding these substances, however, you should carefully consider nondrug alternatives. Many such alternatives, although often time-consuming, are more rewarding and usually contribute more to personal growth than chemically induced experiences do.

The risks associated with drug use extend beyond the personal level. The decision to try any illicit substance encourages illicit drug manufacture and transportation and contributes to the national drug problem. The financial burden of illegal drug use on the U.S. economy is staggering, with an estimated economic cost of around $97.7 billion.[37] This estimate includes substance abuse treatment and prevention costs, other health-care costs, costs associated with reduced job productivity or lost earnings, and social costs such as crime and social welfare. Health-care costs alone are thought to total over $60 billion annually. In addition, roughly one-half of all expenditures to combat crime are related to illegal drugs. The burden of these costs is absorbed primarily by the government (46 percent), followed by those who abuse drugs and members of their households (44 percent). In a study to determine how much money is spent on illegal drugs, the White House Office of National Drug Control Policy (ONDCP) found that between 1988 and 1995, Americans spent $57.3 billion on illicit drugs. These numbers broke down as follows: $38 billion on cocaine, $9.6 billion on heroin, $7 billion on marijuana, and $2.7 billion on other illegal drugs and on the misuse of legal drugs.

Women and Drug Abuse

Approximately 3.8 million U.S. women of all ages, races, and cultures use drugs. It is estimated that 31 percent of U.S. women (over 17 years of age) have used an illicit drug at least once in their lives.[38] Today, approximately 28,000 (66 percent) of AIDS cases among women are related either to injecting drugs or to having sex with a man who injects drugs;

AIDS is now the fourth leading cause of death among women of child-bearing age.[39]

Many women who use drugs have had troubled lives. Studies have found that at least 70 percent of women drug users have been sexually abused by the age of 16. Most of these women had at least one parent who abused alcohol or drugs. Furthermore, these women often have low self-esteem, little self-confidence, and feel powerless. They often feel lonely and are isolated from support networks.

Research has shown that women drug abusers get better when treatment takes care of all their basic needs. Some women need the basic services of food, shelter, and clothing. Other women also need transportation, child care, and parenting training. Good treatment also teaches reading, basic education, and the skills needed to find a job. As a woman's self-esteem increases, her chances of remaining drug-free increase.

········· **WHAT DO YOU THINK?**

What are the societal factors that make getting treatment so difficult for women? Do you think women begin using drugs for reasons that are different from men's? Does society perceive women who abuse substances differently from men? If so, why?

Drugs in the Workplace

NIDA estimates that 9.2 percent of all U.S. workers use dangerous drugs on the job at some time. With approximately 70 to 75 percent of drug users in the United States employed to some degree, the cost to American businesses soars into the billions of dollars annually.[40] Costs are seen in reduced work performance and efficiency, lost productivity, absenteeism and turnover costs, increased health benefits utilization, accidents, and indirect losses stemming from impaired judgment.

Results of National Household Surveys on Drug Abuse indicate that 65.6 percent of full-time workers reported alcohol use within the past month. Some 9.7 percent of full-time workers reported marijuana use within the past year. Part-time employees did not differ much in their use of alcohol and marijuana. The highest rates of illicit drug use among workers are among people in construction, food preparation, and restaurant wait staff. Workers who require a considerable amount of public trust, such as police officers, teachers, and child-care workers, report the lowest use of illicit drugs. In addition, younger employees (18–24 years old) are more likely to report drug use than are older employees (25 years and older). Several other findings concluded that drug users are 1.6 times as likely as nonusers to quit their jobs or to be fired. They are also 1.5 times more likely to be disciplined by their supervisor.[41]

Many employers have instituted drug testing for their employees to counteract the drug epidemic. The use of mandatory drug urinalysis is controversial. Critics argue that such testing violates Fourth Amendment rights of protection from unreasonable search and seizure. Proponents believe the personal inconvenience entailed in testing pales in comparison to the problems caused by drug use in the workplace. Some court decisions have affirmed the right of employers to test their employees for drug use. They contend that Fourth Amendment rights pertain only to employees of government agencies, not to those of private businesses. Most Americans apparently support some type of drug testing for certain types of job categories.

Drug testing is expensive, with costs running as high as $100 per individual test. Moreover, some critics question the accuracy and the reliability of these tests. Both false positives and false negatives can occur. As drug testing becomes more common in the work environment, it is gaining greater acceptance by employees, who see testing as a step to improving safety and productivity.

········· **WHAT DO YOU THINK?**

What do you believe are the moral and ethical issues surrounding drug testing? Are you in favor of drug testing? Should all employees be subjected to drug tests or just those employees in high-risk jobs? Is it the employer's right to conduct drug testing at the worksite?

Solutions to the Problem

Americans are alarmed by the increasing use of illegal drugs, particularly crack and other forms of cocaine. In recent years, we have been constantly warned through the media about this "chemical menace" to our society. Respondents in a poll felt that the most important strategy for fighting drug abuse was educating young people. Other strategies endorsed were working with foreign governments to stop drug trafficking, making a concerted effort to arrest dealers, providing treatment assistance, and arresting drug users.

The most popular antidrug strategies for many years were total prohibition and "scare tactics." Both approaches proved ineffective. Prohibition of alcohol during the 1920s created more problems than it solved, as did prohibition of opiates in 1914. Likewise, prohibition of other illicit drugs has neither eliminated them nor curtailed their trafficking across U.S. borders.

In general, researchers in the field of drug education agree that a multimodal approach to drug education is best. Students should be taught the difference between drug use and abuse. Factual information that is free from scare tactics must be presented; moralizing about drug use and abuse does not work. Programs that teach people to control drugs, as opposed to allowing drugs to control them, are needed, as are programs that teach about the influences of set and setting.

At-risk groups must be targeted for study so that we can better understand the circumstances that make each group more or less prone to drug use. Time, money, and effort by educators, parents, and policymakers are needed to ensure that today's youths are given the love and security essential for building productive and meaningful lives.[42]

Indicators of Drug Abuse

The following is an outline of some of the more common and obvious indicators of drug abuse. It is highly possible for some of these symptoms to exist in a nonuser or for a user not to exhibit warning signs.

Common Symptoms of Drug Abuse
1. Changes in behavior or character
2. Sudden loss of interest in normal activities
3. Dropping grades/skipping class
4. New group of friends
5. Unexplained absences of long duration
6. Poor physical appearance
7. Wearing sunglasses at unusual times, concealing red eyes or dilated pupils
8. Prodrug reading materials, posters, T-shirts, etc.

WHAT TO LOOK FOR
Marijuana
1. Greenish-brown dried plant material in plastic bags or small containers
2. Paraphernalia—rolling papers, pipes, water pipes, roach clips
3. Small dark seeds or stems
4. Excessive reddening of the eyes

5. Increased hunger
6. Odor of burnt leaves on clothing
7. Small holes or burns on shirts

Inhalants
1. Empty glue or spray cans
2. Bags or rags with dry paint, glue, etc., on or in them
3. Dried paint or glue on clothes
4. Running nose and red eyes
5. Unpleasant, chemical breath
6. Increased coughing or salivation

Stimulants
1. Users become talkative, restless, excited
2. Excessive perspiration
3. Various shapes or colors of tablets or capsules
4. Hypodermic needles, cotton balls, spoons
5. Small packets of white powdered substance
6. Mirrors, short straws, single-edge razor blades
7. Chain smoking
8. Long periods without eating or sleeping

Depressants
1. May seem drunk without noticeable alcohol smell
2. Slurred speech, staggering, slowed reactions
3. Strong body odor on person and clothing
4. Pills in various shapes and colors

Opiates
1. Small packets of powder
2. Hypodermic needles, spoons, etc.

3. Small spots of blood on shirt sleeves, clothes, etc.
4. Contracted pupils, bruises, scars along veins
5. Belts or straps used for tourniquets
6. Very sleepy (nod), drowsy, lethargic

Hallucinogens
1. Dream or trancelike state
2. Inappropriate fear or terror reactions
3. Very large pupils
4. Shuddering

If you note several fairly sudden behavior changes in a friend, you may need to get your friend help. To help, try the following:

- Get as much information as you can so you can understand what you and your friend are up against.
- Get some intervention training. Talk to a counselor with special training in chemical dependancy; some offer advice by telephone.
- Confront the user—with other loved ones and a counselor if possible.
- Don't expect the drug abuser to quit without help.
- Offer your support, but make it clear that you expect your friend to undergo therapy.
- Don't believe abusers who say they have learned to control their drug use. Abstinence is the key to any good treatment program.
- Encourage the user to attend support groups such as Narcotics Anonymous or Cocaine Anonymous.

Among the various strategies suggested for combating drug abuse are stricter border surveillance to reduce drug trafficking, longer prison sentences for drug pushers, increased government spending on prevention and enforcement of antidrug laws, and greater cooperation between government agencies and private groups and individuals. All of these approaches will probably help up to a point, but neither alone nor in combination do they offer a total solution to the problem. Drug abuse has been a part of human behavior for thousands of years, and it is not likely to disappear in the near future. For this reason, it is necessary to educate ourselves and to develop the self-discipline necessary to avoid dangerous drug dependencies.

WHAT DO YOU THINK?

Do you feel the public has a social responsibility to fight drug abuse? What is the cost society pays for drug use? Have you ever personally known someone who has suffered because of addiction to drugs? How did you respond?

Taking Charge
Managing Drug Use Behavior

While reading this chapter, you have found that addictions can be devastating, and that even OTC drugs must be used judiciously. A college environment offers many opportunities for young people, most of which are good. Unfortunately, others can be dangerous, including the availability and use of drugs. The following checklist points out some things to watch out for.

CHECKLIST FOR CHANGE

MAKING PERSONAL CHOICES

✓ Are you ready to change or modify your behavior or substance use? Who can help support your decision?

✓ Have you thought about what impact your decision will have on your lifestyle? Are you ready to give up friends, activities, and environments that do not support your efforts?

✓ Are there any known side effects of the medication? What should you do if you experience any side effects?

✓ Are you certain of how often you should take the medication, how long you should take it, and in what dosage?

✓ Do you know if you should avoid any particular foods or beverages while taking the medication?

✓ Does your medication cause any adverse reactions if taken with any other medications, psychoactive drugs, or alcohol?

✓ What drugs are most popular among your peers? What is it about these drugs that makes them popular?

✓ How do you and your peers feel about illicit drug use? Is it condoned or condemned? Has that changed in the last few years? What has led to these feelings?

MAKING COMMUNITY CHOICES

✓ Do you sometimes participate or look the other way when someone you know engages in a behavior that may lead to an addiction?

✓ Do you support policies, such as laws against drunk driving, that serve to protect the community from the effects of addictive behaviors?

✓ Do you know how and where to store your medication properly?

✓ Are there any adverse consequences of long-term use of the medication?

✓ Would you be willing to volunteer to help out at an addiction hotline or community center?

SUMMARY

- Addiction is behavior resulting from compulsion; without the behavior, the addict experiences withdrawal. Addicts have four common symptoms: compulsion, loss of control, negative consequences, and denial.

- The six categories of drugs are prescription drugs, OTC drugs, recreational drugs, herbal preparations, illicit drugs, and commercial preparations. Routes of administration include oral ingestion, injection (intravenous, intramuscular, and subcutaneous), inhalation, inunction, and suppositories.

- Proper drug use begins with creating a drug profile, including knowing the name of the drug, its receptor sites, its main and side effects, possible adverse reactions, methods of administration, potential for addiction and dependency, legality, and possible alternatives. Hazardous drug interactions may occur when a person takes several medications or illegal drugs simultaneously. The most hazardous interactions are synergism, antagonism, inhibition, and intolerance.

- Prescription drugs are administered under medical supervision. Categories include antibiotics, analgesics, prostaglandin inhibitors, sedatives, tranquilizers, antidepressants, and amphetamines. Generic drugs can often be substituted for more expensive brand-name drugs.

- Over-the-counter drug categories include analgesics; cold, cough, allergy, and asthma relievers; stimulants; sleeping aids and relaxants; and dieting aids. Consumers should exercise personal responsibility by reading directions for OTC drugs and asking their pharmacist or doctor if any special precautions are advised when taking these substances.

- People from all walks of life use illicit drugs, although college students report higher usage rates than does the general population. Drug use has declined since the mid-1980s.
- Controlled substances include cocaine and its derivatives, amphetamines, newer-generation stimulants, marijuana,

the opiates, the psychedelics, the deliriants, designer drugs, inhalants, and steroids. Users tend to become addicted quickly to such drugs.

- The drug problem reaches everyone through crime and elevated health-care costs. Women addicts have special problems associated with seeking treatment. Drugs are a major problem in the workplace; workplace drug testing is one proposed solution to this problem.

DISCUSSION QUESTIONS

1. What factors indicate that someone has an addiction? Is it possible for you to tell if someone else is really addicted?
2. Briefly explain the five most common routes of administration for drugs.
3. Differentiate between drug misuse and abuse.
4. Explain the terms *synergism, antagonism,* and *inhibition.*
5. Discuss the precautions of which you need to be aware that pertain to the use of herbal products.
6. Do you think there is such a thing as responsible use of illicit drugs? How would you determine what is legitimate use and illegitimate use?

7. Why do you think that people today feel that marijuana use is not dangerous? What are the arguments in favor of legalizing marijuana? What are the arguments against legalization?
8. If someone has "consensual" sex with another person after lacing his or her drink with a drug, do you think it's a case of rape and should be prosecuted as such?
9. How do you think reports in the media about the use of stimulants and/or steroids by athletes affect the popularity of these drugs?

APPLICATION EXERCISE

Reread the *What Do You Think?* scenario at the beginning of this chapter and answer the following questions:

1. When is it appropriate to self-diagnose and -medicate? What guidelines should you follow when doing so? What would you recommend to Paul if he came to talk about his problem?

2. What is known about the effectiveness of St. John's Wort and the possible side effects and drug interactions? How thoroughly does the FDA regulate herbal remedies? What are some alternative medications that Paul might be prescribed if he were to be treated for depression by a health care provider?

ALCOHOL EFFECTS

① wrecked relationships
② arguements / fights
③ vandalism / thefts #1 in college
④ accidents / injuries
⑤ abuse potential
⑥ assault < verbal
        physical
        rape

A) professor / friends
B) young man / Lyman
C) frat party
d) your girl laura

8

Alcohol, Tobacco, and Caffeine

Unacknowledged Addictions

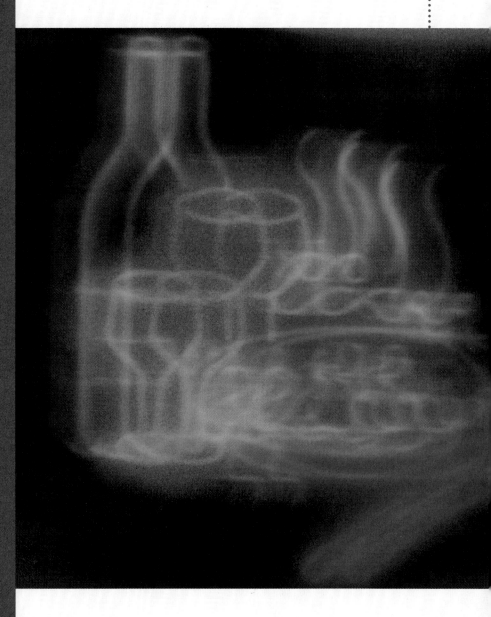

OBJECTIVES

▶ Summarize the alcohol use patterns of college students and discuss overall trends in consumption.

▶ Explain the physiological and behavioral effects of alcohol, including blood alcohol concentration, absorption, metabolism, and immediate and long-term effects of alcohol consumption.

▶ Explain the symptoms and causes of alcoholism, its cost to society, and its effects on the family.

▶ Explain the treatment of alcoholism, including the family's role, varied treatment methods, and whether or not alcoholics can be cured.

▶ Discuss the social issues involved in tobacco use, including advertising and the medical costs associated with tobacco use.

▶ Review how smoking affects a smoker's risk for cancer, cardiovascular disease, and respiratory diseases, and how it adversely affects a fetus's health.

▶ Discuss the risks associated with using smokeless tobacco.

▶ Evaluate the risks to nonsmokers associated with environmental tobacco smoke.

▶ Describe strategies people adopt to quit using tobacco products, including strategies aimed at breaking the nicotine addiction as well as habit.

▶ Compare the benefits and risks associated with caffeine, and summarize the health consequences of long-term caffeine use.

The end of the semester had arrived and David and Shelly decided to have a party at their apartment on campus to celebrate. They invited about 30 friends over and bought two kegs of beer to ensure that there would be plenty for everyone. Figuring this would reduce their liability, David and Shelly had their friends pay $3 for a cup, then they could drink all the beer they wanted for the evening. The party turned out to be a great success until one of their friends, Eric, was found close to dawn, passed out outside the apartment complex. When they tried to wake Eric to bring him inside, they found that he was barely breathing and his face was lying in vomit. Their friend died five hours later.

Who is responsible for Eric's death? What type of precautions could David and Shelly have taken to prevent this from happening? Do any of the other students at the party have any responsibility for this incident? Does the college have any liability in this situation?

WHEN YOU HEAR REFERENCES to the dangers of drugs, what usually comes to mind? Usually the term *drugs* conjures up images of people abusing cocaine, heroin, marijuana, LSD, PCP, and other illegal substances. We conveniently use the word *drugs* to refer to one set of dangerous substances, but we steadfastly refuse to categorize alcohol as a drug, primarily because it is socially accepted. Most of us think of alcohol the way it is portrayed in ads or in the movies: a way of having fun in company, an important adjunct to a romantic dinner or a cozy evening in front of the fireplace. Moderate use of alcohol can enhance celebrations or special times. Research shows that very low levels of use may actually lower some health risks. But you should remember that alcohol is a chemical substance that affects your physical and mental behavior. The tragedies associated with alcohol addiction receive far less attention than cocaine-related deaths, drug busts, and efforts to eradicate marijuana crops. Nevertheless, they are more common and may have devastating effects on people of all ages.

ALCOHOL
An Overview

An estimated 70 percent of Americans consume alcoholic beverages regularly, though consumption patterns are unevenly distributed throughout the drinking population. Ten percent are heavy drinkers, and they account for half of all the alcohol consumed. The remaining 90 percent of the drinking population are infrequent, light, or moderate drinkers.

Alcohol and College Students

Alcohol is the most widely used (and abused) recreational drug in our society. It is also the most popular drug on college campuses, where approximately 85 percent of students consume alcoholic beverages.[1] Some 20 to 25 percent abuse alcohol. Exactly how much alcohol does a typical college student consume? According to a recent survey, the average student consumes approximately five drinks per week, and the number of female drinkers is now close to equaling the number of male drinkers.[2] Colleges and universities have been described as among the "alcohol-drenched institutions." Every year, America's 12 million undergraduates drink 4 billion cans of beer, averaging 55 six-packs apiece, and spend $446 on alcoholic beverages—more than they spend on soft drinks and textbooks combined.[3]

Despite these figures, fewer students are drinking alcohol than in the past. In 1980, 9.5 percent of students nationwide said they abstained from alcohol; in 1997, 19 percent were abstainers.[4] According to the University of Michigan's Institute for Social Research, the percentage of students who report drinking daily also has declined, from 6.5 percent in 1980 to 3.2 percent.[5]

College is a critical time to become aware of and responsible for your drinking. A number of social factors are involved in campus drinking. There is little doubt that drinking is a part of the campus culture and tradition. Students are away from home, often for the first time, and many are

Binge drinking   Drinking for the express purpose of becoming intoxicated; five drinks in a single sitting for men and four drinks in a sitting for women.

excited by their newly found independence. For some students, this new independence and their rite of passage into the college culture are symbolized by the use of alcohol. "Having fun," which often means drinking to simply get drunk, may really be a coping mechanism for stress, boredom, anxiety, or pressures created by academic and social demands.

Students consistently report that their friends drink much more than they do and that average drinking within their own social living group is higher than actual self-reports. Such misinformation may promote or be used to excuse excessive drinking practices among college students. In a survey of students at a large midwestern university, 42 percent reported not having a hangover in the past six months. Yet that same group of surveyed students believed that only 3 percent of their peers had not had a hangover in the past month. Overattending to misbehavior leads to over-perception of misbehavior as the norm. Thus, pressure to misbehave is created because misbehavior allows students to perceive themselves as normal. Efforts to reduce the misperception of what is normal drinking behavior among college students has begun on many college campuses. It is hoped that by providing students with accurate information about their peers and their peers' drinking behavior, it will reduce the pressure for students who feel as though they need to drink, or to drink in excess. (See Health Headlines on pages 188–189.)

Binge drinking or high-risk drinking has become an issue of concern on college campuses. Binge drinking is defined as five drinks in a row by men and four in a row by women on a single occasion. The stakes of binge drinking are high. Students are at increased risk for alcohol-related injuries or death. You may recall the cases of the notorious alcohol poisonings at LSU and MIT in 1997, in which two students poisoned themselves during a tragic night of drinking. An estimated 50 students die annually from alcohol poisonings.

According to a 1997 Harvard School of Public Health study, 42.7 percent of students were found to be binge drinkers, and 20.7 percent were found to be frequent bingers (people who binge drink 3 times or more in a 2-week period) (see Table 8.1).[6] Compared with nonbingers, frequent bingers were more likely to have an array of problems on campus. For example, frequent binge drinkers are 8 times more likely to miss a class, fall behind in their schoolwork, forget where they were or what they did, get hurt or injured, and damage property. Unfortunately, recent studies have confirmed what students have been experiencing for a long time—that binge drinkers cause problems not only for themselves, but also for those around them.[7]

Although everyone is at some risk for alcoholism and alcohol-related problems, college students seem to be particularly vulnerable:

- Alcohol exacerbates their already high risk for suicide, automobile crashes, and falls.

TABLE 8.1
College Student Patterns of Alcohol Use by Gender, 1997

CATEGORY	TOTAL (%)	MEN (%)	WOMEN (%)
Abstainer	19.0	18.4	19.5
Nonbinger	38.3	33.3	41.7
Occasional binger	21.9	24.7	20.1
Frequent binger	20.7	23.7	18.8

Source: H. Wechsler, et al., "Changes in Binge Drinking and Related Problems Among American College Students Between 1993 and 1997," Journal of American College Health 47 (1998): 60.

- Many college and university customs, norms, traditions, and mores encourage certain dangerous practices and patterns of alcohol use.
- University campuses are heavily targeted by advertising and promotions from the alcoholic beverage industry.
- It is more common for college students than their noncollegiate peers to drink recklessly and to engage in drinking games and other dangerous drinking practices.
- College students are particularly vulnerable to peer influences and have a strong need to be accepted by their peers.
- There is institutional denial by college administrators that alcohol problems exist on their campuses.

In an effort to prevent alcohol abuse, many colleges and universities are instituting strong policies against drinking. College and university presidents have formed a leadership group to help curb the problem of alcohol abuse on campuses. Many fraternities have elected to have dry-houses by the year 2000. At the same time, colleges and universities are making more help available to students with drinking problems. Today, both individual and group counseling are offered on most campuses, and more attention is being directed toward the prevention of alcohol abuse. Student organizations such as BACCHUS (Boost Alcohol Consciousness Concerning the Health of University Students) promote responsible drinking and responsible party hosting.

WHAT DO YOU THINK?

Do you think that your campus is a high-binge campus (over 50 percent of students are binge drinkers)? Have you ever had your sleep or studies interrupted or had to babysit a roommate or friend because of their drinking? How did that make you feel?

Are Scare Tactics Effective?

"A safari shirt works well with this classic black pant," one ad says. "The white and red accents from puke don't."

The startling posters are part of a campaign called "Party Smart," started last year by the City of Boston to show college students that "drinking can make anyone look stupid," as the ads put it. The ads can be found around Boston, on billboards and in dormitories, newspapers, and bars. Some images were deemed so disturbing, however, that the city's transportation authority refused to display them on subways and buses.

The advertising company that created the campaign met with about 100 local college students to find out what would work.

"More than leaving school, more than getting arrested, kids said they were afraid of looking like fools in front of their friends," says John J. Dorsey, a spokesman for the Mayor's office. "Most kids felt it was uncool for people to pass out or vomit."

But to critics, Party Smart and other campaigns that warn people of the negative consequences of heavy drinking are scare tactics—"health terrorism," some call it. They argue that the ads are ineffective in reaching students, and that by focusing on the behavior of the minority who drink heavily, the campaign will merely encourage further dangerous drinking.

Campus officials are increasingly advocating an entirely different sort of campaign—one that plays up statistics showing that most students drink responsibly, or don't drink at all. That strategy, known as the "social norms" approach, features advertisements and posters that show smiling students either sitting around talking with one another or participating in such healthful activities as rock climbing, mountain biking, and hiking.

The debate over marketing illustrates how divisive the battle against binge drinking has become. College administrators, health experts, and anti-alcohol groups have not agreed on the best way to combat a behavior that many college presidents say is the No. 1 problem on their campuses.

"I would give you $10,000 if the Party Smart campaign made a dent in binge drinking in the area," says William DeJong, director of the Higher Education Center for Alcohol and Other Drug Prevention, in Newton, Mass., and a supporter of the social-norms approach.

The widely publicized death of an 18-year-old freshman at the Massachusetts Institute of Technology who drank too much at a fraternity pledge event in September 1997 hardly frightened local students into sobriety, he notes. Why, then, would anyone expect a few billboards that show students vomiting to do the trick?

"A campaign that tries to hit people over the head with the possible negative consequences of drinking are not campaign dollars well spent," says Mr. DeJong, an instructor of health communication at Harvard University's School of Public Health. "Today's college students have been hearing since elementary school about the dangers of alcohol abuse, so to have a media campaign that tries to yell at them even louder is not going to have any impact."

He and many other college administrators were initially skeptical of the social-norms approach when Northern Illinois University was the first to experiment with it, in the early 1990s. But it has caught on at many institutions.

This fall, Dartmouth College will begin a newspaper, television, and radio advertising blitz declaring that heavy drinking on the campus is not the norm. It will display posters informing students that 58 percent of their classmates who responded to a campus survey said alcohol was not important for a party, and that 52 percent said they had not gone on a drinking binge in the previous two weeks.

EFFECTS OF ALCOHOL

Alcohol's Chemical Makeup

The intoxicating substance found in beer, wine, liquor, and liqueurs is **ethyl alcohol,** or **ethanol.** It is produced during a process called **fermentation,** whereby plant sugars are broken down by yeast organisms, yielding ethanol and carbon dioxide. Fermentation continues until the solution of plant sugars (called mash) reaches a concentration of 14 percent alcohol. At this point, the alcohol kills the yeast and halts the chemical reactions that produce it.

For beers and ales, which are fermented from malt barley, the process stops when the alcohol concentration is 14 percent. Manufacturers then add other ingredients that dilute the alcohol content of the beverage. Other alcoholic beverages are produced through further processing called **distillation,** during which alcohol vapors are released from the mash at high temperatures. The vapors are then condensed and mixed with water to make the final product.

The **proof** of an alcoholic drink is a measure of the percentage of alcohol in the beverage. "Proof" comes from "gunpowder proof," a reference to the gunpowder test, whereby potential buyers would test the distiller's product by pouring it on gunpowder and attempting to light it. If the alcohol

The University of North Carolina at Chapel Hill will start a campaign—called "2 out of 3, .00 B.A.C." (for blood-alcohol content)—using posters and stickers to tell freshmen that 66 percent of students there drink little or not at all on weekend nights. The campaign is based on a study in which students were given Breathalyzer tests.

Susan Kitchen, vice-chancellor for student affairs at Chapel Hill, hopes that the campaign will "reassure impressionable first-year students, who just left their homes and are eagerly seeking a new family on campus, that they don't have to drink alcohol to find their niche here."

[A student at North Carolina] says that the ads might reach a few impressionable freshmen, but that "most people already have their minds made up on whether they're going to drink or not, long before they get here." He also believes that the university "rigged" the statistics; the number of students who do not drink sounds too high to him . . . Scare tactics don't work. Most people make fun of them," he says. . . .

. . . Last year, MADD began a new campaign, "The Brutal Truth," aimed at reducing underage drinking on college campuses. One poster shows a young man holding his head in his hand, underneath a message telling readers that "alcohol kills more people under 21 than cocaine, marijuana and heroin combined." Another warns that "alcohol consumption contributes to unwanted pregnancies."

Critics say the ads, like so many others, rely too heavily on fear. [Robert Heard, national program director for Mothers Against Drunk Driving, in Irving, Tex.] responds that the messages are based on facts, and that MADD deliberately stayed away from the scare tactics that some groups—including MADD itself—used during the 1980s to combat drunk driving.

Bryan R. Christian, a vice-president at McCann-Erickson Southwest, the Texas advertising agency that designed the "Brutal Truth" ads, says the company wanted to "deliver a rational tone of voice."

"We thought it would have more impact to speak straightforwardly to folks rather than over-scare them," he explains. "The facts are harsh and they're uncomfortable, but they're things you end up having to deal with."

Indeed, critics say that the social-norms campaigns, which feature positive statistics and smiling faces, gloss over the harsh realities of alcohol abuse. Those campaigns may be "well-intentioned," says Richard A. Yoast, director of the Office of Alcohol and Other Drug Abuse at the American Medical Association, in Chicago, "but the reality is that a large number of students do have problems, and the social-norms campaign is simply de-emphasizing that to the point where you don't need to deal with it."

Students themselves say subtle warnings—rather than those that are disturbingly graphic—are the most effective ones.

[A female student] at Boston University, says one of the less graphic Party Smart posters in her dormitory grabbed her attention right away. It puts the viewer in the vantage point of a drunken student facing several classmates who are laughing and pointing at the sight. "I didn't ever want to be in that position," Ms. Seward says. "The way the picture was taken, it brings more of a realistic perception to drinking." . . .

Henry Wechsler, director of college alcohol studies at Harvard's School of Public Health, says any advertising campaign is likely to fail unless it is part of a broader strategy that includes stricter enforcement of alcohol policies.

"Students aren't fools," Mr. Wechsler says. "You can't simply Madison Avenue them out of drinking."

STUDENTS SPEAK UP:
Which strategy do you think is the most effective for curbing alcohol abuse on college campuses—Health Terrorism or the "Social-Norms" Approach?

Source: Excerpted from "When Do Scare Tactics Become 'Health Terrorism'?", September 3, 1999, *The Chronicle of Higher Education.*

Ethyl alcohol (ethanol)   An addictive drug produced by fermentation and found in many beverages.

Fermentation   The process whereby yeast organisms break down plant sugars to yield ethanol.

Distillation   The process whereby mash is subjected to high temperatures to release alcohol vapors, which are then condensed and mixed with water to make the final product.

Proof   A measure of the percentage of alcohol in a beverage.

content was at least 50 percent, the gunpowder would burn; otherwise the water in the product would put out the flame. Thus, alcohol percentage is 50 percent of the given proof. For example, 80 proof whiskey or scotch is 40 percent alcohol by volume, and 100 proof vodka is 50 percent alcohol by volume. The proof of a beverage provides an indication of its strength. Lower-proof drinks will produce fewer alcohol effects than the same amounts of higher-proof drinks.

Most wines are between 12 and 15 percent alcohol, and ales are between 6 and 8 percent. The alcoholic content of beers is between 2 and 6 percent, varying according to state laws and type of beer. Since the early 1980s, many breweries and wineries have been marketing "light" (low-calorie) and alcohol-reduced beers and wines. In an effort to alert consumers to the dangers of alcohol consumption, the government requires that warning labels be placed on alcoholic beverages.

Behavioral Effects

Behavioral changes caused by alcohol vary with the setting and with the individual. Alcohol may make shy people less inhibited and more willing to talk to others. Conversely, it may make a depressed person even more depressed. In people reluctant to share emotions, it may bring out violence and aggression. In many cases, alcohol will do for the drinker what the drinker expects and wants it to do, making it possible for the user to blame his or her inappropriate behavior on the alcohol.

Blood alcohol concentration (BAC) is the ratio of alcohol to total blood volume. It is the factor used to measure the physiological and behavioral effects of alcohol. Despite individual differences, alcohol produces some general behavior effects depending on BAC (see Table 8.2). At a BAC of

0.02, a person feels slightly relaxed and in a good mood. At 0.05, relaxation increases, there is some motor impairment, and a willingness to talk becomes apparent. At 0.08, the person feels euphoric and there is further motor impairment. At 0.10, the depressant effects of alcohol become apparent, drowsiness sets in, and motor skills are further impaired, followed by a loss of judgment. Thus a driver may not be able to estimate distances or speed, and some drinkers lose their ability to make value-related decisions and may do things they would not do when sober. As BAC increases, the drinker suffers increased physiological and psychological effects. All these changes are negative. No skills or functions are enhanced because of alcohol ingestion. Rather, physical and mental functions are all impaired.

People can acquire physical and psychological tolerance to the effects of alcohol through regular use. The nervous system adapts over time, so greater amounts of alcohol are required to produce the same physiological and psychological effects. Some people can learn to modify their behavior so that they appear to be sober even when their BAC is quite high. This ability is called **learned behavioral tolerance.**

TABLE 8.2
Psychological and Physical Effects of Various Blood-Alcohol Concentration Levels*

NUMBER OF DRINKS†	BLOOD-ALCOHOL CONCENTRATION (%)	PSYCHOLOGICAL AND PHYSICAL EFFECTS
1	0.02–0.03	No overt effects, slight mood elevation.
2	0.05–0.06	Feeling of relaxation, warmth; slight decrease in reaction time and in fine-muscle coordination.
3	0.08–0.09	Balance, speech, vision, and hearing slightly impaired; feelings of euphoria, increased confidence; loss of motor coordination.
	0.10	Legal intoxication in most states; some have lower limits.
4	0.11–0.12	Coordination and balance becoming difficult; distinct impairment of mental faculties, judgment.
5	0.14–0.15	Major impairment of mental and physical control; slurred speech, blurred vision, lack of motor skills.
7	0.20	Loss of motor control—must have assistance in moving about; mental confusion.
10	0.30	Severe intoxication; minimum conscious control of mind and body.
14	0.40	Unconsciousness, threshold of coma.
17	0.50	Deep coma.
20	0.60	Death from respiratory failure.

*For each hour elapsed since the last drink, subtract 0.015 percent blood-alcohol concentration, or approximately one drink.
†One drink = one beer (4 percent alcohol, 12 ounces), one highball (1 ounce whiskey), or one glass table wine (5 ounces).
Source: Modified from data given in Ohio State Police Driver Information Seminars and the National Clearinghouse for Alcohol and Alcoholism Information, Rockville, MD.

Absorption and Metabolism

Unlike the molecules found in most other ingestible foods and drugs, alcohol molecules are sufficiently small and fat-soluble to be absorbed throughout the entire length of the gastrointestinal system. A negligible amount of alcohol is absorbed through the lining of the mouth. Approximately 20 percent of ingested alcohol is diffused through the stomach lining into the bloodstream. Nearly 80 percent of the liquid passes through the linings of the upper third of the small intestine. Absorption into the bloodstream is rapid and complete.

How quickly your body will absorb alcohol is influenced by several factors: the alcohol concentration in your drink, the amount of alcohol you consume, the amount of food in your stomach, pylorospasm, and your mood. The higher the concentration of alcohol, the more rapidly it is absorbed in your digestive tract. As a rule, wine and beer are absorbed more slowly than distilled beverages. Carbonated alcoholic beverages are absorbed more rapidly than those containing no sparkling additives, or fizz. Carbonated beverages such as champagne, carbonated wines, and drinks served with mixers cause the pyloric valve—the opening from the stomach into the small intestine—to relax, thereby emptying the contents of the stomach more rapidly into the small intestine. Since the small intestine is the site of the greatest absorption of alcohol, carbonated beverages increase the rate of absorption. On the other hand, if your stomach is full, absorption is slowed because the surface area exposed to alcohol is smaller. A full stomach also retards the emptying of alcoholic beverages into your small intestine.

In addition, the more alcohol you consume, the longer absorption takes. Alcohol can irritate the digestive system, causing a spasm in the pyloric valve (pylorospasm). When the pyloric valve is closed, nothing can move from the stomach to the upper third of the small intestine, so absorption is slowed. If the irritation continues, it can cause vomiting.

Mood is another influence on the rate of absorption, since emotions affect how long it takes for the contents of the stomach to empty into the intestine. Powerful moods, such as stress and tension, are likely to cause the stomach to "dump" its contents into the small intestine. That is why alcohol is absorbed much more rapidly when people are tense than when they are relaxed.

Alcohol is metabolized in the liver, where it is converted by the enzyme alcohol dehydrogenase to acetaldehyde. It is then rapidly oxidized to acetate, converted to carbon dioxide and water, and eventually excreted from the body. Acetaldehyde is a toxic chemical that can cause immediate symptoms such as nausea and vomiting as well as long-term effects such as liver damage. A very small portion of alcohol is excreted unchanged by the kidneys, lungs, and skin.

Like food, alcohol contains calories. Proteins and carbohydrates (starches and sugars) each contain 4 kilocalories (kcal) per gram. Fat contains 9 kcal per gram. Alcohol, although similar in structure to carbohydrates, contains 7 kcal per gram. The body uses the calories in alcohol in the same manner it uses those found in carbohydrates: for immediate energy or for storage as fat if not immediately needed.

A drinker's BAC depends on weight and body fat, the water content in body tissues, the concentration of alcohol in the beverage consumed, the rate of consumption, and the volume of alcohol consumed. Heavier people have larger body surfaces through which to diffuse alcohol; therefore, they have lower concentrations of alcohol in their blood than do thin people after drinking the same amount. Because alcohol does not diffuse as rapidly into body fat as into water, alcohol concentration is higher in a person with more body fat. Because a woman is likely to have more body fat and less water in her body tissues than a man of the same weight, she will be more intoxicated than a man after drinking the same amount of alcohol.

▶ *Alcohol Poisoning*   Alcohol poisoning occurs much more frequently than people realize, and all too often it can cause death. Drinking large amounts of alcohol in a short period of time can cause the blood alcohol level to reach the lethal range relatively quickly. Alcohol, either used alone or in combination with other drugs, is probably responsible for more toxic overdose deaths than any other drug. The scenerios on and between college campuses are quite similar as students try to outdrink each other. At parties, students often consume beer rapidly, seeking that quick high or feeling of numbness or take part in drinking games that penalize the "losers," who are often already intoxicated, by requiring them to take a succession of drinks. But these games can take a turn that can be anything but fun.

Death from alcohol poisoning can be caused by either central nervous system (CNS) and respiratory depression or the inhalation of vomit or fluid into the lungs. The amount of alcohol it takes for a person to become unconscious is dangerously close to the lethal dose. Signs of alcohol poisoning include the following: being unable to be aroused; a weak, rapid pulse; an unusual or irregular breathing pattern; and cool (possibly damp), pale, or bluish skin. If you are with someone who has been drinking heavily and exhibits these conditions, or if you are unsure about the person's condition, call 911 for emergency help right away.

Blood alcohol concentration (BAC)   The ratio of alcohol to total blood volume; the factor used to measure the physiological and behavioral effects of alcohol.

Learned behavioral tolerance   The ability of heavy drinkers to modify their behavior so that they appear to be sober even when they have high BAC levels.

········· **WHAT DO YOU THINK?**

Have you thought that BAC is only based upon the amount of alcohol you drink? What other factors contribute to BAC? Are these factors different for men and women?

▶ *Women and Alcohol*   Body fat is not the only contributor to the differences in alcohol's effects on men and women. Compared to men, women appear to have half as much alcohol hydrogenase, the enzyme that breaks down alcohol in the stomach before it has a chance to get to the bloodstream and the brain. Therefore, if a man and a woman both drink the same amount of alcohol, the woman's BAC will be approximately 30 percent higher than the man's, leaving her more vulnerable to slurred speech, careless driving, and other drinking-related impairments. In female alcoholics, virtually none of the alcohol ingested is broken down in the stomach before it enters the bloodstream.

▶ *Breathalyzer and Other Tests*   The breathalyzer tests used by law enforcement officers are designed to determine BAC based on the amount of alcohol exhaled in the breath. Urinalysis can also yield a BAC based on the concentration of unmetabolized alcohol in the urine. Both breath analysis and urinalysis are used to determine whether a driver is legally intoxicated, but blood tests are more accurate measures. An increasing number of states are requiring blood tests for people suspected of driving under the influence of alcohol. In some states, refusal to take either the breath or the urine test results in immediate revocation of the person's driver's license.

Immediate Effects

The most dramatic effects produced by ethanol occur within the CNS. The primary action of the drug is to reduce the frequency of nerve transmissions and impulses at synaptic junctions. This reduction of nerve transmissions results in a significant depression of CNS functions, with resulting decreases in respiratory rate, pulse rate, and blood pressure. As CNS depression deepens, vital functions become noticeably depressed. In extreme cases, coma and death can result.

Alcohol is a diuretic, causing increased urinary output. Although this effect might be expected to lead to automatic **dehydration** (loss of water), the body actually retains water, most of it in the muscles or in the cerebral tissues. This is because water is usually pulled out of the **cerebrospinal fluid** (fluid within the brain and spinal cord), leading to what is known as mitochondrial dehydration at the cell level within the nervous system. Mitochondria are miniature organs within cells that are responsible for specific functions. They rely heavily upon fluid balance. When mitochondrial dehydration occurs from drinking, the mitochondria cannot carry out their normal functions, resulting in symptoms that include the "morning-after" headaches suffered by some drinkers.

Alcohol is also an irritant to the gastrointestinal system and may cause indigestion and heartburn if taken on an empty stomach. Long-term use of alcohol causes repeated irritation that has been linked to cancers of the esophagus and stomach. In addition, people who engage in brief drinking sprees during which they consume unusually high amounts of alcohol put themselves at risk for irregular heartbeat or even total loss of heart rhythm, which can cause disruption in blood flow and possible damage to the heart muscle.

A **hangover** is often experienced the morning after a drinking spree. The symptoms of a hangover are familiar to most of you who drink: headache, upset stomach, anxiety, depression, thirst, and, in severe cases, an almost overwhelming desire to crawl into a hole and die. People who get hangovers often also smoke too much, stay up too late, or engage in other behaviors likely to leave them feeling unwell the next day. The causes of hangovers are not well known, but the effects of **congeners** are suspected. Congeners are forms of alcohol that are metabolized more slowly than ethanol and are more toxic. Your body metabolizes the congeners after the ethanol is gone from your system, and their toxic by-products are thought to contribute to the hangover. In addition, alcohol upsets the water balance in the body, resulting in excess urination and thirst the next day. Muscle aches, nausea caused by increased production of hydrochloric acid irritating the stomach lining, and muscle aches from overdoing on the drinking spree can all be part of a hangover. It usually takes 12 hours to recover from a hangover. Bed rest, solid food, and aspirin may help relieve the discomforts of a hangover, but unfortunately, nothing cures it but time.

▶ *Drug Interactions*   When you use any drug (and alcohol is a drug), you need to be aware of the possible interactions with any prescription drugs, over-the-counter drugs, or other drugs you are taking or considering taking. Table 8.3 summarizes some possible interactions. Note that alcohol may cause a negative interaction even with aspirin.

Long-Term Effects

Doctors have sobering news for those who think a little alcohol is good for their health. According to a 1994 Harvard Medical School study, anything more than a drink a day may be too much of a good thing. Men who had two to four drinks a week had the lowest rate of death from all causes during an 11-year study. Beyond a drink a day, the risk went up sharply. Those who averaged two or more drinks a day had a death rate that was 63 percent higher than that of nondrinkers.

Researchers found that the lower risk of dying from heart disease was offset by an increase in cancer in those who had more than one drink a day. This new study suggests that the current definition of one to three drinks a day as healthy, moderate drinking should be lowered considerably. The study was conducted only on men, so the results may not hold true for women. However, this should not be taken as a rationale for women to drink more in the name of good health.[8]

▶ *Effects on the Nervous System*   The nervous system is especially sensitive to alcohol. Even people who drink moderately experience shrinkage in brain size and weight and a loss

TABLE 8.3
Drugs and Alcohol: Actions and Interactions

DRUG CLASS/TRADE NAME(S)	EFFECTS WITH ALCOHOL
Antialcohol: Antabuse	Severe reactions to even small amounts: headache, nausea, blurred vision, convulsions, coma, possible death.
Antibiotics: Penicillin, Cyantin	Reduces therapeutic effectiveness.
Antidepressants: Elavil, Sinequan, Tofranil, Nardil	Increased central nervous system (CNS) depression, blood pressure changes. Combined use of alcohol and MAO inhibitors, a specific type of antidepressant, can trigger massive increases in blood pressure, even brain hemorrhage and death.
Antihistamines: Allerest, Dristan	Drowsiness and CNS depression. Impairs driving ability.
Aspirin: Anacin, Excedrin, Bayer	Irritates stomach lining. May cause gastrointestinal pain, bleeding.
Depressants: Valium, Ativan, Placidyl	Dangerous CNS depression, loss of coordination, coma. High risk of overdose and death.
Narcotics: heroin, codeine, Darvon	Serious CNS depression. Possible respiratory arrest and death.
Stimulants: caffeine, cocaine	Masks depressant action of alcohol. May increase blood pressure, physical tension.

Source: Reprinted by permission from Drugs and Alcohol: Simple Facts about Alcohol and Drug Combinations *(Phoenix: DIN Publications, 1988), no. 121.*

of some degree of intellectual ability. The damage that results from alcohol use is localized primarily in the left side of the brain, which is responsible for written and spoken language, logic, and mathematical skills. The degree of shrinkage appears to be directly related to the amount of alcohol consumed. In terms of memory loss, the evidence suggests that having one drink every day is better than saving up for a binge and consuming seven or eight drinks in a night. The amount of alcohol consumed at one time is critical. Alcohol-related brain damage can be partially reversed with good nutrition and staying sober.

▶ *Cardiovascular Effects*   The cardiovascular system is affected by alcohol in a number of ways. Evidence suggests

that the effect of alcohol on the heart is not all bad. Numerous studies have associated light to moderate alcohol consumption (no more than two drinks a day) with a reduced risk of coronary artery disease. Several mechanisms have been proposed to explain how this might happen. The strongest evidence favors an increase in high-density lipoprotein (HDL) cholesterol, which is known as the "good" cholesterol. Studies have shown that drinkers have higher levels of HDL. Another factor that might help is through an *antithrombotic* effect. Alcohol consumption is associated with a decrease in clotting factors that contribute to the development of atherosclerosis.

However, drinking is not recommended as a preventive measure against heart disease because there are many more cardiovascular health hazards than benefits from alcohol consumption. Alcohol contributes to high blood pressure and slightly increased heart rate and cardiac output.

Dehydration   Loss of fluids from body tissues.

Cerebrospinal fluid   Fluid within and surrounding the brain and spinal cord tissues.

Hangover   The physiological reaction to excessive drinking, including such symptoms as headache, upset stomach, anxiety, depression, diarrhea, and thirst.

Congeners   Forms of alcohol that are metabolized more slowly than ethanol and produce toxic by-products.

Cirrhosis   The last stage of liver disease associated with chronic heavy use of alcohol during which liver cells die and damage is permanent.

▶ *Liver Disease*   One of the most common diseases related to alcohol abuse is **cirrhosis** of the liver. It is among the top 10 causes of death in the United States. One result of heavy drinking is that the liver begins to store fat—a condition known as *fatty liver*. If there is insufficient time between drinking episodes, this fat cannot be transported to storage sites and the fat-filled liver cells stop functioning. Continued drinking can cause a further stage of liver deterioration called *fibrosis*, in which the damaged area of the liver develops fibrous scar tissue. Cell function can be partially restored at this stage with proper nutrition and abstinence from alcohol. If the person continues to drink, however, cirrhosis results. At this

ACCESSING YOUR HEALTH ON THE INTERNET

Check out the following Internet sites related to alcohol.

1. *Drinking: A Student's Guide.*   This web site is designed exclusively for student use. It is oriented to answering questions and concerns students have about drinking. An online knowledge test provides immediate feedback about alcohol intake. This web site also provides facts and statistics, guidelines to low-risk drinking, and risk-reduction techniques.

    http//www.glness.com/ndhs

2. *National Institute on Alcohol Abuse and Alcoholism.*   This national government agency provides information on the latest findings in alcohol research, including direct links to statistical information, abstracts, and surveillance reports.

    http//www.niaaa.nih.gov/

3. *NicNet.*   This web site covers a wide range of topics related to tobacco use, including prevention, cessation, policy issues, pipe smokers, cigars, and access to the most current news regarding tobacco.

    http://tobacco.arizona.edu

4. *TIPS (Tobacco Information and Prevention Source).*   The web site provides access to a variety of information regarding tobacco use in the United States, with specific information for and about young people.

    http://www.cdc.gov/tobacco

point, the liver cells die and the damage is permanent. **Alcoholic hepatitis** is a serious condition resulting from prolonged use of alcohol. A chronic inflammation of the liver develops, which may be fatal in itself or progress to cirrhosis.

▶ *Cancer*   Heavy drinkers are at higher risk for certain types of cancer, particularly cancers of the gastrointestinal tract. The repeated irritation caused by long-term use of alcohol has been linked to cancers of the esophagus, stomach, mouth, tongue, and liver. Research has also shown a link between breast cancer and moderate levels of alcohol consumption in women. One compelling report has demonstrated that "drinkers of three or more glasses of alcoholic beverages per day appear to be at greater risk for breast cancer."[9] A 1994 study of male drinkers by the Harvard Medical School showed a 12 percent increased risk for cancer for those who had only one drink a day and 123 percent for those who had two drinks a day. It is unclear how alcohol exerts its carcinogenic effects, though it is thought that it in-

hibits the absorption of carcinogenic substances, permitting them to be taken to sensitive organs.

▶ *Other Effects*   An irritant to the gastrointestinal system, alcohol may cause indigestion and heartburn if ingested on an empty stomach. It also damages the mucous membranes and can cause inflammation of the esophagus, chronic stomach irritation, problems with intestinal absorption, and chronic diarrhea.

Alcohol abuse is a major cause of chronic inflammation of the pancreas, the organ that produces digestive enzymes and insulin. Chronic abuse of alcohol inhibits enzyme production, which further inhibits the absorption of nutrients. Drinking alcohol can block the absorption of calcium, a nutrient that strengthens bones. This should be of particular concern to women, for as women age their risk for osteoporosis (bone thinning and calcium loss) increases. Heavy consumption of alcohol worsens this condition.

Evidence also suggests that alcohol impairs the body's ability to recognize and fight foreign bodies such as bacteria and viruses. The relationship between alcohol and AIDS is unclear, especially since some of the populations at risk for AIDS are populations that are also at risk for alcohol abuse. But any stressor like alcohol with a known effect on the immune system would probably contribute to the development of the disease.

Alcohol and Pregnancy

Of the 30 known teratogens in the environment, alcohol is one of the most dangerous and common. Alcohol can have harmful effects on fetal development. A disorder called **fetal alcohol syndrome (FAS)** is associated with alcohol consumption throughout pregnancy. Alcohol consumed during the first trimester poses the greatest threat to organ development; exposure during the last trimester, when the brain is developing rapidly, is most likely to affect CNS development. FAS is the third most common birth defect and the second leading cause of mental retardation in the United States. The incidence of FAS is estimated to be 1 to 2 in every 1,000 live births. It is the most common preventable cause of mental impairments in the Western world.

FAS occurs when alcohol ingested by the mother passes through the placenta into the infant's bloodstream. Because the fetus is so small, its BAC will be much higher than that of the mother. Thus, consumption of alcohol during pregnancy can affect the infant far more seriously than it does the mother. Among the symptoms of FAS are mental retardation, small head, tremors, and abnormalities of the face, limbs, heart, and brain.

Children with a history of prenatal alcohol exposure, but without all the physical or behavioral symptoms of FAS, may be categorized as having **fetal alcohol effects (FAE).** FAE is estimated to occur three to four times as often as FAS, although it is much less recognized. The signs of FAE in newborns are low birth weight and irritability, and there may be permanent mental impairment. Infants whose mothers habitually consumed more than 3 ounces of alcohol (approximately six drinks) in a short time period when pregnant are at high risk for FAS. Risk levels for babies whose mothers consume smaller amounts are uncertain.

Alcohol can also be passed to a nursing baby through breast milk. For this reason, most doctors advise nursing mothers not to drink for at least four hours before nursing their babies and preferably to abstain altogether.

Several factors determine how alcohol affects individuals; many are related to sound decision making. Irresponsible consumption of alcohol can easily result in disaster.

·········· **WHAT DO YOU THINK?**

Why do we hear so little about FAS in this country when it is the third most common birth defect and second leading cause of mental retardation? Is this a reflection of our society's denial of alcohol as a dangerous drug?

Drinking and Driving

The leading cause of death for all age groups from 5 to 34 years old (including college students) is traffic accidents. Approximately 41 percent of all traffic fatalities are alcohol-related.[10] Nationally, we have approximately 16,600 automobile crashes per year.[11] Unfortunately, college students are overrepresented in alcohol-related crashes. The College Alcohol Study findings indicated that 20 percent of nonbingers, 43 percent of occasional bingers, and 59 percent of frequent bingers reported driving while intoxicated.[12] Furthermore, it is estimated that three out of every ten Americans will be involved in an alcohol-related accident at some time in their lives.[13] Studies show that those involved in car crashes who had been drinking have a 40 to 50 percent higher chance of dying than nondrinkers involved in car crashes.

In 1997, the 16,189 alcohol-related traffic fatalities (ARTFs) represent a 32 percent reduction from the ARTF reported in 1987. From 1987 to 1997, intoxication rates (BAC of 0.10 g/dl or greater) decreased for drivers of all age groups

involved in fatal crashes. The highest intoxication rates in fatal crashes in 1997 were recorded for drivers 21 to 24 years old (26.3 percent), followed by ages 25 to 34 (23.8 percent) and 35 to 44 (22.1 percent). Approximately 1.5 million drivers were arrested in 1996 for driving under the influence of alcohol. This is an arrest rate of 1 for every 122 licensed drivers in the United States.[14]

Several factors probably contributed to these reductions in ARTFs: the enactment of laws raising the drinking age to 21 and stricter enforcement of these laws; increased emphasis on zero tolerance (laws prohibiting those under 21 from driving with *any* detectable BAC); and the educational and other prevention programs designed to discourage drinking and driving. Most states have set 0.10 percent as the BAC at which drivers are considered to be legally drunk. However, 16 states have lowered the standard to 0.08 percent: California, Florida, Alabama, Hawaii, Idaho, Illinois, Kansas, Maine, New Hampshire, New Mexico, North Carolina, Oregon, Utah, Vermont, Virginia, and Washington. Legislators in many other states are trying to follow this lead.[15] National groups such as MADD (Mothers Against Drunk Driving) go as far as tracking drunk driving cases through the court systems to ensure that drunk drivers are punished.

Despite all these measures, the risk of being involved in an alcohol-related automobile crash remains substantial. Researchers have shown a direct relationship between the amount of alcohol in a driver's bloodstream and the likelihood of a crash occurring. A driver with a BAC level of 0.10 percent has approximately 10 times the likelihood of being involved in a car accident as a driver who has not been drinking. At a BAC of 0.15 on weekend nights, the likelihood of dying in a single-vehicle crash is more than 380 times higher than for nondrinkers. Alcohol involvement is highest during nighttime

Alcoholic hepatitis   Condition resulting from prolonged use of alcohol in which the liver is inflamed. It can result in death.

Fetal alcohol syndrome (FAS)   A disorder that may affect the fetus when the mother consumes alcohol during pregnancy. Among its effects are mental retardation, small head, tremors, and abnormalities of the face, limbs, heart, and brain.

Fetal alcohol effects (FAE)   A syndrome describing children with a history of prenatal alcohol exposure but without all the physical or behavioral symptoms of FAS. Among its symptoms are low birth weight, irritability, and possible permanent mental impairment.

(9 P.M. to 6 A.M.) single-vehicle crashes, in which 65 percent of fatally injured passenger vehicle drivers in 1997 had BACs at or over 0.10 percent. Only 25 percent of fatally injured drivers involved in nighttime single-vehicle crashes had no alcohol in their blood. Not only does the time of day increase your risk of being involved in an alcohol-related crash, it also makes a difference whether it is a weekday or weekend. In 1997, 29 percent of all fatal crashes during the week were alcohol-related, compared with 52 percent on weekends.[16]

ALCOHOLISM

Alcohol use becomes **alcohol abuse** or **alcoholism** when it interferes with work, school, or social and family relationships or when it entails any violation of the law, including driving under the influence (DUI).

How, Why, Who?

As with other drug addicts, tolerance, psychological dependence, and withdrawal symptoms must be present to qualify a drinker as an addict. Addiction results from chronic use over a period of time that may vary from person to person. Problem drinkers or irresponsible users are not necessarily alcoholics. The stereotype of the alcoholic on skid row applies to only 5 percent of the alcoholic population. The remaining 95 percent of alcoholics live in some type of extended family unit. They can be found at all socioeconomic levels and in all professions, ethnic groups, geographical locations, religions, and races. You have a 1 in 10 risk of becoming an alcoholic. Moreover, 25 percent of the American population (50 million people) is affected by the alcoholism of a friend or family member. The 1998 National Household Survey on Drug Abuse found that 12 million Americans were heavy drinkers and 33 million were binge drinkers. Studies suggest that the lifetime risk of alcoholism in the United States is about 10 percent for men and 3 percent for women.

Recognition of an alcohol problem is often extremely difficult. Alcoholics themselves deny their problem, often making such statements as, "I can stop any time I want to. I just don't want to right now." Their families also tend to deny the existence of a problem, saying things like, "He really has been under a lot of stress lately. Besides, he only drinks beer." The fear of being labeled a "problem drinker" often prevents people from seeking help.

Women are the fastest-growing component of the population of alcohol abusers. They tend to become alcoholic at a later age and after fewer years of heavy drinking than do male alcoholics. Women at highest risk for alcohol-related problems are those who are unmarried but living with a partner, are in their 20s or early 30s, or have a husband or partner who drinks heavily.

The Causes of Alcoholism

We know that alcoholism is a disease with biological, psychological, and social/environmental components, but we do not know what role each of these components plays in the disease.

predisposes them → all depends on if they drink or not

▶ **Biological and Family Factors** Research into the hereditary and environmental causes of alcoholism has found higher rates of alcoholism among family members of alcoholics. In fact, according to researchers, alcoholism is four to five times more common among the children of alcoholics than in the general population.

Male alcoholics, especially, are more likely than nonalcoholics to have alcoholic parents and siblings. Two distinct subtypes of alcoholism have provided important information about the inheritance of alcoholism. *Type 1 alcoholics* are drinkers who had at least one parent of either sex who was a problem drinker and who grew up in an environment that encouraged heavy drinking. Their drinking is reinforced by environmental events during which there is heavy drinking. Type 1 alcohol abusers share certain personality characteristics. They avoid novelty and harmful situations and are concerned about the thoughts and feelings of others. *Type 2 alcoholism* is seen in males only. These alcoholics are typically the biological sons of alcoholic fathers who have a history of both violence and drug use. Type 2 alcoholics display the opposite characteristics of Type 1 alcoholics. They do not seek social approval, they lack inhibition, and they are prone to novelty-seeking behavior.[17]

A 1984 study found a strong relationship between alcoholism and alcoholic patterns within the family.[18] Children with one alcoholic parent had a 52 percent chance of becoming alcoholics themselves. With two alcoholic parents, the chances of becoming alcoholic jumped to 71 percent. The researchers felt that both heredity and environment were significant factors in the development of alcoholism, but were reluctant to specify precisely how these factors worked.

▶ **Social and Cultural Factors** Although a family history of alcoholism may predispose a person to problems with alcohol, there are numerous other factors that may mitigate or exacerbate that tendency. Furthermore, researchers now believe that social and cultural factors may trigger the affliction for many people who are not genetically predisposed to alcoholism. Some people begin drinking as a way to dull the pain of an acute loss or an emotional or social problem. For example, college students may drink to escape the stress of college life, or problems may trigger a search for an anesthetic. Unfortunately, the emotional discomfort that

Alcohol abuse (alcoholism) Use of alcohol that interferes with work, school, or personal relationships or that entails violations of the law.

CONSUMER HEALTH

Alcohol Advertising

A mother was reading a book about animals to her 3-year-old daughter:

> Mother: *"What does the cow say?"*
> Child: *"Moooo!"*
> Mother: *"Great! What does the cat say?"*
> Child: *"Meow."*
> Mother: *"Oh, you're so smart! What does the frog say?"*
> And this wide-eyed little 3-year-old looked up at her mother and replied, *"Buuuuuuud."*

(Author unknown)

Frogs and lizards, Clydesdale horses, Spuds MacKenzie, and the malt liquor bull. What do they all have in common? They are associated with an alcoholic beverage. Can you name the beverages? Chances are you can name at least some of them. The opening joke is a common one flying around on e-mail these days. Does the Budweiser frog's voice echo in your ears? That is exactly the effect that marketing and advertising departments want to create in consumers—product identification.

Alcohol advertising, including sponsorships, special promotions, and unmeasured media marketing, is a powerful force in this country for teaching young people and adults how to drink, when to drink, where to drink, and what drinking can do for them.[1] A look at some of the biggest sporting events on television reveals the potential impact of a well-placed ad. The Super Bowl, one of the world's most-watched television events, offers a company a captured audience that numbers in the millions. It is in this setting that the Bud Bowl was launched, as well as the ongoing saga of the Budweiser frogs and lizards. Alcohol advertising helps create an environment that suggests that consumption, and possibly even overconsumption, is a normal activ-

ity. While the brewing industry claims that marketing does not influence attitudes, behaviors, or beliefs, it continues to spend $600 million per year on radio and TV ads and another $90 million per year on print ads. The hard liquor industry spends $230 million per year on print ads, its only medium of advertising. While the alcohol industry argues that the main intention of its advertising is to "induce people to switch brands," numerous studies have found that alcohol advertising does contribute to increased consumption of alcohol.[2]

ADVERTISING AND YOUTH

The joke at the start of this article suggests something insidious and frightening: Children remember and identify with clever ads that include cartoon characters, animation, or even cute pets. Children and adolescents are frequently exposed to alcohol ads through television; in fact, by the time people reach the age of 18 they will have seen more than 100,000 beer commercials. Studies show that the more beer commercials children watch, the more they expect to drink when they become adults.[3] Although these advertisements never overtly encourage children to drink, they certainly link the use of alcohol with having a good time, popularity, and/or success. The mere affiliation with major sporting events, which have large young audiences, hints at the positive relationship between alcohol and success. Public health experts are also becoming increasingly concerned about the way alcohol products are marketed in cyberspace. While representatives from the various alcohol companies deny any intentional motive to attract young audiences, more than 35 brands maintain colorful, slick web sites that use games, chat-lines, and cartoon characters to promote their products.[4]

ALCOHOL ADVERTISING AND COLLEGE STUDENTS

The alcohol industry knows a receptive market when it sees it. Each year, college students spend a reported 5.5 billion dol-

lars ($446 per student) on alcohol, consuming some 4 billion cans' worth of alcohol and accounting for 10 percent of total beer sales.[5] For brewers, student drinking spells not just current sales, but future profits as well, because most people develop loyalty to a specific beer between the ages of 18 and 24. To secure this lucrative market, brewers and other alcohol producers spend millions of dollars each year promoting their products to college students. One conservative estimate places annual expenditures for college marketing between $15 million and $20 million.[6] According to one survey, alcohol advertising of local specials in many college newspapers has increased by more than half over the past decade, stymieing college and community efforts to reduce binge drinking.[7]

Needless to say, alcohol and college have long had a symbiotic relationship, whether or not it is wanted. Movies like *Animal House* and special events like Spring Break have helped create a glamourized and almost romanticized vision of college drinking. But recent tragedies associated with binge drinking should remind us that alcohol is anything but romantic.

Sources:

1. "Images About Alcohol," part of the FACE Project, FACE-Truth and Clarity on Alcohol (Clare, MI, 1997).
2. H. Saffer, "Alcohol Advertising and Motor Vehicle Fatalities," *Alcohol Health and Research World,* 20 (1996).
3. J. Grube and L. Wallack, "Television Beer Advertising and Drinking Knowledge, Beliefs, and Intentions Among Schoolchildren," *American Journal of Public Health* 84 (1994): 254–259.
4. S. Schiesel, "On Web, New Threats to Young Are Seen," *New York Times Cyber Times* (online edition), 7 March, 1997.
5. D. Erenberg and G. Hacker, *Last Call: High Risk Bar Promotions That Target College Students,* Center for Science in the Public Interest, Washington, D.C., 1997, 9.
6. Ibid.
7. Ibid., 11.

causes many people to turn to alcohol also ultimately causes them to become even more uncomfortable as the depressant effect of the drug begins to take its toll. Thus, the person who is already depressed may become even more depressed, antagonizing friends and other social supports until they begin to turn away. Eventually, the drinker becomes physically dependent on the drug.

Family attitudes toward alcohol also seem to influence whether or not a person will develop a drinking problem. It has been clearly demonstrated that people who are raised in cultures in which drinking is a part of religious or ceremonial activities or in which alcohol is a traditional part of the family meal are less prone to alcohol dependency. In contrast, in societies in which alcohol purchase is carefully controlled and drinking is regarded as a rite of passage to adulthood, the tendency for abuse appears to be greater.[19]

Certain social factors have been linked with alcoholism as well. These include urbanization, the weakening of links to the extended family and a general loosening of kinship ties, increased mobility, and changing religious and philosophical values. Apparently, then, some combination of heredity and environment plays a decisive role in the development of alcoholism. Certain ethnic and racial groups also have special alcohol abuse problems (see the Health in a Diverse World box).

While no clear evidence exists one way or the other, health officials suspect that a person's attitudes about alcohol use may be influenced by the behavior patterns witnessed while growing up.

········· **WHAT DO YOU THINK?**

How was alcohol used in your family when you were growing up? Was alcohol used only on special occasions or not at all? How much do you think your family's attitudes and behaviors toward alcohol have shaped your behavior?

Effects of Alcoholism on the Family

Only recently have people begun to recognize that it is not only the alcoholic but the alcoholic's entire family that suffers from the disease of alcoholism. Although most research focuses on family effects during the late stages of alcoholism, the family unit actually begins to react early on as the person starts to show symptoms of the disease.

In dysfunctional families, children learn certain rules from a very early age: Don't talk, don't trust, and don't feel. These unspoken rules allow the family to avoid dealing with real problems and real issues.

Dealing with the far-reaching effects of alcoholism strains the alcoholic's entire family. Many families affected by alcoholism have no idea what normal family life is like. Family members unconsciously adapt to the alcoholic's behavior by adjusting their own behavior. To minimize their feelings about the alcoholic or out of love for him or her, family members take on various abnormal roles. Unfortunately, these roles actually help keep the alcoholic drinking. Children in such dysfunctional families generally assume at least one of the following roles:

- *Family hero:* tries to divert attention from the problem by being too good to be true.
- *Scapegoat:* draws attention away from the family's primary problem through delinquency or misbehavior.
- *Lost child:* becomes passive and quietly withdraws from upsetting situations.
- *Mascot:* disrupts tense situations by providing comic relief.

For children in alcoholic homes, life is a struggle. They have to deal with constant stress, anxiety, and embarrassment. Because the alcoholic is the center of attention, the children's wants and needs are often ignored. It is not uncommon for these children to be victims of violence, abuse, neglect, or incest. When these children grow up, they are much more prone to alcoholic behaviors themselves than are children from nonalcoholic families.

In the last decade, we have come to recognize the unique problems of adult children of alcoholics whose difficulties in life stem from a lack of parental nurturing during childhood. Among these problems are an inability to develop social attachments, a need to be in control of all emotions and situations, low self-esteem, and depression.

Fortunately, not all individuals who have grown up in alcoholic families are doomed to have lifelong problems. Many of these people as they mature develop a resiliency in response to their families' problems. They thus enter adulthood armed with positive strengths and valuable career-oriented skills, such as the ability to assume responsibility, strong organizational skills, and realistic expectations of their jobs and others.

Alcohol Availability and Diverse Populations

The impact of alcohol on different ethnic communities is underresearched. In particular, there is very little literature describing the effects of alcohol on Asian/Pacific Islander and American Indian/Alaska Native communities. Most of the available literature on the effects of alcohol in ethnic populations divides ethnic communities into the following five groups: African American, American Indian/Alaska Native, Asian/Pacific Islander, Latino or Hispanic, and White. It should be noted that within these communities, there are often other sociocultural factors involved as well. The major focus of this box is on alcohol availability and advertising in these particular ethnic communities.

ALCOHOL AVAILABILITY

The Trauma Foundation, located in San Francisco, California, has focused a great deal of its attention on the availability of alcohol and related social problems. Part of this work looks at alcohol outlets, which could include liquor stores, package stores, grocery stores, or any establishment that can sell alcohol in the bottle or can for take-out. Research has shown that, on the average, low-income Latino and African American communities have more alcohol outlets than do wealthy White communities. An overconcentration of alcohol outlets may adversely affect the economic and physical health of the community. For example, adding a single outlet in the average Los Angeles County city is estimated to result in about 2.7 more traffic injuries and 3.4 more assaults. In a study of three northern California cities, alcohol outlet density (the number of outlets in a given geographical area) was associated with American youth violence.

Alcohol outlets often display advertisements, which increases the blight associated with alcohol billboards. In one California study, it was found that Latino communities have 5 times as many advertisements as did predominantly White communities. Children walking home from school in Mexican American communities are exposed to 10 to 61 advertisements, depending on the route they take. Many of these advertisements are on the walls of alcohol outlets. While such figures may differ by communities across the country, the relationship is indeed applicable. Such concentrated advertising of alcohol is particularly problematic because alcohol advertising is associated with increased use of alcohol, and alcohol use has been linked with injuries and violence.

AFRICAN AMERICANS

While African Americans use less alcohol overall than do Whites and Latinos, the African-American community as a whole suffers a disproportionate level of alcohol problems. For example, in California, African Americans are more likely to die from alcohol-related homicide than are Whites, Latinos, or "Asian/Other." Also, African-American women suffer more social consequences from alcohol than do White women. Alcoholism is one of the most significant problems in the African-American community. Malt liquor advertisements are targeted almost exclusively at African-American communities. Nearly every inner-city neighborhood is plastered with malt liquor ads projecting images meant to appeal to Blacks.

LATINOS

Latino men consume more alcohol than do White and African-American men. The rates of alcohol-related injuries and death are higher for Latinos than for Whites in California. Among Latinos, 10.15 per 100,000 died in alcohol-related homicides as compared to 2.90 per 100,000 Whites. The circumstances may differ somewhat for women. While 48 percent of Latinas abstained from alcohol, they suffered nearly 3 times as many social consequences as did White women.

ASIANS/PACIFIC ISLANDERS

Research regarding Asians/Pacific Islanders in the United States is sparse; however, studies that have been done generally show that Asians/Pacific Islanders have lower alcohol-related death rates than do other ethnic groups. As a group, Asian Americans and Pacific Islanders also have lower than average rates of alcohol abuse. Asian taboos and community sanctions against excessive alcohol use are thought to protect against alcohol abuse.

AMERICAN INDIANS/ALASKA NATIVES

Alcohol abuse is one of the most widespread and severe health problems for American Indians and Alaska Natives, especially adolescents and young adults. Excessive drinking varies from tribe to tribe but is generally high in both men and women. The rate of alcoholism among American Indians is 2 to 3 times that of the general population, and the death rate from alcohol-related causes is about 8 times higher.

As we look toward the future, the answer to reducing this nation's alcohol-related problems may lie in the availability of alcohol, its pricing, and how it is marketed. State and local officials may need to limit the overconcentration of alcohol outlets in communities and work with the alcohol beverage industry to eliminate promotions that encourage heavy consumption among all ethnic groups.

Source: The Trauma Foundation, Alcohol-Related Injury and Violence; http://www.traumafdn.org/alcohol/ariv/index.html; and E. Hernandez, "The Effects of Alcohol on Latinos in California: A Report for Alcohol Awareness Month. CalPartners Coalition. April 1998.

According to the National Council on Alcoholism and Drug Dependency, in 1996, alcohol-related costs to society were at least $100 billion when health insurance, criminal justice, treatment costs, and lost productivity were factored in. Reportedly, alcoholism is directly and indirectly responsible for over 25 percent of the nation's medical expenses and lost earnings. Well over 50 percent of all child abuse cases are the result of alcohol-related problems. Finally, the costs in emotional health are impossible to measure.[20]

Women and Alcoholism

In the past, women have consumed less alcohol and have had fewer alcohol-related problems than have men. But now, greater percentages of women, especially college-aged women, are choosing to drink and are drinking more heavily. Studies indicate that there are now almost as many female as male alcoholics. However, there appear to be differences between men and women when it comes to alcohol abuse.

Risk factors for drinking problems among *all women* include
- a family history of drinking problems
- peer/spouse pressure to drink
- suffering from depression
- experiencing stress

Risk factors among *young women* include
- college attendance: women in college drink more, and more frequently, than they do after they graduate
- nontraditional, low-status, and part-time jobs, and unemployment
- being single, divorced, or separated

Risk factors among *middle-aged women* include
- loss of social roles (e.g., through divorce, children growing up and leaving the home)
- abuse of prescription drugs
- heavy drinking by spouse
- presence of other disorders, such as depression

Risk factors among *older women* include
- heavy- or problem-drinking spouse
- retirement, with a loss of social networks centered on the workplace

Drinking patterns among *different age groups* also differ, in that
- younger women drink more overall, drink more often, and experience more alcohol-related problems
- middle-aged women are more likely to develop drinking problems in response to a life-changing event
- older women are more likely than are older men to have developed drinking problems within the past 10 years[21]

Until recently, most of the research on treatment issues has been conducted as though everybody were a man. It is estimated that only 14 percent of women who need treatment get it. In one study, women cite potential loss of income, not wanting others to know they may have a problem, inability to pay for treatment, and the fear that treatment would not be confidential as reasons for not seeking treatment.[22] Another major obstacle for women is child care. Most traditional residential treatment centers do not allow women to bring their children with them.

WHAT DO YOU THINK?

Why do you think women appear to be drinking more heavily today than they did in the past? Does society look at men's and women's drinking habits in the same way? Can you think of ways to increase support for women in their recovery process?

RECOVERY

Despite the growing recognition of our national alcohol problem, fewer than 10 percent of alcoholics in the United States receive any care. Factors contributing to this low figure include an inability or unwillingness to admit to an alcohol problem; the social stigma attached to alcoholism; breakdowns in referral and delivery systems (failure of physicians or psychotherapists to follow up on referrals, client failure to follow through with recommended treatments, or failure of rehabilitation facilities to give quality care); and failure of the professional medical establishment to recognize and diagnose alcoholic symptoms among their patients.

Most alcoholics and problem drinkers who seek help have experienced a turning point or dramatic occurrence: a spouse walks out, taking children and possessions; the boss issues an ultimatum to dry out or ship out; the courtroom judge offers the alternatives of prison or a treatment center; a teenage child confesses embarrassment about bringing friends home; a friend or colleague confronts the person about drinking behavior. Regardless of the reasons for seeking help, the alcoholic ready for treatment has, in most cases, reached a low point. The alcoholic has finally recognized that alcohol controls his or her life. The first step on the road to recovery is to regain that control and to begin to assume responsibility for personal actions.

The Family's Role

Family members of an alcoholic sometimes take action before the alcoholic does. They may go to an organization or a treatment facility to seek help for themselves and their relative. An effective method of helping an alcoholic to confront the disease is a process called **intervention.** Essentially, an intervention is a planned confrontation with the alcoholic that involves several family members plus professional counselors. The family members express their love and concern, telling the alcoholic that they will no longer refrain from acknowledging the problem and affirming their support for appropriate treatment. A family intervention is the turning point for a growing number of alcoholics.

Treatment Programs

The alcoholic ready for help has several avenues for treatment: psychologists and psychiatrists specializing in the treatment of alcoholism, private treatment centers, hospitals specifically designed to treat alcoholics, community mental health facilities, and support groups such as Alcoholics Anonymous.

▶ **Private Treatment Facilities** Private treatment facilities have been making concerted efforts to attract patients through radio and television advertising. Upon admission to the treatment facility, the patient is given a complete physical exam to determine whether there are underlying medical problems that will interfere with treatment. Alcoholics who decide to quit drinking will experience withdrawal symptoms, including:

- Hyperexcitability
- Confusion
- Sleep disorders
- Convulsions
- Agitation

- Tremors of the hands
- Brief hallucinations
- Depression
- Headache
- Seizures

In a small percentage, alcohol withdrawal results in a severe syndrome known as **delirium tremens (DTs).** Delirium tremens is characterized by confusion, delusions, agitated behavior, and hallucinations.

For any long-term addict, medical supervision is usually necessary. *Detoxification, the process by which addicts end their dependence on a drug,* is commonly carried out in a medical facility, where patients can be monitored to prevent fatal withdrawal reactions. Withdrawal takes from 7 to 21 days. Shortly after detoxification, alcoholics begin their treatment for psychological addiction. Most treatment facilities keep their patients from three to six weeks. Treatment at

---

Intervention A planned confrontation with an alcoholic in which family members or friends express their concern about the alcoholic's drinking.

Delirium tremens (DTs) A state of confusion brought on by withdrawal from alcohol. Symptoms include hallucinations, anxiety, and trembling.

Alcoholics Anonymous (AA) An organization whose goal is to help alcoholics stop drinking; includes auxiliary branches such as Al-Anon and Alateen.

---

private treatment centers costs several thousand dollars, but some insurance programs or employers will assume most of this expense.

▶ *Family Therapy, Individual Therapy, and Group Therapy* Various individual and group therapies are also available. In family therapy, the person and family members gradually examine the psychological reasons underlying the addiction. In individual and group therapy with fellow addicts, alcoholics learn positive coping skills for use in situations that have regularly caused them to turn to alcohol. On some college campuses, the problems associated with alcohol abuse are so great that student health centers are opening their own treatment programs.

▶ *Other Types of Treatment* Two other treatments are drug and aversion therapy. Disulfiram (trade name: Antabuse) is the drug of choice for treating alcoholics. If alcohol is consumed, the drug causes such unpleasant effects as headache, nausea, vomiting, drowsiness, and hangover. These symptoms discourage the alcoholic from drinking. Aversion therapy is based on conditioning therapy. It works on the premise that the sight, smell, and taste of alcohol will acquire aversive properties if repeatedly paired with a noxious stimulus. For a period of 10 days, the alcoholic takes drugs that induce vomiting when combined with several drinks. These treatments work best in conjunction with some type of counseling.

Alcoholics Anonymous (AA) is a private, nonprofit, self-help organization founded in 1935. The organization, which relies upon group support to help people stop drinking, currently has over 1 million members and has branches all over the world. People attending their first AA meeting will find that no last names are ever used. Neither is anyone forced to speak. Members are taught to believe that their alcoholism is a lifetime problem. They are told that they may never use alcohol again. In meetings, they share their struggles with one another. They talk about the devastating effects alcoholism has had on their personal and professional lives. All members are asked to place their faith and control of the habit into the hands of a "higher power." The road to recovery is taken one step at a time. AA offers specialized meetings for gay, atheist, HIV-positive, and professional individuals with alcohol problems. *12-13 Steps*

Alcoholics Anonymous also has auxiliary groups to help spouses or partners, friends, and children of alcoholics. *Al-Anon* is the group dedicated to helping adult relatives and friends of alcoholics understand the disease and learn how they can contribute to the recovery process. Spouses and other adult loved ones examine their roles in their loved one's alcoholism and alternative behaviors are suggested.

Alateen, another AA-related organization, is designed to help adolescents live with an alcoholic parent or parents. They are taught that they are not at fault for their parents' problems. They learn skills to develop their self-esteem so they can function better socially.

The support gained from talking with others who have similar problems is one of the greatest benefits derived from participation in Al-Anon and Alateen. Many members learn how to exert greater control over their own lives.

Another self-help group is Women for Sobriety. This program was developed in 1975 out of a movement that recognized the differing needs of female alcoholics, who frequently have more severe problems than male alcoholics. Unlike AA meetings, where attendance can be quite large, each Women for Sobriety group has no more than 10 members. Another alternative to AA is Secular Organizations for Sobriety (SOS), which was founded in 1986 for people who cannot accept AA's spiritual emphasis.

Relapse

Success in recovery from alcoholism varies with the individual. A return to alcoholic habits often follows what appears to be a successful recovery. Some alcoholics never recover. Some partially recover and improve other parts of their lives, but remain dependent on alcohol. Many alcoholics refer to themselves as "recovering" throughout their lifetime; they never use the word *cured*.

Roughly 60 percent of alcoholics relapse (resume drinking) within the first three months of treatment. Why is the relapse rate so high? Treating an addiction requires more than getting the addict to stop using; it also requires getting the person to break a pattern of behavior that has dominated his or her life.

People who are seeking to regain a healthy lifestyle must not only confront their addiction, but must also guard against the tendency to relapse. Drinkers with compulsive personalities need to learn to understand themselves and take control. Others need to view treatment as a long-term process that takes a lot of effort beyond attending a weekly self-help group meeting. In order to work, a recovery program must offer the alcoholic ways to increase self-esteem and resume personal growth.

OUR SMOKING SOCIETY

Tobacco use is the single most preventable cause of death in the United States.[23] While tobacco companies continue to publish full-page advertisements refuting the dangers of smoking, nearly 430,000 Americans die each year of tobacco related diseases.[24] This is 50 times as many as will die from all illegal drugs combined. In addition, 10 million will suffer from diseases caused by tobacco. To date, tobacco is known to be the probable cause of about 25 diseases. One in every five deaths in the United States is smoking-related. New studies estimate that about half of all regular smokers die of smoking-related diseases. Therefore, any contention by the tobacco industry that tobacco use is not dangerous is irresponsible and ignores the growing weight of scientific evidence.

In 1998, an estimated 60 million Americans over age 12 smoked cigarettes. This represents a national smoking rate of 27.7 percent.[25] The average age at which Americans begin smoking is 11.6 years, and those who begin smoking this early have only a 15 percent chance of ever quitting.

The desire to model adult behavior plays a major role in teenagers' smoking. In households where one parent smokes, children are 90 percent more likely to take up smoking than are children from households where neither parent smokes. In addition, children whose peers smoke were found to have an 80 percent chance of adopting the habit.

How many teenagers smoke? In 1991, the Youth Risk Behavior Survey (YRBS) indicated that 27.5 percent of teenagers smoked; by 1997, 36.4 percent were current cigarette smokers. Overall, since 1991 cigarette smoking has increased at each grade level surveyed. In addition, teenage males reported a slightly higher (37.7 percent) rate of current cigarette use than did females (34.7 percent).[26] The number of teenagers who become daily smokers before the age of 18 is estimated to be more than 3,000 per day. Every day another 6,000 teens under the age of 18 smoke their first cigarette. The increase in cigarette use is attributed in part to the ready availability of tobacco products through vending machines and the aggressive drive by tobacco companies to entice young people to smoke.

Cigarette smoking in the United States results in untold loss of human potential, with thousands of Americans dying prematurely each year. As you can see in Table 8.4, the age group with the highest percentage of smokers is the 25- to 44-year-old group.

The percentage of Americans who smoke had dropped consistently throughout the 1980s. In fact, the rate reached a percentage of 26.5 in 1990, the lowest recorded in more than 30 years. As noted earlier, by 1995 the smoking rate had gone back up. Today, however, the rate is now under 25 percent, but because of continued population growth, there are 1.5 million more smokers today than there were 20 years ago.[27] So clearly, while inroads have been made, the fight continues.

Tobacco and Social Issues

The production and distribution of tobacco products in the United States and abroad involve many political and economic issues. During the 1980s, tobacco products were one of the United States' top five exports. Tobacco-growing states derive substantial income from tobacco production, and federal, state, and local governments benefit enormously from cigarette taxes.

More recently, nationwide health awareness has led to a decrease in the use of tobacco products among U.S. adults. To compensate for revenue losses, many major tobacco companies have merged with or purchased other corporations that market food or beverage products.

▶ **Advertising** According to estimates, the tobacco industry spends $14 million per day on advertising and promotional

lung cancer most preventable death

100 billion-$ a year for healthcare (50 billion per by non-smokers)

Percentage of Population That Smokes (Age 18 and Older) among Select Groups in the United States

	PERCENTAGE
United States Overall	24.7
Race	
American Indian/Alaska Native	36.2
Asian/Pacific Islander	16.6
Black	25.8
Hispanic	18.3
White	25.6
Age	
18–24	24.8
25–44	28.6
45–64	25.5
>64	13.0
Sex	
Male	27.0
Female	22.6
Education	
>12 years	18.4
12 years	29.5
<12 years	30.4
Income Level	
Below poverty level	32.5
At or above poverty level	23.8

Sources: Office on Smoking and Health, National Center for Chronic Disease Prevention and Health Promotion, 1998; Trends in Cigarette Smoking, American Lung Association, Epidemiology and Statistics Unit, February, 1998.

materials to keep their products in the public eye.[28] With the number of smokers declining by about 1 million each year, the industry must actively recruit new smokers. Campaigns are directed at all age, social, and ethnic groups, but because children and teenagers constitute 90 percent of all new smokers, much of the advertising has been directed toward them. Evidence of product recognition with underage smokers is clear: 86 percent of underage smokers prefer one of the three most heavily advertised brands—Marlboro, Newport, or Camel. One of the most blatant campaigns aimed at young adults was the Joe Camel ad campaign. After R. J. Reynolds introduced this campaign, Camel's market share among underage smokers jumped from 3 to 13.3 percent in 3 years. The company has since agreed to retire the Joe Camel character from their advertising campaigns.

Although the tobacco industry has been denied access to advertising on television and radio since 1970, the tobacco companies continue to find innovative ways in which to gain access to the media. For example, in 1994 Philip Morris and R. J. Reynolds received nearly $40 million in free television

time from their auto-racing sponsorships alone. Advertisements in women's magazines imply that cigarette smoking is a liberating thing to do. These ads have apparently been working. From 1975 through 1988, cigarette sales to women increased dramatically, particularly among 18-to-20-year-old women—the only age group of Americans whose rate of smoking continues to rise. Men are depicted charging over rugged terrain in off-road vehicles or riding bay stallions into the sunset in blatant appeals to a need to feel and appear masculine. *target → college students. chance of a person start smoking after age 23 is almost 0.*

▶ **Financial Costs to Society** The use of tobacco products is costly to all of us in terms of lost productivity and lost lives. In 1996, smoking-related illnesses cost the nation more than $100 billion. The economic burden of tobacco use was more than $50 billion in medical expenditures (these costs include hospital, physician, and nursing home expenditures; prescription drugs; and home health-care expenditures) and $50 billion in indirect costs (absentism, added cost of fire insurance, training costs to replace employees who die prematurely, disability payments, and so on).[29] Based on these figures, smoking costs each American approximately $398 per year. *most of cost is put on non-smokers*

College Students and Smoking

College and university students are especially vulnerable when they are placed in a new, often stressful social and academic environment. For many, the college years are their initial taste of freedom from daily parental supervision. Smoking may begin earlier, but most college students are a part of the significant age group in which people initiate smoking and become hooked. Recently, researchers at the Harvard School of Public Health surveyed 30,000 students (14,521 in 1993 and 15,103 in 1997) and were stunned to find an increase in smoking rates among college students. Long-held beliefs have indicated that increased education is associated with a decreased likelihood of smoking. This study, however, showed that smoking among college students increased 28 percent between 1993 and 1997, which challenges that belief. In addition, the 1997 study showed that more than a quarter of the student smokers began smoking in college.[30]

Apparently, 18- to 24-year-olds have become the new target for tobacco advertisers. The tobacco industry has set up very aggressive marketing promotions in bars, at music festivals, and the like, specifically targeted to this age group. Additionally, modeling and peer influence have an impact on smoking initiation. The potential impact for modeling and peer influence is heightened when one considers that while over half of campuses consider themselves smoke-free, they do permit smoking in residence hall rooms, student centers, and cafeterias, and many sell tobacco products in campus stores and student lounges.

A common perception on many college campuses is that students are not interested in smoking cessation efforts or that students perceive themselves to be occasional smokers who

- *lawsuits → Flordia, Reynolds + Phillip Morris*
- *Mississippi sued on behalf of non-smokers*
  $280 billion settlement

can quit whenever they want. However, the Harvard Study found that 50 percent of students had tried to quit in the past year, a rate much higher than the 30 percent of adults who try to quit. It is important that colleges and universities engage in antismoking efforts, have stricter control over tobacco advertising, provide smoke-free residence halls, and provide greater accessibility to smoking cessation programs.

> ·········· **WHAT DO YOU THINK?**
>
> Do you think the United States could ever be smoke-free? What are the greatest barriers to a smoke-free society? Would the economic impact on the tobacco industry be offset by the economic impact on the health-care industry?

TOBACCO AND ITS EFFECTS

Tobacco is available in several forms: Cigarettes, cigars, and pipes are used for burning and inhaling tobacco. Snuff is a finely ground form of tobacco that can be inhaled, chewed, or placed against the gums. Chewing tobacco, also known as "smokeless tobacco," is placed between the gums and teeth for sucking or chewing.

The chemical stimulant nicotine is the major psychoactive substance in all these tobacco products. In its natural form, nicotine is a colorless liquid that turns brown upon oxidation (exposure to oxygen). When tobacco leaves are burned in a cigarette, pipe, or cigar, nicotine is released and inhaled into the lungs. Sucking or chewing a quid of tobacco releases nicotine into the saliva, and the nicotine is then absorbed through the mucous membranes in the mouth.

Smoking is the most common form of tobacco use. Smoking delivers a strong dose of nicotine to the user, along with an additional 4,000 chemical substances. Among these chemicals are various gases and vapors that carry particulate matter in concentrations that are 500,000 times greater than the most air-polluted cities in the world.[31]

Particulate matter condenses in the lungs to form a thick, brownish sludge called tar. Tar contains various carcinogenic (cancer-causing) agents such as benzopyrene and chemical irritants such as phenol. Phenol has the potential to combine with other chemicals to contribute to the development of lung cancer.

In healthy lungs, millions of tiny hairlike tissues called cilia sweep away foreign matter. Once the foreign material is swept up and collected by the cilia, it can be expelled from the lungs by coughing. Nicotine impairs the cleansing function of the cilia by paralyzing them for up to one hour following the smoking of a single cigarette. Tars and other solids in tobacco smoke are thus allowed to accumulate and irritate sensitive lung tissue.

Tar and nicotine are not the only harmful chemicals in cigarettes. In fact, tars account for only 8 percent of the components of tobacco smoke. The remaining 92 percent is made up of various gases, the most dangerous of which is carbon monoxide. In tobacco smoke, the concentration of carbon monoxide is 800 times higher than the level considered safe by the U.S. Environmental Protection Agency (EPA). In the human body, carbon monoxide reduces the oxygen-carrying capacity of the red blood cells by binding with the receptor sites for oxygen. Smoking thus diminishes the capacity of the circulatory system to carry oxygen, causing oxygen deprivation in many body tissues.

The heat from tobacco smoke, which can reach 1,616 degrees Fahrenheit, is also harmful to the smoker. Inhaling hot gases and vapors exposes sensitive mucous membranes to irritating chemicals that weaken the tissues and contribute to the development of cancers of the mouth, larynx, and throat.

Filtered cigarettes designed to reduce levels of gases such as hydrogen cyanide and hydrocarbons may actually deliver more hazardous carbon monoxide to the user than do nonfiltered brands. Some smokers use low-tar and nicotine products as an excuse to smoke more cigarettes. This practice is self-defeating, because such smokers wind up exposing themselves to more harmful substances than they would if they smoked regular-strength cigarettes.

Clove cigarettes contain about 40 percent ground cloves (a spice) and about 60 percent tobacco. Many users mistakenly believe that these products are made entirely of ground cloves and that smoking them eliminates the risks associated with tobacco. In fact, clove cigarettes contain higher levels of tar, nicotine, and carbon monoxide than do regular cigarettes. In addition, the numbing effect of eugenol, the active ingredient in cloves, allows smokers to inhale the smoke more deeply.

Cigars. Those big stogies that we see celebrities and government figures puffing on these days are really nothing more than tobacco fillers wrapped in more tobacco. Since 1991, cigar sales in the United States have increased 250 percent, and we have been witness to what many refer to as a growing cigar culture. This growing fad has sparked the creation of special upscale smoking lounges and is especially popular among young men and women. This trend is fueled in part by the efforts of the tobacco industry to glamorize cigars and the willingness of famous celebrities to be photographed puffing on one. Among women, the industry seems to have tapped into an impulse among some to be slightly outrageous and to be liberated from old restrictions and stereotypes. Lost in this new fad is the perception among many people that cigars are safer than cigarettes, when in fact nothing could be further from the truth.[32] Though most premium cigars contain only pure tobacco and no additives, the smoke from cigars contains 23 poisons and 43 carcinogens. Clearly, as shown in Table 8.5, any argument about the safety of cigars is, well, a smokescreen.

Smoking as little as one cigar per day can increase the risk of several cancers, including cancer of the oral cavity (lip, tongue, mouth, and throat), esophagus, larynx, and lungs. Daily cigar smoking, especially for people who inhale, also increases the risk of heart disease (cigar smokers double their

TABLE 8.5

A Comparison between Filter Cigarettes and Cigars Shows a Marked Difference in Quantities

	FILTER CIGARETTE	REGULAR CIGAR
Weight	Approx. 0.68 g	Approx. 0.8 g
Nicotine	0.5–1.4 mg	1.7–5.2 mg
Tar	0.5–18 mg	16–110 mg
Carbon monoxide	0.5–18 mg	90–120 mg

Source: Downloaded from Youth Media Network, "No Such Thing as a Safe Smoke!" (1998): http://www.ymn.org/

risk of heart attack and stroke) and a type of lung disease known as chronic obstructive pulmonary disease (COPD). Smoking one or two cigars doubles the risk for oral cancers and esophageal cancer, compared with someone who has never smoked.

A common question asked is whether cigars are addictive. Most cigars have as much nicotine as several cigarettes, and regardless of whether a smoker inhales or not, nicotine is highly addictive. When cigar smokers inhale, nicotine is absorbed as rapidly as it is with cigarettes. For those cigar smokers who don't inhale, nicotine is still absorbed through the mucous membranes in the mouth, although more slowly.

Physiological Effects of Nicotine

Nicotine is a powerful central nervous system stimulant that produces a variety of physiological effects. Its stimulant action in the cerebral cortex produces an aroused, alert mental state. Nicotine also stimulates the adrenal glands, increasing the production of adrenaline. The physical effects of nicotine stimulation include increased heart and respiratory

• *aroused state*

Snuff   A powdered form of tobacco that is sniffed and absorbed through the mucous membranes in the nose or placed inside the cheek and sucked.

Chewing tobacco   A stringy type of tobacco that is placed in the mouth and then sucked or chewed.

Nicotine   The stimulant chemical in tobacco products.

Tar   A thick, brownish substance condensed from particulate matter in smoked tobacco.

Carbon monoxide   A gas found in cigarette smoke that binds at oxygen receptor sites in the blood.

Nicotine poisoning   Symptoms often experienced by beginning smokers; they include dizziness; diarrhea; lightheadedness; rapid, erratic pulse; clammy skin; nausea; and vomiting.

rate, constriction of blood vessels, and subsequent increased blood pressure because the heart must work harder to pump blood through the narrowed vessels. *short lived*

Nicotine decreases the stomach contractions that signal hunger. It also decreases blood sugar levels. These factors, along with decreased sensation in the taste buds, reduce appetite. For this reason, many smokers eat less than nonsmokers do and weigh, on average, 7 pounds less than nonsmokers. Beginning smokers usually feel the effects of nicotine with their first puff. These symptoms, called **nicotine poisoning,** include dizziness, lightheadedness, rapid, erratic pulse, clammy skin, nausea, vomiting, and diarrhea. The effects of nicotine poisoning cease as soon as tolerance to the chemical develops. Medical research indicates that tolerance develops almost immediately in new users, perhaps after the second or third cigarette. In contrast, tolerance to most other drugs, such as alcohol, develops over a period of months or years.

> ········· **WHAT DO YOU THINK?**
>
> Because nicotine is so highly addictive, should it be regulated as a controlled substance? Should more resources be directed toward treatment of nicotine addiction?

HEALTH HAZARDS OF SMOKING

Cigarette smoking adversely affects the health of every person who smokes. Each pack of cigarettes has a warning label alerting smokers to some of the dangers. Smoking has been estimated to be responsible for almost 19 percent of all U.S. deaths each year—that's almost one out of every five deaths. Each day cigarettes contribute to over 1,000 deaths from cancer, heart disease, and respiratory diseases.

Cancer

The American Cancer Society estimates that tobacco smoking is the cause of approximately 30 percent of all deaths from cancer and of more than 85 to 90 percent of all cases of lung cancer. Lung cancer is the leading cause of cancer deaths in the United States. It is estimated that there will be 171,500 *new* cases of lung cancer in the United States in 1998 alone, and 160,100 Americans will *die* of lung cancer in 1998. Less than 10 percent of lung cancers occur among nonsmokers.[33]

Lung cancer can take from 10 to 30 years to develop. The outlook for victims of this disease is poor. Most lung cancer is not diagnosed until it is fairly widespread in the body; at that point, the five-year survival rate is only 13 percent. When a

easiest to prevent

malignancy is diagnosed and recognized while still localized, the five-year survival rate rises to 47 percent.

If you are a smoker, your risk of developing lung cancer is dependent on several factors. First, the number of cigarettes you smoke per day is important. Someone who smokes two packs a day is 15 to 25 times more likely to develop lung cancer than a nonsmoker. If you started smoking in your teens, you have a greater chance of developing lung cancer than people who started later. If you inhale deeply when you smoke, you also increase your chances of developing the disease. Occupational or domestic exposure to other irritants, such as asbestos and radon, will also increase your likelihood of developing lung cancer.[34]

Tobacco is linked to other cancers as well. Cigarette smoking increases the risk of pancreatic cancer by 70 percent. Smokers can reduce those odds by 30 percent if they quit for 11 years or more.[35] Cancers of the lip, tongue, salivary glands, and esophagus are five times more likely to occur in smokers than in nonsmokers. Smokers are also more likely to develop kidney, bladder, and larynx cancers.

5 yrs. → 13%

Cardiovascular Disease

Half of all tobacco-related deaths occur as a result of some form of heart disease.[36] Smokers have a 70 percent higher death rate from heart disease than nonsmokers do, and heavy smokers have a 200 percent higher death rate than moderate smokers do. In fact, smoking cigarettes poses as great a risk for developing heart disease as high blood pressure and high cholesterol levels do.

Smoking contributes to heart disease by adding the equivalent of 10 years of aging to the arteries.[37] One possible explanation for this is that smoking increases the development of atherosclerosis, the buildup of fatty deposits in the heart and major blood vessels. For unknown reasons, smoking decreases blood levels of HDLs (high-density lipoproteins), which help protect against heart attacks. Smoking also contributes to **platelet adhesiveness,** or the sticking together of red blood cells that is associated with blood clots. The oxygen deprivation associated with smoking decreases the oxygen levels supplied to the heart and can weaken tissues. Smoking also contributes to irregular heart rhythms, which can lead to a sudden heart attack. Both carbon monoxide and nicotine in cigarette smoke can precipitate angina attacks (pain spasms in the chest when the heart muscle does not get the blood supply it needs).

▶ **Stroke** Smokers are twice as likely to suffer strokes as nonsmokers. A stroke occurs when a small blood vessel in the brain bursts or is blocked by a blood clot, denying oxygen and nourishment to vital portions of the brain. Depending on the area of the brain supplied by the vessel, the stroke can result in paralysis, loss of mental functioning, or death. Smoking contributes to strokes by raising blood pressure, thereby increasing the stress on vessel walls. Platelet adhesiveness contributes to clotting. Five to 15 years after they have

quit →
risk goes ↓ 50% in 1 yr.

stopped smoking, the risk of stroke for ex-smokers is the same as that for people who have never smoked.

▶ **Risks for Women** Women who take oral contraceptives (birth control pills) and who smoke cigarettes increase their risk of heart attack several times. In a recent study, for pill users who smoked 10 or more cigarettes a day, the risk for a heart attack was 20 times higher than for women who did not smoke and did not use the pill.[38] Oral contraceptives increase the risk of developing blood clots, which can block already narrowing arteries in women with atherosclerosis, a disease that smokers are at increased risk for developing. For these reasons, smoking while taking oral contraceptives also increases the risk of peripheral vascular disease and stroke.

Respiratory Disorders

The respiratory system is quickly impaired by smoking. Smokers can feel the impact of their smoking in a relatively short period of time—they are more prone to breathlessness, chronic cough, and excess phlegm production than nonsmokers their age. Smokers tend to miss work one-third more often than nonsmokers do, primarily because of respiratory diseases. Cigarette smokers are up to 18 times more likely than nonsmokers to die of diseases of the lungs. Cigarette smokers have higher death rates from emphysema and chronic bronchitis and more frequently have impaired lung function and other symptoms of lung disease than do nonsmokers.[39]

Chronic bronchitis is the presence of a productive cough that persists or reoccurs frequently. It may develop in smokers because their inflamed lungs produce more mucus and constantly try to rid themselves of this mucus and foreign particles. The effort to do so results in the "smoker's hack," the persistent cough experienced by most smokers. Smokers are more prone than nonsmokers to respiratory ailments such as influenza, pneumonia, and colds.

Emphysema is a chronic disease in which the alveoli (the tiny air sacs in the lungs) are destroyed, impairing the lungs' ability to obtain oxygen and remove carbon dioxide. As a result, breathing becomes difficult. Whereas healthy people expend only about 5 percent of their energy breathing, people with advanced emphysema expend nearly 80 percent of their energy breathing. A simple movement such as rising from a seated position may be painful and difficult for the emphysema patient. Since the heart has to work harder to do even the simplest tasks, it may become enlarged and the person may die from heart damage. There is no known cure for emphysema. Approximately 80 percent of all cases of emphysema are related to cigarette smoking.

Other Health Effects

Gum disease is three times more common in smokers than in nonsmokers. Smokers also lose significantly more teeth than do nonsmokers, despite any efforts to practice good oral hygiene.[40] Smokers are also likely to use more medications than are nonsmokers. Nicotine and the other ingredients in cigarettes interfere with the metabolism of drugs: nicotine speeds up the process by which the body uses and eliminates drugs, so that medications become less effective. The smoker may therefore have to take a higher dosage of a drug or take it more frequently.

Despite attempts by the tobacco advertisers to make smoking appear sexy, a number of recent studies have found that smokers are about two times as likely as nonsmokers to suffer from some form of impotence. The problem occurs when toxins in cigarette smoke damage blood vessels, thereby reducing arterial blood flow. Restriction of blood flow to the penis leads to an inadequate erection. It is thought that impotence could be a possible indicator of oncoming cardiovascular disease.

Despite all that we know about its long-term effects, more and more young people continue to put their health at risk. Why?

············ **WHAT DO YOU THINK?**

Identifying the long-term health hazards of tobacco use seems to have little effect on smoking initiation. What more immediate effects of smoking might help deter people from tobacco use?

Women and Smoking

Women who smoke have an increased risk of cancer, heart disease, and problems associated with reproductive organs. The risk of cervical cancer, for instance, is higher in women who smoke than in those who don't. A woman reduces her risk dramatically when she quits.

According to a recent study, cigarettes are more dangerous to women than to men; women are more likely to develop lung cancer and to do so with fewer cigarettes. Already lung cancer has surpassed breast cancer as the most common cause of cancer death in women.

The risk of heart disease for women who smoke more than 25 cigarettes per day is 500 percent higher than it is for nonsmokers. Even smoking one to four cigarettes per day doubles a woman's risk for heart attack.

Smoking appears to cause women to begin menopause one to two years early. But former smokers start their menopause at about the same age as do women who have

never smoked. Smoking also contributes to osteoporosis, a condition involving bone loss that particularly afflicts women. Current female smokers aged 35 and older are more than 10 times as likely to die of emphysema or chronic bronchitis than male smokers.

▶ *Smoking and Pregnancy* Each year in the United States, approximately 50,000 miscarriages are attributed to smoking during pregnancy. On average, babies born to mothers who smoke weigh less than those born to nonsmokers, and low birth weight is correlated with many developmental problems. Pregnant women who stop smoking in the first three or four months of their pregnancies give birth to higher-birth-weight babies than do women who smoke throughout their pregnancies. Infant mortality rates are also higher among babies born to smokers.

Maternal smoking has long been linked to the increased risk of **sudden infant death syndrome (SIDS)**. SIDS, or "crib-death," occurs when an infant, usually under 1 year of age, dies during its sleep for no apparent reason. The increased risk is associated with how much the mother smokes. Passive smoke has also been associated with significant increases in the risk of SIDS. This risk is increased in normal-weight infants, about twofold with passive smoke exposure, and about threefold when the mother smokes both during the pregnancy and after the baby is born. Infants who are born to mothers who smoke during pregnancy have more episodes of apnea and excessive sweating. We do not know exactly how smoking affects the infant during the pregnancy, but it has been suggested that smoking may influence the development of the nervous system.

One study found that daughters of women who smoked during pregnancy are four times more likely to begin smoking

Platelet adhesiveness Stickiness of red blood cells associated with blood clots.

Emphysema A chronic lung disease in which the tiny air sacs in the lungs are destroyed, making breathing difficult.

Sudden infant death syndrome (SIDS) Death that occurs without apparent cause in babies under two years of age; some cases may be associated with tobacco use by the mother during pregnancy.

during adolescence and to continue smoking than the daughters of women who did not smoke while pregnant. The study suggests that nicotine, which crosses the placental barrier, may affect the female fetus during an important period of development so as to predispose the brain to the addictive influence of nicotine more than a decade later.[41]

SMOKELESS TOBACCO

Smokeless tobacco is used by approximately 5 million U.S. adults. Most users are teenage (20 percent of male high school students) and young adult males, who are often emulating a professional sports figure or a family member. There are two types of smokeless tobacco—chewing tobacco and snuff. Chewing tobacco comes in the form of loose leaf, plug, or twist. Chewing tobacco contains tobacco leaves treated with molasses and other flavorings. The user places a "quid" of tobacco in the mouth between the teeth and gums and then sucks or chews the quid to release the nicotine. Once the quid becomes ineffective, the user spits it out and inserts another. Dipping is another method of using chewing tobacco. The dipper takes a small amount of tobacco and places it between the lower lip and teeth to stimulate the flow of saliva and release the nicotine. Dipping rapidly releases the nicotine into the bloodstream.

Snuff can come in either a dry or moist powdered form or sachets (tea bag-like pouches) of tobacco. The most common placement of snuff is inside the cheek. In European countries, inhaling dry snuff is more common than in the United States.[42]

Risks of Smokeless Tobacco

Smokeless tobacco is just as addictive as cigarettes due to its nicotine content. There is nicotine in all tobacco products, but smokeless tobacco contains more nicotine than do cigarettes. Holding an average-sized dip or chew in your mouth for 30 minutes gives you as much nicotine as smoking four cigarettes. A two-can-a-week snuff dipper gets as much nicotine as a one-and-a-half-pack-a-day smoker.

One of the major risks of chewing tobacco is leukoplakia, a condition characterized by leathery white patches inside the mouth produced by contact with irritants in tobacco juice. Smokeless tobacco contains 10 times the amount of cancer-producing substances found in cigarettes and 100 times more than the Food and Drug Administration allows in foods and other substances used by the public. Between 3 and 17 percent of diagnosed leukoplakia cases develop into oral cancer.

Users of smokeless tobacco are 50 times more likely to develop oral cancers than are nonusers. Warning signs of oral cancers include: lumps in the jaw or neck area; color changes or lumps inside the lips; white, smooth, or scaly patches in the mouth or on the neck, lips, or tongue; a red spot or sore on the lips or gums or inside the mouth that does not heal in two weeks; repeated bleeding in the mouth; difficulty or abnormality in speaking or swallowing.

The lag time between first use and contracting cancer is shorter for smokeless tobacco users than for smokers because absorption through the gums is the most efficient route of nicotine administration. A growing body of evidence suggests that long-term use of smokeless tobacco also increases the risk of cancer of the larynx, esophagus, nasal cavity, pancreas, kidney, and bladder. Moreover, many smokeless tobacco users eventually "graduate" to cigarettes.

Chewers and dippers do not face the specific hazards associated with heat and smoke, but they do run other tobacco-related risks. The stimulant effects of nicotine may create the same circulatory and respiratory problems for chewers as for smokers. Chronic smokeless tobacco use also results in delayed wound healing, peptic ulcer disease, and reproductive disturbances.

Smokeless tobacco also impairs the senses of taste and smell, causing the user to add salt and sugar to food, which may contribute to high blood pressure and obesity. Some smokeless tobacco products contain high levels of sodium (salt), which also contributes to high blood pressure. In addition, dental problems are common among users of smokeless tobacco. Contact with tobacco juice causes receding gums, tooth decay, bad breath, and discolored teeth. Damage to both the teeth and jawbone can contribute to early loss of teeth. Users of all tobacco products may not be able to use the vitamins and other nutrients in food effectively. In some cases, vitamin supplements may be recommended by a physician.

ENVIRONMENTAL TOBACCO SMOKE

As the population of nonsmokers rises, so does the demand for the right to breathe clean air. Although fewer than 30 percent of Americans are smokers, air pollution from smoking in public places continues to be a problem. Environmental tobacco smoke (ETS) is divided into two categories: mainstream smoke and sidestream smoke (also called secondhand smoke). Mainstream smoke refers to smoke drawn through tobacco while inhaling; **sidestream smoke** refers to smoke from the burning end of a cigarette or to smoke exhaled by a smoker. People who breathe smoke from someone else's smoking product are said to be *involuntary* or *passive* smokers. Nearly 9 out of 10 nonsmoking Americans are exposed to environmental tobacco smoke. Measurable levels of nicotine were found in the blood of 88 percent of all nontobacco users. This documents the widespread exposure of people in the United States to ETS.[43]

Although involuntary smokers breathe less tobacco than active smokers do, they still face risks from exposure to tobacco smoke. Sidestream smoke actually contains more carcinogenic substances than the smoke that a smoker inhales. According to the American Lung Association, sidestream smoke has about 2 times more tar and nicotine, 5 times more carbon monoxide, and 50 times more ammonia than mainstream smoke. Each year, exposure to ETS causes an estimated 3,000 nonsmoking Americans to die of lung cancer.[44] The Environmental Protection Agency (EPA) has designated secondhand tobacco smoke a *group A cancer-causing agent* that is even worse than other group A threats such as benzene, arsenic, and radon. The EPA has no power to regulate levels of indoor tobacco smoke, but officials believe that the agency's recommendations carry weight with employers and local governments. There is also evidence that sidestream smoke poses an even greater risk for death due to heart disease than for death due to lung cancer.[45]

Sidestream smoke is estimated to cause more deaths per year than any other environmental pollutant. The risk of dying because of exposure to passive smoking is 100 times greater than the risk that requires the EPA to label a pollutant as carcinogenic and 10,000 times greater than the risk that requires the labeling of a food as carcinogenic.[46]

Lung cancer and heart disease are not the only risks involuntary smokers face. Exposure to ETS in children increases the risk of their suffering from lower respiratory tract infections. An estimated 300,000 children are at greater risk of pneumonia and bronchitis as a result of their exposure to ETS.[47] Children exposed to sidestream smoke have a greater chance of developing other respiratory problems, such as cough, wheezing, asthma, and chest colds, along with a decrease in pulmonary performance. The greatest effects of sidestream smoke are seen in children under the age of five. Children exposed to sidestream smoke daily in the home

miss 33 percent more school days and have 10 percent more colds and acute respiratory infections than those not exposed. A recent study found that 31.2 percent of children are exposed to cigarette smoke daily in the home. This study found wide regional, income, and education differences: children of high-income, high-education-level parents in California are exposed far less than are children of low-income, low-education-level parents in the Midwest.[48]

Cigarette, cigar, and pipe smoke in enclosed areas present other hazards to nonsmokers. An estimated 10 to 15 percent of nonsmokers are extremely sensitive (hypersensitive) to cigarette smoke. These people experience itchy eyes, difficulty in breathing, painful headaches, nausea, and dizziness in response to minute amounts of smoke. The level of carbon monoxide in cigarette smoke contained in enclosed places is 4,000 times higher than the standard recommended by the EPA for a definition of clean air.

Efforts to reduce the hazards associated with passive smoking have been gaining momentum in recent years. Groups such as GASP (Group Against Smokers' Pollution) and ASH (Action on Smoking and Health) have been working since the early 1970s to reduce smoking in public places. In response to their efforts, some 44 states have enacted laws limiting or restricting smoking in public places such as restaurants, theaters, bowling alleys, public schools, airports, and bus depots.[49] The federal government has restricted smoking in all government buildings. Hotels and motels now set aside rooms for nonsmokers, and car rental agencies designate certain vehicles for nonsmokers. Since 1990, smoking has been banned on all domestic airline flights. During 1994, McDonald's banned smoking in 1,400 of its company-owned fast-food restaurants and 20 major-league baseball parks went smokeless.[50]

.... **WHAT DO YOU THINK?**

If environmental tobacco smoke presents health hazards to nonsmokers, whose rights should have precedence: smokers or nonsmokers? Do nonsmoking areas in restaurants and businesses eliminate the problem of ETS, or do they placate nonsmokers by providing an area of reduced exposure to tobacco smoke?

Tobacco and Politics

It has been at least 30 years since the government began warning that tobacco use was hazardous to the health of the nation. Today the tobacco industry is under fire, with 46 states having sued to recover health-care costs related to treating smokers. In 1997, the tobacco industry and attorneys general from nearly 40 states reached an historic settlement. Major tobacco companies agreed to pay $368 billion over 25 years and $15 billion a year thereafter, to settle smoking-related lawsuits filed by states. These funds would be used to finance antismoking campaigns, to permit federal regulation of tobacco, and to pay fines if tobacco use by minors did not

Leukoplakia   A condition characterized by leathery white patches inside the mouth produced by contact with irritants in tobacco juice.

Environmental tobacco smoke (ETS)   Smoke from tobacco products, including sidestream and mainstream smoke.

Mainstream smoke   Smoke that is drawn through tobacco while inhaling.

Sidestream smoke   The cigarette, pipe, or cigar smoke breathed by nonsmokers; also called secondhand smoke.

decline. In return, the industry would be protected against most tobacco-related lawsuits and the awarding of punitive damages. In addition, the Food and Drug Administration (FDA) would have regulatory control over the way cigarettes are manufactured and packaged. The settlement, which required congressional approval, died in the Senate after the price escalated and the tobacco companies withdrew their support for the legislation.

New tobacco litigation in 1998 had 46 states suing to recover health-care costs related to treating smokers. This deal did not require congressional approval and in November 1998, a settlement was reached. In its final phases, some public health advocates criticized the proposed settlement and felt the attorneys general may have thrown in the towel. Key provisions of the settlement are as follows:

- It will cost the tobacco companies about $200 billion over the first 25 years.
- The industry will pay $1.5 billion over 10 years to support antismoking measures, including education and advertising. An additional $250 million will fund research to determine the most effective ways to stop kids from smoking.
- The industry will be barred from billboard advertising.
- All outdoor advertising on public transit systems and in arenas, stadiums, shopping malls, and video game arcades is banned.
- The agreement bans youth access to free samples, proof-of-purchase gifts, and the sale and distribution of "branded" merchandise, such as T-shirts, hats and other items bearing tobacco brand names or logos.
- Cartoon characters, such as Joe Camel, considered particularly appealing to young children, are prohibited from use in advertising.
- Tobacco company sponsorship of sporting events, particularly those with high youth attendance, is severely restricted.
- The industry will agree not to market cigarettes to children and not misrepresent the health effects of cigarettes.[51–53]

Although this legislation is the largest obstacle faced by the tobacco industry, it's not the only battle they are fighting. Other states and communities are advocating for stricter tobacco control. In recent years, a number of states have imposed extra taxes on cigarette sales in an effort to discourage use. The monies are then used for various purposes, including prevention and cessation programs and school health programs. For example, the state of California passed Proposition 10, which requires an extra 50-cent tax on a packet of cigarettes. According to the proposition, the $750 million raised annually will be used to create programs for children under the age of 5 and to educate pregnant women on the dangers of smoking. Two other community-based programs, ASSIST (American Stop Smoking Intervention Study) and IMPACT (Initiatives to Mobilize for the Prevention and Control of Tobacco Use) are tobacco control initiatives that are targeted at the local level. These measures are focused on creating legislation that would help prohibit the sale of tobacco to minors and assist with enforcement.

QUITTING

⅓ try and quit 90% go back

Quitting smoking isn't easy. To stop smoking requires breaking an addiction and a habit. Smokers must break the physical addiction to nicotine. And they must break the habit of lighting up at certain times of the day.

From what we know about successful quitters, quitting is often a lengthy process involving several unsuccessful attempts before success is finally achieved. Even successful quitters suffer occasional slips, emphasizing the fact that quitting smoking is a dynamic process that occurs over time.

Breaking the Nicotine Addiction

Nicotine addiction may be one of the toughest addictions to overcome. Smokers' attempts to quit lead to withdrawal symptoms. Symptoms of **nicotine withdrawal** include irritability, restlessness, nausea, vomiting, and intense cravings for tobacco.

▶ *Nicotine Replacement Products*   Nontobacco products that replace depleted levels of nicotine in the bloodstream have helped some people stop using tobacco. The two most common nicotine-replacement products are nicotine chewing gum and the nicotine patch, both of which are available over the counter. The FDA has recently approved a nicotine nasal spray to help cigarette smokers stop smoking.

Some patients use a prescription chewing gum containing nicotine, called Nicorette, to help them reduce their nicotine consumption over time. Under the guidance of a physician, the user chews between 12 and 24 pieces of gum per day for up to six months. Nicorette delivers about as much nicotine as a cigarette does, but because it is absorbed through the mucous membrane of the mouth, it doesn't produce the same rush as inhaling a cigarette does. Users experience no withdrawal symptoms and fewer cravings for nicotine as the dosage is reduced until they are completely weaned.

There is some controversy surrounding the use of nicotine replacement gum. Opponents believe that it substitutes one addiction for another. Successful users counter that it is a valid way to help break a deadly habit without suffering the unpleasant withdrawal symptoms and cravings that often lead ex-smokers to resume smoking.

The nicotine patch, first marketed in 1991, is the hottest new method for those attempting to quit smoking. It is generally used in conjunction with a comprehensive smoking-behavior cessation program. A small, thin 24-hour patch placed on the smoker's upper body delivers a continuous flow of nicotine through the skin, helping to relieve the body's cravings. The patch is worn for 8 to 12 weeks under the guidance of a physician. During this time, the dose of nicotine is gradually reduced until the smoker is fully weaned from nicotine. Occa-

Nicotine withdrawal   Symptoms including nausea, headaches, and irritability, suffered by smokers who cease using tobacco.

sional side effects include mild skin irritation, insomnia, dry mouth, and nervousness. The patch costs the equivalent of two packs of cigarettes a day—about four dollars—and some insurance plans will pay for it.

Analysis of 17 studies involving 5,098 people, the nicotine patch was at least twice as effective as placebo (fake) patches. At the end of treatment periods lasting at least four weeks, 27 percent of the nicotine patch wearers were free of cigarettes versus 13 percent of placebo patch users. Six months later, 22 percent of the nicotine patch users were abstinent compared to only 9 percent of the placebo users. The study also showed that the patch was effective with or without intensive counseling.[54]

The nasal spray, which requires a prescription, is much more powerful and reaches the bloodstream faster than the gum or the patch. Patients are warned to be careful not to overdose; as little as 40 milligrams of nicotine taken at once could be lethal

to some people. It has been reported that the spray is somewhat unpleasant for people to use. The FDA has advised that it should be used for no more than 3 months and never for more than 6 months, so that smokers don't find themselves as dependent on nicotine in spray form as they were on nicotine from cigarettes. The FDA also advises that no one who experiences nasal or sinus problems, allergies, or asthma should use it. For many smokers, the road to quitting includes some type of antismoking plan. One of the American Cancer Society's approaches is shown in the Skills for Behavior Change box on page 212.

Benefits of Quitting

According to the American Cancer Society, many tissues damaged by smoking can repair themselves. As soon as smokers stop, their bodies begin the repair process (see Figure 8.1).

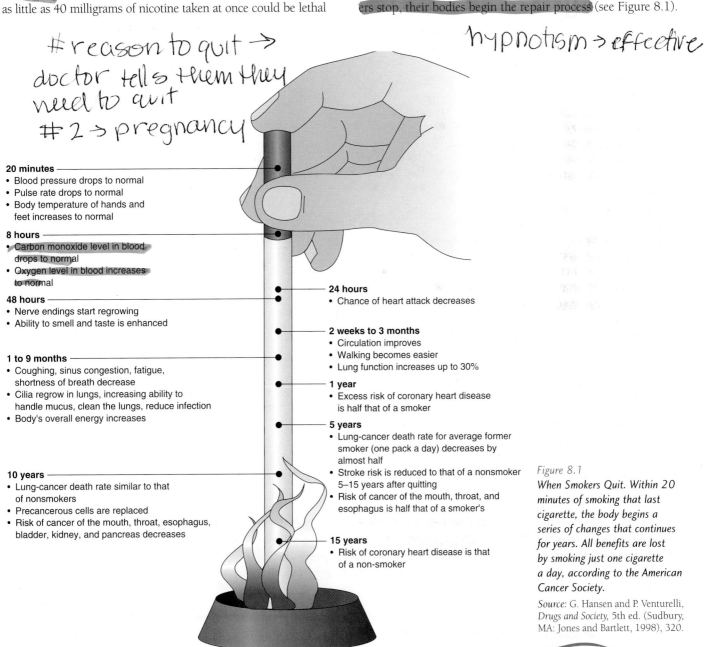

reason to quit → doctor tells them they need to quit
#2 → pregnancy

hypnotism → effective

20 minutes
- Blood pressure drops to normal
- Pulse rate drops to normal
- Body temperature of hands and feet increases to normal

8 hours
- Carbon monoxide level in blood drops to normal
- Oxygen level in blood increases to normal

48 hours
- Nerve endings start regrowing
- Ability to smell and taste is enhanced

1 to 9 months
- Coughing, sinus congestion, fatigue, shortness of breath decrease
- Cilia regrow in lungs, increasing ability to handle mucus, clean the lungs, reduce infection
- Body's overall energy increases

10 years
- Lung-cancer death rate similar to that of nonsmokers
- Precancerous cells are replaced
- Risk of cancer of the mouth, throat, esophagus, bladder, kidney, and pancreas decreases

24 hours
- Chance of heart attack decreases

2 weeks to 3 months
- Circulation improves
- Walking becomes easier
- Lung function increases up to 30%

1 year
- Excess risk of coronary heart disease is half that of a smoker

5 years
- Lung-cancer death rate for average former smoker (one pack a day) decreases by almost half
- Stroke risk is reduced to that of a nonsmoker 5–15 years after quitting
- Risk of cancer of the mouth, throat, and esophagus is half that of a smoker's

15 years
- Risk of coronary heart disease is that of a non-smoker

Figure 8.1

When Smokers Quit. Within 20 minutes of smoking that last cigarette, the body begins a series of changes that continues for years. All benefits are lost by smoking just one cigarette a day, according to the American Cancer Society.

Source: G. Hansen and P. Venturelli, *Drugs and Society,* 5th ed. (Sudbury, MA: Jones and Bartlett, 1998), 320.

SKILLS FOR BEHAVIOR CHANGE

Developing a Plan to Kick the Habit

There is no magic cure that can help you stop. Take the first step to quitting. Answer this question: Why do I want to stop smoking?

Write your reasons in the space below. Once you have prepared your list, cut it out and carry it with you. Memorize it. Every time you are tempted to smoke, go over your reasons for stopping.

My Reasons for Stopping

1. _____
2. _____
3. _____
4. _____
5. _____

DEVELOP A PLAN; CHANGE SOME HABITS

Over time, smoking becomes a strong habit. Often, daily events such as finishing a meal, talking on the phone, drinking coffee, and chatting with friends trigger your urge to smoke. Breaking the link between the trigger and your smoking will help you stop. Think about the times and places you usually smoke. What could you do instead of smoking at those times?

Things to Do Instead of Smoking

1. _____
2. _____
3. _____

THE BOTTOM LINE: COMMIT YOURSELF

There comes a time when you have to say good-bye to your cigarettes.

- Pick a day to stop smoking.
- Fill out a "Stop Smoking Contract."
- Have a family member or friend sign the contract.

THEN

- Throw away all your cigarettes, lighters, and ashtrays at home and at work. You will not need them again.
- Be prepared to feel the urge to smoke. The urge will pass whether or not you smoke. Use the FOUR Ds to fight the urge:

  Delay

  Deep breathing

  Drink water

  Do something else

- Keep "mouth toys" handy: lifesavers, gum, straws, and carrot sticks can help.
- If you've had trouble stopping before, ask your doctor about nicotine chewing gum.

- Tell your family and friends that you've stopped smoking.
- Put "NO SMOKING" signs in your car, work area, and house.
- Give yourself a treat for stopping. Go to a movie, go out to dinner, or buy yourself a gift.

FOCUS ON THE POSITIVES

Now that you have stopped smoking, your mind and your body will begin to feel better. Think of the good things that have happened since you stopped. Can you breathe easier? Do you have more energy? Do you feel good about what you've done?

Use the space below to list the good things about not smoking. Carry them with you. Look at them when you have the urge to smoke.

_____
_____
_____
_____
_____
_____
_____
_____

Source: Reprinted by permission from *Smart Move! A Stop Smoking Guide.* © 1996, American Cancer Society, Inc.

Within eight hours, carbon monoxide and oxygen levels return to normal, and "smoker's breath" disappears. Within a few days of quitting, the mucus clogging airways is broken up and eliminated. Circulation and the senses of taste and smell improve within weeks. Many ex-smokers who have kicked the cigarette habit say they have more energy, sleep better, and feel more alert. By the end of one year, the risk for lung cancer and stroke decreases. In addition, smokers reduce considerably their risks of developing the following cancers: mouth, throat, and esophagus; larynx; pancreatic; bladder; and cervical. They also reduce their risk of developing or causing the following conditions: peripheral artery disease, chronic obstructive lung disease, coronary heart disease, ulcers, and low-birth-weight babies. Within two years, the risk for heart attack drops to near normal. At the end of 10 smoke-free years, the ex-smoker can expect to live out his or her normal life span.

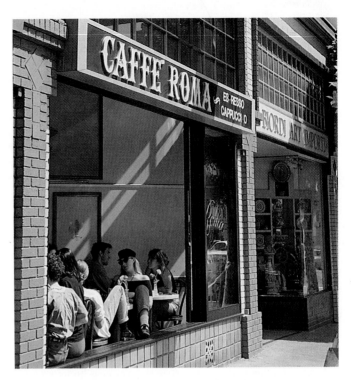

What new medications are available to help people stop smoking? Should insurance pay for smoking cessation programs or medications? What situations often lead to relapse when someone is trying to stop smoking or chewing tobacco?

CAFFEINE

Caffeine is the most popular and widely consumed drug in the United States. Almost half of all Americans drink coffee every day, and many others use caffeine in some other form, mainly for its well-known "wake-up" effect. Drinking coffee is legal, even socially encouraged. Many people believe caffeine is a nondrug item and not really addictive. Besides, it tastes good. Coffee and other caffeine-containing products seem harmless; with no cream or sugar added, they are calorie-free and therefore a good way to fill yourself up if you are dieting. If you share these attitudes, you should think again, because research in the last decade has linked caffeine to certain health problems.

Caffeine is a drug derived from the chemical family called xanthines. Two related chemicals, *theophylline* and *theobromine,* are found in tea and chocolate, respectively. The xanthines are mild central nervous system stimulants. They enhance mental alertness and reduce feelings of fatigue. Other stimulant effects include increases in heart muscle contractions, oxygen consumption, metabolism, and urinary output. These effects are felt within 15 to 45 minutes of ingesting a caffeine-containing product.

Side effects of the xanthines include wakefulness, insomnia, irregular heartbeat, dizziness, nausea, indigestion, and sometimes mild delirium. Some people also experience heartburn. As with some other drugs, the user's psychological outlook and expectations will influence the stimulant effects of xanthine-containing products.

Different products contain different concentrations of caffeine. A 5-ounce cup of coffee contains between 60 and 180 milligrams of caffeine. Caffeine concentrations vary with the brand of the beverage and the strength of the brew. Small chocolate bars contain up to 15 milligrams of caffeine and theobromine.

Caffeine   A stimulant found in coffee, tea, chocolate, and some soft drinks.

Xanthines   The chemical family of stimulants to which caffeine belongs.

Caffeinism   Caffeine intoxication brought on by excessive caffeine use; symptoms include chronic insomnia, irritability, anxiety, muscle twitches, and headaches.

Coffeehouses and coffee kiosks have become commonplace in every town and city, airports, hospitals, and many businesses. Yet, it's important to remember that caffeine, like all drugs, can have adverse effects.

Caffeine Addiction

As the effects of caffeine begin to wear off, users may feel let down, mentally or physically depressed, exhausted, and weak. To counteract these effects, people commonly choose to drink another cup of coffee. Habitually engaging in this practice leads to tolerance and psychological dependence. Until the mid-1970s, caffeine was not medically recognized as addictive. Chronic caffeine use and its attendant behaviors were called "coffee nerves." This syndrome is now recognized as *caffeine intoxication,* or **caffeinism.** Symptoms of caffeinism include chronic insomnia, jitters, irritability, nervousness, anxiety, and involuntary muscle twitches. Withdrawing the caffeine may compound the effects and produce severe headaches. (Some physicians ask their patients to take a simple test for caffeine addiction: Don't consume anything containing caffeine, and if you get a severe headache within four hours, you are addicted.) Because caffeinism meets the requirements for addiction—tolerance, psychological dependence, and withdrawal symptoms—it can be classified as addictive.

Although you would have to drink between 67 and 100 cups of coffee in a day to produce a fatal overdose of caffeine, you may experience sensory disturbances after consuming only 10 cups of coffee within a 24-hour period. These symptoms include tinnitus (ringing in the ears), spots before the eyes, numbness in arms and legs, poor circulation, and visual hallucinations. Because 10 cups of coffee is not an extraordinary amount for many people to drink within a 24-hour period, caffeine use clearly poses health threats.

The Health Consequences of Long-Term Caffeine Use

Long-term caffeine use has been suspected of being linked to a number of serious health problems, ranging from heart disease and cancer to mental dysfunction and birth defects. However, based on information available, no strong evidence exists to suggest that moderate caffeine use (less than 500 milligrams daily, which is approximately 5 cups of coffee) produces harmful effects in healthy, nonpregnant people.

It appears that caffeine does not cause long-term high blood pressure and has not been linked to strokes. Nor is there any evidence of a relationship between coffee and heart disease.[55] However, people who suffer from irregular heartbeat are cautioned against the use of caffeine because the resultant increase in heart rate might be life-threatening. Coffee is also considered a gastric irritant that can contribute to ulcers. Both decaffeinated and caffeinated coffee products contain ingredients that can irritate the stomach lining and thus can be harmful to people with stomach ulcers.

For years, caffeine consumption was linked with fibrocystic breast disease, a condition characterized by painful, noncancerous lumps in the breast. Reports claim that caffeine promotes cyst formation in female breasts. Although these conclusions have been challenged, many clinicians advise patients with mammilary cysts to avoid caffeine. In addition, some reports indicate that very high doses of caffeine given to pregnant laboratory animals can cause stillbirths or offspring with low birthweights or limb deformations. Studies have found that moderate consumption of caffeine (less than 300 milligrams per day) did not significantly affect human fetal development.[56] Mothers are usually advised to avoid or at least reduce caffeine use during pregnancy.

WHAT DO YOU THINK?

Have you ever experienced caffeinism? Do you ingest caffeinated substances because you like their taste or because you are looking for a lift? Have you ever felt any ill effects after avoiding caffeinated beverages for a period of time?

Taking Charge
Managing Alcohol, Tobacco and Caffeine

After reading this chapter, you should have a better understanding of the potential dangers of what many people consider to be recreational drugs. Being aware of the threats inherent in alcohol, tobacco, and caffeine consumption will make you more thoughtful when you are confronted with these substances. Use the following questions to help you answer some tough questions about your relationship with these drugs.

CHECKLIST FOR CHANGE

MAKING PERSONAL CHOICES

✓ Can you distinguish between a social drinker and a problem drinker?

✓ Can you distinguish between a problem drinker and an alcoholic?

✓ Do you feel comfortable with how you currently use alcohol? Would you like to change any of your current drinking behaviors?

✓ Do you know what resources are available to help yourself or others who might be experiencing a problem with alcohol?

✓ Have you established responsible drinking guidelines for yourself?

✓ Have you identified your smoking habits?

✓ Have you ever tried to quit smoking? If so, do you know how and where to get support that you will need? You can start by calling your local chapter of the American

Cancer Society or community hospital to discover what programs are being offered.

✓ Begin by tapering off. For a period of one to two weeks, cut down or change to a lower-nicotine brand. Stop carrying matches, and don't buy a new pack of cigarettes until you finish the one you're smoking.

✓ Set a quit date and announce to friends and family when you are going to stop.

✓ Stop. A week before you quit, cut your cigarette consumption down to a few cigarettes per day. Smoke these few cigarettes in the late day or evening.

✓ Continue to seek support from support group or program members, and when you quit, treat yourself to something nice.

✓ If you fail to stop despite your best efforts, don't beat yourself up. Try again soon.

✓ Cut your caffeine consumption gradually. Cut down by one serving a day every few days.

✓ Mix caffeinated products with decaffeinated products, gradually increasing the proportion of the latter until caffeinated products are eliminated.

✓ Cut down on caffeine before you give up nicotine, because caffeine is metabolized faster in smokers than in nonsmokers.

✓ Find satisfying alternatives to coffee-associated behaviors.

SUMMARY

- Alcohol is a central nervous system depressant used by 70 percent of all Americans and 85 percent of all college students; 42.7 percent of college students are binge drinkers. While consumption trends are slowly creeping downward, college students are under extreme pressure to consume alcohol.

- Alcohol's effect on the body is measured by the blood alcohol concentration (BAC), the ratio of alcohol to total blood volume. The higher the BAC, the greater the impaired judgment and coordination and drowsiness. Some negative consequences associated with alcohol use and college students are lower grade point averages, academic problems, dropping out of school, unplanned sex, hangovers, and injury. Long-term effects of alcohol overuse include damage to the nervous system, cardiovascular damage, liver disease, and increased risk for cancer. Use during pregnancy can cause fetal alcohol effects (FAE) or fetal alcohol syndrome (FAS). Alcohol is also a causative factor in traffic accidents.

- Alcohol use becomes alcoholism when it interferes with school, work, or social and family relationships or entails violations of the law. Causes of alcoholism include biological and family factors and social and cultural factors. Alcoholism has far-reaching effects on families, especially on children. Children of alcoholics have problematic childhoods and generally take those problems into adulthood.

- Recovery is problematic for alcoholics. Most alcoholics do not admit to a problem until reaching a major life crisis or having their families intervene. Treatment options include detoxification at private medical facilities, therapy (family, individual, or group), and programs like Alcoholics Anonymous. Most alcoholics relapse (60 percent

within three months) because alcoholism is a behavioral addiction as well as a chemical addiction.

- The use of tobacco involves many social issues, including advertising targeted at youth and women, the largest growing populations of smokers. Health care and lost productivity resulting from smoking cost the nation about $100 billion.

- The health hazards of smoking include markedly higher rates of cancer, heart and circulatory disorders, respiratory diseases, and gum diseases. Smoking while pregnant presents risks for the fetus, including miscarriage or low birthweight.

- Smokeless tobacco contains more nicotine than do cigarettes and dramatically increases risks for oral cancer and other oral problems.

- Environmental tobacco smoke (sidestream smoke) puts nonsmokers at risk for elevated rates of cancer and heart disease according to an EPA study. While many businesses and local governments have responded by banning smoking, the tobacco industry contends that flaws in the study make it invalid.

- Quitting is complicated by the dual nature of smoking: Smokers must kick a chemical addiction as well as a habit. Nicotine replacement products (gum and the patch) are available to help wean smokers off nicotine. Several therapy methods can help smokers break the habit of lighting up.

- Caffeine is a widely used central nervous system stimulant. No long-term ill-health effects have been proven, although caffeine may produce withdrawal symptoms for chronic users who try to quit.

DISCUSSION QUESTIONS

1. When it comes to drinking alcohol, how much is too much? When you see a friend having "too many" drinks at a party, what actions do you normally take? What actions could you take?
2. What are some of the most common negative consequences college students experience as a result of their drinking? What are secondhand binge effects?
3. Describe a social drinker, a problem drinker, and an alcoholic. What factors may cause someone to slip from being a social drinker to being an alcoholic? What effect does alcoholism have on an alcoholic's family?

4. Discuss the varied forms in which you can ingest tobacco. In each form, how do chemicals enter your system? What are the physiological effects of nicotine?
5. Discuss the varied risks of smokeless tobacco. Do you think that smokeless tobacco should be banned from major-league baseball, as it was from the minor leagues?
6. After learning about the potential problems associated with caffeine use, have you considered altering the amount you consume?

APPLICATION EXERCISE

Reread the *What Do You Think?* scenario at the beginning of the chapter and answer the following questions.

1. From what you have learned in this chapter, what are ways David and Shelly might have been able to prevent this tragedy?

2. What are some steps Eric could have taken to prevent this tragic situation?
3. What are some possible signs Eric might have been exhibiting at BACs of 0.11 to 0.12, 0.20, and 0.40?

OBJECTIVES

▶ Examine the factors that influence your dietary decisions and discuss how you can change old eating habits, including appropriate use of the Food Guide Pyramids, eating nutrient-dense foods, and other factors.

▶ Describe the major essential nutrients, indicating what purpose they serve in maintaining your overall health, as well as exploring many of the controversies that surround these substances.

▶ Discuss the role of food as a form of medicine and the facts surrounding some of our newer foods and food supplements and their roles in health and well-being.

▶ Distinguish among the various forms of vegetarianism, discussing possible health benefits and risks from these dietary alternatives.

▶ Discuss issues surrounding gender and nutrition and explain the implications of some of these issues for your own dietary behaviors.

▶ Discuss the unique problems that college students may have when trying to eat healthy foods and the actions they can take to ensure compliance with the food pyramid.

▶ Explain some of the food safety concerns facing Americans as well as persons from other regions of the world.

Nutrition
Eating for Optimum Health

Tim is an avid fitness enthusiast who runs 5 to 10 miles daily, lifts weights 3 to 4 times per week, and constantly talks about his quest for the perfect body. He criticizes anyone who puts mayonnaise or butter on bread, eats any form of meat, and/or eats any kind of fast food. He constantly worries about his food intake and the "fuel" that is supplying his body.

Do you consider Tim to be a healthy person? How would you assess Tim's dietary behaviors? What factors may have contributed to his attitudes and beliefs? What aspect of his behavior would you want to change? Why? If you were to describe someone with healthy eating behaviors, what would that person be like? What kind of person do you like to associate with when it comes to eating behaviors?

ODAY, WE FACE DIETARY CHOICES and nutritional challenges that our grandparents never dreamed of— exotic foreign foods; dietary supplements; artificial sweeteners; no-fat, low-fat, and artificial-fat alternatives; cholesterol-free, high-protein, high-carbohydrate, and low-calorie products—thousands of alternatives bombard us daily. Caught in the cross fire of advertised claims by the food industry and advice provided by health and nutrition experts, most of us find it difficult to make wise dietary decisions. Just when we think we have the answers, a new research study tells us that what we thought was true probably wasn't.

A study of more than 2,000 college student dietary practices has indicated that students often face considerable difficulty planning their own menus for eating healthfully and having the resources to prepare balanced meals.[1] While this study provides a somewhat gloomy forecast of college student eating habits, a subsequent study of approximately 1,300 students and their nonstudent counterparts indicated that college students and graduates tended to practice more healthful habits and made more healthful food choices than did non-students in their area.[2] Many of the eating behaviors from both of these studies appeared to mirror eating patterns and behaviors that these students learned in their homes. In this chapter, we take a closer look at how we got to where we are today in the nutritional arena.

HEALTHY EATING

Eating is one activity that most of us take for granted. We assume that we will have sufficient food to get us through the day and rarely are we forced to eat things that we do not like for the sake of staying alive. In fact, although we have all undoubtedly experienced **hunger** before mealtime, few of us have ever experienced the type of hunger that continues for days and threatens our survival.

ideally we should eat when the body tells us to.

If our **appetite** for food is stimulated, we may want to eat something because it looks or smells good, even though we are not actually hungry. Finding the right balance between eating to maintain body functions (eating to live) and eating to satisfy our appetites (living to eat) is a problem for many of us.

Social pressures, including family traditions, social events that involve eating, and busy work schedules, can also influence our diets. Although our ancestors typically sat down to three large meals per day, they also labored heavily in the fields or at other work and burned off many of those calories. Today, eating three large meals per day combined with an inactive lifestyle is a recipe for weight gain.

Cultural factors also play a role in how we eat. People from Middle-eastern cultures tend to eat more rice, fruits, and vegetables than does the typical American. Native Japanese eat more fish. Clearly, each culture has both healthy and unhealthy eating habits. *rewards; social events*

Nutrition is the science that investigates the relationship between physiological function and the essential elements of the foods we eat. With our overabundance of food, our vast number of choices, a media that "primes" us to want the tasty morsels we see advertised and our easy access to almost every

health problems

Hunger The feeling associated with the physiological need to eat. *physical*

Appetite The desire to eat; normally accompanies hunger, but is more psychological than physiological.

Nutrition The science that investigates the relationship between physiological function and the essential elements of foods we eat.

Nutrients The constituents of food that sustain us physiologically: proteins, carbohydrates, fats, vitamins, minerals, and water.

Calorie A unit of measure that indicates the amount of energy we obtain from a particular food.

nutrient (proteins, carbohydrates, fats, vitamins, minerals, and water), Americans should have few nutritional problems. But nutritionists believe that our "diets of affluence" are responsible for many of our diseases and disabilities. Heart disease, certain types of cancer, hypertension (high blood pressure), cirrhosis of the liver, tooth decay, and chronic obesity continue to be major health risks.

·········· WHAT DO YOU THINK?

Think about your own eating habits. Do you eat significant amounts of red meats and dairy products? Are you a vegetarian? Would you be happy with a veggie-laden salad and some wheat bread for your evening meal or do you crave a hot, meat-and-potatoes dining experience? Why do you think you feel the way you do? How did your family eat when you were growing up?

Responsible Eating

Americans consume more calories per person than does any other group of people in the world. A **calorie** is a unit of measure that indicates the amount of energy we obtain from a particular food. Calories are eaten in the form of *proteins, fats,* and *carbohydrates,* three of the basic nutrients necessary for

life. Three other nutrients, *vitamins, minerals,* and *water,* are necessary for bodily function but do not contribute any calories to our diets.

Excess calorie consumption is a major factor in our tendency to be overweight. However, it is not so much the quantity of food we eat that is likely to cause weight problems and resultant diseases as it is the relative proportion of nutrients in our diets and our lack of physical activity. The high concentration of fats in the American diet, particularly saturated fats (largely animal fats), appears to increase our risk for heart disease. In fact, most diet-related diseases are a result of increased consumption of fat and excess caloric consumption. Over the years, several federal agencies have worked to modify the average American's diet through a series of dietary goals and guidelines.

calories/day < 11-12 hundred females
< 13-15 hundred males

The Food Guide Pyramid

Recent changes in the way we think about food groups and eating were consolidated with the development of the Food Guide Pyramid, promoted by the United States Department of Agriculture (USDA). Recently revised, the pyramid is designed to illustrate graphically the importance of grains, cereals, vegetables, and fruits compared to meat, fish, poultry, dairy products, and other foods. Figure 9.1 shows the American Food Guide Pyramid, including recommended servings. The following examples show the equivalent of one serving

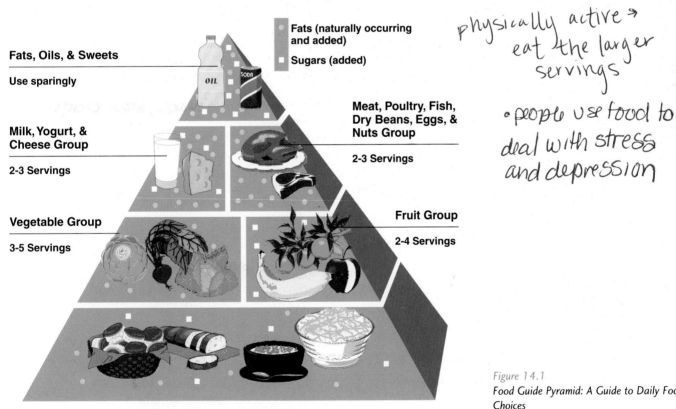

physically active → eat the larger servings

• people use food to deal with stress and depression

Figure 14.1

Food Guide Pyramid: A Guide to Daily Food Choices

Source: U.S. Department of Agriculture, 1993.

Ethnic Food Guide Pyramids

As the world becomes more global, we are becoming increasingly aware of other cultures' customs and cuisines. While the standard American Food Guide Pyramid is applicable to the American lifestyle, other cultures embrace different nutritional needs. In some cases, this is because of access to different types of foods due to climate and terrain; in other cases, it may be because of different customs and traditions. For this reason, food guide pyramids have been created for a variety of populations. For example, the Latin American Diet Pyramid emphasizes fruits, vegetables, beans, and grains, as shown in the illustration. Notice that specific portions are not provided for each category. The color key, instead, specifies which types of foods should be eaten at specific intervals. For the Latin diet, fruits, vegetables, beans, grains, and nuts are to be eaten at every meal. Fish and shellfish, plant oils, dairy,

and poultry are to be eaten daily or less frequently, and eggs, meats, and sweets are to be eaten on occasion, or in small quantities.

The Mediterranean Diet Pyramid emphasizes daily consumption of carbohydrates such as breads, pasta, couscous, polenta, grains, and potatoes; also to be eaten daily, but slightly higher on the pyramid, are fruits, beans and nuts, and vegetables; still higher in the daily category are olive oil (in varying amounts), cheese, and yogurt. Foods to be eaten a few times per week, from bottom to top, are fish, poultry, eggs, and sweets. Red meats should be eaten only a few times per month. Wine can be consumed in moderation.

The Asian pyramid places the most emphasis on rice, grains, fruits, vegetables, legumes, nuts, seeds, and vegetable oils. Dairy, fish, and shellfish are daily options. However, sweets, eggs, and poultry are recommended weekly, and meats, monthly.

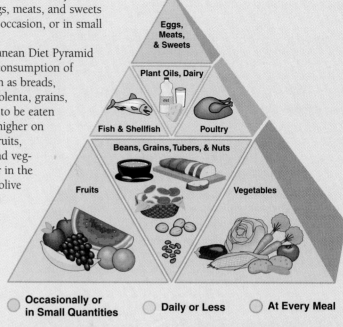

Despite the recommendations for the various cultures, these are not necessarily recommended for the American diet. Each pyramid is applicable to its specific population. Each population has its specific needs. These pyramids accommodate both.

Source: www.intelihealth.com, John Hopkins Health Information.

---

from each of the major food groups. The Health in a Diverse World box presents information about some new ethnic Food Guide Pyramids.

Breads, Cereals, Rice, and Pasta Group (6–11 servings)

- 1 slice of bread or medium dinner roll
- ½ hamburger bun, hot dog bun, bagel, or English muffin
- ½ cup cooked rice, pasta, or other grains
- 6 saltines (the small squares) or snack crackers or 3 ring pretzels
- 1 ounce ready-to-eat cereal
- ½ cup cooked cereal
- 3 cups popped popcorn

- 1 tortilla, pancake, or waffle square
- 3 graham cracker squares or small, unfrosted cookies

Fruit Group (2–4 servings)

- whole fruit such as medium apple, banana, or orange
- ½ cup of raw, cooked, or canned fruit
- ¾ cup of fruit juice
- ½ cup canned fruit
- ¼ cup dried fruit

Vegetable Group (3–5 servings)

- 1 cup leafy raw vegetables
- ½ cup chopped fresh, frozen, or canned vegetables
- ¾ cup fresh, frozen, or canned juice
- ¼ cup dried vegetables

Meat, Poultry, Fish, Dry Beans, Eggs, and Nuts Group (2–3 servings)

- 2–3 ounces lean, trimmed, and baked or roasted meat, fish, or poultry

The following can substitute for 1 ounce of meat:

- 2 tablespoons peanut butter or other nut/seed butter
- ¼ cup nuts
- ½ cup cooked legumes
- 3 oz. tofu
- 1 egg

Milk, Yogurt, and Cheese (2 servings; 3 servings for pregnant and breast-feeding women and teens; 4 servings for teens who are pregnant or breast-feeding)

- 1 cup of milk or yogurt
- 1½ oz. of natural cheese
- 2 oz. processed cheese
- ½ cup cottage cheese
- 1½ cups ice cream, ice milk, or frozen yogurt
- 1 cup sauces or puddings made with milk

Today's Dietary Guidelines

With so many changes in the field of nutrition science, the federal government revised its Dietary Guidelines for Americans in January of 1998 (see Figure 9.2). A summary of these changes follows:

- *Alcohol, in moderation, has health benefits.* For women, moderation refers to one drink a day, preferably with a meal. This dose of alcohol has been consistently linked to higher levels of HDL, or "good" cholesterol, and fewer heart attacks than those among people who never drink.
- *Vegetarianism is healthful.* The USDA acknowledges for the first time that a vegetarian diet is beneficial to health.
- *Hydrogenated polyunsaturated fats should be limited.* Cut back on foods containing trans-fatty acids, such as margarines and shortenings.
- *Vitamin and mineral supplements are no substitute for a variety of foods.* In general, it is better to combine foods, especially those that act synergistically with each other, than it is to take supplements. The exceptions include calcium, folate, and vitamin D.
- *Sugar and salt should be used sparingly.* Although much of the information about related ill-health effects, hyperactivity, and other problems associated with excess sugar is not true, sugar is a major source of excess calories in the average American's diet. While the negative effects of salt may be overexaggerated, there are individuals who react hypertensively to excess sodium.

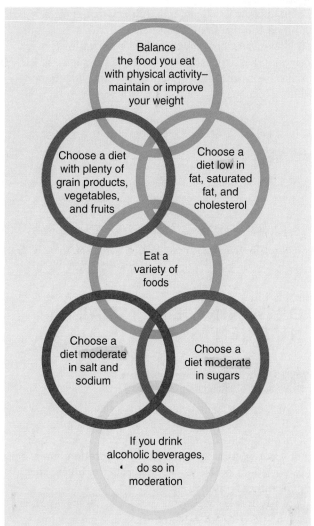

Figure 9.2

Dietary Guidelines for Americans

Source: U.S. Department of Agriculture, 1998.

- *Weight should not increase with age.* Because of increasing levels of information about the relationship between weight gain and premature health risks, maintaining a stable weight throughout life is recommended.

Making the Pyramid Work for You

Many people are overwhelmed by their first glance at the pyramid. Most of you are probably saying to yourselves, "I'd have to eat like Babe the pig, and I'd end up looking the part!" Don't despair. Consider a serving size: an ounce of ready-to-eat cereal, half a small hamburger bun or bagel, four to five potato chips, or one slice of bread. A normal bowl of cereal has three to four ounces of cereal. It is really quite easy to get all the servings in this group that you need. It is generally recommended that you try to consume these foods throughout the day.

Many people are duped into thinking that granola is a health food and that bran muffins are better than bagels or bread. Sometimes these products are loaded with fat, sugar, and calories. Read the labels on packaged products and opt for reduced-fat, whole-grain products when trying to meet pyramid requirements.

········· **WHAT DO YOU THINK?**

Which food groups from the Food Guide Pyramid are you most likely to eat adequate amounts of during a typical day? Which ones, if any, are you most likely to skimp on? What are some simple changes that you could make right now in your diet to help you comply with pyramid recommendations? Why is it more difficult for you to eat some of these food groups than others?

OBTAINING ESSENTIAL NUTRIENTS

Water: A Crucial Nutrient

If you were to go on a survival trip, which would you take with you—food or water? The average person can go for weeks without certain vitamins and minerals before experiencing serious deficiency symptoms. **Dehydration,** however, can cause serious problems within a matter of hours; after a few days without water, death is likely.

Between 50 and 60 percent of our total body weight is water. The water in our system bathes cells, aids in fluid and electrolyte balance, maintains pH balance, and transports molecules and cells throughout the body. Water is the major component of the blood, which carries oxygen and nutrients to the tissues and is responsible for maintaining cells in working order.

64 oz. per day

Most experts believe that six to eight glasses of water per day are necessary. Because of high concentrations of water in most of the foods we consume, however, the actual number of glasses needed each day is somewhat less than this for the average person. Individual needs vary drastically according to dietary factors, age, size, environmental temperature and humidity levels, exercise, and the effectiveness of the individual's system. Certain diseases, such as diabetes or cystic fibrosis, cause victims to lose fluids at a rate necessitating a higher volume of fluid intake.

Many believe that bottled water is healthier than city water. In most instances, this is not the case. Have your current water source tested if in doubt.

limited intake *water is need in almost 100% of what we do.*

Proteins

Next to water, **proteins** are the most abundant substances in the human body. Proteins are major components of nearly every cell and have been called the "body builders" because of

their role in the development and repair of bone, muscle, skin, and blood cells. Proteins are also the key elements of the antibodies that protect us from disease, of enzymes that control chemical activities in the body, and of hormones that regulate bodily functions. Moreover, proteins aid in the transport of iron, oxygen, and nutrients to all of the body's cells and supply another source of energy to body cells when fats and carbohydrates are not readily available. In short, adequate amounts of protein in the diet are vital to many body functions and to your ultimate survival.

Whenever you consume proteins, your body breaks them down into smaller molecules known as **amino acids,** which link together like beads in a necklace to form 20 different combinations. Nine of these combinations are termed **essential,** meaning that although the body needs them for growth and repair, it must receive them from the diet.

Dietary protein that supplies all of the essential amino acids is called **complete (high quality) protein.** Typically, protein from animal products is complete. When we consume foods that contain protein but are deficient in some of the essential amino acids, the total amount of protein that can be synthesized from other amino acids is decreased. For proteins to be complete, they must also be present in digestible form and in amounts proportional to body requirements.

Proteins from plant sources are often **incomplete proteins** in that they are missing one or two of the essential amino acids. Nevertheless, it is relatively easy for the non-meat-eater to combine plant foods effectively and to eat complementary sources of plant protein. An excellent example of this mutual supplementation process is eating peanut butter on whole-grain bread. Although each of these foods is deficient in

4 cal/gram • 8 essential potroteins

Dehydration   Abnormal depletion of body fluids; a result of lack of water.

Proteins   The essential constituents of nearly all body cells. Proteins are necessary for the development and repair of bone, muscle, skin, and blood, and are the key elements of antibodies, enzymes, and hormones.

Amino acids   The building blocks of protein.

Essential amino acids   Eight of the basic nitrogen-containing building blocks of protein that we must obtain from foods to ensure our personal health.

Complete (high-quality) proteins   Proteins that contain all of the eight essential amino acids.

Incomplete proteins   Proteins that are lacking in one or more of the essential amino acids.

Carbohydrates   Basic nutrients that supply the body with the energy needed to sustain normal activity.

Simple sugars   A major type of carbohydrate which provides short-term energy.

Complex carbohydrates   A major type of carbohydrate which provides sustained energy.

essential amino acids, eating them together provides high-quality protein.

Plant sources of protein fall into three general categories: *legumes* (beans, peas, peanuts, and soy products), *grains* (whole grains, corn, and pasta products), and *nuts* and seeds. Certain vegetables, such as leafy green vegetables and broccoli, also contribute valuable plant proteins. Mixing two or more foods from each of these categories during the same meal will provide all of the essential amino acids necessary to ensure adequate protein absorption. People who are not interested in obtaining all of their protein from plants can combine incomplete plant proteins with complete low-fat animal proteins such as chicken, fish, turkey, and lean red meat. Low-fat or nonfat cottage cheese, skim milk, egg whites, and nonfat dry milk all provide high-quality proteins and have few calories and little dietary fat.

Just as you need to make sure you eat enough protein, you also need to make sure not to have too much protein. Eating too much protein, particularly animal protein, can put added stress on the liver and kidneys. It also may increase calcium excretion in urine, which can elevate the risk of osteoporosis and bone fractures.[3]

Recently, some low-calorie diets that practically eliminate carbohydrates and focus on eating large quantities of protein have reemerged in the popular press. While diets that deviate from a balanced nutritional approach are almost certainly flawed, most won't do serious damage for a short period of time. However, for people who have kidney or liver problems or suffer from fluid imbalances or problems, high-protein diets should be avoided.

Situations that might warrant extra protein consumption include cases in which a person is fighting off a serious infection, recovering from surgery or blood loss, or recovering from burns. In these instances, proteins that are lost to cellular repair may need to be replaced.

The average American consumes more than 100 grams of protein daily, and about 70 percent of this comes from high-fat animal flesh and dairy products.[4] The recommended protein intake for the average man is only 63 grams, and the average woman needs only 50 grams. The typical recommendation is that, in a 2,000-calorie diet, about 10 percent of calories should come from protein, 60 percent from carbohydrates, and less than 30 percent from fat. The excess is stored as extra calories, leading to extra fat. See Figure 9.3 to determine your own recommended daily allowance (RDA) for protein.

Carbohydrates, 4cal/gram

Carbohydrates supply us with the energy needed to sustain normal daily activity. In fact, carbohydrates can actually be metabolized more quickly and efficiently than can proteins. Carbohydrates are a quick source of energy, being easily converted to glucose, the fuel for the body's cells. These foods also play an important role in the functioning of the internal

• main source of energy

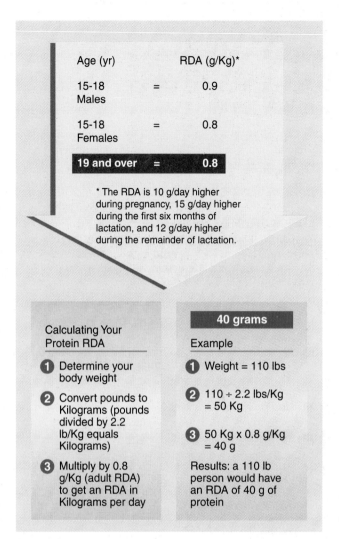

Figure 9.3

Calculating Your Protein RDA

Source: Adapted by permission of Wadsworth Publishing Company from p. 198 of *Nutrition Concepts and Controversies*, 6th ed., by Eva Hamilton, Eleanor Whitney, and Frances Sizer. Copyright 1994 by West Publishing Company. All rights reserved.

organs, the nervous system, and the muscles. They are the best source of energy for endurance athletics because they provide both an immediate and a time-released energy source as they are digested easily and then consistently metabolized in the bloodstream.

There are two major types of carbohydrates: **simple sugars,** which are found primarily in fruits, and **complex carbohydrates,** which are found in grains, cereals, dark green leafy vegetables, yellow fruits and vegetables (carrots, yams), *cruciferous* vegetables (such as broccoli, cabbage, and cauliflower), and certain root vegetables, such as potatoes. Most of us do not get enough complex carbohydrates in our daily diets.

A typical diet contains large amounts of simple sugars. The most common form is *glucose*. Eventually, the human

[handwritten: simple sugars give negative effect on athletic performance]

ACCESSING YOUR HEALTH ON THE INTERNET

Check out the following Internet sites related to nutrition:

1. *U.S. Department of Agriculture (USDA).* A full discussion of the USDA Dietary Guidelines for Americans.

   http://www.nalusda.gov/fnic/dga/dga95/cover.html

2. *American Dietetic Association (ADA).* Provides information on a full range of dietary topics, including sports nutrition, healthful cooking, and nutritional eating; also links to scientific publications and information on scholarships and public meetings.

   http://www.eatright.org

3. *U.S. Food and Drug Administration (FDA).* Provides information for consumers and professionals in the areas of food safety, supplements, and medical devices and links to other sources of nutrition and food information.

   http://www.fda.gov

4. *Food and Drug Administration's Center for Food Safety and Applied Nutrition.* Reviews key elements of food safety and congressional hearings, as well as consumer advice.

   vm.cFsan.fda.gov/list.html

5. *Tufts Health and Nutrition Information on Line.* Excellent site for review of nutritional advice on the Web. Complete with search engine.

   http://navigator.tufts.edu

body converts all types of simple sugars to glucose to provide energy to cells. In its natural form, glucose is sweet and is obtained from substances such as corn syrup, honey, molasses, vegetables, and fruits. *Fructose* is another simple sugar found in fruits and berries. Glucose and fructose are **monosaccharides** and contain only one molecule of sugar.

Disaccharides are combinations of two monosaccharides. Perhaps the best-known example is common granulated table sugar (known as sucrose), which consists of a molecule of fructose chemically bonded to a molecule of glucose. Lactose, found in milk and milk products, is another form of disaccharide, formed by the combination of glucose and galactose (another simple sugar). Disaccharides must be broken down into simple sugars before they can be used by the body.

Controlling the amount of sugar in your diet can be difficult because sugar, like sodium, is often present in food products in which you might not expect to find it. Such diverse items as ketchup, Russian dressing, Coffee-Mate, and Shake 'n' Bake derive between 30 and 65 percent of their

calories from sugar. Reading labels carefully before purchasing food products is a must.

Polysaccharides are complex carbohydrates formed by the combining of long chains of saccharides. Like disaccharides, they must be broken down into simple sugars before they can be utilized by the body. There are two major forms of complex carbohydrates: *starches* and *fiber,* or **cellulose.**

Starches make up the majority of the complex carbohydrate group. Starches in our diets come from flours, breads, pasta, potatoes, and related foods. They are stored in body muscles and the liver in a polysaccharide form called **glycogen.** When the body requires a sudden burst of energy, it breaks down glycogen into glucose.

▶ *Carbohydrates and Athletic Performance* In the last decade, carbohydrates have become the "health foods" of athletes. Many fitness enthusiasts consume concentrated sugary foods or drinks before or during athletic activity, thinking that the sugars will provide extra energy. However, in some situations, they may actually be counterproductive.

One possible problem involves the gastrointestinal tract. If your intestines react to activity (or the nervousness before competition) by moving material through the small intestine more rapidly than usual, undigested disaccharides and/or unabsorbed monosaccharides will reach the colon, which can result in a very inopportune bout of diarrhea.

Consuming large amounts of sugar during exercise can also have a negative effect on hydration. Concentrations exceeding 24 grams of sugar per 8 ounces of fluid can delay stomach emptying and hence absorption of water. Some fruit juices, fruit drinks, and other sugar-sweetened beverages have more than this amount of sugar.

Marathon runners and other people who require reserves of energy for demanding tasks often attempt to increase stores of glycogen in the body by a process known as *carbohydrate loading.* This process involves modifying the nature of both workouts and diet, usually during the week or so before competition. The athlete trains very hard early in the week while eating small amounts of carbohydrates. Right before competition, the athlete dramatically increases intake of carbohydrates to force the body to store increased levels of glycogen, to be used during endurance activities (such as the last miles of a marathon).

▶ *The Myth of Sugar and Hyperactivity* Contrary to early media reports, extensive research done in the last decade indicates that sugars *do not* cause hyperactivity.[5] In well-controlled dietary challenge studies, consumption of sugar has not been shown to have negative effects on motor activity, spontaneous behavior, performance in psychological tests, learning, memory, attention span, or problem-solving ability.

[handwritten: takes more energy to consume than what it gives to the body.]

Fiber

The role fiber plays in promoting nutrition and health has been a controversial subject in recent years. Often referred

[handwritten: fiber → digestive track clean]

to as "bulk" or "roughage," fiber is the indigestible portion of plant foods that helps move foods through the digestive system and softens stools by absorbing water. It also helps control weight by creating a feeling of fullness without adding extra calories. In spite of all the fiber advocates, the average American consumes only about 12 grams of fiber a day, about half the recommended daily amount of 25 grams.[6,7] *Insoluble fiber,* which is found in bran, whole-grain breads and cereals, and most fruits and vegetables, is associated with these gastrointestinal benefits and has also been found to reduce the risk for several forms of cancer. *Soluble fiber* appears to be a factor in lowering blood cholesterol levels, thereby reducing risk for cardiovascular disease. Major sources of soluble fiber in the diet include oat bran, dried beans (such as kidney, garbanzo, pinto, and navy beans), and some fruits and vegetables.

The best way to increase your dietary fiber is to eat more complex carbohydrates, such as whole grains, fruits, vegetables, dried peas and beans, nuts, and seeds. As with most nutritional advice, however, too much of a good thing can pose problems. Sudden increases in dietary fiber may cause flatulence (intestinal gas), cramping, or a bloated feeling. Consuming plenty of water or other liquids may reduce such side effects.

Current research supports many benefits of fiber, including the following:[8]

- *Protection against colon and rectal cancer.* One of the leading causes of cancer deaths in the United States, colorectal cancer is much rarer in countries having diets high in fiber and low in animal fat. Several studies have supported the theory that fiber-rich diets, particularly those including insoluble fiber, prevent the development of precancerous growths.
- *Protection against breast cancer.* Research into the effects of fiber on breast-cancer risks is very inconclusive. However, some studies have indicated that wheat bran (rich in insoluble fiber) reduces blood-estrogen levels, which may affect the risk for breast cancer. Another theory is that people who eat more fiber have proportionally

less fat in their diets and that this is what reduces overall risk.
- *Protection against constipation.* Insoluble fiber, consumed with adequate fluids, is the safest, most effective way to prevent or treat constipation. Fiber also helps produce gas, which in turn may initiate a bowel movement.
- *Protection against diverticulosis. Diverticulosis* is a condition in which tiny bulges or pouches form on the large intestinal wall. These bulges become irritated and cause chronic pain if under strain from constipation. Insoluble fiber helps to reduce constipation and added pain.
- *Protection against heart disease.* Many studies have indicated that soluble fiber (as in oat bran, barley, and fruit pectin) helps reduce blood cholesterol, primarily by lowering LDL ("bad") cholesterol. Whether this reduction is a direct effect or occurs instead through the displacement of fat calories by fiber calories in a high-fiber diet or through intake of other nutrients, such as iron, remain in question.
- *Protection against diabetes.* Some studies have suggested that soluble fiber improves control of blood sugar and can reduce the need for insulin or medication in people with diabetes.
- *Protection against obesity.* Because most high-fiber foods are high in carbohydrates and low in fat, they help control caloric intake.

Most experts believe that Americans should double their current consumption of dietary fiber—to 20 to 30 grams per day for most people and perhaps to 40 to 50 grams for others. To do this, the following steps are recommended:

1. Eat a variety of foods.
2. Eat at least five servings of fruits and vegetables and three to six servings of whole-grain breads, cereals, and legumes per day throughout the day.
3. Eat less processed food.
4. Eat the skins of fruits and vegetables.
5. Get your fiber from foods rather than pills or powders. Pills and powders do not supply enough essential nutrients.
6. Spread out your fiber intake.
7. Drink plenty of liquids—at least 64 ounces of water daily.

Fats reduce - don't eliminate

Fats (or *lipids*) are another group of basic nutrients. Fats play a vital role in the maintenance of healthy skin and hair, insulation of the body organs against shock, maintenance of body temperature, and the proper functioning of the cells themselves. Fats make our foods taste better and carry the fat-soluble vitamins A, D, E, and K to the cells. They also provide a concentrated form of energy in the absence of sufficient amounts of carbohydrates.

Although moderate consumption of fats is essential to health maintenance, overconsumption can be dangerous. The

---

Monosaccharide A simple sugar that contains only one molecule of sugar.

Disaccharide A combination of two monosaccharides.

Polysaccharide A complex carbohydrate formed by the combination of long chains of saccharides.

Cellulose Fiber, a major form of complex carbohydrates.

Glycogen The polysaccharide form in which glucose is stored in the liver.

Fats Basic nutrients composed of carbon and hydrogen atoms; needed for the proper functioning of cells, insulation of body organs against shock, maintenance of body temperature, and healthy skin and hair.

most common form of fat circulating in the blood is the **triglyceride,** which makes up about 95 percent of total body fat. When we consume too many calories, the excess is converted into triglycerides in the liver, which are stored throughout our bodies.

The remaining 5 percent of body fat is composed of substances such as **cholesterol,** which can accumulate on the inner walls of arteries, causing a narrowing of the channel through which blood flows. This buildup, called **plaque,** is a major cause of *atherosclerosis* (hardening of the arteries). Current thinking is that the actual amount of circulating cholesterol itself is not as important as the ratio of total cholesterol to a group of compounds called **high-density lipoproteins (HDLs).** Lipoproteins are the transport facilitators for cholesterol in the blood. High-density lipoproteins are capable of transporting more cholesterol than are **low-density lipoproteins (LDLs).** Whereas LDLs transport cholesterol to the body's cells, HDLs apparently transport circulating cholesterol to the liver for metabolism and elimination from the body. People with a high percentage of HDLs therefore appear to be at lower risk of cholesterol-clogged arteries. Regular vigorous exercise plays a part in reducing cholesterol by increasing high-density lipoproteins.

Fat cells consist of chains of carbon and hydrogen atoms. Those that are unable to hold any more hydrogen in their chemical structure are labeled **saturated fats.** They generally come from animal sources, such as meats and dairy products, and are solid at room temperature. **Unsaturated fats,** which come from plants and include most vegetable oils, are generally liquid at room temperature and have room for additional hydrogen atoms in their chemical structure. The terms *monounsaturated fat* and *polyunsaturated fat* refer to the relative number of hydrogen atoms that are missing. Peanut and olive oils are high in monounsaturated fats, whereas corn, sunflower, and safflower oils are high in polyunsaturated fats. There is currently a great deal of controversy about which type of unsaturated fat is most beneficial. Although polyunsaturated fats were favored by nutritional researchers in the early 1980s, today many researchers believe that polyunsaturates may decrease beneficial HDL levels while reducing LDL levels. Monounsaturated fats seem to lower only LDL levels and thus are the "preferred" fats of the 1990s.

▶ *Reducing Fat in Your Diet* Finding the best ways to cut fat in your diet is largely dependent on you. The following basic guidelines are a good place to start to reduce your fat intake:

- *Know what you are putting in your mouth.* No more than 10 percent of your total calories should come from saturated fat, and no more than 30 percent should come from all forms of fat.
- *Choose fat-free or low-fat versions of cakes, cookies, crackers, or chips.*

- *Use olive oil for baking and sautéing.*
- *Whenever possible, use liquid, diet, or whipped margarine: they have far less trans-fatty acids than solid fat has.*
- *Choose lean meats, fish, or poultry. Remove skin. Broil or bake whenever possible. Drain off fat after cooking.*
- *Choose fewer cold cuts, bacon, sausage, hot dogs, and organ meats.*
- *Select nonfat dairy products whenever possible.*
- *When cooking, use substitutes for butter, margarine, oils, sour cream, mayonnaise, and salad dressings.*
- *Remember to think of your food intake as an average over a day or a couple of days. If you have a high-fat breakfast or lunch, have a low-fat dinner to balance it.*

▶ **Trans-Fatty Acids: Still Bad?** Since 1961, Americans have shown that they have heeded the dire warnings about cholesterol and saturated fat by decreasing their intake of butter by over 43 percent and substituting margarine, which became known as the "better butter" after reports labeled unsaturated fats the "heart-healthy" alternative. But a widely publicized study in 1990 questioned the benefits of margarine; it indicated that margarine contains fats that raise blood cholesterol at least as much as the saturated fat in butter does.[9] The culprits? **Trans-fatty acids,** fatty acids having unusual shapes, are produced when polyunsaturated oils are *hydrogenated,* a process in which hydrogen is added to unsaturated fats to make them more solid and resistant to chemical change.[10] Besides raising cholesterol levels, trans-fatty acids have been implicated in the development of certain types of cancer.[11,12]

While the 1990 study pointed an accusing finger at the potential "bad" margarine, researchers Walter Willet and Albert Ascherio of the Harvard School of Public Health provided a resounding "wake-up call" for those of us who have faithfully avoided butter in favor of the healthier margarine alternative. According to their analysis of several fat studies, the trans-fatty acids found in margarine may not just be potentially harmful; they may in fact pose an even greater risk for heart disease than does eating saturated fat villains such as butter and lard.[13] But before you dash out and fill your refrigerator with butter, remember that Willet and Ascherio's research is also controversial. Researchers backed by the American Heart Association say that butter, which contains both cholesterol and saturated fat, is still worse than margarine.

Vitamins

Vitamins are potent, essential, organic compounds that promote growth and help maintain life and health. Every minute of every day, vitamins help maintain your nerves and skin, produce blood cells, build bones and teeth, heal wounds, and convert food energy to body energy. And they do all of this without adding any calories to your diet.

Age, heat, and other environmental conditions can destroy vitamins in food. Vitamins can be classified as either *fat soluble,* meaning that they are absorbed through the intestinal tract with the help of fats, or *water soluble,* meaning that they are easily dissolved in water. Vitamins A, D, E, and K are fat soluble; B complex vitamins and vitamin C are water soluble. Fat-soluble vitamins tend to be stored in the body. Water-soluble vitamins are generally excreted (see Table 9.1 on pages 228–229).

Despite all of the media suggestions to the contrary, few Americans suffer from true vitamin deficiencies if they eat a diet containing all of the food groups at least part of the time. Nevertheless, Americans continue to purchase large quantities of vitamin supplements. For the most part, vitamin supplements are unnecessary and, in certain instances, may even be harmful. Overuse of vitamin supplements can lead to a toxic condition known as **hypervitaminosis.**

*calcium

Minerals

Minerals are the inorganic, indestructible elements that aid physiological processes within the body. Without minerals, vitamins could not be absorbed. Minerals are readily excreted and are usually not toxic. **Macrominerals** are those minerals that the body needs in fairly large amounts: sodium, calcium, phosphorus, magnesium, potassium, sulfur, and chloride. **Trace minerals** include iron, zinc, manganese, copper, iodine, and cobalt. Only trace amounts of these minerals are needed, and serious problems may result if excesses or deficiencies occur. Specific types of minerals are listed in Table 9.2 on pages 230–231.

Although minerals are necessary for body function, there are limits on the amounts of each that we should consume. Americans tend to overuse or underuse certain minerals.

▶ *Sodium*   Sodium is necessary for the regulation of blood and body fluids, for the successful transmission of nerve impulses, for heart activity, and for certain metabolic functions. However, we consume much more sodium every day than we need. The RDA subcommittee recommended that sodium be restricted to no more than 2,400 milligrams per day; less is better. The most common form of sodium in the American diet comes from table salt. However, table salt accounts for only 15 percent of sodium intake. The remainder of dietary sodium comes from the water we drink and from highly processed foods that are infused with sodium to enhance flavor. Many fast-food entrees and convenience entrees have 500 to 1,000 milligrams of sodium per serving.

Many experts believe that there is a link between excessive sodium intake and hypertension (high blood pressure). Although this theory is controversial, researchers recommend that hypertensive Americans cut back on sodium consumption to reduce their risk for cardiovascular disorders.[14] Osteoporosis researchers are confirming that high sodium intake may increase calcium loss in the urine, thus increasing your risk for debilitating fractures as you age.

▶ *Calcium*   The issue of calcium consumption has gained national attention with the rising incidence of osteoporosis among elderly women. Although calcium plays a vital role in building strong bones and teeth, muscle contraction, blood clotting, nerve impulse transmission, regulating heartbeat, and fluid balance within cells, most Americans do not consume the 1,200 milligrams of calcium per day established by the RDA.

Because calcium intake is so important throughout your life for a strong bone structure, it is critical that you consume the minimum required amounts each day. Over half of our calcium intake usually comes from milk, one of the highest

---

Triglyceride   The most common form of fat in the body; excess calories consumed are converted into triglycerides and stored as body fat.

Cholesterol   A form of fat circulating in the blood that can accumulate on the inner walls of arteries.

Plaque   Cholesterol buildup on the inner walls of arteries, causing a narrowing of the channel through which blood flows; a major cause of atherosclerosis.

High-density lipoproteins (HDLs)   Compounds that facilitate the transport of cholesterol in the blood to the liver for metabolism and elimination from the body.

Low-density lipoproteins (LDLs)   Compounds that facilitate the transport of cholesterol in the blood to the body's cells.

Saturated fats   Fats that are unable to hold any more hydrogen in their chemical structure; derived mostly from animal sources; solid at room temperature.

Unsaturated fats   Fats that do have room for more hydrogen in their chemical structure; derived mostly from plants; liquid at room temperature.

Trans-fatty acids   Fatty acids that are produced when polyunsaturated oils are hydrogenated to make them more solid.

Vitamins   Essential organic compounds that promote growth and reproduction and help maintain life and health.

Hypervitaminosis   A toxic condition caused by overuse of vitamin supplements.

Minerals   Inorganic, indestructible elements that aid physiological processes.

Macrominerals   Minerals that the body needs in fairly large amounts.

Trace minerals   Minerals that the body needs in only very small amounts.

TABLE 9.1
A Guide to the Vitamins

VITAMIN	BEST SOURCES	CHIEF ROLES
Water-soluble vitamins		
Thiamin 1.5 mg (RDA + RDI)	Meat, pork, liver, fish, poultry, whole-grain and enriched breads, cereals, pasta, nuts, legumes, wheat germ, oats.	Helps enzymes release energy from carbohydrate; supports normal appetite and nervous system function.
Riboflavin 1.7 mg (RDA + RDI)	Milk, dark green vegetables, yogurt, cottage cheese, liver, meat, whole-grain or enriched breads and cereals.	Helps enzymes release energy from carbohydrate, fat, and protein; promotes healthy skin and normal vision.
Niacin 20 mg NE (RDA + RDI)	Meat, eggs, poultry, fish, milk, whole-grain and enriched breads and cereals, nuts, legumes, peanuts, nutritional yeast, all protein foods.	Helps enzymes release energy from energy nutrients; promotes health of skin, nerves, and digestive system.
Vitamin B_6 2.0 mg (RDA + RDI)	Meat, poultry, fish, shellfish, legumes, whole-grain products, green, leafy vegetables, bananas.	Protein and fat metabolism; formation of antibodies and red blood cells; helps convert tryptophan to niacin.
Folate 400 mcg (DFE + RDA)	Green, leafy vegetables, liver, legumes, seeds.	Red blood cell formation; protein metabolism; new cell division; prevents neural tube defects.
Vitamin B_{12} 2.4 mg (RDA)	Meat, fish, poultry, shellfish, milk, cheese, eggs, nutritional yeast.	Helps maintain nerve cells; red blood cell formation; synthesis of genetic material.
Pantothenic acid 5–7 mg (AI)	Widespread in foods.	Coenzyme in energy metabolism.
Biotin 30 mcg (AI)	Widespread in foods.	Coenzyme in energy metabolism; fat synthesis; glycogen formation.
Vitamin C (ascorbic acid) (RDI + RDA) = 60 mg	Citrus fruits, cabbage-type vegetables, tomatoes, potatoes, dark green vegetables, peppers, lettuce, cantaloupe, strawberries, mangos, papayas.	Synthesis of collagen (helps heal wounds, maintains bone and teeth, strengthens blood vessels); antioxidant; strengthens resistance to infection; helps body's absorption of iron.
Fat-soluble vitamins		
Vitamin A 5,000 IU	*Retinal:* fortified milk and margarine, cream, cheese, butter, eggs, liver. *Carotene:* spinach and other dark leafy greens, broccoli, deep orange fruits (apricots, peaches, cantaloupe) and vegetables (squash, carrots, sweet potatoes, pumpkin).	Vision, growth and repair of body tissues; reproduction; bone and tooth formation; immunity; cancer protection; hormone synthesis.
Vitamin D 400 IU (RDA + RDI)	Self-synthesis with sunlight, fortified milk, fortified margarine, eggs, liver, fish.	Calcium and phosphorus metabolism (bone and tooth formation); aids body's absorption of calcium.
Vitamin E 30 IU (RDA + RDI)	Vegetable oils, green leafy vegetables, wheat germ, whole-grain products, butter, liver, egg yolk, milk fat, nuts, seeds.	Protects red blood cells; antioxidant; stabilization of cell membranes.
Vitamin K 70–140 µg	Bacterial synthesis in digestive tract, liver, green, leafy, and cabbage-type vegetables, milk.	Synthesis of blood-clotting proteins and a blood protein that regulates blood calcium.

DEFICIENCY SYMPTOMS	TOXICITY SYMPTOMS
Beriberi, edema, heart irregularity, mental confusion, muscle weakness, low morale, impaired growth.	Rapid pulse, weakness, headaches, insomnia, irritability.
Eye problems, skin disorders around nose and mouth.	None reported, but an excess of any of the B vitamins can cause a deficiency of the others.
Pellagra: skin rash on parts exposed to sun, loss of appetite, dizziness, weakness, irritability, fatigue, mental confusion, indigestion.	Flushing, nausea, headaches, cramps, ulcer irritation, heartburn, abnormal liver function, low blood pressure.
Nervous disorders, skin rash, muscle weakness, anemia, convulsions, kidney stones.	Depression, fatigue, irritability, headaches, numbness, damage to nerves, difficulty walking.
Anemia, heartburn, diarrhea, smooth tongue depression, poor growth.	Diarrhea, insomnia, irritability, may mask a vitamin B_{12} deficiency.
Anemia, smooth tongue, fatigue, nerve degeneration progressing to paralysis.	None reported.
Rare; sleep disturbances, nausea, fatigue.	Occasional diarrhea.
Loss of appetite, nausea, depression, muscle pain, weakness, fatigue, rash.	None reported.
Scurvy, anemia, atherosclerotic plaques, depression, frequent infections, bleeding gums, loosened teeth, pinpoint hemorrhages, muscle degeneration, rough skin, bone fragility, poor wound healing, hysteria.	Nausea, abdominal cramps, diarrhea, breakdown of red blood cells in persons with certain genetic disorders, deficiency symptoms may appear at first on withdrawal of high doses.
Night blindness, rough skin, susceptibility to infection, impaired bone growth, abnormal tooth and jaw alignment, eye problems leading to blindness, impaired growth.	Red blood cell breakage, nosebleeds, abdominal cramps, nausea, diarrhea, weight loss, blurred vision, irritability, loss of appetite, bone pain, dry skin, rashes, hair loss, cessation of menstruation, growth retardation.
Rickets in children; osteomalacia in adults; abnormal growth, joint pain, soft bones.	Raised blood calcium, constipation, weight loss, irritability, weakness, nausea, kidney stones, mental and physical retardation.
Muscle wasting, weakness, red blood cell breakage, anemia, hemorrhaging, fibrocystic breast disease.	Interference with anticlotting medication, general discomfort.
Hemorrhaging.	Interference with anticlotting medication; may cause jaundice.

Values vary (increase) among women who are pregnant or lactating.

Sources: Adapted by permission of Wadsworth Publishing Company from pp. 152–153 of Personal Nutrition, *2d ed., by Marie Boyle and Gail Zyla. Copyright 1991 by West Publishing Company. All rights reserved; National Academy Press Website under "Reading Room," at http://www.Nap.edu. (1999)*

TABLE 9.2
A Guide to the Minerals

MINERAL	SIGNIFICANT SOURCES	CHIEF FUNCTIONS IN THE BODY
Calcium RDA = 800–1,200 mg + RDI = 1,000 mg	Milk and milk products, small fish (with bones), tofu, greens, legumes.	Principal mineral of bones and teeth; involved in muscle contraction and relaxation, nerve function, blood clotting, blood pressure.
Phosphorus RDA = 1,000 mg	All animal tissues.	Part of every cell; involved in acid-based balance.
Magnesium RDA = 400 mg	Nuts, legumes, whole grains, dark green vegetables, seafoods, chocolate, cocoa.	Involved in bone mineralization, protein synthesis, enzyme action, normal muscular contraction, nerve transmission.
Sodium RDA = 500 mg DRV = 2,400 mg	Salt, soy sauce; processed foods; cured, canned, pickled, and many boxed foods.	Helps maintain normal fluid and acid-base balance.
Chloride RDA = 750 mg	Salt, soy sauce; processed foods.	Part of stomach acid, necessary for proper digestion, fluid balance.
Potassium RDA = 2,000 mg DRV = 3,500 mg	All whole foods: meats, milk, fruits, vegetables, grains, legumes.	Facilitates many reactions including protein synthesis, fluid balance, nerve transmission, and contraction of muscles.
Iodine RDA = 150 µg RDI = 150 µg	Iodized salt, seafood.	Part of thyroxine, which regulates metabolism.
Iron RDA = 18 mg RDI = 18 mg	Beef, fish, poultry, shellfish, eggs, legumes, dried fruits.	Hemoglobin formation; part of myoglobin; energy utilization.
Zinc RDA = 15 mg RDI = 15 mg	Protein-containing foods: meats, fish, poultry, grains, vegetables.	Part of many enzymes; present in insulin; involved in making genetic material and proteins, immunity, vitamin A transport, taste, wound healing, making sperm, normal fetal development.
Copper RDA = 2 mg RDI = 2 mg	Meats, drinking water.	Absorption of iron; part of several enzymes.
Fluoride 1.5–4.0 mg	Drinking water (if naturally fluoride-containing or fluoridated), tea, seafood.	Formation of bones and teeth; helps make teeth resistant to decay and bones resistant to mineral loss.
Selenium 50–70 µg	Seafood, meats, grains.	Helps protect body compounds from oxidation.
Chromium 50–200 µg	Meats, unrefined foods, fats, vegetable oils.	Associated with insulin and required for the release of energy from glucose.
Molybdenum 75–250 µg	Legumes, cereals, organ meats.	Facilitates, with enzymes, many cell processes.
Manganese 2.0–5.0 mg	Widely distributed in foods.	Facilitates, with enzymes, many cell processes.

DEFICIENCY SYMPTOMS	TOXICITY SYMPTOMS
Stunted growth in children; bone loss (osteoporosis) in adults.	Excess calcium is excreted except in hormonal imbalance states.
Unknown.	Can create relative deficiency of calcium.
Weakness, confusion, depressed pancreatic hormone secretion, growth failure, behavioral disturbances, muscle spasms.	Not known.
Muscle cramps, mental apathy, loss of appetite.	Hypertension (in salt-sensitive persons).
Growth failure in children, muscle cramps, mental apathy, loss of appetite.	Normally harmless (the gas chlorine is a poison but evaporates from water); disturbed acid-base balance; vomiting.
Muscle weakness, paralysis, confusion; can cause death; accompanies dehydration.	Causes muscular weakness; triggers vomiting; if given into a vein, can stop the heart.
Goiter, cretinism.	Very high intakes depress thyroid activity.
Anemia: weakness, pallor, headaches, reduced resistance to infection, inability to concentrate.	Iron overload: infections, liver injury.
Growth failure in children, delayed development of sexual organs, loss of taste, poor wound healing.	Fever, nausea, vomiting, diarrhea.
Anemia, bone changes (rare in human beings).	Unknown except as part of a rare hereditary disease (Wilson's disease).
Susceptibility to tooth decay and bone loss.	Fluorosis (discoloration of teeth).
Anemia (rare).	Digestive system disorders.
Diabetes-like condition marked by inability to use glucose normally.	Unknown as a nutrition disorder. Occupational exposures damage skin and kidneys.
Unknown.	Enzyme inhibition.
In animals: poor growth, nervous system disorders, abnormal reproduction.	Poisoning, nervous system disorders.

Because we have less information about minerals than about vitamins, RDA recommendations are estimates of minimum requirements.

Source: Adapted by permission of Wadsworth Publishing Company from pp. 178–179 of Personal Nutrition, *2d ed., by Marie Boyle and Gail Zyla; and pp. 298–300 of* Nutrition Concepts and Controversies, *5th ed., by Eva Hamilton, Eleanor Whitney, and Frances Sizer. Copyright 1994 by West Publishing Company. All rights reserved.*

sources of dietary calcium. New, calcium-fortified orange juice provides a good way to get calcium if you are not a milk drinker. Many green, leafy vegetables are good sources of calcium, but some contain oxalic acid, which makes their calcium harder to absorb. Spinach, chard, and beet greens are not particularly good sources of calcium, whereas broccoli, cauliflower, and many peas and beans offer good supplies (pinto beans and soybeans are among the best). Many nuts, particularly almonds, brazil nuts, and hazelnuts, and seeds such as sunflower and sesame contain good amounts of calcium. Molasses is fairly high in calcium. Some fruits—such as citrus fruits, figs, raisins, and dried apricots—have moderate amounts. Bone meal is not a recommended calcium source due to possible contamination.

Of interest to those of you who drink carbonated soft drinks is the fact that the added phosphoric acid (phosphate) in these drinks can cause you to excrete extra calcium, which may result in calcium being pulled out of your bones. Calcium/phosphorous imbalances may lead to kidney stones and other calcification problems as well as to increased atherosclerotic plaque.

We also know that sunlight increases the manufacture of vitamin D in the body, and is therefore like having an extra calcium source because vitamin D improves absorption of calcium. Stress, on the other hand, tends to contribute to calcium depletion. It is generally best to take calcium throughout the day, consuming protein, vitamin D, and vitamin C-containing foods with it for optimum absorption. Experts vary on which type of supplemental calcium is most readily and efficiently absorbed, although bone meal, aspartate, or citrate salts of calcium are among those most often recommended. The best way to obtain calcium, like all the other nutrients, is to consume it as part of a balanced diet.

▶ **Iron** Iron is a problem mineral for millions of people. Although it is found in every cell of all living things, many humans have difficulty getting enough iron in their daily diets. Females aged 19 to 50 need about 18 milligrams per day, and males aged 19 to 50 need about 10 milligrams. Iron deficiencies can lead to **anemia,** a problem resulting from the body's inability to produce hemoglobin, the bright red, oxygen-carrying component of the blood. When this occurs, body cells receive less oxygen, and carbon dioxide wastes are removed less efficiently. These problems cause a person to feel tired and run down. Anemia can be caused by accidents, cancers, ulcers, and other conditions, but iron deficiency is a common cause. Generally, women are more likely than men to suffer from iron deficiency problems, partly because they typically eat less than men, and their diets therefore contain less iron. Also, because blood loss is the major reason for iron depletion, women having heavy menstrual flows may be prone to iron deficiency. Another problem with iron deficiency is that the immune system becomes less effective, which can lead to increased risk of illness.

Recently, researchers have speculated that too much iron in the body may increase the risk for heart disease. They point to the low risk for heart disease in premenopausal women and the striking rise in risk in postmenopausal women as a possible indicator of such an association. An important study in 1992 indicated that men who consume high-iron diets also appear to be at increased risk. But this research is preliminary; since this early study, research about the relationship between iron and CVD has been inconclusive.[15] Blood donors and pregnant women may need to increase iron intake. A less common problem, iron toxicity, is caused by too much iron in the blood.

THE MEDICINAL VALUE OF FOOD

The old adage "you are what you eat" has become a motto by which to live. This is supported by the increased interest in the *benefits* of foods and food products that has recently emerged. These beneficial foods have been coined **"Functional Foods,"** based on the ancient belief that eating the right foods may not only prevent disease, but also actually cure disease. This perspective is gaining increased credibility among the scientific community.

This positive regard is due primarily to results from two major studies, the *Dietary Approaches to Stop Hypertension (DASH) Study,* and the *Dietary Intervention Study (DIS),* both of which provide compelling evidence that diet may be as effective as drugs in bringing borderline hypertension back to the normal range. It may also play a role in reducing cholesterol and controlling insulin-dependent diabetes.[16]

In these clinically controlled trials, subjects were assigned to two groups: treatment and control. In the treatment group, subjects had to follow recommended diets, which were low in fats and high in fiber and fruits. The control group followed typical American dietary intervention. In each study, subjects in the treatment groups had significantly improved health indicators (blood pressure, cholesterol, and blood glucose in the DIS study), which reflected the potential benefits of diet in improving health and treating disease.

Information from leading nutritional experts at the Linus Pauling Institute at Oregon State University summarized other research that provides compelling evidence that certain nutrients may have a powerful impact on some of the world's lead-

Anemia Iron deficiency disease that results from the body's inability to produce hemoglobin.

Functional Foods Foods believed to be beneficial and/or serve to prevent disease.

ing health problems, especially heart disease. Some of the major findings from studies in this field include:[17]

- Elderly men and women with the highest plasma levels of vitamin C had a 47 percent lower risk of dying from heart disease.
- Vitamin C supplementation substantially improved blood vessel relaxation in patients with heart disease, diabetes, hypertension, and other illnesses, and was shown to relieve the pain of angina pectoris.
- Daily intake of about 100 to 200 international units of vitamin E was associated with a substantially lowered risk of heart disease.
- Daily intake of 400 to 800 international units of vitamin E was associated with a 75 percent decrease of second, nonfatal heart attacks in heart disease patients.

Much of this research focuses on the beneficial effects of a class of nutrients known as *antioxidants*.

Antioxidants eat a balanced diet

One of the components of fruits and vegetables that has been heavily promoted in the 1990s is antioxidants. These nutrients have been touted as doing everything from protecting DNA to preventing some forms of cancers. The public, responding to these reports, has been consuming these products in droves, a trend that has many health experts alarmed. While no one disputes that antioxidants, the most common of which are vitamins C and E, are beneficial to the body, the "more is better" approach may be quite harmful and may in fact cause health problems for those who consider themselves most health-conscious.[18] A recent British study of 30 healthy men and women showed that taking a daily 500-milligram supplement of Vitamin C had both positive and negative effects on DNA. Similarly, a widely cited Finnish study of 29,000 men reported that for those who smoked a pack of cigarettes a day and took daily beta carotene supplements, risk of lung cancer actually increased by 18 percent over those who took no supplement.[19] Newer research on the benefits of the antioxidant compound *lycopene,* found in tomatoes and tomato-based products, indicates a possible beneficial effect as a prostate and lung cancer protector. If this seemingly conflicting information leaves you confused, you are not alone.

According to the experts, the answer is moderation. "Antioxidants should always be taken as part of a well-balanced mixture, either as a diet or as a supplement, and not singly," says Dr. John R. Smythies, a researcher at the University of California–San Diego and author of *Every Person's Guide to Antioxidants*.[20] Smythies, like many other experts, advocates for balance in intake and advises that adults take 500 milligrams of daily vitamin C and 400 to 800 I.U. of vitamin E, plus 10 milligrams of beta carotene. (Other antioxidant researchers might go to 1,000 milligrams of vitamin C for the general population and more vitamin E for anyone who exercises intensely for more than an hour each day.[21] Other

experts, such as Dr. Balz Frei at the Linus Pauling Institute, indicate that the "200 rule" might be the best option. This recommendation calls for fruits and vegetables in the diet and a supplement of 200 milligrams of vitamin C, 200 international units of vitamin E, and 200 micrograms of selenium, along with 400 micrograms of folate and 3 milligrams of vitamin B_6.[22] It is believed that these combinations will reduce the body's overproduction of free radicals, those unstable molecules that can damage healthy cells and turn low-density lipoproteins into artery-clogging compounds.[23] However, even the lowering of free radicals is controversial. Many believe that free radicals are beneficial and work to kill germs in the same way they kill other cells. From this standpoint, killing off free radicals may result in lowering your resistance to harmful pathogens.

Since there is no ideal solution, the best rule of thumb continues to be to check your daily diet for the presence of necessary nutrients and try to get antioxidants from fruits and vegetables. (See Table 9.3 for a listing of common sources of antioxidants.) While antioxidants may be beneficial, a conservative regimen will maximize their benefits.

TABLE 9.3
Antioxidant Options for Your Daily Diet

Beta-carotene	Apricots, cantaloupe, carrots, collard greens, fennel, kale, mustard greens, peaches, pumpkin, red pepper, romaine lettuce, spinach, sweet potatoes, Swiss chard, winter squash
Vitamin C	Broccoli, Brussels sprouts, cantaloupe, cauliflower, citrus fruits, green pepper, kiwi, papaya, peaches, red cabbage, red pepper, strawberries, potatoes
Vitamin E	Wheat germ, seeds, nuts, dark green leafy vegetables, avocados, peanuts, sweet potatoes
Lycopene	Tomatoes, apricots, guava, pink grapefruit, mango, oranges, peaches, papaya, watermelon
Lutein/zexanthin	Dark leafy green vegetables, especially spinach and broccoli
Flavonoids	Apples, citrus fruits, flaxseed, lentils, onions, peanuts, rice, soybeans, blueberries, cranberries, currants, olive oil, red wine, green tea, chamomile tea, black tea
Polyphenols	Chocolate, coffee, grapes, nuts, oranges, strawberries, green tea, black tea, red wine

Folate

In 1998, the Food and Drug Administration (FDA) took a major dietary plunge by mandating *folate* fortification of all bread, cereal, rice, and macaroni products sold in the United States. This practice, which will boost folate intake by an average of about 100 micrograms daily, is expected to decrease the number of infants born with spina bifida and other neural tube defects.

Folate is a form of vitamin B that is believed to decrease blood levels of *homocysteine,* an amino acid that has been linked to vascular diseases. Homocysteine is created as a result of the breakdown of methionine, an amino acid found in meat and other protein-laden foods. Two B vitamins—folate and B_6—are believed to control homocysteine levels.[24] When intake of folate and B_6 is low, homocysteine levels rise in the blood. Recent studies indicate that when the level of homocysteine rises, arterial walls and blood platelets become sticky, which encourages clotting. (Note: Homocysteine levels tend to rise with age, smoking, and menopause.) When clots develop in areas already narrowed by atherosclerosis, a heart attack or stroke is likely.

Although the amount of folate needed to protect the heart has not been determined, many older adults have jumped on the folate bandwagon, taking daily folate supplements of up to 800 micrograms. Recently, a new *dietary folate equivalent (DFE)* was established to distinguish folate in food from its synthetic counterpart, *folic acid.* As a food additive or a supplement, folic acid is absorbed about twice as efficiently as is folate. The DFE for folate in women aged 19 or over is approximately 400 micrograms, with higher levels for pregnant or lactating women. (See Table 9.1 on pages 228–229 for daily recommendations of other B vitamins.) The potential dangers of taking too much folate include a potential masking of B_{12} deficiencies and resulting problems, ranging from nerve damage, immunodeficiency problems, anemia, fatigue, and headache, to constipation, diarrhea, weight loss, gastrointestinal disturbances, and a host of neurological symptoms.[25]

GENDER AND NUTRITION

Men and women differ in body size, body composition, and overall metabolic rates. They therefore have differing needs for most nutrients throughout the life cycle (see tables on vitamin and mineral requirements) and face unique difficulties in keeping on track with their dietary goals. Some of these differences have already been discussed. However, there are some diet/nutrition factors that need further consideration.

Different Cycles, Different Needs

From menarche to menopause, women undergo cyclical physiological changes that can have dramatic effects on metabolism, nutritional needs, and efforts to stick to a nutritional plan. For example, during the menstrual cycle, many women report significant food cravings that may cause them to overconsume. Later in women's lives, with the advent of menopause, nutritional needs again change rather dramatically. With depletion of the hormone estrogen, the body's need for calcium to ward off bone deterioration becomes pronounced. Women must pay closer attention to their exercise patterns and to getting enough calcium through diet or dietary supplements or run the risk of severe osteoporosis (see Chapter 13 for a more complete description of this disease).

Changing the Meat and Potatoes Man

Although men do not have the same cyclical patterns and dietary needs as women, they do suffer from a heritage of dietary excesses that are difficult to change. The "meat and potatoes" kind of guy has been part of the American way since our earliest agrarian years. Consider the following:

- Men who eat red meat as a main dish five or more times a week have four times the risk of colon cancer of men who eat red meat less than once a month.
- Heavy red meat eaters are more than twice as likely to get prostate cancer and nearly 5 times more likely to get colon cancer.
- For every 3 servings of fruits or vegetables per day men can expect a 22 percent lower risk of stroke.
- High fruit and vegetable diets may lower the risk of lung cancer in smokers from 20 times the risk of non-smokers to "only" ten times the risk. They may also protect against oral, throat, pancreas, and bladder cancers, all of which are more common in smokers.
- The fastest-rising malignancy in the U.S. is cancer of the lower esophagus, particularly in white men. While obesity seems to be a factor, fruits and vegetables are the protectors. (The average American male eats less than 3 servings/day, although 5–9 servings is recommended. Women average 3–7 servings/day.)

Is there something in the meat that makes it inherently bad? By eating so much protein a person fills up sooner and never gets around to the fruits and vegetables. Thus, any potential protective factors may be lost.

Folate   A type of vitamin B that is believed to decrease levels of homocysteine, an amino acid that has been linked to vascular diseases.

Recommended Dietary Allowances (RDAs)   The average daily intakes of energy and nutrients considered adequate to meet the needs of most healthy people in the United States under usual conditions.

Adequate Intakes (AIs)   Best estimates of nutritional needs.

Nutritional needs of men and women vary a great deal depending on a number of factors, including levels of fitness, hormonal changes, and age. These metabolic differences need to be taken into consideration when eating for maximal energy.

······ **WHAT DO YOU THINK?**

Think about the women that you know who seem to have weight problems. What are their ages? What factors may have influenced them to have more problems keeping weight off than you may have? What advantages, if any, do men have in controlling their eating behaviors and managing their weight?

Determining Nutritional Needs

Determining the right amount of a nutrient that people of different ages, sex, activity level, or physical condition must obtain daily is no easy task. Since the early 1940s various special national committees have been working on policies to provide sound advice for Americans.

▶ *Recommended Dietary Allowances—Adequate Intake* For more than 50 years, a document called the **"Recommended Dietary Allowances (RDAs)"** has been the gold standard for nutrient intake in the United States.[26] Established by the Committee on Dietary Allowances, the RDAs are the average daily intakes of energy and nutrients considered adequate to

meet the needs of most healthy people in the United States under usual conditions. Revised every 5 years, the RDAs reflect the fact that a person's actual level of need for a nutrient can be influenced by age, sex, body size, growth, and reproductive status. Thus, pregnant and lactating women have their own set of RDAs. Today, RDAs are based on the quantity necessary to provide health benefits. When evidence doesn't support an RDA, **Adequate Intakes (AIs)** are used as the best estimates of nutritional needs.

▶ *Daily Values, RDIs, and DRVs* From the RDAs came the more familiar U.S. RDA (U.S. Recommended Daily Allowances) established by the Food and Drug Administration (FDA). The U.S. RDAs were set as maximum values to account for potential nutrient loss during absorption, cooking, and storage of food. People followed the U.S. RDAs for years until the entire system was overhauled and made even more specific for consumers. In 1993, the FDA supplemented most U.S. RDAs with "% Daily Values," a set of standard values purported to represent the nutrient needs of the typical consumer. Daily Values are made up of two sets of reference values. The first, the Reference Daily Intake (RDI), reflects the average daily allowances for proteins, vitamins, and minerals based on the RDA. The second, the Daily Reference Values (DRV), is for nutrients and food components, such as fat and fiber, that do not have an established RDA but are highly correlated with health. At the same time the new Daily Values were issued, the FDA also issued a new food label that is now familiar to most consumers (see Figure 9.4 on page 236). Some of the RDIs and DRVs are included with the Daily Value information now found on food labels.

······ **WHAT DO YOU THINK?**

Of all of the nutrients discussed in this section, which one do you worry about not getting enough in your diet the most? What is the basis for your worry? Are you planning to take any action to make sure your daily intake is adequate? What steps will you take?

VEGETARIANISM

For aesthetic, animal rights, economic, personal, health, cultural, or religious reasons, some people choose specialized diets. Between 5 and 15 percent of all Americans today claim to be some form of vegetarian. Normally, vegetarianism provides a superb alternative to our high-fat, high-calorie, meat-based cuisine, but, without proper information, vegetarians can also have dietary problems.

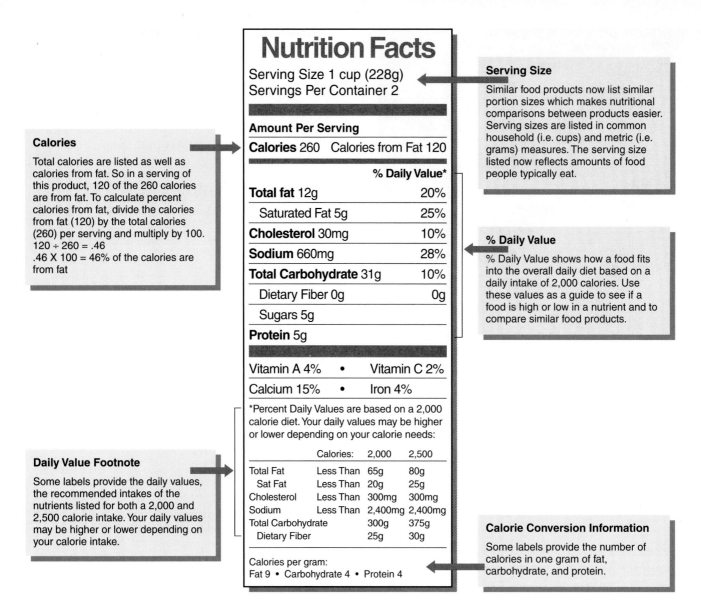

Nutrition Facts

Serving Size 1 cup (228g)
Servings Per Container 2

Amount Per Serving

Calories 260   Calories from Fat 120

	% Daily Value*
Total fat 12g	20%
Saturated Fat 5g	25%
Cholesterol 30mg	10%
Sodium 660mg	28%
Total Carbohydrate 31g	10%
Dietary Fiber 0g	0g
Sugars 5g	
Protein 5g	

Vitamin A 4%	•	Vitamin C 2%
Calcium 15%	•	Iron 4%

*Percent Daily Values are based on a 2,000 calorie diet. Your daily values may be higher or lower depending on your calorie needs:

	Calories:	2,000	2,500
Total Fat	Less Than	65g	80g
Sat Fat	Less Than	20g	25g
Cholesterol	Less Than	300mg	300mg
Sodium	Less Than	2,400mg	2,400mg
Total Carbohydrate		300g	375g
Dietary Fiber		25g	30g

Calories per gram:
Fat 9 • Carbohydrate 4 • Protein 4

Calories

Total calories are listed as well as calories from fat. So in a serving of this product, 120 of the 260 calories are from fat. To calculate percent calories from fat, divide the calories from fat (120) by the total calories (260) per serving and multiply by 100.
120 ÷ 260 = .46
.46 X 100 = 46% of the calories are from fat

Serving Size

Similar food products now list similar portion sizes which makes nutritional comparisons between products easier. Serving sizes are listed in common household (i.e. cups) and metric (i.e. grams) measures. The serving size listed now reflects amounts of food people typically eat.

% Daily Value

% Daily Value shows how a food fits into the overall daily diet based on a daily intake of 2,000 calories. Use these values as a guide to see if a food is high or low in a nutrient and to compare similar food products.

Daily Value Footnote

Some labels provide the daily values, the recommended intakes of the nutrients listed for both a 2,000 and 2,500 calorie intake. Your daily values may be higher or lower depending on your calorie intake.

Calorie Conversion Information

Some labels provide the number of calories in one gram of fat, carbohydrate, and protein.

Figure 9.4
The New Food Label

Source: Reprinted by permission from Darlene Zimmerman, M.S., R.D., "Hungry for a New Food Label?" *Weight Watchers Thinline* (published by The WW Group Inc.), July–August 1994, 9.

The term **vegetarian** means different things to different people. Strict vegetarians, or *vegans,* avoid all foods of animal origin, including dairy products and eggs. Far more common are *lacto-vegetarians,* who eat dairy products but avoid flesh foods. Their diet can be low in fat and cholesterol, but only if they consume skim milk and other low- or nonfat products. *Ovo-vegetarians* add eggs to their diet, while *lacto-ovo-vegetarians* eat both dairy products and eggs. *Pesco-vegetarians* eat fish, dairy products, and eggs, while *semivegetarians* eat chicken, fish, dairy products, and eggs. Some people in the semivegetarian category prefer to call themselves "non-red-meat eaters."

Generally, people who follow a balanced vegetarian diet have lower weights, better cholesterol levels, fewer problems with irregular bowel movements (constipation and diarrhea), and a lower risk of heart disease than do nonvegetarians. Some preliminary evidence suggests that vegetarians may also have a reduced risk for colon and breast cancer. Whether these lower risks are due to the vegetarian diet per se or to some combination of lifestyle variables remains unclear.

Although in the past vegetarians often suffered from vitamin deficiencies, today's vegetarian is usually extremely adept at combining the right types of foods to ensure proper nutrient intake. People who eat dairy products and small

[handwritten notes:] religious financial social animal rights

amounts of chicken or fish are seldom nutrient-deficient; in fact, while vegans typically get 50 to 60 grams of protein per day, lacto-ovo vegetarians normally consume between 70 and 90 grams per day, well beyond the RDA. Vegan diets may be deficient in vitamins B_2 (riboflavin), B_{12}, and D. Riboflavin is found mainly in meat, eggs, and dairy products; but broccoli, asparagus, almonds, and fortified cereals are also good sources. Vitamins B_{12} and D are found only in dairy products and fortified products such as soy milk. Vegans are also at risk for calcium, iron, zinc, and other mineral deficiencies, but these nutrients can be obtained from supplements. Strict vegans have to pay much more attention to what they eat than the average person does, but by eating complementary combinations of plant products, they can receive adequate amounts of essential amino acids. Eating a full variety of grains, legumes, fruits, vegetables, and seeds each day will help to keep even the strictest vegetarian in excellent health. Pregnant women, the elderly, the sick, and children who are vegans need to take special care to ensure that their diets are adequate. People who are on heavy aerobic exercise programs (over three hours per week) may need to increase their protein consumption.

The Vegetarian Pyramid

Dr. Arlene Spark, a nutritionist at New York Medical College, devised a food guide pyramid in 1994 that conveys all the essentials of a vegetarian diet. Modeled after the Food Guide Pyramid discussed earlier in this chapter, the vegetarian version clarifies what people who don't eat meat need to do to stay healthy. The vegetarian pyramid defines the following categories. We include examples of single servings of foods in each category.

Grains and Starchy Vegetables Group (6–11 servings/day)

- 1 slice bread
- ½ roll or bagel
- 1 tortilla (6")
- 1 ounce cold cereal
- ½ cup cooked cereal, rice, or pasta
- 3–4 crackers
- 3 cups popcorn
- ½ cup corn
- 1 medium potato
- ½ cup green peas

Vegetarian   A term with a variety of meanings: *vegans* avoid all foods of animal origin; *lacto-vegetarians* avoid flesh foods but eat dairy products; *ovo-vegetarians* avoid flesh foods but eat eggs; *lacto-ovo-vegetarians* avoid flesh foods but eat both dairy products and eggs; *pesco-vegetarians* avoid meat but eat fish, dairy products, and eggs; *semivegetarians* eat chicken, fish, dairy products, and eggs.

Vegetable Group (3 + servings/day)

- ½ cup cooked or chopped raw vegetables
- 1 cup raw leafy vegetables
- ¾ cup vegetable juice

Fruit Group (2–4 servings/day)

- 1 medium whole piece of fruit
- ½ cup canned, chopped, or cooked fruit
- ¾ cup fruit juice

Milk and Milk Substitutes Group (3 servings/day for preteens and 4 for teens; 2–4 servings/day for adults)

- 1 cup milk or yogurt
- 1 cup calcium- and vitamin B_{12}-fortified soy milk
- 1½ ounces hard cheese
- 1½ ounces calcium- and vitamin B_{12}-fortified soy cheese

Meat/Fish Substitutes Group (2–3 servings/day)

- 1 cup cooked dry beans, peas, or lentils
- 2 eggs
- 8 ounces bean curd or tofu
- ½ cup shelled nuts
- 3–4 tablespoons peanut butter
- 3–4 tablespoons tahini
- ⅓ to ½ cup seeds

Vegans Must Consume Daily:

- 3–5 teaspoons vegetable oil + 1 tablespoon blackstrap molasses + 1 tablespoon brewer's yeast

········· **WHAT DO YOU THINK?**

Why are so many people today becoming vegetarians? How easy is it to be a vegetarian on your campus? What concerns about vegetarianism would you be likely to have, if any?

IMPROVED EATING FOR THE COLLEGE STUDENT

College students often face a challenge when trying to eat healthy foods. Some students live in dorms and do not have their own cooking or refrigeration facilities. Others live in crowded apartments where everyone forages in the refrigerator for everyone else's food. Still others eat at university food services where food choices may be limited. Most students have time constraints that make buying, preparing, and eating healthy food a difficult task. In addition, many lack the financial resources needed to buy many foods that their parents purchased while they lived at home. What's a student to do? The following sections provide advice for some of the particular problems you may face.

Fast Foods: Eating on the Run

If your campus is like many others across the country, you've probably noticed a distinct move toward fast-food restaurants in your student unions so that they now resemble the food courts found in most major shopping malls. These new eating centers fit student's needs for a fast bite of food at a reasonable rate between classes and also bring in money to your school.

You should recognize that not all fast foods are created equal and not all of them are bad for you. Even at the often-maligned burger chains, menus are healthier than ever before and offer excellent choices for the discriminating eater. The key word here is *discriminating*. It really is possible to eat healthy food if you follow these suggestions:

- Ask for nutritional analyses of items. Most fast-food chains now have them.
- Order it "your way"—avoid mayonnaise or sauces and other add-ons. Some places even have fat-free mayonnaise if you ask.
- Hold the cheese.
- Order single, small burgers rather than large, high-calorie, bacon- or cheese-topped choices.
- Order salads and be careful how much dressing you put on. Try the vinegar and oil or low-fat alternative dressings. Stay away from eggs and other high-fat add-ons such as bacon bits.
- When ordering a chicken sandwich, order the skinless broiled version rather than the deep-fried version.
- Check to see what type of oil is used to cook fries if you must have them. Avoid lard-based or other saturated fat products.
- Order the wheat buns/bread and ask them to hold the butter.
- Avoid fried foods in general, including hot apple pies and other crust-based fried foods.
- Opt for spots where foods tend to be broiled rather than fried.

For the best and worst fast-food selections, see the Consumer Health feature.

When Funds Are Short

Balancing the need for adequate nutrition with the many other activities that are part of college life can become a difficult task. However, if you take the time to plan healthy diets, you may find that you are eating better, enjoying eating more, and actually saving money.

In addition, you can take these steps to help ensure a quality diet:

- Buy fruits and vegetables in season whenever possible for their lower cost, higher nutrient quality, and greater variety.

- Use coupons and specials whenever possible.
- Whenever possible, shop at discount warehouse food chains; capitalize on no-frills products.
- Plan ahead and avoid extra trips to the store. Make a list and stick to it.
- Purchase meats and other products in volume, freezing portions for future needs. Or purchase small amounts of meats and other expensive proteins and combine them with beans and plant proteins for lower total cost, lower calories, and lower fat.
- Cook large meals and freeze smaller portions.
- Drain off extra fat after cooking. Save juices for use in soups and in other dishes.
- If you find that you have no money for food, talk to someone at your county/city health department. Although they often restrict subsidies such as food stamps for full-time students, they may know of some alternative ways for you to get assistance.

········ **WHAT DO YOU THINK?**

What problems cause you the most difficulty when you try to eat more healthful foods? Are these problems that you noted in your family, too, or are they unique to your current situation as a student? What actions can you take that would help improve your current eating practices?

FOOD SAFETY

As we become increasingly worried that the food we put in our mouths may be contaminated with potentially harmful bacteria, insects, worms, or other not-so-nice substances, the food industry has come under fire. To convince us that our products are safe for consumption, some manufacturers have come up with "new and improved" ways of protecting our foods. How well do they work?

Food-Borne Illnesses

In increasing numbers, Americans are becoming sick from what they eat, and many of these sicknesses are life-threatening. Scientists estimate, based on several studies conducted over the past 10 years, that food-borne pathogens sicken between 6.5 and 81 million people and cause some 9,000 deaths in the United States annually.[27]

Symptoms of food-borne illnesses vary tremendously and usually include one or several symptoms: diarrhea, nausea, cramping, and vomiting. Depending on the virulence of the pathogen ingested and the amount that actually gets into your system, symptoms may appear as early as 30 minutes after eating contaminated food, or they may take several days or

What's Good on the Menu?

While some restaurants do offer hints for health-conscious diners, you're on your own most of the time. To help you order wisely, here are lighter options and high-fat pitfalls. "Best" choices have fewer than 30 grams of fat, a generous meal's worth for an active, medium-sized woman. "Worst" choices have up to 100 grams of fat.

FAST FOOD

Best
Grilled chicken sandwich
Roast beef sandwich
Single hamburger
Salad with light vinaigrette

Worst
Bacon burger
Double cheeseburger
French fries
Onion rings

Tips
Order sandwiches without mayo or "special sauce." Avoid deep-fried items like fish fillets, chicken nuggets, and French fries.

ITALIAN

Best
Pasta with red or white clam sauce
Spaghetti with marinara or tomato-and-meat sauce

Worst
Eggplant parmigiana
Fettuccine alfredo
Fried calamari
Lasagna

Tips
Stick with plain bread instead of garlic bread made with butter or oil. Ask for the waiter's help in avoiding cream- or egg-based sauces.

CHINESE

Best
Hot-and-sour soup
Stir-fried vegetables
Shrimp with garlic sauce
Szechuan shrimp
Wonton soup

Worst
Crispy chicken
Kung pao chicken
Moo shu pork
Sweet-and-sour pork

Tips
Share a stir-fry; help yourself to steamed rice. Ask for vegetables steamed or stir-fried with less oil. Order moo shu vegetables instead of pork. Avoid fried rice, breaded dishes, and items loaded with nuts.

SANDWICHES

Best
Ham and Swiss cheese
Roast beef
Turkey

Worst
Tuna salad
Reuben
Submarine

Tips
Ask for mustard; hold the mayo and cheese. See if turkey-ham is available.

MEXICAN

Best
Bean burrito (no cheese)
Chicken fajitas

Worst
Beef chimichanga
Chile relleno
Quesadilla
Refried beans

Tips
Choose soft tortillas with fresh salsa, not guacamole. Special-order grilled shrimp, fish, or chicken. Ask for beans made without lard or fat.

BREAKFAST

Best
Hot or cold cereal with 2% milk
Pancakes or French toast with syrup
Scrambled eggs with hash browns and plain toast

Worst
Belgian waffle with sausage
Sausage and eggs with biscuits and gravy
Ham and cheese omelette with hash browns and toast

Tips
Ask for whole-grain cereal or shredded wheat with 1% milk or whole-wheat toast without butter or margarine. Order omelettes without cheese, fried eggs without bacon or sausage.

SEAFOOD

Best
Broiled bass, halibut, or snapper
Grilled scallops
Steamed crab or lobster

Worst
Fried seafood platter
Blackened catfish

Tips
Order fish broiled, baked, grilled, or steamed—not pan-fried or sauteed. Ask for lemon instead of tartar sauce. Avoid creamy and buttery sauces.

Source: Health 10 (November/December 1996): 79.

---

weeks to develop. Most of the time, symptoms occur between 5 and 8 hours after eating and last only a day or two. For certain populations, however, such as the very young or very old or persons with AIDS or other severe illnesses, food-borne illnesses can be fatal.

Several factors may be contributing to the emergence of increasing numbers of food-borne illnesses. According to Michael T. Osterholm, Ph.D., state epidemiologist in Minneapolis,[28] the movement away from a traditional meat-and-potato American diet to "heart-healthy" eating—increasing

How to Avoid Food-Borne Illnesses in the Home

Part of the responsibility for preventing food-borne illness lies with consumers, for over 30 percent of all such illnesses result from unsafe handling of food at home.

- When shopping, pick up your packaged and canned foods first and save frozen foods and perishables such as meat, poultry, and fish till the last. Try to put these foods in separate plastic bags so that drippings don't run onto other foods in your cart, contaminating them.
- Check for cleanliness at the salad bar and meat and fish counters. For instance, cooked shrimp lying on the same small bed of ice as raw fish can easily be contaminated.

- When shopping for fish, buy from markets that get their supplies from state-approved sources; stay clear of vendors who sell shellfish from roadside stands or the back of trucks. If you're planning to harvest your own shellfish, check the safety of the water in the area.
- Remember that most cuts of meat, fish, and poultry should be kept in the refrigerator no more than one or two days. They shouldn't be in the grocery store meat counter beyond their dated shelf life, either. If your fish smells particularly "fishy" and your meat has a dark or greenish tinge to it, use caution. Check the shelf life of all products before buying. If expiration dates are close, freeze or eat immediately.
- Leftovers should be eaten within three days.
- Keep hot foods hot and cold foods cold.
- Use a thermometer to ensure that meats are completely cooked. Remember that the rarer the steak, the greater the number of bacteria swarming on the plate. Beef and

lamb should be cooked to at least 140°F, pork to 150°F, and poultry to 165°F. Don't eat poultry that is pink inside.
- Fish is done when the thickest part becomes opaque and the fish flakes easily when poked with a fork.
- Cooked food should never be left standing on the stove or table for more than two hours. Disease-causing bacteria grow in temperatures between 40°F and 140°F. Cooked foods that have been left standing in this temperature range for more than two hours should be thrown away.
- Never thaw frozen foods at room temperature. Put in the refrigerator for a day to thaw, or thaw in cold water, changing the water every 30 minutes.
- Wash your hands with soap and water between courses when preparing food, particularly after handling meat, fish, or poultry. Wash the countertop and all utensils before using them for other foods.

---

consumption of fruits and vegetables and grains—has lead to increasing demand for fresh foods that are not in season most of the year. Today, depending on the season, up to 70 percent of the fruits and vegetables consumed in the United States come from Mexico alone. The upshot is that a visit to developing countries isn't necessary to be stricken with food-borne "traveler's diarrhea" because the produce does the traveling.[29] Although we are told when we travel to developing countries, "boil it, peel it, or don't eat it," we bring these foods into our kitchens, often without even basic washing.[30] One of the ways food becomes contaminated is that it has been watered with contaminated water, fertilized with "organic" fertilizers (animal manure), and not subjected to the same rigorous pesticide regulations as American-raised produce. To give you an idea of the implications of this, studies have shown that E. coli (a lethal bacterial pathogen) can survive in cow manure for up to 70 days and can multiply in foods grown with manure unless heat or additives such as salt or preservatives are used to kill the microbes.[31] There are essentially no regulations that say farmers can't use animal manure in growing their crops.

Key factors associated with the increasing spread of food-borne diseases include:[32]

- *Globalization of the food supply:* Because the food supply is distributed worldwide, the possibility of exposure to pathogens native to remote regions of the world is greater.
- *Inadvertent introduction of pathogens into new geographic regions:* One theory is that cholera was introduced into waters off the coast of the southern United States when a cargo ship discharged contaminated ballast as it came into harbor. Other pathogens may enter into aquatic life in a similar manner.
- *Exposure to unfamiliar food-borne hazards:* Travellers, refugees, and immigrants who are in foreign countries are exposed to food-borne hazards, and in the course of traveling, bring them home with them.
- *Changes in microbial populations:* Changing microbial populations can lead to the evolution of new pathogens. As a result, new virulence factors develop for old pathogens, or antibiotic resistance to the pathogens develops, making diseases more difficult to treat.

- *Increased susceptibility of varying populations:* People are becoming more vulnerable to disease. The numbers of highly susceptible persons are expanding worldwide.
- *Insufficient education about food safety:* Increased urbanization, industrialization, and travel, combined with more people eating out, increase the risk of unsafe food handling and more risk of illness.

Irradiation

Food irradiation involves treating foods with gamma radiation from radioactive cobalt, cesium, or some other source of X-rays. The killing effect on microorganisms rises with the power of the rays, which are measured in rads (radiant energy absorbed).[33] Irradiation lengthens food products' shelf life and prevents microorganism and insect contamination. Because this results in less waste, the food industry can make higher profits while charging consumers lower prices. It is also claimed that irradiation will reduce the need to use many of the toxic chemicals now used to preserve foods and prevent contamination from external contaminants.

The following foods have already received approval for irradiation by the Food and Drug Administration: fresh produce such as strawberries, potatoes, and other perishable foods; poultry and some seafood (in which salmonella is a serious problem); and pork (to kill off the parasite trichina). Many spices and herbs have been irradiated for years, and grains, vegetables, and frozen foods are already targeted for irradiation in the near future.

The long-term side effects of irradiation are unknown. Although irradiation doesn't actually make your food radioactive, it does damage its molecular structure, creating new substances known as free radicals. Free radicals have been implicated in certain types of cancers, and diseases of the liver and kidney in animal studies, but, to date, no studies of the toxicity of irradiated foods on humans have been done. While the health effects of irradiated food may not be known for many years, the long-term impact of the proliferation of radioactive material on our environment must be considered.

Food Additives

Additives generally help to reduce the risk of food-borne illness (i.e., nitrates added to cured meats), prevent spoilage, and enhance the ways foods look and taste. Additives also are used to enhance nutrient value, especially when the benefits are so great for the general public. A deficiency can be a terrible public health problem, and a solution is relatively easy to administer.

One of the newest additives to our daily food is folate, which is produced by plants and yeasts. Folate is believed to offer many health benefits, including but not limited to reducing the risk of neural tube defects, certain anemias, cervical dysplasia, and heart attacks. The best sources of folate are fruits and vegetables, particularly beans, spinach, and broccoli. Many multivitamin supplements also supply this amount. Recently, the Public Health Service took the recommendation one step further by approving the addition of folate to flour.

Although the FDA regulates additives by effectiveness, ability to detect them in foods, and safety, there are continued questions about those additives put into foods intentionally and those that get in unintentionally before or after processing.

Intentional Food Additives:

- *Antimicrobial agents:* Substances like salt, sugar, nitrates, and others that tend to make foods less hospitable for microbes.
- *Antioxidants:* Substances that preserve color and flavor by reducing loss due to exposure to oxygen. Vitamin C and E are among those antioxidants believed to play a role in reduced cancer and cardiovascular disease. BHA and BHT are additives that also are antioxidant in action.
- *Artificial colors*
- *Nutrient additives*

Indirect Food Additives:

- *Substances that inadvertently get into food products from packaging and or handling.*
- *Dioxins:* Found in coffee filters, milk containers, and frozen foods.
- *Methylene chloride:* Found in decaffeinated coffee.
- *Hormones:* Bovine growth hormone (BGH) found in animal meat.

Food Allergies

Once believed to be a rare event, approximately 5 percent of all children in the United States, and more than 10 percent of all adults may have an allergic reaction to something they eat. Typical culprits include milk, eggs, peanuts, soybeans, tree nuts, fish and shellfish, and wheat. Reactions can range from minor rashes to severe swelling in the mouth, tongue, and throat to violent vomiting and diarrhea, and, occasionally, death. Emergency rooms and hospitals throughout the country report rapid increases in the number of incidents tied to food allergies.

Food allergies occur when a person's body views a specific food, usually a protein, as an invader or a threat. The body's immune system kicks into high gear and tries to rid the body of the problem by using typical immune system

---

Food irradiation   Treating foods with gamma radiation from radioactive cobalt, cesium, or some other source of X-rays to kill microorganisms.

Food allergies   Overreaction by the body to normally harmless proteins, which are perceived as allergens. In response, the body produces antibodies, triggering allergic symptoms.

TABLE 9.4
Eight Foods That Cause 90 Percent of Allergic Reactions

FOOD	OVERVIEW/KEY POINTS	TIPS
Milk	A common allergy among children. Avoid all milk products, including butter, cheeses, and yogurt. Several other commonly used ingredients can cause problems, i.e., caseinates (listed as ammonium, calcium, magnesium, potassium, or sodium caseinate), whey, and anything with lactose in the name.	Look for kosher symbols: Kosher dietary law prohibits the mixture of milk and meat. Kosher foods that include dairy products are marked with a D. Foods made with dairy-products equipment are marked D. E.
Eggs	Whether you're allergic to the egg white or the yolk, the entire egg is off limits. Some typical ingredients that include egg are albumin, globulin, livetin, ovalbumin, ovomucin, ovovittelin, and simplesse.	If you need an egg substitute for baking, try mixing 1½ Tbsp. water with ½ Tbsp. oil and 1 tsp baking powder for each egg.
Peanuts	Peanuts and other legumes are a big source of allergies for many children. Peanuts *are* a common ingredient.	Check cookie and other baked-good labels and remember that peanut oil is used in many Thai and Chinese dishes.
Soybeans	While allergy to soybeans is rare in adults, a lot of children can't stomach the legume. Many processed foods contain soybean products.	Watch out for ingredients such as hydrolyzed plant protein, natural flavorings, vegetable gum, and vegetable starch—all of which are code names for *soy*.
Tree nuts	Unlike peanuts, all other nuts grow in trees. A reaction to one or more of them is the most common form of allergy there is. Nuts are found in many foods, from barbecue sauce to crackers and ice cream.	Look out for marzipan, an almond paste used in many desserts.
Fish	People who are allergic to one kind of fish must stay away from all fish since the allergen that causes the reaction is similar throughout fish species.	Look out for fish products in Worcestershire sauce and Caesar salad, and surimi, fish muscle used in imitation seafoods.
Shellfish	Allergic reactions to shellfish are occasional in kids and common in adults, coming on suddenly. Watch out for seafoods and Asian foods, which sometimes include small amounts of shellfish for flavoring.	Kosher foods do not contain any pork or shellfish.
Wheat	Wheat can be replaced with other grains, such as rye, oats, barley corn, buckwheat, amaranth, greens that are ground into flour, and quinoa, a ricelike grain.	For baking, try replacing 1 cup wheat flour with other grains, such as 1⅓ cup rice flour, 1 cup barley flour, or use a combination of ¾ cup amaranth plus ¼ cup either arrowroot, tapioca, or potato starch.

Source: American Dietetic Association.

helpers. The first signs are typically rapid breathing or wheezing, hives, rash, eczema, or a chronic runny nose. More dramatic symptoms include facial swelling or respiratory problems related to *anaphylactic reaction,* which require a shot of epinephrine, a hormone that stimulates the heart and relieves overt symptoms.

Once diagnosed with a food allergy, the key is to find a nutrition specialist (with a degree or academic training in nutrition) who can help you make necessary dietary adjustments. See Table 9.4 for a listing of possible foods that cause allergies and tips on how to reduce your reactions. Also, remember that many apparent reactions to foods are really not allergic reactions per se. Included among this group are:

- **Food intolerance,** which occurs in people who lack certain digestive chemicals and suffer adverse effects when they consume certain substances because their bodies

Food intolerance   Adverse effects resulting when people who lack the digestive chemicals needed to break down certain substances eat those substances.

Genetic Engineering at a Grocer Near You

It started simply enough in the mid-1990s with a tomato called *FlavrSavr* that was resistant to blight, kept longer on the shelves, had more vitamin C, and tasted sweeter than previous generations. Next came new strains of beans and grains genetically engineered to have more protein, caffeine-free coffee beans, strawberries packed with extra natural sugars, and potatoes that soak up less grease when fried. Many saw this as the sign of a new wave, a seemingly endless stream of new foods genetically engineered to outperform those foods we've come to know . . . and love. Known as *Genetically Modified Organisms,* or *GMOs,* these foods represent a process of genetic engineering in which scientists break fundamental genetic barriers between species. Through a process in which genes of nonrelated species are spliced together using viruses, antibiotic-resistant genes, bacteria, and other agents, the most desirable traits are merged to create a super species.

One of the most noteworthy examples of the GMO process, the genetic engineering of a hardier corn, also garnered a great deal of controversial attention. By splicing DNA from the common soil bacterium *Bacillus thuringiensis* into the genes of corn, scientists have created a plant that produces the same toxin as the corn borer, a mothlike pest that can destroy the corn crops it infests. When the corn borer eats the genetically altered corn, the toxin kills it, potentially saving farmers billions of dollars and dramatically increasing crop yields. Today, more than 25 percent of the U.S. corn crop comes from genetically engineered seed.

However, just as the agricultural community thought a major problem had been solved, and as GMO corn producers were building steam, Dr. John Losey from Cornell University reported a disturbing finding. His research showed that when the larvae of the monarch butterfly also ate the corn, they, too, died or produced stunted, deformed butterflies. Environmental groups, quick to point out that what happens in the simplest species in nature also may be a harbinger of what may happen in humans, signaled an alarm, about ALL genetically modified organisms.

In recent years, controversy over GMOs has grown. Proponents of GMOs argue that these new products will make agriculture more sustainable, will help address world hunger issues by increasing crop yields, will reduce the threats from some pests and diseases, and will improve overall public health. In addition, farmers cite the cost efficiency of GMOs. Opponents retaliate with the following concerns:

- Unpredictable mutations of the genetic code, causing new diseases, viruses, and bacteria
- Side effects from new toxins and allergens in foods that people will be unable to trace without proper labeling
- Increased used of chemicals on crops, resulting in increased contamination of the food supply, waterways, and soil
- Continued rise in resistance to antibiotics
- Disturbance of ecological balance and natural selection processes

Currently, there are increasing concerns over GMO's affect on the global population. Consumer action has temporarily halted a new GMO, known as the "Terminator Seed," from being marketed in many regions of the world. This seed was designed to produce crops only once; hence, no seeds from adult plants are carried over to grow foods the next year, creating a perpetual new market of buyers during each planting season. Environmentalists argued that such a seed could cross-pollinate with other plants, causing massive destruction of the plant world as we know it. In addition, England, Australia, and several European Union countries have passed legislation requiring that genetically altered foods be labeled as such to allow consumers the right to choose whether they wish to eat GMO foods. Other countries, such as Japan, are fighting to ban the use of such products.

Labeled "Frankenstein Foods" by the British tabloids, GMOs have only recently begun to be examined by the American media. In the United States, consumer protection groups argue that people have a right to know whether the foods they eat have been genetically engineered and whether they pose any threats. Currently, no such labeling exists in the United States, and as many as four dozen commonly consumed GMO foods may already be on the market. For example, as many as 500,000 dairy cows per year are treated with recombinant Bovine Growth Hormone (rBGH), leading to questions over the potential transfer of the hormone to humans and related side-effects. Many states are actively lobbying to restrict rBGH use or to eliminate it completely.

STUDENTS SPEAK UP:

Do you think the benefits of GMO foods outweigh the arguments against them? Are you aware of what is in the foods you eat?

Sources: Gordon Conway, Rockefeller Foundation. The Rockefeller Foundation and Plant Biotechnology. "Cost and Benefit Analysis of GMOs," June 24, 1999. M. J. Friedrich, "Genetically Enhanced Rice to Help Fight Malnutrition," *JAMA,* 282 (16), October 27, 1999. Richard Heinberg, "Cloning the Buddha: The Moral Impact of Biotechnology," First Quest Edition, Wheaton, IL: The Theosophical Publishing House, 1999. Donna Mitten, Rob MacDonald, and Dirk Klonus, "Regulation of Foods Derived from Genetically Engineered Crops," *Current Opinion in Biotechnology,* 10 (1999): 298–302.

Special acknowledgement: This Health Headlines was researched and co-written by Ms. Monica Hunsberger, Oregon State University.

have difficulty breaking them down. One of the most common examples is lactose intolerance, experienced by people who do not have the digestive chemicals needed to break down the lactose in milk.

- *Reactions to food additives,* such as sulfites and MSG.
- *Reactions to substances occurring naturally in some foods,* such as tyramine in cheese, phenylethylamine in chocolate, caffeine in coffee, and some compounds in alcoholic beverages.
- *Food-borne illnesses.*
- *Unknown reactions* in people who have adverse symptoms that they attribute to foods and that may actually go away when treated as allergies but for which there is no evidence of a physiological basis for the reactions.[34]

Organic Foods

Mounting concerns about food safety have caused many people to try to protect themselves by refusing to buy processed foods and mass-produced agricultural products. Instead, they purchase foods that are **organically grown**—foods reported to be pesticide- and chemical-free. Though they are sold at premium prices, many of these products are of only average quality. They are probably not worth the money, according to most experts, for several reasons. First, whether food has been exposed to pesticides at some time in the production cycle is not as important as the residual pesticides in the food at the time you consume it. Obviously, too much of anything is potentially harmful, but if a "nonorganic" food has been sprayed and the poison has since evaporated, changed into a nontoxic compound, or been diluted below the point at which it can do any harm, the food may be no more harmful than a product labeled as "organic."[35] Second, even though so-called organic foods generally claim to be pesticide-free, tests indicate that many contain pesticide residues in the same amounts as nonorganic foods.[36] These residues may be the result of pesticide drift from neighboring farms and water supplies, sneak sprays by unscrupulous producers, or soils that have residue from previous growers.

The bottom line is what is really in the food, not whether it is labeled as "organic," "natural," or "healthy." In fact, these labels are often placed on foods that are far from healthy and may actually be of very low quality. Although the ideals upon which the organic movement was founded are sound, more testing and regulation are needed before people can be assured that what they are paying high prices for is the real unadulterated thing—a pesticide-free product.

Organically grown   Foods that are grown without use of pesticides or chemicals.

Taking Charge ....
Managing Your Eating Behavior

Let's face it. Eating for health is not easy. It takes knowledge, careful thought and analysis, and the ability to put it all together and make the best decision for your own lifestyle and personal goals within certain budgetary limits. There are no shortcuts, and, as researchers sift through studies showing conflicting results, what is true today may turn out to be false tomorrow. But by paying attention; reading; seeking help from reputable, trained professionals; and planning ahead, you can increase your own nutritional health.

CHECKLIST FOR CHANGE

MAKING PERSONAL CHOICES

✓ *Eat lower on the food chain.* Substitute fruits, vegetables, nuts, or grains for animal products at least once a day.

✓ *Eat lean.* Pay attention to labels, assess your food intake, and balance high-fat meals with low-fat meals. Choose leaner cuts and bake, grill, boil, or broil whenever possible.

- *Increase your consumption of fruits and vegetables.* Use the real thing instead of juices.
- *Combine foods for optimum nutrition.* Identify the best ways to combine grains, beans, fruits, vegetables, nuts, and other foods.
- *Practice responsible consumer safety.* Avoid unnecessary chemicals and buy, prepare, and store foods prudently to avoid food-borne illness.
- *Keep dietary foods in balance.* Consume appropriate amounts of fats, carbohydrates, proteins, vitamins, minerals, amino acids, fatty acids, and water.
- *Pay attention to changing nutrient needs.* Remain informed about new, reputable sources of information concerning specific nutrient benefits and hazards.

MAKING COMMUNITY CHOICES

- Pay attention to the types of eating establishments available on your campus. If you don't have the options you think you should, take action. Involve your student newspaper and student organizations, talk with food service representatives, involve your student health service, and solicit the support of key people on campus.
- If you patronize certain food establishments, review the food choices. Tell them when they are doing a good job and request other options.

SUMMARY

- Recognizing that we eat for more reasons than just survival is the first step toward changing our health. The Food Guide Pyramid provides guidelines for healthy eating.
- The major nutrients that are essential for life and health include water, proteins, carbohydrates, fiber, fats, vitamins, and minerals.
- Experts are now becoming interested in the role of food as medicine and in the benefits of food, called "functional foods." These foods may play an important role in improving certain conditions, such as hypertension.
- Men and women have differing needs for most nutrients throughout the life cycle because of their different body size and composition.
- Vegetarianism can provide a healthy alternative for those wishing to cut fat from their diets or wanting to reduce

animal consumption. The vegetarian pyramid provides dietary guidelines to help vegetarians obtain needed nutrients.

- College students face unique challenges in eating healthfully. Learning to make better choices at fast-food restaurants, eat healthily when funds are short, and eating nutritionally in the dorm are all possible when you use the knowledge contained in this chapter.
- Food-borne illnesses, food irradiation, food allergies, and other food-safety and health concerns are becoming increasingly important to health-wise consumers. Recognition of potential risks and active steps taken to prevent problems are part of a sound nutritional plan.

DISCUSSION QUESTIONS

1. What are several factors that may influence the dietary patterns and behaviors of the typical college student? What factors have been the greatest influences on your eating behaviors?
2. What are the six major food groups on the new Food Guide Pyramid? What groups might you find it difficult to get enough servings from? What can you do to increase/decrease your intake of selected food groups? What can you do to remember the six groups?
3. Distinguish between the different types of vegetarianism.
4. What are the major functional foods discussed in this chapter? What are their reported benefits, if any?
5. What are the major problems that many college students face when trying to eat the right foods? List five actions that you and your classmates could take immediately to improve your eating.

APPLICATION EXERCISE

Reread the *What Do You Think?* scenario at the beginning of the chapter and answer the following questions.

1. Critique Tim's behavior and attitude. What suggestions could you make to help him? How could you make these suggestions in a way that won't offend him?

2. If someone ate a high-fat diet, was 70 years old and never sick, would you want to change them?

OBJECTIVES

▶ Describe those factors that place people at risk for problems with obesity. Indicate which factors are within your control and those that are not.

▶ Describe the options that are available for determining body content assessment. Indicate which are the most reliable and the possible shortcomings of each.

▶ Discuss the roles of exercise, dieting, nutrition, lifestyle modification, fad diets, and other strategies of weight control.

▶ Indicate why so many diets fail, and describe the most effective methods of weight management.

▶ Describe the three major eating disorders and explain the health risks of these conditions.

Managing Your Weight

Finding a Healthy Balance

IF YOU'VE NEVER MET A DESSERT you didn't like, you are probably like many Americans who feel trapped in the perennial "battle of the bulge." In spite of all the proactive messages that suggest we live in an era dedicated to diet and exercise, numerous studies on eating patterns suggest that Americans are doing worse with each progressive decade. In fact, according to the most recent of a series of National Health and Nutrition Examination Surveys (NHANES III) conducted by the Centers for Disease Control and Prevention, 33 percent of adults in the United States were found to be clinically obese, with dramatic increases in prevalence shown over the past three decades.[1,2] Findings indicate that on any given day, nearly 40 percent of American women and 24 percent of men over the age of 20 are trying to lose weight, yet many will fail or they will end up shedding pounds, only to gain it all back within a few short months.[3,4] An even more alarming trend of increasing obesity has emerged among young children. Health experts estimate that 22 percent of today's children and adolescents are obese, an increase of 15 percent since the 1970s.[5] Equally disturbing is the corresponding rise in the incidence of eating disorders among young people.

Obesity is a major public health problem that needs to be addressed. The threats to life and overall health and happiness are staggering. In fact, officials estimate that more than 300,000 lives are lost each year to conditions directly related to obesity, and perhaps many more deaths are indirectly related to a history of obesity throughout a person's life.[6] The estimated annual health-care cost due to obesity in the United States is believed to exceed $70 billion.[7]

This chapter is designed to help you better understand what *underweight, normal weight, overweight,* and *obesity* really mean and why weight control is essential to your overall health and well-being. It also provides a mechanism for understanding the relationship between weight and health and suggests strategies for controlling your own weight.

BODY IMAGE

Most of us think of the obsession with thinness as a phenomenon of recent years. Beginning with supermodel Twiggy in the 1960s and continuing with supermodel Kate Moss in

Images in the media, whether of supermodels or popular film or television stars, can leave a person questioning the "ideal" body.

Minority Populations: At Greater Risk for Obesity

Anyone who has ever traveled extensively has probably noted that in some places, rotund people seem to abound, while in other areas, thin is definitely "in." NHANES III provided even more credence to the argument that some groups seem to have more obese and overweight individuals than do others. Consider the following:

- Those in the lowest socioeconomic (SES) classes have nearly five times the rate of obesity as those in the highest socioeconomic classes.
- Groups with the highest proportion of overweight people were black, non-Hispanic women (49%) and Mexican American women (47%).
- While more women of color were obese, it is important to note that the averages of whites (up 9% to 33% of total) and nonwhites (up 4% among black women and 7% for Mexican American women) have increased since a similar study was done in the 1980s. White men also showed a steep increase in obesity rates.
- In some Native American communities, up to 70 percent of all adults are dangerously overweight.
- There may be a greater tolerance in some cultures for larger body size, and in some, bigger is actually better.
- Cultures with lower SES tend to eat more high-fat, high-calorie foods and fewer fruits and vegetables than higher SES groups

In a study of racial differences, obesity, and risk for breast cancer, it was found that:

- There were significant racial differences in body weight and body mass, with black women twice as likely as white women to be moderately obese and more than six times as likely to have a body mass index greater than or equal to 32.3, the cutpoint for severe obesity.
- Twenty-six percent of black women, as compared with 7 percent of white women, are severely obese.

In yet another study of physical activity and minority women, it was found that:

- Black and Hispanic women demonstrated lower rates of physical activity than did white women. In fact, black women have the highest rates of physical inactivity compared with white and Hispanic women. As many as 46 percent of non-Hispanic black women were physically inactive (defined as having done no exercise or physically active hobbies in the previous 2 weeks), and 44 percent of Hispanic women reported similar levels of no activity.
- Reported barriers to activity among these groups included safety, availability of exercise areas, and cost, as well as personal motivation, lack of time, and health concerns.

Sources: Adapted from the *Boston Globe,* from Alison Bass, "Record Obesity Levels Found," *Boston Globe,* 20 July 1995, 1, 10; Beth Jones, Kasl Stanislav, Mary McCrea Curnen, Patricia Owens, and Robert Dubrow, "Severe Obesity as an Explanatory Factor for Black/White Difference in Stage at Diagnosis of Breast Cancer," *American Journal of Epidemiology* 146 (1997): 394–404; Amy Eyler, Elizabeth Baker, LaChenna Cromer, Abby King, Ross Brownson, and Rebecca Donatelle, "Physical Activity and Minority Women: A Qualitative Study," *Health Education and Behavior* 25 (1998): 640–652.

the 1990s, the thin look seems to dominate fashion ads. But the thin look has been around for a long time. Anorexia nervosa, an eating disorder, has been defined as a psychiatric disorder since 1873. During the Victorian era, corsets were used to achieve unrealistically tiny waists. By the 1920s, it was common knowledge that obesity was linked to poor health.

Today, beautiful female models in size 4 clothes and underweight Miss Americas exemplify the "ideal" body. In addition, public health warnings that being overweight increases our risks of heart disease, certain cancers, and a number of other disorders can send a panic through people when their weight isn't what they think it should be. Sadly, increasing numbers of elementary school children, adolescents, teens, and adults have become so preoccupied with trying to be like the size 4 models that they make themselves sick trying to get to some magical weight or clothes size.

Determining the Right Weight for You

Knowing what weight is right for you depends on a wide range of variables, not the least of which is your body structure, height, the distribution of the weight that you carry, and the ratio of fat to lean tissue in your body. In fact, your weight is often a very deceptive indicator of whether or not you are obese. Many extremely lean, muscular athletes carry a tremendous amount of weight and would be considered overweight based on traditional height-weight charts. Many young women think that they are the right weight based on charts, yet they are shocked when they discover that 35 to 40 percent of their weight is body fat!

In an attempt to resolve some of the misinterpretation of the traditional height-weight charts, the Department of Agriculture and the Department of Health and Human Services devised one weight table for both men and women that allows for the variations in body structure, the distribution of

Body image #1
Dieting trend for cosmetic reasons

weight, and weight gains in middle age (see Table 10.1). Weights at the lower end of the range are recommended for individuals with a low ratio of muscle and bone to fat; those at the upper end are advised for people with more muscular builds.

Redefining Obesity

Obesity generally is defined as an accumulation of fat (*adipose tissue*) beyond what is considered normal for a person's age, sex, and body type. Historically, nutritionists have defined *overweight* as being between 1 and 19 percent above your ideal weight, based on the height-weight tables. If you slipped over that 19, you were labeled *obese*. In an attempt to clarify obesity even further, experts labeled people who were 20 to 40 percent above their ideal weight as *mildly obese* (90% of the obese fit into this category). Those 41 to 99 percent above their ideal weight have been described as *moderately obese* (about 9%–10% of the obese), and those who are 100 percent or more above their ideal weight are identified as *severely, morbidly,* or *grossly overweight* (about 1% of the obese.) Even the terminology (e.g., gross obesity) speaks volumes about the way society views this group of individuals.[8]

TABLE 10.1
Healthy Weight Ranges for Men and Women

HEIGHT WITHOUT SHOES	WEIGHT* WITHOUT CLOTHES
4'10"	91–119
4'11"	94–124
5'0"	97–128
5'1"	101–132
5'2"	104–137
5'3"	107–141
5'4"	111–146
5'5"	114–150
5'6"	118–155
5'7"	121–160
5'8"	125–164
5'9"	129–169
5'10"	132–174
5'11"	136–179
6'0"	140–184
6'1"	144–189
6'2"	148–195
6'3"	152–200
6'4"	156–205
6'5"	160–211
6'6"	164–216

*In pounds
Source: Dietary Guidelines for Americans, 1995, USDA.

TABLE 10.2
General Ratings of Body Fat Percentages by Age and Gender

RATING	MALES (AGES 18–30) (PERCENT)	FEMALES (AGES 18–30) (PERCENT)
Athletic*	6–10	10–15
Good	11–14	16–19
Acceptable	15–17	20–24
Overfat	18–19	25–29
Obese	20 or over	30 or over

*The ratings in the athletic category are general guidelines for those athletes, such as gymnasts and long-distance runners, whose need for a "competitive edge" in selected sports may compel them to try to lose as much weight as possible. However, for the average person, such low body fat levels should be approached with caution.

The difficulty with defining *obesity* lies in determining what is normal. To date, there are no universally accepted standards for the most "desirable" or "ideal" body weight or *body composition* (the ratio of lean body mass to fat body mass). While sources vary slightly, men's bodies should contain between 11 and 15 percent total body fat and women should be within the range of 18 to 22 percent body fat. At various ages and stages of life, these ranges also vary (see Table 10.2), but generally, when men exceed 20 percent body fat and women exceed 30 percent body fat, they have slipped into the hole from which it is hard to emerge—obesity.

Why the difference between men and women? Much of it may be attributed to the normal structure of the female body and to sex hormones. As mentioned earlier, when considering how much or how little fat a person should have, it is important to think of body composition in terms of lean body mass and body fat. Lean body mass is made up of the structural and functional elements in cells, body water, muscle, bones, and other body organs such as the heart, liver, and kidneys. Body fat is composed of two types: essential fat and storage fat. Essential fat is necessary for normal physiological functioning, such as nerve conduction. Essential fat makes up approximately 8 to 17 percent of total body weight in men and approximately 12–15 percent of total body weight in women. *Storage fat,* the part that many of us are always trying to shed, makes up the remainder of our fat reserves. It accounts for only a small percentage of total body weight for very lean people and between 5 and 25 percent of body weight of most American adults.

Too Little Fat?

Although most of us continually try to reduce our body fat, there are levels below which we dare not go. A minimal amount of body fat is necessary for insulation of the body, for cushioning between parts of the body and vital organs, and for maintaining body functions. In men, this lower limit is approximately 3 to 4 percent. Women should generally not go below 8 percent. Excessively low body fat in females may lead to amenorrhea, a disruption of the normal menstrual cycle. The critical level of body fat necessary to maintain normal menstrual flow is believed to be between 8 and 13 percent, but there are numerous exceptions to this rule and many additional factors that affect the menstrual cycle. Under extreme circumstances, such as starvation diets and certain diseases, the body often utilizes all available fat reserves and begins to break down muscle tissue as a last-ditch effort to obtain nourishment. The key is to find a level at which you are not at high risk for health problems and at which you are comfortable with your appearance.

ASSESSING YOUR BODY CONTENT

Today, most weight control authorities believe that getting on the scale to determine your weight and then looking at where you fall on some arbitrary chart may be more harmful than helpful. Determining weight status in such ways may lead many to think they are overly fat when they are not, or that they are okay when, in fact, they may be at risk. A number of measures exist for calculating body content, and some provide a very precise reading or calculation of your body fat. Others are less sophisticated but are based on factors that have been identified as key indicators for assessing body content.

Body Mass Index

In recent years, **body mass index (BMI)** has emerged as the medical standard used to define obesity. BMI is an index of the relationship of height and weight and is one of the most accurate indicators of a person's health risk due to excessive weight, rather than "fatness" per se.

Although many people recoil in fright when they see that they have to convert pounds to kilograms and inches to meters to calculate BMI, it really is not as difficult as it may seem. To get your kilogram weight, just divide your weight in pounds (without shoes or clothing) by 2.2. To convert your height to meters squared, divide your height in inches (without shoes) by 39.4, then square this result. Sounds pretty easy and it actually is. Once you have these basic values, calculat-

ing your BMI involves dividing your weight in kilograms by your height in meters squared.

$$BMI = \frac{Weight\ (in\ lbs) \div 2.2\ (to\ determine\ weight\ in\ kg)}{(Height\ (in\ inches) \div 39.4)^2\ (to\ determine\ height\ in\ meters\ squared)}$$

Healthy weights have been defined as those associated with BMIs of 19 to 25, the range of lowest statistical health risk.[9] A BMI greater than 27 indicates obesity and potentially significant health risks.[10] The desirable range for females is between 21 and 23; for males, it is between 22 and 24.[11] (see Figure 10.1). The secret lies in establishing a healthful weight

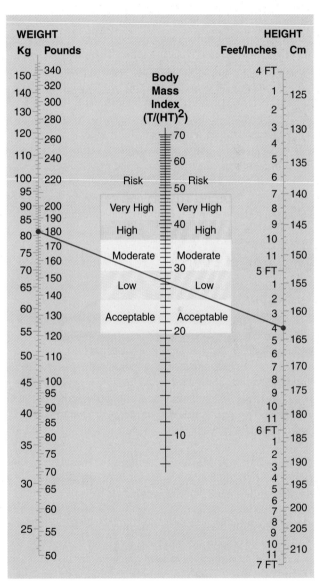

Figure 10.1

Are you overweight? To find out if your current level of fatness increases your chances of dying early, angle a pencil on the edge of a piece of paper from your weight (on the left) to your height (on the right). Read your risk where the pencil crosses the center line.

Obesity   A weight disorder generally defined as an accumulation of fat beyond that considered normal for a person's age, sex, and body type.

Body mass index (BMI)   A technique of weight assessment based on the relationship of weight to height.

at a young age and maintaining it—a task easier said than done. The U.S. Dietary Guidelines for Americans encourages a weight gain of no more than 10 pounds after reaching adult height and endorses small weight losses of one-half to 1 pound per week, if needed, as well as smaller weight losses of 5 to 10 percent to make a difference toward health.[12]

Waist-to-Hip Ratio

Another useful measure that has been in the news lately is the *waist-to-hip ratio*, a measure of regional fat distribution. Research has shown that excess fat in the abdominal area poses a greater health risk than does excess fat in the hips and thighs and is associated with a number of disorders, including high blood pressure, diabetes, heart disease, and certain types of cancer. A waist-to-hip ratio greater than 1.0 in men and 0.8 in women indicates increased health risks.[13] Therefore, knowing where your fat is being carried may be more important than knowing your total fat content. Work in this area has generally found that men and postmenopausal women tend to store fat in the upper regions of their body, particularly in the abdominal area. Premenopausal women usually store their fat in lower regions of their bodies, particularly the hips, buttocks, and thighs.[14] In fact, waist measurement alone may be a viable way to assess fat distribution. Some research suggests that a waistline greater than 40 inches (102 cm) in men and 35 inches (88 cm) in women may be an indicator of greater health risk.[15]

Measures of Body Fat

▶ *Hydrostatic Weighing Techniques*   From a clinical perspective, the most accurate method of measuring body fat is through **hydrostatic weighing techniques.** This method measures the amount of water a person displaces when completely submerged. Because fat tissue has a lower density than muscle or bone tissue, a relatively accurate indication of actual body fat can be computed by comparing a person's underwater and out-of-water weights. Although this method may be subject to errors, it is one of the most sophisticated techniques currently available.

▶ *Pinch and Skinfold Measures*   Perhaps the most commonly used method of body fat determination is the **pinch test.** Numerous studies have determined that the triceps area (located in the back of the upper arm) is one of the most reliable areas of the body for assessing the amount of fat in the subcutaneous (just under the surface) layer of the skin. In making this assessment, a person pinches a fold of skin just behind the triceps with the thumb and index finger. It is important to pinch only the fat layer and not the triceps muscle. After selecting a spot for measure, the person assesses the distance between the thumb and index finger. If the size of the pinch appears to be thicker than 1 inch, the person is generally considered overfat. Another technique, the **skinfold caliper test,** resembles the pinch test but is much more accurate. In this procedure, a person pinches folds of skin at various points on the body with the thumb and index finger. This technique uses a specially calibrated instrument called a *skinfold caliper* to take a precise measurement of the fat layer. Besides the triceps area, the points most often used in these measurements are the biceps area (front of the arm), the subscapular area (upper back), and the iliac crest (hip). Once these data points are assessed, special formulas are employed to arrive at a combined prediction of total body fat. In the hands of trained technicians, this procedure can be fairly accurate. However, the heavier a person is, the more prone this technique is to error. For chronically obese people, difficulties in assessment are magnified because of problems with distinguishing between flaccid muscles and fat. Also, most currently available calipers do not expand far enough to obtain accurate measurements on the moderately obese (20 to 40 percent overweight) or the morbidly obese (more than 50 percent overweight). Additional errors in skinfold assessments may occur as a result of failure to account for certain age, sex, and ethnic differences in calibrations.

▶ *Girth and Circumference Measures*   Another common method of body fat assessment is the use of **girth and circumference measures.** Diagnosticians use a measuring tape to take girth, or circumference, measurements at various body sites. These measurements are then converted into constants, and a formula is used to determine relative percentages of body fat. Although this technique is inexpensive, easy to use, and commonly performed, it is not as accurate as many of the other techniques listed here.

▶ *Soft-Tissue Roentgenogram*   A relatively new technique for body fat determination, the **soft-tissue roentgenogram,** involves injecting a radioactive substance into the body and allowing this substance to penetrate muscle (lean) tissue so distinctions between fat and lean tissue can be made by means of imaging.

▶ *Bioelectrical Impedance Analysis*   Another method of determining body fat levels, **bioelectrical impedance analysis (BIA),** involves sending a small electric current through the subject's body. The amount of resistance to the current, along with the person's age, sex, and other physical characteristics, is then fed into a computer that uses special formulas to determine the total amount of lean and fat tissue.

▶ *Total Body Electrical Conductivity*   One of the newest (and most expensive) assessment techniques is **total body electrical conductivity (TOBEC),** which uses an electromagnetic force field to assess relative body fat. Although based on the same principle as impedance, this assessment requires much more elaborate, expensive equipment, and therefore is not practical for most people.

Although all of these methods can be useful, they can also be inaccurate and even harmful unless the testers are skillful and well trained.

Calculate your BMI using the formula provided. If possible, try to have your percentage body fat tested with calipers or one of the other methods listed. Which value is most important to you? Why? How are they similar?

RISK FACTORS FOR OBESITY

The rate of obesity in the United States is rising as we head into a new century. While in the early 1990s, 1 in 8 American adults were found to be obese, the century closes with 1 in 5 American adults considered obese. The rates of obesity are climbing at almost epidemic proportions.[16]

For many of us, the reason for obesity is quite simple: If you take in more calories than you burn up, you will gain weight. If you do this throughout your life, you will become increasingly obese.

Although the calorie explanation of obesity is certainly valid, it offers only one possible reason for a person's weight problem. Research *has* identified a number of factors that contribute to obesity that may offer some answers.

Heredity

▶ *Body Type and Genes*   Many scientists have explored the role of heredity in determining human body shapes. Some

Hydrostatic weighing techniques   Methods of determining body fat by measuring the amount of water displaced when a person is completely submerged.

Pinch test   A method of determining body fat whereby a fold of skin just behind the triceps is pinched between the thumb and index finger to determine the relative amount of fat.

Skinfold caliper test   A method of determining body fat whereby folds of skin and fat at various points on the body are grasped between thumb and forefinger and measured with calipers.

Girth and circumference measures   A method of assessing body fat that employs a formula based on girth measurements of various body sites.

Soft-tissue roentgenogram   A technique of body fat assessment in which radioactive substances are used to determine relative fat.

Bioelectrical impedance analysis (BIA)   A technique of body fat assessment in which electrical currents are passed through fat and lean tissue.

Total body electrical conductivity (TOBEC)   Technique using an electromagnetic force field to assess relative body fat.

researchers cite statistics showing that 80 percent of children having two obese parents are also obese.[17]

▶ *Twin Studies*   Studies of identical twins who were separated at birth and raised in different environments have provided us with some of the most conclusive evidence to date that obesity may be an inherited trait. Whether raised in family environments with fat or thin family members, twins with obese natural parents tend to be obese in later life.[18] According to another study, sets of identical twins who were separated and raised in different families and who ate widely different diets still grew up to weigh about the same.[19]

These studies contain the strongest evidence yet that the genes a person inherits are the major factor determining overweight, leanness, or average weight. Although the exact mechanics remain unknown, it is believed that genes set metabolic rates, influencing how the body handles calories. Some experts believe that this genetic tendency may contribute as much as 25 to 40 percent of the reason for being overweight.[20]

▶ *Specific Obesity Genes?*   In the past decade, more and more research has pointed to the existence of a special "fat gene." The most promising candidate is the *Ob* gene (for obesity), which is believed to disrupt the body's "I've had enough to eat" signaling system and may prompt individuals to keep eating past the point of being comfortably full. Research on Pima Indians, who have an estimated 75 percent obesity rate and nine in ten who are overweight, seems to point to an Ob gene that is a "thrifty gene." It is theorized that because their ancestors had to struggle through centuries of famine, their ancestor's basal metabolic rates slowed, allowing them to store precious fat for survival. They may have passed these genes on to their children, explaining the lower metabolic rates found in Pimas today and their greater propensity for obesity.[21] Scientists have found that they can manipulate mice genes and construct an Ob gene that will invariably lead to fatness in mice and to the development of diabetes II. Many suspect a human counterpart to this gene, but an actual gene formation has yet to be found. In addition, the (Beta)-3 adrenergic-receptor gene has been identified and found in human beings and mice. When mutated, it is thought to impede the body's ability to burn fat.[22]

Although the 1994 discovery of the Ob gene has provided fertile ground for speculation, researchers have since further refined their theories to focus on a protein that the Ob gene may produce, known as Leptin, and a new leptin receptor in the brain. According to these studies, leptin is the chemical that signals the brain when you are full and need to stop eating.[23,24] Although obese people have adequate amounts of leptin and working leptin receptors, they do not seem to work properly.

Another group of scientists appear to have isolated a more direct route to appetite suppression, a protein called GLP-1, which is known to slow down the passage of food through the intestines to allow the absorption of nutrients.

Are New Diet Drugs Safe for Consumption?

Not quite two years after the Food and Drug Administration (FDA) pulled the appetite suppressants fenfluramine and desfenfluramine (Redux) off the market because of serious risks to consumers, a list of newer and supposedly better and safer diet drugs has been unveiled. Some are still in clinical trials; others are already being marketed in Europe and the United States. Despite the problems of and negative publicity about past "diet miracles," consumers seem undaunted and ready to try the next ones.

One of the newest families of drugs in the fat-fighting war is those on leptin, a protein hormone produced by the body's fat cells. After noting that mice injected with the hormone lost large amounts of weight, it wasn't long before human trials were under way. Although it may be a couple of years before leptin-based drugs are approved by the FDA and become available to the public, initial results seem promising. Given by injection, one such drug produces significant weight loss, with few apparent side effects, except for irritation at the site of the injection.

Another new drug, Orlistat (market name, *Xenical*), produced by Hoffman-LaRoche was approved in May 1999 and hit the diet marketplace with immediate success. Although concerns exist that this medication may have unforeseen negative side effects, much like Redux, such has not been the case thus far. In fact, few side effects have shown up in animal or human studies conducted in some of the 17 countries where the medication has been available for two to three years. The key to this good news may be that very little of the drug is actually absorbed in the body. Unlike Redux, Orlistat doesn't work by reducing appetite. Instead, it interferes with the intestinal enzymes that break down dietary fat into an absorbable form. In short, Orlistat turns normal fat into a substance similar to Olestra, the substance used in many foods on the market today. Much like Olestra, significant amounts of fat found in the foods are flushed right through the digestive system. One of the most significant side effects, however, is that beneficial nutrients, such as vitamins A, D, E, and K, are also flushed. Therefore the FDA requires labels on Orlistat recommending that users take a multivitamin with these nutrients at least two hours before or after taking the drug. Other negative side effects include large, greasy stools; flatulence; diarrhea, sometimes uncontrollable; a condition known as "anal leakage"; and staining. While this may not be enough to prevent some people from using Orlistat, the fact that weight loss itself is slow and difficult to maintain may be a more important deciding factor.

Another newly approved diet drug, Meridia, works by regulating two chemical messengers involved in appetite control: serotonin and norepinephrine. Meridia also has side effects, such as severe elevation of blood pressure in some people.

In spite of the rather weak overall results and some negative side effects, the rush for these drugs is already on. In its first four weeks on the market, Orlistat alone sold over 95,600 prescriptions. Some analysts suggest that, given time, Orlistat may overtake Viagra, another wildly popular drug, in total sales.

Although the newest drugs do not offer the initial promise of rapid weight loss, as did Redux and fenfluramine, pharmaceutical companies remain highly motivated to discover, test, and bring dietary drugs to market. With over 70 million certifiably obese individuals and millions of more prospective weight-loss candidates awaiting proven products, the market is eager . . . and vulnerable. One of the greatest concerns involving all of these newer diet drugs is that health is often superceded by the frenzy to lose weight. Orlistat serves as the perfect example. Intended only for the very obese, Orlistat should be used only under a doctor's supervision and as part of a well-monitored regimen of weight loss and exercise. Yet, even before it was approved for sale in the United States, Orlistat was available on-line from companies in countries throughout the world.

For many, a few pounds lost each year is not exactly what they have in mind. These individuals may be especially vulnerable to weight-loss scams or to sales of untested drugs from abroad. Clearly, the jury is out on the safest of these medications. The best advice for weight loss continues to be exercise more, eat less, and make sure you include enough fruits and vegetables in your dietary regimen.

STUDENTS SPEAK UP:

Why do you think people are willing to compromise their health and put up with the unpleasant side effects of diet drugs just to lose weight?

When scientists injected GLP-1 into the brains of hungry rats, the rats stopped eating immediately.[25] It is speculated that leptin and GLP-1 might play complementary roles in weight control. An understanding of genetic factors in obesity has resulted in much research for diet drugs, as discussed in the Health Headlines box.

Hunger, Appetite, and Satiety

Theories abound concerning the mechanisms that regulate food intake. Some sources indicate that the hypothalamus (the part of the brain that regulates appetite) closely monitors levels of certain nutrients in the blood. When these levels begin to fall, the brain signals us to eat. In the obese person, it is possible that the monitoring system does not work properly and that the cues to eat are more frequent and intense than they are in people of normal weight.

Other sources indicate that thin people may send more effective messages to the hypothalamus. This concept, known as **adaptive thermogenesis,** states that thin people can often consume large amounts of food without gaining weight because the appetite center of their brains speeds up metabolic activity to compensate for the increased consumption. Older studies have indicated the possibility that specialized types of fat cells, called **brown fat cells,** may send signals to the brain, which controls the thermogenesis response.

The hypothesis that food tastes better to obese people, thus causing them to eat more, has largely been refuted. Scientists do distinguish, however, between hunger and appetite. Obese people may be more likely than thin people to satisfy their appetite and eat for reasons other than simple hunger.

In some instances, the problem with overconsumption may be more related to **satiety** than to appetite or hunger. People generally feel satiated, or full, when they have satisfied their nutritional needs and their stomach signals "no more." For undetermined reasons, obese people may not feel full until much later than thin people.

appetite → learned

Developmental Factors

Some obese people may have excessive numbers of fat cells. This type of obesity, **hyperplasia,** usually begins to develop in early childhood and perhaps, due to the mother's dietary habits, even prior to birth. The most critical periods for the development of hyperplasia seem to be the last two to three months of fetal development, the first year of life, and between the ages of 9 and 13. Parents who allow their children to eat without restrictions and to become overweight may be setting their children up for a lifelong excess of fat cells. Central to this theory is the belief that the number of fat cells

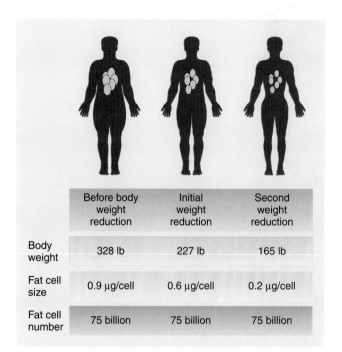

	Before body weight reduction	Initial weight reduction	Second weight reduction
Body weight	328 lb	227 lb	165 lb
Fat cell size	0.9 µg/cell	0.6 µg/cell	0.2 µg/cell
Fat cell number	75 billion	75 billion	75 billion

Figure 10.2

The figure depicts one person at various stages of weight loss. Note that, according to theories of hyperplasia, the number of fat cells remains constant but their size decreases.

in a person's body does not increase appreciably during adulthood. However, the ability of each of these cells to swell and shrink, known as **hypertrophy,** does carry over into adulthood. Weight gain may be tied to both the number of fat cells in the body and the capacity of each individual cell to enlarge.

An average-weight adult has approximately 25 billion to 30 billion fat cells, a moderately obese adult about 60 billion to 100 billion, and an extremely obese adult as many as 200 billion.[26] People who add large numbers of fat cells to their bodies in childhood may be able to lose weight by decreasing the size of each cell in adulthood, but the large numbers of cells remain, and with the next calorie binge, they fill up and sabotage weight-loss efforts (see Figure 10.2). Additional research must be conducted to determine the accuracy of these theories.

Setpoint Theory

In 1982, nutritional researchers William Bennett and Joel Gurin presented a highly controversial theory concerning the difficulty some people have in losing weight. Their theory, known as the **setpoint theory,** states that a person's body has a setpoint of weight at which it is programmed to be comfortable. If your setpoint is around 160 pounds, you will gain and lose weight fairly easily within a given range of that point. For example, if you gain 5 to 10 pounds on vacation, it will be fairly easy to lose that weight and remain around the 160-pound mark for a long period of time. Through a process of

---

Adaptive thermogenesis   Theoretical mechanism by which the brain regulates metabolic activity according to caloric intake.

Brown fat cells   Specialized type of fat cell that affects the ability to regulate fat metabolism.

Satiety   The feeling of fullness or satisfaction at the end of a meal.

Hyperplasia   A condition characterized by an excessive number of fat cells.

Hypertrophy   The ability of fat cells to swell and shrink.

Setpoint theory   A theory of obesity causation that suggests that fat storage is determined by a thermostatic mechanism in the body that acts to maintain a specific amount of body fat.

adaptive thermogenesis, the body actually tries to maintain what it thinks its best weight might be. Some people have equated this point with the **plateau** that is sometimes reached after a person on a diet loses a certain amount of weight. The setpoint theory proposes that after losing a predetermined amount of weight, the body will actually sabotage additional weight loss by slowing down metabolism. Proponents of this theory argue that it is possible to raise one's setpoint over time by continually gaining weight and failing to exercise. Conversely, reducing caloric intake and exercising over a long period of time can slowly decrease one's setpoint. Exercise may be the most critical factor in readjusting your setpoint, although diet may also be important.

This theory remains controversial. In fact, it has prompted nutritional experts to look more carefully at popular methods of weight loss. If the setpoint theory is correct, a low-calorie or starvation diet, besides being dangerous, may cause the body to protect the dieter from "starvation" by slowing down metabolism and making weight loss more difficult.

Endocrine Influence

Over the years, many people have attributed obesity to problems with their **thyroid glands.** They claimed that an underactive thyroid impeded their ability to burn calories. Most authorities agree, however, that only 3 to 5 percent of the obese population have a thyroid problem.

Psychosocial Factors → environmental

In mainstream America, eating tends to be a focal point of people's lives, and the comfort foods of childhood may provide a salve for painful social pressures. Eating is essentially a social ritual associated with companionship, celebration, and enjoyment. The intimate dinner for two, the office party complete with snacks, and the picnic at the beach all center on eating. Is it any wonder that for many people the social emphasis on the eating experience is a major obstacle to successful dieting? time of day / upbringing / availability of food

Eating Cues

At least one major factor in our preoccupation with food is the pressure placed on us by the highly sophisticated, heavily advertised "eating" campaigns launched by the food industry. According to the USDA, the food and restaurant industries spend $40 billion a year on ads designed to entice hungry people to forgo fresh fruit and sliced vegetables for Ring Dings and Happy Meals.[27] The average child, says psychologist Kelly Brownell, head of the Yale University Center for Eating and Weight Disorders, watches 10,000 food ads a year on TV. "And they're not seeing commercials for brussels sprouts," Brownell complains. "They're seeing soft drinks, candy bars, sugar-coated cereals and fast food."[28]

An increasing percentage of the foods we eat are from fast-food restaurants. This is unfortunate because (1) fast food is high in calories, fat, sodium, and carbohydrates; (2) it tends to get eaten, even though portions are often much bigger than they should be; and (3) it tends to be eaten quickly, so there isn't enough time for the "I'm full" signal to get to your brain before the last bite of food is eaten.[29] This is a particular problem for college students who now face the temptation of fast-food courts right on campus.

Metabolic Changes

Even when completely at rest, the body needs a certain amount of energy. The amount of energy your body uses at complete rest is known as your **basal metabolic rate (BMR).** About 60 to 70 percent of all the calories you consume on a given day go to support your basal metabolism. So if you are consuming about 2,000 calories per day, between 1,200 and 1,400 of those calories are burned without your doing any significant physical activity. But unless you exert yourself enough to burn the remaining 600 to 800 calories, you will gain weight. Your BMR can fluctuate considerably, with several factors influencing whether it slows down or speeds up. In general, the younger you are, the higher your BMR. BMR is highest during infancy, puberty, and pregnancy, when

11,00 → female / 1300 → male / calories

bodily changes are most rapid. BMR is also influenced by body composition. Muscle tissue is highly active—even at rest—compared to fat tissue. In essence, the more lean tissue you have, the greater your BMR and the more fat tissue you have, the lower your BMR. Men have a higher BMR than women do, at least partly because of their greater tendency toward lean tissue.

Age is another factor that may greatly affect BMR. After the age of 30, your BMR slows down by about 1 to 2 percent a year. Therefore, people over 30 commonly find that they must work harder to burn off an extra helping of ice cream than they did when they were in their teens. A slower BMR, coupled with priorities (family and career) that come before fitness and weight, puts many middle-aged people's weight in jeopardy.

The body has a number of self-protective mechanisms that signal BMR to speed up or slow down. In starvation situations, the body tries to protect itself by slowing down BMR to conserve precious energy. Thus, when people repeatedly resort to extreme diets, it is believed that their bodies "reset" their BMRs at lower rates. **Yo-yo diets,** in which people repeatedly gain weight and then starve themselves to lose the weight, lowering their BMR in the process, are doomed to failure. When they begin to eat again after the weight loss, they have a BMR that is set lower, making it almost certain that they will regain the weight they just lost. After repeated cycles of such dieting/regaining, these people find it increasingly hard to lose weight and increasingly easy to regain it, so they become heavier and heavier.

According to a recent study by Kelly Brownell of Yale University, middle-aged men who maintained a steady weight (even if they were overweight) had a lower risk of heart attack than men whose weight cycled up and down in a yo-yo pattern. Brownell found that smaller, well-maintained weight losses are more beneficial for reducing cardiovascular risk than larger, poorly maintained weight losses.[30]

In addition, new research supports the theory that by increasing your *muscle mass,* you will increase your metabolism and burn more calories each time you exercise (see Chapter 11).

Plateau   That point in a weight-loss program at which the dieter finds it difficult to lose more weight.

Thyroid gland   A two-lobed endocrine gland located in the throat region that produces a hormone that regulates metabolism.

Basal metabolic rate (BMR)   The energy expenditure of the body under resting conditions at normal room temperature.

Yo-yo diet   Cycles in which people repeatedly gain weight, then starve themselves to lose weight. This lowers their BMR, which makes regaining weight even more likely.

Although a great many more people work out on a regular basis, a great many people continue to lead sedentary lifestyles, putting themselves at risk for obesity and cardiovascular diseases.

Lifestyle

Of all the factors affecting obesity, perhaps the most critical is the relationship between activity levels and calorie intake. Obesity rates are rising. According to a recent Centers for Disease Control survey, 58 percent of U.S. adults said that they exercised sporadically or not at all. Inactivity was especially marked among blacks, Hispanics, low-income people, and the unemployed.[31] Meanwhile, physical education classes in schools throughout the country are the victims of budget cuts and an apparent disinterest in physical fitness.

You probably know someone who seems to be able to eat you under the table and does not appear to exercise more than you do, yet never seems to gain weight. If you were to follow this person around for a typical day and monitor the level and intensity of activity, you might find that although the person's schedule may not include strenuous exercise, it probably includes a high level of activity. Walking up a flight of stairs rather than taking the elevator, speeding up the pace while mowing the lawn, and doing housework vigorously all burn extra calories. (Actually, it may even go beyond that. In studies of calorie burning by individuals placed in a controlled respiratory chamber environment where calories consumed, motion, and overall activity were measured, it was found that some people are better fat burners than others. It is possible that low fat burners may not produce as many of the enzymes needed to convert fat to energy. Or they may not have as many blood vessels supplying fatty tissue, making it tougher for them to deliver fat-burning oxygen.)

Clearly, any form of activity that helps your body burn additional calories helps you maintain your weight. In fact, in a study conducted at Stanford University in 1987, a group of men who lost weight through exercise were far more

• perception of self
• exercise

successful at keeping the weight off than were a similar group who lost weight through dieting.

Gender and Obesity

Throughout a woman's life, issues of appearance and beauty dominate her surroundings. Only recently have researchers begun to understand just how significant the quest for beauty and the perfect body really is.

Of increasing interest is another emerging problem seen in both young men and women, known as **social physique anxiety (SPA),** in which the desire to "look good" has a destructive and sometimes disabling effect on one's ability to function effectively in relationships and interactions with others. Although there are many manifestations of this form of anxiety, in some cases, it may mean that these people spend a disproportionate amount of time "fixating" on their bodies, working out, and performing tasks that are ego-centered and self-directed, rather than focusing on interpersonal relationships and general tasks.[32] Overweight and obesity are clear risks for this problem, and experts speculate that it may also be a contributing factor to eating-disordered behaviors.

Researchers have determined that being severely overweight in adolescence may predetermine one's social and economic future—particularly if you happen to be female. Researchers found that obese women complete about half a year less schooling, are 20 percent less likely to get married, and earn $6,710 on average less per year than their slimmer counterparts. Obese women also have rates of household poverty 10 percent higher than those of women who are not overweight. In contrast, the study found that overweight men were 11 percent less likely to be married than thinner men but suffer few adverse economic consequences.

Compared with men, women have a lower ratio of lean body mass to fatty mass, in part due to differences in bone size and mass, muscle size, and other variables. For all ages after sexual maturity, men have higher metabolic rates, making it easier for them to burn off excess calories than it is for women. Women also face greater potential for weight fluctuation due to hormonal changes, pregnancy, and other conditions that increase the likelihood of weight gain. Also, as a group, men are more socialized into physical activity from birth. Strenuous activity in both work and play are encouraged for men, while women's roles have typically been more sedentary and required a lower level of caloric expenditure to complete.

Not only are women more vulnerable to weight gain, but also pressures to maintain and/or lose weight make them more likely to take dramatic measures to lose weight. The predominance of eating disorders among women and the greater numbers of women than men taking diet pills is just one indicator of the female obsession with being thin and beautiful. However, males are also victims. As the male image becomes more associated with the body-builder shape and size, eating disorders, exercise addictions, and other maladaptive responses among men are on the increase.

MANAGING YOUR WEIGHT

At some point in our lives, almost all of us will go on a diet. Considering what we've discussed in this chapter, many of us will meet with mixed success and we will be left scratching our heads and wondering why we can't seem to find the diet that works. It has been well documented that hypocaloric (low-calorie) diets produce only temporary losses and may actually produce disordered binge eating or related problems.[33] Although the repeated bouts of restrictive dieting may not be physiologically harmful, the sense of failure that we get each time we try and fail may have far-reaching psychological costs.[34] Drugs and intensive counseling have contributed to positive weight losses, but even then, weight is often regained after treatment.

The failure to produce lasting weight loss and the subsequent reduction of self-esteem have led some health professionals to focus on optimizing psychological and physical health rather than on weight loss.[35] Goals of modern weight-management programs should focus on the following:

- Helping people establish tolerable, enjoyable, and stable eating and exercise patterns
- Focusing on small gains and benefits to health and well-being initially; later focusing on long-term functional improvements, improvements in energy, and reduced risk from disease
- Establishing maintainable goals
- Making a lifetime commitment to a healthful lifestyle that includes exercise, food choices, and stress management
- Seeking continued support from professionals and loved ones
- Improving access to low-cost, healthful foods and broadening one's perspective on food possibilities
- Deemphasizing food as a central focus and learning to enjoy other activities that bring joy
- Becoming a wise food consumer

Whether dieting for vanity or for your health, it's important to begin by finding a program of exercise and healthy eating behaviors that will work for you now and in the long term.

What Is a Calorie?

A *calorie* is a unit of measure that indicates the amount of energy we obtain from a particular food. One pound of body fat contains approximately 3,500 calories. So each time you consume 3,500 calories more than your body needs to maintain weight, you gain a pound. Conversely, each time your body expends an extra 3,500 calories, you lose a pound. The two ways to lose weight, then, are to lower caloric intake (through improved eating habits) and to increase exercise (expending more calories). The best strategy is to go slow, set short-term goals, and stick to them.

Exercise

Approximately 90 percent of the daily calorie expenditures of most people occurs as a result of the **resting metabolic rate (RMR).** The RMR is slightly higher than the BMR; it includes the BMR plus any additional energy expended through daily sedentary activities, such as food digestion, sitting, studying, or standing. The **exercise metabolic rate (EMR)** accounts for the remaining 10 percent of all daily calorie expenditures; it refers to the energy expenditure that occurs during physical exercise. If we increase the level and intensity of our physical activity to moderate or heavy, however, our EMR may be 10 to 20 times greater than typical resting metabolic rates and can contribute substantially to weight loss.

Increasing BMR, RMR, or EMR levels will help burn calories. An increase in the intensity, frequency, and duration of your daily exercise levels may have significant impact on your total calorie expenditure.

Physical activity makes a greater contribution to BMR when large muscle groups are used. The energy spent on physical activity is the energy used to move the body's muscles—the muscles of the arms, back, abdomen, legs, and so on—and the extra energy used to speed up heartbeat and respiration rate. The number of calories spent depends on three factors:

1. The amount of muscle mass moved.
2. The amount of weight being moved.
3. The amount of time the activity takes.

Lose 1-2 per week MAX.

Social physique anxiety (SPA)   The desire to look good has a destructive effect on a person's ability to function effectively socially.

Resting metabolic rate (RMR)   The energy expenditure of the body under BMR conditions plus other daily sedentary activities.

Exercise metabolic rate (EMR)   The energy expenditure that occurs during exercise.

An activity involving both the arms and the legs burns more calories than one involving only the legs, an activity performed by a heavy person burns more calories than one performed by a lighter person, and an activity performed for 40 minutes requires twice as much energy as the same activity performed for only 20 minutes. Thus, obese persons walking for 1 mile burn more calories than slim people walking the same distance. It may also take overweight people longer to walk the mile, which means that they are burning energy for a longer time and therefore expending more overall calories than are thin walkers.

.... **WHAT DO YOU THINK?**

Which of the methods for weight reduction discussed above do you think offers the lowest risk and the greatest chance for success?

Changing Your Eating Habits

Before you can change a given behavior, you must first determine what causes that behavior. Why do you suddenly find yourself at the refrigerator door eating everything in sight? Why do you take that second and third helping of potatoes or dessert when you know that you should be trying to lose weight? *Eating triggers*

Once you recognize the factors that cause you to eat, removing the triggers or substituting other activities for them will help you develop more sensible eating patterns. Here are some examples of substitute behaviors:

1. When eating dinner, turn off all distractions, including the television and radio.
2. Replace snack breaks or coffee breaks with exercise breaks.
3. Instead of gulping your food, force yourself to chew each bite slowly.
4. Vary the time of day when you eat. Instead of eating by the clock, do not eat until you are truly hungry.
5. If you find that you generally eat all that you can cram on a plate, use smaller plates.
6. If you find that you are continually seeking your favorite foods in the cupboard, stop buying them. Or place them in a spot that is very inconvenient to reach.

After recording your daily intake for a week, you will be able to devise a list of substitutes that are geared toward your particular eating behaviors.

.... **WHAT DO YOU THINK?**

Do you eat because it's time or because you are really hungry? Do you know what real hunger feels like? Chart your eating behaviors for the next 2 to 3 days. Each time you find yourself "grazing" for food or drink, ask yourself (1) whether you are really hungry and (2) what triggered you to eat.

Calorie intake vs. calorie expenditure
-500 less than
Ave. 2000-2500 per day (cal)

Selecting a Weight Management Plan

To be successful in your weight-loss efforts, you must plan for success. Don't try to lose 40 pounds in four months; instead, try to lose a healthy 1 to 2 pounds during the first week, and then continue with this slow and steady regimen. Reward yourself when you lose pounds, and if you binge and go off your nutrition plan, get right back on it the next day, without self-recrimination.

Additional weight-loss strategies include the following:

- Seek assistance from reputable sources in selecting a dietary plan that is easy to follow and includes adequate amounts of basic nutrients.
- Seek reliable information from registered dieticians, some physicians (not all have strong backgrounds in nutrition), health educators, and exercise physiologists with nutritional backgrounds, or any other health professionals with an understanding of nutrition.
- Avoid quick weight-loss programs that promise miracle results.
- If you join a weight-loss program, ask about your adviser's credentials and assess the nutrient value of the prescribed diet.

- Assess any diet program in terms of its compatibility with your likes and dislikes, budget, and lifestyle.

Keep in mind that dietary programs that ask you to change your behavior radically or that ask you to sacrifice everything you enjoy is doomed to failure. Give yourself the opportunity to make choices so you can give yourself the opportunity to succeed.

Ultimately, the decision to practice responsible weight management is yours. To be successful, you must choose a combination of exercise and eating that fits your needs and lifestyle. Find a workable plan, stick to it, and you will succeed.

"Miracle" Diets

Fasting, starvation diets, and other forms of **very low calorie diets (VLCDs)** have been shown to cause significant health risks. Typically, when you deprive your body of food for prolonged periods, your body makes adjustments to save you from inevitable organ shutdown. It begins to deplete its energy reserves to obtain necessary fuels. One of the first reserves the body turns to to maintain its supply of glucose is lean, protein tissue. As this occurs, you lose weight rapidly, because protein contains only half as many calories per pound as fat. At the same time, significant water stores are lost. Over time, the body begins to run out of liver tissue, heart muscle, blood, and so on, as these readily available substances are burned to supply energy. Only after the readily available proteins from these sources are depleted will your body begin to burn fat reserves. In this process, known as **ketosis,** the body adapts to prolonged fasting or carbohydrate deprivation by converting body fat to ketones, which can be used as fuel for some brain cells. Within about 10 days after the typical adult begins a complete fast, the body has used many of its energy stores and death may occur.

In very low calorie diets, powdered formulas are usually given to patients under medical supervision. These formulas have daily values of from 400 to 700 calories plus vitamin and mineral supplements. Although these diets may be beneficial for people who have failed at all conventional weight-loss methods and who face severe threats to their health that are complicated by their obesity, they should never be undertaken without strict medical supervision. Problems associated with fasting, VLCDs, and other forms of severe calorie deprivation include blood sugar imbalances, cold intolerance, constipation, decreased BMR, dehydration, diarrhea, emotional problems, fatigue, headaches, heart irregularity, ketosis, kidney infections and failure, loss of lean body tissue, weakness, and weight gain due to the yo-yo effect and other variables.

Very low calorie diets (VLCDs)   Diets with caloric value of 400 to 700 calories.

Ketosis   A condition in which the body adapts to prolonged fasting or carbohydrate deprivation by converting body fat to ketones, which can be used as fuel for some brain activity.

Anorexia nervosa   Eating disorder characterized by excessive preoccupation with food, self-starvation, and/or extreme exercising to achieve weight losses.

Bulimia nervosa   Eating disorder characterized by binge eating followed by inappropriate compensating measures taken to prevent weight gain.

Dieter Beware!

The market is flooded with diet options that claim miraculous results. From diet plans that profess to guide you toward rapid weight reduction to products that promise to melt your fat away, the array of choices is mind-numbing. Whether you are considering a diet program or a diet product, beware!

Some of the recent fad diets have helped people lose weight successfully. Diets such as "The Zone" and the Atkins diet can legitimately claim success. However, are these diets safe, effective, and long lasting? Probably not. First of all, both of these diets encourage those following them to eat very high protein and extremely low carbohydrate diets. According to the U.S. Dietary Guidelines, these programs essentially eliminate important nutrients from our daily diet. Even fruits and vegetables are largely off-limits because of their high fructose

levels. In addition to eliminating key foods and food groups, these diets encourage eating patterns that differ from what people are used to, so the likelihood of maintaining these eating patterns after the weight loss has been achieved is unlikely.

A number of other diets, such as Optifast, Nutri/System, and Jenny Craig, are programs that provide prepackaged foods during the weight-loss phase of the diet. Although clients benefit from weekly meetings or sessions with non-professional counselors, what happens when these sessions are finished and the prepackaged foods are no longer available? The likelihood of their maintaining the weight loss once they return to eating supermarket foods is uncertain.

In addition to these diet plans, which are only a sampling of what is available, there are myriad products that promise easy and effective weight loss, including:

- *Diet patches:* These have not been proved either safe or effective.
- *"Fat blockers":* These claim to absorb fat; however, these claims are, thus far, unfounded.
- *"Start blockers":* Although this product claims to hinder digestion of

starches, this has not been proved. In addition, negative side effects include nausea, vomiting, stomach pains, and diarrhea.
- *Spirulina:* This species of blue algae, which has been touted as a weight-loss supplement, has no documented record of success.
- *"Magnet" diet pills:* The assertion that this product "flushes fat out of the body" has not been verified. In fact, the Federal Trade Commission is suing several marketers of this product.
- *Glucomanan:* This plant root, advertised as "The Weight Loss Secret That's Been in the Orient for Over 500 Years," has no scientific evidence to back up this claim.

So, if you are tempted by the big, bold advertisements that feature phrases that describe weight loss products or programs as being "easy," "effortless," "guaranteed," "miraculous," "magical," "a breakthrough," or an "ancient remedy," read between the lines, and remember, "If it sounds too good to be true . . . it is!"

Source: Thrive Online, Weight Loss Products, "How to Evaluate," weightcontro@thrive.com DHHS Publication, no. (FDA) 92-1189.

Trying to Gain Weight

Although trying to lose weight poses a major challenge for many of us, there is a smaller group of people who, for a variety of metabolic, hereditary, psychological, and other reasons, can't seem to gain weight no matter how hard they try. If you are one of these individuals, determining the reasons for your difficulty in gaining weight is a must. Once you know what is causing you to have a daily caloric deficit, there are several things that you can do to help yourself gain extra weight:

- Control your exercise. Cut back if you are doing too much, slow down, and keep a careful record of calories burned.
- Eat more. Obviously, you are not taking in enough calories to support whatever is happening in your body. Eat more frequently, spend more time eating, eat the high-calorie foods first if you tend to fill up fast, and always start with the main course. Put extra spreads such as peanut butter, cream cheese, or cheese on your foods.

Make your sandwiches with extra-thick slices of bread and add more filling. Take seconds whenever possible and eat high-calorie snacks during the day.
- Supplement your diet with high-calorie drinks that have a healthy balance of nutrients.
- Relax. Many people who are underweight operate at high gear most of the time. Slow down, get more rest, and control stress.

EATING DISORDERS

Throughout our lives, most of us wage a running battle with food. For an increasing number of people, particularly young women, an obsessive relationship with food develops into a persistent, chronic eating disorder known as **anorexia nervosa,** a condition characterized by deliberate food restriction and severe, life-threatening weight loss, or **bulimia nervosa** or a variation know as **binge eating disorder (BED),** which involve frequent bouts of binge eating followed by purging, or self-induced vomiting, laxative abuse, or excessive exercise.[36] In the United States more than 10 million people, 90 percent of whom are women, meet the established criteria for one of these disorders, and the numbers appear to be on the increase.[37] Many more suffer from minor forms of these conditions. (See Table 10.3 for a list of the newest eating-disorder criteria.)

Anorexia Nervosa

Anorexia involves self-starvation motivated by an intense fear of gaining weight along with an extremely distorted sense of one's own body image. When anorexia occurs in childhood, failure to gain weight in a normal growth pattern may be the key indicator; later, this typically results in actual weight loss. Nearly 1 percent of girls in late adolescence meet the full criteria for anorexia; many others suffer from significant symptoms.

Usually anorectics achieve their weight loss through initial reduction in total food intake, particularly of high-calorie

~~tooth~~ decay •hair loss
Voluntary

TABLE 10.3
DSM-IV Eating Disorder Criteria

Anorexia

According to the DSM-IV, people who meet the criteria for anorexia nervosa experience all of the following symptoms:

- Refusal to maintain the minimum body weight for one's height and age.
- Intense fear of gaining weight even though underweight.
- Disturbed perception of one's body weight or size.
- In post-pubescent women, the absence of at least three consecutive menstrual cycles. (In some women, the loss of periods precedes any significant weight loss.)

Bulimia

People with bulimia experience all of the following:

- Recurrent episodes of consuming much larger amount of food than most people would during a similar time period (this is usually about two hours) and a sense of loss of control over eating during each episode.
- Accompanying attempts to compensate for eating binges by vomiting, abusing laxatives or other drugs or by fasting or excessive exercise.
- Both the binge eating and purging occur at least twice a week for three months.
- A negative perception of one's shape and weight.

Source: From DSM-IV, reported in "Treating Eating Disorders," Harvard Women's Health Watch, May 1996, 4–5. Reprinted with permission from the Diagnostic and Statistical Manual of Mental Disorders, Fourth Edition. Copyright 1994 American Psychiatric Association.

---

foods, eventually leading to restrictions in intake of almost all foods. What they do eat, they often purge, or get rid of, through vomiting or the use of laxatives. Although they lose weight, anorectics never seem to be able to feel "thin enough" and are constantly identifying body parts that are "too fat."

Bulimia Nervosa

Bulimics are binge eaters who take inappropriate measures, such as secret vomiting, to lose the calories/weight that they have just acquired. Up to 3 percent of adolescents and young female adults are bulimic, with male rates being about 10 percent of the female rate. Bulimics also have an obsession with their bodies, weight gain, and how they appear to others. Unlike anorectics, bulimics are often "hidden" from the public eye, as their weight may only vary slightly or be within a normal range. Effective treatment appears to be more likely with bulimia than with anorexia.

iox more common in women in men

Binge Eating Disorder

Binge eating disordered individuals also binge eat like their bulimic counterparts; unlike bulimics, however, people with BED do not take excessive measures to lose the weight that they gain. Often they are clinically obese, and they tend to binge much more often than the typical obese person who spaces his or her eating over a more normal daily eating pattern.

Who's at Risk?

Disordered eating patterns are the result of many factors other than an addiction to food or low self-esteem. Often, they are partially the result of poor self-concept, but other factors, such as a perceived lack of control in their lives, may trigger these problems. To win social approval by maintaining a thin body and to gain control of some aspects of their lives, anorectics or bulimics take rigid control over eating.

Sufferers tend to be women from white middle class or upper class families in which there is undue emphasis on achievement, body weight, and appearance. Contrary to popular thinking, however, eating disorders span social class, gender, race, and ethnic backgrounds and are present in countries throughout the world. In addition, increasing numbers of males suffer from various forms of eating disorders.

Some studies have shown possible associations between identical twins, and others have pointed to the large numbers

---

Binge eating disorder (BED) Eating disorder characterized by recurrent binge eating. However, BED sufferers do not take excessive measures to lose the weight gained during binges.

of eating disordered persons who have a mother or sister with the disease. Many persons with disordered eating patterns also suffer from other problems: 50 percent suffer from clinical depression, 25 percent are alcoholics, and large numbers have other problems, such as compulsive stealing, gambling, or other addictions.[38]

Treatment for Eating Disorders

Because eating disorders are the result of many factors, spanning many years of development, there are no quick or simple solutions to the problems. Treatment often focuses on reducing the threat to life; once the patient is stabilized, long-term therapy involves family, friends, and other significant people in the individual's life. Therapy focuses on the psycho-logical, social, environmental, and physiological factors that have led to the problem. Support groups often help the family and the individual gain understanding and emotional support and learn self-development techniques designed to foster positive reactions and actions.

········· WHAT DO YOU THINK?

Which groups or individuals on your campus appear to be at greatest risk? What social factors might encourage this? Why do you think society tends to overlook eating disorders in males? What programs or services on your campus are available for someone with an eating disorder?

Taking Charge ··································

Taking Control of Your Weight

Controlling your weight will be a lifelong struggle. Finding a way to gain control over food, to modify your behaviors, and to prioritize exercise in your life are important steps. To ensure success, you must make a real change in the way you eat and consider it a lifelong commitment rather than a diet. You need to set a realistic goal. Ask yourself, why do I want to meet this goal? Then set out a plan to reach your goal. Each person must find his or her own best strategy, recognize potential difficulties, and work to modify behaviors to help bring his or her weight under control. Your school and community have resources to help. If in doubt, ask your instructor or find out where you can gain assistance from your student health center. Some of the following suggestions may help you get started.

CHECKLIST FOR CHANGE

MAKING PERSONAL CHOICES

✓ Design your plan for your needs. Your plan must fit your personality, your priorities, and your work and recreation schedules. It should allow for sufficient rest and relaxation.

✓ Plan for nutrient-dense foods. Attempt to get the most from the foods you eat by selecting foods with high nutritional value.

✓ Balance food intake throughout the day. Rather than gorging yourself at one main meal, you are probably better off eating several smaller meals throughout the day.

✓ Plan for plateaus. If you prepare yourself psychologically for plateaus you will be less likely to become discouraged. Exercise is probably the critical factor in getting past a plateau.

✓ Chart your progress. Think in terms of weekly weigh-ins to avoid frustration. After all, it is long-range success you are after.

✓ Chart your setbacks. Rather than thinking in terms of failure and punishment, think in terms of temporary setbacks and how to accommodate them. By carefully recording your emotional states when eating, eating habits, environmental cues, and feelings, you may determine why you needed that ice cream cone or why you chose a pizza instead of a salad.

✓ Become aware of your feelings of hunger and fullness. For many of us, eating is time-dependent, and we stop eating only when the food is gone (the "clean your plate" syndrome).

✓ Accept yourself. For many people, this is the most important aspect of successful weight management. It is important to keep your weight in perspective. Unless you feel good about who you are inside, exterior changes will not help you very much.

✓ Exercise, exercise, exercise. Although we would all like to wish away our extra pounds, losing weight requires hard work and concentration. Different people benefit from different types of activities. Select an exercise program that you consider fun, not a daily form of punishment for overeating. It is important to remember that every little effort contributes toward long-term results.

SUMMARY

- Overweight, obesity, and weight-related problems appear to be on the rise in the United States. Obesity is now defined in terms of fat content rather than in terms of weight alone.

- There are many different methods of assessing body fat. BMI is one of the most commonly accepted measures of your weight based on your height. Body fat percentages give you a more accurate indication of how fat versus lean you really are.

- Many factors contribute to your risk for obesity. Included among these factors are genetics, developmental factors, your setpoint, endocrine influences, psychosocial factors, eating cues, lack of awareness, metabolic changes,

lifestyle, and gender. Women often have considerably more difficulty with weight loss.

- Exercise, dieting, diet pills, and other strategies are used to maintain or lose weight. However, sensible eating behavior and adequate exercise probably offer the best options.

- Eating disorders consist of severe disturbances in eating behaviors, unhealthy efforts to control body weight, and abnormal attitudes about body and shape. Anorexia nervosa, bulimia nervosa, and binge eating disorder are the three main eating disorders. Eating disorders occur mainly in adolescent and young adult women in industrialized countries.

DISCUSSION QUESTIONS

1. Discuss the pressures, if any, you feel to improve your personal body image. Do these pressures come from TV shows, movies, ads, and other external sources or from concern for your personal health?

2. List the risk factors for obesity. Evaluate which seem to be most important in determining whether you will be obese in middle age.

3. Create a plan to help someone lose the "Freshman 15" over the summer vacation. Assume that the person is male, 180 pounds, and has 15 weeks to lose the excess weight.

4. Differentiate among the three eating disorders. Then give reasons why females might be more prone to anorexia and bulimia than might males.

APPLICATION EXERCISE

Reread the *What Do You Think?* scenario at the beginning of the chapter and answer the following questions:

1. Why is Jeff the kind of person who probably shouldn't go on blind dates?

2. What are the possible long-term consequences of Jeff's behavior on Donna? Have you ever been in a situation like this?

11

OBJECTIVES

▶ Describe the benefits of regular physical activity, including improved cardio-respiratory fitness, muscular fitness, bone mass, weight control, stress management, mental health, and lifespan.

▶ Describe the components of an aerobic exercise program and how to determine proper exercise frequency, intensity, and duration.

▶ Describe the different stretching exercises designed to improve flexibility.

▶ Compare the various types of resistance exercise programs, including the methods of providing external resistance and intended physiological benefits.

▶ Describe common fitness injuries, suggest ways to prevent injuries, and list the treatment process.

▶ Summarize the key components of a personal fitness program.

Personal Fitness

Improving Your Health through Exercise

To this point, Shawn hadn't been very physically active throughout his life. While in high school he didn't enjoy the physical education classes because he didn't have the fitness level needed for most of the competitive activities like basketball and soccer. Now 20 years old and a sophomore in college, Shawn typically drives his car to campus rather than walking the six blocks from his apartment. Shawn's idea of a complete meal is a large pepperoni pizza delivered to his door, and washed down with a large soda. To relax, he'll play one of the many computer games he owns. Recently Shawn saw a TV show that described the adverse health effects of the sedentary lifestyle—obesity, high blood pressure, increased risk of heart disease, and colon cancer. He realized that he has made some poor choices and was determined to no longer be a couch potato.

Now that Shawn is ready to live a more active lifestyle, how should he begin? After years of not exercising, with what types of exercises should he begin? Should Shawn see his family physician before he starts his exercise program? How long will he need to continue a physical activity program before he notices the positive effects of regular exercise?

ORE THAN 30 YEARS AGO, the President's Council on Physical Fitness was created because of concerns about the low fitness levels of American children. Participation in regular fitness activity gradually increased during the 1970s and 1980s, but has leveled off in recent years. Research indicates that your physical activity level as a child is a good predictor of your physical activity level as an adult.[1] But if you weren't active in your childhood or adolescence, don't despair. College is an excellent place to make a break with the past and develop exercise habits that can increase both the quality and duration of your life. Especially when combined with a healthy diet, regular physical activity combats obesity and reduces your risk of heart disease, high blood pressure, diabetes, and colon cancer.[2] Regular physical activity improves more than 50 different physiological, metabolic, and psychological aspects of human life[3]—which is why more and more Americans are getting serious about exercising.

BENEFITS OF REGULAR PHYSICAL ACTIVITY

Physical activity is any force exerted by skeletal muscles that results in energy usage above the level used when the body's systems are at rest.[4] Among adults, higher levels of physical activity have been associated with a lower risk of coronary heart disease (the leading cause of death in the United States for both men and women), diabetes, and osteo-

porosis.[5] The recent Surgeon General's report on Physical Activity and Health[6] indicates that physical activity need not be strenuous in order to achieve health benefits (see Figure 11.1), and that women and men of all ages benefit from a moderate amount of *daily* physical activity.

Regular physical activity has been linked to lower incidences of high blood pressure (hypertension), cancers of the colon and reproductive organs, bone fractures as a result of osteoporosis,[7] and psychological disorders such as depression and anxiety.[8] A recent study reported that regular exercise (4 hours a week or more) beginning in adolescence and continuing into adulthood can significantly reduce the risk of breast cancer in women 40 and younger.[9]

Many of the risk factors for coronary artery disease, hypertension, and osteoporosis first appear during childhood and adolescence.[10] As many as 60 percent of American children exhibit at least one of the adult risk factors for coronary artery disease by the age of 12.[11] Fortunately, if identified during childhood, adolescence, or young adulthood, many of these risks can be reduced through exercise and modifications in diet.

bone mass - lower chlorestral

Systolic blood pressure The pressure in the arteries during a heartbeat; abnormal if consistently 160 mm Hg or above.

Diastolic blood pressure The pressure in the arteries during the period between heartbeats; abnormal if consistently 95 mm Hg or above.

Osteoporosis A disease characterized by low bone mass and deterioration of bone tissue, which increase fracture risk.

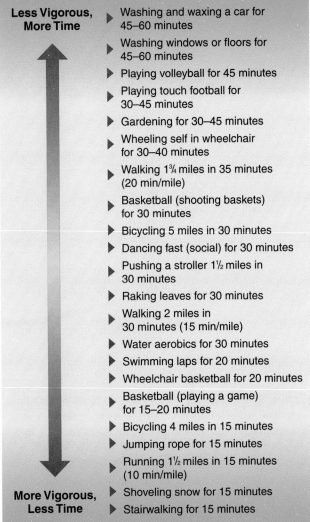

Less Vigorous, More Time
Washing and waxing a car for 45–60 minutes
Washing windows or floors for 45–60 minutes
Playing volleyball for 45 minutes
Playing touch football for 30–45 minutes
Gardening for 30–45 minutes
Wheeling self in wheelchair for 30–40 minutes
Walking 1¾ miles in 35 minutes (20 min/mile)
Basketball (shooting baskets) for 30 minutes
Bicycling 5 miles in 30 minutes
Dancing fast (social) for 30 minutes
Pushing a stroller 1½ miles in 30 minutes
Raking leaves for 30 minutes
Walking 2 miles in 30 minutes (15 min/mile)
Water aerobics for 30 minutes
Swimming laps for 20 minutes
Wheelchair basketball for 20 minutes
Basketball (playing a game) for 15–20 minutes
Bicycling 4 miles in 15 minutes
Jumping rope for 15 minutes
Running 1½ miles in 15 minutes (10 min/mile)
Shoveling snow for 15 minutes
Stairwalking for 15 minutes
More Vigorous, Less Time

Figure 11.1

A moderate amount of physical activity is roughly equivalent to physical activity that uses approximately 150 calories (kcal) of energy per day, or 1,000 calories per week. Some activities can be performed at various intensities: the suggested durations correspond to expected intensity of effort.

Source: Surgeon General's Office, "A Report of the Surgeon General: Physical Activity and Health," 1996 U.S. Department of Health and Human Services.

Improved Cardiorespiratory Fitness

Cardiorespiratory fitness is a health-related component of physical fitness that relates to the ability of the circulatory and respiratory systems to supply oxygen to the body during sustained physical activity. Long-term participation in a regular program of *aerobic* (with oxygen) exercise will improve the efficiency of these systems through *hypertrophy* (increased size) of the heart muscle, enabling more blood to be pumped with each stroke, and an increased number of *capillaries* (small arteries) in trained skeletal muscles, which permit a greater volume of blood to flow to active skeletal muscles.

The major change in the respiratory system from aerobic exercise is an increase in the maximum amount of oxygen that is inspired and distributed to the active muscles.[12]

▶ **Reduced Risk of Heart Disease**   Your heart is a muscle made up of highly specialized tissue. Because muscles become stronger and more efficient with use, regular exercise strengthens the heart. A stronger, more efficient heart is better able to meet the ordinary and extraordinary demands of life.

▶ **Prevention of Hypertension**   Hypertension, the medical term for abnormally high blood pressure, is a significant risk factor for cardiovascular disease and stroke. Hypertension is particularly prevalent among adult African Americans, who experience it approximately 1.5 times more frequently than do white adults.[13] If your resting **systolic blood pressure** is consistently 160 millimeters of mercury (mm Hg) or higher, your risk of coronary heart disease is four times greater than normal. If your resting **diastolic blood pressure** regularly exceeds 95 mm Hg, your risk of heart disease is six times greater than normal.[14] Low to moderate exercise training lowers both systolic and diastolic blood pressure by about 10 mm Hg in people with mild to moderate hypertension.[15] Regular physical activity can also reduce both systolic and diastolic blood pressure in people with normal and high blood pressures.[16]

▶ **Improved Blood Lipid and Lipoprotein Profile**   Lipids are fats that circulate in the bloodstream and are stored in various places in your body. Regular exercise is known to reduce the levels of low-density lipoproteins (LDLs—"bad cholesterol") while increasing the number of high-density lipoproteins (HDLs—"good cholesterol") in the blood. Higher HDL levels are associated with lower risk for artery disease because they remove some of the "bad cholesterol" from artery walls and hence prevent clogging. The net effect of these two physiological responses to exercise is a diminished risk of cardiovascular disease.

Improved Bone Mass

A common affliction in older adults is **osteoporosis,** a disease characterized by low bone mass and deterioration of bone tissue, which increase fracture risk. Osteoporosis is more common among women than among men for at least three reasons: Women live longer than men, women have lower peak bone mass than men, and women lose bone mass at an accelerated rate after menopause as their estrogen levels decrease.[17] (See the Reality Check box on page 268.)

One of the physical activities recommended most frequently to women wanting to improve their bone health is walking. While walking is an excellent activity for overall fitness, there is currently no evidence that casual walking

The Facts about Osteoporosis

While osteoporosis is a threat to both men and women later in life, the threat is more imminent for women due to the loss of estrogen after menopause. This is why it is critical that women begin protecting themselves early by building strong bones and muscles. Some useful facts about osteoporosis that will help you gain perspective on how you can help yourself today are:

✓ 25 million Americans have osteoporosis.
✓ Half of the women ages 50 and up are expected to have a degree of osteoporosis.
✓ One-third of the men ages 75 and older are expected to have osteoporosis.
✓ Caucasians are at greatest risk of osteoporosis.
✓ Bone fractures can be early indicators of osteoporosis.
✓ Osteoporosis is responsible for stooped posture and loss of height.
✓ By advanced age, women lose between 35 percent and 50 percent of their bone mass, and men, 20 percent to 35 percent.
✓ Weight-bearing exercise can help slow bone loss.

✓ Walking, jogging, running, and stair climbing help build bone mass.
✓ Weight lifting (resistance training) is recommended for preventing bone loss.
✓ Activities that use arm strength, such as tennis and volleyball, help build bone mass.
✓ A combination of strength training and weight-bearing exercises is an ideal preventative measure against osteoporosis.

Source: Mayo Clinic Health Letter, October 1997.

---

can significantly increase bone mass in healthy women.[18] Bone, like other human tissues, responds to the demands placed upon it, and unless the mechanical stresses placed on bone by a particular physical activity exceed the level of stress the bone has adapted to, there is no stimulus to increase bone mass.[19] Women (and men) have much to gain by remaining physically active as they age—bone mass levels have been found to be significantly higher among active than among sedentary women.[20] However, it appears that the full benefit of exercise can only be achieved when proper hormone levels (estrogen in women, testosterone in men) are present. Regular exercise, when combined with a balanced diet containing adequate calcium, will help maintain bone mass, although this benefit is more difficult to achieve as we age.

Strength in joints
flexibility & range of motion   reproducing bone mass

Improved Weight Control

For many people, the desire to lose weight is the main purpose for starting an exercise program. Level of physical activity does have a direct effect upon metabolic rate, even raising it for a few hours following a vigorous workout. According to the American College of Sports Medicine, if you are planning to lose weight through exercise alone, without decreasing the amount of food you eat, you'll have to exercise frequently (at least four days a week) for extended time periods (at least 50 minutes per workout).[21] A more effective method for losing weight combines regular endurance-type exercises with a moderate decrease (about 500 to 1,000 calories per day) in food intake. Decreasing daily caloric intake beyond this range ("severe dieting") appears to decrease metabolic rate by up to 20 percent, making weight loss more difficult.

lose, gain, or maintain
500 1,000   even

Improved Health and Life Span

▶ *Prevention of Diabetes*   Non-insulin-dependent diabetes is a complex disorder that is known to affect an estimated 8 million Americans (approximately 3 percent of the U.S. population), with twice that number thought to have diabetes but not know it.[22] The greatest predisposing factors for this type of diabetes are obesity, increasing age, and a family history of diabetes; lesser risk factors include high blood pressure and high cholesterol.[23] Physicians suggest exercise combined with weight reduction and proper diet for the management of this form of diabetes. A large epidemiological study found that for every 2,000 calories of energy expended during leisure-time activities, the incidence of diabetes was reduced by 24 percent. Perhaps the most encouraging finding was that the protective effect of exercise was greatest among those individuals who were at the highest risk for non-insulin-dependent diabetes.[24]

▶ *Increased Longevity*   Experts have long debated the relationship between exercise and longevity. For decades, most research failed to show that we could increase our life expectancy through exercise alone. Then, a landmark study conducted at the Institute for Aerobics Research in Texas found that exercise does increase longevity. More than 13,000 white middle- to upper-middle-class men and women aged 20 to 80 were followed for eight years to discover how physical fitness relates to death rates. Participants were assigned fitness levels based upon their age, sex, and results of exercise tests. The death rate in the least physically fit group was more than three times higher than the death rate in the most fit group. Participants who changed from a sedentary lifestyle to one that included a brisk 30- to 60-minute

Reduced risk of disease and new dimensions for living are among the benefits of physical fitness that are available to people of all ages and capabilities.

walk each day experienced significant increases in their life expectancies.[25]

▶ **Improved Immunity to Disease**   Research suggests that regular moderate exercise makes people less susceptible to disease, but that this potential benefit may depend upon whether they perceive exercise as pleasurable or stressful.[26] For example, athletes engaging in marathon-type events or very intense physical training programs have been shown to be at increased risk of upper respiratory tract infections (e.g., colds and flu).[27] In a study of 2,300 marathon runners, those who ran more than 60 miles per week suffered twice as many upper respiratory tract infections as those who ran fewer than 20 miles per week.[28]

Just how exercise alters immunity is not well understood. We do know that brisk exercise temporarily increases the number of white blood cells (WBCs), the blood cells responsible for fighting infection. Generally speaking, the less fit the person and the more intense the exercise, the greater the increase in WBCs.[29] After brief periods of exercise (without injury), the number of WBCs typically returns to normal levels within one to two hours. After exercise bouts lasting

Physical fitness   A set of attributes related to the ability to perform normal physical activity.

Exercise training   The systematic performance of exercise at a specified frequency, intensity, and duration to achieve a desired level of physical fitness.

longer than 30 minutes, WBCs may be elevated for 24 hours or more before returning to normal levels.[30]

Improved Mental Health and Stress Management

Regular vigorous exercise has been shown to "burn off" the chemical by-products released by our nervous system during normal response to stress. Elimination of these biochemical substances reduces our stress levels by accelerating the neurological system's return to a balanced state.

Regular exercise also improves physical appearance by toning and developing muscles and, in combination with dieting, reducing body fat. Feeling good about personal appearance can provide a tremendous boost to self-esteem. At the same time, as people come to appreciate the improved strength, conditioning, and flexibility that accompany fitness, they often become less obsessed with physical appearance.[31]

·········· **WHAT DO YOU THINK?**

Do you know your resting heart rate? Blood pressure? Cholesterol level? Who could provide you with this information? Based upon what you've read, what are the health benefits you'd like to achieve as the result of regular physical activity?

Improved Physical Fitness

Physical fitness can be defined as a set of attributes related to the ability to perform moderate-to-vigorous levels of physical activity without excessive fatigue and the capability of maintaining this level of function throughout life. The individual fitness components are listed and described in Table 11.1 on page 270. **Exercise training** is the systematic performance of exercise at a specified frequency, intensity, and duration to achieve a desired level of physical fitness.[32]

Although physical fitness has many facets, it is most commonly measured by four interdependent components: (1) cardiorespiratory fitness, (2) flexibility, (3) muscular strength and endurance, and (4) body composition.

To be considered physically fit, you generally need to attain (and then maintain) certain minimum standards for each component that have been established by exercise physiologists and other fitness experts. Some people have physical limitations that make achieving one or more of these standards impossible. That doesn't mean they can't attain physical fitness. For example, a woman who needs to use a wheelchair may be unable to run or walk a mile, as is required in some fitness tests, but can achieve physical fitness by playing wheelchair basketball. Our definition of physical fitness should be adapted to address individual differences in capabilities.

TABLE 11.1
Major Components of Physical Fitness

Cardiorespiratory fitness	Ability to sustain moderate-intensity whole-body activity for extended time periods.
Muscular strength and endurance	Maximum force applied with a single muscle contraction. Ability to perform repeated high-intensity muscle contractions.
Flexibility	Range of motion at a joint or series of joints.
Body composition	A composite of total body mass, fat mass, fat-free mass, and fat distribution.

Source: American College of Sports Medicine, "ACSM Position Stand on the Recommended Quantity and Quality of Exercise for Developing and Maintaining Cardiorespiratory and Muscular Fitness and Flexibility in Adults," Medicine and Science in Sports and Exercise 30 (1998): 975–991.

WHAT DO YOU THINK?

Which of the key aspects of physical fitness do you currently possess? Which ones would you like to improve or develop? What types of activities will you do to improve your fitness level?

IMPROVING CARDIORESPIRATORY FITNESS

The number of walkers, joggers, bicyclists, step aerobics participants, and swimmers is tangible evidence of Americans' increased awareness of the most important aspect of physical fitness: **cardiorespiratory fitness,** which refers to the ability of the circulatory and respiratory systems to supply oxygen during sustained physical activity.

The primary category of physical activity known to improve cardiorespiratory endurance is **aerobic exercise.** The term *aerobic* means "with oxygen" and describes any type of exercise, typically performed at moderate levels of intensity for extended periods of time, that increases your heart rate. **Aerobic capacity** (commonly written as $VO_{2\,max}$) is defined as the maximum volume of oxygen consumed by the muscles during exercise.

To measure your maximal aerobic capacity, an exercise physiologist or physician will typically have you exercise on a treadmill. He or she will initially ask you to walk or run

at an easy pace, and then, at set time intervals during this **graded exercise test,** will gradually increase the workload (i.e., a combination of running speed and the angle of incline of the treadmill) to the point of maximal exertion. Generally, the higher your cardiorespiratory endurance level, the more oxygen you can transport to exercising muscles and the longer you can maintain a high intensity of exercise prior to exhaustion.

According to the exercise testing guidelines of the American College of Sports Medicine, maximal aerobic capacity treadmill tests should not be conducted on men over 40 or women over 50 without a prior comprehensive physical examination and permission from their physicians.[33]

Aerobic Fitness Programs

Researchers tell us that a physically active lifestyle is the key to improved cardiovascular health, but what level of activity is required to improve aerobic fitness? There are numerous variables in any particular aerobic activity, but for healthy young adults, aerobic activity that works your heart at a moderate intensity (approximately 70 percent of your maximum heart rate, or about 140 to 160 beats per minute) for prolonged periods of time (20 to 60 minutes of continuous activity) will improve your fitness level.

The most beneficial aerobic exercises are total body activities involving all the large muscle groups of your body, for example, swimming, cross-country skiing, or rowing. If you have been sedentary for quite a while, simply initiating a physical activity program may be the hardest task you'll face. Don't be put off by the next-day soreness you are likely to feel in your long-dormant muscles. The key is to begin your exercise program at a very low intensity, progress slowly . . . and stay with it! For example, if you choose an aerobic fitness program that involves jogging, you'll need several weeks of workouts combining walking and jogging before you will reach a fitness level that enables you to jog continuously for 15 to 20 minutes.

You will need to adjust the frequency, intensity, and duration of your aerobic activity program to accommodate your initial level of cardiorespiratory fitness. As you progress, add to

Cardiorespiratory fitness The ability of the heart, lungs, and blood vessels to supply oxygen to skeletal muscles during sustained physical activity.

Aerobic exercise Any type of exercise, typically performed at moderate levels of intensity for extended periods of time (typically 20 to 30 minutes or longer), that increases heart rate.

Aerobic capacity The current functional status of a person's cardiovascular system; measured as $VO_{2\,max}$.

Graded exercise test A test of aerobic capacity administered by a physician, exercise physiologist, or other trained person; two common forms are the treadmill running test and the stationary bike test.

What's New in the World of Exercise?

Although we have been exhorted to exercise for much of the twentieth century, researchers and scientists continue to examine the world of fitness and exercise to determine the true impact of too much exercise, too little exercise, and the wrong and right types of exercise. Two recent studies cast an interesting light on exercise benefits for individual health

The first, a study of 2,428 adults over a six-year period, examined the risks that those of us who are out of shape face when we suddenly decide to don exercise clothes, lace up the shoes, and hit the exercise trail. The research team studied heart-rate changes in the first minute after exercise among patients who had previous symptoms of heart disease. They found that people whose hearts took longer to slow down, or recover, after exercise were nearly four times more likely to die during the six-year study period than were participants with normal recovery times. While just 26 percent of all people in the study had abnormal recovery times, these people constituted 56 percent of all deaths during the course of the study. In addition, the study indicated that people who demonstrated good heart-rate recovery are more likely to benefit from heart surgery and other corrective

procedures in the event of cardiovascular problems.

Results of the study indicate that people who have high blood pressure, are obese, take heart medications, and are out of condition physically face significant risks of heart failure when they begin unsupervised, strenuous physical activity. For someone out of shape, getting back into shape should be viewed as a serious behavioral change. Efforts to lose weight, reduce blood pressure, and work up to high-energy expenditures should be done gradually and under a doctor's supervision. Although this has long been the recommended plan of action, this study confirmed the importance of following that plan. Most important, however, the study helped identify heart-rate recovery as a significant indicator of benefits and risks.

The second of the landmark studies was an epidemiological study of the exercise behavior patterns of over 14,000 female participants in the Nurses' Health Study. Although physical activity has long been associated with the reduced risk of coronary heart disease, little has been known about the benefits of certain types of exercise, particularly for women. Walking, in particular, has long been believed to be highly beneficial and often has been recommended as part of a rehabilitation program for people recovering from heart problems and other serious illnesses, but questions still arose about its specific benefits. Until the Nurses' Health Study, the role of walking in the battle against heart disease had not been carefully analyzed, despite being the most common form of exercise among women.

In the Nurses' Health Study, women's risk factors and exercise behaviors were

assessed every two years for a period of 14 years. Results of the study provide compelling evidence of the benefits of walking. It indicated that brisk walking may, in fact, be just as beneficial for the reduction of cardiovascular disease as vigorous exercise. Results suggested that a regimen of brisk walking for a total of three or more hours per week (an average of 30 minutes per day) could reduce the risk of coronary events by 30 percent to 40 percent. Increasing this time provided even greater benefits. This is in line with the most recent recommendations from the Centers for Disease Control and Prevention, the American College of Sports Medicine, and the Surgeon General's Report on Physical Activity and Health.

The implications are clear. What we have long suspected is true: Walking makes good sense! It is relatively available to everyone, requires no special equipment, can be done alone or in groups, and may be less damaging to joints over time than repetitive running or other strenuous activities. So put on those walking shoes, and let's get going!!

STUDENTS SPEAK UP:

What is the significance of these two studies? How are they related to each other? What can you do to apply their findings to your own personal health behavior?

Sources: M. S. Lauer, E. Blackstone, F. J. Pashkow, C. Snader, and C. Cole. "Heart-Rate Recovery Immediately after Exercise as a Predictor of Mortality," *The New England Journal of Medicine,* 341 (1999):1351–1357; J. E. Manson et al., "A Prospective Study of Walking as Compared with Vigorous Exercise in the Prevention of Coronary Heart Disease in Women," *The New England Journal of Medicine.* 341 (1999):650–659.

---

your exercise load by increasing exercise duration or intensity, but do not increase both at the same time.

▶ *Determining Exercise Frequency* If you are a newcomer to regular physical activity, the frequency of your aerobic exercise bouts should be at least three times per week. The surgeon general's recommendation is for moderate amounts of *daily*

physical activity.[34] As your fitness level improves, your goal should be to exercise 20 to 30 minutes per day, five days a week. Figure 11.2 on page 272 provides some guidelines for various activity levels.

▶ *Determining Exercise Intensity* Your aerobic exercise program should employ activities of moderate intensity that use

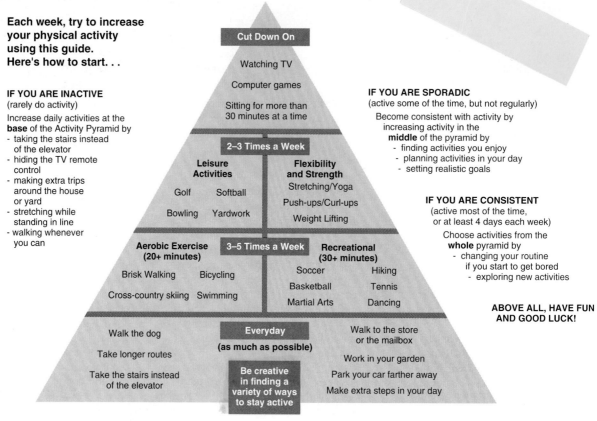

Each week, try to increase your physical activity using this guide. Here's how to start...

IF YOU ARE INACTIVE
(rarely do activity)
Increase daily activities at the **base** of the Activity Pyramid by
- taking the stairs instead of the elevator
- hiding the TV remote control
- making extra trips around the house or yard
- stretching while standing in line
- walking whenever you can

IF YOU ARE SPORADIC
(active some of the time, but not regularly)
Become consistent with activity by increasing activity in the **middle** of the pyramid by
- finding activities you enjoy
- planning activities in your day
- setting realistic goals

IF YOU ARE CONSISTENT
(active most of the time, or at least 4 days each week)
Choose activities from the **whole** pyramid by
- changing your routine if you start to get bored
- exploring new activities

ABOVE ALL, HAVE FUN AND GOOD LUCK!

Cut Down On
Watching TV
Computer games
Sitting for more than 30 minutes at a time

2–3 Times a Week

Leisure Activities
Golf   Softball
Bowling   Yardwork

Flexibility and Strength
Stretching/Yoga
Push-ups/Curl-ups
Weight Lifting

Aerobic Exercise (20+ minutes)
Brisk Walking   Bicycling
Cross-country skiing   Swimming

3–5 Times a Week

Recreational (30+ minutes)
Soccer   Hiking
Basketball   Tennis
Martial Arts   Dancing

Everyday (as much as possible)
Walk the dog
Take longer routes
Take the stairs instead of the elevator
Be creative in finding a variety of ways to stay active
Walk to the store or the mailbox
Work in your garden
Park your car farther away
Make extra steps in your day

Figure 11.2
Guidelines for Various Activity Levels
Source: Copyright © 1996. Institute for Research and Education, HealthSystem Minnesota.

---

large muscle groups and can be maintained for prolonged periods of time. The measure of such a workout is your **target heart rate,** which is a percentage of your maximum heart rate. To calculate target heart rate, subtract your age from 220 for females or from 226 for males. The result is your maximum heart rate. You determine your target heart rate by calculating a desired percentage of maximum heart rate, often 60 percent. If you are a 20-year-old woman, your maximum heart rate is 200 (220 – 20). Your 60-percent target heart rate would be 120 (200 × .60). People in poor physical condition should set a target heart rate between 40 and 50 percent of maximum. As your condition improves, you can gradually increase your target heart rate. Increases should be made in small increments: Increase from 40 to 45 percent; then from 45 to 50 percent. Because of the potential risks and adherence-to-exercise problems associated with high-intensity activity (> 80% of maximum heart rate), moderate-intensity activity of longer duration is suggested for adults who are not training for competitive athletics.[35]

Once you know your target heart rate, you can determine how close you are to this value during your workout. You'll need to stop exercising briefly in order to measure your heart rate. To take your pulse, lightly place your index and middle fingers (don't use your thumb) over one of the carotid arteries in your neck (along either side of your Adam's apple), or over one of the radial arteries (thumb side) of your wrist.

Be sure to start counting your pulse immediately after you stop exercising, as your heart rate will decrease quickly. Using a watch or clock, take your pulse for six seconds and multiply this number by 10 (just add a zero to your count) to get the number of beats per minute (bpm). Your pulse should be within a range of about 5 bpm above or below your target heart rate. If necessary, increase or decrease the pace or intensity of your workout to achieve your target heart rate.

A target heart rate of 70 percent of maximum is sometimes called the "conversational level of exercise" because you are able to talk with a partner while exercising.[36] If you are a novice and you are breathing so hard that talking is difficult, your intensity of exercise is too high. If you can sustain a conversational level of aerobic exercise for 20 to 30 minutes, you will improve your cardiorespiratory fitness.

▶ *Determining Exercise Duration*   Duration refers to the number of minutes of activity performed during any one session. The Centers for Disease Control and Prevention (CDC) and the American College of Sports Medicine (ACSM) suggest that every adult engage in 20 to 60 minutes of continuous or intermittent (if intermittent, bouts of at least 10-minute duration) moderate-intensity physical activity over the course of most days of the week.[37] One way to meet the CDC/ACSM daily activity recommendation is to walk 2 miles briskly.

The lower the intensity of the activity, the longer the duration you'll need to get the same caloric expenditure. For example, a 180-pound man will expend 288 calories per hour of playing golf if he carries his clubs, but will burn 805 calories per hour if he is cross-country skiing.[38] Your goal should be to expend 300 to 500 calories per exercise session, with an eventual weekly goal of 1,500 to 2,000 calories.

Since many of the health benefits associated with cardiorespiratory fitness activities take about one year of regular exercise to achieve, you shouldn't expect an immediate reduction in your risk of cardiovascular disease when you start an exercise program.[39] However, any low-to-moderate-intensity physical activity, even if it does not meet all the cardiorespiratory exercise characteristics mentioned in this chapter, will benefit your overall health almost from the start.

ACCESSING YOUR HEALTH ON THE INTERNET

Check out the following Internet sites related to fitness.

1. *FitnessZone.* Up-to-date information on health and fitness. Includes a personal fitness profiler and a nationwide gym and health club locator.

   http://www.fitnesszone.com

2. *ACSM Online.* A link with the American College of Sports Medicine and all their resources.

   http://www.acsm.org/

3. *NetSweat.com.* An all-encompassing site with links to numerous fitness-related sites.

   http://www.netsweat.com

········· **WHAT DO YOU THINK?**

Calculate your maximum heart rate. Pick an intensity of exercise that suits your fitness level, for example, 60 percent, 70 percent, or 80 percent of your maximum heart rate. Using a familiar physical activity and monitoring your pulse, experiment by exercising at three different intensities. Do you notice any difference in the way you felt while exercising? Afterward?

IMPROVING YOUR FLEXIBILITY

Flexibility is a measure of the range of motion, or the amount of movement possible, at a particular joint. Improving your range of motion through stretching exercises will enhance your efficiency of movement and your posture. In addition, flexibility exercises have been shown to be effective in reducing the incidence and severity of musculo-tendinous injuries.[40] A regular program of stretching exercises can enhance psychological as well as physical well-being.

Types of Stretching Exercises

Flexibility is enhanced by the controlled stretching of muscles that act on a particular joint. The primary strategy is to decrease the resistance to stretch (tension) within a tight muscle that you have targeted for increased range of motion. To do this, you repeatedly stretch the muscle and its two tendons of attachment to elongate them.

The three major types of stretching techniques are static, proprioceptive neuromuscular facilitation (PNF), and ballistic. **Static stretching** techniques involve the slow, gradual stretching of a muscle and its tendons, holding the muscle or muscle group at a point of mild discomfort (a burning sensation is felt within the muscle), followed by the slow return to the starting position. When static stretching is done properly, it stimulates the tension receptors to allow the muscle being stretched to relax and permit the muscle to be stretched to greater length.[41] **Proprioceptive neuromuscular facilitation (PNF)** techniques have been shown to be superior to other stretching techniques for improving flexibility; unfortunately, PNF techniques in their original form are quite complex and a certified athletic trainer or physical therapist may be required to help you perform them correctly. Several PNF techniques (e.g., hold/relax, contract/relax) have been modified and simplified to the point that they can be performed with an exercise partner or even alone. With PNF techniques, a 6-second contraction of the muscle to be stretched is followed by an

Target heart rate Calculated as a percentage of maximum heart rate (220 minus age); heart rate (pulse) is taken during aerobic exercise to check if exercise intensity is at the desired level (e.g., 70 percent of maximum heart rate).

Flexibility The measure of the range of motion, or the amount of movement possible, at a particular joint.

Static stretching Techniques that gradually lengthen a muscle to an elongated position (to the point of discomfort) and hold that position for 10 to 30 seconds.

Proprioceptive neuromuscular facilitation (PNF) stretching Techniques that involve the skillful use of alternating muscle contractions and static stretching in the same muscle.

assisted stretch of 10 to 30 seconds' duration.[42] **Ballistic stretching** involves repeated bouncing motions, during which the muscle and tendon are rapidly stretched and returned to resting length. This process can be likened to taking a rubber band between two fingers, rapidly pulling it apart, and then releasing the tension, again and again. And just as a rubber band can snap in your fingers, if you apply too much tension, the muscle fibers being stretched in this way can be torn during these rapid movements. The risk of injury with ballistic stretching is so high that this type of stretching is no longer recommended for improving flexibility.

Of the three types of flexibility exercises, static stretches are probably the most commonly used. A major goal of static stretching is to cause permanent elongation of the targeted muscle or muscle group, thus permitting greater range of motion at a given joint. With static stretching, the end position is held for 10 to 30 seconds, and each of the major muscle groups should be stretched at least four times in close succession for optimal improvement. To achieve this goal, a comprehensive stretching program must be performed a minimum of two to three days a week.[43]

> ········· **WHAT DO YOU THINK?**
>
> Why is it so important to have good flexibility throughout life? What are some situations in which improved flexibility would help you perform daily activities with less effort? What specific actions will you take to improve your flexibility?

IMPROVING MUSCULAR STRENGTH AND ENDURANCE

Muscular strength refers to the amount of force a muscle is capable of exerting. The most common way to assess strength in a resistance exercise program is to measure the maximum amount of weight you can lift one time. This value is known as the **one repetition maximum,** and is written as **1RM. Muscular endurance** is defined as a muscle's ability to exert force repeatedly without fatiguing. The more repetitions of a certain resistance exercise you can perform successfully (e.g., a bench press of one-half your body weight), the greater your muscular endurance.

Principles of Strength Development

There are three key principles to understand if you intend to maximize muscular strength and endurance benefits from your **resistance exercise program.**[44] Unless you follow these principles, you are likely to be disappointed in the results of your program.

▶ *The Tension Principle*   The key to developing strength is to create tension within a muscle. The more tension you can create in a muscle, the greater your strength gain will be. The most common recreational way to create tension in a muscle is by lifting weights. While weight lifting is one method of producing tension in a muscle, any activity that creates muscle tension—for example, riding a bike up a hill—will result in greater strength.

▶ *The Overload Principle*   The overload principle is the most important of the three key principles for improving muscular strength. Everyone begins a resistance training program with an initial level of strength. To increase that level of strength, you must regularly create a degree of tension in your muscles that is greater than they are accustomed to. This overloading of your muscles will cause your muscles to adapt to the new level of overload. As your muscles respond to a regular program of overloading by getting larger (**hypertrophy**), they become capable of generating more tension. Figure 11.3 illustrates how a continual process of overload and adaptation to the overload improves strength.

Some women avoid resistance exercise because they fear that they'll develop large "bulky" muscles, while others are frustrated because their weight-lifting efforts in the gym don't produce the same results as in their male friends. The main reason for this difference is the hormone *testosterone*. Before puberty, testosterone levels in blood are similar for both boys and girls. During adolescence, testosterone in men increases about tenfold to its adult level; testosterone in women remains at prepubertal levels throughout adulthood. Women's muscles will hypertrophy from regular exercise but typically not to the same degree as in adult males. The difference in

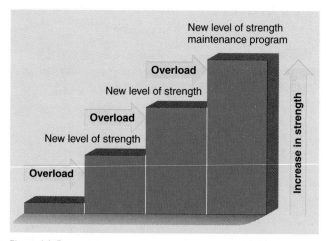

Figure 11.3

The overload principle contributes to an increase in strength. Notice that once the muscle has adapted to the original overload, a new overload must be placed on the muscle for subsequent gains in strength to occur.

Source: From Philip A. Sienna, *One Rep Max: A Guide to Beginning Weight Training,* Fig. 2.1, 8. Copyright © 1989. Wm. C. Brown Communications, Inc., Dubuque, Iowa. Reprinted by permission of Times Mirror Higher Education Group, Inc., Dubuque, Iowa. All rights reserved.

maximum attainable hypertrophy between men and women is not currently known.[45]

▶ *The Specificity of Training Principle*   This principle refers to the manner in which a specific body system responds to the physiological demands placed upon it. According to the specificity principle, the effects of resistance exercise training are specific to the area of the body being exercised. If the overload you impose is designed to improve strength in the muscles of your chest and back, the response to that demand (overload) will be improved strength in those muscles only.

Methods of Providing Resistance

There are four commonly used methods of applying resistance to develop strength and endurance.

▶ *Body Weight Resistance*   Many different techniques can be used to develop skeletal muscle fitness without relying on resistance equipment. Most of these methods use part or all of your body weight to offer the resistance during exercise. These types of resistance activities are convenient—no special equipment is needed—and are generally sufficient to improve muscle tone and maintain the level of muscular strength created by this type of overload. But they do not help you to make significant strength gains.   *chin ups pull ups*

▶ *Fixed Resistance*   Fixed resistance exercises provide a constant amount of resistance throughout the full range of movement. Barbells and dumbbells provide fixed resistance because their weight (amount of resistance) does not change as you exercise. The advantages of fixed resistance exercise include the portability and low cost of barbells and dumbbells, the common availability of fixed resistance exercise machines at university recreation/fitness facilities and health clubs, and

Most college campuses now have some type of recreation facility available to students and staff interested in getting or staying fit.

the existence of numerous exercises designed to strengthen all the major muscle groups in the body.

▶ *Variable Resistance*   Variable resistance equipment alters the resistance encountered by a muscle at various joint angles so that the effort by the muscle is more consistent throughout the full range of motion. Variable resistance machines are typically single-station devices (e.g., Nautilus, Hammer Strength), but some have multiple stations at which muscles of the upper and lower extremities can be exercised (e.g., Soloflex). While some of these machines are expensive and permanently placed, there are also inexpensive, portable forms sold for home use.   *range of motion = flexibility → machines*

▶ *Accommodating Resistance*   With accommodating resistance devices, the resistance changes according to the amount of force generated by the individual. There is no external weight to move or overcome. Resistance is provided by having the exerciser perform at maximal level of effort, while the exercise machine controls the speed of the exercise and does not allow any faster motion. The body segment being exercised must move at a rate faster than or equal to the set speed to encounter resistance.[46]

Getting Started

When beginning a resistance exercise program, remember to consider your age, fitness level, and the personal goals you would like to achieve. Strength training exercises are done in a *set*, or a single series of multiple repetitions using

Ballistic stretching   Techniques that employ the repetitive, rapid stretching of muscles with no holding of the stretch at a terminal position; not recommended because of the risk of injury to muscle and/or tendon.

Muscular strength   The amount of force that a muscle is capable of exerting.

One repetition maximum (1RM)   The amount of weight/resistance that can be lifted/moved one time, but not twice; a common measure of strength.

Muscular endurance   A muscle's ability to exert force repeatedly without fatiguing.

Resistance exercise program   A regular program of exercises designed to improve muscular strength and endurance in the major muscle groups.

Hypertrophy   Increased size (girth) of a muscle.

the same resistance. Current research tells us that for healthy people of all ages (and for many individuals with chronic illnesses), single set resistance programs of up to 15 repetitions per exercise, performed a minimum of two days per week, are recommended. Each of your workout sessions should include 8 to 10 different resistance exercises that involve the major muscle groups of the upper and lower extremities and the trunk. Somewhat surprisingly, single-set resistance programs have been recently recommended by the American College of Sports Medicine[47] for the majority of the United States population because they produce most of the health and fitness benefits associated with much more time consuming, traditional multiple-set programs (e.g., 3 sets of 10 repetitions of each exercise three days per week). Table 11.2 contains the essential information required to begin your program to build muscular strength and muscular endurance.

Remember that resistance training exercises cause microscopic damage (tears) to muscle fibers, and the rebuilding process that increases the size and capacity of the muscle takes about 24 to 48 hours. Thus resistance training exercise programs should include at least one day of rest and recovery between workouts before overloading the same muscles again. *muscular strength gain → 60-70% of your 1RM*

sets - 3 reps. 5-8

TABLE 11.2
Resistance Training Program Guidelines

- Resistance training should be an integral part of an adult fitness program and of sufficient intensity to enhance strength, muscular endurance, and maintain fat-free mass (FFM).

- Resistance training should be progressive in nature, individualized, and provide a stimulus (overload) to all major muscle groups in the body.

- One set of 8 to 10 different resistance exercises that condition the major muscle groups 2 to 3 days per week is recommended.

- Most healthy individuals should complete one set of 8 to 12 repetitions for each selected exercise; for older (50 to 60 years of age and above) and more frail persons, one set of 10 to 15 repetitions may be more appropriate.

- The goal of this type of resistance training program is to develop and maintain a significant amount of muscle mass, endurance, and strength to contribute to overall fitness and health throughout the life span.

- If sufficient time is available, multiple-set resistance exercise regimens using heavier weights and fewer repetitions will result in greater strength gains and fitness benefits.

Source: American College of Sports Medicine, "ACSM Position Stand on the Recommended Quantity and Quality of Exercise for Developing and Maintaining Cardiorespiratory and Muscular Fitness and Flexibility in Adults," Medicine and Science in Sports and Exercise 30 (1998): 975–991.

What types of resistance equipment can you currently access? Based on what you've read, what specific actions can you take to increase your muscular strength? Muscular endurance? How would you measure your improvement?

BODY COMPOSITION

Body composition is a fifth and final component of a comprehensive fitness program. Body composition parameters that can be influenced by regular physical activity include total body mass, fat mass, fat-free mass, and regional fat distribution.[48] Body composition is significantly different between women and men; women have a higher percentage of fat mass than do men, and significantly lower percentages of fat-free mass (muscle and bone are of primary interest) and bone mineral density.[49]

The context for inclusion of body composition in the discussion of physical fitness relates to weight control. The most successful weight-loss programs are those that combine diet and exercise. If your main reason for participating in a regular exercise program is to lose weight, then you'll need to combine diet with at least three workouts per week that expend 250 to 300 kcal per session (at least 30 to 45 minutes of continuous low-to-moderate intensity activity, depending on your body weight) in order to see reductions in your total body mass and fat mass.[50]

FITNESS INJURIES

Overtraining is the most frequent cause of injuries associated with fitness activities. Enthusiastic but out-of-shape beginners often injure themselves by doing too much activity too soon. One strategy to prevent overuse injury to a particular muscle group or body part is to vary your fitness activities throughout the week to give muscles and joints a rest. Establishing realistic but challenging fitness goals can help you maintain a high level of motivation while ensuring that you do not overdo it.

Causes of Fitness-Related Injuries

There are two basic types of injuries stemming from participation in fitness-related activities: overuse and traumatic. **Overuse injuries** occur because of cumulative, day-after-day stresses placed on tendons, bones, and ligaments during exercise. The forces that occur normally during physical activity are not enough to cause a ligament sprain or muscle strain, but when these forces are applied on a daily basis for weeks

rest

Shopping for a Personal Trainer

Personal trainers were once considered a luxury that only the wealthy could afford. That's no longer true. Many people today find personal trainers to be a valuable source of education and inspiration that helps them maintain their fitness regimen safely and consistently. The role of a personal trainer is to help you design a safe and effective fitness program that will fit your lifestyle. Your fitness program includes your exercise routine, and your nutritional program, and, if you are looking to lose weight, he or she can help you work toward that goal as well.

But how do you find the right personal trainer for you? One that will fit your budget and your lifestyle? One that is qualified and knowledgeable? Find answers to the following questions:

- What is the trainer's overall philosophy? Does it correspond to your personal beliefs?
- Is the trainer certified and/or registered as a personal trainer?
- How many years has the trainer been in practice?
- Does the trainer have a background in exercise physiology, anatomy, and injury prevention?
- Can the trainer provide a list of references?
- Is the trainer affiliated with a fitness center?
- Is the equipment at the training facility well maintained?
- Does the trainer know CPR?
- Does the trainer require permission from your doctor before designing your program?
- Does the trainer keep a written record of your routine and progress?
- Does the trainer vary your routine and keep up with the latest advances in fitness?
- Can the trainer help you establish short- and long-terms goals?
- Does the trainer have liability insurance?
- Does the trainer listen to your needs and show flexibility to accommodate them?
- Is the trainer located somewhere that is easily accessible?
- Are the trainer's rates affordable?

If you are able to answer these questions to your satisfaction, then, chances are, you have found a trainer who will help you make a difference in your life.

Sources: Intelihealth: Home to Johns Hopkins Health Information, "Hiring a Personal Trainer," http://www.intelihealth.com; TotalFitness Guide.com, "Tips to Finding the Personal Trainer or Massage Therapist That's Right for You," http://www.totalfitnessguide.com/fitnesstips3.htm

---

or months they can result in an injury. Common sites of overuse injuries are the leg, knee, shoulder, and elbow joints.

Traumatic injuries, which occur suddenly and violently, typically by accident, are the second major type of fitness-related injuries. Typical traumatic injuries are broken bones, torn ligaments and muscles, contusions, and lacerations. If your traumatic injury causes a noticeable loss of function and immediate pain or pain that does not go away after 30 minutes, you should have a physician examine it. Many people today are turning to personal trainers to help them avoid injuries or work around injuries they have developed from past exercise routines. (See the Consumer Health box.)

Overuse injuries   Injuries that result from the cumulative effects of day-after-day stresses placed on tendons, muscles, and joints.

Traumatic injuries   Injuries that are accidental in nature; they occur suddenly and violently (e.g., fractured bones, ruptured tendons, and sprained ligaments).

Prevention

For personal fitness activities, the function of your exercise clothing is far more important than the fashion statement it makes. For some types of physical activity, you will need clothing that allows maximal body heat dissipation—for example, light-colored nylon shorts and mesh tank top while running in hot weather. For other types, you will need clothing that permits significant heat retention without getting you sweat-soaked—for example, layers of polypropylene and/or wool clothing while cross-country skiing.

▶ *Appropriate Footwear*   When you are purchasing running shoes, look for several key components. Biomechanics research has revealed that running is a "collision" sport—that is, the runner's foot collides with the ground with a force three to five times the runner's body weight with each stride.[51] The force not absorbed by the running shoe is transmitted upward into the foot, leg, thigh, and back. Our bodies are able to absorb forces such as these, but may be injured by the cumulative effects of repetitive impacts (e.g., running 40 miles per week). Therefore, the ability of running shoes to absorb shock is a critical factor to consider when you are sampling shoes at the store.

Women Athletes and Knee Injuries

Since the passing of Title IX in 1972, opportunities for female athletes have consistently grown. In the past decade, however, that growth has been nothing short of remarkable. Women's college basketball now rivals its male counterpart in many parts of the country; professional women's basketball leagues have been greeted with success; and who can ignore the fervor that was created by the U.S. Women's Soccer Team in the summer of 1999 as they played before sellout crowds in some of the largest athletic venues in the United States, on their way to winning the Women's World Cup Soccer title.

As women continue to raise the bar in the world of sports, we learn more and more about their potential. At the same time, however, we also learn more about their tendencies toward injury. As athletic achievement for women has grown, an unsettling injury pattern also has arisen. Although medical experts are unsure of the reasons, female athletes appear to be more susceptible to knee injuries, particularly injuries to their anterior cruciate ligaments (ACLs). Recent studies indicate that women are anywhere from five to eight times more likely than men to suffer painful, disabling ACL injuries at some point in their lives.

The ACL is a strand of soft tissue that, along with other ligaments, muscles, and tendons, helps stabilize the knee joint. It's role in pivoting, jumping, and sudden changes of direction is critical. Once it is damaged, mobility is often reduced. This ligament is most severely compromised when women partake in contact sports, such as soccer, basketball, and volleyball, although injuries have occurred in noncontact activities as well.

Once injured, the ACL must be repaired surgically and requires months of painful rehabilitation for any chance of a return to normal athletic levels. Even with therapy, ACL injuries can predispose people to later bouts of immobility, injuries due to lingering instability, and various forms of arthritis.

Why are we seeing this trend? Does the explanation lie in the fact that female participation itself has increased, or are female athletes truly more susceptible to these injuries? A number of hypotheses, ranging from physiological and anatomical differences to hormonal variances, have been suggested and are being explored further.

Many researchers in sports medicine suspect that musculoskeletal differences serve as the basic reason for the greater risk of ACL injury. According to the American Academy of Orthopedic Surgeons, the answers lie in physiological differences between males and females. Female athletes are thought to be at a disadvantage because of an imbalance in strength between the hamstring muscles, behind the thigh, and the quadriceps muscles in front of the thigh. When these two muscle groups work together, they act antagonistically to protect each other and supporting ligature, including that around the knee, from damage. Some researchers suggest that women tend to have underdeveloped or weak hamstrings, which results in increased stress placed on the ACL, particularly during unusual movements. In addition, during actions such as jumping and landing, it is felt that women tend to land more straight-legged and more flat-footed, a tendency related to weaker thigh muscles. In contrast, men often have much-stronger quadriceps and hamstrings and tend to bend the knees and cushion the shock when jumping, thereby causing less stress on supporting structures. Thus, in women who are underexercised or have a severe imbalance between their quadriceps and hamstrings, the risk of ACL injury increases. In addition to lower muscle strength, sports medicine officials speculate that structural characteristics, such as wider hips, put greater pressure on the inside of the knee and less on the leg muscle.

Another hypothesis is that women are more prone to ACL injuries during ovulation, when increased estrogen works to reduce the production of collagen, the body's connective tissue. Orthopedic surgeon Dr. Edward M. Wojtys put this theory to the test by evaluating the injuries of 40 young women with acute ACL injuries. He discovered that a majority of these women did in fact sustain their injuries during ovulation, encouraging the need for further investigation.

So, what can women do to protect themselves from ACL injuries? At this point, Dr. Wojtys says that there is no evidence that hormone supplements will protect women against ACL injuries. For the time being, however, doctors advise women to get involved in sports at an early age and partake in weight training and other types of conditioning that will build the hamstring muscles. When knee injuries do occur, they must be taken seriously and treated with rest, ice, compression, and elevation (RICE). If pain doesn't subside, a visit to an orthopedic surgeon may be necessary.

Sources: Johns Hopkins Health website, Health News Zone, http://www.intelihealth.com, "Keeping in the Game: Young Women and Their Knees"; *The Doctor's Guide to Medical and Other News,* "Link Found Between Menstrual Cycle and Knee Injuries," June 25, 1997.

The midsole of a running shoe must absorb impact forces, but must also be flexible. One method used to evaluate the flexibility of the midsole is to hold the shoe between the index fingers of your right and left hand. When you push on both ends of the shoe with your fingers, the shoe should bend easily at the midsole. If the force exerted by your index fingers cannot bend the shoe, its midsole is probably too rigid and may cause irritation of your Achilles tendon, among other problems.[52] Other basic characteristics of running shoes include: a rigid plastic insert within the heel of the shoe (known as a heel counter) to control the movement of your heel; a cushioned foam pad surrounding the heel of the shoe to prevent Achilles tendon irritation; and a removable thermoplastic innersole that customizes the fit of the shoe by using your body heat to mold it to the shape of your foot. Shoes are the runner's most essential piece of equipment, so carefully select appropriate footwear before you start a running program.

Shoe companies also sell cross-training shoes to help combat the high cost of having to buy separate pairs of running shoes, tennis shoes, weight-training shoes, and so on. Although the cross-training shoe can be used for participation in several different fitness activities by the novice or recreational athlete, a distance runner who runs 25 or more miles per week needs a pair of specialty running shoes in order to prevent injury.

▶ **Appropriate Exercise Equipment** For some activities, there is specialized protective equipment that will reduce your chances of injury. In tennis, for example, the use of proper equipment helps prevent the general inflammatory condition known as tennis elbow. Excessive racquet string tension, repetitive use of the forearm muscles during hours of daily practice, and poor flexibility cause this problem in experienced tennis players.

Eye injuries can occur in virtually all fitness-related activities, though the risk of injury is much greater in some activities than in others. As many as 90 percent of the eye injuries resulting from racquetball and squash are preventable with the use of appropriate eye protection—for example, goggles with polycarbonate lenses.[53] One-eyed participants should wear polycarbonate prescription or nonprescription eyeglasses for all recreational activities.[54]

Nearly 100 million people in the United States ride bikes for pleasure, fitness, or competition. Head injuries used to account for 85 percent of all deaths attributable to bicycle accidents; however, the wearing of bike helmets has significantly reduced the number of skull fractures and facial injuries among recreational cyclists.[55] Bicycle helmets that meet the standards established by the American National Standards Institute (ANSI) and the Snell Memorial Foundation (SNELL) should be worn by all cyclists.

········· **WHAT DO YOU THINK?**

Given your activity level, what are some injury risks that you are exposed to on a regular basis? What changes can you make in your equipment or clothing to reduce these risks?

Common Overuse Injuries

Body movements in physical activities such as running, swimming, and bicycling are highly repetitive, so participants are susceptible to overuse injuries. In fitness activities, the joints of the lower extremities (foot, ankle, knee, and hip) tend to be injured more frequently than the upper-extremity joints (shoulder, elbow, wrist, and hand). Three of the most

common injuries from repetitive overuse during exercise are plantar fasciitis, "shin splints," and "runner's knee."

▶ **Plantar Fasciitis** Plantar fasciitis is an inflammation of the plantar fascia, a broad band of dense, inelastic tissue (fascia) that runs from the heel to the toe on the bottom of your foot. The main function of the plantar fascia is to protect the nerves, blood vessels, and muscles of the foot from injury. In repetitive, weight-bearing fitness activities such as walking and running, the plantar fascia may become inflamed. Common symptoms of this condition are pain and tenderness under the ball of the foot, at the heel, or at both locations.[56] The pain of plantar fasciitis is particularly noticeable during your first steps out of bed in the morning. If not treated properly, this injury may progress in severity to the point that weight-bearing exercise is too painful to endure. Uphill running is not advised for anyone suffering from this condition, since each uphill stride severely stretches (and thus irritates) the already inflamed plantar fascia. This injury can often be prevented by regularly stretching the plantar fascia prior to exercise and by wearing athletic shoes with good arch support and shock absorbency.

▶ **Shin Splints** A general term for any pain that occurs below the knee and above the ankle is shin splints. More than 20 different medical conditions have been identified within the broad description of shin splints. Problems range from stress fractures of the tibia (shinbone) to severe inflammation in the muscular compartments of the lower leg, which can interrupt the flow of blood and nerve supply to the foot. The most common type of shin splints occurs along the inner side of the tibia and is usually a combination of a muscle irritation and irritation of the tissues that attach the muscles to the bone in this region. Typically, there is pain and swelling along the middle one-third of the posteromedial tibia in the soft tissues, not the bone.

Sedentary people who start a new weight-bearing exercise program are at the greatest risk for shin splints, though well-conditioned aerobic exercisers who rapidly increase their distance or pace may also develop shin splints.[57] Running is the most frequent cause of shin splints, but those who do a great deal of walking (e.g., mail carriers, waitresses) may also develop this injury.

To help prevent shin splints, wear athletic shoes that have good arch support and shock absorbency. If the severity of this lower-leg condition increases to the point that you cannot comfortably complete your desired fitness activity, see your physician.

▶ **Runner's Knee** An overuse condition known as runner's knee describes a series of problems involving the muscles, tendons, and ligaments about the knee. The most common problem identified as runner's knee is abnormal movement of the patella (kneecap).[58] Women are more commonly affected by this condition than are men because their wider pelvis makes abnormal lateral pull on the patella by the muscles that act at the knee more likely. In women (and some men), this causes irritation to the cartilage on the back side of the patella as well as to the nearby tendons and ligaments.

The main symptom of this kind of runner's knee is the pain experienced when downward pressure is applied to the patella after the knee is straightened fully. Additional symptoms may include swelling, redness, and tenderness around the patella, and a dull, aching pain felt in the center of the knee.[59] If you have these symptoms in your knee, your physician will probably recommend that you stop running for a few weeks and reduce daily activities that put compressive forces on the patella until you no longer have any pain around your kneecap.

Treatment

First-aid treatment for virtually all personal fitness injuries involves **RICE: r**est, **i**ce, **c**ompression, and **e**levation. *Rest,* the first component of this treatment, is required to eliminate the risk of further irritation of the injured body part. *Ice* is applied to relieve the pain of the injury and to constrict the blood vessels in order to slow and stop any internal or external bleeding associated with the injury. Never apply ice cubes, reusable gel ice packs, chemical cold packs, or other forms of cold directly to your skin. Instead, place a layer of wet toweling or elastic bandage between the ice and your skin. Ice should be applied to a new injury for approximately 20 minutes every hour for the first 24 to 72 hours. *Compression* of the injured body part can be accomplished with a 4- or 6-inch-wide elastic bandage; this applies indirect pressure to damaged blood vessels to help stop bleeding. Be careful, though, that the compression wrap does not interfere with normal blood flow. A throbbing, painful hand or foot is an indication that the compression wrap was applied too tightly and should be loosened. *Elevation* of the injured extremity above the level of your heart also helps to control internal or external bleeding by making the blood flow uphill to reach the injured area.

Exercising in the Heat

Exercising in warm temperatures may increase your risk for a heat-related injury. If you are in good physical condition and wear appropriate clothing for outdoor physical activities, you can safely withstand a wide range of temperatures and humidity levels. Heat stress, which includes several potentially fatal illnesses resulting from excessive core body temperatures, should be a concern when you are exercising in warm, humid weather. In these conditions, your body's rate of heat production often exceeds its ability to cool itself.

You can help prevent heat stress by following certain precautions. First, proper acclimatization to hot and/or humid climates is essential. The process of heat acclimatization, which increases your body's cooling efficiency, requires about 10 to 14 days of gradually increased activity in the hot environment. Second, heat stress can be prevented by avoiding dehydration, accomplished through proper fluid replacement during and following exercise. Third, wear clothing appropriate for the fitness activity and the environment. Finally, use common sense when exercising in hot and humid conditions.

Regardless of your form of exercise, any physical exertion in the heat carries with it the risk of heat exhaustion or heat stroke.

The three different heat stress illnesses are progressive in their level of severity: heat cramps, heat exhaustion, and heat stroke. The least serious problem, heat-related muscle cramps (**heat cramps**), is easily prevented by adequate fluid replacement and a diet that includes the electrolytes lost during sweating (sodium and potassium). **Heat exhaustion** is caused by excessive water loss resulting from intense or prolonged exercise or work in a warm and/or humid environment. Symptoms of heat exhaustion include nausea, headache, fatigue, dizziness and faintness, and, paradoxically, "goosebumps" and chills. If you are suffering from heat exhaustion, your skin will be cool and moist. Heat exhaustion is actually a mild form of shock, in which the blood pools in the arms and legs away from the brain and major organs of the body, causing nausea and fainting. **Heat stroke,** often called sunstroke, is a life-threatening emergency condition having a 20 to 70 percent death rate.[60] Heat stroke occurs during vigorous exercise when the body's heat production significantly exceeds your body's cooling capacities. Body core temperature can rise from normal (99.6°F) to 105°F to 110°F within minutes after the body's cooling mechanism shuts down. With no cooling taking place, rapidly increasing core temperatures can cause brain damage, permanent disability, and death. Common signs of heat stroke are dry, hot, and usually red skin; very high body temperature; and a very rapid heart rate.

Heat stress illnesses may occur in situations in which the danger is not obvious. Serious or fatal heat strokes may result from prolonged sauna or steam baths, prolonged total immersion in a hot tub or spa, or by exercising in a plastic or rubber head-to-toe "sauna suit." If, while exercising, you experience any of the symptoms mentioned here, you should stop exercising immediately, move to the shade or a cool spot to rest, and drink large amounts of cool fluids.[61]

Regarding the best type of cool fluids to drink, the American College of Sports Medicine (ACSM) found little evidence of differences in human performance during exercise sessions lasting less than one hour when drinking plain water or "sports drinks" (carbohydrate-electrolyte drinks).[62] However, a recent study comparing the benefits of ingesting water or a sports drink suggests otherwise. In a laboratory study requiring intense stationary bicycling (50 minutes of high-level activity followed by a 9- to 12-minute long "sprint to the finish"), subjects' cycling performance improved by 6 percent when they drank enough water to replace about 80 percent of the fluid they lost as sweat. Better yet, their performances improved by 12 percent when they consumed a similar amount of a sports drink.[63] During intense exercise lasting longer than one hour, ACSM recommends drinking fluids that contain 4 percent to 8 percent carbohydrates (to delay muscular fatigue) and a small amount of sodium (to improve taste and promote fluid retention). Fluid intake *following* physical activity is also very important to prevent dehydration— be sure to drink at least a pint of fluid (your choice!) for every pound of body weight lost during your exercise session.

Exercising in the Cold

When you exercise in cool to cold weather, especially in windy conditions, your body's rate of heat loss is frequently greater than its rate of heat production. Under these conditions, **hypothermia**—a potentially fatal condition resulting from abnormally low body core temperature, which occurs when body heat is lost faster than it is produced—may result. Hypothermia can occur as a result of prolonged, vigorous exercise (e.g., snowboarding or rugby) in 40°F to 50°F temperatures, particularly if there is rain, snow, or a strong wind.

RICE Acronym for the standard first-aid treatment for virtually all traumatic and overuse injuries: rest, ice, compression, and elevation.

Heat cramps Muscle cramps that occur during or following exercise in warm/hot weather.

Heat exhaustion A heat stress illness caused by significant dehydration resulting from exercise in warm/hot conditions; frequent precursor to heat stroke.

Heat stroke A deadly heat stress illness resulting from dehydration and overexertion in warm/hot conditions; can cause body core temperature to rise from normal to 105°F to 110°F in just a few minutes.

Hypothermia Potentially fatal condition caused by abnormally low body core temperature.

In mild cases of hypothermia, as your body core temperature drops from the normal 99.6°F to 93.2°F, you will begin to shiver. Shivering—the involuntary contraction of nearly every muscle in your body—is designed to increase your body temperature by using the heat given off by muscle activity. During this first stage of hypothermia, you may also experience cold hands and feet, poor judgment, apathy, and amnesia.[64] Shivering ceases in most hypothermia victims as their body core temperatures drop to between 87°F and 90°F, a sign that the body has lost its ability to generate heat. Death from hypothermia usually occurs at body core temperatures between 75°F and 80°F.

To prevent hypothermia, follow these commonsense guidelines: analyze weather conditions and your risk of hypothermia before you undertake your planned outdoor physical activity, remembering that wind and humidity are as significant as temperature; use the "buddy system"—that is, have a friend join you for your cold-weather outdoor activities; wear layers of appropriate clothing to prevent excessive heat loss (e.g., polypropylene or woolen undergarments, a windproof outer garment, and wool hat and gloves); and finally, don't allow yourself to become dehydrated.[65]

> **········ WHAT DO YOU THINK?**
>
> Given what you've read about the symptoms of common fitness injuries, are you currently developing any overuse injuries? If so, what specific actions can you take to prevent these problems from getting more serious?

PLANNING YOUR FITNESS PROGRAM

You now know that regular physical activity and exercise can help you avoid preventable diseases and add to both the quality and length of your life. If you are currently active, you are more aware of the benefits of regular physical activity and should be motivated to continue your efforts. If you are sedentary or sporadically active, you realize that you should not delay one day longer in making the behavioral changes necessary to improve your fitness level. (See the Skills for Behavior Change box on page 282.)

Identifying Your Fitness Goals

Before you initiate a fitness program, analyze your personal needs, limitations, physical activity likes and dislikes, and daily schedule. If you have inherited no major risks for fatal or debilitating diseases, your specific goal may be to achieve (or maintain) healthy levels of body fat, cardiovascular fitness, muscular strength and endurance, or flexibility/mobility.

Once you become committed to regular physical activity and exercise, you will observe gradual changes and note progress toward your goals. Unfortunately, you can't get fit for

Starting an Exercise Routine

Beginners often start their exercise programs too rigorously. The most successful exercise program is one that is realistic and appropriate for your skill level and needs. Be realistic about the amount of time you will need to get into good physical condition. Perhaps the most significant factor early on in an exercise program is personal comfort. You'll need to experiment to find an activity that you truly enjoy. Be open to exploring new activities and new exercise equipment.

Start slow as a beginning exerciser. For the sedentary, first-time exerciser, any type and amount of physical activity will be a step in the right direction. If you are extremely overweight or out of condition, you might only be able to walk for five minutes at a time. Don't be discouraged; you're on your way!

Make only one life change at a time. Success at one major behavioral change will encourage you to make other positive changes.

Have reasonable expectations for yourself and your fitness program. Many people become exercise dropouts because their expectations were too high to begin with. Allow sufficient time to reach your fitness goals.

Choose a specific time to exercise and stick with it. Learning to establish priorities and keeping to a schedule are vital steps toward improved fitness. Experiment by exercising at different times of the day to learn what schedule works best for you.

Exercise with a friend. Reneging on an exercise commitment is much more difficult if you exercise with someone else. Partners can motivate and encourage one another, provided they remember that the rate of progress will not be the same for them both.

Make exercise a positive habit. Usually, if you are able to practice a desired activity for three weeks, you will be able to incorporate it into your lifestyle.

Keep a record of your progress. Include various facts about your physical activities (duration, intensity) and chronicle your emotions and personal achievements as you progress.

Take lapses in stride. Physical deconditioning—a decline in fitness level—occurs at about the same rate as physical conditioning. First, renew your commitment to fitness, and then restart your exercise program.

a couple of years while you're young and expect the positive changes to last the rest of your life. You must become committed to fitness for the long haul—to establish a realistic schedule of diverse exercise activities that you can maintain and enjoy throughout your life.

Designing Your Fitness Program

Once you commit yourself to becoming physically active, you must decide what type of fitness program is best suited to your needs. Good fitness programs are designed to improve or maintain cardiorespiratory fitness, flexibility, muscular strength and endurance, and body composition. A comprehensive program could include a warm-up period of easy walking followed by stretching activities to improve flexibility, then selected strength development exercises, followed by performance of an aerobic activity for 20 minutes or more, and concluding with a cool-down period of gentle flexibility exercises.

The greatest proportion of your exercise time should be spent developing cardiovascular fitness, but you should not exclude the other components. Choose an aerobic activity you think you will like. Many people find **cross training**—alternate-day participation in two or more aerobic activities

(i.e., jogging and swimming)—less monotonous and more enjoyable than long-term participation in only one aerobic activity. Cross training is also beneficial because it strengthens a variety of muscles, thus helping you avoid overuse injuries to muscles and joints.

Responding to the exercise boom, fitness equipment manufacturers have made it easy for you to participate in a variety of activities. Most colleges and universities now have recreation centers where students can use stair-climbing machines, stationary bicycles, treadmills, rowing machines, and ski-simulators.

WHAT DO YOU THINK?

You now have the ability to design your own fitness program. What two activities would you select for a cross-training program? Do the activities you selected exercise different major muscle groups?

Cross training Regular participation in two or more types of exercises (e.g., swimming and weight lifting).

Taking Charge
Managing Your Fitness Behaviors

The decision to be physically fit is an easy one to make but not always easy to put into action. Physical fitness should be enjoyable.

Do you think you need to improve your fitness level? Is your endurance where it should be for someone of your age and sex? Endurance, however, is only one aspect of fitness. Do you need to improve in the other areas as well? Begin by making a list of your favorite physical activities that might increase strength, flexibility, and cardiorespiratory fitness. Your list may include walking, yardwork, bicycling, swimming, or weight lifting. Choose which you would like to make part of a regular routine. Then identify specific times to exercise. If time is tight for you, consider how exercise could become part of your daily activities. For example, maybe you could leave for class a few minutes earlier than usual and walk instead of driving or taking a shuttle bus. Then do it!

CHECKLIST FOR CHANGE

MAKING COMMUNITY CHOICES

✓ Does your college have facilities for exercise? Are there special student rates? What hours are those facilities available?

✓ What community exercise facilities does your hometown have?

✓ What opportunities are available for you to volunteer at a local exercise facility? Have you considered volunteering to help out low-income individuals? Why or why not?

SUMMARY

- The physiological benefits of regular physical activity include reduced risk of heart attack, prevention of hypertension, improved blood profile, improved skeletal mass, improved weight control, prevention of diabetes, increased life span, improved immunity to disease, improved mental health and stress management, and improved physical fitness.

- An aerobic exercise program improves cardiorespiratory fitness. Exercise frequency begins with three days per week and eventually moves up to five. Exercise intensity involves working out at your target heart rate. Exercise duration should increase to 30 to 45 minutes.

- Flexibility exercises should involve static stretching exercises performed in sets of four or more repetitions held for 10 to 30 seconds at least two to three days a week in order for progress to be made.

- The key principles for developing muscular strength and endurance are the tension principle, the overload principle, and the specificity of training principle. Resistance training programs include fixed, variable, and accommodating resistance.

- Fitness injuries are generally caused by overuse or trauma; the most common are plantar fasciitis, shin splints, and runner's knee. Limited prevention can be achieved with proper footwear and equipment. Exercise in the heat or cold requires special precautions.

- Planning your fitness program involves setting goals and designing a program to achieve these goals.

DISCUSSION QUESTIONS

1. What are the key components of a physical fitness program? What types of things might you need to consider when beginning a fitness program?

2. Why is stretching vital to improving personal flexibility?
3. Identify at least four physiological and psychological benefits of physical fitness. What is the significance of

the latest fitness report from the Surgeon General's office? How might it help more people realize the benefits of physical fitness?

4. Your roommate has decided to start running first thing in the morning. What advice would you give your roommate to make sure he or she does it properly?

APPLICATION EXERCISE

Reread the *What Do You Think?* scenario at the beginning of the chapter and answer the following questions.

1. Assume for a moment that you are Shawn, thinking about starting an exercise program after a period of inactivity. Create an outline for a three-month program that starts slow and gradually progresses.

2. One of the hardest obstacles for Shawn will be breaking his old habits: driving instead of walking, watching TV, playing computer games, and eating unhealthy foods. What advice would you give Shawn to help him break his habits?

OBJECTIVES

▶ Describe the anatomy and physiology of the heart and circulatory system and the importance of healthy heart functioning.

▶ Review the various types of heart disease, factors that contribute to their development, current diagnostic and treatment options, as well as the importance of fundamental lifestyle modifications aimed at prevention.

▶ Discuss the controllable risk factors for cardiovascular disease, Examine your own risk profile and determine those you can and cannot control.

▶ Discuss the issues surrounding cardiovascular disease risk and disease burden from the perspective of women and persons from diverse backgrounds.

▶ Discuss some of the newer methods of diagnosing and treating cardiovascular disease, and the importance of being a wise health-care consumer.

▶ Define cancer and discuss how it develops.

▶ Discuss the probable causes of cancer, including biological causes, occupational and environmental causes, lifestyle, psychological causes, chemicals in foods, viral causes, medical causes, and combined causes.

▶ Understand and act appropriately in response to self-exams, medical exams, and symptoms related to different types of cancers is an important element of successful cancer survival.

▶ Discuss cancer detection and treatment, including radiation therapy, chemotherapy, immunotherapy, and other common methods of detection and treatment in use today.

12

Cardiovascular Disease and Cancer

Reducing Your Risks

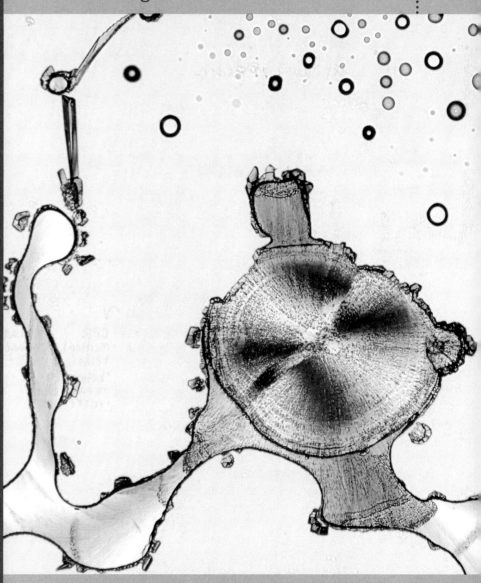

# of diagnosis is constant
# of death's is less

#1 cause of death

DESPITE THE MANY ADVANCES in medical technology, heart disease and cancer continue to be two of the leading causes of death in the United States. **Cardiovascular diseases (CVDs),** in fact, account for over 42 percent of all deaths, nearly three times the rate of the second greatest killer, cancer, and more than the number of deaths caused by all other diseases combined. In fact, since 1900, CVD has been the number one killer in the United States in every year but one, 1918, when a killer strain of influenza struck.[1]

Despite these gloomy statistics, there is reason for optimism. Medical scientists have made tremendous progress in fighting cardiovascular diseases and cancer. The death rate (numbers per 100,000 persons) from cardiovascular disease has declined by more than 25 percent during the last decade, even though numbers of deaths have held fairly constant.[2]

Although it is impossible to place a monetary value on human life, the economic burden of cardiovascular disease on our society is overwhelming. In 1998, cardiovascular diseases will have cost us in excess of $275 billion.[3] This figure includes the cost of physician and nursing services, hospital and nursing home services, medications, and lost productivity of the victim resulting from disability. Likewise, cancer's price tag has been estimated at $107 billion, which includes direct medical costs (total of all health expenditures), indirect morbidity costs (cost of lost productivity due to illness), and indirect mortality costs (cost of lost productivity due to premature death).[4]

You can reduce your risk for CVD and cancer by taking steps to change certain behaviors. For example, controlling

high blood pressure and reducing your intake of saturated fats and cholesterol are two things you can do to lower your chances of heart attack. By maintaining your weight, decreasing your intake of sodium, exercising, not smoking, and changing your lifestyle to reduce stress, you can lower your blood pressure and reduce your risk of cancer. You can also monitor the levels of fat and cholesterol in your blood and adjust your diet to prevent your arteries from becoming clogged. As combinations of these risk factors seem to increase your risk even more than by just adding them together, reducing several risk factors can have a dramatic effect. By understanding how your body works, you will have a better chance of understanding your risks and of changing your behaviors to reduce them.

• CPR
• medical tech. *• education* *• change in diet • exercise*
• better treatment
• more EMT's

UNDERSTANDING YOUR CARDIOVASCULAR SYSTEM

The **cardiovascular system** is the network of elastic tubes through which blood flows as it carries oxygen and nutrients to all parts of the body. It includes the *heart, lungs, arteries, arterioles* (small arteries), and *capillaries* (minute blood vessels). It also includes *venules* (small veins) and *veins,* the blood vessels though which blood flows as it returns to the heart and lungs.

Under normal circumstances, the human body contains approximately 6 quarts of blood. This blood transports nutrients, oxygen, waste products, hormones, and enzymes throughout the body. It also regulates body temperature,

15-20 thousand miles of blood vessels

cellular water levels, and acidity levels of body components, and aids in bodily defense against toxins and harmful micro-organisms. An adequate blood supply is essential to health and well-being.

How does the heart ensure that blood is constantly recirculated to body parts? The four chambers of the heart work together to achieve this (see Figure 12.1). The two upper chambers of the heart, called **atria,** or auricles, are large collecting chambers that receive blood from the rest of the body. The two lower chambers, known as **ventricles,** pump the blood out again. Small valves regulate the steady, rhythmic flow of blood between chambers and prevent inappropriate backwash. The *tricuspid valve,* located between the right atrium and the right ventricle; the *pulmonary (pulmonic) valve,* between the right ventricle and the pulmonary artery; the *mitral valve,* between the left atrium and left ventricle; and the *aortic valve,* between the left ventricle and the aorta, permit blood to flow in only one direction.[5]

Heart activity depends on a complex interaction of biochemical, physical, and neurological signals. The following is a simplified version of the steps involved in heart function:

1. Deoxygenated blood enters the right atrium after having been circulated through the body.
2. From the right atrium, blood moves to the right ventricle and is pumped through the pulmonary artery to the lungs, where it receives oxygen.
3. Oxygenated blood from the lungs then returns to the left atrium of the heart.
4. Blood from the left atrium is forced into the left ventricle.

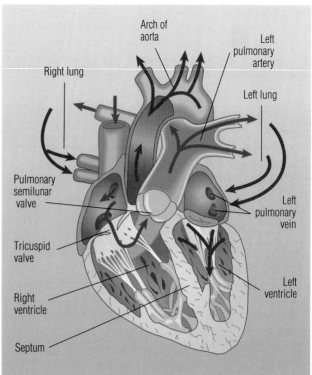

Figure 12.1
Anatomy of the Heart

5. The left ventricle pumps blood through the aorta to all body parts.

Different types of blood vessels are required for different parts of this process. **Arteries** carry blood away from the heart—except for pulmonary arteries, which carry deoxygenated blood to the lungs, where it picks up oxygen and gives off carbon dioxide. As they branch off from the heart, the arteries divide into smaller blood vessels called **arterioles,** and then into even smaller blood vessels called **capillaries.** Capillaries have thin walls that permit the exchange of oxygen, carbon dioxide, nutrients, and waste products with body cells. The carbon dioxide and waste products are transported to the lungs and kidneys through **veins** and venules (small veins).

For the heart to function properly, the four chambers must beat in an organized manner. This is governed by an electrical impulse that directs the heart muscle to move when the impulse moves across it, which results in a sequential contraction of the four chambers. This signal starts in a small bundle of highly specialized cells, the **sinoatrial node (SA node),** located in the right atrium. The SA node serves as a form of natural pacemaker for the heart.[6] People with damaged or nonfunctional natural pacemaker activity must often have a mechanical pacemaker inserted to ensure the smooth passage of blood through the sequential phases of the heart beat.

The average adult heart at rest beats 70 to 80 times per minute, although a well-conditioned heart may beat only 50 to

Cardiovascular diseases (CVDs)   Diseases of the heart and blood vessels.

Cardiovascular system   A complex system consisting of the heart and blood vessels that transports nutrients, oxygen, hormones, and enzymes throughout the body and regulates temperature, the water levels of cells, and the acidity levels of body components.

Atria   The two upper chambers of the heart, which receive blood.

Ventricles   The two lower chambers of the heart, which pump blood through the blood vessels.

Arteries   Vessels that carry blood away from the heart to other regions of the body.

Arterioles   Branches of the arteries.

Capillaries   Minute blood vessels that branch out from the arterioles; their thin walls allow for the exchange of oxygen, carbon dioxide, nutrients, and waste products with body cells.

Veins   Vessels that carry blood back to the heart from other regions of the body.

Sinoatrial node (SA node)   Node serving as a form of natural pacemaker for the heart.

60 times per minute to achieve the same results. When overly stressed, a heart may beat over 200 times per minute, particularly in an individual who is overweight or out of shape. A healthy heart functions more efficiently and is less likely to suffer damage from overwork than is an unhealthy one.

········· **WHAT DO YOU THINK?**

What risk factors for heart disease do you currently have? What is your current resting heart rate? What actions can you start taking today to reduce your risk of CVD?

TYPES OF CARDIOVASCULAR DISEASES

Although most of us associate cardiovascular disease with heart attacks, there are actually a number of different types of cardiovascular system diseases (see Figure 12.2). Current efforts are aimed at preventing and treating the most common types of cardiovascular diseases:

- Atherosclerosis (fatty plaque buildup in arteries).
- Coronary heart disease (CHD).
- Chest pain (angina pectoris).
- Irregular heartbeat (arrhythmia).
- Congestive heart failure (CHF).
- Congenital and rheumatic heart disease.
- Stroke (cerebrovascular accident).

Prevention and treatment of these diseases range from changes in diet and lifestyle to use of medications and surgery.

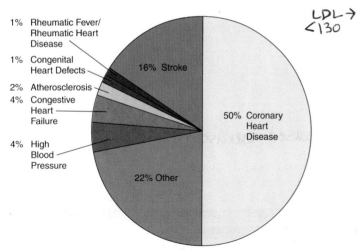

1% Rheumatic Fever/Rheumatic Heart Disease
1% Congenital Heart Defects
2% Atherosclerosis
4% Congestive Heart Failure
4% High Blood Pressure
16% Stroke
50% Coronary Heart Disease
22% Other

Figure 12.2

Percentage Breakdown of Deaths from Cardiovascular Diseases

Source: CDC/NCHS and the American Heart Association.

[handwritten notes:]
LDL → <130
cholesterol < 200 – 220 doubles risk
LDL < 130 – ↑ higher risk
HDL > 35 – ↑ lower risk
triglycerides < 200 – ↑ higher risk

Atherosclerosis

Historically, **atherosclerosis** has been referred to as a general term for thickening and hardening of the arteries, a condition that underlies many of the ischemic heart diseases. Atherosclerosis is actually a type of **arteriosclerosis** and is characterized by deposits of fatty substances, cholesterol, cellular waste products, calcium, and *fibrin* (a clotting material in the blood) in the inner lining of the artery. The resulting buildup is referred to as **plaque**.[7] Often, atherosclerosis is referred to as a *coronary artery disease (CAD)* because of the resultant damage done to coronary arteries.

Atherosclerotic plaque tends to occur primarily in large and medium-sized elastic and muscluar arteries and can lead to ischemia (decrease in blood flow or blockage of blood flow) of the heart, brain, or extremities. Plaque may be present throughout a person's lifetime, with the earliest formation, known as a "fatty streak," being fairly common in infants and young children.[8]

Initially, it was thought that plaque developed in "response to injury" and tended to collect at sites of injury. Many scientists believe that the process of plaque buildup begins because the protective inner lining of the artery (*endothelium*) became damaged and fats, cholesterol, and other substances in the blood tend to aggregate in these damaged areas. High blood pressure surges, elevated cholesterol and *triglyceride* levels in the blood, and cigarette smoking have been the main suspects in this injury to artery walls. As a result of national campaigns aimed at reducing dietary fats, millions of people report cutting down on animal fat and dairy products. However, despite massive lifestyle changes and the use of cholesterol-lowering drugs, cardiovascular diseases continue to be the leading cause of death in the United States, Europe, and most of Asia.[9]

Atherosclerosis is now believed to be an *inflammatory disease*, with numerous factors contributing to plaque formation.[10] Among these culprits are elevated and modified low-density lipoprotein, free radicals caused by cigarette smoking, hypertension, diabetes mellitus, and certain infectious microorganisms, such as *herpesviruses* or *Chlamydia pneumoniae,* and a combination of these and other factors.[11] The bottom line is that while elevated cholesterol continues to be important in approximately 50 percent of patients with cardiovascular diseases,[12] other factors need to be taken into consideration, particularly those that cause inflammation and subsequent injury within the artery walls.[13]

Coronary Heart Disease

Of all the major types of CVD, CHD is the single greatest killer. In fact, this year well over 1,200,000 people will suffer from one of the major forms of coronary attack, and one-third of them will die from one.[14] A **myocardial infarction (MI),** or **heart attack,** involves a blockage of normal blood supply to an area of the heart. This condition is often brought on by a **coronary thrombosis,** or blood clot in the

anywhere in the heart muscle - blockage

*heart attack symptoms
sweating   nervous
nautious   pain left shoulder*

coronary artery, or through an atherosclerotic narrowing that becomes closed.

When blood does not flow readily, there is a corresponding decrease in oxygen flow. If the heart blockage is extremely minor, the otherwise healthy heart will adapt over time by utilizing small unused or underused blood vessels to reroute needed blood through other areas. This system, known as **collateral circulation,** is a form of self-preservation that allows a damaged heart muscle to heal.

When heart blockage is more severe and the body is unable to adapt on its own, outside lifesaving support is critical. The hour following a heart attack is believed to be the most critical period because over 40 percent of heart attack victims die within this time. These are sudden deaths caused by cardiac arrest, usually resulting from *ventricular fibrillation,* or irregular, inefficient heartbeats.

WHAT DO YOU THINK?

Based on new evidence that atherosclerosis may begin as early as in the womb and infancy, what implications are there for parents? Sexually active, non-monogymous parents? What risk factors might typical college-aged students have for plaque formation? What should new CVD prevention guidelines look like if these new theories are true?

females - tendancy to not show early signs & symptoms of heart attacks.

Atherosclerosis   A general term for thickening and hardening of the arteries.

Arteriosclerosis   Characterized by deposits of fatty substances, cholesterol, cellular waste products, calcium, and fibrin in the inner lining of an artery.

Plaque   Buildup of deposits in the arteries.

Myocardial infarction (MI)   Heart attack.

Heart attack   A blockage of normal blood supply to an area in the heart.

Coronary thrombosis   A blood clot occurring in the coronary artery.

Collateral circulation   Adaptation of the heart to partial damage accomplished by rerouting needed blood through unused or underused blood vessels while the damaged heart muscle heals.

Ischemia   Reduced oxygen supply to the heart.

Angina pectoris   Severe chest pain occurring as a result of reduced oxygen flow to the heart.

Arrhythmia   An irregularity in heartbeat.

Fibrillation   A sporadic, quivering pattern of heartbeat resulting in extreme inefficiency in moving blood through the cardiovascular system.

Angina Pectoris

As a result of atherosclerosis and other circulatory impairments, the heart's oxygen supply is often reduced, a condition known as **ischemia.** Individuals with ischemia often suffer from varying degrees of **angina pectoris,** or chest pains. In fact, an estimated 7,200,000 Americans (more women than men) suffer from mild to crushing forms of chest pain each day.[15] Many people experience short episodes of angina whenever they exert themselves physically. Symptoms may range from a slight feeling of indigestion to a feeling that the heart is being crushed. Generally, the more serious the oxygen deprivation, the more severe the pain. Although angina pectoris is not a heart attack, it does indicate underlying heart disease.

Currently, there are several methods of treating angina. In mild cases, rest is critical. The most common treatments for more severe cases involve using drugs that affect (1) the supply of blood to the heart muscle or (2) the heart's demand for oxygen. Pain and discomfort are often relieved with *nitroglycerin,* a drug used to relax (dilate) veins, thereby reducing the amount of blood returning to the heart and thus lessening its workload. Patients whose angina is caused by spasms of the coronary arteries are often given drugs called *calcium channel blockers.* These drugs prevent calcium atoms from passing through coronary arteries and causing heart contractions. They also appear to reduce blood pressure and to slow heart rates. *Beta blockers* are the other major type of drugs used to treat angina. The chemical action of beta blockers serves to control potential overactivity of the heart muscle.

Arrhythmias

An **arrhythmia** is an irregularity in heartbeat. It may be suspected when a person complains of a racing heart in the absence of exercise or anxiety; *tachycardia* is the medical term for this abnormally fast heartbeat. On the other end of the continuum is *bradycardia,* or abnormally slow heartbeat. When a heart goes into **fibrillation,** it exhibits a totally sporadic, quivering pattern of beating resulting in extreme inefficiency in moving blood through the cardiovascular system. If untreated, this condition may be fatal. Not all arrhythmias are life-threatening. In many instances, excessive caffeine or nicotine consumption can trigger an arrhythmia episode. However, severe cases may require treatment to prevent serious complications.

caused - exercise   nicoteu, caffiene & contibrt

Congestive Heart Failure (CHF)

When the heart muscle is damaged or overworked and lacks the strength to keep blood circulating normally through the body, its chambers are often taxed to the limit. CHF affects over 5 million Americans and dramatically increases risk of premature death.[16] Patients who have been afflicted with rheumatic fever, pneumonia, or other cardiovascular problems (particularly after heart surgery) in the past often have weakened heart muscles. In addition, the walls of the heart and the blood vessels may be damaged from previous radiation or chemotherapy treatments for cancer. These weakened muscles respond poorly when stressed, blood flow out of the heart through the arteries is diminished, and the return flow of blood through the veins begins to back up, causing congestion in the tissues. This pooling of blood causes enlargement of the heart and decreases the amount of blood that can be circulated. Fluid begins to accumulate in other body areas, such as in the vessels in the legs and ankles or the lungs, causing swelling or difficulty in breathing. Today, CHF is the single most frequent cause of hospitalization in the United States.[17] If untreated, congestive heart failure will result in death. Most cases respond well to treatment that includes *diuretics* (water pills) for relief of fluid accumulation; drugs, such as *digitalis,* that increase the pumping action of the heart; and drugs called *vasodilators* that expand blood vessels and decrease resistance, allowing blood to flow more easily and making the heart's work easier.

Congenital and Rheumatic Heart Disease

Approximately 1 out of every 125 children is born with some form of **congenital heart disease** (disease present at birth). These forms may range from slight murmurs caused by valve irregularities, which some children outgrow, to serious complications in heart function that can be corrected only with surgery. Their underlying causes are unknown but are believed to be related to hereditary factors. The prognosis for children with congenital heart defects is better than ever before.

Rheumatic heart disease can cause similar heart problems in children. It is attributed to rheumatic fever, an inflammatory disease that may affect many connective tissues of the body, especially those of the heart, the joints, the brain, or the skin, and which is caused by an unresolved *streptococcal infection* of the throat (strep throat). In a small number of cases, this infection can lead to an immune response in which antibodies attack the heart as well as the bacteria. Many of the 75,000 annual operations on heart valves in the United States are related to rheumatic heart disease.[18]

Stroke

Like heart muscle, brain cells must have a continuous adequate supply of oxygen in order to survive. A **stroke** (also called a cerebrovascular accident) occurs when the blood supply to the brain is cut off. Strokes may be caused by a **thrombus** (blood clot), an **embolus** (a wandering clot), or an **aneurysm** (a weakening in a blood vessel that causes it to bulge and, in severe cases, burst). Figure 12.3 illustrates these blood vessel disorders. Stroke killed more than 160,000 Americans in 1997 and accounted for 1 in 14 of our total deaths, surpassed only by CHD and cancer.[19] On average, someone suffers a stroke every 53 seconds, with someone dying every 3 minutes.[20]

When any of these events occurs, the result is the death of brain cells, which do not have the capacity to heal or regenerate. Strokes may cause speech impairments, memory

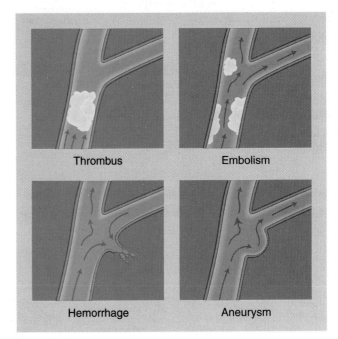

Figure 12.3
Common Blood Vessel Disorders

loss, and loss of motor control. Although some strokes affect parts of the brain that regulate heart and lung function and kill within minutes, others are mild and cause only temporary dizziness or slight weakness or numbness. About one in ten major strokes is preceded (days, weeks, or months before) by one of these mild forms of strokes, called **transient ischemic attacks (TIAs).** These are often indications of an impending major stroke. Knowing the warning signs or symptoms of stroke may help you or a loved one get medical attention earlier, when treatment may be more effective. Among the most common symptoms are:

- Sudden weakness or numbness of the face, arm, or leg on one side of the body or
- Sudden dimness or loss of vision, particularly in only one eye.
- Loss of speech, or trouble talking or understanding speech.
- Sudden, severe headaches with no known cause.
- Unexplained dizziness, unsteadiness, or sudden falls, especially along with any of the previous symptoms.

CONTROLLING YOUR RISKS FOR CARDIOVASCULAR DISEASES

In a recent study, researchers reported that one way to determine those most at risk of dying prematurely of heart disease is to determine how quickly a person's heartbeat returns to normal after exercise. It was found that for those with normal hearts, the heartbeat is restored to normal quickly after exertion. However, for those with heart disease, the heart's recovery time was much slower. The purpose of this study was to determine the heart risk of those patients who have symptoms of heart disease. While there is no specific treatment for this event, doctors state that reducing other risk factors that contribute to heart disease reduces the risk of death.[21]

Knowing the factors that contribute to cardiovascular disease can lead to health-promoting lifestyle changes. Different risks can have a compounded effect when combined. For example, if you have high blood pressure, smoke cigarettes, have a high cholesterol level, and have a family history of heart disease, you run a much greater risk of having a heart attack than does someone with only one of these risks.

Risks You Can Control

Factors that increase the risk for cardiovascular disease fall into two categories: those that can be controlled and those that cannot. As you read about each factor, ask yourself whether it applies to you.

▶ **Stop Smoking** In 1984, the surgeon general of the United States asserted that smoking was the greatest risk factor for heart disease. The risk for cardiovascular disease is 70 percent greater for smokers than for nonsmokers. Smokers who have a heart attack are more likely to die suddenly (within one hour) than are nonsmokers. Available evidence also indicates that chronic exposure to environmental tobacco smoke (ETS or passive smoking) increases the risk of heart disease by as much as 30 percent.[22]

Although we do not fully understand how cigarette smoking damages the heart, there are two plausible explanations. One theory states that nicotine increases heart rate, heart output, blood pressure, and oxygen use by heart muscles. Because the carbon monoxide in cigarette smoke

Congenital heart disease Heart disease that is present at birth.

Rheumatic heart disease A heart disease caused by untreated streptococcal infection of the throat.

Stroke A condition occurring when the brain is damaged by disrupted blood supply.

Thrombus Blood clot.

Embolus Blood clot that is forced through the circulatory system.

Aneurysm A weakened blood vessel that may bulge under pressure and, in severe cases, burst.

Transient ischemic attacks (TIAs) Mild form of stroke; often an indicator of impending major stroke.

ACCESSING YOUR HEALTH ON THE INTERNET

Check out the following Internet sites related to cardiovascular health and cancer.

1. *American Heart Association.* Home page for the leading private organization dedicated to heart health. This site provides information, statistics, and resources regarding cardiovascular care, including an opportunity to test your own risk for CVD.

   http://www.amhrt.org

2. *Johns Hopkins Cardiac Rehabilitation Home Page.* Information about prevention of heart disease and rehabilitation from CVDs from one of the best cardiac care centers in the United States, including information about programs available to help individuals stop smoking, lose weight, lower blood pressure and blood cholesterol, and reduce emotional stress.

   www.jhbmc.jhu.edu/cardiology/rehab/rehab.html

3. *American Cancer Society.* Home page for the leading private organization dedicated to cancer prevention. This site provides information, statistics, and resources regarding cancer.

   http://www.cancer.org

4. *International Cancer Information Center.* Sponsored by the National Cancer Institute, this site is designed to be a comprehensive information resource on cancer for patients and health professionals.

   http://cancernet.nci.nih.gov

displaces oxygen in heart tissue, the heart is forced to work harder to obtain sufficient oxygen. The other theory states that chemicals in smoke damage the lining of the coronary arteries, allowing cholesterol and plaque to accumulate more easily. This additional buildup constricts the vessels, increasing blood pressure and causing the heart to work harder.

When people stop smoking, regardless of how long or how much they've smoked, their risk of heart disease declines rapidly.[23] Three years after quitting, the risk of death from heart disease and stroke for people who smoked a pack a day or less is almost the same as for people who never smoked. Quitting today will also raise your HDL levels, reducing your risks even further.[24]

▶ *Cut Down on Fats and Cholesterol* Researchers now realize that high-fat diets are even more dangerous than previously thought. Fatty diets not only raise cholesterol levels slowly over time, but also can send the body's blood-clotting system into high gear and make the blood sludgy in just a few hours, increasing the risk for heart attack. Studies indicate that fatty foods apparently trigger production of factor VII, a blood-clotting substance. Switching to a low-fat diet promptly eliminates the risk of clotting.[25]

A fatty diet also increases the amount of cholesterol in the blood, contributing to atherosclerosis. In past years, cholesterol levels of between 200 and 250 milligrams per 100 milliliters of blood (mg/dl) were considered normal. Recent research indicates that levels between 180 and 200 mg/dl are more desirable for reducing the risk for CVD. Cholesterol comes in two varieties: **low-density lipoproteins (LDLs)** and **high-density lipoproteins (HDLs).** Scientists used to think that the critical question was whether a person had more of the "good" HDLs than the "bad" LDLs. But now according to scientists, what may really count is the HDL component Lp(a). The more of this protective protein a person has, it seems, the lower the risk for heart disease.[26]

A study published in 1996 in the *Journal of the American Medical Association* has raised questions about the role of cholesterol in increased risk for CVD among the elderly. Researchers studied 997 people whose cholesterol was measured as part of a longitudinal (covering several years) study of older Americans. Results indicated that there was no association between elevated total serum cholesterol and any outcome, including myocardial infarction.[27] Although it should be noted that this was just one study, it does challenge the screening for cholesterol and treatment of high cholesterol levels in the elderly as possibly unnecessary.

▶ *Cut Back on Overall Triglycerides*   As people get older, their triglyceride and cholesterol levels tend to rise. Although some CVD patients have elevated triglyceride levels, a causal link between high triglyceride levels and CVD has yet to be established. It may be that high triglyceride levels do not directly cause atherosclerosis but rather are among the abnormalities that speed its development. It is also important to remember not to reduce fat consumption too greatly, because some fat is necessary to overall health.

▶ *Monitor Your Cholesterol Levels*   If a blood test reveals that you have a high level of total cholesterol (more than 240 mg/dl), the first thing you should do is to have the test retaken to make sure that the reading is accurate. If your total cholesterol level is still high, you should request that a lipoprotein analysis be done to determine the level of LDLs and HDLs in your blood.

Lipoprotein analysis, which also requires that you fast for 12 hours, measures the level of three substances: total cholesterol, HDL, and triglycerides. The level of LDL is derived using a standard formula: LDL = Total cholesterol − HDL − (Triglycerides ÷ 5).

In general, LDL is more closely associated with cardiovascular risks than is total cholesterol. However, most authorities agree that by looking only at LDL, we ignore the positive effects of HDL. Perhaps the best method of evaluating risk is to

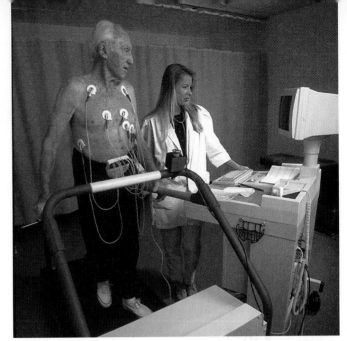

Extensive research and testing has helped us understand the functioning of the heart, what puts it at risk, and what we need to do to take care of it.

→ *nicotene increases heart rate*
→ *chemicals from cig. line the artiries*

examine the *ratio* of HDL to total cholesterol or the percentage of HDL in total cholesterol. If the percentage of HDL is less than 35, the risk increases dramatically. The ratio of HDL to total cholesterol can be controlled either by lowering LDL levels or by raising HDL levels. The best way to lower LDL levels is to reduce your dietary intake of the major sources of saturated fat. However, in extreme cases medications can also be used.

▶ *Control Your Blood Pressure*   **Hypertension** refers to sustained high blood pressure. If it cannot be attributed to any specific cause, it is known as **essential hypertension.** Approximately 90 percent of all cases of hypertension fit this category. **Secondary hypertension** refers to hypertension caused by specific factors, such as kidney disease, obesity, or tumors of the adrenal glands. In general, the higher your blood pressure, the greater your risk for CVD. Hypertension is known as the "silent killer," because it usually has no symptoms. Although hypertension affects nearly 61 million Americans, 20 percent of them don't know they have the condition, and only one-third of those who are aware of it have it under control.[28]

Blood pressure is measured in two parts and is expressed as a fraction—for example, 110/80, or 110 over 80. Both values are measured in *millimeters of mercury* (mm Hg). The first number refers to **systolic pressure,** or the pressure being applied to the walls of the arteries when the heart contracts, pumping blood to the rest of the body. The second value is **diastolic pressure,** or the pressure applied to the walls of the arteries during the heart's relaxation phase. During this phase, blood is reentering the chambers of the heart, preparing for the next heartbeat.

Normal blood pressure varies for different individuals depending on weight, age, physical condition and for different groups of people, such as women and minorities. As a rule, men have a greater risk for high blood pressure than women have until age 55, when their risks become about equal. At age 75 and over, women are more likely victims of high blood pressure than are men.[29] For the average person, 110 over 80 is a normal blood pressure level. If your blood pressure exceeds 140 over 90, you probably need to take steps to lower it. See Table 12.1 for a summary of blood pressure values and what they mean.

TABLE 12.1
Blood Pressure Values and What They Mean to You

CLASSIFICATION	SYSTOLIC READING	DIASTOLIC READING	ACTIONS
Normal	Below 130	Below 85	Recheck in two years.
High normal	130–139	85–89	Recheck in one year.
Mild hypertension	140–159	90–99	Check in two months.
Moderate hypertension	160–179	100–109	See physician within a month.
Severe hyptertension	180 or above	110 or above	See physician immediately.

Note: Systolic and diastolic values are based on an average of two or more readings taken at different times.
Source: Adapted from "Fifth Report of the Joint National Committee on Detection, Evaluation, and Treatment of High Blood Pressure," Archives of Internal Medicine 153 (25 January 1993): 154–183 (published by the American Medical Association); and American Heart Association.

▶ **Exercise** & Diet   According to the American Heart Association, and the U.S. Surgeon General, inactivity is a definite risk factor for CVD.[30,31] Even modest levels of low-intensity physical activity are beneficial if done regularly and long term. Such activities include walking for pleasure, gardening, housework, and dancing.

▶ **Lose Weight**   Like exercise, diet and obesity are believed to play a role in CVD. Researchers are not certain whether high-fat, high-sugar, high-calorie diets are a direct risk for CVD or whether they invite risk by causing obesity, which forces the heart to strain to push blood through the many miles of capillaries that supply each pound of fat. In fact, people who are overweight or obese are more likely to develop heart disease and stroke even if they have no other risk factors. If you're overweight, losing even 5 to 10 pounds can make a difference, especially if you're an "apple" (that means you're thicker around your waist than around your hips and thighs) rather than a "pear" (thicker around your hips and thighs). Your waist measurement divided by your hip measurement should be less than 0.9 (for men) and less than 0.8 (for women).[32,33]

▶ **Control Diabetes Risks**   Diabetics, particularly those who have taken insulin for a number of years, appear to run an increased risk for the development of CVD. In fact, CVD is the leading cause of death among diabetic patients. Because overweight people have a higher risk for diabetes, distinguishing between the effects of the two conditions is difficult. Diabetics also tend to have elevated blood fat levels, increased atherosclerosis, and a tendency toward deterioration of small blood vessels, particularly in the eyes and extremities.

▶ **Manage Stress**   Some scientists have noted a relationship between CVD risk and a person's stress level, behavior habits, and socioeconomic status. These factors may affect established risk factors. For example, people under stress may start smoking or smoke more than they otherwise would.[34] Other studies have challenged the apparent link between emotional stress and heart disease.

Researcher-physician Robert S. Eliot demonstrated that approximately one out of five people has an extreme cardiovascular reaction to stressful stimulation. These people experience alarm and resistance so strongly that, when under stress, their bodies produce large amounts of stress chemicals, which in turn cause tremendous changes in the cardiovascular system, including remarkable increases in blood pressure. These people are called *hot reactors*. Although their blood pressure may be normal when they are not under stress—for example, in a doctor's office—it increases dramatically in response to even small amounts of everyday stress.

Cold reactors are those who are able to experience stress without reacting with harmful cardiovascular responses. Cold reactors may internalize stress, but their perceptions about the

Low-density lipoproteins (LDLs)   Compounds that facilitate the transport of cholesterol in the blood to the body's cells.

High-density lipoproteins (HDLs)   Compounds that facilitate the transport of cholesterol in the blood to the liver for metabolism and elimination from the body.

Hypertension   Sustained elevated blood pressure.

Essential hypertension   Hypertension that cannot be attributed to any cause.

Secondary hypertension   Hypertension caused by specific factors, such as kidney disease, obesity, or tumors of the adrenal glands.

Systolic pressure   The upper number in the fraction that measures blood pressure, indicating pressure on the walls of the arteries when the heart contracts.

Diastolic pressure   The lower number in the fraction that measures blood pressure, indicating pressure on the walls of the arteries during the relaxation phase of heart activity.

stressful events lead them to a nonresponse state in which their cardiovascular system remains virtually unaffected.[35] New research indicates that people who have an underlying predisposition toward a *toxic core* personality (in other words, who are chronically hostile and hateful) may be at greatest risk for a CVD event.

Risks You Cannot Control

There are, unfortunately, some risk factors for CVD that you cannot prevent or control. The most important are:

- *Heredity:* Having a family history of heart disease appears to increase risks significantly.
- *Age:* The risk for CVD increases with age for both sexes.
- *Gender:* Men are at much greater risk for CVD until old age. Women under 35 have a fairly low risk unless they have high blood pressure, kidney problems, or diabetes. Using oral contraceptives while smoking also increases risk. Hormonal factors appear to reduce risk for women, although after menopause or after estrogen levels are otherwise reduced (e.g., hysterectomy), women's LDL levels tend to go up, increasing their risk for CVD. (For a more detailed discussion of the gender factor, see the next section.)
- *Race:* African Americans are at 45 percent greater risk for hypertension and thus a greater risk for CVD than are whites. In addition, African Americans have a worse chance of surviving heart attacks, as discussed in the Health in a Diverse World box.

WHAT DO YOU THINK?

Which do you think is your biggest CVD risk factor right now? What is your second biggest risk factor? List four actions that you can take this week to reduce these two risk factors. Who can you get to help you in your attempt to change your health behaviors?

WOMEN AND CARDIOVASCULAR DISEASE

Since 1970, cardiovascular diseases have been the single leading cause of death for men and women in the United States.[36] While men tend to have more heart attacks and to have them earlier in life than do women, some interesting trends in survivability have emerged.

Risk Factors for Heart Disease in Women

Premenopausal women are unlikely candidates for heart attacks, except for those who suffer from diabetes, high blood pressure, or kidney disease, or who have a genetic predisposition to high cholesterol levels. Family history and smoking can also increase the risk for premenopausal women.

▶ **The Estrogen Element**   Once her estrogen production drops with menopause, a woman's chances of developing CVD rise rapidly. A 60-year-old woman has the same heart attack risk as a 50-year-old man. By her late 70s, a woman has the same heart attack risk as a man her age. To date, much of this changing risk has been attributed to the aging process, but some preliminary evidence indicates that hormones may play a bigger role than once thought. Recent results from the *Postmenopausal Estrogen/Progestin Interventions (PEPI)* study, a longitudinal study of how various hormone replacement therapies (HRTs) affect cardiovascular risks, indicate that HRT may reduce CVD by as much as 12 to 25 percent. In this study, HRT seemed to reduce a woman's risk for CVD by raising HDL cholesterol levels and lowering LDL cholesterol levels. Even when their total blood cholesterol levels are higher than men's, women may be at less risk because they typically have a higher percentage of HDL.[37]

But that's only part of the story. It's true that women aged 25 and over tend to have lower cholesterol levels than do men of the same age. But when they reach 45, things change. Most men's cholesterol levels become more stable, while both LDL and total cholesterol levels in women start to rise. The gap widens further beyond age 55.[38]

Before age 45, women's total blood cholesterol levels average below 220 mg/dl. By the time she is 45 to 55, the average woman's blood cholesterol rises to between 223 and 246 mg/dl. Studies of men have shown that for every 1 percent drop in cholesterol, there is a 2 percent decrease in CVD risk.[39] If this holds true for women, prevention efforts focusing on dietary interventions and exercise may significantly help postmenopausal women.

Symptoms of Heart Disease in Postmenopausal Women

Postmenopausal women often do not display the same extreme symptoms of heart disease that men do. The first sign of heart disease in men is generally a myocardial infarction. In women, the first sign is usually uncomplicated angina pectoris. Because chest discomfort rather than pain is the common manifestation of angina in women, and because angina has a much more favorable prognosis in women than in men, many physicians ignore the condition in their female patients or treat it too casually.

A heart attack also shows different signs in women than in men. In men, a heart attack usually manifests itself as crushing chest pain radiating to the arm. But in women, a heart attack can feel like severe abdominal pain or indigestion.

Hormone replacement therapies (HRTs)   Therapies that replace estrogen in postmenopausal women.

HEALTH IN A DIVERSE WORLD

Disparity in CVD Risks

Cardiovascular disease is not an "equal opportunity" disease. In fact, when it comes to risk of attack and eventual mortality, there are huge disparities based on gender, race, and age. Consider the following:

- Approximately 85 percent of those who die from CVD are age 65 and older.

Source: American Heart Association, *Heart and Stroke Facts, 1998.*

- More women die of CVD each year than do men.
- In 1997, CHD death rates were 124.4 for white males and 133.1 for black males (7% higher) at all ages and stages of life.
- In 1997, CHD death rates for white females were 60.3 for white females and 81.6 for black females (35.3% higher) at all ages and stages of life.
- For ages 35 to 74, the age-adjusted death rate from CHD for black

women is more than 71 percent higher than that of white women.

- Blacks are 60 percent more likely to suffer a stroke than are whites, and are two and a half times more likely to die of a stroke than are whites.
- A family history of diabetes, gout, high blood pressure, or high cholesterol increases one's risk of heart disease. Blacks have an increased risk of these familial risk factors, increasing their overall risk for CVD.

Cholesterol levels by race, age 20 and over

53% of non-Hispanic white females	higher than 200 mg/dL
47% of non-Hispanic black females	higher than 200 mg/dL
43% of Mexican Americans	higher than 200 mg/dL
27% of Asian/Pacific Islanders	higher than 200 mg/dL
28% of Indian/Alaska Natives	higher than 200 mg/dL

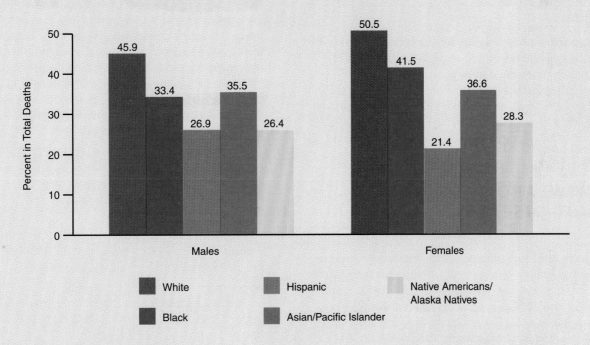

Deaths from Cardiovascular Disease
United States: 1996 Mortality, Final Data
Source: 1999 Heart and Stroke Statistical Update, American Heart Association

Neglect of Heart Disease Symptoms in Women

Research has suggested three main reasons for the widespread neglect of the signs of heart disease in women: (1) physicians may often be gender-biased in their delivery of health care, tending to concentrate on women's reproductive organs rather than on the whole woman; (2) physicians tend to view male heart disease as a more severe problem because men have traditionally had a higher incidence of the disease; and (3) women decline major procedures more often than men do. Other possible explanations for the diagnostic and therapeutic difficulties women with heart disease encounter include:[40]

- Delay in diagnosing a possible heart attack.
- The complexity involved in interpreting chest pain in women.
- Typically less aggressive treatment of women heart attack victims.
- Their older age, on average, and more frequent co-morbidities (other diseases/problems).
- Their coronary arteries are often smaller than men's, making surgical or diagnostic procedures more difficult technically.
- Their increased incidence of postinfarction angina and heart failure.

Although there is much debate about whether women have actually been ignored by past research concerning cardiovascular diseases, at least one study points out that the differences in treatment of suspected acute cardiac ischemia in men cannot be applied directly to women. More importantly, at least one study suggests that these differences may reflect overtreatment of men rather than undertreatment of women.[41]

NEW WEAPONS AGAINST HEART DISEASE

The victim of a heart attack today has a variety of options that were not available a generation ago. Medications designed to strengthen heartbeat, control irregularities in rhythm, and relieve pain are widely prescribed. Triple and quadruple bypasses and angioplasty have become relatively commonplace procedures in hospitals throughout the nation. A great deal of information is available about the care and treatment of disease; much of it can be confusing. The Consumer Health box can help you wade through the process.

Techniques of Diagnosing Heart Disease

Several techniques are used to diagnose heart disease, including electrocardiogram, angiography, and positron emission tomography scans. An **electrocardiogram (ECG)** is a record of the electrical activity of the heart measured during a stress test. Patients walk or run on treadmills while their hearts are monitored. A more accurate method of testing for heart disease is **angiography** (often referred to as *cardiac catheterization*), in which a needle-thin tube called a *catheter* is threaded through blocked heart arteries, a dye is injected, and an X-ray is taken to discover which areas are blocked. A more recent and even more effective method of measuring heart activity is **positron emission tomography,** also called a **PET scan,** which produces three-dimensional images of the heart as blood flows through it. During a PET scan, a patient receives an intravenous injection of a radioactive tracer. As the tracer decays, it emits positrons that are picked up by the scanner and transformed by a computer into color images of the heart.

Newer tests that are now performed at many medical centers include:

- *Radionuclide imaging* (includes such tests as thallium test, MUGA scan, and acute infarct scintigraphy). These tests involve injecting substances called radionuclides into the bloodstream. Computer-generated pictures can then show them in the heart. These tests can show how well the heart muscle is supplied with blood, how well the heart's chambers are functioning, and which part of the heart has been damaged by a heart attack.
- *Magnetic resonance imaging* (also called MRI or NMR). This test uses powerful magnets to look inside the body. Computer-generated pictures can show the heart muscle, identify damage from a heart attack, diagnose certain congenital heart defects, and evaluate disease of larger blood vessels such as the aorta.
- *Digital cardiac angiography* (also called DCA or DSA). This modified form of computer-aided imaging records pictures of the heart and its blood vessels.

Electrocardiogram (ECG)   A record of the electrical activity of the heart measured during a stress test.

Angiography   A technique for examining blockages in heart arteries. A catheter is inserted into the arteries, a dye is injected, and an X-ray is taken to find the blocked areas. Also called cardiac catheterization.

Positron emission tomography (PET scan)   Method for measuring heart activity by injecting a patient with a radioactive tracer that is scanned electronically to produce a three-dimensional image of the heart and arteries.

Coronary bypass surgery   A surgical technique whereby a blood vessel is implanted to bypass a clogged coronary artery.

Angioplasty   A technique in which a catheter with a balloon at the tip is inserted into a clogged artery; the balloon is inflated to flatten fatty deposits against artery walls, allowing blood to flow more freely.

CONSUMER HEALTH

Personal Advocacy and Heart-Smart Behaviors

If you or a loved one must face a CVD crisis, it is important to act with knowledge, strength, and assertiveness. Following these suggestions may help ensure that you feel comfortable with your choices.

1. *Know your rights as a patient.* Ask about the relative risks and costs of various diagnostic tests. Some procedures, particularly angiography, may pose significant risks for the elderly, those who have had a history of TIAs, or those who have had chemotherapy or other treatments which may have damaged blood vessels. Ask for test results and an explanation of any abnormalities.

2. *Find out about informed consent procedures, living wills, durable power of attorney, organ donation, and other legal issues before you are sick.* Having someone shove a clipboard in your face and ask you if life support can be terminated in case of a problem is one of the great horrors of many people's hospital experiences. If you aren't prepared, this can be an unnecessary emotional burden.

3. *Ask about alternative procedures.* If possible, seek a second opinion at a health-care facility that is unrelated to your present one (in other words, get at least two opinions from doctors who are not in the same group and who cannot read each other's diagnoses). New research indicates that doctors may not use drug treatments as aggressively as they could and that drug treatments may be as effective as major bypass or open heart surgeries. There is always the possibility that another treatment may be better for you.

4. *Remain with your loved one as his or her "personal advocate."* If your loved one is weak and unable to ask questions, ask questions for him or her. Ask questions about new medications that are being given, new tests that are being run, and other potentially risky procedures that may be undertaken during the course of treatment or recovery. If your loved one is being removed from intensive care or other closely monitored areas prematurely, ask if the hospital is taking this action to comply with DRGs (established limits of treatment for certain conditions) and if this action is warranted. Most hospitals have waiting areas or special rooms that family members can use to stay close to a patient. Exercise your rights to this option.

5. *Monitor the actions of health-care providers.* In an attempt to control costs by means of managed care, some hospitals are hiring nursing aides and other untrained personnel to perform duties previously performed by registered nurses. Ask about the patient-to-nurse ratio, and make sure that people monitoring you or your loved ones have appropriate credentials.

6. *Be kind to and considerate of your care provider.* One of the most stressful jobs any person can be entrusted with is care of a critically ill person after a major cardiac event. Although questions are appropriate, be as tactful and considerate as possible, even though your emotions may be running high. Nurses often carry a disproportionate responsibility for the care of patients during critical times. They are often forced to carry a higher than necessary patient load. Try to remain out of their way, ask questions as necessary, and report any irregularities in care to the supervisor in charge.

7. *Be patient with the patient.* The pain, suffering, and fears associated with a cardiac event often cause otherwise nice people to act in not-so-nice ways. Be patient, helpful, and allow time for the patient to get his or her rest. Talk with the patient about how he or she is feeling, and about his or her concerns, fears, etc. Do not ignore his or her concerns in an attempt to ease your own anxieties.

Angioplasty versus Bypass Surgery

During the 1980s, coronary bypass surgery seemed to be the ultimate technique for treating patients who had coronary blockages or who had suffered heart attacks. In coronary bypass surgery, a blood vessel taken from another site in the patient's body (usually the *saphenous vein* in the leg or the *internal mammary artery*) is implanted to transport blood by bypassing blocked arteries. Recently, experts have begun to question the effectiveness of bypass operations, particularly for elderly people. Bypass patients typically spend up to 7 days in the hospital to recuperate from the surgery. The average cost of the procedure itself is well over $35,000, and the additional intensive care treatments and follow-ups often result in total medical bills that are closer to $100,000. Death rates are generally much lower at medical centers where surgical teams and intensive care teams see large numbers of patients.[42]

A procedure called angioplasty (sometimes called balloon angioplasty) is associated with fewer risks and is believed by many experts to be more effective than bypass surgery in selected cardiovascular cases. This procedure is similar to angiography. A needle-thin catheter is threaded through blocked heart arteries. The catheter has a balloon at the tip, which is inflated to flatten fatty deposits against the artery walls, allowing blood to flow more freely. Angioplasty patients are generally

·repeated·

The Top Heart Disease and Stroke Advances of 1999

Although heart disease continues to be the leading cause of death in the United States, actual rates of heart disease have declined substantially in recent decades. Improvements in drugs, surgical techniques, diagnostic techniques, emergency response systems, and dietary practices have contributed greatly to this reduction. Every year we know more about the functioning of the heart, and this knowledge has helped promote preventive behaviors as well as increases in longevity among those who have experienced a major or minor heart or stroke event. As we enter the twenty-first century, health officials look back on 1999 as another significant year in the fight against heart disease and stroke. While the list of potential advances for 1999 is long, there are ten that lead the list as significant steppingstones into the next century. Several on the list reflect the great strides being made in genetic research. All will be major factors in determining new prevention, intervention, and treatment strategies for heart disease and stroke.

- *High Blood Pressure Gene:* Discovery of a gene that produces a special protein receptor that appears to serve as a "master regulator of the body's handling of salt" provides researchers with greater insight into the causes of an inherited form of high blood pressure in children. A defective gene results in the receptor sticking in the "on" position, which causes the kidneys to retain salt, leading to increases in blood pressure.
- *Congenital Heart Defects:* A genetic defect has been identified as the cause of DiGeorge syndrome, a condition marked by malformations of the heart and face. Identification of this missing gene, called UFD1, may provide clues to the prevention and treatment of congenital heart defects.
- *New Diagnostic Testing:* A special process called microarray analysis can be used to detect missing or defective genes more quickly than ever before. Using this process, researchers found a genetic defect in people with Tangier disease, a blood-fat disorder caused by a shortage of HDL, the good cholesterol that carries fat from tissues. This knowledge may help researchers learn more about raising HDL levels for millions of individuals.
- *Reducing "Stunning":* Scientists have found the cause of "stunning," a condition in which the heart's pumping action is severely weakened and that often strikes after heart attacks or heart surgery. The problem has been traced to a genetic flaw that affects a protein, troponin I, needed for normal heart contractions.
- *Tissue Growth:* As a result of remarkable advances in tissue engineering, scientists have successfully grown heart valves in the laboratory. These new home-grown valves may eventually replace the mechanical valves and preserved pig valves commonly used now.
- *Diabetes Link:* A link between diabetes and CVD has resulted in diabetes joining smoking, high blood pressure, high cholesterol, and lack of exercise as a risk factor for heart disease and stroke. It is now believed that diabetes increases the risk of dying of heart attack, stroke, heart failure, or kidney failure by threefold.
- *New Uses for an Old Drug:* A study of 10,000 heart and diabetes patients found that a standard high blood pressure drug, ramipril, can reduce the risk of death from a wide range of circulatory problems and may help prevent atherosclerosis.
- *New Clot Busters:* Experimental blood clot busters were shown to prevent brain damage and disability from stroke if given within three to six hours of the attack.
- *New Imaging Procedures:* New ultra-fast CT imaging and magnetic resonance angiography (MRA), which uses magnets and radio waves to view the inside of arteries, offer exciting new means of noninvasive diagnosis of artery blockage.
- *Robotic Surgery:* Preliminary studies on the use of robotics in bypass surgery provide hope for safer options. Operating through three small holes in the chest, robotic arms mimic the actions of a surgeon working the controls. The use of robotics provides greater steadiness, eliminates human error, and increases the potential for microsurgery. The method was tested on 15 people in 1999.

When these findings are coupled with new knowledge about diet,* exercise, and other intervention techniques, scientists are optimistic about even greater gains in reducing death rates from CVD in the years ahead.

STUDENTS SPEAK UP:

Do you think heart disease and stroke will ever be eliminated? Why do the above accomplishments provide people with such hope?

*Special Note: In June 1999, the Federal government released its first *Clinical Guidelines on the Identification, Evaluation, and Treatment of Overweight and Obesity in Adults.* Key recommendations from this report are that physicians should use three main measures in evaluating weight and risk: (1) body mass index (BMI), (2) the presence of risk factors for disease and conditions associated with obesity, and (3) waist circumference. For more details on this information, see the Heart Memo reference below and/or refer to the web site specified at the bottom of this page. *Source:* Heart Memo (1999), National Institutes of Health, National Heart, Lung, and Blood Institute.

Sources: Dr. Claude Lenfant and Dr. Phillip Gorden, "Diabetes Mellitus: A Major Risk Factor for Cardiovascular Disease," National Institutes of Health, National Heart, Lung, and Blood Institute, News Release, September 1, 1999; *Live Healthier, Live Longer* web site at http://rover.hnlbi.nih.chd; American Heart Association, "Gene Discoveries Among Top 10 Research Advances in Heart Disease and Stroke for 1999," *AHA News Release,* December 30, 1999.

awake but sedated during the procedure and spend only one or two days in the hospital after treatment. Most people can return to work within five days. In about 30 percent of all angioplasty patients, the treated arteries become clogged again within six months. Some patients may undergo the procedure as many as three times within a five-year period. Some surgeons argue that given angioplasty's high rate of recurrence, bypass may be a more effective method of treatment.

New research suggests that in many instances, drug treatments may be just as effective in prolonging life as the invasive surgical techniques, but it is critical that doctors follow an aggressive drug treatment program and that patients comply with the doctors' drug orders.[43]

Aspirin for Heart Disease

Research has indicated that the use of low-dose aspirin (325 milligrams daily or every other day) is beneficial to heart patients due to its blood-thinning properties. It has even been advised as a preventive strategy for individuals with no current heart disease symptoms. However, major problems associated with aspirin use are gastrointestinal intolerance and a tendency for some people to have difficulty with blood clotting, and these factors may outweigh its benefits in these cases. Although the findings concerning the overall benefits of using aspirin to treat or prevent heart disease are inconclusive, the research seems promising.[44]

Thrombolysis

Whenever a heart attack occurs, prompt action is the key factor in the patient's eventual prognosis. When a coronary artery gets blocked, the heart muscle doesn't die immediately, but time determines how much damage occurs. If a victim gets to an emergency room and is diagnosed fast enough, a form of reperfusion therapy called **thrombolysis** can sometimes be performed. Thrombolysis involves injecting an agent

---

Thrombolysis Injection of an agent to dissolve clots and restore some blood flow, thereby reducing the amount of tissue that dies from ischemia.

Cancer A large group of diseases characterized by the uncontrolled growth and spread of abnormal cells.

Neoplasm A new growth of tissue that serves no physiological function resulting from uncontrolled, abnormal cellular development.

Tumor A neoplasmic mass that grows more rapidly than surrounding tissue.

Malignant Very dangerous or harmful; refers to a cancerous tumor.

Benign Harmless; refers to a noncancerous tumor.

Biopsy Microscopic examination of tissue to determine if a cancer is present.

---

such as TPA (tissue plasminogen activator) to dissolve the clot and restore some blood flow, thereby reducing the amount of tissue that dies from ischemia.[45] These drugs must be used within one to three hours of a heart attack for best results.

• early prevention•
• right after a heart attack—3 hrs.—

AN OVERVIEW OF CANCER

During 1998, approximately 564,800 people died of cancer, a much-feared disease that is the second-leading cause of death in the United States. Put into perspective, this means that each day of the year more than 1,500 people die of one of the multiple types of cancer that affect humans. While cancer deaths pose an ominous threat, it is important to note that although more than 2.5 million people will be diagnosed with cancer in a year, and many will experience emotional and physical pain, nearly 4 in 10 will be alive 5 years after diagnosis. Many will be considered "cured," meaning that they have no subsequent cancer in their systems 5 years after diagnosis and can expect to live a long and productive life.[46]

When adjusted for normal life expectancy (factors such as dying of heart disease, accidents, etc.), a relative 5-year survival of 60 percent is seen for all cancers.[47] Some cancers that only a few decades ago presented a very poor outlook are often cured today: acute lymphocytic leukemia in children, Hodgkin's disease, Burkitt's lymphoma, Ewing's sarcoma (a form of bone cancer), Wilms' tumor (a kidney cancer in children), testicular cancer, and osteogenic (bone) sarcoma are among the most remarkable indicators of progress in treatment techniques.

What Is Cancer?

Cancer is the name given to a large group of diseases characterized by the uncontrolled growth and spread of abnormal cells. It may seem hard to understand how normal, healthy cells become cancerous, but if you think of a cell as a small computer, programmed to operate in a particular fashion, the process will become clearer. Under normal conditions, healthy cells are protected by a powerful overseer, the immune system, as they perform their daily functions of growing, replicating, and repairing body organs. When something interrupts normal cell programming, however, uncontrolled growth and abnormal cellular development results in a new growth of tissue serving no physiologic function called a **neoplasm.** This neoplasmic mass often forms a clumping of cells known as a **tumor.**

Not all tumors are **malignant** (cancerous); in fact, most are **benign** (noncancerous). Benign tumors are generally harmless unless they grow in such a fashion as to obstruct or crowd out normal tissues or organs. A benign tumor of the brain, for instance, is life-threatening when it grows in a manner that causes blood restriction and results in a stroke. The only way to determine whether a given tumor or mass is benign or malignant is through **biopsy,** or microscopic examination of cell development.

Benign and malignant tumors differ in several key ways. Benign tumors are generally composed of ordinary-looking cells enclosed in a fibrous shell or capsule that prevents their spreading to other body areas. Malignant tumors are usually not enclosed in a protective capsule and can therefore spread to other organs. This process, known as **metastasis,** makes some forms of cancer particularly aggressive in their ability to overcome bodily defenses. By the time they are diagnosed, malignant tumors have frequently metastasized throughout the body, making treatment extremely difficult. Unlike benign tumors, which merely expand to take over a given space, malignant cells invade surrounding tissue, emitting clawlike protrusions that disrupt chemical processes within healthy cells. More specifically, malignant cells disturb the ribonucleic acid (RNA) and deoxyribonucleic acid (DNA) within the normal cells. Tampering with these substances, which control cellular metabolism and reproduction, produces **mutant cells** that differ in form, quality, and function from normal cells.

fastest growing cancer - skin cancer

WHAT CAUSES CANCER?

Most research supports the idea that cancer is caused by both *external* (chemicals, radiation, and viruses) and *internal* (hormones, immune conditions, and inherited mutations) factors. Causal factors may act together or in sequence to initiate or promote cancer development.[48] We do not know why some people have malignant cells in their body but never develop cancer, while others may take 10 years or more to develop cancer, or not get it at all. Scientists have proposed several theories for the cellular changes that produce cancer.

One theory of cancer development proposes that cancer results from some spontaneous error that occurs during cell reproduction. Perhaps cells that are overworked or aged are more likely to break down, causing genetic errors that result in mutant cells.

Another theory suggests that cancer is caused by some external agent or agents that enter a normal cell and initiate the cancerous process. Numerous environmental factors, such as radiation, chemicals, hormonal drugs, immunosuppressant drugs (drugs that suppress the normal activity of the immune system), and other toxins, are considered possible **carcinogens** (cancer-causing agents); perhaps the most common carcinogen is the tar in cigarettes. This theory of environmental carcinogens obviously has profound implications for our industrialized society. As in most disease-related situations, the greater the dose or the exposure to environmental hazards, the greater the risk of disease. People who are forced to work, live, and pass through areas that have high levels of environmental toxins may, in fact, be at greater risk for several types of cancers.[49]

A third theory came out of research on certain viruses that are believed to cause tumors in animals. This research led to the discovery of **oncogenes,** suspected cancer-causing

genes that are present on chromosomes. Although oncogenes are typically dormant, scientists theorize that certain conditions such as age, stress, and exposure to carcinogens, viruses, and radiation may activate these oncogenes. Once activated, they begin to grow and reproduce in an out-of-control manner.

There is still a great deal that remains unanswered about the oncogene theory of cancer development. Scientists are uncertain whether only people who develop cancer have oncogenes or whether we all have **protooncogenes,** genes that can become oncogenes under certain conditions. Many **oncologists** (physicians who specialize in the treatment of malignancies) believe that the oncogene theory may lead to a greater understanding of how individual cells function and may bring us closer to developing an effective treatment for cancerous cells. Many factors are believed to contribute to cancer development. Experts believe that combining risk factors can dramatically increase a person's risk for cancer.

Lifestyle Factors

Over the years, an emerging pattern of higher risks for cancer among persons who engage (or do not engage) in selected lifestyle variables has captured national attention. In particular, diet, sedentary lifestyle, consumption of alcohol and cigarettes, stress, and other health-related behaviors have provided fertile ground for speculation about risks. Many of the studies supporting these purported risks show associations with lifestyle risks, but they have not been shown conclusively to be a causal role in cancer development.

Likewise, colon and rectal cancer appears to occur more frequently among persons with a high-fat, low-fiber diet; in those who don't eat enough fruits and vegetables; and in those who are inactive; yet we can't say that these behaviors actually will cause cancer. For now, there is compelling evidence that certain actions are clearly associated with a greater than average risk of developing diseases. In any of these situations, apparent increases in risk provide fertile ground for behavior modification.

Biological Factors

Some early cancer theorists believed that we inherit a genetic predisposition toward certain forms of cancer.[50] Recent research conducted by the University of Utah indicates that a gene for breast cancer exists. To date, however, the research in this area remains inconclusive. Although a rare form of eye cancer does appear to be passed genetically from mother to child, most cancers are not genetically linked. It is possible that we can inherit a tendency toward a cancer-prone, weak immune system or, conversely, that we can inherit a cancer-fighting potential. Both possibilities are considered rather remote at this time. But the complex interaction of hereditary predisposition, lifestyle, and environment on the development

• *when you add risk factors, chances multiply*

of cancer makes the likelihood of determining a single cause fairly remote.

Cancers of the breast, stomach, colon, prostate, uterus, ovaries, and lungs do appear to run in families. For example, a woman runs a much higher risk of having breast cancer if her mother or sisters (primary relatives) have had the disease, particularly if they had the disease at a young age. Hodgkin's disease and certain leukemias show similar familial patterns. Whether these familial patterns are attributable to genetic susceptibility or to the fact that people in the same families experience similar environmental risks remains uncertain.

Gender also affects the likelihood of developing certain forms of cancer. For example, breast cancer occurs primarily among females, although men do occasionally get breast cancer. Obviously, factors other than heredity and familial relationships affect which sex develops a particular cancer. In the 1950s and 1960s, for example, women rarely contracted lung cancer. But with increases in the number of women who smoked and the length of time they had smoked, lung cancer became the leading cause of cancer deaths for American women in the 1980s and continues to be the leading cause of cancer death in women. Lifestyle is clearly a critical factor in the interaction of variables that predispose a person toward cancer. Although gender plays a role in certain cases, other variables are probably more significant.

Occupational/Environmental Factors

Various occupational hazards are known to cause cancer when exposure levels are high or exposure is prolonged. Overall, however, workplace hazards account for only a small percentage of all cancers. One of the most common occupational carcinogens is asbestos, a fibrous substance once widely used in the construction, insulation, and automobile industries. Nickel, chromate, and chemicals such as benzene, arsenic, and vinyl chloride have definitively been shown to be carcinogens for humans. Also, people who routinely work with certain dyes and radioactive substances

Metastasis Process by which cancer spreads from one area to different areas of the body.

Mutant cells Cells that differ in form, quality, or function from normal cells.

Carcinogens Cancer-causing agents.

Oncogenes Suspected cancer-causing genes present on chromosomes.

Protooncogenes Genes that can become oncogenes under certain conditions.

Oncologists Physicians who specialize in the treatment of malignancies.

may have increased risks for cancer. Working with coal tars, as in the mining profession, or working near inhalants, as in the auto-painting business, is also hazardous. Those who work with herbicides and pesticides also appear to be at higher risk, although the evidence is inconclusive to date for low-dose exposures. Several federal and state agencies are responsible for monitoring such exposures and ensuring that businesses comply with standards designed to protect workers.

▶ *Radiation: Ionizing and Nonionizing* Ionizing radiation—radiation from X-rays, radon, cosmic rays, and ultraviolet radiation (primarily UVB radiation)—is the only form of radiation proven to cause human cancer. (See the section on skin cancer.) Some studies have shown that living near nuclear power plants increases risks. Others show that persons living in these areas have no greater risk than living elsewhere.[51,52]

Although nonionizing radiation produced by radio waves, cell phones, microwaves, computer screens, televisions, electric blankets, and other products has been a topic of great concern in recent years, research has not proven excess risk to date. Data supporting claims of such risk are inconclusive.[53]

Social and Psychological Factors

Many researchers claim that social and psychological factors play a major role in determining whether a person gets cancer. Stress has been implicated in increased susceptibility to several types of cancers. A number of therapists have established preventive treatment centers where the primary focus is on "being happy" and "thinking positive thoughts."

Although orthodox medical personnel are skeptical of overly simplistic cancer prevention centers that focus on humor and laughter, we cannot rule out the possibility that negative emotional states contribute to disease development. People who are under chronic, severe stress, who suffer from depression or other persistent emotional problems, appear to have a higher rate of cancer development than their healthy counterparts.

Although psychological factors may play a part in cancer development, exposure to substances such as tobacco and alcohol in our social environment are far more important. The American Cancer Society states that cigarette smoking is responsible for 30 percent of all cancer deaths—87 percent of all lung cancer deaths. Heavy consumption of alcohol has been related to cancers of the mouth, larynx, throat, esophagus, and liver. These cancers show up even more frequently in people whose heavy drinking is accompanied by smoking. The negative effects of smoking are not just concerns for the active smoker. Environmental (passive) tobacco smoke (ETS) causes an estimated 3,000 deaths from lung cancer, 40,000 deaths from heart disease, up

TABLE 12.2
Cancer Prevention and Diet

TYPE	DECREASES RISK	INCREASES RISK	PREVENTABLE BY DIET
Lung	Vegetables, fruits	Smoking; some occupations	33–50%
Stomach	Vegetables, fruits; food refrigeration	Salt; salted foods	66–75%
Breast	Vegetables, fruits	Obesity; alcohol	33–50%
Colon/rectum	Vegetables; physical activity	Meat; alcohol; smoking	66–75%
Mouth/throat	Vegetables, fruits; physical activity	Salted fish; alcohol; smoking	33–50%
Liver	Vegetables	Alcohol; contaminated food	33–66%
Cervix	Vegetables, fruits	Smoking	10–20%
Esophagus	Vegetables, fruits	Deficient diet; smoking; alcohol	50–75%
Prostate	Vegetables	Meat or meat fat; dairy fat	10–20%
Bladder	Vegetables, fruits	Smoking; coffee	10–20%

Sources: World Cancer Research Fund, American Institute for Cancer Research.

to 300,000 respiratory problems, and countless deaths among nonsmokers. Cancers of the mouth and throat pose significant risks for smokers.[54]

Chemicals in Foods

Among the food additives suspected of causing cancer is sodium nitrate, a chemical used to preserve and give color to red meat. Research indicates that the actual carcinogen is not sodium nitrate but nitrosamines, substances formed when the body digests the sodium nitrates. Sodium nitrate has not been banned, primarily because it kills the bacterium botulism, which is the cause of the highly virulent food-borne disease known as botulism. It should also be noted that the bacteria found in the human intestinal tract may contain more nitrates than a person could ever take in from eating cured meats or other nitrate-containing food products. Nonetheless, concern about the carcinogenic properties of nitrates has led to the introduction of meats that are nitrate-free or that contain reduced levels of the substance.

Much of the concern about chemicals in foods today centers on the possible harm caused by pesticide and herbicide residue left on foods by agricultural practices. While some of these chemicals cause cancer at high doses in experimental animals, the very low concentrations found in some foods are well within established government safety levels. Continued research regarding pesticide and herbicide use is essential for maximum food safety and the continuous monitoring of agricultural practices is necessary to ensure a safe food supply.

FDA–food regulation

Viral Factors

The chances of becoming infected with a "cancer virus" are very remote. Over the years, several forms of virus-induced cancers have been observed in laboratory animals and there is some indication that human beings display a similar tendency toward virally transmitted cancers. Evidence that the herpes-related viruses may be involved in the development of some forms of leukemia, Hodgkin's disease, cervical cancer, and Burkitt's lymphoma has surfaced in recent years. The Epstein-Barr virus, associated with mononucleosis, may also contribute to cancer development. Cervical cancer has also been linked to the human papillomavirus, the virus that causes genital warts.[55]

Although research is inconclusive, many scientists believe that selected viruses may help to provide an *opportunistic* environment for subsequent cancer development. It is likely that a combination of immunological bombardment by viral or chemical invaders and other risk factors substantially increases the risk of cancer.

Medical Factors

In some cases, medical treatment increases a person's risk for cancer. One famous example is the widespread use of the prescription drug diethylstilbestrol (DES) during the years 1940 to 1960 to control problems with bleeding during pregnancy and to reduce the risk of miscarriage. It was not until the 1970s that the dangers of this drug became apparent. Although DES caused few side effects in the millions of women who took it, their daughters were found to have an increased risk for cancers of the reproductive organs.

Some scientists claim that the use of estrogen replacement therapy among postmenopausal women is dangerous because it increases the risks for uterine cancer. Others believe that because estrogen is critical to the prevention of osteoporosis and heart disease in aging women, its use should not be curtailed.

How do we determine whether a given factor is a "risk factor" for a disease? Although we have never shown a causal relationship between lung cancer and smoking, the evidence supporting such a relationship is strong. Must we have a "causal" link clearly established before we begin to warn consumers about risk? Can you think of apparent dietary risks for cancer that appeared to be conclusive but have since been refuted? How does the consumer know who or what to believe?

TYPES OF CANCERS

As we said earlier, the term *cancer* refers not to a single disease but to hundreds of different diseases. However, four broad classifications of cancer are made according to the type of tissue from which the cancer arises. *5yr. 40% survival rate*

Classifications of Cancer

▶ **Carcinomas** Epithelial tissues (tissues covering body surfaces and lining most body cavities) are the most common sites for cancers. Carcinoma of the breast, lung, intestines, skin, and mouth are examples. These cancers affect the outer layer of the skin and mouth as well as the mucous membranes. They metastasize through the circulatory or lymphatic system initially and form solid tumors.

▶ **Sarcomas** Sarcomas occur in the mesodermal, or middle, layers of tissue—for example, in bones, muscles, and general connective tissue. They metastasize primarily via the blood in the early stages of disease. These cancers are less common but generally more virulent than carcinomas. They also form solid tumors.

▶ **Lymphomas** Lymphomas develop in the lymphatic system—the infection-fighting regions of the body—and metastasize through the lymph system. Hodgkin's disease is one type of lymphoma. Lymphomas also form solid tumors.

▶ **Leukemia** Cancer of the blood-forming parts of the body, particularly the bone marrow and spleen, is called leukemia. A nonsolid tumor, leukemia is characterized by an abnormal increase in the number of white blood cells.

The seriousness and general prognosis of a particular cancer are determined through careful diagnosis by trained oncologists. Once laboratory results and clinical observations have been made, cancers are rated by level and stage of development. Those diagnosed as "carcinoma in situ" are localized and are often curable. Cancers that are given higher level or stage ratings have spread farther and are less likely to be cured. Figure 12.4 shows the most common sites of cancer and the number of deaths annually from each type of cancer.

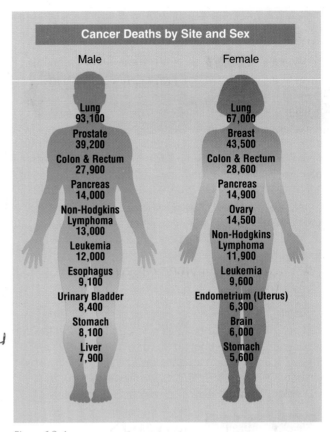

Cancer Deaths by Site and Sex

Male	Female
Lung 93,100	Lung 67,000
Prostate 39,200	Breast 43,500
Colon & Rectum 27,900	Colon & Rectum 28,600
Pancreas 14,000	Pancreas 14,900
Non-Hodgkins Lymphoma 13,000	Ovary 14,500
Leukemia 12,000	Non-Hodgkins Lymphoma 11,900
Esophagus 9,100	Leukemia 9,600
Urinary Bladder 8,400	Endometrium (Uterus) 6,300
Stomach 8,100	Brain 6,000
Liver 7,900	Stomach 5,600

Figure 12.4

Leading Sites of New Cancer Cases and Deaths—1998 Estimates

Source: Reprinted by permission of the American Cancer Society, Inc., from *Cancer Facts and Figures 1998*.

Lung Cancer

Although lung cancer rates have dropped among white males during the last decade, the incidence among white females (particularly young teens) and black males and females continues to rise. Lung cancer caused an estimated 160,100 deaths in 1998. In 1987, for the first time, more women died from lung cancer than from breast cancer, which for over 40 years had been the major cause of cancer deaths in women. Today, lung cancer continues to be the leading cancer killer for both men and women.[56]

Symptoms of lung cancer include a persistent cough, blood-streaked sputum, chest pain, and recurrent attacks of pneumonia or bronchitis. Treatment depends on the type and stage of the cancer. Surgery, radiation therapy, and chemotherapy are all treatment options. If the cancer is localized, surgery is usually the treatment of choice. If the cancer has spread, surgery is used in combination with radiation and chemotherapy. Unfortunately, despite advances in medical technology, survival rates for lung cancer have improved only slightly over the past decade. Just 13 percent of lung cancer patients live five or more years after diagnosis. These rates improve to 47 percent with early detection, but only

15 percent of lung cancers are discovered in their early stages of development.[57]

▶ **Prevention** Smokers, especially those who have smoked for over 20 years, and people who have been exposed to certain industrial substances such as arsenic and asbestos or to radiation from occupational, medical, or environmental sources are at the highest risk for lung cancer. The American Cancer Society estimated that in 1998, 175,000 cancer deaths were caused by tobacco use and an additional 19,000 cancer deaths were related to alcohol use, frequently in combination with tobacco use.[58] Exposure to sidestream cigarette smoke, known as *environmental tobacco smoke* or ETS, increases the risk for nonsmokers. Some researchers have theorized that as many as 90 percent of all lung cancers could be avoided if people did not smoke.

#1 preventable cancer

Breast Cancer

About 1 out of 8 women will develop breast cancer at some time in her life. Although this oft-repeated ratio has frightened many women, it represents a woman's lifetime risk. Thus, not until the age of 80 does a woman's risk of breast cancer rise to 1 in 8.[59] Here is the risk at earlier ages:

Birth to 39: 1 in 227
40–59: 1 in 25
60–79: 1 in 15
Birth to death: 1 in 8

increases w/ age

In 1998, approximately 178,700 women in the United States were diagnosed with breast cancer for the first time. About 1,600 new cases of breast cancer were diagnosed in men in 1998. About 43,900 women (and 400 men) will die, making breast cancer the second leading cause of cancer death for women.[60] According to the most recent data, mortality rates are falling in white women but not in black. The decline in whites rates may be due to earlier diagnosis and improved treatment as numerous studies have shown that early detection increases survival and treatment options.

Warning signals of breast cancer include persistent breast changes such as a lump, thickening, swelling, dimpling, skin irritation, distortion, retraction or scaliness of the nipple, nipple discharge, pain, or tenderness. Risk factors for breast cancer may vary considerably.[61] Typically, risk factors include being over the age of 40, having a primary relative (a grandmother, mother, or sister) who had breast cancer, never having had children or having breast-fed, having your first child after age 30, having had early menarche, having had a late age of menopause, lengthy exposure to cyclic estrogen, and having a higher education and socioeconomic status. International variability in breast cancer incidence rates correlate with differences in diet, with more affluent societies having significantly higher cancer rates. However, it is important to note that a causal role for dietary factors has not been firmly established.[62,63]

Although risk factors are useful tools, they do not always adequately predict individual susceptibility. However, because of increased awareness, better diagnostic techniques, and improved treatments, breast cancer victims have a better chance of surviving today than they did in the past. The five-year survival rate for victims of localized breast cancer (which includes all women living five years after diagnosis, whether the patient is in remission, disease-free, or under treatment) has risen from 72 percent in the 1940s to 97 percent today. These statistics vary dramatically, however, based on when the cancer is first detected. Survival after a diagnosis of breast cancer continues to decline beyond 5 years. Sixty-seven percent of women diagnosed with breast cancer survive 10 years, and 56 percent survive 15 years.[64]

▶ **Prevention** A recent study of the role of exercise in reducing the risk for breast cancer has generated excitement in the scientific community. The study, involving 1,090 women who were 40 or younger (545 with breast cancer and 545 without) analyzed subjects' exercise patterns since they began menstruating. The risk of those who averaged four hours of exercise a week since menstruation was 58 percent lower than that of women who did no exercise at all. The good news was that subjects did not have to be avid joggers to have reduced risk. Among the activities reported were team sports, individual sports, dance, exercise classes, swimming, walking, and a variety of other activities. Researchers speculated that exercise may protect women by altering the production of the ovarian hormones estrogen and progesterone during menstrual cycles.[65]

Regular self-examination (see Figure 12.5) and mammography offer the best hope for early detection of breast cancer. Recommendations for when a woman should obtain her first baseline mammogram are included in the American Cancer Society guidelines. It is important to note that there is tremendous controversy over the cost effectiveness and usefulness of getting a mammogram before the age of 40. In addition, the American Cancer Society and National Cancer Institute waged a controversial debate in 1997 over the appropriate recommendations for women in their 40s, with the ACS recommending mammograms every one to two years and the NCI against the recommendation. Eventually, after much public debate and review of results of recent studies, both the ACS and NCI agreed on the more frequent mammograms and its merits in early detection. Many health professionals recommend that if you have any of the risk factors listed above, are prone to fibrous breasts, and are excessively worried about your own condition, a mammogram may be warranted.

International differences in breast cancer incidence seem to correlate with variations in diet, especially fat intake, although a causal role for these dietary factors has not been firmly established. Sudden weight gain has also been implicated in increased risk. Exciting new research about the BRCA1 and BRCA2 susceptibility genes for breast cancer is also in progress, although screening in the general population for these genes is not yet recommended.

How to Examine Your Breasts

Do you know that 95% of breast cancers are discovered first by women themselves? And that the earlier the breast cancer is detected, the better the chance for a complete cure? Of course, most lumps or changes are not cancer. But you can safeguard your health by making a habit of examining your breasts once a month – a day or two after your period or, if you're no longer menstruating, on any given day. And if you notice anything changed or unusual – a lump, thickening, or discharge – contact your doctor right away.

How to Look for Changes

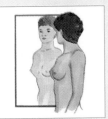

Step 1
Sit or stand in front of a mirror with your arms at your side. Turning slowly from side to side, check your breasts for
• changes in size or shape
• puckering or dimpling of the skin
• changes in size or position of one nipple compared to the other

Step 2
Raise your arms above your head and repeat the examination in Step 1.

Step 3
Gently press each nipple with your fingertips to see if there is any discharge.

How to Feel for Changes

Step 1
Lie down and put a pillow or folded bath towel under your left shoulder. Then place your left hand under your head. (From now on you will be feeling for a lump or thickening in your breasts.)

Step 2
Imagine that your breast is divided into quarters.

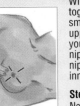

Step 3
With the fingers of your right hand held together, press firmly but gently, using small circular motions to feel the inner, upper quarter of your left breast. Start at your breastbone and work toward the nipple. Also examine the area around the nipple. Now do the same for the lower, inner portion of your breast.

Step 4
Next, bring your arm to your side and feel under your left armpit for swelling.

Step 5
With your arm still down, feel the upper, outer part of your breast, starting with your nipple and working outwards. Examine the lower, outer quarter in the same way.

Step 6
Now place the pillow under your right shoulder and repeat all the steps using your left hand to examine your right breast.

▶ *Treatment*   Today, women with breast cancer (and people with nearly any other type of cancer) have many decisions to make in determining the best treatment options available for them. Fortunately, there are services available to help you get the best information, even if you live in a fairly remote area of the country. The important thing to remember is that in most instances, taking the time to thoroughly check out your physician's track record and his or her philosophy on the best treatment is always a good idea. Is his or her treatment recommendation consistent with that of the major cancer centers in the country? Check out the doctors' credentials and the past experiences of patients who have seen this doctor and the surgeon who will perform your biopsy and other surgical techniques. If possible, seek a facility that has a significant number of breast cancer patients, does many surgeries, is regarded as a "teaching facility" for new oncologists, treats large numbers of patients, has the "latest and greatest" in terms of technology, and is highly regarded by past patients. Often, cancer support groups can give you invaluable information and advice. Treatments range from the simple lumpectomy to radical mastectomy to various combinations of radiation or chemotherapy. Figure 12.6 on page 306 reviews these options. Remember that it is always a good idea to seek more than one opinion before making a decision.

········ WHAT DO YOU THINK?

Why do you think there is such a big difference between mammography screening rates for varied ethnic groups? What actions could be taken to change such disparities? Why do you think so many women fail to be tested for breast cancer? Do you think men are better at seeking recommended screenings for cancers? Why or why not?

Colon and Rectum Cancers

Although colon and rectum cancers are the third leading cause of cancer deaths, with an estimated 47,700 deaths from colon cancer and 8,800 deaths from rectal cancer in 1998, many people are unaware of their potential risk. Bleeding from the rectum, blood in the stool, and changes in bowel habits are the major warning signals. People who are over the age of 40, who are obese, who have a family history of colon and rectum cancer, a personal or family history of polyps (benign growths) in the colon or rectum, or inflammatory bowel problems such as colitis run an increased risk. Diets high in fats or low in fiber may also increase risk, although

Figure 12.5

The illustration demonstrates breast self-examination—the 10-minute habit that could save your life.

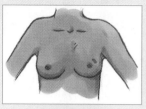

Lumpectomy
Performed when tumor is in earliest localized stages. Prognosis for recovery is better than 95 percent. Only tumor itself is removed. Some physicians may also remove normal tissue in surrounding area.

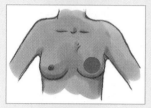

Simple mastectomy
Removal of breast and underlying tissue. Prognosis for full recovery better than 80 percent.

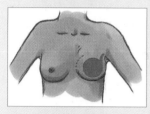

Modified radical mastectomy
Breast and lymph nodes in immediate area removed. Prognosis for full recovery dependent on level of spread.

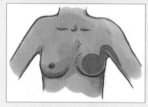

Radical mastectomy
Removal of breast, lymph nodes, pectoral muscles, all fat and underlying tissue. Prognosis for recovery may be as low as 60 percent dependent on level of spread.

Figure 12.6

The illustration depicts selected surgical procedures for diagnosed breast cancer. These surgeries are typically followed by radiation treatment and/or chemotherapy.

recent studies have raised serious questions about whether a high-fiber diet makes any difference in cancer reduction.[66]

Because colorectal cancer tends to spread slowly, the prognosis is quite good if it is caught in the early stages. Treatment often consists of radiation or surgery. Chemotherapy, although not used extensively in the past, is today a possibility. A permanent *colostomy,* the creation of an abdominal opening for the elimination of body wastes, is seldom required for people with colon cancer and even less frequently for those with rectum cancer.

Prostate Cancer *2nd leading cause in men*

Cancer of the prostate is the most common type of cancer in males today, after skin cancer. In 1998, 184,500 new cases of prostate cancer were diagnosed, and from these, about 39,200 men will die. Prostate cancer is the second leading cause of cancer death. Most signs and symptoms of prostate cancer are nonspecific—that is, they mimic the signs of infection or enlarged prostate. Symptoms include weak or inter-

rupted urine flow or difficulty starting or stopping the urine flow; the need to urinate frequently; pain or difficulty in urinating; blood in the urine; and pain in the lower back, pelvis, or upper thighs. Many males mistake these symptoms for other nonspecific conditions such as infections and delay treatment.

Fortunately, even with so many generalized symptoms, most prostate cancers are detected while they are still localized and tend to progress slowly. Because most men detect cancer in their late 60s and early 70s, it is likely that they will die of other causes before prostate cancer leads to their deaths. For this reason, health-care groups are beginning to question the cost-effectiveness and necessity of prostate surgeries and other costly procedures that may have little real effect on life expectancy. Prostate patients have an average five-year survival rate of 80 percent. Because the incidence of prostate cancer increases with age, every man over the age of 40 should have an annual prostate examination. In addition, the American Cancer Society recommends that men aged 50 and older have an annual prostate-specific antigen (PSA) test.

Skin Cancer: Sun Bathers Beware
- fastest growing -

The sun is the primary cause of nearly 1 million cases of skin cancer in the United States this year. In fact, skin cancer is the most common cancer in the United States today, accounting for nearly 2 percent of all cancer deaths.[67] While most people don't die from the highly treatable *basal* or *squamous cell* skin cancers, the highly virulent **malignant melanoma** has become the most frequent cancer in women ages 25 to 29 and runs second only to breast cancer in women ages 30 to 34.

In spite of these grisly statistics, over 60 percent of all Americans 25 years and under report that they are "working on a tan" at some point during the year. In spite of this love of the sun, fewer than 1 in 3 sunbathers bother to wear UVB-thwarting lotions.

Basal and squamous cell carcinomas can be a recurrent annoyance, showing up most commonly on the face, ears, neck, arms, hands, and legs as warty bumps, colored spots, or scaly patches. In the most serious cases, surgery is often required to remove these moles, but they are seldom life threatening. In striking contrast is the insidious melanoma, an invasive killer that quickly spreads to regional organs and potentially throughout the body, accounting for over 75 percent of all skin cancer deaths. Risks increase dramatically among whites after age 20.[68] In 1998, about 41,600 Americans will develop melanoma and 7,300 will die.[69] Often, these moles start as normal-looking growths, but quickly become asymmetrical in shape, developing an uneven, scalloped, or notched border. They may vary in color from tan to deeper brown, to reddish black, black, or deep bluish, and they may or may not bleed if bumped. Typically, they are about the size of a pencil eraser; however, sizes may vary dramatically. Most important, they spread so quickly that by the time a person has them checked, they are often difficult, if not impossible, to treat. A simple *ABCD* rule outlines the warning

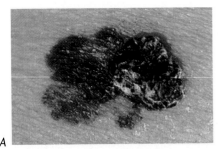
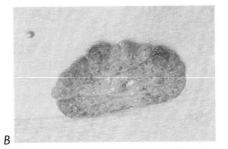
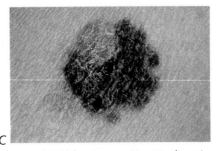

A   B   C

Prevention of skin cancer includes keeping a careful watch for any new pigmented growths and for changes to any moles. Melanoma symptoms, as shown in photos A and C, include scalloped edges, asymmetrical shapes, discoloration, and an increase in size.

signals of melanoma: *A* is for asymmetry. One half of the mole does not match the other half. *B* is for border irregularity. The edges are ragged, notched, or blurred. *C* is for color. The pigmentation is not uniform. *D* is for diameter greater than 6 millimeters. Any or all of these symptoms should cause you to visit a physician.

Treatment of skin cancer depends on the seriousness of the condition. Surgery is used in 90 percent of all cases. Radiation therapy, *electrodesiccation* (tissue destruction by heat), and *cryosurgery* (tissue destruction by freezing) are also common forms of treatment. For melanoma, treatment may involve surgical removal of the regional lymph nodes, radiation, or chemotherapy.

Testicular Cancer

Testicular cancer is currently one of the most common types of solid tumors found in males entering early adulthood. Those between the ages of 17 and 34 are at greatest risk. There has been a steady increase in tumor frequency over the past several years in this age group.[70]

Although the exact cause of testicular cancer is unknown, several possible risk factors have been identified. Males with undescended testicles appear to be at greatest risk for the disease. In addition, some studies indicate that there may be a genetic influence.

In general, testicular tumors are first noticed as a painless enlargement of the testis or as an apparent thickening in testicular tissue. Because this enlargement is often painless, it is extremely important that all young males practice regular testicular self-examination. This is done by placing the index and middle fingers of both hands on the underside of the testicle and the thumbs on top. Gently roll the testicle between your thumb and fingers. If a suspicious lump or thickening is found, medical follow-up should be sought immediately. It is best to perform an exam after a bath or

shower, as the heat causes the testicles to descend and the scrotal skin to relax.

Ovarian Cancer   age 40 - ↑

Ovarian cancer is the fourth leading cause of cancer death for women, killing nearly 15,000 in 1998. Because its symptoms are often nonspecific (vague feelings of stomach bloating, digestive irregularities, unusual amounts of gas or stomachaches), it often goes undiagnosed in its early stages. The most common sign is enlargement of the abdomen (or a feeling of bloating) in women over the age of 40. Other symptoms include vague digestive disturbances, such as gas and stomach aches that persist and cannot be explained.[71]

The risk for ovarian cancer increases with age, with the highest rates found in women in their 60s. Women who have never had children are twice as likely to develop ovarian cancer as are those who have. This is because the main risk factor appears to be exposure to the reproductive hormone estrogen. Women who have multiple pregnancies or use oral contraceptives, both of which inhibit estrogen, are at lower risk. In addition, having one or more primary relatives (mother, sisters, grandmothers) who have had the disease appears to increase individual risk.

▶ *Prevention*   A pivotal Yale University study indicated that diet may also play a role in ovarian cancer.[72] Researchers found that when comparing 450 Canadian women with newly diagnosed ovarian cancer with 564 demographically similar, healthy women, the women without ovarian cancer had a diet lower in saturated fat. Such results, particularly when combined with cardiovascular risks and other health risks, may provide yet another reason to hold the fat—or at least cut down on your overall intake. increase fiber

To protect yourself, annual thorough pelvic examinations are important. Pap tests, although useful in detecting cervical cancer, do not reveal ovarian cancer. Women over the age of 40 should have a cancer-related checkup every year. Transvaginal ultrasound and a tumor marker, CA125, may assist in diagnosis but are not recommended for routine screening.[73] If you have any of the symptoms of ovarian cancer and they persist, see your doctor. If they continue to persist, get a second opinion.

Malignant melanoma   A virulent cancer of the melanin (pigment-producing portion) of the skin.

Endometrium (Uterine) Cancer

In 1998, an estimated 36,100 new cases of uterine cancer were diagnosed in the United States. Most uterine cancers develop in the body of the uterus, usually in the endometrium (lining). The rest develop in the cervix, located at the base of the uterus. The overall incidence of early-stage uterine cancer—that is, cervical cancer—has increased slightly in recent years in women under the age of 50.[74] In contrast, invasive, later-stage forms of the disease appear to be decreasing. Much of this apparent trend may be due to more effective regular screenings of younger women using the Pap test, a procedure in which cells taken from the cervical region are examined for abnormal cellular activity. Although these tests are very effective for detecting early-stage cervical cancer, they are less effective for detecting cancers of the uterine lining and are not effective at all for detecting cancers of the fallopian tubes or ovaries.[75]

Risk factors for cervical cancer include early age of first intercourse, multiple sex partners, cigarette smoking, and certain sexually transmitted diseases, such as the herpes virus and the human papillomavirus. For endometrial cancer, a history of infertility, failure to ovulate, obesity, and treatment with tamoxifen or unopposed estrogen therapy appear to be major risk factors.[76]

Early warning signs of uterine cancer include bleeding outside the normal menstrual period or after menopause or persistent unusual vaginal discharge. These symptoms should be checked by a physician immediately.[77]

Leukemia

Leukemia is a cancer of the blood-forming tissues that leads to proliferation of millions of immature white blood cells. These abnormal cells crowd out normal white blood cells (which fight infection), platelets (which control hemorrhaging), and red blood cells (which prevent anemia). As a result, symptoms such as fatigue, paleness, weight loss, easy bruising, repeated infections, nosebleeds, and other forms of hemorrhaging occur. In children, these symptoms can appear suddenly.[78]

Leukemia can be acute or chronic in nature and can strike both sexes and all age groups. Chronic leukemia can develop over several months and have few symptoms. Although many people believe that leukemia is a childhood disease, leukemia struck many more adults (26,500) than children (2,200) in 1998.[79] The 5-year survival rate for patients with leukemia is 38 percent, due partly to very poor survival for patients with some types of leukemia. Over the last 30 years, however, there has been a dramatic improvement in survival of patients with acute lymphocytic leukemia—from a five-year survival rate of 4 percent for people diagnosed in the early 1960s to 28 percent in the early 1970s to 52 percent in the mid-1980s. In children, the improvement has been from 4 percent to 80 percent.[80]

FACING CANCER

While heart disease mortality rates have declined steadily over the past 50 years, cancer mortality rates have increased consistently in the same period. Based on current rates, about 83 million—or one in three of us now living—will eventually develop cancer. Many factors have contributed to the rise in cancer mortality, but the increase in the incidence of lung cancer is probably the most important reason. Despite these gloomy predictions, recent advancements in the diagnosis and treatment of many forms of cancer have reduced much of the fear and mystery that once surrounded this disease.

Detecting Cancer

The earlier a person is diagnosed as having cancer, the better the prospect for survival. Various high-tech diagnostic techniques exist to detect cancer, including the following:

- New high-technology diagnostic imaging techniques have replaced exploratory surgery for some cancer patients. Magnetic resonance imaging (MRI) is one example of such technology. In MRI, a huge electromagnet is used to detect hidden tumors by mapping the vibrations of the various atoms in the body on a computer screen. Com-

Pap test A procedure in which cells taken from the cervical region are examined for abnormal cellular activity.

Magnetic resonance imaging (MRI) A device that uses magnetic fields, radio waves, and computers to generate an image of internal tissues of the body for diagnostic purposes without the use of radiation.

Computerized axial tomography (CAT scan) A machine that uses radiation to view internal organs not normally visible on X-rays.

Prostate-specific antigen (PSA) An antigen found in prostate cancer patients.

Radiotherapy The use of radiation to kill cancerous cells.

Chemotherapy The use of drugs to kill cancerous cells.

puterized axial tomography scanning (CAT scan) uses X-rays to examine parts of the body. In both of these painless, noninvasive procedures, cross-section pictures can show a tumor's shape and location more accurately than can conventional X-rays.

- *Prostatic ultrasound* (a rectal probe using ultrasonic waves to produce an image of the prostate) is currently being investigated as a potential means to increase the early detection of prostate cancer. Recently, prostatic ultrasound has been combined with a blood test for **prostate-specific antigen (PSA)**, an antigen found in prostate cancer patients. Although the reliability of PSA tests for screening has been questioned, it appears to show promise.

Such medical techniques, along with regular self-examinations and checkups, play an important role in the early detection and secondary prevention of cancer.

Regardless of insurance status, individuals must be actively involved in their own cancer detection. Figure 12.7 shows the Seven Warning Signals of cancer. If you notice any of these signals, and they don't appear to be related to anything else, you should see a doctor immediately. For example, difficulty swallowing may be due to a cold or flu. But if you are otherwise symptomless and the difficulty continues, you should see a doctor. Refer to Table 12.3 on page 310 for the American Cancer Society's recommendations for early detection of cancer.

New Hope in Cancer Treatments

Although cancer treatments have changed dramatically over the last 20 years, surgery, in which the tumor and sur-

Increased awareness about cancer has resulted in positive strides toward a cure, but the fight is far from over.

rounding tissue are removed, is still common. Today's surgeons tend to remove less surrounding tissue than previously and to combine surgery with either **radiotherapy** (the use of radiation) or **chemotherapy** (the use of drugs) to kill cancerous cells.

Radiation works by destroying malignant cells or stopping cell growth. It is most effective in treating localized cancer masses. Unfortunately, in the process of destroying malignant cells, radiotherapy also destroys some healthy cells. In addition, in recent years, many scientists have come to suspect that radiotherapy may increase the risks for other types of cancers. Despite these qualifications, radiation continues to be one of the most common and effective forms of treatment.

When cancer has spread throughout the body, it is necessary to use some form of chemotherapy. Currently, over 50 different anticancer drugs are in use, some of which have excellent records of success. A chemotherapeutic regimen including four anticancer drugs in combination with radiation therapy has resulted in remarkable survival rates for some cancers, including Hodgkin's disease. Ongoing research into new drug development will result in compounds that are less toxic to normal cells and more potent against tumor cells. Current research indicates that some tumors may actually be resistant to certain forms of chemotherapy and that the treatment drugs do not reach the core of the tumor. Scientists are currently working to circumvent resistance to chemotherapeutic drugs and to make tumor cells more vulnerable throughout treatment.

Cancer's Seven Warning Signals

1 Changes in bowel or bladder habits.

2 A sore that does not heal.

3 Unusual bleeding or discharge.

4 Thickening or lump in breast or elsewhere.

5 Indigestion or difficulty in swallowing.

6 Obvious change in a wart or mole.

7 Nagging cough or hoarseness.

If you have a warning signal, see your doctor.

Figure 12.7
Cancer's Seven Warning Signals

TABLE 12.3

Summary of American Cancer Society Recommendations for the Early Detection of Cancer in Asymptomatic People

SITE	RECOMMENDATION
Cancer-related checkup	A cancer-related checkup every 3 years for people aged 20–40 and every year for people age 40 and older. This exam should include health counseling and, depending on a person's age, might include examination for cancers of the thyroid, oral cavity, skin, lymph nodes, testes, and ovaries, as well as for some nonmalignant diseases.
Breast	Women 40 and older should have an annual mammogram, an annual clinical breast exam (CBE) performed by a health-care professional, and should perform monthly breast self-examination. The CBE should be conducted close to the scheduled mammogram. Women ages 20–39 should have a clinical breast exam performed by a health-care professional every 3 years and should perform monthly breast self-examination.
Colon and rectum	Men and women aged 50 and older should follow *one* of the examination schedules below: • A fecal occult blood test every year and a flexible sigmoidoscopy every 5 years.* • A colonoscopy every 10 years.* • A double-contrast barium enema every 5 to 10 years.* *A digital rectal exam should be done at the same time as a sigmoidoscopy, colonoscopy, or double-contrast barium enema. People who are at moderate or high risk for colorectal cancer should talk with a doctor about a different testing schedule.
Prostate	Both the prostate-specific antigen (PSA) blood test and the digital rectal examination should be offered annually, beginning at age 50, to men who have a life expectancy of at least 10 years and to younger men who are at high risk. Men in high-risk groups, such as those with a strong familial predisposition (e.g., two or more affected first-degree relatives), or African Americans may begin at a younger age (e.g., 45 years).
Uterus	**Cervix:** All women who are or have been sexually active or who are 18 and older should have an annual Pap test and pelvic examination. After three or more consecutive satisfactory examinations with normal findings, the Pap test may be performed less frequently. Discuss the matter with your physician. **Endometrium:** Women at high risk for cancer of the uterus should have a sample of endometrial tissue examined when menopause begins.

Source: American Cancer Society, Cancer Facts and Figures 1998.

Whether used alone or in combination, radiotherapy and chemotherapy have possible side effects, including extreme nausea, nutritional deficiencies, hair loss, and general fatigue. Long-term damage to the cardiovascular system and many other systems of the body can be significant. It is important that you discuss these matters fully with your doctors. The Skills for Behavior Change box offers advice on how to talk to your doctor about your cancer.

Among the most promising new treatments are:[81]

• An estrogen-blocking drug called *tamoxifen* is used to treat women who have breast cancer that is estrogen positive, or grows more rapidly when estrogen levels are high. This drug is often an alternative to chemotherapy for many women with breast cancer.

• **Immunotherapy** is a new technique designed to enhance the body's own disease-fighting systems to help control cancer.

• Research on the effectiveness of *gene therapy* has moved into early clinical trials. Scientists have found hopeful signs of a virus carrying genetic information that makes the cells it infects susceptible to an antiviral drug.

• Researchers are testing compounds that may have the ability to inhibit tumors from forming new blood vessels, a process known as *angiogenesis*.

Immunotherapy A process that stimulates the body's own immune system to combat cancer cells.

Talking with Your Doctor about Cancer

Anytime there is the suspicion of cancer, the person involved is likely to react with great anxiety, fear, and anger. Emotional distress is sometimes so intense that the person involved is unable to serve as his or her own best advocate in making critical health-care decisions. If you find it difficult to know what to ask your doctor on a routine exam, imagine how hard it would be to discuss life or death options for yourself or a loved one. Having a list of important questions to ask when you appear at the doctor's office may help tremendously. By actively challenging, questioning, and letting the physician know your wishes, difficult decisions may become easier.

You may want answers to the following questions:

- What kind of cancer do I have? What stage is it in? Based on my age and stage, what type of prognosis do I have?
- What are my treatment choices? Which do you recommend? Why?
- What are the expected benefits of each kind of treatment?
- What are the long- and short-term risks and possible side effects?
- Would a clinical trial be appropriate for me? (Clinical trials are research studies designed to answer specific questions and to find better ways to prevent or treat cancer. Often new cancer-fighting treatments are used.)

If surgery is recommended, you may want to ask these questions:

- What kind of operation will it be and how long will it take? What form of anesthesia will be used? How many similar procedures has this surgeon done in the last month? What is his or her success rate?
- How will I feel after surgery? If I have pain, how will you help me?
- Where will the scars be? What will they look like? Will they cause disability?

- Will I have any activity limitations after surgery? What kind of physical therapy, if any, will I have? When will I get back to normal activities?

If radiation is recommended, you may want to ask these questions:

- Why do you think this treatment is better than my other options?
- How long will I need to have treatments and what will the side effects be in the short and long term? What body organs/systems may be damaged?
- What can I do to take care of myself during therapy? Are there services available to help me?
- What is the long-term prognosis for people my age with my type of cancer using this treatment?

If chemotherapy is recommended, you may want to ask these questions:

- Why do you think this treatment is better than my other options?
- Which drug combinations pose the least risks and most benefits?
- What are the short- and long-term side effects on my body?
- What are my options?

- Scientists have identified various steps in what is termed the *cancer pathway*. These include oncogene actions, hormone receptors, growth factors, metastasis, and angiogenesis. Preliminary studies are underway to "design" compounds (*rational drug design*) aimed at specific molecules along the cancer pathway with the intent of inhibiting actions at these various steps.
- Cell mutations can cause increased production of destructive enzymes that allow them to invade surrounding tissues and penetrate blood vessels to travel to other parts of the body.
- *Neoadjuvant chemotherapy* (giving chemotherapy to shrink the cancer and then removing it surgically) has been tried against various types of cancers. This is a promising new treatment approach.

In addition, psychosocial and behavioral research has become increasingly important as health professionals seek the answers to questions concerning complex life-style factors that appear to influence risks for cancer as well as the survivability of patients with particular psychological and mental health profiles. Also, health-care practitioners have become more aware of the psychological needs of patients and families and have begun to tailor treatment programs to meet the diverse needs of different people.

Life After Cancer

Heightened public awareness and an improved prognosis for cancer victims have made the cancer experience less threatening and isolating than it once was.

Assistance for the cancer patient is more readily available than ever before. Cancer support groups, cancer information workshops, and low-cost medical consultation are just a few of the forms of assistance now offered in many communities. Increasing efforts in cancer research, improvements in diagnostic equipment, and advances in treatment provide hope for the future.

Taking Charge
Managing Your Health

As students in college, you may feel invincible, with threats of cancer and cardiovascular disease seeming to be an unnecessary and unwarranted concern. At this point in your life, chances are good that these threats are not imminent; however, it is not too early to start working toward preventing these illnesses from becoming factors in your life. You may find the following checklists to be helpful reminders.

CHECKLIST FOR CHANGE

MAKING PERSONAL CHOICES

✓ Determine your hereditary risk. If it is high, outline the steps that you can take to reduce your overall risk.

✓ Know about the normal CVD risk changes that occur with age. Take the extra steps needed to minimize your risks as you age.

✓ If you smoke, quit. If you don't smoke, don't start.

✓ Find out what your cholesterol level is, including your HDL and LDL levels.

✓ Reduce saturated fat in your diet and take steps to reduce your triglyceride and cholesterol levels.

✓ Get out and exercise.

✓ Control your blood pressure. Monitor it regularly, and see your doctor if you are hypertensive.

✓ Lose weight if you are overweight.

✓ Control your stress levels.

✓ Avoid excessive sunlight.

✓ Avoid excessive alcohol consumption.

✓ Do not use smokeless tobacco.

✓ Properly monitor estrogen use. While estrogen therapy does seem to lower women's risk for heart disease and osteoporosis, it should not be undertaken without careful discussion between a woman and her physician.

✓ Avoid occupational exposures to carcinogens. Exposure to several different industrial agents increases the risk for various cancers.

✓ Eat your fruits and vegetables. Eat at least five servings of fruits and vegetables every day to reduce your risk.

MAKING COMMUNITY CHOICES

✓ Take a class in CPR. Your local Red Cross likely offers them, and your college may as well. Be prepared to offer bystanders CPR.

✓ Consider becoming an Emergency Medical Technician (EMT). You don't have to make a career of it; however, you could be prepared to save people in your dorm, or your office building, and your community.

✓ Does your community have any major sources of carcinogens (toxic waste dumps, chemical factories, etc.)? What precautions are taken to ensure that any environmental risks are reduced?

✓ Does your community have cancer support groups that you could join if you are found to have cancer? Where would you find out about such support?

SUMMARY

• The cardiovascular system consists of the heart and circulatory system and is a carefully regulated, integrated network of vessels that supply the body with the nutrients and oxygen necessary to perform daily functions.

• Cardiovascular diseases include atherosclerosis (hardening of the arteries), heart attack, angina pectoris, arrhythmias, congestive heart failure, congenital and rheumatic heart disease, and stroke. These combine to be the leading cause of death in the United States today.

• Risk factors for cardiovascular disease include cigarette smoking, high blood fat and cholesterol levels, hypertension, lack of exercise, high-fat diet, obesity, diabetes, and emotional stress. Some factors, such as age, gender, and heredity, are risk factors that are not under your control.

Many of these factors have a compounded effect when combined.

- Women have a unique challenge in controlling their risk for CVD, particularly after menopause, when estrogen levels are no longer sufficient to be protective.
- New methods developed for treating heart blockages include coronary bypass surgery and angioplasty.
- Cancer is a group of diseases characterized by uncontrolled growth and spread of abnormal cells.

- Several probable causes of cancer have been identified. Biological factors include inherited genes and gender. Occupational and environmental hazards are carcinogens present in people's home or work environments.
- Early diagnosis affects your survival rate. Self-exams for breast, testicular, and skin cancer, and knowledge of the Seven Warning Signals of cancer aid early diagnosis.
- New types of cancer treatments include various combinations of radiotherapy, chemotherapy, and immunotherapy.

DISCUSSION QUESTIONS

1. List the different types of CVDs. Compare and contrast their symptoms, risk factors, prevention, and treatment.
2. What are the major indicators that CVD poses a particularly significant risk to people your age? To the elderly? To people from selected minority groups?
3. Discuss the role exercise, stress management, dietary changes, checkups, sodium reduction, and other factors can play in reducing your risk of CVD.
4. Describe some of the diagnostic and treatment alternatives for CVD. If you had a heart attack today, which treatment would you prefer? Explain why.
5. What is the difference between a benign and a malignant tumor?

6. List the likely causes of cancer. Do any of these causes put you at greater risk? What can you do to reduce this risk?
7. What are the symptoms of lung, breast, prostate, and testicular cancer? What can you do to increase your chances of surviving these cancers or reduce your risks of getting them?
8. Discuss the Seven Warning Signals of cancer. What could signal that you have cancer instead of a minor illness? How soon should you seek treatment for any of the warning signs?

APPLICATION EXERCISE

Reread the *What Do You Think?* scenario at the beginning of the chapter and answer the following questions.

1. Consider Beth's case in the chapter opener. Is her situation typical of people you know? Why do you think so many young Americans deny their risk for CVD?

2. As a friend of either Beth or Sedrick, what advice might you give?

13

Infectious and Noninfectious Conditions

Risks and Responsibilities

WHAT DO YOU THINK?

Gayle and Patrick have been in a monogamous marriage for seven years. During a medical checkup, Gayle finds that she is HIV positive. Because she has not been sexually active outside her marriage and has never injected drugs, received a blood transfusion, or been hospitalized, she is quite certain that Patrick must have infected her. When she calls the local health clinic to discover if Patrick has been tested for HIV, they tell her that this information is confidential. She does not want to confront Patrick for fear that he may not be infected and she will have to explain her own infection.

What do you think Gayle should do? What would you do in a similar situation? What laws does your state have regarding partner notification for HIV, AIDS, and other sexually transmitted infections?

EVERY MOMENT OF EVERY DAY, you are in constant contact with microscopic organisms that have the ability to make you sick, at the very least, or cause death. These disease-causing agents, known as **pathogens,** are found in the air you breathe, in the foods you eat, and on nearly every object or person with whom you come in contact. Although new varieties of pathogens arise all the time, scientific evidence indicates that many pathogens have existed for as long as there has been life on the planet. In spite of our best efforts to eradicate these diseases, they are a continuing menace to all people, regardless of age, gender, lifestyle, ethnic background, and socioeconomic status.

The news isn't all bad, however. Even though we are bombarded by potential pathogenic threats, our immune systems are remarkably adept at protecting us. *Endogenous microorganisms* are those that live in peaceful coexistence with their human host most of the time. For people in good health and whose immune systems are functioning properly, endogenous organisms are usually harmless. But in sick people, or those with weakened immune systems, these normally harmless pathogenic organisms can cause serious health problems. *Exogenous microorganisms* are organisms that do not normally inhabit the body. When they do, however, they are apt to produce an infection and/or illness. The more easily these pathogens are able to gain a foothold in the body and sustain themselves, the more **virulent** or aggressive they may be in causing disease. Several factors influence your susceptibility to diseases.

ASSESSING YOUR DISEASE RISKS

Today we recognize that most diseases are **multifactorial,** or caused by the interaction of several factors from inside and outside the person. For a disease to occur, the *host* must be susceptible, meaning that the immune system must be in a weakened condition; an *agent* capable of transmitting a disease must be present; and the *environment* must be hospitable to the pathogen in terms of temperature, light, moisture, and other requirements. Other risk factors also apparently increase or decrease levels of susceptibility.

Risk Factors You Can't Control

Uncontrollable risk factors are those that increase your susceptibility and over which you may have little or no control. Some of the most common factors are:

▶ *Heredity*   Perhaps the single greatest factor influencing your longevity is your parents' longevity. Being born into a family in which heart disease, cancer, or other illnesses are prevalent seems to increase your risk. Some people having a close relative who is a diabetic become diabetic themselves even though they take precautions, watch their weight, and exercise regularly. Still other diseases are caused by direct chromosomal inheritance. **Sickle cell anemia,** an inherited blood disease that primarily affects African Americans, is often transmitted to the fetus if both parents carry the sickle cell trait.

It is often unclear whether hereditary diseases occur as a result of inherited chromosomal traits or inherited insufficiencies in the immune system.

▶ *Aging*   After the age of 40 we become more vulnerable to most of the chronic diseases. Moreover, as we age, our immune systems respond less efficiently to invading organisms, increasing our risk for infection and illness. The same flu that produces an afternoon of nausea and diarrhea in a younger person may cause days of illness or even death in an older person. The very young are also at risk for many diseases, particularly if they are not vaccinated against them.

▶ *Environmental Conditions*   Unsanitary conditions and the presence of drugs, chemicals, and hazardous pollutants and wastes in our food and water probably have a great effect on our immune systems. That **immunological competence**—the body's ability to defend itself against pathogens—is weakened in such situations has been well documented.[1]

▶ *Organism Resistance*   Some organisms, such as the food-borne organism **botulism,** are particularly virulent, and even tiny amounts may make the most hardy of us ill. Other organisms have mutated and are resistant to our bodies' defenses as well as other conventional treatments designed to protect us. Still other, newer forms of pathogens pose unique challenges for our immune systems—ones that our bodily defenses are ill-adapted to fight.

Risk Factors You Can Control

Although our degree of control over risk factors for disease may vary according to our socioeconomic condition, cultural upbringing, geographic location, and a host of other variables, we all have some degree of personal control over certain risk factors for disease. Too much stress, inadequate nutrition, a low physical fitness level, lack of sleep, misuse or abuse of legal and illegal substances, personal hygiene, high-risk behaviors, and other variables significantly increase the risk for a number of diseases. These variables are discussed individually in various chapters of this text. Several of these controllable risk factors are noted with an asterisk in the following list. These factors influence your response to pathogens:[2]

- Dosage, virulence, and portal of entry of agent
- Age at time of infection
- Preexisting level of immunity*
- Nature and vigor of immune response*
- Genetic factors controlling immune response
- Nutritional status of host*

Airborne pathogens can be transmitted easily and unknowingly which is why many public places take special precautions to ensure the health and safety of patrons.

- Preexisting diseases*
- Personal habits: smoking, alcohol, exercise, drugs*
- Dual infection or superinfection with other agents
- Psychological factors (e.g., motivation, emotional status, and so on)

········ **WHAT DO YOU THINK?**

If you were to list your own risk factors for infectious diseases, what would they be? What actions can you take to reduce your risks?

Pathogen   A disease-causing agent.

Virulent   Said of organisms able to overcome host resistance and cause disease.

Multifactorial disease   Disease caused by interactions of several factors.

Sickle cell anemia   Genetic disease commonly found among African Americans; results in organ damage and premature death.

Immunological competence   Ability of the immune system to defend the body from pathogens.

Botulism   A resistant food-borne organism that is extremely virulent.

Autoinoculation   Transmission of a pathogen from one part of your body to another.

THE PATHOGENS
Routes of Invasion

Pathogens enter the body in several ways. They may be transmitted by direct contact between infected persons, such as during sexual relations, kissing, or touching, or by indirect contact, such as by touching an object the infected person has had contact with. The hands are probably the greatest source of infectious disease transmission. You may also **autoinoculate** yourself, or transmit a pathogen from one part of your body to another. For example, you may touch a sore on your lip that is teeming with viral herpes and then transmit the virus to your eye when you subsequently scratch your itchy eyelid.

Pathogens are also transmitted by *airborne contact,* either through inhaling the droplet spray from a sneeze or breathing in air that carries a particular pathogen, or you may become the victim of *food-borne infection* if you eat something contaminated by microorganisms. Recent episodes of food poisoning from *salmonella* bacteria found in certain foods and *E. coli* bacteria found in undercooked beef have raised concerns about the safety of our food supply in the United States and forced many food handlers to make sure that their burgers and chicken are cooked to the proper organism-killing temperatures. Recently, labels were introduced that caution consumers to cook meats thoroughly, to wash utensils, and to take other food-handling precautions.

Your best friend may be the source of *animal-borne pathogens.* Dogs as well as cats, livestock, and wild animals can spread numerous diseases through their bites or feces or by carrying infected insects into your living areas. Although **interspecies transmission** of diseases (diseases passed from humans to animals and vice versa) is rare, it does occur. *Water-borne diseases* are transmitted directly from drinking water and indirectly from foods washed or sprayed with water containing their pathogens. These pathogens can also invade your body if you wade or swim in contaminated streams, lakes, and reservoirs.

Bacteria

Bacteria are single-celled organisms that are plantlike in nature but lack chlorophyll (the pigment that gives plants their green coloring). There are three major types of bacteria: cocci, bacilli, and spirilla. Bacteria may be viewed under a standard light microscope.

Although there are several thousand species of bacteria, only approximately 100 cause diseases in humans. In many cases, it is not the bacteria themselves that cause disease but rather the poisonous substances, called **toxins,** that they produce. The following are the most common bacterial infections:

▶ *Staphylococcal Infections* One of the most common forms of bacterial infection is the staph infection. **Staphylococci** are normally present on our skin at all times and usually cause few problems. But when there is a cut or break in the **epidermis,** or outer layer of the skin, staphylococci may enter and cause a localized infection. If you have ever suffered from acne, boils, styes (infections of the eyelids), or infected wounds, you have probably had a staph infection.

At least one staph-caused disorder, **toxic shock syndrome,** is potentially fatal. Media reports in the early 1980s indicated that the disorder was exclusive to menstruating women, particularly those who used high-absorbency tampons and left them inserted for prolonged periods of time. Although most cases of toxic shock syndrome have occurred in menstruating women, the disease was first reported in 1978 in a group of children and continues to be reported in people recovering from wounds, surgery, or other injury.

To reduce the likelihood of contracting toxic shock syndrome, take the following precautions: (1) avoid superabsorbent tampons except during the heaviest menstrual flow; (2) change tampons at least every four hours; and (3) use napkins at night instead of tampons.

▶ *Streptococcal Infections* Another common form of bacterial infection is caused by microorganisms called **streptococci.** A "strep throat" (severe sore throat characterized by white or yellow pustules at the back of the throat) is the typical streptococcal problem. Scarlet fever (characterized by acute fever, sore throat, and rash) and rheumatic fever (said to "lick the joints and bite the heart") are serious streptococcal infections.

▶ *Pneumonia* In the late nineteenth century and early twentieth century, **pneumonia** was one of the leading causes of death in the United States. This disease is characterized by chronic cough, chest pain, chills, high fever, fluid accumulation, and eventual respiratory failure. One of the most common forms of pneumonia is caused by bacterial infection and responds readily to antibiotic treatment in the early stages. Other forms are caused by the presence of viruses, chemicals, or other substances in the lungs. In these types of pneumonia, treatment may be more difficult.

▶ *Legionnaire's Disease* This bacterial disorder gained widespread publicity in 1976, when several Legionnaires at the American Legion convention in Philadelphia contracted the disease and died before the invading organism was isolated and effective treatment devised. Although one of the lesser-known diseases, the water-borne nature of this disease has led to several recent outbreaks in the United States.[3] The symptoms are similar to those for pneumonia, which sometimes makes identification difficult. In people whose resistance is lowered, particularly the elderly, delayed identification can have serious consequences.

▶ *Tuberculosis* One of the leading fatal diseases in the United States in the early 1900s, **tuberculosis (TB),** or "White Death" was largely controlled by the mid-1900s through improved sanitation, isolation of infected persons, and treatment with drugs such as *rifampin* or *isoniazid*. In fact, the number of reported cases in 1985 reached an all-time low of about 22,000 cases. But during the last decade, deteriorating social conditions, including overcrowding and poor sanitation, and the failure to isolate active cases have led to an epidemic of tuberculosis in some U.S. communities; there are nearly 45,000 active cases in the United States today. Newer strains of *drug-resistant* tuberculosis make this new epidemic potentially more devastating than previous outbreaks.[4] Globally, tuberculosis kills 2.9 million persons a year and drug-resistant forms pose a potentially devastating threat in certain countries of the world, such as India and Pakistan.[5]

Tuberculosis is caused by bacterial infiltration of the respiratory system. It is transmitted from person to person by the breathing of air infected by coughing or sneezing, but it is normally fairly difficult to catch. In fact, you need, on average, to be in contact with the disease eight hours a day for six straight months, and even then, the chances of getting it are only about 50 percent. Many people infected with TB are contagious without actually showing any symptoms themselves. The average healthy person is not at high risk; however, those who may be fighting other diseases, such as some of the HIV-related diseases, may be at increased risk. Symptoms include persistent coughing, weight loss, fever, and spitting up blood. A quick test can usually detect TB. TB can usually be treated and made noncontagious within two weeks and can often be cured within six months. The usual test involves a superficial injection of weakened tuberculosis bacteria just under the skin. If the site of the injection becomes red or swells within 48 hours, a positive test result is recorded, indicating that the person may be infected. Confirming tests, including a chest X-ray, are done before a diagnosis is made. Treatment includes rest, careful infection-control procedures, and drugs.

▶ *Periodontal Diseases* Diseases of the tissue around the teeth, called **periodontal diseases,** affect three out of four adults over 35. Improper home tooth care, including lack of flossing and poor brushing habits, and the failure to obtain

professional dental care regularly lead to increased bacterial growth, caries (tooth decay), and gum infections. If left untreated, permanent tooth loss may result.

····· **WHAT DO YOU THINK?**

Why do you think we are experiencing increases in many infectious diseases today? Why are some bacterial agents becoming more resistant to current treatment regimens? What can be done to reduce the spread of infectious diseases such as tuberculosis? What can you do to reduce your own risks?

Viruses

Viruses are the smallest of the pathogens, being approximately 1/500th the size of bacteria. Because of their tiny size, they are visible only under an electron microscope and were therefore not identified until this century. By the 1960s, viruses were being effectively grown outside the body in tissue cultures.[6]

Essentially, a virus consists of a protein structure that contains either *ribonucleic acid (RNA)* or *deoxyribonucleic acid (DNA)*. It is incapable of carrying out the normal cell functions of respiration and metabolism. It cannot reproduce on its own and can only exist in a parasitic relationship with the cell it invades.

Drug treatment for viral infections is limited. Drugs powerful enough to kill viruses also kill the host cells, although there are some drugs available that block stages in viral reproduction without damaging the host cells.

We have another form of virus protection within our own bodies. When exposed to certain viruses, the body begins to produce a protein substance known as **interferon.** Interferon does not destroy the invading microorganisms but sets up a protective mechanism to aid healthy cells in their struggle against the invaders. Although interferon research is promising, it should be noted that not all viruses stimulate interferon production.

▶ *The Common Cold* Colds are responsible for more days lost from work and more uncomfortable days spent at work than any other ailment.

Caused by any number of viruses (some experts claim there may be over 100 different viruses responsible for the common cold), colds are **endemic** (always present to some degree) among peoples throughout the world. Current research indicates that otherwise healthy people carry cold viruses in their noses and throats most of the time. These viruses are held in check until the host's resistance is lowered. It is possible to "catch" a cold—from the airborne droplets of another person's sneeze or from skin-to-skin or mucous membrane contact—though recent studies indicate that the hands may be the greatest avenue of cold and other viral transmission.

Interspecies transmission When diseases are passed from humans to animals or from animals to humans.

Bacteria Single-celled organisms that may be disease-causing.

Toxins Poisonous substances produced by certain microorganisms that cause various diseases.

Staphylococci Round, gram-positive bacteria, usually found in clusters.

Epidermis The outermost layer of the skin.

Toxic shock syndrome A potentially life-threatening bacterial infection that is most common in menstruating women.

Streptococci Round bacteria, usually found in chain formation.

Pneumonia Bacterially caused disease of the lungs.

Tuberculosis (TB) A disease caused by bacterial infiltration of the respiratory system.

Periodontal diseases Diseases of the tissue around the teeth.

Viruses Minute parasitic microbes that live inside another cell.

Interferon A protein substance produced by the body that aids the immune system by protecting healthy cells.

Endemic Describing a disease that is always present to some degree.

The best rule of thumb is to keep your resistance level high. Sound nutrition, adequate rest, stress reduction, and regular exercise appear to be your best bets in helping you fight off infection. Also, avoiding people with newly developed colds (colds appear to be most contagious during the first 24 hours of onset) is advisable. Once you contract a cold, bed rest, plenty of fluids, and aspirin for relief of pain and discomfort are the tried-and-true remedies for adults. Children should not be given aspirin for colds or the flu because of the possibility that this may lead to a potentially fatal disease known as *Reye's syndrome.*

▶ *Influenza*   In otherwise healthy people, **influenza,** or flu, is usually not serious. Symptoms, including aches and pains, nausea, diarrhea, fever, and coldlike ailments, generally pass very quickly. (See Figure 13.1 for a comparison of cold and flu symptoms.) However, in combination with other disorders, or among the elderly (people over the age of 65), those with respiratory or heart disease, or the very young (children under the age of 5), the flu can be very serious.

To date, three major varieties of flu virus have been discovered, with many different strains existing within each variety. The "A" form of the virus is generally the most virulent, followed by the "B" and "C" varieties. Although if you con-

tract one form of influenza you may develop immunity to it, you will not necessarily be immune to other forms of the disease. There is little that can be done to treat flu patients once the infection has become established. Some vaccines have proved effective preventives for certain strains of flu virus, but they are totally ineffective against others. In spite of minor risks, it is recommended that people over the age of 65, pregnant women, people with heart disease, and those with certain other illnesses be vaccinated.

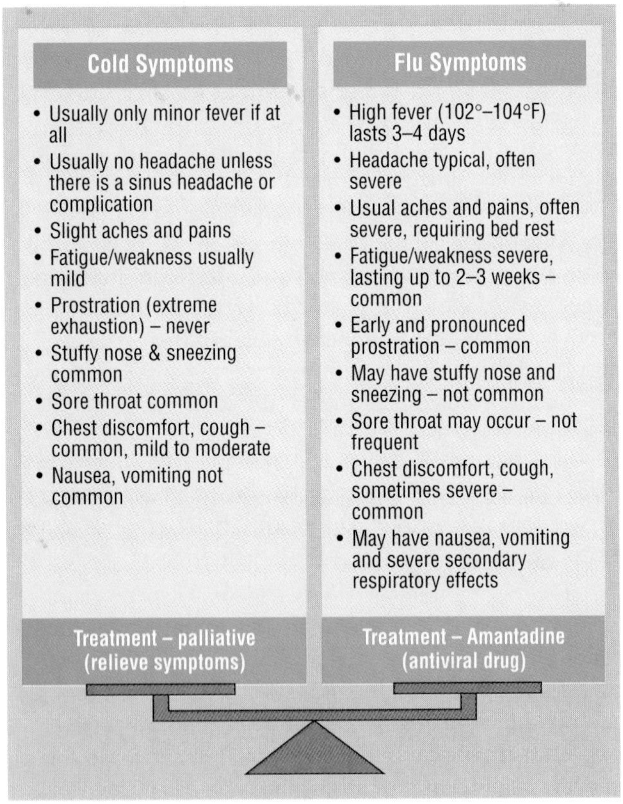

▶ *Infectious Mononucleosis*   This affliction of college-aged students is often jokingly referred to as the "kissing disease." The symptoms of mononucleosis, or "mono," include sore throat, fever, headache, nausea, chills, and a pervasive weakness or tiredness in the initial stages. As the disease progresses, lymph nodes may become increasingly enlarged, and jaundice, spleen enlargement, aching joints, and body rashes may occur.

Caused by the *Epstein-Barr virus,* mononucleosis is readily detected through a *monospot test,* a blood test that measures the percentage of specific forms of white blood cells. Because many viruses are caused by transmission of body fluids, many people once believed that young people passed the disease on by kissing. Although this is still considered a possible cause, mononucleosis is not believed to be highly contagious. Multiple cases among family members are rare, as are cases between intimate partners.

Treatment of mononucleosis is often a lengthy process that involves bed rest, balanced nutrition, and medications to control the symptoms of the disease. Gradually, the body develops a form of immunity to the disease and the person returns to normal activity levels.

▶ *Hepatitis*   One of the most highly publicized viral diseases is **hepatitis,** generally defined as a virally caused inflammation of the liver. It is characterized by symptoms that include fever, headache, nausea, loss of appetite, skin rashes, pain in the upper right abdomen, dark yellow (with brownish tinge) urine, and the possibility of jaundice (the yellowing of the whites of the eyes and the skin). Currently, there are seven known forms of hepatitis, with the following three indicating the highest rate of incidence.

- *Hepatitis A:* An acute, self-limiting infection that is contracted through the fecal-oral route, such as ingesting shellfish taken from sewage-infected waters.
- *Hepatitis B:* A disease that is spread primarily through bodily fluids, particularly during unprotected sex, puts the infected person at risk of chronic liver disease or a form of liver cancer. One of the fastest growing sexually transmitted infections in the United States, with over 300,000 new cases per year, most people recover within 6 months, although some can become chronic carriers.
- *Hepatitis C:* Long referred to as non-A–non-B hepatitis, hepatitis C infections are on an epidemic rise in many

Cold Symptoms	Flu Symptoms
• Usually only minor fever if at all	• High fever (102°–104°F) lasts 3–4 days
• Usually no headache unless there is a sinus headache or complication	• Headache typical, often severe
• Slight aches and pains	• Usual aches and pains, often severe, requiring bed rest
• Fatigue/weakness usually mild	• Fatigue/weakness severe, lasting up to 2–3 weeks – common
• Prostration (extreme exhaustion) – never	• Early and pronounced prostration – common
• Stuffy nose & sneezing common	• May have stuffy nose and sneezing – not common
• Sore throat common	• Sore throat may occur – not frequent
• Chest discomfort, cough – common, mild to moderate	• Chest discomfort, cough, sometimes severe – common
• Nausea, vomiting not common	• May have nausea, vomiting and severe secondary respiratory effects
Treatment – palliative (relieve symptoms)	Treatment – Amantadine (antiviral drug)

[handwritten note:] 100 x's more infectious than HIV

Figure 13.1

Cold or flu? Weighing your symptoms may answer your questions.

Source: Adapted from *National Institutes of Health Bulletin* and H. Sheldon, *Introduction to Human Diseases* (Philadelphia: W. B. Saunders, 1992).

regions of the world, as resistant forms are emerging. Hepatitis C has gained notoriety in recent years as incidence rates have grown considerably. The most disturbing factor of this disease is its manifestation after a prolonged period of time without symptoms or any hint of infection.

In the United States, hepatatis continues to be a major threat in spite of a safe blood supply and massive efforts at education about hand washing (hepatitis A), and safer sex (primarily hepatitis B). Treatment of all the forms of viral hepatitis is somewhat limited.

▶ *Mumps* Until 1968, mumps was a common viral disorder among children. That year a vaccine became available and the disease seemed to be largely under control, with reported cases declining from 80 per 100,000 people in 1968 to less than 2 per 100,000 people in 1984. But today the incidence of mumps, as well as of many other childhood diseases, is on the increase nationally.[7] Failure to vaccinate children due to public apathy, misinformation, and social and economic conditions is responsible for the rise. Approximately one-half of all mumps infections are not apparent because they produce only minor symptoms. Large numbers of mumps cases are never reported, so actual incidence rates may be higher than indicated. Typically, there is an incubation period of 16 to 18 days, followed by symptoms caused by the lodging of the virus in the glands of the neck. The most common symptom is the swelling of the parotid (salivary) glands. One of the greatest dangers associated with mumps is the potential for sterility in men who contract the disease in young adulthood. Also, some victims suffer hearing loss.

▶ *Chicken Pox* Caused by the *herpes zoster varicella* virus, chicken pox produces the characteristic symptoms of fever and tiredness 13 to 17 days after exposure, followed by skin eruptions that itch, blister, and produce a clear fluid. The virus is present in these blisters for approximately one week. Symptoms are generally mild, and immunity to subsequent

Influenza A common viral disease of the respiratory tract.

Hepatitis A virally caused disease in which the liver becomes inflamed, producing such symptoms as fever, headache, and jaundice.

Measles A viral disease that produces symptoms including an itchy rash and a high fever.

German measles (rubella) A milder form of measles that causes a rash and mild fever in children and may cause damage to a fetus or a newborn baby.

Fungi A group of plants that lack chlorophyll and do not produce flowers or seeds; several microscopic varieties are pathogenic.

Protozoa Microscopic, single-celled organisms.

infection appears to be lifelong. Although a vaccine for chicken pox is now available, many believe that it is not necessary and fail to vaccinate their children. Many children still contract the disease. Scientists believe that after the initial infection, the virus goes into permanent hibernation and, for most people, there are no further complications. For a small segment of the population, however, the zoster virus may become reactivated. Blisters will develop, usually on only one side of the body and tending to stop abruptly at the midline. Cases in which the disease covers both sides of the body are far more serious. This disease, known as *shingles,* affects over 5 percent of the population each year. More than half the sufferers are over 50 years of age.

▶ *Measles* Technically referred to as *rubeola,* **measles** is a viral disorder that often affects young children. Symptoms, appearing about 10 days after exposure, include an itchy rash and a high fever. **German measles (rubella),** is a milder viral infection that is believed to be transmitted by inhalation, after which it multiplies in the upper respiratory tract and passes into the bloodstream. It causes a rash, especially on the upper extremities. It is not generally a serious health threat and usually runs its course in three to four days. The major exceptions to this rule are among newborns and pregnant women. Rubella can damage a fetus, particularly during the first trimester, creating a condition known as congenital rubella, in which the infant may be born blind, deaf, retarded, or with heart defects. Immunization has reduced the incidence of both measles and German measles. Infections in children not immunized against measles can lead to fever-induced problems such as rheumatic heart disease, kidney damage, and neurological disorders.

Other Pathogens

▶ *Fungi* Hundreds of species of **fungi,** multi- or unicellular primitive plants, inhabit our environment and serve useful functions. Moldy breads, cheeses, and mushrooms used for domestic purposes pose no harm to humans. But some species of fungi can produce infections. *Candidiasis* (a vaginal yeast infection), athlete's foot, ringworm, and jock itch are examples of fungal diseases. Keeping the affected area clean and dry plus treatment with appropriate medications will generally bring prompt relief from these infections.

▶ *Protozoa* **Protozoa** are microscopic, single-celled organisms that are generally associated with tropical diseases such as African sleeping sickness and malaria. Although these pathogens are prevalent in the developing countries of the world, they are largely controlled in the United States. The most common protozoal disease in the United States is *trichomoniasis,* an infection discussed further in the sexually transmitted infections section of this chapter. A common water-borne protozoan disease in many regions of the country is *giardiasis.* Persons who drink or are exposed to the giardia

Body Piercing and Tattooing: Risks to Health

One look around college campuses and other enclaves for young people reveals a trend that, while not necessarily new, has been growing in recent years. We're talking, of course, about body piercing and tattooing, also referred to as forms of "body art." For decades, tattoos appeared to be the sole propriety of bikers, military guys, and general roughnecks; and in many people's eyes, they represented the rougher, seedier part of society. Body piercing, on the other hand, was virtually nonexistent in our culture except for pierced ears, which didn't really appear until the latter part of the twentieth century. Even then, pierced ears were limited, for the most part, to women.

Various forms of body embellishment, or body art, however, can be traced throughout human history when people "dressed themselves up" to attract attention or be viewed as acceptable by their peers. Examinations of cultures throughout the world, both historic and contemporary, provide evidence of the use of body art as a medium of self- and cultural expression. Ancient cultures often used body piercing as a mark of royalty or elitism. Egyptian pharaohs underwent rites of passage by piercing their navels. Roman soldiers demonstrated manhood by piercing their nipples.

But why the surge in popularity in current society, particularly among young people? Today, young and old alike are getting their ears and bodies pierced in record numbers, in such places as the eyebrows, tongues, lips, noses, navels, nipples, genitals, and just about any place possible. Many people view the trend as a fulfillment of a desire for self-expression, as this University of Wisconsin-Madison student points out:

" . . . The nipple [ring] was one of those things that I did as a kind of empowerment, claiming my body as my own and refuting the stereotypes that people have about me. . . . The tattoo was kind of a lark and came along the same lines and I like it too. . . . [T]hey both give me a secret smile."

Whatever the reason, tattoo artists are doing a booming business in both their traditional artistry of tattooing as well as in the "art" of body piercing. Amidst the "oohing" and "aahing" over the latest artistic additions, however, the concerns over health risks from these procedures have been largely ignored. Despite the warnings from local health officials and federal agencies, the popularity of piercings and tattoos has grown.

The most common health-related problems associated with tattoos and body piercing include skin reactions, infections, and scarring. The average healing times for piercings depend on the size of the insert, location, and the person's overall health. Facial and tongue piercings tend to heal more quickly than piercings of areas not commonly exposed to open air or light and which are often

---

pathogen may suffer symptoms of intestinal pain and discomfort weeks after infection.

▶ *Parasitic Worms* **Parasitic worms** are the largest of the pathogens. Ranging in size from the relatively small pinworms typically found in children to the relatively large tapeworms found in all forms of warm-blooded animals, most parasitic worms are more a nuisance than a threat. Of special note today are the new forms of worm infestations commonly associated with eating raw fish in Japanese sushi restaurants. Cooking fish and other foods to temperatures sufficient to kill the worms or their eggs is an effective means of prevention.

▶ *Prions* One of the newest and more frightening pathogens to infect humans and animals in recent years is a self-replicating, protein-based *agent* that has been labeled as a **prion,** or unconventional virus. Believed to be the underlying cause of *spongiform* diseases, such as Mad Cow disease, this agent systematically destroys brain cells. A discussion of Prion-based diseases occurs later in this chapter.

YOUR BODY'S DEFENSES

Although all of the pathogens described in the preceding section pose a threat if they take hold in your body, the chances that they will take hold are actually quite small. To do so, they must overcome a number of effective barriers, many of which were established in your body before you were born.

Physical and Chemical Defenses

Perhaps our single most critical early defense system is the skin. Layered to provide an intricate web of barriers, the skin allows few pathogens to enter. **Enzymes,** complex proteins manufactured by the body that appear in body secretions such as sweat, provide additional protection, destroying microorganisms on skin surfaces by producing inhospitable pH levels. Microorganisms that flourish at a selected pH will be weakened or destroyed as these changes occur. A third protection is our frequent slight elevations in body tempera-

teeming with bacteria, such as the genitals. Because the hands are great germ transmitters, "fingering" of pierced areas poses a significant risk for infection.

Of greater concern, however, is the potential transmission of dangerous pathogens that any puncture of the human body exacerbates. The use of unsterile needles—which can cause serious infections and can transmit HIV, hepatitis B and C, tetanus, and a host of other diseases—poses a very real risk. Body piercing and tattooing are performed by body artists, unlicensed "professionals" who generally have learned their trade from other body artists. Laws and policies regulating body piercing and tattooing vary greatly by state. While some states don't allow tattoo and body-piercing parlors, others may regulate them carefully, and still others provide few regulations and standards by which parlors have to abide. Standards for safety usually include minimum age of use, standards of sanitation, use of aseptic techniques, sterilization of equipment, informed risks, instructions for skin care, record keeping, and recommendations for dealing with adverse reactions. Because of the varying degree of standards regulating this business and the potential for transmission of dangerous pathogens, anyone who receives a tattoo, body piercing, or permanent make-up tattoo cannot donate blood for one year.

Anyone who does opt for tattooing or body piercing should remember the following:

- Look for clean, well-lit work areas, and ask about sterilization procedures.
- Before having the work done, watch the artist at work. Tattoo removal is expensive and often undoable. Make sure the tattoo is one you can live with.
- Right before piercing or tattooing, the body area should be carefully sterilized and the artist should wear new latex gloves and touch nothing else while working.
- Packaged, sterilized needles should be used only once and then discarded. A piercing gun should not be used because it cannot be sterilized properly.
- Only jewelry made of noncorrosive metal, such as surgical stainless steel, niobium, or solid 14-karat gold, is safe for new piercing.
- Leftover tattoo ink should be discarded after each procedure.
- If any signs of pus, swelling, redness, or discoloration persist, remove the piercing object and contact a physician.

STUDENTS SPEAK UP:

How do you explain the popularity of tattoos and body piercings among young people today? What are the pros and cons of this trend?

Sources: M. L. Armstrong and K. P. Murphy, "Adolescent Tattooing and Body Piercing." *The Prevention Researcher.* Integrated Research Services, Eugene, Oregon. 5 (1998):3, p. 5; Center for Food Safety and Applied Nutrition, "Tattoos and Permanent Makeup," Office of Cosmetics Fact Sheet, U.S. Food and Drug Administration, February (1995), web site: http://vm.cfsan.fda.gov/~dms/cos-204.html; Marilynn Larkin, "Tattooing in the 90s: Ancient Art Requires Care and Caution," *FDA Consumer,* U.S. Food and Drug Administration, October (1993), web site: http://vm.cfsan.fda.gov/~dms/cos-204.html

ture, which create an inhospitable environment for many pathogens. Only when there are cracks or breaks in the skin can pathogens gain easy access to the body.

The linings of the body provide yet another protection against pathogens. Mucous membranes in the respiratory tract and other linings of the body trap and engulf invading organisms. *Cilia,* hairlike projections in the lungs and respiratory tract, sweep unwanted invaders toward body openings, where they are expelled. Tears, nasal secretions, ear wax, and other secretions found at body entrances contain enzymes designed to destroy or neutralize invading pathogens. Finally, any invading organism that manages to breach these initial lines of defense faces a formidable specialized network of defenses thrown up by the immune system.

The Immune System: Your Body Fights Back

Immunity is a condition of being able to resist a particular disease by counteracting the substance that produces the disease. Any substance capable of triggering an immune response is called an **antigen.** An antigen can be a virus, a bacterium, a fungus, a parasite, or a tissue or cell from another individual. When invaded by an antigen, the body responds by forming substances called **antibodies** that are matched to the specific

Parasitic worms   The largest of the pathogens, most of which are more a nuisance than a threat.

Prions   One of the newest, more frightening pathogens to infect humans and animals in recent years. This is a self-replicating protein-based agent that systematically destroys brain cells.

Enzymes   Organic substances that cause bodily changes and destruction of microorganisms.

Antigen   Substance capable of triggering an immune response.

Antibodies   Substances produced by the body that are individually matched to specific antigens.

antigen much as a key is matched to a lock. Antibodies belong to a mass of large molecules known as *immunoglobulins,* a group of nine chemically distinct protein substances, each of which plays a role in neutralizing, setting up for destruction, or actually destroying antigens. Once an antigen breaches the body's initial defenses, the body begins a careful process of antigen analysis. It considers the size and shape of the invader, verifies that the antigen is not part of the body itself, and then begins to produce a specific antibody to destroy or weaken the antigen. This process, which is much more complex than described here, is part of a system called *humoral immune responses.* Humoral immunity is the body's major defense against many bacteria and bacterial toxins.

Cell-mediated immunity is characterized by the formation of a population of lymphocytes that can attack and destroy the foreign invader. These lymphocytes constitute the body's main defense against viruses, fungi, parasites, and some bacteria. Key players in this immune response are specialized groups of white blood cells known as *macrophages* (a type of phagocytic, or cell-eating, cell) and *lymphocytes,* other white blood cells in the blood, lymph nodes, bone marrow, and certain glands.

Two forms of lymphocytes in particular, the *B-lymphocytes* (B-cells) and *T-lymphocytes* (T-cells), are involved in the immune response. There are different types of B-cells, named according to the area of the body in which they develop. Most are manufactured in the soft tissue of the hollow shafts of the long bones. T-cells, in contrast, develop and multiply in the thymus, a multilobed organ that lies behind the breastbone. T-cells assist your immune system in several ways. *Regulatory T-cells* help direct the activities of the immune system and assist other cells, particularly B-cells, to produce antibodies. Dubbed "helper Ts," these cells are essential for activating B-cells, other T-cells, and macrophages. Another form of T-cell, known as the "killer Ts" or "cytotoxic Ts," directly attacks infected or malignant cells. Killer Ts enable the body to rid itself of cells that have been infected by viruses or transformed by cancer; they are also responsible for the rejection of tissue and organ grafts. The third type of T-cells, "suppressor Ts," turns off or suppresses the activity of B-cells, killer Ts, and macrophages. Suppressor Ts circulate in the bloodstream and lymphatic system, neutralizing or destroying antigens, enhancing the effects of the immune response, and helping to return the activated immune system to normal levels. After a successful attack on a pathogen, some of the attacker T- and B-cells are preserved as *memory T- and B-cells,* enabling the body to quickly recognize and respond to subsequent attacks by the same kind of organism at a later time. Thus macrophages, T- and B-cells, and antibodies are the key factors in mounting an immune response.

Once people have survived certain infectious diseases, they become immune to those diseases, meaning that in all probability they will not develop them again. Upon subsequent attack by the disease-causing microorganism, their memory T- and B-cells are quickly activated to come to their defense. Immunization works on the same principle. Vaccines containing an attenuated (weakened) or killed version of the disease-causing microorganism or containing an antigen that is similar to but not as dangerous as the disease antigen are administered to stimulate the person's immune system to produce antibodies against future attacks—without actually causing the disease.

▶ *Autoimmune Diseases* Although white blood cells and the antigen-antibody response generally work in our favor by neutralizing or destroying harmful antigens, the body sometimes makes a mistake and targets its own tissue as the enemy, builds up antibodies against that tissue, and attempts to destroy it. This is known as *autoimmune* disease (*auto* means "self"). Common examples of this type of disease are rheumatoid arthritis, lupus erythematosus, and myasthenia gravis.

In some cases, the antigen-antibody response completely fails to function. The result is a form of *immune deficiency syndrome. Acquired immune deficiency syndrome* (AIDS), which we will discuss later in this chapter, is a case in point.

Fever

If an infection is localized, pus formation, redness, swelling, and irritation often occur. These symptoms indicate that the invading organisms are being fought systematically. Another indication is the development of a fever, or a rise in body temperature above the norm of 98.6°F. Fever is frequently caused by toxins secreted by pathogens that interfere with the control of body temperature. Although this elevated temperature is often harmful to the body, it is also believed to act as a form of protection. Elevations of body temperature by even 1 or 2 degrees provide an environment that destroys some types of disease-causing organisms. Also, as body temperature rises, the body is stimulated to produce more white blood cells which destroy more invaders.

Pain

Although pain is not usually thought of as a defense mechanism, it plays a valuable role in the body's response to invasion. Pain is generally a response to injury. Pain may be either direct, caused by the stimulation of nerve endings in an

Referred pain Pain that is present at one point, but the source of pain is elsewhere.

Vaccination Inoculation with killed or weakened pathogens or similar, less dangerous antigens in order to prevent or lessen the effects of some disease.

Acquired immunity Immunity developed during life in response to disease, vaccination, or exposure.

Natural immunity Immunity passed to a fetus by its mother.

affected area, or **referred pain,** meaning it is present in one place while the source is elsewhere. Most pain responses are accompanied by inflammation. Pain tends to be the earliest sign that an injury has occurred and often causes the person to slow down or stop the activity that was aggravating the injury, thereby protecting against further damage. Because it is often one of the first warnings of disease, persistent pain should not be overlooked.

Vaccines: Bolstering Your Immunity

Our natural defense mechanisms are our strongest allies in the battle against disease. There are periods in our life, however, when either invading organisms are too strong or our own natural immunity is too weak to protect us from catching a given disease. It is at such times that we need outside assistance in developing immunity to an invading organism. Such assistance is generally provided in the form of a **vaccination,** which, as we said earlier, consists of killed or weakened versions of disease microorganisms or of antigens that are similar to but far less dangerous than the disease microorganism. Vaccines are given orally or by injection, and this form of artificial immunity is termed **acquired immunity,** in contrast to **natural immunity,** which a mother passes to her fetus via their shared blood supply.

Today, depending on the virulence of the organism, vaccines containing live, weakened, or dead organisms are given

to people for a variety of diseases. In some instances, if a person is already weakened by other diseases, vaccination may provoke an actual mild case of the disease. The 1998 schedule for childhood vaccinations is in Table 13.1.

EMERGING AND RESURGENT DISEASES

Although our immune systems are remarkably adept at responding to a host of challenges, they are threatened by an army of microbes that is so diverse, so virulent, and so insidious, that the invaders appear to be gaining ground. As society and our environment change, the potential for exposure to these threats increases dramatically. According to the World Health Organization's 1996 *World Health Report,* trends such as the aging of the population (the young and old are particularly vulnerable), the urbanization of developing countries, poverty, environmental pollution, globalization of the food supply, and crumbling health-care systems bode very badly for the future. Table 13.2 on page 326 identifies some of the contributors to the emergence and resurgence of infectious diseases, as indicated by the Centers for Disease Control's national prevention programs. For information on what is being done to address the spread of disease, see the Health in a Diverse World box on page 327.

TABLE 13.1
Recommended Childhood Immunization Schedule

VACCINE	BIRTH	2 MOS	4 MOS	6 MOS	12 MOS	15 MOS	18 MOS	4–6 YRS	11–12 YRS	14–16 YRS
Hepatitis B (HepB)	HepB-1	HepB-2		HepB-3						
Diphtheria, Tetanus, Pertussis		DTP	DTP	DTP	DTP or DTaP at ≥15 months			DTP or DTaP	Td	
Haemophilus influenzae type b (Hib)		Hib	Hib	Hib	Hib					
Polio		OPV	OPV	OPV				OPV		
Measles, Mumps, Rubella					MMR			MMR or	MMR	
Varicella zoster (VZV)					VZV	VZV	VZV			

Mothers who have tested positive for hepatitis B should consult their doctors about their infant's vaccinations.
HepB vaccine recommended at 11–12 years of age for children not previously vaccinated.
VZV recommended at 11–12 years of age for children not previously vaccinated, and who lack a reliable history of chicken pox. Children under 13 years of age should receive a single dose; persons 13 years of age and older should receive 2 doses 4–8 weeks apart.
Source: "Recommended Childhood Immunization Schedule, United States" (Washington, D.C.: American Academy of Pediatrics, 1998).

TABLE 13.2
Factors Contributing to Emergent/Resurgent Disease Spread and Possible Solutions

CONTRIBUTING FACTORS	POSSIBLE SOLUTIONS
Hardier bugs: Tiny size, adaptability, resistant strains, misuse of antibiotics	Increase pharmaceutical efforts, new drug development, selective use of new drugs; improve vaccination rates; fund new research.
Failure to prioritize public health initiatives on national level	Increase government funding; improve efforts aimed at prevention and intervention. (Less than 1% of the federal budget goes to prevention programs.)
Explosive population growth: Resource degradation, overcrowding, land use atrocities, increased urbanization	Population control, wise use of natural resources, environmental controls, reduced deforestation and increased pollution prevention efforts.
International travel	Education or risk reduction, restrict unvaccinated populations; improve air quality/venting on commercial airlines.
Human behaviors, particularly IV drug use and risky sexual behavior	Educate about risky behaviors; provide incentives for improved behaviors; increase personal motivation.
Vector management failures: Widespread overuse/misuse of pesticides and antimicrobial agents that hasten resistance	Manage pesticide use; focus on pollution prevention; regulate and enforce laws
Food and water contamination; globalization of food supply and centralized processing	Control population growth; animal controls; food controls, improved environmental legislation, food safety, and enforcement, pollution prevention.
Complacency/apathy	Education—Develop "we" mentality rather than "me" mentality; provide alternatives.
Poverty	Government support; international aide for vaccination programs. early diagnosis, and treatment; care for disadvantaged.
War/mass refugee migration, famine, disasters	Government intervention; international aid.
Aging of population	Support for prevention/intervention against controllable age-related health problems.
Irrigation, deforestation, and reforestation projects that alter habitats of disease-carrying insects and animals	Improved techniques for conservation, responsible use of resources, policies and programs that protect environment.
Increased human contact with tropical rainforests and other wilderness habitats that are reservoirs for insects and animals that harbor unknown infectious agents	Increased regulation to reduce human impact, more research to study better ways of human/environmental interaction.

Sources: Authors, plus information found in "Preventing Emerging Infectious Diseases: A Strategy for the 21st Century," U.S. Department of Health and Human Services, Centers for Disease Control and Prevention, Atlanta, 1998, 3.

Tiny Microbes: Lethal Threats

In the 1950s and 1960s scientists thought that with an arsenal of antibiotics and infection control practices, they would conquer infectious diseases. They know better now.[8] Today's arsenal of antibiotics appears to be increasingly ineffective, with penicillin-resistant strains of diseases on the rise as microbes are able to outlast and outsmart even the best of our antibiotic weapons.[9,10] Old scourges are back, and new ones are emerging, wreaking havoc from remote Third World villages to the modern First World cities.[11] Consider the following:

- *Mad Cow Disease:* Known as *bovine spongiform encephalopathy (BSE),* or *mad cow disease,* the disease is thought to have been transmitted when cows were fed a protein-based substance to help them put on weight and grow faster. Failure to treat this protein by-product sufficiently to kill the BSE organism left it to proliferate in and eventually infect the cows to which it was fed. The disease is believed to be transmitted to humans through the meat of these slaughtered cows. Research continues into a possible link between BSE and *Creutzfeld-Jakobs disease,* a disease in humans noted by progressively worsening neurological damage and possible death.

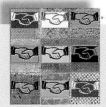

CDC Targets Emerging Disease Threats

In the early 1990s, the Institute of Medicine (IOM) of the National Academy of Sciences published a report entitled, "Emerging Infections: Microbial Threats to Health in the United States." This report emphasized the intimate links between U.S. health and international health, and served as a basis for the emergence of a concerted international effort for prevention and control of disease threats. In 1994, the Centers for Disease Control and Prevention (CDC) published a document, "Addressing Emerging Infectious Disease Threats: A Prevention Strategy for the U.S.," which called for immediate action to stem the tide of diseases around the world. It outlined ten priority areas, with a focus on improving surveillance, conducting applied research, rebuilding the public health infrastructure, and enhancing prevention of emerging diseases. In 1997,

funds became available to implement about one-third of these priority areas. These activities were accomplished in partnership with federal, state, and local agencies; universities; private industries; foreign governments; the World Health Organization (WHO); and many non-government groups. Goals of this program include the following:

Goal 1: Surveillance and Response This goal is designed to detect, investigate, and monitor emerging pathogens; the diseases they cause; and the factors influencing their emergence. It also calls for improving surveillance nationally and internationally in an effort to act quickly and appropriately when emerging infections threaten. Countries in all regions of the world will participate in a global system for surveillance and response that includes surveillance for infectious agents that are resistant to antimicrobial drugs.

Goal 2: Applied Research This goal is designed to integrate laboratory science and epidemiology to optimize public health practice. It includes funding for research on such things as evaluating the role of prescribing practices in the development of antimicrobial drug re-

sistance, assessing the impact of food preparation, handling guidelines, and so forth.

Goal 3: Prevention and Control This goal is designed to enhance communication of public health information about emerging diseases and ensure prompt implementation of prevention strategies. It focuses on improving methods of delivering health education about risks, and on developing and implementing guidelines for the prevention of opportunistic infections, particularly in immunosuppressed persons.

Goal 4: Infrastructure and Training This goal is designed to strengthen local, state, and federal public health infrastructures to support surveillance and implement prevention and control programs. It focuses on state-of-the-art training in diagnostic evaluation and testing for medical laboratory personnel to ensure accurate diagnosis and surveillance of emerging infections.

Source: "Preventing Emerging Infectious Diseases: A Strategy for the 21st Century," U.S. Department of Health and Human Services, Centers for Disease Control and Prevention, Atlanta, 1998.

- *Dengue and Dengue Hemorrhagic Fever: Dengue* (Den) viruses are the most widespread arthropod viruses in the world and are transmitted by mosquitoes. Dengue symptoms include flulike nausea, aches, and chronic fatigue and weakness. As urban areas become increasingly infected with mosquitoes, nearly 1.5 billion people, including about 600 million children, are at risk. A more serious form of the disease, *dengue hemorrhagic fever,* can kill children in 6 to 12 hours, as the virus causes capillaries to leak and spill precious fluid and blood into surrounding tissue.
- *Ebola:* The Ebola virus is concentrated mostly in portions of Africa and is spread by overcrowded, unsanitary conditions. The virus causes fever and massive internal hemorrhaging. In 1995, an outbreak in Zaire killed 245 of the 316 people infected, forcing massive quarantine of the region.
- *Cryptosporidium:* In 1993, the United States was shaken by the largest waterborne coccidian protozoan disease

outbreak ever recognized in this country, as this once obscure intestinal parasite (*Cryptosporidium*) infected the municipal water supply of Milwaukee, Wisconsin, causing many deaths and illness for hundreds of thousands of people and over 4,500 hospitalizations. Exactly how the water supply became infected remains in question; however, the fact that humans, birds, and animals can carry the infective agent opens the door for many possible routes.
- *Escherichia coli 0157:H7:* In the past decade, a rash of food-borne deaths and illnesses have been traced to the consumption of foods contaminated with *E. coli* bacteria. Once thought to be limited to uncooked meats, recent infections found in apple juice were apparently the result of cows defecating in areas under trees where wind-fall apples are picked up for juice. While *E. coli* organisms continue to pose threats to humans, simple changes in the way cattle are fed prior to slaughter may

reduce risks, as will careful cleaning and preparation of foods.

- *Cholera:* Cholera, an infectious disease transmitted through fecal contamination of foods or water supplies, has been extremely rare in the United States for most of this century. Recent epidemic outbreaks in the Western Hemisphere (over 900,000 cases), however, have started to affect the United States. Until we control these epidemics, prevention of infection from outside visitors to the United States will be difficult.

- *Hantavirus:* Transmitted via rodent feces, this virus was responsible for many deaths in the desert southwestern United States in 1994 before experts were able to identify the culprit. Victims were believed to have come into contact with this organism through breathing the virus-laden dust created in rodent-infested homes. Today, cases of hantavirus have been noted in over 20 states, and vaccines are being developed to counteract it.

- *Flesh-Eating Strep:* The stuff of science fiction, this organism caused waves of hysteria in the United States in 1994 as hospital patients fell prey to a form of streptococcus that slowly invaded and killed tissue in healing wounds. Our then-current arsenal of drugs was too weak to fight the microbe, until a highly potent, newer form of antibiotic was found to stop the invader.

SEXUALLY TRANSMITTED INFECTIONS

Sexually transmitted infections (STIs) have been with us since our earliest recorded days on earth. In spite of our best efforts to eradicate them, prevent them, and control their spread, they continue to increase, affecting millions more Americans than previously thought, according to the first new STI estimate in a decade.[12] Today, there are more than 20 known types of STIs. Once referred to as "venereal diseases" and then "sexually transmitted diseases," the most current terminology is believed to be broader in scope and more reflective of the number and types of these communicable diseases. More virulent strains and more antibiotic-resistant forms spell trouble for at-risk populartions in the days ahead.

The most common STI is **human papilloma virus,** the disease-causing agent in genital warts. The CDC report reveals that there are currently 5.5 million annual cases of this virus, which has a suspected link to cervical cancer and may be responsible for problems with sterility. Recent research has also implicated chlamydia with the development of coronary artery diseases.

In many victims, early symptoms of an STI are mild and unrecognizable. (See Figure 13.2 for signs that may indicate the presence of an STI.) Left untreated, some of these infections can have grave consequences, such as sterility, blindness, central nervous system destruction, disfigurement, and even

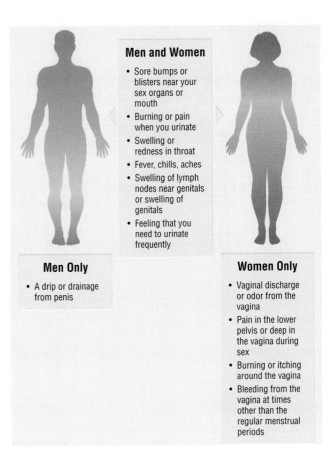

Men and Women
- Sore bumps or blisters near your sex organs or mouth
- Burning or pain when you urinate
- Swelling or redness in throat
- Fever, chills, aches
- Swelling of lymph nodes near genitals or swelling of genitals
- Feeling that you need to urinate frequently

Men Only
- A drip or drainage from penis

Women Only
- Vaginal discharge or odor from the vagina
- Pain in the lower pelvis or deep in the vagina during sex
- Burning or itching around the vagina
- Bleeding from the vagina at times other than the regular menstrual periods

Figure 13.2
Common signs or symptoms of an STI.

death. Infants born to mothers carrying the organisms for these infections are at risk for a variety of health problems.

As with many of the communicable diseases, much of the pain, suffering, and anguish associated with STIs can be eliminated through education, responsible action, simple preventive strategies, and prompt treatment.

Possible Causes

Several reasons have been proposed to explain the present high rates of STIs. The first relates to the moral and social stigma associated with these infections. Shame and embarrassment often keep infected people from seeking treatment. Unfortunately, these people usually continue to be sexually active, thereby infecting unsuspecting partners. People who are uncomfortable discussing sexual issues may also be less likely to use and/or ask their partners to use condoms as a means of protection against STIs and/or pregnancy.

Another reason proposed for the STI epidemic is our casual attitude about sex. Bombarded by media hype that glamorizes easy sex, many people take sexual partners without considering the consequences. Others are pressured into sexual relationships they don't really want. Generally, the more sexual partners a person has, the greater the risk for contracting an STI.

Ignorance about the infections themselves and an inability to recognize actual symptoms or to acknowledge that a person may be asymptomatic yet still have the infection are also factors behind the STI epidemic.

Modes of Transmission

Sexually transmitted infections are generally spread through some form of intimate sexual contact. Sexual intercourse, oral-genital contact, hand-genital contact, and anal intercourse are the most common modes of transmission. More rarely, pathogens for STIs are transmitted mouth to mouth or, even more infrequently, through contact with fluids from body sores. While each STI is a different infection caused by a different pathogen, all STI pathogens prefer dark, moist places, especially the mucous membranes lining the reproductive organs. The majority of these organisms is susceptible to light, excess heat, cold, and dryness, and many die quickly on exposure to air. (The toilet seat is not a likely breeding ground for most bacterial or viral STIs!) Although most STIs are passed on by sexual contact, other kinds of close contact, such as sleeping on the sheets used by someone who has pubic lice, may also cause you to get an STI.

Like other communicable infections, STIs have both pathogen-specific incubation periods and periods of time during which transmission is most likely, called periods of communicability.

Chlamydia

In 1997, **chlamydia,** a disease that often has no symptoms, topped the list of the most commonly reported infections in the United States. Tracked officially for the first time by the CDC, this so-called silent epidemic spoke loudly and clearly, with over 500,000 new cases. Chlamydia was more commonly reported among women, striking 398,488 in 1997, while gonorrhea and AIDS were reported more by men.[13] Public health officials believe that the actual number of cases are probably higher because these figures represent only those cases reported. Like most STIs, chlamydia is not biased in whom it chooses to infect, crossing socioeconomic, racial, educational, and other artificial lines with great ease. College students account for over 10 percent of the infected numbers, and these numbers seem to be increasing yearly.

The name of the disease is derived from the Greek verb *chlamys,* meaning "to cloak," because, unlike most bacteria, chlamydia can only live and grow inside other cells. Although many people classify chlamydia as either *nonspecific* or *nongonococcal urethritis (NGU),* a person may have NGU without having the organism for chlamydia.

In males, early symptoms may include painful and difficult urination, frequent urination, and a watery, puslike discharge from the penis. Symptoms in females may include a yellowish discharge, spotting between periods, and occasional spotting after intercourse. Females are especially prone to be asymptomatic; over 70 percent do not realize they have the disease until secondary damage occurs.

The secondary damage resulting from chlamydia is serious in both sexes. Male victims can suffer damage to the prostate gland, seminal vesicles, and bulbourethral glands as well as arthritislike symptoms and damage to the blood vessels and heart. In females, secondary damage from chlamydia may include inflammation that damages the cervix or fallopian tubes, causing sterility, and damage to the inner pelvic structure, leading to pelvic inflammatory disease (PID). If an infected woman becomes pregnant, she has a high risk for miscarriages and stillbirths. Chlamydia may also be responsible for one type of **conjunctivitis,** an eye infection that affects not only adults but also infants, who can contract the disease from an infected mother during delivery. Untreated conjunctivitis can cause blindness.

Chlamydia can be controlled through responsible sexual behavior and familiarity with the early symptoms of the infection. If detected early enough, chlamydia is easily treatable with antibiotics such as tetracycline, doxycycline, or erythromycin.

Sexually transmitted infections (STIs) Infectious diseases transmitted via some form of intimate, usually sexual, contact.

Human papilloma virus (HPV) The disease-causing agent in genital warts.

Chlamydia Bacterially caused STI of the urogenital tract.

Conjunctivitis Serious inflammation of the eye caused by any number of pathogens or irritants; can be caused by STDs such as chlamydia.

Pelvic inflammatory disease (PID) Term used to describe various infections of the female reproductive tract.

Pelvic Inflammatory Disease (PID)

Pelvic inflammatory disease (PID) is actually not one infection but a term used to describe a number of infections of the uterus, fallopian tubes, and ovaries. Although PID is often the result of an untreated sexually transmitted infection, especially chlamydia and gonorrhea, it is not actually an STI. Nonsexual causes of PID are also common, including excessive vaginal douching, cigarette smoking, and substance abuse.

Women make over 2 million visits to private physicians each year for PID symptoms, which may include acute inflammation of the pelvic cavity, severe pain in the lower abdomen, menstrual irregularities, fever, nausea, painful intercourse, tubal pregnancies, and severe depression.[14] The major consequences of untreated PID are infertility, ectopic pregnancy, chronic pelvic pain, and recurrent upper genital infections. Risk factors include young age at first sexual intercourse, multiple sex partners, high frequency of sexual intercourse, and change of sexual partners within the last 30 days.

Gonorrhea

Gonorrhea is one of the most common STIs in the United States, being surpassed only by chlamydia in number of cases. Although over 2 million new cases of gonorrhea are reported annually in the United States, a significant number probably go unreported. Caused by the bacterial pathogen, *Neisseria gonorrhoea,* this infection primarily infects the linings of the urethra, genital tract, pharynx, and rectum. It may be spread to the eyes or other body regions via the hands or body fluids. Most victims are males between the ages of 20 and 24, with sexually active females between the ages of 15 and 19 also at high risk.[15]

In males, a typical symptom is a white milky discharge from the penis accompanied by painful, burning urination two to nine days after contact. This is usually enough to send most men to their physician for treatment. Only about 20 percent of all males with gonorrhea are asymptomatic.

In females, the situation is just the opposite. Only about 20 percent of all females experience any form of discharge, and few develop a burning sensation upon urinating until much later in the course of the infection (if ever). The organism can remain in the woman's vagina, cervix, uterus, or fallopian tubes for long periods with no apparent symptoms other than an occasional slight fever. Thus a woman can be unaware that she has been infected and that she may be infecting her sexual partners.

Upon diagnosis, an antibiotic regimen using penicillin, tetracycline, spectiomycin, ceftriaxone, or other drugs is begun. A penicillin-resistant form of gonorrhea may require a particularly strong combination of antibiotics. Treatment is generally completely effective within a short period of time if the infection is detected early.

If the infection goes undetected in a woman, it can spread throughout the genital-urinary tract to the fallopian tubes and ovaries, causing sterility, or at the very least, severe inflammation and PID symptoms. If an infected woman becomes pregnant, the infection can cause conjunctivitis in her infant. To prevent this, physicians routinely administer silver nitrate or penicillin preparations to the eyes of newborn babies.

Untreated gonorrhea in the male may spread to the prostate, testicles, urinary tract, kidney, and bladder. Blockage of the vasa deferentia due to scar tissue formation may cause sterility. In some cases, the penis develops a painful curvature during erection.

Syphilis Direct Contact

Syphilis, the other well-known sexually transmitted infection, is also caused by a bacterial organism, the spirochete known as *Treponema pallidum*. Because it is extremely delicate and dies readily upon exposure to air, dryness, or cold, the organism is generally transferred only through direct sexual contact. Typically, this means contact between sexual organs during intercourse, but in rare instances, the organism enters the body through a break in the skin, through deep kissing in which body fluids are exchanged, or through some other transmission of body fluids.

Syphilis is called the "great imitator" because its symptoms resemble those of several other infections. Only an astute physician who has reason to suspect the presence of the infection will order the appropriate tests for a diagnosis. Syphilis generally progresses through several distinct stages.

▶ *Primary Syphilis* The first stage of syphilis, particularly for males, is often characterized by the development of a sore known as a chancre (pronounced "shank-er"), located most frequently at the site of the initial infection. This chancre is usually about the size of a dime and is painless, but it is oozing with bacteria. Usually the chancre appears between three to four weeks after contact.

In males, the site of the chancre tends to be the penis or scrotum because this is the site where the organism first makes entry into the body. But, if the infection was contracted through oral sex, the sore can appear in the mouth, throat, or other "first contact" area. In females, the site of infection is often internal, on the vaginal wall or high on the cervix. Because the chancre is not readily apparent, the likelihood of detection is not great. In both males and females, the chancre will completely disappear in three to six weeks.

▶ *Secondary Syphilis* From a month to a year after the chancre disappears, secondary symptoms may appear, including a rash or white patches on the skin or on the mucous membranes of the mouth, throat, or genitals. Hair loss may occur, lymph nodes may become enlarged, and the victim may run a slight fever or develop a headache. In rare cases, sores develop around the mouth or genitals. As during the active chancre phase, these sores contain infectious bacteria, and contact with them may spread the infection. In some people, symptoms follow a textbook pattern; in others, there are no symptoms at all. In a few cases, there may be arthritic pain in the joints. Because symptoms vary so much and because the symptoms that do appear are so far removed from previous sexual experience that the victim seldom connects the two, the infection often goes undetected even at this second stage. Symptoms may persist for a few weeks or months and then disappear, leaving the victim thinking that all is well.

▶ **Latent Syphilis**   The syphilis spirochetes begin to invade body organs after the secondary stage. There may be periodic reappearance of previous symptoms, including the presence of infectious lesions, for between two and four years after the secondary period. After this period, the infection is rarely transmitted to others, except during pregnancy, when it can be passed on to the fetus. The child will then be born with congenital syphilis, which can cause death or severe birth defects such as blindness, deafness, or disfigurement. Because in most cases the fetus does not become infected until after the first trimester, treatment of the mother during this period will usually prevent infection of the fetus.

In some instances, a child born to an infected mother will show no apparent signs of the infection at birth but, within several weeks, will develop body rashes, a runny nose, and symptoms of paralysis. *Congenital syphilis* is usually detected before it progresses much further. But sometimes the child's immune system will ward off the invading organism, and further symptoms may not surface until the teenage years. Fortunately, most states protect against congenital syphilis by requiring prospective marriage partners to be tested for syphilis prior to obtaining a marriage license.

In addition to causing congenital syphilis, latent syphilis, if untreated, will continue to progress, infecting more and more organs until the infection reaches its final stage, late syphilis.

▶ **Late Syphilis**   Most of the horror stories concerning syphilis involve the late stages of the infection. Years after syphilis has entered the body and progressed through the various organs, its net effects become clearly evident. Late-stage syphilis indications may include heart damage, central nervous system damage, blindness, deafness, paralysis, premature senility, and, ultimately, insanity.

▶ **Treatment for Syphilis**   Treatment for syphilis resembles that for gonorrhea. Because the organism is bacterial, it is treated with antibiotics, usually penicillin, benzathine penicillin G, or doxycycline. Blood tests are administered to determine the exact nature of the invading organism, and the doses

of antibiotics are much stronger than those taken by the typical gonorrhea patient. The major obstacle to treatment is misdiagnosis of this "imitator" infection.

Pubic Lice

Often called crabs, pubic lice are more annoying than dangerous. Pubic lice are small parasites that are usually transmitted during sexual contact. They prefer the dark, moist regions of the body and, during sex, move easily from partner to partner. They have an affinity for pubic hair, attaching themselves to the base of these hairs, where they deposit their eggs (nits). Between one and two weeks later, these nits develop into adults that lay eggs and migrate to other body parts, thus perpetuating the cycle. Treatment includes washing clothing, furniture, and linens that may harbor the eggs. It usually takes two to three weeks to kill all larval forms. Although sexual contact is the most common mode of transmission, you can become infested with pubic lice from lying on sheets that an infected person has slept on. Sleeping in hotel and dormitory rooms in which blankets and sheets are not washed regularly or sitting on toilet seats where the nits or larvae have been dropped and lie in wait for a new carrier may put you at risk.

Venereal Warts

Venereal warts (also known as genital warts or condylomas) are caused by a small group of viruses known as *human papilloma viruses* (HPVs). A person becomes infected when an HPV penetrates the skin and mucous membranes of the genitals or anus through sexual contact. The virus appears to be relatively easy to catch. The typical incubation period is from six to eight weeks after contact. Many people have no apparent symptoms, particularly if the warts are located inside the reproductive tract. Others may develop a series of itchy bumps on the genitals, which may range in size from a small pinhead to large cauliflowerlike growths that can obstruct normal urinary or reproductive activity. On dry skin (such as on the shaft of the penis), the warts are commonly small, hard, and yellowish-gray, resembling warts that appear on other parts of the body.

Venereal warts are of two different types: (1) *full-blown genital warts* that are noticeable as tiny bumps or growths, and (2) the much more prevalent *flat warts* that are not usually visible to the naked eye.

▶ **Risks of Venereal Warts**   Many venereal warts will eventually disappear on their own. Others will grow and generate unsightly flaps of irregular flesh on the external genitalia. Although these flaps may be a source of embarrassment, they typically do not cause serious problems. If they grow large enough to obstruct urinary flow or become irritated by clothing or sexual intercourse, they can cause significant problems.

The greatest threat from venereal warts may lie in the apparent relationship between them and a tendency for

---

Gonorrhea   Second most common STD in the United States; if untreated, may cause sterility.

Syphilis   One of the most widespread STDs; characterized by distinct phases and potentially serious results.

Chancre   Sore often found at the site of syphilis infection.

Pubic lice   Parasites that can inhabit various body areas, especially the genitals; also called "crabs."

Venereal warts   Warts that appear in the genital area or the anus; caused by the human papilloma viruses (HPVs).

---

dysplasia, or changes in cells that may lead to a precancerous condition. Exactly how HPV infection leads to cervical cancer is uncertain. What is known is that within five years after infection, 30 percent of all HPV cases will progress to the precancerous stage. Of those cases that become precancerous and are left untreated, 70 percent will eventually result in actual cancer. In addition, venereal warts may pose a threat to a pregnant woman's unborn fetus if the fetus is exposed to the virus during birth. Cesarean deliveries may be considered in serious cases. Treatment for venereal warts may take several forms, including drugs and surgery.

Candidiasis (Moniliasis)

Unlike many of the other sexually transmitted infections, which are caused by pathogens that come from outside the body, the yeastlike fungus caused by the *Candida albicans* organism normally inhabits the vaginal tract in most women. Only under certain conditions will these organisms multiply to abnormal quantities and begin to cause problems.

The likelihood of **candidiasis** (also known as moniliasis) is greatest if a woman has diabetes, if her immune system is overtaxed or malfunctioning, if she is taking birth control pills or other hormones, or if she is taking broad-spectrum antibiotics. All of the above factors decrease the acidity of the vagina, making conditions more favorable for the development of a yeastlike infection.

Symptoms of candidiasis include severe vaginal itching, a white cheesy discharge, swelling of the vaginal tissue due to irritation, and a burning sensation. These symptoms are often collectively called **vaginitis**. When this microbe infects the mouth, whitish patches form, and the condition is referred to as thrush. This monilial infection also occurs in males and is easily transmitted between sexual partners.

Candidiasis strikes at least half a million American women a year. Antifungal drugs applied on the surface or by suppository usually cure the infection in just a few days. For approximately 1 out of 10 women, however, nothing seems to work, and the organism returns again and again. In patients with this chronically recurring infection, symptoms are often aggravated by contact of the vagina with soaps, douches, perfumed toilet paper, chlorinated water, and spermicides. Tight-fitting jeans and pantyhose can provide the combination of moisture and irritant the organism thrives on.

Trichomoniasis

Unlike many of the other STIs, **trichomoniasis** is caused by a protozoan. Although as many as half of the men and women in the United States may have this organism present, most remain free of symptoms until their bodily defenses are weakened. Both men and women may transmit the infection, but women are the more likely candidates for infection. The "trich" infection may cause a foamy, yellowish discharge with an unpleasant odor that may be accompanied by a burning sensation, itching, and painful urination. These symptoms are most likely to occur during or shortly after menstruation, but they can appear at any time or be absent altogether in an infected woman. Although usually transmitted by sexual contact, the "trich" organism may be easily spread by toilet seats, wet towels, or other items that have discharged fluids on them. You can also contract trichomoniasis by sitting naked on the bench of the dressing room of your local health spa or locker room. Treatment includes oral metronidazole, usually given to both sexual partners to avoid the possible "ping-pong" effect of repeated cross-infection so typical of the STIs.

General Urinary Tract Infections

Although *general urinary tract infections (UTIs)* can be caused by various factors, some forms are sexually transmitted. Any time invading organisms enter the genital area, there is a risk that they may travel up the urethra and enter the bladder. Similarly, organisms normally living in the rectum, urethra, or bladder may travel to the sexual organs and eventually be transmitted to another person.

You can also get a UTI through autoinoculation (transmission to yourself by yourself). This frequently occurs during the simple task of wiping yourself after defecating. Wiping from the anus forward may transmit organisms found in feces to the vaginal opening or to the urethra. Contact between the hands and the urethra and between the urethra and other objects are also common means of autoinoculation of bacterial and viral pathogens. Women, with their shorter urethras, are more likely to contract UTIs. Treatment depends on the nature and type of pathogen.

Herpes

Herpes is a general term for a family of infections characterized by sores or eruptions on the skin. Herpes infections range from mildly uncomfortable to extremely serious. One subcategory, *herpes simplex,* is caused by a virus. Herpes simplex virus type 1 (HSV-1) causes cold sores and fever blisters. It is believed that four out of five adult Americans have herpes

---

Candidiasis Yeastlike fungal disease often transmitted sexually.

Vaginitis Set of symptoms characterized by vaginal itching, swelling, and burning.

Trichomoniasis Protozoan infection characterized by foamy, yellowish discharge and unpleasant odor.

Genital herpes STD caused by herpes simplex virus type 2.

Acquired immune deficiency syndrome (AIDS) Extremely virulent sexually transmitted disease that renders the immune system inoperative.

simplex type 1 (also called orofacial herpes) and that one out of six has genital herpes.[16]

Genital herpes, caused by *herpes simplex virus type 2,* is one of the most widespread STIs in the world. Typically, genital herpes is characterized by distinct phases. First, the herpes virus enters the body through the mucous membranes of the genital area. Once these organisms invade, the victim will experience the *prodromal (precursor) phase,* which is characterized by a burning sensation and redness at the site of the infection. This phase is typically followed by the formation of a small blister filled with a clear fluid containing the virus. If you pick at this blister or otherwise spread this clear fluid by your hands, you can autoinoculate other body parts. Particularly dangerous is the possibility of spreading the infection to your eyes this way because a herpes lesion on the eye may cause blindness.

Over a period of days, this unsightly blister will crust, dry, disappear, and the virus will travel to the base of an affected nerve supplying the area and become dormant. Only when the victim becomes overly stressed, when diet is inadequate, when the immune system is overworked, or when there is excessive exposure to sunlight or other stressors will the virus reactivate (at the same site every time) and begin the blistering cycle all over again. This cyclical recurrence can be painful, unsightly, and, most importantly, highly contagious. Fluids from these blisters may readily be transmitted to sexual partners. Through oral sex, herpes simplex type 2 may be transmitted to the mouth. Symptoms are similar to those of herpes simplex type 1. Figure 13.3 summarizes the herpes cycle.

Genital herpes is especially serious in pregnant women because of the danger of infecting the baby as it passes through the vagina during birth. For that reason, many physicians recommend cesarean deliveries for infected women. Additionally, women who have a history of genital herpes also appear to have a greater risk of developing cervical cancer.

Although there is no cure for herpes at present, certain drugs have shown some success in reducing symptoms. Unfortunately, they only seem to work if the infection is confirmed during the first few hours after contact. The effectiveness of other treatments, such as L-lysine, is largely unsubstantiated to date. Although lip balms and cold-sore medications may provide temporary anesthetic relief, it is useful to remember that rubbing anything on a herpes blister may spread herpes-laden fluids to other body parts.

▶ *Preventing Herpes* If you are worried about contracting herpes, there are several precautions that you should take:

- Avoid any form of kissing if you notice a sore or blister on your partner's mouth. Kiss no one, not even a peck on the cheek, if you know that you have a herpes lesion. Allow a bit of time after the sores go away before you start kissing again.
- Be extremely cautious if you have casual sexual affairs. Not every partner will feel obligated to tell you that he or she may have a problem.

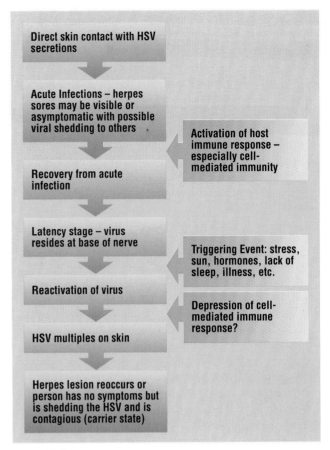

Figure 13.3

The Herpes Cycle

Source: Adapted by permission of Lippincott-Raven Publishers from "Sexually Transmitted Diseases in the 1990s," *STD Bulletin* 11 (1992): 4.

- Wash your hands immediately with soap and water after any form of sexual contact.
- If you have herpes, reduce the risk of a herpes episode by avoiding excessive stress, sunlight, or whatever else appears to trigger a herpes outbreak in you.
- If you have questionable sores or lesions, seek medical help at once.
- Since the herpes organism dies quickly upon exposure to air, toilet seats, soap, and similar sources are not likely means of transmission.
- If you have herpes, be responsible in your sexual contacts with others. If you have herpes lesions that might put your partner at risk, let that person know.

HIV/AIDS

Although deaths due to **acquired immune deficiency syndrome (AIDS)** have decreased in the United States in the last 3 to 4 years, HIV/AIDS continues to be a significant global health threat. Since 1981, when AIDS was first recognized,

47 million people in the world have become infected with **human immunodeficiency virus (HIV)**, the virus that causes AIDS; 14 million of these people have died.[17] In the United States, as of December 1997, 641,086 men, women, and children with AIDS have been reported to the Centers for Disease Control and Prevention (CDC), and at least 390,000 have died.[18] The CDC estimates that at least 40,000 new infections occur each year in the United States, despite the fact that more is known today than ever before about HIV prevention.

The estimated number of cases worldwide show a disturbing lack of progress in HIV prevention. According to the Joint United Nations Programme on HIV/AIDS, in 1997, there were 16,000 new infections each day.[19]

A Shifting Epidemic

[handwritten: 1970's–1980's Europe → cat disease San Fran → sheep disease]

Under old definitions, people with HIV were diagnosed as having AIDS only when they developed blood infections, the cancer known as Kaposi's sarcoma, or any of 21 other indicator diseases, most of which were common in males. The CDC expanded the definition under pressure from AIDS activists and women's groups, who charged that the CDC was ignoring AIDS symptoms peculiar to injecting drug users (IDUs) and women, thereby making it difficult for these people to obtain health insurance payments and federally funded health benefits. Thus, the new definition added pulmonary tuberculosis, recurrent pneumonia, and invasive cervical cancer to the indicator list. Perhaps the most significant new indicator, however, was a drop in the level of the body's master immune cells, called CD4s, to 200 per cubic millimeter (that's one-fifth the level in a healthy person). It is estimated that over 220,000 Americans have this low CD4 count and don't know it.[20]

AIDS cases have been reported state by state throughout the United States since the early 1980s as a means of tracking the disease. Today, the CDC recommends that all states extend their reporting requirements to also include HIV infection (not just AIDS). Because of medical advances in treatment and increasing numbers of HIV-infected persons who do not progress to AIDS, it is believed that AIDS incidence statistics may not provide a true picture of the epidemic, the long-term costs of treating HIV-infected individuals, and other key information. Currently, only 33 states mandate that those who test positive for the HIV antibody be reported.[21] Although there is significant pressure to mandate reporting in all states, there is controversy over implementing such a mandate. Many believe that once we begin to mandate reporting of HIV-positive tests, many people will refuse to be tested, even though they may suspect that they are infected.

.... **WHAT DO YOU THINK?**

If you knew that your name and vital statistics would be "on file" and reported to public health officials if you tested positive for HIV, would you be as likely to go in for the HIV test to begin with? Do you favor mandatory reporting of this information? Why or why not?

Women and AIDS

[handwritten: 4 to 10 x's more likley]

Homosexuals, IDUs, prostitutes, children, promiscuous heterosexual males, Haitians, and other groups all had their turn in discussions of HIV and the AIDS epidemic during the 1980s. Now there is increasing realization that HIV is not an infection that certain groups get because of inherent group characteristics; it is an equal-opportunity pathogen that can attack anyone who engages in certain high-risk behaviors.

Recently, the focus has finally fallen on the 51 percent of the population that was long ignored: women. These are a few of the facts that have emerged:[22,23]

- From 1985 through 1997, the proportion of AIDS cases among American women increased from 7 percent to 22 percent.
- From 1994 through 1997, women accounted for a greater proportion of HIV than AIDS diagnoses (28 percent of all HIV diagnoses versus 17 percent of all AIDS diagnoses).
- Women in the age group of 13- to 24-year-olds accounted for 44 percent of new HIV cases in 1997.
- Most women with AIDS were infected through heterosexual exposure to HIV, followed by injection drug use (sharing needles).
- Women of color are disproportionately affected by HIV; African-American and Hispanic women together account for 76 percent of AIDS cases reported to date among women in the United States, while comprising less than 25 percent of all U.S. women.
- AIDS is the leading cause of death among African-American women ages 25 to 44, and is the fourth leading cause of death among all American women in this age group.

Compounding the problems of women with HIV are serious deficiencies in our health and social service systems, including inadequate treatment for women addicts and lack of access to child care, health care, and social services for families headed by single women. Women with HIV/AIDS are of special interest because they are the major source of infection in infants. Virtually all new HIV infections among children in the United States are attributable to perinatal transmission of HIV.

How HIV Is Transmitted

HIV typically enters one person's body when another person's infected body fluids (semen, vaginal secretions, blood, etc.) gain entry through a breach in body defenses. Mucous membranes of the genital organs and the anus provide the easiest route of entry. If there is a break in the mucous membranes (as can occur during sexual intercourse, particularly anal intercourse), the virus enters and begins to multiply.

Human immunodeficiency virus (HIV)   The slow-acting virus that causes AIDS.

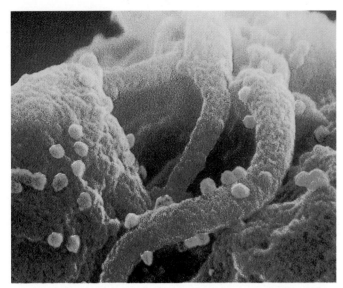

Viruses attach themselves to host cells and inject their own DNA or RNA in order to reproduce new cells. Some viruses run their course before expiring. Others, such as HIV shown here, are more long-term and destructive.

After initial infection, the HIV typically begins to multiply rapidly in the body, invading the bloodstream and cerebrospinal fluid. It progressively destroys helper T-lymphocytes, weakening the body's resistance to disease. The virus also changes the genetic structure of the cells it attacks. In response to this invasion, the body quickly begins to produce antibodies.

Despite some rather hysterical myths, HIV is not a highly contagious virus. Countless studies of people living in households with a person with HIV/AIDS have turned up no documented cases of HIV infection due to casual contact. Other investigations provide overwhelming evidence that insect bites do not transmit HIV.

▶ *Engaging in High-Risk Behaviors*   AIDS is not a gay disease, or a disease of minority groups, or Haitians, or any other class of people. It is a disease of certain high-risk behaviors. Anyone at any time who engages in unprotected sex with a person who has engaged in high-risk behaviors is at risk. Promiscuous sex—in males and females of all ages, races, ethnic groups, sexual orientations, and socioeconomic conditions—is the greatest threat. If you don't exchange body fluids, you won't get the disease. If you decide to be intimate, use a condom. The following activities are high-risk behaviors.

▶ *Exchange of Body Fluids*   The exchange of HIV-infected body fluids during vaginal and anal intercourse is the greatest risk factor. Substantial research evidence indicates that blood, semen, and vaginal secretions are the major fluids of concern. Although the virus was found in 1 person's saliva (out of 71 people in a study population), most health officials state that saliva is not a high-risk body fluid unless blood is present. But the fact

that the virus has been found in saliva does provide a good rationale for using caution when engaging in deep, wet kissing.

Initially, public health officials also included breast milk in the list of high-risk fluids because a small number of infants apparently contracted HIV while breast-feeding. Subsequent research has indicated that HIV transmission could have been caused by bleeding nipples as well as by actual consumption of breast milk and other fluids. Infection through contact with feces and urine is believed to be highly unlikely though technically possible.

▶ *Receiving a Blood Transfusion prior to 1985*   A small group of people became infected with HIV as a result of having received a blood transfusion before 1985, after which the Red Cross and other blood donation programs implemented a stringent testing program for all donated blood. Today, because of these massive screening efforts, the risk of receiving HIV-infected blood is almost non-existent.

▶ *Injecting Drugs*   A significant percentage of cases of AIDS in the United States are believed to be the result of sharing or using HIV-contaminated needles and syringes. While illegal drug users are the people we usually think of as being in this category, it is important to remember that others may also share needles—for example, diabetics who inject insulin or athletes who inject steroids. People who share needles and also engage in sexual activities with members of high-risk groups, such as those who exchange sex for drugs, increase their risks dramatically.

▶ *Mother-to-Infant Transmission (Perinatal)*   Approximately one in three of the children who have contracted AIDS received the virus from their infected mothers while in the womb or while passing through the vaginal tract during delivery.

Symptoms of HIV Disease

A person may go for months or years after infection by HIV before any significant symptoms appear. The incubation time varies greatly from person to person. Children have shorter incubation periods than do adults. Newborns and infants are particularly vulnerable to AIDS because human beings do not become fully immunocompetent (that is, their immune system is not fully developed) until they are 6 to 15 months old. New information suggests that some very young children show the "adult" progression of AIDS. In adults who receive no medical treatment, the average length of time it takes the virus to cause the slow, degenerative changes in the immune system that are characteristic of AIDS is 8 to 10 years. During this time, the person may experience a large number of opportunistic infections (infections that gain a foothold when the immune system is not functioning effectively). Colds, sore throats, fever, tiredness, nausea, night sweats, and other generally non-life-threatening conditions commonly appear.

CONSUMER HEALTH

Home Tests for HIV Infection

Since May 1996, most national pharmacies have sold FDA-approved home testing kits for HIV. The *Home Access HIV-1 Test System* is available for $40, and includes an easy-to-use lancet for drawing blood, a card for the sample, and a prepaid shipping envelope. All results are anonymous, using code numbers instead of names, and are available in 7 days. Trained counselors are available by phone for more results, information, and follow-up.

An analysis of HIV home sample collection test data collected from manufacturers during the first year of availability in the United States was published in the *Journal of the American Medical Association.** Results indicated that during that time period, 174,316 tests were performed. Of that number, 97 percent called the manufacturer to learn their test results. Less than 1 percent (0.9%) tested positive for HIV. Test users were predominantly white men, aged 25 to 34 years.

This study supported the view that home testing encourages persons to be tested who might not otherwise because of concerns about lack of confidentiality. Almost 60 percent of the survey participants had never before been tested for HIV. However, considering the fact that over 16 million HIV tests are performed each year in the United States, the overall effect of home tests may not be significant.

When home tests initially became available, some opposed them because of concerns about telephone counseling.

This study showed that 23 percent of those who tested positive for HIV already had a follow-up care source, and 65 percent accepted referrals; however, 5 percent of HIV-positive callers hung up without counseling. For those who hung up, no follow-up information was available.

For those who do not want to go to locations where their results may go on file, home tests may be a reasonable solution. Some researchers believe that the home tests "may pave the way for the approval of other technologies, such as 1-step rapid HIV tests." Such tests will be able to provide results in 10 to 15 minutes without the need for a laboratory; in fact, this could allow consumers the option of performing the test, then interpreting the results at home.

Source: *B. M. Bransom, "Home Sample Collection Tests for HIV Infection," *Journal of the American Medical Association* 280 (1998): 1699–1701.

Testing for HIV Antibodies

Once antibodies have begun to form in reaction to the presence of HIV, a blood test known as the **ELISA** test may detect their presence. If sufficient antibodies are present, the ELISA test will be positive. When a person who previously tested *negative* (no HIV antibodies present) has a subsequent test that is *positive,* seroconversion is said to have occurred. In such a situation, the person would typically take another ELISA test, followed by a more expensive, more precise test known as the **Western blot** to confirm the presence of HIV antibodies.

As testing for HIV antibodies has been perfected, scientists have explored various ways of making it easier for individuals to be tested. Part of the reason health officials make the distinction between *reported* and *actual* cases of HIV infection is because it is believed that many people who may actually be HIV positive avoid being tested. One suspected reason is fear of knowing the truth. Another possible reason for avoiding testing is the fear of recriminations from employers, insurance companies, and medical staff if a positive test becomes known to others. Yet, immediate treatment for someone in the early stages of HIV disease is critical; therefore, early detection and reporting is important. The Consumer Health box discusses the latest product designed to alleviate individual concerns.

New Hope and Treatments

New high-powered, anti-HIV drugs have slowed the progression from HIV to AIDS and have prolonged life expectancies in many AIDS patients. In the United States, AIDS fell from being the eighth leading cause of death in 1996 to being the fourteenth leading cause of death in 1997.[24] While the drugs currently available in the United States are responsible for this encouraging news, advocates for AIDS patients say the medications still cost too much money and still cause too many side effects.

Current treatment regimens have focused on combinations of selected drugs, with the protease inhibitors leading the pack. Protease inhibitors are a promising new class of antiretroviral therapies for the treatment of HIV infection. They act to prevent the production of virus in chronically infected cells that HIV has already invaded. In effect, the older drugs work by preventing the virus from infecting new cells and the protease inhibitors work by preventing infected cells from reproducing new HIV.

Protease inhibitors have proven very difficult to manufacture, and some have failed while others are successful. Side effects vary from person to person, and getting the right dose is critical for effectiveness. All of the protease drugs seem to work best in combination with other therapies. These combination treatments are still quite experimental, and no combination has proven to be absolute for all people as yet. Also, as with other antiviral treatments, resistance to the drugs can develop. Individuals that may already have a resistance to AZT may not be able to use a protease-AZT combination. This can pose a problem for many people who have been taking the common drugs, who may find their options for combination therapy limited. The truth remains that although these drugs provide new hope and longer survival rates for people living with HIV, we are still a long way from a cure.

Preventing HIV Infection

Although scientists have been searching for a vaccine to protect people from HIV infection since 1983, they have had no success so far. The only effective prevention strategies closely relate to the means by which people contract HIV. Do not engage in risky behaviors.

HIV infection and AIDS are not uncontrollable conditions. You can reduce your risks by the choices you make in sexual behaviors and the responsibilities you take for your health and for that of your loved ones.

NONINFECTIOUS DISEASES

Typically, when we think of the major ailments and diseases affecting Americans today, we think of "killer" diseases such as cancer and heart disease. Clearly, these diseases make up the major portion of our life-threatening diseases—

ELISA Blood test that detects presence of antibodies to HIV virus.

Western blot More precise test than the ELISA to confirm presence of HIV antibodies.

Idiopathic Of unknown cause.

Dyspnea Chronic breathlessness.

Chronic obstructive pulmonary diseases (COPDs) A collection of chronic lung diseases including asthma, emphysema, and chronic bronchitis.

Allergy Hypersensitive reaction to a specific antigen or allergen in the environment in which the body produces excessive antibodies to that antigen or allergen.

Histamines Chemical substances that dilate blood vessels, increase mucous secretions, and produce other allergy-like symptoms.

---

accounting for nearly two-thirds of all deaths. Although these diseases capture much of the media attention, other forms of chronic disease often cause substantial pain, suffering, and disability. Fortunately, the majority of these diseases can be prevented, or relief of symptoms is possible.

To prevent the development of certain noninfectious and chronic diseases, we must identify the major common characteristics of these diseases. They are usually not transmitted by any pathogen or by any form of personal contact. They often develop over a long period of time, and they cause progressive damage to human tissues. Although these conditions normally do not result in death, they do lead to illness and suffering for many people. Lifestyle and personal health habits are often implicated as underlying causes; however, there are a number of "newer" maladies that seem to defy conventional wisdom about causation. For those known maladies and **idiopathic** (unknown cause) disorders, education, reasonable changes in lifestyles, pharmacological agents, and public health efforts aimed at research, prevention, and control can minimize the effects of these diseases.

Chronic Lung Diseases

Chronic lung diseases pose a serious and significant threat to Americans today. Collectively, they have become the fourth leading cause of death, with most sufferers living with a condition known as chronic **dyspnea,** or chronic breathlessness. Chronic lung disease can result in major disability and lack of function as the lungs fill with mucus, become susceptible to bacterial or viral infections, or cause acute stress on the heart as they struggle to get valuable oxygen. Among the more deadly of the chronic lung diseases are the **chronic obstructive pulmonary diseases (COPDs):** asthma, emphysema, and chronic bronchitis. Other, lesser known chronic lung diseases also cause significant health risks.

▶ *Allergy-Induced Problems* An **allergy** occurs as a part of the body's attempt to defend itself against a specific *antigen* or *allergen* by producing specific *antibodies*. When foreign pathogens such as bacteria or viruses invade the body, the body responds by producing antibodies to destroy these invading antigens. Under normal conditions, the production of antibodies is a positive element in the body's defense system. However, for unknown reasons, in some people the body overreacts by developing an overly elaborate protective mechanism against relatively harmless allergens or antigens. The resultant *hypersensitivity reaction* to specific allergens or antigens in the environment is fairly common. Most commonly, these allergic responses occur as a reaction to environmental antigens such as molds, animal dander (hair and dead skin), pollen, ragweed, or dust. Once excessive antibodies to these antigens are produced, they trigger the release of **histamines,** chemical substances that dilate blood vessels, increase mucous secretions, cause tissues to swell, and produce other allergylike symptoms, particularly in the respiratory system (see Figure 13.4 on page 338).

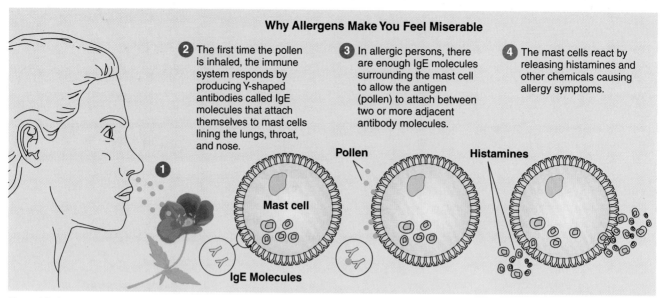

Why Allergens Make You Feel Miserable

2 The first time the pollen is inhaled, the immune system responds by producing Y-shaped antibodies called IgE molecules that attach themselves to mast cells lining the lungs, throat, and nose.

3 In allergic persons, there are enough IgE molecules surrounding the mast cell to allow the antigen (pollen) to attach between two or more adjacent antibody molecules.

4 The mast cells react by releasing histamines and other chemicals causing allergy symptoms.

1

Pollen

Histamines

Mast cell

IgE Molecules

Figure 13.4

Steps of an Allergy Response

Allergies tend to become progressively worse with time and with increased exposure to allergens. If allergic responses become chronic in nature, treatment becomes difficult. Many people take allergy shots to reduce the severity of their symptoms with some success. In most cases, once the offending antigen has disappeared, allergy-prone people suffer few symptoms. Although allergies can cause numerous problems, one of the most significant effects is on the immune system.

▶ *Hay Fever* Perhaps the best example of a chronic respiratory disease is **hay fever.** Usually considered to be a seasonally related disease (most prevalent when ragweed and flowers are blooming), hay fever is common throughout the world. Hay fever attacks, which are characterized by sneezing and itchy, watery eyes and nose, cause a great deal of misery for countless people. Hay fever appears to run in families, and research indicates that lifestyle is not as great a factor in developing hay fever as it is in other chronic diseases. Instead, an overzealous immune system and an exposure to environmental allergens including pet dander, dust, pollen from various plants, and other substances appear to be the critical factors that determine vulnerability. For those people who are unable to get away from the cause of their hay fever response, medical assistance in the form of injections or antihistamines may provide the only possibility of relief.

▶ *Asthma* Unfortunately, for many persons who suffer from allergies such as hay fever, their condition often becomes complicated by the development of one of the major COPDs: asthma, emphysema, or bronchitis. **Asthma** is characterized by attacks of wheezing, difficulty in breathing, shortness of breath, and coughing spasms. Although most asthma attacks

are mild and non-life-threatening, they can trigger bronchospasms (contractions of the bronchial tubes in the lungs) that are so severe that without rapid treatment, death may occur. Between attacks, most people have few symptoms.

A number of things can trigger an attack, including air pollutants; particulate matter, such as wood dust; and indoor air pollutants, such as sidestream smoke from tobacco, and allergens, such as dust mites, cockroach saliva, and pet dander. Stress is also believed to trigger an asthmatic attack in some individuals.[25]

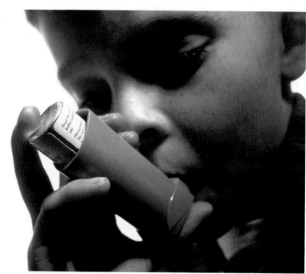

Although a number of new medications are available to relieve the symptoms of asthma sufferers, the marked increase of this respiratory problem in young children has officials worried.

SKILLS FOR BEHAVIOR CHANGE

Keys to Asthma Prevention

Although asthma rates continue to increase internationally, there is much that individuals and communities can do to reduce risk:

- Work with local leaders to reduce air pollution in your communities. Regulations on the burning of household and yard trash, field burning, use of wood-burning stoves, and sidestream smoke from cigarettes, all known triggers for asthma attacks, should be analyzed and revised.
- Purchase a good air filter in the home and clean furnace filters regularly. Clean houses often, using a high-suction vacuum rather than a broom to reduce dust particles in suspended air.
- Wash pillows regularly to avoid pesty mites and other debris inside the pillows. Use pillow protectors and mattress protectors, which keep dust mites and other critters out of your face and trapped inside the pillow or mattress. Don't purchase used mattresses, as they may be teeming with mites.
- Avoid having cats or dogs that are known for high dander production in the home. If you must have these pets, keep them off your bed and wash them and their bedding weekly. Vacuum their hair regularly.
- Have asthma medications handy and know where you left them in case of an emergency.
- Keep your home clean and pest-free; cockroaches and other vermin have enzymes in their saliva or particles on their body that may trigger allergic reactions.
- Keep mold concentrations low by using antimold cleaners or by running a dehumidifier to keep moisture levels down.
- Avoid mowing the lawn or excessive outdoor exposure to pollen during high-pollen times. Your local news station often provides pollen warnings. If you must be outdoors, wear a pollen mask.
- Get adequate amounts of exercise to keep your lungs functioning well.
- Avoid smokers.
- If you have a fireplace or wood-burning stove, check it regularly to make sure that it is not spewing out smoke and particulate matter.
- Let people close to you know that you are asthmatic and educate them about what to do if you have an asthmatic attack. Understanding and knowledge are two of the greatest tools that the health consumer has. Make sure your loved ones have access to information.

Although anyone can develop asthma, some trends have been noted. For example, in childhood, asthma strikes more boys than girls; in adulthood, it strikes more women than men. Also, the asthma rate is 50 percent higher among African Americans than whites, and four times as many African Americans die of asthma than do whites. Midwesterners appear to be more prone to asthma than are people from other areas of the country. In recent years, concern over the rise in incidence of asthma has grown considerably. How serious is the problem? Consider these points:

- Asthma has become the most common chronic disease of childhood.
- Asthma is the number one cause of hospitalization and absenteeism.

- Asthma affects over 15 million Americans, including 5 million children.
- The number of asthma sufferers has increased more than 62 percent since the 1980s.
- The death toll from asthma has nearly doubled since 1980, to more than 5,000 persons per year.

People with asthma fall into one of two distinctly different types of asthma development. The most common type, known as *extrinsic (or slow onset) asthma,* is most commonly associated with allergic triggers. This type tends to run in families and begins to develop in childhood. Often, by adulthood, a person has few episodes, or the disorder completely goes away. *Intrinsic asthma* also may have allergic triggers, but the main difference is that any unpleasant event or stimulant may trigger an attack. A common form of extrinsic asthma is *exercise-induced asthma (EIA),* which may or may not have an allergic connection. Some athletes have no other allergies, yet live with asthma. Cold, dry air is believed to exacerbate EIA; thus, keeping your lungs moist and warming up prior to working out may reduce risk. The warm, moist air around a swimming pool is one of the best environments for asthmatics. Preventive measures are identified in the Skills for Behavior Change box.

Hay fever   A chronic respiratory disorder that is most prevalent when ragweed and flowers bloom.

Asthma   A chronic respiratory disease characterized by attacks of wheezing, shortness of breath, and coughing spasms.

▶ **Emphysema**   If you have ever seen someone hooked up to an oxygen tank and struggling to breathe while climbing a flight of stairs or listened to someone gasping for air for no apparent reason, you have probably witnessed an emphysemic episode. **Emphysema** involves the gradual destruction of the **alveoli** (tiny air sacs) of the lungs. As the alveoli are destroyed, the affected person finds it more and more difficult to exhale. The victim typically struggles to take in a fresh supply of air before the air held in the lungs has been expended. The chest cavity gradually begins to expand, producing the barrel-shaped chest characteristic of the chronic emphysema victim.

The exact cause of emphysema is uncertain. There is, however, a strong relationship between the development of emphysema and long-term cigarette smoking and exposure to air pollution. Victims of emphysema often suffer discomfort over a period of many years. In fact, studies have shown that lung function decline may begin well before the age of 50 and that the early morning "smoker's cough" may signal that the damage has already begun.[26] Inadequate oxygen supply, com-

bined with the stress of overexertion on the heart, eventually takes its toll on the cardiovascular system and leads to premature death.

▶ **Chronic Bronchitis**   Although often dismissed as "smoker's cough" or a bad case of the common cold, **chronic bronchitis** may be a serious, if not life-threatening, respiratory disorder. In this ailment, the bronchial tubes become so inflamed and swollen that normal respiratory function is impaired. Symptoms of chronic bronchitis include a productive cough and shortness of breath that persist for several weeks over the course of the year. Cigarette smoking is the major risk factor for this disease, although fumes, dust, and particulate matter in the air are also contributing factors.

WHAT DO YOU THINK?

Which of the respiratory diseases described in this section do you or your family have problems with? Why do you think that COPDs tend to be among the leading causes of death in the United States? Why do you think the incidence of COPDs, as a group, is increasing? What actions can you and/or the people in your community take to reduce risks/problems from these diseases?

NEUROLOGICAL DISORDERS

Headaches

Almost all of us have experienced the agony of at least one major headache in our lives. In fact, over 80 percent of women and 65 percent of men experience headaches on a regular basis.[27] Headaches may result from dilated blood vessels within the brain, underlying organic problems, or excessive stress and anxiety. The following are the most common forms of headaches and the most effective methods of treatment.

▶ **Tension Headache**   Tension headaches, also referred to as muscular contraction headaches, are generally caused by muscle contractions or tension in the neck or head. This tension may be caused by actual strain placed on neck or head muscles due to overuse, static positions held for long periods of time, or tension triggered by stress. Recent research indicates that tension headaches may be a product of a more "generic mechanism" in which chemicals deep inside the brain may cause the muscular tension, pain, and suffering often associated with an attack. Triggers for this chemical assault may be red wine, lack of sleep, fasting, menstruation, or other factors. Symptoms may vary in intensity and duration. Relaxation, hot water treatment, and massage have surfaced as the new "holistic treatments," while aspirin, Tylenol, Aleve, and Advil are the old standby forms of pain relief. Although such painkillers may bring temporary relief of symptoms, it is believed that, over time, the drugs may dull the brain's own pain-killing weapons and result in more headaches rather than fewer.

▶ *Migraine Headache*   **Migraine** is not just a name for an unusually bad headache; it is a specific diagnosis, involving pain that begins on one side of the head, often accompanied by nausea and sensitivity to light and sounds. Many migraine sufferers experience the sensation of an "aura" in their visual field, typically some form of disturbance such as flashing lights or blind spots, along with numbness or weakness on one side of the body or slurred speech,[28] all signals of an ensuing bad headache. Most people report pain behind or around one eye and always on the same side of the head—a pain that can last for hours or days and then disappear. A migraine can strike at any time, although the hormonal changes around menstruation and ovulation often seem to set off migraines in women, who are three times more likely to get migraines as are men. Migraines can occur in children as young as 2 years, with incidences peaking from the mid-20s through middle age and then trailing off around age 55.[29]

Although migraines are believed to run in families, and the hormonal influences seem to be well established, findings about other forms of migraine "triggers" seem to be highly speculative at best. Patients report that migraines can be triggered by emotional stress, the weather, certain foods, lack of sleep, and a litany of other causes. When tested under laboratory settings, however, much of this evidence is inconclusive. Migraines occur when blood vessels in the membrane that surrounds the brain dilate. Historically, treatments have centered on reversing or preventing this dilation, with the most common treatment derived from the rye fungus *ergot*. Today, many of these fast-acting ergot compounds are available by nasal spray, vastly increasing the speed of relief to patients. However, ergot drugs have many side effects, the least of which may be that they are habit forming, causing users to wake up with "rebound" headaches each morning after use.[30]

When true migraines occur, relaxation is only minimally effective as a treatment. Often, strong pain-relieving drugs prescribed by a physician are necessary. In 1994, the FDA approved Imitrex, a new drug tailor-made for migraines that works for about 80 percent of those who try it. But the cost of a single dose is a stunning $14 per pill and second doses are often needed. In addition, its side effects make Imitrex inappropriate for anyone having uncontrolled high blood pressure or heart disease. Recently, treatment with lidocaine has also shown promising results, and newer drugs called triptans, such as Zomig, Amerge, and Maxalt are now available. All triptans, however, are cleared from the body in a few hours and the migraine sometimes returns.[31]

▶ *Secondary Headaches*   Secondary headaches arise as a result of some other underlying condition. A good example is a person with a severe sinus blockage that causes pressure in the sinus cavity. This pressure may induce a headache. Hypertension, allergies, low blood sugar, diseases of the spine, the common cold, poorly fitted dentures, problems with eyesight, and other types of pain or injury can trigger this condition. Relaxation and pain relievers such as aspirin are of little help in treating secondary headaches. Rather, medications or other therapies designed to relieve the underlying organic cause of the headache must be included in the treatment regimen.

Seizure Disorders

The word **epilepsy** is derived from the Greek *epilepsia*, meaning "seizure." Approximately 1 percent of all Americans suffer from some form of seizure-related disorder. These disorders are generally caused by abnormal electrical activity in the brain and are characterized by loss of control of muscular activity and unconsciousness. Symptoms vary widely from person to person.

There are several forms of seizure disorders, the most common forms of which are:

- *Grand mal, or major motor seizure:* These seizures are often preceded by a shrill cry or a seizure aura (body sensations such as ringing in the ears or a specific smell or taste that occurs prior to a seizure). Convulsions and loss of consciousness generally occur and may last from 30 seconds to several minutes or more. Keeping track of the length of time elapsed is one aspect of first aid.
- *Petit mal, or minor seizure:* These seizures involve no convulsions. Rather, a minor loss of consciousness that may go unnoticed occurs. Minor twitching of muscles may take place, usually for a shorter time than the duration of grand mal convulsions.
- *Psychomotor seizure:* These seizures involve both mental processes and muscular activity. Symptoms may include mental confusion and a listless state characterized by such activities as lip smacking, chewing, and repetitive movements.

Emphysema   A respiratory disease in which the alveoli become distended or ruptured and are no longer functional.

Alveoli   Tiny air sacs of the lungs.

Chronic bronchitis   A serious respiratory disorder in which the bronchial tubes become so inflamed and swollen that respiratory function is impaired.

Migraine   A condition characterized by localized headaches that result from alternating dilation and constriction of blood vessels.

Epilepsy   A neurological disorder caused by abnormal electrical brain activity; can be accompanied by altered consciousness or convulsions.

- *Jacksonian seizure:* This is a progressive seizure that often begins in one part of the body, such as the fingers, and moves to other parts, such as the hand or arm. Usually only one side of the body is affected.

Improvements in medication and surgical interventions to reduce some causes of seizures are among the most promising treatments today.

GENDER-RELATED DISORDERS

Fibrocystic Breast Condition

Fibrocystic breast condition is a common, noncancerous problem among women in the United States. Symptoms range in severity from a small palpable lump to large masses of irregular tissue found in both breasts. The underlying causes of the condition are unknown. Although some experts believe it to be related to hormonal changes that occur during the normal menstrual cycle, many women report that their conditions neither worsen nor improve during their cycles. In fact, in most cases, the condition appears to run in families and to become progressively worse with age, irrespective of pregnancy or other hormonal disruptions. Although the majority of these cyst formations consists of fibrous tissue, some are filled with fluid. Treatment often involves removal of fluid from the affected area or surgical removal of the cyst itself.

Premenstrual Syndrome (PMS)

Premenstrual syndrome (PMS) is a syndrome describing a series of characteristic symptoms that occur prior to menstruation in some women. PMS is characterized by as many as 150 possible physical and emotional symptoms that vary from person to person and from month to month. These symptoms usually appear a week to 10 days preceding the menstrual period and affect between 20 and 40 percent of U.S. women of menstruating age to some degree. They include depression, tension, irritability, headaches, tender breasts, bloated abdomen, backache, abdominal cramps, acne, fluid retention, diarrhea, and fatigue. It is believed that women who have PMS develop a predictable pattern of symptoms during the menstrual cycle and that the severity of their symptoms may be influenced by external factors, such as stress.

Women usually experience PMS for the first time after the age of 20, and it may remain a regular part of their reproductive life unless they seek treatment. For many women, the first day of their period brings immediate relief. For others, the depressive symptoms persist all month and are only heightened prior to the menstrual period.

Most authorities believe that the most plausible cause of PMS is a hormonal imbalance related to the rise in estrogen levels preceding the menstrual period. This theory is substantiated by the fact that women with PMS who are given prescriptions for progesterone often experience relief of symptoms. Critics of this theory argue that controlled research has not yet been conducted on the effects of progesterone on PMS.

Common treatments for PMS include hormonal therapy in addition to drugs and behaviors designed to relieve the symptoms. These include aspirin for pain, diuretics for fluid buildup, decreases in caffeine and salt intake, increases in complex carbohydrate intake, stress reduction techniques, and exercise.

Endometriosis

Whether the incidence of **endometriosis** is on the rise in the United States or whether the disorder is simply attracting more attention is difficult to determine. Victims of endometriosis tend to be women between the ages of 20 and 40. Symptoms include severe cramping during and between menstrual cycles, irregular periods, unusually heavy or light menstrual flow, abdominal bloating, fatigue, painful bowel movements with periods, painful intercourse, constipation, diarrhea, menstrual pain, infertility, and low back pain.

Although much remains unknown about the causes of endometriosis, we do know that the disease is characterized by the abnormal growth and development of endometrial tissue (the tissue lining the uterus) in regions of the body other than the uterus. Among the most widely accepted theories concerning the causes of endometriosis are the transmission of endometrial tissue to other regions of the body during surgery or through the birthing process; the movement of menstrual fluid backward through the fallopian tubes during menstruation; and abnormal cell migration through body-fluid movement. Women with cycles shorter than 27 days and those with flows lasting over a week are at increased risk. The more aerobic exercise a woman engages in and the earlier she starts, the less likely she is to develop endometriosis.

Fibrocystic breast condition   A common, noncancerous condition in which a woman's breast contain fibrous or fluid-filled cysts.

Premenstrual syndrome (PMS)   A series of physical and emotional symptoms that may occur in women prior to their menstrual periods.

Endometriosis   Abnormal development of endometrial tissue outside the uterus resulting in serious side effects.

Hysterectomy   Surgical removal of the uterus.

Insulin   A hormone produced by the pancreas; required by the body for the metabolism of carbohydrates.

Diabetes mellitus   A disease in which the pancreas fails to produce enough insulin or the body fails to use insulin effectively.

Hyperglycemia   Elevated blood sugar levels.

Uterine Fibroids

Severe abdominal cramps. Incontinence. Infertility. Excessive bleeding. All symptoms of a disorder that can shake a woman, her family, and friends.

Uterine fibroids are noncancerous growths that can develop in a woman's uterus and that occur in 20 percent to 25 percent of all women. Fibroids are most common in women aged 30 to 40, but they can occur at any age. They also tend to occur more frequently and grow more quickly in black women than in white women. Symptoms include the following:

- Changes in menstruation
  - ✓ Excessive bleeding
  - ✓ Longer or more frequent periods
  - ✓ Excessive menstrual cramps
  - ✓ Vaginal bleeding at times other than menstruation
  - ✓ Anemia

- Pain
  - ✓ In the abdomen or lower back, usually a dull, heavy ache, but may be sharp
  - ✓ During sex

- Pressure
  - ✓ Difficulty in urinating or frequent urination
  - ✓ Constipation, rectal pain, or difficult bowel movements
  - ✓ Abdominal cramps

- Miscarriage and infertility

Many women develop small fibrous growths in their uterus and experience few problems. They may live their entire lives unaware of these growths. For others, however, the fibroids may grow over a period of time into masses large enough to place pressure on internal organs or interfere with normal functioning. They may even be the cause of infertility in some women.

The options available to women with fibroids fall into two categories: surgical or nonsurgical. Women beyond child-bearing age and with tolerable symptoms may opt to let nature take its course. Medication may also help to shrink the fibroids before the onset of menopause. Women who opt for surgery also have a couple of choices: a hysterectomy or a myomectomy. A hysterectomy is the removal of the uterus, the cervix, and surrounding tissue, including the fibroids. A myomectomy is the removal of only the fibroids, with everything else left intact.

Fibroids can be detected during an annual pelvic exam and verified by an ultrasound or other methods, such as a laparoscopy, magnetic resonance imaging (MRI), or computerized tomography (CT) scans when a more detailed image is necessary. Paying attention to changes or unusual events with the menstrual cycle and paying attention to general body health are important components of every woman's prevention profile.

Source: "Uterine Fibroids," a pamphlet from the American College of Obstetricians and Gynecologists, 409 12th Street SW, Washington, D.C. 20024–2188.

Treatment of endometriosis ranges from bed rest and reduction in stressful activities to **hysterectomy** (the removal of the uterus) and/or the removal of one or both ovaries and the fallopian tubes. Recently, physicians have been criticized by some segments of the public for being too quick to select hysterectomy as the treatment of choice. More conservative treatments that involve dilation and curettage, surgically scraping endometrial tissue off the fallopian tubes and other reproductive organs, and combinations of hormone therapy have become more acceptable in most regions of the country. Hormonal treatments include gonadotropin-releasing hormone (GnRH) analogs, various synthetic progesterone-like drugs (Provera), and oral contraceptives.

········ WHAT DO YOU THINK?

Which of the preceding health problems do you think causes the most problems for women in the United States? Are these problems related to stigma associated with the condition, the condition's physiological effects, or are they psychological in nature? What actions should be taken to increase awareness and understanding of these conditions?

DIGESTION-RELATED DISORDERS

Diabetes

In healthy people, the *pancreas*, a powerful enzyme-producing organ, produces the hormone **insulin** in sufficient quantities to allow the body to use or store glucose (blood sugar). When this organ fails to produce enough insulin to regulate sugar metabolism or when the body fails to use insulin effectively, a disease known as **diabetes mellitus** occurs. Diabetics exhibit **hyperglycemia,** or elevated blood sugar levels, and high glucose levels in their urine. Other symptoms include excessive thirst, frequent urination, hunger, tendency to tire easily, wounds that heal slowly, numbness or tingling in the extremities, changes in vision, skin eruptions, and, in women, a tendency toward vaginal yeast infections. Each year an average of 650,000 new cases are identified, with rapidly rising incidence rates in recent decades. Diabetes mellitus is among the leading causes of death in America and is a major contributor to cardiovascular disease (CVD), blindness, and renal failure.

The more serious form, known as type I (insulin-dependent) diabetes, is an autoimmune disease in which the immune system destroys the insulin-making beta cells, and it usually begins early in life.[32] Type I diabetics typically must depend on insulin injections or oral medications for the rest of their lives because insulin is not present in their bodies. Adult-onset (noninsulin-dependent), or type II diabetes, in which insulin production is deficient, tends to develop in later life. These diabetics can often control the symptoms of their disease, with minimal medical intervention, through a regimen of proper diet, weight control, and exercise. They may be able to avoid oral medications or insulin indefinitely.

Justationable diabetis → found in preg. woman

▶ *Risk Factors*   Diabetes tends to run in families, and a tendency toward being overweight, coupled with inactivity, dramatically increases a person's risk. Older persons and mothers of babies weighing over 9 pounds also run an increased risk. Approximately 80 percent of all patients are overweight at the time of diagnosis. Weight loss and exercise are important factors in lowering blood sugar and improving the efficiency of cellular use of insulin. Both can help to prevent overwork of the pancreas and the development of diabetes. People who develop diabetes today have a much better prognosis than did those who developed diabetes just 20 years ago.

▶ *Controlling Diabetes*   Most physicians attempt to control diabetes with a variety of insulin-related drugs. Most of these drugs are taken orally, although self-administered hypodermic injections are prescribed when other treatments are inadequate. Recent breakthroughs in individual monitoring and the implanting of insulin monitors and insulin infusion pumps that regulate insulin intake "on demand" have provided many diabetics with the opportunity to lead normal lives. Other diabetics have found that they can help to control their diabetes by eating foods that are rich in complex carbohydrates, low in sodium, and high in fiber; by losing weight; and by getting regular exercise.

Lactose Intolerance

As many as 50 million Americans are unable to eat dairy products such as milk, cheese, ice cream, and other foods that the rest of us take for granted. These people suffer from a malady known as **lactose intolerance,** meaning that they have lost the ability to produce the digestive enzyme lactase, which is necessary for the body to convert milk sugar (lactose) into glucose. That cold glass of milk has now become a source of stomach cramping, diarrhea, nausea, gas, and related symptoms. Lactose intolerance, however, need not be a death knell for future dairy product consumption. Once diagnosed, lactose intolerance can be treated by introducing low-lactose or lactose-free foods into the diet. Through trial and error, individuals usually find that they can tolerate one type of low-lactose food better than others. In addition to learning to eat lower lactose-laden foods, some people find that they can

purchase special products that contain the missing lactase and thus eat these foods without serious side effects.

Colitis and Irritable Bowel Syndrome (IBS)

Ulcerative colitis is a disease of the large intestine in which the mucous membranes of the intestinal walls become inflamed. Victims with severe cases may have as many as 20 bouts of bloody diarrhea a day. Colitis can also produce severe stomach cramps, weight loss, nausea, sweating, and fever. Although some experts believe that colitis occurs more frequently in people with high stress levels, this theory is controversial. Hypersensitivity reactions, particularly to milk and certain foods, have also been considered as a possible cause. It is difficult to determine the cause of colitis because the disease goes into unexplained remission and then recurs without apparent reason. This pattern often continues over periods of years and may be related to the later development of colorectal cancer. Because the cause of colitis remains unknown, treatment focuses exclusively on relieving the symptoms. Increasing fiber intake and taking anti-inflammatory drugs, steroids, and other medications designed to reduce inflammation and soothe irritated intestinal walls have been effective in relieving symptoms.

Many people develop a condition related to colitis known as **irritable bowel syndrome (IBS),** in which nausea, pain, gas, diarrhea attacks, or cramps occur after eating certain foods or when a person is under unusual stress. IBS symptoms commonly begin in early adulthood. Symptoms may vary from week to week and can fade for long periods of time only to return. The cause of IBS is unknown, but researchers suspect that people with IBS have digestive systems that are overly sensitive to what they eat and drink, to stress, and to certain hormonal changes. They may also be more sensitive to pain signals from the stomach. Stress management, relaxation techniques, regular activity, and diet can bring IBS under control in the vast majority of cases.

Diverticulosis

Diverticulosis occurs when the walls of the intestine become weakened for undetermined reasons and small pea-sized bulges develop. These bulges often fill with feces and, over time, become irritated and infected, causing pain and discomfort. If this irritation persists, bleeding and chronic obstruction may occur, either of which can be life-threatening. If you have a persistent pain in the lower abdominal region, seek medical attention at once.

Peptic Ulcers

An ulcer is a lesion or wound that forms in body tissue as a result of some form of irritant. A **peptic ulcer** is a chronic ulcer that occurs in the lining of the stomach or the section of the small intestine known as the *duodenum*. It has been thought to be caused by the erosive effect of digestive juices on these tissues. The lining of these organs becomes irritated, the protective covering of mucus is reduced, and the gastric acid begins to digest the dying tissue, just as it would a piece of food. Typically, this irritation causes pain that disappears when the person eats, but returns about an hour later.

In 1994, the National Institutes of Health (NIH) announced that a common bacteria, *Helicobacter pylori,* may be the cause of most ulcers, and called for the use of powerful antibiotics to treat the disorder, which affects over 4 million Americans every year. This was a dramatic departure from the typical treatment using acid-reducing drugs. The new treatment recommends a two-week course of antibiotics and antacids in ulcer cases in which excess stomach acid or overuse of drugs such as aspirin and ibuprofen have caused an irritation. The good news is that by treating ulcers with germ-killing drugs, the ulcers appear less likely to recur. People with ulcers should avoid high-fat foods, alcohol, and substances such as aspirin that may irritate organ linings or cause increased secretion of stomach acids and thereby exacerbate this condition. In some cases, surgery has been necessary to relieve persistent symptoms.

Arthritis can cause a great degree of discomfort, often interfering with the simplest of tasks or the most delicate.

MUSCULOSKELETAL DISEASES

Arthritis

Called the "nation's primary crippler," **arthritis** strikes one in seven Americans, or over 38 million people. Symptoms range from the occasional tendinitis of the weekend athlete to the horrific pain of rheumatoid arthritis.

Osteoarthritis, also known as degenerative joint disease, is a progressive deterioration of bones and joints that has been associated with the "wear and tear" theory of aging. More recent research indicates that as joints are used, they release enzymes that digest cartilage while other cells in the cartilage try to repair the damage. When the enzymatic breakdown overpowers cellular repair, the pain and swelling characteristic of arthritis may occur. Weather extremes, excessive strain, and injury often lead to osteoarthritis flare-ups. But a specific precipitating event does not seem to be necessary.

Although age and injury are undoubtedly factors in the development of osteoarthritis, heredity, abnormal use of the joint, diet, abnormalities in joint structure, and impaired blood supply to the joint may also contribute. Osteoarthritis of the hands seems to have a particularly strong genetic component. Extreme disability as a result of osteoarthritis is rare. However, when joints become so distorted that they impair activity, surgical intervention is often necessary. Joint replacement and bone fusion are common surgical repair techniques. For most people, anti-inflammatory drugs and pain relievers such as aspirin and cortisone-related agents ease discomfort. In some sufferers, applications of heat, mild exercise, and massage may also relieve the pain.

Rheumatoid arthritis is an autoimmune disease involving chronic inflammation that can occur at any age, but most commonly appears between the ages of 20 and 45. It is three times more common among women than among men during early adulthood but equally common among men and women in the over-70 age group. Symptoms include stiffness, pain, and swelling of multiple joints, often including the joints of the hands and wrists, and can be gradually progressive or sporadic, with occasional unexplained remissions.

Lactose intolerance   The inability to produce lactose, an enzyme needed to convert milk sugar into glucose.

Ulcerative colitis   An inflammatory disorder that affects the mucous membranes of the large intestine, producing bloody diarrhea.

Irritable bowel syndrome (IBS)   Nausea, pain, gas, or diarrhea caused by certain foods or stress.

Diverticulosis   A condition in which bulges form in the walls of the intestine; results in irritation and infection of the intestine.

Peptic ulcer   Damage to the stomach or intestinal lining, usually caused by digestive juices.

Arthritis   Painful inflammatory disease of the joints.

Osteoarthritis   A progressive deterioration of bones and joints that has been associated with the "wear and tear" theory of aging.

Rheumatoid arthritis   A serious inflammatory joint disease.

Treatment of rheumatoid arthritis is similar to that for osteoarthritis. Emphasis is placed on pain relief and attempts to improve the functional mobility of the patient. In some instances, immunosuppressant drugs are given to reduce the inflammatory response.

Fibromyalgia

Although there are many diseases today that seem to defy our best medical tests and treatments, one that is particularly frustrating is **fibromyalgia,** a chronic, painful, rheumatoid-like disorder that affects as many as 5 to 6 percent of the general population. Persons with fibromyalgia experience an array of symptoms including headaches, dizziness, numbness and tingling, itching, fluid retention, chronic joint pain, abdominal or pelvic pain, and even occasional diarrhea. Suspected causes have ranged from sleep disturbances, stress, emotional distress, viruses, and autoimmune disorders; however, none have been proven in clinical trials. Because of fibromyalgia's multiple symptoms, it is usually diagnosed only after myriad tests have ruled out other disorders. The American College of Rheumatology identifies the major diagnostic criteria as:[33]

- History of widespread pain of at least 3 months' duration in the axial skeleton as well as in all four quadrants of the body
- Pain in at least 11 of 18 paired tender points on digital palpation of about 4 kilograms of pressure

What is known is that the disease primarily affects women in their 30s and 40s, and that it can be extremely debilitating due to the unrelieved pain, feelings of bloating or swelling, and fatigue that victims may suffer. Many people with fibromyalgia also become depressed and report chronic fatigue-like symptoms.

Treatment for fibromyalgia varies based on the severity of symptoms. Typically, adequate rest, stress management, relaxation techniques, dietary supplements and selected herbal remedies, and pain medications are prescribed. Avoidance of extreme temperatures, which may exacerbate symptoms, is also recommended.

Systemic Lupus Erythematosus (SLE)

Lupus is a disease in which the immune system attacks the body, producing antibodies that destroy or injure organs such as the kidneys, brain, and heart. The symptoms vary from mild to severe and may disappear for periods of time. A butterfly-shaped rash covering the bridge of the nose and both cheeks is common. Nearly all SLE sufferers have aching joints and muscles, and 60 percent of them develop redness and swelling that moves from joint to joint. The disease affects 1 in 700 Caucasians but 1 in 250 African Americans; 90 percent of all victims are females. Extensive research has not yet found a cure for this sometimes fatal disease.

Low Back Pain

Approximately 80 percent of all Americans will experience low back pain at some point during their lifetimes. Although some of these low back pain (LBP) episodes may result from muscular damage and be short-lived and acute, others may involve dislocations, fractures, or other problems with spinal vertebrae or discs and be chronic or require surgery. Low back pain is epidemic throughout the world. It is the major cause of disability for people aged 20 to 45 in the United States, who suffer more frequently and severely from this problem than older people do.[34]

Back injuries are the most frequently mentioned complaints in injury-related lawsuits, and result in high medical and rehabilitation bills, costing businesses and industries in the United States over $50 billion annually in direct and indirect costs.[35]

▶ **Preventing Back Pain and Injury** To prevent back pain, you must be knowledgeable about what area of the spinal column is most at risk and attempt to protect that area as much as possible. Almost 90 percent of all back problems occur in the lumbar spine region (lower back). You can avoid many problems by consciously attempting to maintain good posture. Other preventive hints include the following:

- Purchase a firm mattress and avoid sleeping on your stomach.
- Avoid high-heeled shoes, which often tilt the pelvis forward.
- Control your weight.
- Lift objects with your legs, not your back.
- Buy a good chair for doing your work, preferably one with lumbar support.
- Move your car seat forward so that your knees are elevated slightly.
- Warm up before exercising.
- Strengthen abdominal and back muscles.

OTHER MALADIES

During the last decade, numerous afflictions have surfaced that seem to be products of our times. Some of these health problems relate to specific groups of people, some are due to technological advances, and some are unexplainable. Still other diseases have been present for many years and continue to cause severe disability (see Table 13.3). Among the

Fibromyalgia A chronic, painful rheumatoidlike disorder that can be highly painful and difficult to diagnose.

Lupus A disease in which the immune system attacks the body, producing antibodies that destroy or injure organs such as the kidneys, brain, and heart.

TABLE 13.3
Other Modern Afflictions

DISEASE	DESCRIPTION	TREATMENT
Parkinson's disease	A disease affecting 1.5 million American men and women; most over the age of 55. Symptoms include tremors, rigidity, slowed movement, loss of autonomic movements, and difficulty walking.	Unknown cause makes prevention difficult. Tranquilizers are useful in controlling nerve responses.
Multiple sclerosis	Disease that affects 250,000 Americans each year, women more than men. Precise cause uncertain. Symptoms include vision problems, tingling and numbness in extremities, chronic fatigue, and neurological impairments.	Medication to control symptoms and slow progression of the disease. Stress management may be helpful.
Cystic fibrosis	Inherited disease occurring in 1 out of every 1,600 births. Characterized by pooling of large amounts of mucus in lungs, digestive disturbances, and excessive sodium excretion. Results in premature death.	Most treatments are geared toward relief of symptoms. Antibiotics are administered for infection. Recent strides in genetic research suggest better treatments and potential cure in the near future.
Sickle cell disease	Inherited disease affecting 8–10 percent of all African Americans. Disease affects hemoglobin, forming sickle-shaped red blood cells that interfere with oxygenation. Results in severe pain, anemia, and premature death.	Reduce stress and attend to minor infections immediately. Seek genetic counseling.
Cerebral palsy	Disorder characterized by the loss of voluntary control over motor functioning. Believed to be caused by a lack of oxygen to the brain at birth, brain disorders or an accident before or after birth, poisoning, or brain infections.	Follow preventive actions to reduce accident risks; improved neonatal and birthing techniques.
Graves' disease	A thyroid disorder characterized by swelling of the eyes, staring gaze, and retraction of the eyelid. Can result in loss of sight. The cause is unknown and it can occur at any age.	Medication may help control symptoms. Radioactive iodine supplements also may be administered.

conditions that have received the most attention in recent years are chronic fatigue syndrome and disorders related to the use of video display terminals.

Chronic Fatigue Syndrome (CFS)

Fatigue is a subjective condition in which people feel tired before they begin activities, lack the energy to accomplish tasks that require sustained effort and attention, or become abnormally exhausted after normal activities. To many Americans, such symptoms are all too common. In the late 1980s, however, a characteristic set of symptoms including chronic fatigue, headaches, fever, sore throat, enlarged lymph nodes, depression, poor memory, general weakness, nausea, and symptoms remarkably similar to mononucleosis were noted in several U.S. clinics. Despite extensive testing, no viral cause has been found to date.[36]

Today, in the absence of a known pathogen, many researchers believe that the illness, now commonly referred to as chronic fatigue syndrome (CFS), may have strong psychosocial roots. According to Harvard psychiatrist Arthur Barsky, our heightened awareness of health makes some of us scrutinize our bodies so carefully that the slightest deviation becomes amplified. The more we focus on our body and on our perception of our health, the worse we feel.[37]

The diagnosis of chronic fatigue syndrome depends on two major criteria and eight or more minor criteria. The major criteria are debilitating fatigue that persists for at least six months and the absence of diagnoses of other illnesses that could cause the symptoms. Minor criteria include headaches, fever, sore throat, painful lymph nodes, weakness, fatigue after exercise, sleep problems, and rapid onset of these symptoms.

Repetitive Stress Injuries (RSIs)

The Bureau of Labor Statistics estimates that 25 percent of all injuries in the labor force that result in lost work time are due to **repetitive stress injuries (RSIs).** These injuries are estimated to cost employers over $22 billion a year in worker's compensation and an additional $85 billion in related costs, such as absenteeism.

One of the most common RSIs is **carpal tunnel syndrome,** a product of both the information age and the age of technology in general. Hours spent typing at the computer, flipping groceries through computerized scanners, or other jobs "made simpler" by technology can result in irritation to the median nerve in the wrist, causing numbness, tingling, and pain in the fingers and hands. Although carpal tunnel syndrome risk can be reduced by proper placement of the keyboard, wrist pads, and other techniques, RSIs are often overlooked until significant damage has been done. Better education and ergonomic workplace designs can eliminate many injuries of this nature.

> **Repetitive stress injury (RSI)** An injury to nerves, soft tissue, or joints due to the physical stress of repeated motions.
>
> **Carpal tunnel syndrome** A common occupational injury in which the median nerve in the wrist becomes irritated, causing numbness, tingling, and pain in the fingers and hands.

Taking Charge ....
Managing Your Disease Risks

Infectious diseases pose serious challenges in the United States, as well as throughout the world. In particular, sexually transmitted infections, including HIV infection, present an increasing health risk to our nation's youth. Nearly all infectious diseases can be prevented by practicing safe and responsible behaviors. In addition, many non-infectious diseases can be prevented, or their onset delayed, by adopting positive personal health habits.

CHECKLIST FOR CHANGE

MAKING PERSONAL CHOICES

- ✓ Be aware of factors that can threaten your health status.
- ✓ Know your disease and immunization history.
- ✓ Take the proper precautions to protect yourself from exposure to infectious pathogens.
- ✓ Know the health status of your intimate partners.
- ✓ Communicate openly and honestly with your partners about your feelings regarding sexual intimacy.
- ✓ If you have an infectious disease that can be spread through casual contact, remember to wash your hands frequently.
- ✓ Avoid traveling to places where outbreaks of infectious diseases have not been controlled.
- ✓ Follow a healthy routine of sleep, nutrition, and exercise.

- ✓ Follow safe measures when involved with someone with an infectious disease.
- ✓ Cook foods at their appropriate temperatures.
- ✓ Assess your level of risk for acquiring an STI, including HIV infection.
- ✓ Respect the rights and needs of individuals affected by an infectious disease.
- ✓ How much individual responsibility should we each accept for chronic diseases we could have prevented? Do you have any lifestyle or personal health habits that could cause a chronic disease?
- ✓ What actions can you take today to reduce your own risks for the diseases and disorders discussed in this chapter? Which concern you most?

✓ Does your student health service offer testing for STIs? How about HIV? If not, is there a local free clinic where you could be tested for STIs or HIV?

✓ Does your local school system offer a sex education curriculum, including discussion about how to stop the spread of HIV?

✓ If you worked for a government agency charged with helping people improve their personal health habits, what approaches would you take?

✓ Do you think the strategy of raising the cost of cigarettes is discouraging their use?

✓ What role should businesses play in improving employee health? Should businesses be held liable for situations in which employees get carpal tunnel syndrome or experience lower back problems?

SUMMARY

- The major uncontrollable risk factors for contracting infectious diseases are heredity, age, environmental conditions, and organism resistance. The major controllable risk factors are stress, nutrition, fitness level, sleep, hygiene, avoidance of high-risk behaviors, and drug use.

- The major pathogens are bacteria, viruses, fungi, protozoa, prions, and parasitic worms.

- Your body uses a number of defense systems to keep pathogens from invading. The skin is our major protection, helped by enzymes. The immune system increases antibodies to destroy antigens. In addition, fever and pain play a role in defending the body.

- Sexually transmitted infections are spread through intercourse, oral sex, anal sex, hand–genital contact, and, sometimes, mouth-to-mouth contact. Major STIs include chlamydia, pelvic inflammatory disease, gonorrhea, syphilis, pubic lice, venereal warts, candidiasis, trichomoniasis, and herpes.

- Acquired immune deficiency syndrome (AIDS) is caused by the human immunodeficiency virus (HIV). HIV is not confined to certain high-risk groups. Your risk for AIDS can be cut by deciding not to engage in risky sexual activities.

- Chronic lung diseases include allergies, hay fever, asthma, emphysema, and chronic bronchitis. Allergies are part of the body's natural defense system.

- Headaches may be caused by a variety of factors, the most common of which are tension, dilation and/or con-

traction of blood vessels in the brain, chemical influences on muscles and vessels that cause inflammation and pain, and underlying physiological and psychological disorders.

- Several modern maladies affect only women. Fibrocystic breast condition is a common, noncancerous build-up of irregular tissue. Premenstrual syndrome (PMS) is the name given to a wide variety of syndromes that appear to be related to the menstrual cycle. Endometriosis is the build-up of endometrial tissue in regions of the body other than the uterus.

- Pathogens, problems in enzyme or hormone production, anxiety or stress, functional abnormalities, and other problems are often listed as probable causes or digestive disorders.

- Musculoskeletal diseases such as arthritis, lower back pain, repetitive stress injuries, and other problems cause significant pain and disability in millions of people. Age, occupation, gender, posture, abdominal strength, and psychological factors contribute to the development of lower back problems.

- Chronic fatigue syndrome (CFS), and repetitive stress injuries (such as carpal tunnel syndrome) have emerged in the past decade as major chronic maladies. CFS is associated with depression. Repetitive stress injuries are preventable by proper equipment placement and usage.

DISCUSSION QUESTIONS

1. What is a pathogen? What are the similarities and differences between pathogens and antigens? What are the uncontrollable risk factors that can threaten your health? What factors are controllable? What can be done to limit the effects of either type of risk factor?

2. How have social conditions among the poor and homeless increased the risks for certain diseases, such as tuberculosis, influenza, and hepatitis? Why are these conditions challenges to the efforts of public health officials?

3. What is the difference between active and natural immunity?
4. Identify five sexually transmitted infections. What are their symptoms? How do they develop? What are their potential long-term risks?
5. Why might it be inappropriate to identify groups as at high risk for HIV infection? Why might HIV infection be better referred to as a sexually *transmissible* infection than as a sexually transmitted infection?
6. What are some of the major noninfectious chronic diseases affecting Americans today? Do you think there is a pattern in the types of diseases that we get? What are the common risk factors?
7. List the common respiratory diseases affecting Americans. Which of these diseases has a genetic basis? An environ-

mental basis? An individual basis? What, if anything, is being done to prevent, treat, and/or control each of these conditions?
8. Do you believe that PMS is a disorder or disease, or simply a catch-all name for many naturally occurring events in the menstrual cycle?
9. What are the medical risks of fibrocystic breast condition and endometriosis? How can they be treated?
10. Describe the symptoms and treatment of diabetes.
11. How can you tell whether your stomach is reacting to final exams or telling you that you have a serious medical condition?

APPLICATION EXERCISE

Reread the *What Do You Think?* scenario at the beginning of this chapter and answer the following questions:

1. What was your initial reaction to the scenario presented in the chapter opener?
2. What are some legal issues that could arise or that already exist regarding all infectious diseases, including

STIs? Should you be able to "sue" someone who flagrantly spreads an infectious disease? Why or why not?
3. What services exist on your campus for people living with HIV infection or AIDS? What services focus on informing people about sexually transmitted infections?

14

Life's Transitions

The Aging Process

Grow old along with me!
The best is yet to be,
The last of life, for which the first was made . . .
—Robert Browning, *Rabbi Ben Ezra*

In a society that seems to worship youth, researchers have finally begun to offer some good—even revolutionary—news about the aging process: Growing old doesn't have to mean a slow slide to disability, loneliness, and declining physical and mental health. Health promotion, disease prevention, and wellness-oriented activities can prolong vigor and productivity, even among those who haven't always had model lifestyles or given healthful habits priority. In fact, getting older may actually mean getting better in many ways—particularly socially, psychologically, and intellectually.

Who you are as you age and the manner in which you view aging (either as a natural part of living or as an inevitable move toward disease and death) are important factors in how successfully you will adapt to life's transitions. If you view these transitions as periods of growth, as changes that will lead to improved mental, emotional, spiritual, and physical phases in your development as a human being, your journey through even the most difficult times may be easier.

Aging has traditionally been described as the patterns of life changes that occur in members of all species as they grow older. Some believe that it begins at the moment of conception. Others contend that it starts at birth. Still others believe that true aging does not begin until we reach our 40s. Perhaps our traditional definitions of aging need careful reexamination.

REDEFINING AGING

Discrimination against people based on age is known as **ageism.** When directed against the elderly, this type of discrimination carries with it social ostracism and negative portrayals of older people.

The study of individual and collective aging processes, known as **gerontology,** explores the reasons for aging and the ways in which people cope with and adapt to this process. Gerontologists have identified several types of age-related characteristics that should be used to determine where a person is in terms of biological, psychological, social, legal, and functional life-stage development:[1]

- *Biological age* refers to the relative age or condition of the person's organs and body systems. Arthritis and other chronic conditions often accelerate the aging process.
- *Psychological age* refers to a person's adaptive capacities, such as coping abilities and intelligence, and to the person's awareness of his or her individual capabilities, self-efficacy, and general ability to adapt to a given situation.
- *Social age* refers to a person's habits and roles relative to society's expectations. People in a particular life stage usually share similar tastes in music, television shows, and politics.
- *Legal age* is probably the most common definition of age in the United States. Legal age is based on chronological years and is used to determine such things as voting rights, driving privileges, drinking age, eligibility for Social Security payments, and a host of other rights and obligations.
- *Functional age* refers to the ways in which people compare to others of a similar age. It is difficult to separate func-

—today more than ever the elderly are active—

In most cases, you need look no further than your family tree to get an idea of the effects aging will have on you.

tional aging from many of the other types of aging, particularly chronological and biological aging.

What Is Successful Aging?

Contemporary gerontologists have begun to analyze the vast majority of people who continue to live full and productive lives throughout their later years. They have devised several categories for specific age-related characteristics. People aged 65 to 74 are viewed as the **young-old;** those aged 75 to 84 are the **middle-old** group; those 85 and over are classified as the **old-old.**

You should note that chronological age is not the only component to be considered when objectively defining *aging*. The question is not how many years a person has lived, but how much life the person has packed into those years. This *quality-of-life index,* combined with the inevitable chronological process, appears to be the best indicator of the "aging gracefully" phenomenon. Most experts today agree that the

---

Aging The patterns of life changes that occur in members of all species as they grow older.

Ageism Discrimination based on age.

Gerontology The study of our individual and collective aging processes.

Young-old People aged 65 to 74.

Middle-old People aged 75 to 84.

Old-old People 85 and over.

---

best way to experience a productive, full, and satisfying old age is to take appropriate action to lead a productive, full, and satisfying life prior to old age.

WHAT DO YOU THINK?

What factors influence the aging process? Which of these factors do you have the power to change through the behaviors that you engage in right now?

The Elderly: A Growing Population

By the year 2010, a whole generation of 1960s' bead-wearing, tie-dye flaunting "flower children," who once proclaimed that no one over 30 could be trusted, will be turning 65. While the 65 and older group makes up one in 8 of all Americans today, it will include one in 6 by the year 2020 and one in 5 by 2050.[2] By 2020, this nation's elderly population is expected to swell to 53.2 million—a 63 percent increase over the current elderly population of 33 million.[3] (See Figure 14.1 on page 354.)

According to researchers at the National Institute on Aging, "the aging of the 75 million-strong baby boomer generation could have an impact on our society of equal magnitude to that of immigration at the turn of the century."[4] Representatives of the American Association of Retired Persons (AARP) state that, "As children, boomers strained the educational system. As workers, they competed fiercely for jobs. Now, as they age, they're going to put a tremendous strain on health and social services.[5]

HEALTH ISSUES FOR AN AGING SOCIETY

The concerns of government officials over the impending growth in the elderly population center around meeting their financial and medical needs. According to the latest statistics, life expectancy for a person born in 1997 is 76.5 years, about 29 years longer than a child born in 1900.[6] Whereas people aged 65 and older made up 13 percent of the U.S. population in 1992, they are projected to make up over 21 percent of the population by 2030. Where will these elderly people live? How will they pay for their medical costs? These and other questions pose many challenges for all of us.

Health Care Costs

As people live longer, the chances of developing a costly chronic disease increases. As our technology improves, chronic illnesses that once were fatal may now be treated successfully

everyone would live 115-120 yrs. old if there were no lifestyles threats

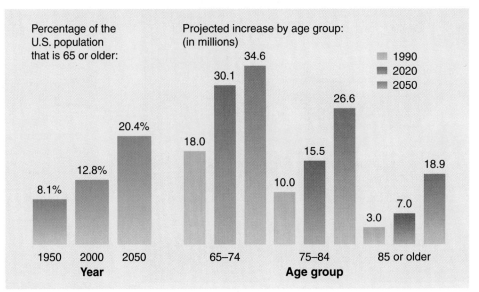

Figure 14.1

Our Aging Population

Source: U.S. Census Bureau, as shown in *USA Today*, 21 May 1996, 4A.

[handwritten: 38% of health care housing]

for several years. Projected future costs from these dual contributors are staggering.

Will working Americans be willing to pay an increased share of the health care costs for people on fixed incomes who cannot pay for themselves? If not, what will become of these people? Perhaps most important, who will ultimately pay?

········· **WHAT DO YOU THINK?**

Do you currently have health insurance? If not, why not? What do you think people over 65 would do if they were suddenly without Medicare? Should elderly Americans be left out of the health insurance industry because they are high risk? Why are the aging of the population and the impending difficulties with health care costs and access important to everyone? What actions could you take to reduce the possibility of high-cost problems later in your life?

▶ *Housing and Living Arrangements* With the costs of owning and maintaining a home slowly moving beyond the reach of the average American, housing problems for low-income elderly people are becoming more acute. Contrary to popular opinion, only about 1 percent of all people between the ages of 65 and 74, 5 percent of those between 75 and 84, and 15 percent of those over 85 are forced to seek nursing-home care. Increasing numbers of the elderly are remaining in their own homes and/or living with family members until their final hospitalizations.[7] (See Figure 14.2.)

▶ *Ethical and Moral Considerations* At the present time, the implications for an already overburdened health-care delivery system are staggering. Questions have already surfaced regarding the efficacy of hooking a terminally ill older person up to costly machines that may prolong life for a few

weeks or months but overtax our health-care resources. Will future generations be forced to devise a set of criteria for deciding who will be helped and who will not? Understanding the process of aging and knowing what actions you can take to prolong your healthy years are a part of our collective responsibility.

THEORIES ON AGING

Biological Theories

Of the various theories about the biological causes of aging, the following are among the most commonly accepted.

[handwritten: most pop.]

- *The wear-and-tear theory* states that, like everything else in the universe, the human body wears out. Inherent in this theory is the idea that the more you abuse your body, the faster it will wear out. Fortunately, today's elderly can achieve high levels of fitness without having to be a marathoner. Strength training, walking, gardening, vigorous shopping, and other activities allow even the most out of shape to improve.

- *The cellular theory* states that at birth we have only a certain number of usable cells, and these cells are genetically programmed to divide or reproduce only a limited number of times. Once these cells reach the end of their reproductive cycle, they begin to die and the organs they make up begin to show signs of deterioration. The rate of deterioration varies from person to person, and the impact of the deterioration depends on the system involved.

- *The autoimmune theory* attributes aging to the decline of the body's immunological system. Studies indicate that as we age, our immune systems become less effective in fighting disease. Eventually, bodies that are subjected to

[handwritten: financial burden]

[handwritten: - Social Security Issues - 2025 - will run out]

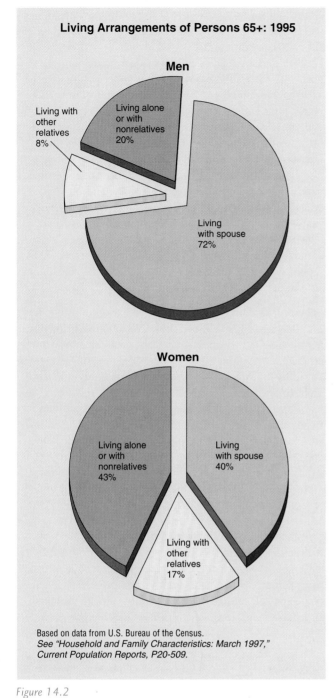

Living Arrangements of Persons 65+: 1995

Men

Living with other relatives 8%

Living alone or with nonrelatives 20%

Living with spouse 72%

Women

Living alone or with nonrelatives 43%

Living with spouse 40%

Living with other relatives 17%

Based on data from U.S. Bureau of the Census.
See "Household and Family Characteristics: March 1997,"
Current Population Reports, P20-509.

Figure 14.2

Living Arrangements of Persons 65+: 1995

Source: Based on data from U.S. Bureau of the Census. See "Household and Family Characteristics: March 1997," *Current Population Reports.*

too much stress, lack of sleep, and so on, especially if these are coupled with poor nutrition, begin to show signs of disease and infirmity. In some instances, the immune system appears to lose control and to turn its protective mechanisms inward, actually attacking the person's own body. Some gerontologists believe that the condition increases in frequency and severity with age.

• *The genetic mutation theory* proposes that the number of cells exhibiting unusual or different characteristics increases with age. Proponents of this theory believe that aging is related to the amount of mutational damage within the genes. The greater the mutation, the greater the chance that cells will not function properly, leading to eventual dysfunction of body organs and systems.

Psychosocial Effects on Aging

Numerous psychological and sociological factors also have a strong influence on the manner in which people age. Psychologists Erik Erikson and Robert Peck have formulated theories of personality development that encompass the human life span and emphasize adaptation and adjustment in self-development. In his developmental model, Erikson states that people must progress through eight critical stages during their lifetimes. If a person does not receive the proper stimulus or develop effective methods of coping with life's turmoil from infancy onward, problems are likely to develop later in life. According to this theory, attitudes, behaviors, and beliefs related to maladjustments in old age are often a result of problems encountered in earlier stages of a person's life.

Peck focuses much of his developmental theory on the crucial issues of middle and old age. He argues that during these periods people face a series of increasingly stressful tasks. Those who are poorly adjusted psychologically or who have not developed appropriate coping skills are likely to undergo a painful aging process.

A key element in the theories of both Erikson and Peck is the incorporation of age-related factors into lifelong behavior patterns. Both suggest that a combination of psychosocial and biological factors and environmental "trigger mechanisms" causes each of us to age in a unique manner.

CHANGES IN THE BODY AND MIND

In order to assess the typical aging process, we should probably ask ourselves what we can reasonably expect to happen to our bodies as we grow older.

Typical Physical Changes

Although the physiological consequences of aging differ in their severity and timing from person to person, there are standard changes that occur as a result of the aging process.

▶ *The Skin* As a normal consequence of aging, the skin becomes thinner and loses elasticity, particularly in the outer surfaces. Fat deposits, which add to the soft lines and shape of the skin, begin to diminish. Starting at about age 30, lines develop on the forehead as a result of smiling, squinting, and other facial expressions. These lines become more pronounced, with added "crow's-feet" around the eyes, during the 40s. During a person's 50s and 60s, the skin begins to sag and lose color, leading to pallor in the 70s. Body fat in underlying layers of skin continues to be redistributed away from the limbs and extremities into the trunk region of the body. Age spots become more numerous because of excessive pigment accumulation under the skin, particularly in those with heavy sun exposure.

▶ **Bones and Joints**   Throughout the life span, bones are continually changing because of the accumulation and loss of minerals. By the third or fourth decade of life, mineral loss from bones becomes more prevalent than mineral accumulation, resulting in a weakening and porosity (diminishing density) of bony tissue. This loss of minerals (particularly calcium) occurs in both sexes, although it is much more common in females. Loss of calcium can contribute to **osteoporosis,** a condition characterized by weakened, porous, and fractured bones.

Although many people consider osteoporosis a disease of the elderly, it is actually a progressive disorder that may already have begun to affect you. When you hear of osteoporosis, you may envision a slumped over individual with a characteristic "dowager's hump" in the upper back, but this is the rare extreme of the condition. As described in Chapter 11, bone loss occurs over many years and may be without symptoms until actual fractures occur or are diagnosed via X-rays. The spine, hips, and wrists are the most common sites of fractures, though other bones of the body may be involved.[8]

In the United States, osteoporosis affects over 25 million Americans and causes 1.5 million fractures annually. Of these fractures, about 250,000 occur at the hip. An estimated 12 to 20 percent of patients with hip fractures die within one year.[9] Several risk factors for developing osteoporosis have been identified:

- *Gender:* Women have a four times greater risk than men have. Their peak bone mass is lower than men's, and they experience an accelerated rate of bone loss after menopause.
- *Age:* After the third and fourth decade of life, all individuals lose bone mass and are more susceptible.
- *Low bone mass:* Low bone mass is one of the strongest predictors of osteoporosis. Measurement of bone density is an important aspect of risk assessment.
- *Early menopause:* The early occurrence of menopause, whether natural or caused by surgery, means that the positive effects of estrogen are lost for a longer period of time. (Decreases in sex hormones—estrogen in females and testosterone in males—appear to increase risk for the disease.) Menstrual disturbances, such as those caused by anorexia or bulimia or excessive exercise, may similarly result in an early loss of bone mass.
- *Thin, small-framed body:* Petite, thin women usually have a relatively low peak bone mass and are therefore at greater risk for osteoporosis.

- *Race:* Whites and Asians are at higher risk of developing osteoporosis than are blacks because blacks have heavier bone density on average.
- *Lack of calcium:* A lifetime of low calcium intake (well below the RDA and below the natural loss of calcium of 300 to 400 milligrams per day) may result in low peak bone mass and above-average loss of bone mass throughout adulthood.
- *High sodium consumption:* Increasingly, sodium has been implicated in calcium excretion/loss.
- *Lack of physical activity:* Immobilized, bedridden, or very inactive people usually have less muscle and bone mass.
- *Cigarette smoking:* Though the mechanism is not clear, smoking is linked to the development of osteoporosis.
- *Alcohol and/or caffeine:* Abuse of these substances is also linked to the development of osteoporosis.
- *Heredity:* Unidentified hereditary factors may play a role in the development of osteoporosis.

The goal of both treatment and prevention of osteoporosis is to decrease the likelihood and severity of bone fractures. Currently accepted treatments of established osteoporosis include adequate calcium intake, daily weight-bearing exercises approved by a physician, fall-prevention measures, and use of the hormones estrogen (in those not at high risk for certain forms of cancer) and calcitonin. A National Dairy Council study has shown that increasing calcium intake to 1,380 milligrams per day—an amount that exceeds the current RDA for calcium—both reduces bone loss and increases bone mineralization in women aged 58 to 77. Other therapies for osteoporosis, such as various metabolites of vitamin D and bisphosphonates, are under investigation.

Although the vitamin industry would like all of us to take megadoses of calcium every day, the preferred source of calcium is a nutritionally balanced diet. Dairy products, including milk, yogurt, and cheese, are the best sources of dietary calcium; canned fish, certain dark green leafy vegetables (such as kale and broccoli), legumes, calcium-enriched grain products, and fortified fruit juices may also be good sources.

▶ **The Head**   With age, features of the head enlarge and become more noticeable. Increased cartilage and fatty tissue cause the nose to grow a half-inch wider and another half-inch longer. Earlobes get fatter and grow longer, while overall head circumference increases one-quarter of an inch per decade, even though the brain itself shrinks. The skull becomes thicker with age.

▶ **The Urinary Tract**   At age 70, the kidneys can filter waste from the blood only half as fast as they could at age 30. The need to urinate more frequently occurs because the bladder's capacity declines from 2 cups of urine at age 30 to 1 cup at age 70.

One problem often associated with aging is **urinary incontinence,** which ranges from passing a few drops of

Macular Degeneration

Today, age-related macular degeneration, or AMD, is one of the leading causes of disability and premature blindness among elder Americans. Although degrees of disability vary, over one-fourth of those over the age of 65 and one-third of those over 80 experience some degree of AMD.

AMD occurs when the macula (the most light-sensitive part of the retina) begins to deteriorate, meaning that the person affected begins to lose vision, particularly straight-ahead vision and the ability to distinguish fine details. As a result, persons with AMD might not be able to drive a car due to difficulties in seeing details right in front of them. They also may not be able to distinguish faces sitting across the table from them.

There is little that can be done for those with AMD. A new device, however, developed at Johns Hopkins Wilmer Eye Institute, offers some promise. Called the low-vision enhancement system (LVES) and worn like a pair of goggles, it helps a person focus on objects that might otherwise be a blur, such as the television set, a newspaper, or other objects.

There are some controllable risk factors for AMD. Some studies have shown that smoking may increase risk, possibly because it compromises the eye's blood supply or interferes with the beneficial effects of certain molecules that prevent cell damage. Another apparent risk, prolonged exposure to glaring sunlight in the summer months of the year, seems to increase risks for the most serious forms of AMD. In addition, preliminary studies indicate that diets rich in carotenoids (the pigments found in yellow, orange, red, and dark green fruits and vegetables) may reduce one's risk. Other studies, however, show no apparent benefit and, in fact, suggest the potential for actual harm.

Regardless of cause, AMD poses a significant burden for an aging population. The alarming numbers of elderly persons suffering from this disease poses significant concern for gerontologists. Will AMD cause more and more adults to lose independence long before their other body systems begin to fail? Is this disease preventable? If so, the general public needs to be educated about the risks, and sun-lovers need to be aware that there is another reason to protect themselves from the sun. Taking steps to reduce risks for this problem is an important part of a healthy lifestyle.

Source: "New Ways to Protect Your Vision," *The Johns Hopkins Medical Letter—Health after 50,* 10 (1998): 3.

---

urine while laughing or sneezing to having no control over when and where urination takes place. Although exact estimates vary, as many as 19 percent of older men and 38 percent of older women have some degree of urinary incontinence.[10]

However, incontinence is not an inevitable part of the aging process. Most cases are caused by highly treatable underlying neurological problems that affect the central nervous system, or by medications, infections of the pelvic muscles, weakness in the pelvic walls, or other problems. When the problem is treated, the incontinence usually vanishes.[11]

Incontinence poses major social, physical, and emotional problems for the elderly. Embarrassment and fear of wetting oneself may cause an older person to become isolated. Prolonged wetness and the inability to properly care for oneself can lead to irritation, infections, or other problems. Fortunately, there are many treatments for this problem. Drug therapy can slow bladder contractions, increase bladder capacity, contract or relax the bladder sphincter, and increase fluid output. Surgery to repair the pelvic floor is often successful in stress incontinence. Artificial devices that slow urine flow, improvements in access to toilet facilities, rigid schedules for urination, and many newer treatments have also shown promise.

▶ **The Heart and Lungs** Resting heart rate stays about the same during a person's life, but the stroke volume (the amount of blood the muscle pushes out per beat) diminishes as heart muscles deteriorate. Vital capacity, or the amount of air that moves when you inhale and exhale at maximum effort, also declines with age. Exercise can do a great deal to reduce potential deterioration in heart and lung function.

▶ **Eyesight** By the age of 30, the lens of the eye begins to harden, causing specific problems by the early 40s. The lens begins to yellow and loses transparency, while the pupil of the eye begins to shrink, allowing less light to penetrate. Activities such as reading become more difficult, particularly in dim light. By age 60, depth perception declines and farsightedness often develops. A need for glasses usually develops in the 40s that evolves into a need for bifocals in the 50s and trifocals in the 60s. **Cataracts** (clouding of the lens) and **glaucoma** (elevation of pressure within the eyeball)

Osteoporosis A degenerative bone disorder characterized by increasingly porous bones.

Urinary incontinence The inability to control urination.

Cataracts Clouding of the lens that interrupts the focusing of light on the retina, resulting in blurred vision or eventual blindness.

Glaucoma Elevation of pressure within the eyeball, leading to hardening of the eyeball, impaired vision, and possible blindness.

Understanding Erectile Dysfunction

Not until former senator Bob Dole grabbed the nation's attention with his "tell-all" advertisements did so many people (willingly or unwillingly) become aware of a problem experienced by many men, yet rarely discussed openly. Erectile dysfunction, or ED, is a condition in which men either have trouble getting or keeping an erection. Although some people may feel uncomfortable with the subject matter of Senator Dole's commercials, and a number of others question his judgment in making them, there's no doubt that putting such a visible and recognizable face on the problem has helped shed light on ED and eliminate the shame that has often accompanied the disorder.

Just how common is this little-known problem? ED is believed to affect 1 in 3 men in the United States, a rate that increases with age, with over half of all men between the ages of 40 and 70 experiencing some form of ED. Clearly, issues of privacy, concern over image, and the fact that males are often more reluctant to seek health care for health problems have contributed to the shroud of secrecy that has long engulfed ED, as well as most other sexual dysfunctions. The fact that there was no readily available treatment until recently also may have contributed to the silence of ED sufferers.

Now, however, as more is known about the causes of ED, more men are willing to seek help for impotency problems. For years, many men lived with the secret, fearing there was little that could be done and afraid to admit to the problem. In recent years, it has become more and more clear that the majority of all ED cases actually stem from various medical conditions, from medications being taken for various health conditions, and from lifestyle factors such as alcohol, tobacco, psychoactive drugs, and stress. Sometimes ED is a temporary reaction to these contributors, and sometimes it can be chronic. The following list identifies the rate of occurrence of ED for a sample of medical conditions, many of which are more common in older men.

For many people living with ED, once the underlying cause is eliminated or reduced, the ability to have or maintain an erection often improves. In addition, the development of Viagra, a drug designed to improve or restore function, has helped men resume active sexual lives even more quickly. Like any medication, however, Viagra is not free of side effects or possible risks. Also, it is important to note that lifestyle changes, such as reduction in alcohol use, stress management, elimination of illicit drug use, and careful monitoring of potential drug interactions from prescription drugs, should be the first steps in solving ED problems. For persistent ED problems and those that seem unrelated to lifestyle behaviors, it is best to consult with a doctor to determine possible underlying causes.

STUDENTS SPEAK UP:

Why do you think people are so reluctant to admit to ED? How do you think the advent of Viagra has changed the public's acceptance of ED?

Condition	Rate of Occurrence
Cardiovascular disease	8 in 10 men who have circulation difficulties
	2 in 3 men who've had a heart attack
	1 in 2 men who've had coronary artery bypass surgery
Diabetes	3 in 4 men
High blood pressure	1 in 7 men
Depression	9 in 10 men
Spinal injuries or trauma	1 in 4 men
Prostate surgery	7 in 10 men (particularly in the weeks immediately following surgery)

become more likely. There may eventually be a tendency toward color blindness, especially for shades of blue and green.

▶ **Hearing**   The ability to hear high-frequency consonants (for example, s, t, and z) diminishes with age. Much of the actual hearing loss is in the ability to distinguish not normal conversational tones but extreme ranges of sound.

▶ **Sexual Changes**   As men age, they experience notable changes in sexual functioning. The following changes generally occur:

1. The ability to obtain an erection is slowed.
2. The ability to maintain an erection is diminished.
3. The length of the refractory period between orgasms increases.
4. The angle of the erection declines with age.
5. The orgasm itself grows shorter in duration.

Women also experience several changes:

1. Menopause usually occurs between the ages of 45 and 55. Women may experience such symptoms as hot flashes, mood swings, weight gain, development of facial hair, and other hormone-related problems.

Ginkgo Biloba— Miracle for that Failing Memory?

Do you ever think you are losing it mentally? If you are like millions of people, young and old, you have occasional lapses in both short- and long-term memory. At certain times in your life, particularly at menopause for women, and after the age of 50, many people report declines in their ability to remember things that happened in the near or far periods of their life. For many of us, it could be that we are so stressed by all that we have to do, we can't focus on any one thing. Regardless of the cause of your memory problems, a new herbal remedy, known as ginkgo biloba, has been touted as "the thinking person's supplement." One need only go the local drugstore to see shelves of enticing packages with the Ginkgo label, all promising to keep you as sharp as a tack.

According to a report by Varro Tyler, Ph.D., a leading expert on herbal supplements, "ginkgo won't work for everyone. . . . In fact, the group for which studies have shown that ginkgo improves short-term memory and concentration consists of people with impaired blood flow to the brain. As people age, it becomes more common for the arteries leading to the brain to become clogged or narrowed. That results in decreased blood flow to brain cells, which, in turn, can cause short-term memory loss and problems concentrating. Ginkgo appears to help by acting as a blood thinner, which improves circulation." According to Dr. Tyler, there is no scientific evidence that ginkgo is effective in improving the memories of those with no impairment.

Many experts believe that ginkgo poses little threat. However, among those who are already taking aspirin or other blood-thinning substances, such as vitamin E or coumadin or other medicines, there may be a risk of hemorrhage if you are injured in an accident, require emergency surgery, or have other risks. Should you run out and buy ginkgo biloba? A good night's sleep would probably be a wiser and cheaper alternative.

Source: "Some Straight Thinking about Ginkgo," *Tufts University Health and Nutrition Letter* 15 (1997): 8.

---

2. The walls of the vagina become less elastic, and the epithelium thins, making painful intercourse more likely.
3. Vaginal secretions, particularly during sexual activity, diminish.
4. The breasts decrease in firmness. Loss of fat in various areas leads to fewer curves, with a decrease in the soft lines of the body contours.

While such physiological changes may be somewhat discouraging to some people, a recent study by the National Council on Aging indicates that despite these changes, older Americans continue to be sexually active. The findings of the study refute long-held beliefs that sexual desire decreases as we age. Results indicate that nearly half of Americans over age 60 engage in sexual activity at least once a month and 4 out of 10 would like to have sex more frequently than they currently do.[12] With the advent of drugs designed to treat sexual dysfunction, such as Viagra, many older adults may get their wishes.

▶ **Body Comfort** Because of the loss of body fat, thinning of the epithelium, and diminished glandular activity, elderly people experience greater difficulty in regulating body temperature. This change means that their ability to withstand extreme cold or heat may be very limited, thus increasing the risks of hypothermia, heatstroke, and heat exhaustion.

WHAT DO YOU THINK?

Of the health conditions listed in this section, which ones can you prevent? Which ones can you delay? What actions can you take now to protect yourself from these problems?

Mental Changes

▶ **Intelligence** Recent research has demonstrated that much of our previous knowledge about elderly intelligence was based on inappropriate testing procedures. Given an appropriate length of time, elderly people may learn and develop skills in a similar manner to younger people. Researchers have also determined that what many elderly people lack in speed of learning they make up for in practical knowledge—that is, the "wisdom of age."

▶ **Memory** Have you ever wondered why your grandfather seems unable to remember what he did last weekend even though he can graphically depict the details of a social event that occurred 40 years earlier? This phenomenon is not unusual among the elderly. Research indicates that although short-term memory may fluctuate on a daily basis, the ability

ACCESSING YOUR HEALTH ON THE INTERNET

Check out the following Internet sites related to life's transitions:

1. *Administration on Aging.*   A link to the Health and Human Services agency dedicated to addressing the health needs of the elderly.

    http://www.aoa.dhhs.gov/

2. *SeniorCom.*   Home page to a link to numerous resources for senior citizens, including chat rooms, databases, and services dedicated to assisting the aging.

    http://www.senior.com/

3. *Project on Death in America.*   A site dedicated to helping people understand and transform the culture of dying and bereavement in the United States, including links to numerous organizations and sites with related information.

    http://www.soros.org/death.html

4. *Hospice Web.*   A link to numerous resources for and information about hospice care, including a link to similar resources and a listing of hospices around the country.

    http://www.teleport.com/~hospice/

to remember events from past decades seems to remain largely unchanged in many elderly people.

▶ *Flexibility versus Rigidity*   Having lived through a multitude of experiences and having faced diverse joys, sorrows, and obstacles, the typical elderly person has developed unique methods of coping with life. These unique adaptive variations make for interesting differences in how the elderly confront the many changes brought on by the aging process.

▶ *Depression*   Some research indicates that depression may be the most common psychological problem facing older adults. However, the rate of major depression is actually lower among older people than among younger adults.

▶ *Senility: Getting Rid of Ageist Attitudes*   The elderly have often been the victims of ageist attitudes. People who were chronologically old were often labeled "senile" whenever they displayed memory failure, errors in judgment, disorientation, or erratic behaviors. Today scientists recognize that these same symptoms can occur at any age and for various reasons, including disease or the use of OTC and prescription drugs. When the underlying problems are corrected, the memory loss and disorientation also improve. Currently, the term

senility is seldom used except to describe a very small group of organic disorders.

▶ *Alzheimer's Disease*   Dementias are progressive brain impairments that interfere with memory and normal intellectual functioning. Although there are many types of dementia, one of the most common forms is **Alzheimer's disease.** In November 1994, the announcement that former president Ronald Reagan has Alzheimer's disease dramatized the Alzheimer patient's struggle for those who had not yet experienced its effects on a relative or friend. Attacking over 4 million Americans, and killing over 100,000 of them every year, this disease is one of the most painful and devastating conditions that families can endure. It kills its victims twice: First through a slow loss of their personhood (memory loss, disorientation, personality changes, and eventual loss of the ability to function as a person), and then as their bodily systems gradually succumb to the powerful impact of neurological problems.

Currently, Alzheimer's afflicts an estimated 1 in 10 people over the age of 65 and 1 in 5 people over the age of 85. These numbers are certain to increase. It is estimated to cost society over $100 billion a year currently.[13] With the U.S. population gradually aging, the economic burden of the future seems even more dismal.

Named after Alois Alzheimer, a German neuropathologist who recorded it as early as 1906, Alzheimer's refers to a degenerative disease of the brain in which nerve cells stop communicating with one another. Ordinarily, brain cells communicate by releasing chemicals that allow the cells to receive and transmit messages for various types of behavior. In Alzheimer's patients, the brain doesn't produce enough of these chemicals, cells can't communicate, and eventually the cells die.

This degeneration happens in the sections of the brain that affect memory, speech, and personality, leaving the parts that control other bodily functions, such as heartbeat and breathing, working just fine. It all happens in a slow, progressive manner, and it may be as long as 20 years before you notice symptoms. Alzheimer's is generally detected first by families, who note unusual memory losses and personality changes in their loved ones. Medical tests rule out underlying causes, and certain neurological tests help confirm the likelihood of this disease.

Alzheimer's disease is characteristically diagnosed in three stages. During the *first stage,* symptoms include forgetfulness, memory loss, impaired judgment, increasing inability to handle routine tasks, disorientation, lack of interest in one's surroundings, and depression. These symptoms accelerate in the *second stage,* which also includes agitation and restlessness (especially at night), loss of sensory perceptions, muscle twitching, and repetitive actions. Many patients become depressed and there is a tendency to be combative and aggressive. In the *final stage,* disorientation is often complete. The person becomes completely dependent on others for eating, dressing, and other activities. Identity loss and speech problems are common symptoms. Eventually, control of bodily functions may be lost.

Once Alzheimer's disease strikes, the victim's life expectancy is cut in half. Tragically, there is little that can be done at present to treat the disorder.

Current research is looking into genetic predisposition, malfunction of the immune system, a slow-acting virus, chromosomal or genetic defects, and neurotransmitter imbalance, among other possibilities.

[handwritten: use your mind activity]

[handwritten: high correlation between education level & not getting Alzheimers.]

HEALTH CHALLENGES OF THE ELDERLY

The elderly are disproportionately victimized by a number of problems; some are brought on by failing health (see Table 14.1), and others are societally induced. Other problems result when people do not develop the ability to cope properly with life's hurdles. Still other problems come from a perceived loss of control over the circumstances of their lives by the elderly—who watch loved ones die, are forced to retire, face problems with personal health, and confront an uncertain economy on a fixed income.

Alcohol Use and Abuse

[handwritten: older alcoholics - much more severe]

Although the elderly are often believed to be at high risk for alcoholism, exact numbers in this area are difficult to obtain. Some early studies reported incidence rates of 2 to 10 percent, but the exact percentages are controversial today. However, if you are prone to alcoholism in your younger and middle years, the chances are great that you will continue with these patterns of abuse in your older years. The old alcoholic is probably no more common in American society than the young alcoholic. Often, when people think they see a drunken older person they may really be seeing a confused older person who has taken too many different prescription medications.

Men tend to have higher risks for alcoholism at all ages. Alcohol abuse is five times more common among elderly men than among elderly women. Yet as many as half of all elderly men and an even higher proportion of elderly women don't drink at all. Those who do drink do so less than younger persons, consuming only five to six drinks weekly.

Senility A term associated with loss of memory and judgment and orientation problems occurring in a small percentage of the elderly.

Alzheimer's disease A chronic condition involving changes in nerve fibers of the brain that results in mental deterioration.

TABLE 14.1
Top 10 Health Problems of Older Americans

TOP 10 CAUSES OF DEATH	TOP 10 CHRONIC CONDITIONS
Diseases of the heart	Arthritis
Malignant neoplasms (cancer)	High blood pressure
Cerebrovascular diseases and stroke	Hearing impairment
Chronic obstructive pulmonary diseases/emphysema	Diseases of the heart
Pneumonia and influenza	Cataracts
Diabetes mellitus	Limb deformities or impairments
Unintentional injuries	Chronic sinusitis
Alzheimer's disease	Diabetes
Kidney disease	Tinnitus (ringing of the ears)
Bloodstream infections	Visual impairment

Source: "Healthy Aging/Healthy Living—START NOW," American Association for World Health, 1999.

Most drinking among the elderly is social drinking, and may, in fact, be much less of a problem than previously thought.

Prescription Drug Use

It is extremely rare for elderly people to use illicit drugs, but some do overuse, and grow dependent upon prescription drugs. Beset with numerous aches, pains, and inexplicable as well as diagnosable maladies, some elderly people take between four and six prescription drugs a day.

Anyone who combines different drugs runs the risk of dangerous drug interactions. The risks of adverse effects are even greater for people with circulation impairments and declining kidney and liver functions. Elderly people displaying symptoms of these drug-induced effects, which may include bizarre behavior patterns or an appearance of being out of touch, are often misdiagnosed as being senile rather than examined for underlying causes and treated.

Over-the-Counter Remedies

Although today's elderly appear to be more receptive to medical treatment than the elderly of previous generations, a substantial segment of the over-60 population avoid orthodox medical treatment, viewing it as only a last resort. This is becoming increasingly true as Medicare coverage becomes less and less adequate and the elderly are forced to pay greater amounts of their medical bills out of their own resources. The poor are particularly prone to turn to folk medicine and over-the-counter (OTC) preparations as cheaper, less intimidating alternatives.

PREVENTIVE ACTIONS FOR HEALTHY AGING

There are many things that you can do now to prolong your life and improve the quality of your life. There are some factors, however, that should be emphasized, particularly in light of the potential to delay the seemingly inevitable changes that will occur due to aging. Each of the following should make up a regular part of your younger years in order to provide for healthier older years.

Improving Fitness

If you're basically a sedentary person, just about any kind of moderate-intensity exercise that gets your heart beating faster and increases strength and/or flexibility is important to your physical health. Getting moving and keeping moving is a must, no matter what the activity is.

It is never too late to get started. Even if you're in your 60s or 70s, exercise can increase life expectancy by improving circulation, reducing blood pressure, and reducing overall risks. Age-associated loss of muscle mass, or **sarcopenia,** is a direct result of loss of muscle strength. With regular strength training, you can increase your muscle mass, keep your metabolism up, strengthen your bones, prevent osteoporosis, and in general feel better and function more efficiently. Strength training has been shown to improve balance and physical functioning and helps you feel more secure in your physical abilities.

Eating for Healthy Older Years

Clearly, we need more of certain nutrients as we age, and we must use prudence in selecting our food choices. Key nutrients for the elderly to consider—and for you to consider along the way—include:

- *Calcium:* Although we know that bone mass is relatively stable in young adults, bone loss tends to increase in women, particularly in the hip region, shortly before menopause. During perimenopause and menopause, this bone loss accelerates rapidly, with an average of about 3 percent skeletal mass loss per year over an approximate 5-year period. With this loss of mass comes an increased risk for fracture and disability.
- *Vitamin D:* It has been well documented that vitamin D is necessary for adequate calcium absorption, yet most people do not know that as people age, particularly in their 50s and 60s, they do not absorb vitamin D from foods as readily as they did in their younger years. If

For many, the secret to aging well is to stay active and enjoy the company of good friends.

vitamin D is unavailable, calcium levels are also likely to be lower.
- *Protein:* As the elderly become more concerned about cholesterol levels and fatty foods, budgets shrink, and cooking interest decreases, one nutrient that often takes the "hit" is protein. Many elderly cut back on protein to a point that is below the recommended daily amount. Because protein is necessary for muscle mass, protein insufficiencies can spell problems. Although there are other nutrients, including vitamin E, folic acid (folate), iron, potassium, and vitamin B-12, that are important to the aging process, most of these are readily available in any diet that follows food pyramid recommendations.

Caring for the Elderly

According to the most recent census data, elderly women fill a disproportionate place in American society. Because women live seven years longer than men on average, elderly women are more likely than elderly men to be living alone. Further, they are more likely to experience poverty and multiple chronic health problems, a situation referred to as **comorbidity.** Consequently, more elderly women than men are likely to need assistance from children, other relatives, friends, and neighbors.

Women have usually been the primary caregivers for elderly Americans. A national survey found that 72 percent of primary caregivers were women, and 60 percent of these were wives of the person who was receiving care.[14] Research also indicates that women spend more hours than do men (38 hours versus 27 hours per week) in caregiving activities and that women perform a wider range of activities than do men. Regardless of the time spent, caregiving is a difficult and stressful experience for both women and men. **Respite care,** or care that is given by someone who relieves the primary caregiver, should be available to ease the burden of the primary caregiver. As the population ages and more elderly people are in need of care, the importance of the caregiver in maintaining health and well-being will become even more important.

> **········ WHAT DO YOU THINK?**
>
> Why are women so often the primary caregivers for their aging spouses and other family members? What potential problems can such caregiving cause for women? How can women best learn to cope with the stresses and strains of caregiving?

UNDERSTANDING DEATH

Throughout history, humans have attempted to determine the nature and meaning of death. The questioning continues today.

Confrontations with death elicit different feelings depending on many factors, including age, religious beliefs, family orientation, health, personal experience with death, and the circumstances of the death itself. To cope effectively with dying, we must address the individual needs of those involved as they face the final transition in life.

Defining Death

Dying is the process of decline in body functions resulting in the death of an organism. **Death** can be defined as the "final cessation of the vital functions" and also refers to a state in which these functions are "incapable of being restored."[15] This definition has become more significant as medical and scientific advances have made it increasingly possible to postpone death.

Sarcopenia Age-related loss of muscle mass.

Comorbidity The presence of a number of diseases at the same time.

Respite care The care provided by substitute caregivers to relieve the principal caregiver from his or her continuous responsibility.

Dying The process of decline in body functions resulting in the death of an organism.

Death The "final cessation of the vital functions" and the state in which these functions are "incapable of being restored."

In response to legal and ethical questions related to death and dying, a presidential commission developed the Uniform Determination of Death Act in 1981, which was endorsed by the American Medical Association, the American Bar Association, and the National Conference for Commissioners on Uniform State Laws. This act, which has been adopted by several states, reads as follows: "An individual who has sustained either (1) irreversible cessation of circulatory and respiratory functions, or (2) irreversible cessation of all functions of the entire brain, including the brainstem, is dead. A determination of death must be made in accordance with accepted medical standards."[16]

The concept of "brain death," defined as the irreversible cessation of all functions of the entire brain stem, has gained increasing credence. As the Ad Hoc Committee of the Harvard Medical School defined it in 1968, brain death occurs when the following criteria are met:

- Unreceptivity and unresponsiveness—that is, no response even to painful stimuli.
- No movement for a continuous hour after observation by a physician and no breathing after three minutes off a respirator.
- No reflexes, including brainstem reflexes; pupils are fixed and dilated.
- A "flat" EEG for at least 10 minutes.
- All of these tests repeated at least 24 hours later with no change.
- Certainty that hypothermia (extreme loss of body heat) and depression of the central nervous system caused by use of drugs such as barbiturates are not responsible for these conditions.[17]

The Harvard report provides useful guidelines; however, the definition of *death* and all its ramifications continue to concern us.

> **········ WHAT DO YOU THINK?**
>
> How long do you think you will live? Do you have concerns about the quality of your life up until you die? What can you do now and in the future to help guarantee not only a long life but a healthy quality of life?

Denying Death

We can look at our attitudes toward death as falling on a continuum. At one end of the continuum, death is viewed as the mortal enemy of humankind. Both medical science and religion have promoted this idea of death. At the other end of the continuum, death is accepted and even welcomed.[18] For people whose attitudes fall at this end, death is a passage to a better state of being. But most of us perceive ourselves to be in the middle of this continuum. From this perspective, death is a bewildering mystery that elicits fear and apprehension as well as profoundly influences our attitudes, beliefs, and actions throughout our lives.

Contemporary Western Death Attitudes

"The contemporary view of death in the West is that every death is contingent, a matter of chance, and that, in principle, there is no reason why any particular injury or disease cannot be overcome."

Our present Western culture differs significantly from those that preceded it. We are living in a "death-denying" period. To understand this designation, we must look at the parameters of contemporary death attitudes. Four major factors influence the different attitudes toward death among cultures:

- Exposure to death
- Life expectancy
- Perceived control over the forces of nature
- Understanding of what it is to be a human being

EXPOSURE TO DEATH

The experience that one has with bereavement and death is usually a limiting factor with respect to death attitudes. Having never lost a loved one will play a major role in the attitude development toward death. In many countries, children grow up with the presence of uncontrolled threats to mortality, such as earthquakes, volcanic eruptions, chemical and nuclear disasters, and continuous war. In most Western settings, children grow up protected from death. However, even in the West exposure varies. Where a person lives and the experiences that one encounters play a major role in the formula in developing attitudes about death.

LIFE EXPECTANCY

Today more than ever before, we have seemingly been able to deny death as a result of better sanitation and food supplies, and improved medical care. We are living longer in years and in quality. When individuals die young, it is viewed as though that person was cheated out of life.

CONTROL OVER THE FORCES OF NATURE

One's view of the world and the perceived control of it help to shape attitudes toward death. A person's perceived control over the forces of nature will take a part in shaping views about death. Persons who believe they can be "protected" from nature have less respect for the power of nature over life.

SENSE OF THE INDIVIDUAL PERSON

The meaning of what it is to be a person seems to be the most important element in the development of attitudes toward death. Those who believe that each life is unique will perceive the end of that life as a different order of loss than those who perceive that a life has meaning only within a whole.

Source: Dr. John D. Morgan, King's College, 266 Epworth Avenue, London, Ontario; Tel. 519–342–7946; Jmorgan@julian.uwo.ca; Wwdc.com/deaths/attitudes.html

---

In the United States, there is a high level of discomfort associated with death and dying. As a result, we may avoid speaking about death in an effort to limit our own discomfort. You may wish to deny death if you

- avoid people who are grieving after the death of a loved one so you won't have to talk about it
- fail to validate a dying person's frightening situation by talking to the person as if nothing were wrong
- substitute euphemisms for the word *death* (a few examples are "passing away," "no longer with us," or "going to a better place")
- give false reassurances to people who are dying by saying things like "everything is going to be okay"
- shut off conversation about death by silencing people who are trying to talk about it
- do not touch people who are dying

Although some experts indicate that death denial has always been a predominant characteristic of our society, we must keep in mind that social attitudes change over time.

It is therefore important to understand the climate in which our parents and grandparents developed their perceptions so we can understand their reactions to death as well as our own.

THE PROCESS OF DYING

Dying is a complex process that includes physical, intellectual, social, spiritual, and emotional dimensions. Accordingly, we must consider the process of dying from several perspectives.

Coping Emotionally with Death

Science and medicine have enabled us to understand changes associated with growth, development, aging, and social roles throughout the life span, but they have not revealed the nature of death. This may partially explain why the transition from life to death evokes so much mystery and emotion.

Much of our knowledge about reactions to dying stems from the work of Elisabeth Kübler-Ross, a major figure in modern **thanatology,** the study of death and dying. In 1969, Kübler-Ross published *On Death and Dying,* a sensitive analysis of the reactions of terminally ill patients. This pioneering work encouraged the development of death education as a discipline and prompted efforts to improve the care of dying patients. In her book, Kübler-Ross identified five psychological stages that terminally ill patients often experience as they approach death: denial, anger, bargaining, depression, and acceptance. The health care profession immediately embraced this "stage theory" and hastily applied it in clinical settings. However, research evidence supporting the concept of stages of grief is neither extensive nor convincing. Although it is normal to grieve when a severe loss has been sustained, some people never go through this process and instead remain emotionally calm. Others may pass back and forth between the stages.

A summation of the five stages follows.

- *Denial:* ("Not me, there must be a mistake.") This is usually the first stage, experienced as a sensation of shock and disbelief. A person intellectually accepts the impending death but rejects it emotionally. The patient is too confused and stunned to comprehend "not being" and thus rejects the idea. Within a relatively short time, the anxiety level may diminish, enabling the patient to sort through the powerful web of emotions.
- *Anger:* ("Why me?") Anger is another common reaction to the realization of imminent death. The person becomes angry at having to face death when others, including loved ones, are healthy and not threatened. The dying person perceives the situation as "unfair" or "senseless" and may be hostile to friends, family, physicians, or the world in general.
- *Bargaining:* ("If I'm allowed to live, I promise . . .") This stage generally occurs at about the middle of the progression toward acceptance of death. During this stage, the dying person may resolve to be a better person in return for an extension of life or may secretly pray for a short reprieve from death in order to experience a special event, such as a family wedding or birth.
- *Depression:* ("It's really going to happen to me and I can't do anything about it.") Depression eventually sets in as vitality diminishes and the patient begins to experience distressing symptoms with increasing frequency. The patient's deteriorating condition becomes impossible

for him or her to deny, and feelings of doom and tremendous loss may become unbearably pervasive. Feelings of worthlessness and guilt are also common in this depressed state because the dying person may feel responsible for the emotional suffering of loved ones and the arduous but seemingly futile efforts of caregivers.

- *Acceptance:* ("I'm ready.") This is often the final stage. The patient stops battling with emotions and becomes very tired and weak. The need to sleep increases, and wakeful periods become shorter and less frequent. With acceptance, the patient does not "give up" and become sullen or resentfully resigned to death, but rather becomes passive. According to one dying patient, the acceptance stage is "almost void of feelings . . . as if the pain had gone, the struggle is over, and there comes a time for the final rest before the long journey."[19] As he or she lets go, the dying person may no longer welcome visitors and may not wish to engage in conversation. Death usually occurs quietly and painlessly while the victim is unconscious.

Some of Kübler-Ross's contemporaries consider her stage theory to be too neat and orderly. Subsequent research has indicated that the experiences of dying people do not fit easily into specific stages and that patterns vary from person to person. Even if it is not accurate in all its particulars, however, Kübler-Ross's theory offers valuable insights for those seeking to understand or deal with the process of dying.

········· **WHAT DO YOU THINK?**

Do you agree with Elisabeth Kübler-Ross's stages of dying? How might the environment in which you die play an influencing role on these stages?

Social Death

The need for recognition and appreciation within a social group is nearly universal. Although the size and nature of the social group may vary widely, the need to belong exists in all of us. Loss of value or of appreciation by others can lead to **social death,** an irreversible situation in which a person is not treated like an active member of society. Dramatic examples of social death include the exile of nonconformists from their native countries or the excommunication of dissident members of religious orders. More often, however, social death is inflicted by avoidance of social interaction. Numerous studies indicate that people are treated differently when they are dying. The isolation that accompanies social death in terminally ill patients may be promoted by the following common behaviors:

- The dying person is referred to as if he or she were already dead.
- The dying person may be inadvertently excluded from conversations.
- Dying patients are often moved to terminal wards and are given minimal care.

Thanatology   The study of death and dying.

Social death   An irreversible situation in which a person is not treated like an active member of society.

- Bereaved family members are avoided, often for extended periods, because friends and neighbors are afraid of feeling uncomfortable in the presence of grief.
- Medical personnel may make degrading comments about patients in their presence.[20]

A decrease in meaningful social interaction often strips dying and bereaved people of recognition as valued members of society at a time when belonging is critical. Some dying people choose not to speak of their inevitable fate in an attempt to make others feel more comfortable and thus preserve vital relationships.

Coping with Loss

The losses resulting from the death of a loved one may be extremely difficult to cope with. The dying person, as well as close family and friends, frequently suffers emotionally and physically from the impending loss of critical relationships and roles. Words used to describe feelings and behavior related to losses resulting from death include *bereavement, grief, grief work,* and *mourning.* These terms are related but not identical. Understanding them may help you to comprehend the emotional processes associated with loss and the cultural constraints that often inhibit normal coping behavior (see Figure 14.3).

Bereavement is generally defined as the loss or deprivation experienced by a survivor when a loved one dies. Because relationships vary in type and intensity, reactions to losses also vary. The death of a parent, a spouse, a sibling, a child, a friend, or a pet will result in different kinds of feelings. In the lives of the bereaved or of close survivors, "holes" will be left by the loss of loved ones. Time and courage are necessary to fill these spaces.

When a person experiences a loss that cannot be openly acknowledged, publicly mourned, or socially supported, coping may be much more difficult. This type of grief is referred to as **disenfranchised grief.**[21] This might happen for those who miscarry, are mentally retarded, or are close friends rather than relatives of the deceased. It may also include those relationships that are not socially approved, such as with extramarital lovers or homosexual couples.

A special case of bereavement occurs in old age. Loss is an intrinsic part of growing old. The longer we live, the more losses we are likely to experience. These losses include physical, social, and emotional losses as our bodies deteriorate and more and more of our loved ones die. The theory of *bereavement overload* has been proposed to explain the effects of multiple losses and the accumulation of sorrow in the lives of some elderly people. This theory suggests that the gloomy outlook, disturbing behavior patterns, and apparent apathy that characterize these people may be related more to bereavement overload than to intrinsic physiological degeneration in old age.[22]

Grief is a mental state of distress that occurs in reaction to significant loss, including one's own impending death, the death of a loved one, or a quasi-death experience. Grief reactions include any adjustments needed for one to "make it through the day" and may include changes in patterns of eating, sleeping, working, and even thinking.

The term **mourning** is often incorrectly equated with the term *grief.* As we have noted, *grief* refers to a wide variety of feelings and actions that occur in response to bereavement. *Mourning,* in contrast, refers to culturally prescribed and accepted time periods and behavior patterns for the expression of grief. In Judaism, for example, "sitting *shivah*" is a designated mourning period of seven days that involves prescribed rituals and prayers. Depending on a person's relationship with the deceased, various other rituals may continue for up to a year.

By accepting dying as a part of the continuum of life, many people are able to make necessary readjustments after the death of a loved one. This holistic concept, which accepts dying as a part of the total life experience, is shared by both believers and nonbelievers.

What Is "Normal" Grief?

Grief responses vary widely from person to person. This common grief reaction can include the following symptoms:

- Periodic waves of physical distress lasting from 20 minutes to an hour.
- A feeling of tightness in the throat.
- Choking and shortness of breath.
- A frequent need to sigh.
- A feeling of emptiness in the abdomen.

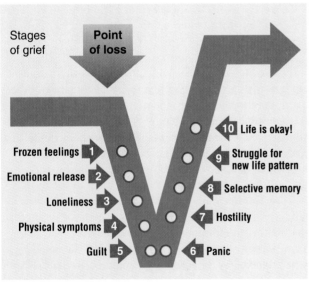

Figure 14.3

The diagram shows the stages of grief. People react differently to losses, but most eventually adjust. The common stages of grief and relief are depicted. Generally, the stronger the social support system, the smoother the progression through the stages of grief.

A significant loss can be particularly difficult for children.

- A feeling of muscular weakness.
- An intense feeling of anxiety that is described as actually painful.

When an Infant or a Child Dies

The death of a child is terribly painful for the whole family. However, for several reasons, the siblings of the deceased child have a particularly hard time with **grief work**, which is the process of integrating the reality of the loss with everyday life. Bereaved children usually have limited experience with death and therefore have not yet learned how to deal with major loss. Children may feel uncomfortable talking about death, and they may also receive less social support and sympathy than do the parents of the deceased child. Because so

---

Bereavement   The loss or deprivation experienced by a survivor when a loved one dies.

Disenfranchised grief   Grief concerning a loss that cannot be openly acknowledged, publicly mourned, or socially supported.

Grief   The mental state of distress that occurs in reaction to significant loss, including one's own impending death, the death of a loved one, or a quasi-death experience.

Mourning   The culturally prescribed behavior patterns for the expression of grief.

Grief work   The process of integrating the reality of the loss with everyday life.

Quasi-death experiences   Losses or experiences that resemble death in that they involve separation, termination, significant loss, a change of personal identity, and grief.

Hospice   A concept of care for terminally ill patients designed to maximize the quality of life.

---

much attention and energy are devoted to the deceased child, the surviving children may also feel emotionally abandoned by their parents.

Quasi-Death Experiences

Social and emotional support for the bereaved in the aftermath of death is supported by many cultures. Typically, however, there is little support for many other significant losses in life. Losses that in many ways resemble death and that may carry with them a heavy burden of grief include an abduction or kidnapping, a divorce, the loss of a romance or an intimate friendship, retirement, or ending an athletic career. These **quasi-death experiences**[23] resemble death in that they involve separation, termination, loss, and a change in identity or self-perception. If grief results from these losses, the pattern of the grief response will probably follow the same course as responses to death.

TAKING CARE OF BUSINESS

Caring for dying people and dealing with the practical and legal questions surrounding death can be difficult and painful. The problems of the dying person and the bereaved loved ones involve a wide variety of psychological, legal, social, spiritual, economic, and interpersonal issues.

Hospice Care: Positive Alternatives

Since the mid-1970s, **hospice** programs have grown from a mere handful to more than 2,500, available in nearly every community. The Robert Wood Johnson Foundation, a leading health-care philanthropy, has launched a $12-million initiative to improve care for the dying. Also, the American Medical Association has made the training of physicians in end-of-life care one of its top priorities.

The primary goals of the hospice program are to relieve the dying person's pain, to offer emotional support to the dying person and loved ones, and to restore a sense of control to the dying person, the family, and friends. Although home care with maximum involvement by loved ones is emphasized, hospice programs are under the direction of cooperating physicians, coordinated by specially trained nurses, and fortified with the services of counselors, clergy, and trained volunteers. Hospital inpatient beds are available if necessary. Hospice programs usually include the following characteristics:

1. The patient and family constitute the unit of care, because the physical, psychological, social, and spiritual problems of dying confront the family as well as the patient.
2. Emphasis is on symptom control, primarily the alleviation of pain. Curative treatments are curtailed as requested by

the patient, but sound judgment must be applied to avoid a feeling of abandonment.

3. There is overall medical direction of the program, with all health care being provided under the direction of a qualified physician.
4. Services are provided by an interdisciplinary team because no one person can provide all the needed care.
5. Coverage is provided 24 hours a day, 7 days a week, with emphasis on the availability of medical and nursing skills.
6. Carefully selected and extensively trained volunteers are an integral part of the health-care team, augmenting staff service but not replacing it.
7. Care of the family extends through the bereavement period.
8. Patients are accepted on the basis of their health needs, not their ability to pay.

Despite the growing number of people considering the hospice option, many people prefer to go to a hospital to die. Others choose to die at home, without the intervention of medical staff or life-prolonging equipment. Each dying person and his or her family should decide as early as possible what type of terminal care is most desirable and feasible. This will allow time for necessary emotional, physical, and financial preparations. *—Costly—*

Making Funeral Arrangements

Anthropological evidence indicates that all cultures throughout history have developed some sort of funeral ritual. For this reason, social scientists agree that funerals somehow assist survivors of the deceased in coping with their loss.

In the United States, with its diversity of religious, regional, and ethnic customs, funeral patterns vary. In some faiths, prior to body disposal, the deceased may be displayed to formalize last respects and increase social support to the bereaved. This part of the funeral ritual is referred to as a wake or viewing. The body of the deceased is usually embalmed prior to viewing to retard decomposition and minimize offensive odors. The funeral service may be held in a church, in a funeral chapel, or at the burial site. Some people choose to replace the funeral service with a simple memorial service held within a few days of the burial. Social interaction associated with funeral and memorial services is valuable in helping survivors cope with their losses.

Common methods of body disposal include burial in the ground, entombment above ground in a mausoleum, cremation, and anatomical donation. Expenses involved in body disposal vary according to the method chosen and the available options. It should be noted that if burial is selected, an additional charge may be assessed for a burial vault. Burial vaults—concrete or metal containers that hold the casket—are required by most cemeteries to limit settling of the gravesite as the casket disintegrates and collapses. The actual container for the body or remains of the dead person is only one of many things that must be dealt with when a person dies. There are many other decisions concerning the funeral ritual that can be burdensome for survivors.

Pressures on Survivors

Stress related to funeral ritual varies culturally as well as individually. A great number of decisions have to be made, usually within 24 hours. These decisions relate to the method and details of body disposal, the type of memorial service, display of the body, the site of burial or body disposition, the cost of funeral options, organ donation decisions, ordering of floral displays, contacting friends and relatives, planning for the arrival of guests, choosing markers, gathering and submitting obituary information to newspapers, printing of memorial folders, as well as numerous other details. Even though funeral directors are available to facilitate decision making, the bereaved may experience undue stress, especially in the event of a sudden death. In our society, people who make their own funeral arrangements can save their loved ones from having to deal with unnecessary problems. Even making the decision regarding the method of body disposal can greatly reduce the stress on survivors.

Wills

The issue of inheritance is a controversial one in some families and should be resolved before the person dies in order to reduce both conflict and needless expense. Unfortunately, many people are so intimidated by the thought of making a will that they never do so and die **intestate** (without a will). This is tragic, especially because the procedure involved in establishing a legal will is relatively simple and inexpensive. In addition, if you don't make up a will before you die, the courts (as directed by state laws) will make up a will for you. Legal issues, rather than your wishes, will preside.

In some cases, other types of wills may substitute for the traditional legal will. One of these alternative forms is the **holographic will**, written in the handwriting of the **testator** (person who leaves a will) and unwitnessed. Caution should be taken concerning alternatives to legally written and witnessed wills because they are not honored in all states. And holographic wills are contestable in court. Think of the parents who never approved of their child living with someone

Intestate   The situation in which a person dies without having made a will.

Holographic will   A will written in the testator's own handwriting and unwitnessed.

Testator   A person who leaves a will or testament at death.

SKILLS FOR BEHAVIOR CHANGE

Funeral Etiquette

Sometimes, going to a funeral can be uncomfortable. We often don't know enough about funerals to know what is socially acceptable behavior. This information should provide you with a guide for modern funeral practices and customs, and is only intended as a guide for those that might have questions.

THE FUNERAL SERVICE

The family or closest living friends or relatives generally specify the type of service for the deceased. The service is usually held at a place of worship or at a funeral home. The presence of friends at this time is an acknowledgment of friendship and support.

DRESS

Wearing colorful clothing is no longer inappropriate for relatives and friends. The key here is dignity and respect for the family and the occasion.

CONDOLENCES

The death of someone you love creates a confusing and emotional time for the family members. No matter what your means of expressing your sympathy, it is important to identify yourself to the family.

FLOWERS

Sending a floral tribute is a very appropriate way of expressing your condolences to the family of the deceased.

MEMORIAL DONATIONS

A memorial contribution to a specific cause or charity can be appreciated as much as flowers. The family may have expressed a preference as to the charity or cause they wish to support.

SYMPATHY CARDS

Sending a card of sympathy, even if you are only an acquaintance, is appropriate. It means a great deal to the family members to know they are in good thoughts.

TELEPHONE CALL

Speaking to the family may also give you the opportunity to offer your services and let them know that you really care. They may wish to discuss their recent loss. Talking about the deceased and being a good listener can be very comforting to both you and the person to whom you are talking.

VISITATION

Visitation provides a time and place for friends to offer their expressions of sorrow and sympathy. It is often better than approaching the subject at the office or grocery store. Also, when the funeral service is over, the survivors often feel very alone in dealing with their feelings. It is important that they know you are still there. Keep in touch.

SYMPATHY EXPRESSIONS

Simple statements of condolence can be very useful when addressing survivors of the deceased.

"I'm sorry."

"My sympathy to you."

"It was good to know (name of deceased)."

"My sympathy to you and your family."

The family member in return may say . . .

"Thanks for coming."

"Come see me when you can."

"It is so nice to know that so many people cared."

Source: Adapted from the Ontario Funeral Service Association, 1994.

---

outside a marriage: They can successfully challenge the holographic will in court.

Organ Donation

Another decision concerns organ donation. Organ transplant techniques have become so refined, and the demand for transplant tissues and organs has become so great, that many people are being encouraged to donate these "gifts of life" upon their death. Uniform donor cards are available through the National Kidney Foundation, donor information is printed on the backs of drivers' licenses, and many hospitals have in-cluded the opportunity for organ donor registration as a part of their admission procedures. Although some people are opposed to organ transplants and tissue donation, others experience a feeling of personal fulfillment from knowing that their organs may extend and improve someone else's life after their own deaths.

·········· WHAT DO YOU THINK?

What can you do to assure that your wishes will be carried out at the time of your death?

The Walter Payton story served as a reminder that even the best health practices can't prevent certain conditions or disorders and placed even greater emphasis on the importance of organ donation.

LIFE-AND-DEATH DECISION MAKING

Life-and-death decisions are serious, complex, and often expensive. We will not attempt to present the "answers" to death-related moral and philosophical questions. Instead, we offer topics for your consideration. We hope that discussion of the needs of the dying person and the bereaved will help you to make difficult decisions in the future. A few issues that are problematic or controversial are the questions concerning the right to die, the concept of rational suicide, and euthanasia.

The Right to Die

Few people would object to a proposal for the right to a dignified death. Going beyond that concept, however, many people today believe that they should be allowed to die if their condition is inevitably terminal and their existence is dependent on mechanical life support devices or artificial feeding or hydration systems.

As long as a person is conscious and competent, he or she has the legal right to refuse treatment, even if this decision will hasten death. However, when a person is in a coma or is otherwise incapable of speaking on his or her own behalf, medical personnel and administrative policy will dictate treatment. This issue has evolved into a battle involving personal freedom, legal rulings, health care administration policy, and physician responsibility. The living will was developed to assist in solving conflicts among these people and agencies.

Cases have been reported in which the wishes of people who have signed a living will (or advanced directive) indicating their desire not to receive artificial life support were not honored by their physician or medical institution. This problem can be avoided by choosing both a physician and a hospital that will carry out the directives of the living will.

Many legal experts suggest that you take the following steps to assure that your wishes are carried out:

1. *Get specific:* Rather than signing an advanced directive (that only speaks in generalities), fill out a directive that permits you to make specific choices about a variety of procedures under six different circumstances. It is also essential to attach that document to a completed copy of the standard advance directive for your state.
2. *Get an agent:* You may want to appoint a family member or friend to act as your agent, or *proxy,* by making out a form known as either a durable power of attorney for health care or a health-care proxy.
3. *Discuss your wishes:* Discuss your wishes in detail with your proxy and your doctor. Going over the situations described in the form will give them a clear idea of just how much you are willing to endure to preserve your life.
4. *Deliver the directive:* Distribute several copies, not only to your doctor and your agent but also to your lawyer and to immediate family members or a close friend. Make sure *someone* knows to bring a copy to the hospital in the event you are hospitalized.[24]

Rational Suicide

Although exact numbers are not known, medical ethicists, experts in rational suicide, and specialists in forensic medicine (the study of legal issues in medicine) estimate that thousands of terminally ill people decide to kill themselves rather than endure constant pain and slow decay every year. To these people, the prospect of an undignified death is unacceptable. But does anyone have the right to end his or her life? This issue has been complicated by advances in death prevention techniques that allow terminally ill patients to exist in an irreversible disease state for extended periods of time. Medical personnel, clergy, lawyers, and patients all must struggle with this ethical dilemma.

Dyathanasia is a form of "mercy killing" in which someone plays a passive role in the death of a terminally ill person. This passive role may include the withholding of life-prolonging treatments or withdrawal of life-sustaining medical support, thereby allowing the person to die. Euthanasia is often referred to as "mercy killing." The term **active euthanasia**

Dyathanasia The passive form of "mercy killing" in which life-prolonging treatments or interventions are not offered or are withheld, thereby allowing a terminally ill person to die naturally.

Active euthanasia "Mercy killing" in which a person or organization knowingly acts to hasten the death of a terminally ill person.

Passive euthanasia The intentional withholding of treatment that would prolong life.

has been given to end the life of a person (or animal) that is suffering greatly and has no chance of recovery. An example might be a lethal injection, or the administration of carbon monoxide. **Passive euthanasia** refers to the intentional withholding of treatment that would prolong life.

In 1990, a physician in Michigan by the name of Dr. Jack Kevorkian started a one-person campaign to try to force the medical profession to change its position regarding assisted death. Since that time, Kevorkian has assisted many terminally ill patients in dying and until recently, had escaped conviction despite being taken into court several times for his actions. Kevorkian has argued that the Hippocratic oath is not binding. He believes that the present situations in our society demand a shift in the thinking and practices that medicine has had throughout most of human history. He believes that acceptance of euthanasia, specifically physician-assisted death, to be one of those changes. On November 20, 1998 Dr. Kevorkian took his argument to prime time, as the CBS News program "60 Minutes" broadcast Kevorkian's latest case of assisting a terminally ill patient with ending his life. This time, however, the courts determined that Jack Kevorkian's

methods had gone too far and, in early 1999, Kevorkian was convicted of murder and sentenced to prison.

Over the years, Dr. Kevorkian's actions have focused a great deal of attention on the issue, causing many to speculate on the merits of physician-assisted suicide. A study in Michigan revealed that a greater number of physicians were in favor of legalizing assisted suicide than were against it.[25] In a similar study in Oregon it was found that physicians have a more favorable attitude toward legalized physician-assisted suicide, are more willing to participate, and are currently participating in greater numbers than other surveyed groups in the United States.[26] In both studies, a sizable minority of physicians had a number of reservations about the practical applications of the law.

WHAT DO YOU THINK?

Are there any end-of-life situations in which you would ask a physician to help you die? Why or why not? Do you believe people should have the right to ask a physician to help them die?

Taking Charge
Dealing with the Aging Process

The question of how to best take responsible action to promote your potential for a full, productive life is not an easy one to answer. There are many obstacles to overcome, some of which may be totally beyond your control. There is no one right way to age. Most people who do age successfully, however, pay attention to their physical, spiritual, emotional, mental, and social well-being.

CHECKLIST FOR CHANGE

MAKING PERSONAL CHOICES

✓ Keep active mentally. For some people, mentally active equals socially active. Take time for quiet reflection, concentrated thought, and idle musing.

✓ Have regular medical checkups. One of the best ways to protect yourself against major health problems at any age is to take care of seemingly minor problems early.

✓ Develop a sense of self. Maintaining a sense of yourself as a worthwhile, productive member of society can be a challenge in the face of changes that appear to diminish individual prestige.

✓ Learn to accept help when you need it.

✓ Make optimal use of your time and energy. It would be foolish to assume that, as you age, your energy levels and reserves of strength will continue to be the same.

- Make an honest evaluation of your personal weaknesses and strengths. Once you have made this evaluation, make a conscious effort to improve in weak areas wherever possible.

- Take positive steps now to plan for a secure retirement.

- Become familiar with services that are available to assist the elderly in need of help.

- Do not allow yourself to stagnate. The willingness to encounter change and undertake new activities can add pleasure to life at any age. Similarly, stagnation can occur at any age.

- Do you have a will prepared? Do you update it regularly?

- Have you completed a directive to physicians?

- If you had died yesterday, would your loved ones have known what plans you had for your funeral, body disposal, and asset distribution? What steps can you take to make sure such information is known?

- What coping techniques will you turn to if someone you know dies? Do you think you would be able to help someone else who is dealing with a loss?

MAKING COMMUNITY CHOICES

- What community services are available to promote health at each of the different levels and stages of life? What services are available for children? For young adults? For people in their middle years? Older years?

- What services do you think are needed to help people achieve optimal health through the years?

- Do you keep up with the federal government's plans for Social Security and Medicare? Have you taken the time to learn how these programs will affect you in the future?

- What community support is available to help people cope with the death of a loved one? For example, are there widow or widower support groups?

- What are your state's laws regarding directives to physicians?

- Is physician-assisted suicide legal in your state? Are any laws pending regarding rational suicide?

SUMMARY

- Aging can be defined in terms of biological age, psychological age, social age, legal age, or functional age.

- The growing numbers of elderly (people age 65 and older) will have a growing impact on our society in terms of economy, health care, housing, and ethical considerations.

- Two broad groups of theories—biological and psychosocial—purport to explain the physiological and psychological changes that occur with aging.

- Aging changes the body and mind in many ways. Physical changes occur in the skin, bones and joints, head, urinary tract, heart and lungs, senses, sexual functioning, and temperature regulation. Major physical concerns are osteoporosis and urinary incontinence. The elderly maintain a high level of intelligence and memory. Potential mental problems include depression and Alzheimer's disease.

- Special challenges for the elderly include alcohol abuse, prescription drug and OTC interactions, questions about vitamin and mineral supplementation, and issues regarding caregiving.

- Exercise and healthful eating habits can increase life expectancy and improve the quality of life in your later years.

- *Death* can be defined biologically in terms of the final cessation of vital functions. Various classes of death include cell death, local death, somatic death, apparent death, functional death, and brain death.

- Death is a multifaceted process and individuals may experience emotional stages of dying including denial, anger, bargaining, depression, and acceptance. Social death results when a person is no longer treated as living. Grief is the state of distress felt after loss.

- Practical and legal issues surround dying and death. Decisions should be made in advance of death through wills and organ donation cards.

- The right to die by rational suicide involves ethical, moral, and legal issues. Dyathanasia involves passive help in suicide for a terminally ill patient; euthanasia involves direct help.

DISCUSSION QUESTIONS

1. Discuss the various definitions of aging. At what age would you place your parents for each category?

2. As the elderly population grows, what implications are there for you? Would you be willing to pay higher

taxes to support government social programs for the elderly?

3. List the major physiological changes that occur with aging. Which of these, if any, can you change?

4. Explain the major health challenges that the elderly may face. What advice would you give to your grandparents before they took a prescription or OTC drug?

5. Discuss why so many of us deny death. How could death become a more acceptable topic to discuss?

6. What are the stages that terminally ill patients theoretically experience? Do you agree with the five-stage theory? Explain why or why not.

7. Compare and contrast the hospital experience with hospice care. What must one consider before arranging for hospice care?

8. Debate whether or not rational suicide should be legalized for the terminally ill. What restrictions would you include in a law?

APPLICATION EXERCISE

Reread the *What Do You Think?* scenario at the beginning of the chapter and answer the following questions.

1. Should Ed be able to request rational suicide? If so, when should the suicide occur? As soon as his symptoms start to get intolerable? As soon as Ed feels regular pain?

2. If Ed had made out a directive to physicians asking for assisted suicide 10 years ago, before he had married and had three children, should that document still be used? Or should his children's or wife's request to keep him alive longer be considered? In other words, is the patient the only person who should have a say in the matter?

15

Environmental Health

Thinking Globally, Acting Locally

OBJECTIVES

▶ Identify the problems associated with current levels of global population growth.

▶ Discuss the major causes of air pollution, including photochemical smog and acid rain, and the global consequences of the accumulation of greenhouse gases and of ozone depletion.

▶ Identify sources of water pollution and the specific chemical contaminants often found in water.

▶ Describe the physiological consequences of noise pollution.

▶ Distinguish between municipal solid waste and hazardous waste.

▶ Discuss the health concerns associated with ionizing and nonionizing radiation.

When the children living on the St. Regis Mohawk reservation in New York began experiencing headaches, nausea, and eye irritation, pollution from production plants next to the reservation were suspected as the cause. The tribe formed a group called Mohawks Agree on Safe Health (MASH) to investigate the effects of industrial pollution on human health and the entire ecosystem of the reservation. They found underlying philosophical differences on economic development and the environment: "The industry's model is based on resource extraction, pollution, and profit; the tribe's, on spiritual, social, and cultural relationships with the natural world." In 1994, the tribe entered into a 5-year cooperative agreement with the U.S. Agency for Toxic Substances and Disease Registry to conduct community and health professional environmental health education in response to these problems.

What factors put environmental groups and big business at odds with each other? What can we as individuals do to stop pollution and its attendant problems? Why do you think some groups are at greater risk of exposure to hazardous chemicals? What can be done about these disparities?

HUMAN HEALTH, WELL-BEING, AND SURVIVAL of all living things are ultimately dependent on the health and integrity of the planet on which we live. Americans' concern about the environment has intensified since the initial outpouring of interest on the first Earth Day in 1970. Today, most citizens are interested in the health effects of global warming and depletion of the ozone layer; increasing problems with air, water, and solid waste pollution; deforestation; endangered species; population control; and the impact of too many people on dwindling natural resources. *Pollution prevention* and *environmental protection* are household words, as school children discuss these major issues in classrooms across the country and media specials portray the potential threat of too little action done too late. Vice President Al Gore, one of the first high-ranking leaders to make the environment his number one priority, has stated that the public needs to know more about environmental pollution and the government needs to include more environmental health activities in its plan for the twenty-first century.[1] In response to public and political concerns, there has been a surge in federal and state regulations along with a multibillion dollar national infrastructure—but there remains doubt as to the effectiveness of that infrastructure in reducing environmental health risks.[2] This chapter reviews some of the major global environmental issues that affect us today and that will affect us in the generations to come.

OVERPOPULATION

Our most challenging environmental problem is population growth. The anthropologist Margaret Mead wrote, "Every human society is faced with not one population problem but two: how to beget and rear enough children and how not to beget and rear too many."[3]

The world population is increasing at unprecedented numbers. The United Nations projects that the world population will grow from 6.1 billion in the year 2000 to 9.4 billion in 2050.[4] While the world population is expanding, the earth's resources to support that population are not expanding. Population experts believe that many areas of the world are already struggling with "demographic fatigue," and that the most critical environmental challenge today is to slow the population growth of the world.[5]

The population explosion is not distributed equally around the world. The United States and western Europe have the lowest birth rates. At the same time, these two regions produce more grain and other foodstuffs than their populations consume. Countries that can least afford a high birth rate in economic, social, health, and nutritional terms are the ones with the most rapidly expanding populations.

The vast bulk of population growth in developing countries is occurring in urban areas. Third World cities' populations are doubling every 10 to 15 years, overwhelming their governments' attempts to provide clean water, sewage facilities, adequate transportation, and other basic services. Every week, the population of the world's urban centers grows by more than one million.[6] As early as 1964, researcher Ronald Wraith described the Third World giant city plagued by pollution and shantytowns as, "megalopolis—the city running riot with no one able to control it."[7] In 1800, London was the only city in the world with one million people; today, 14 cities in the world each have populations over 10 million.[8]

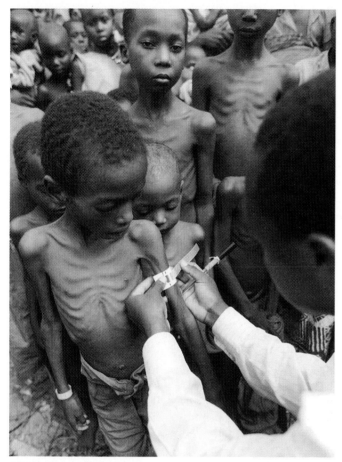

A burgeoning worldwide population puts a strain on valuable resources and leaves many parts of the world unable to meet the needs of its citizens.

As the global population expands, so does the competition for the earth's resources. Environmental degradation caused by loss of topsoil, pesticides, toxic residues, deforestation, global warming, air pollution, acid rain, a rapidly expanding population, and increasing poverty is exerting heavy pressure on natural resources and the capacity of natural resources to support human life and world health.[9]

Overpopulation threats are more evident in developing countries in Latin America, Africa, and Asia. The country projected to have the largest increase in population is India, which is projected to add another 600 million people by the year 2050, surpassing China as the most populous country in the world.[10] These projections could change, however, if the governments are not able to cope with population growth along with increased resource and economic demands. For example, the AIDS epidemic has stabilized in industrial countries to an adult infection rate of under 1 percent, but countries such as Zimbabwe, Botswana, and Zambia may lose one-fifth or more of their adult population within the next decade to AIDS.[11] The loss of a significant part of the work force may have devastating economic as well as health consequences. Diseases such as

AIDS are not the only threats to countries with unstable population growth. As governments strain to support their growing numbers, they are at increased risk to any new or increased demands on resources.

The combination of falling economic levels and rising grain prices due to grain scarcity has frequently led to famine in these areas. An estimated 40,000 children under the age of five die each day in these countries from severe nutritional deprivation and related infectious diseases.[12] Between 1993 and 1994, world carryover stocks of grain dropped by 57 million tons, one of the largest drops since the 1989 drop, which followed the drought-decimated 1988 grain harvest.[13]

We can begin to do our part by recognizing that the United States consumes far more energy and raw materials per person than does any other nation on earth. Many of these resources come from other countries, and our consumption is depleting the resource balances of those countries. Therefore, we must start by living environmentally conscious lives.

Perhaps the simplest course of action we can take is to control our own reproductivity. The concept of zero population growth (ZPG) was born in the 1960s. Proponents of this idea believed that each couple should produce only two offspring. When the parents die, the two offspring are their replacements, and the population stabilizes.

The continued preference for large families in many developing nations is caused by such factors as high infant mortality rates; the traditional view of children as "social security" (they not only work from a young age to assist families in daily survival but also support parents when they are too old to work); the low educational and economic status of women; and the traditional desire for sons that keeps parents of several daughters reproducing until they get male offspring. Education may be the single biggest contribution toward zero population growth. As education levels of women increase, fertility rates drop. Moreover, some developing nations feel that overpopulation is not as great a problem as the inequitable distribution of wealth and resources, both within their countries and worldwide. For all these reasons, demographers contend that broad-based social and economic changes will be necessary before a stabilization in population growth rates can occur.

WHAT DO YOU THINK?

How would you react to government-imposed restrictions on family size in the United States? Can you think of government programs or policies that seem to actually reward Americans for having children? Is it better to give tax breaks to couples who have large families, or would it be better to tax couples more when they choose to have several children? Do you favor mandatory limitations on births in developing countries?

AIR POLLUTION

Although we often assume that the air we breathe is safe, the daily impact of a growing population makes clean air more difficult to find. Concern about air quality prompted Congress to pass the Clean Air Act in 1970 and to amend it in 1977 and again in 1990. The object was to develop standards for six of the most widespread air pollutants that seriously affect health: sulfur dioxide, particulates, carbon monoxide, nitrogen dioxide, ozone, and lead.

Sources of Air Pollution

▶ *Sulfur Dioxide* **Sulfur dioxide** is a yellowish-brown gas that is a by-product of burning fossil fuels. Electricity generating stations, smelters, refineries, and industrial boilers are the main source points. In humans, sulfur dioxide aggravates symptoms of heart and lung disease, obstructs breathing passages, and increases the incidence of such respiratory diseases as colds, asthma, bronchitis, and emphysema. It is toxic to plants, destroys some paint pigments, corrodes metals, impairs visibility, and is a precursor to acid rain, which we discuss later in this chapter.

▶ *Particulates* **Particulates** are tiny solid particles or liquid droplets that are suspended in the air. Cigarette smoke releases particulates. They are also by-products of some industrial processes and the internal combustion engine. Particulates can in and of themselves irritate the lungs and can additionally carry heavy metals and carcinogenic agents deep into the lungs. When combined with sulfur dioxide, they exacerbate respiratory diseases. Particulates can also corrode metals and obscure visibility. Numerous scientific studies have found significant links between exposure to air particulate concentrations at or below current standards and adverse health effects, including premature death.[14]

▶ *Carbon Monoxide* **Carbon monoxide** is an odorless, colorless gas that originates primarily from motor vehicle emissions. Carbon monoxide interferes with the blood's ability to absorb and carry oxygen and can impair thinking, slow reflexes, and cause drowsiness, unconsciousness, and death. Many people have purchased home monitors to test for carbon monoxide.

▶ *Nitrogen Dioxide* **Nitrogen dioxide** is an amber-colored gas emitted by coal-powered electrical utility boilers and by motor vehicles. High concentrations of nitrogen dioxide can be fatal. Lower concentrations increase susceptibility to colds and flu, bronchitis, and pneumonia. Nitrogen dioxide is also toxic to plant life and causes a brown discoloration of the atmosphere. It is a precursor of ozone, and, along with sulfur dioxide, of acid rain.

▶ *Ozone* Ground-level **ozone** is a form of oxygen that is produced when nitrogen dioxide reacts with hydrogen chloride. These gases release oxygen, which is altered by sunlight to produce ozone. In the lower atmosphere, ozone irritates the mucous membranes of the respiratory system, causing coughing and choking. It can impair lung functioning, reduce resistance to colds and pneumonia, and aggravate heart disease, asthma, bronchitis, and pneumonia. This ozone corrodes rubber and paint and can injure or kill vegetation. It is also one of the irritants found in smog. The natural ozone found in the upper atmosphere (sometimes called "good" ozone), however, serves as a protective membrane against heat and radiation from the sun. We will discuss this atmospheric layer, called the ozone layer, later in the chapter.

▶ *Lead* **Lead** is a metal pollutant that is found in paint, batteries, drinking water, pipes, and dishes with lead-glazed bases. The elimination of lead from gasoline and auto exhaust in the 1970s was one of the great public health accomplishments of all time. Although stricter standards for all of the above prevail, almost one million children in the United States had elevated blood lead levels in 1997.[15] Lead affects the circulatory, reproductive, and nervous systems. It can also affect the blood and kidneys and can accumulate in bone and other tissues. Lead is particularly detrimental to children and fetuses. It can cause birth defects, behavioral abnormalities, and decreased learning abilities.

▶ *Hydrocarbons* Although not listed as one of the six major air pollutants in the Clean Air Act, hydrocarbons encompass a wide variety of chemical pollutants in the air. Sometimes known as *volatile organic compounds* (VOCs), **hydrocarbons** are chemical compounds containing different combinations of carbon and hydrogen. The principal source of polluting hydrocarbons is the internal combustion engine. Most automobile engines emit hundreds of different types of hydrocarbon compounds. By themselves, hydrocarbons seem to cause few problems, but when they combine with sunlight and other pollutants, they form such poisons as formaldehyde, various ketones, and peroxyacetylnitrate (PAN), all of which are respiratory irritants. Hydrocarbon combinations such as benzene and benzopyrene are carcinogenic. In addition, hydrocarbons play a major part in the formation of smog.

Photochemical Smog

Photochemical smog is a brown, hazy mix of particulates and gases that forms when oxygen-containing compounds of nitrogen and hydrocarbons react in the presence of sunlight. Photochemical smog is sometimes called *ozone pollution* because ozone is created when vehicle exhaust reacts with sunlight. Such smog is most likely to develop on days when there is little wind and high traffic congestion. In most cases, it forms in areas that experience a **temperature inversion,** a weather condition in which a cool layer of air is trapped under a layer of warmer air, preventing the air from circulating. When gases such as the hydrocarbons and nitrogen oxides are released into the cool air layer, they cannot escape, and thus they remain suspended until wind conditions move away the warmer air layer. Sunlight filtering through the air causes chemical changes in the hydrocarbons and nitrogen oxides, which results in smog. Smog is more likely to be produced in valley regions blocked by hills or mountains—for example, the Los Angeles basin, Denver, and Tokyo.

The most noticeable adverse effects of exposure to smog are difficulty in breathing, burning eyes, headaches, and nausea. Long-term exposure to smog poses serious health risks, particularly for children, the elderly, pregnant women, and people with chronic respiratory disorders such as asthma and emphysema.

Acid Rain

Acid rain is precipitation that has fallen through acidic air pollutants, particularly those containing sulfur dioxides and nitrogen dioxides. This precipitation, in the form of rain, snow, or fog, has a more acidic composition than does unpolluted precipitation. When introduced into lakes and ponds, acid rain gradually acidifies the water. When the acid content of the water reaches a certain level, plant and animal life cannot survive. Ironically, lakes and ponds that are acidified become a crystal-clear deep blue, giving the illusion of beauty and health.

▶ *Sources of Acid Rain*   More than 95 percent of acid rain originates in human actions, chiefly the burning of fossil fuels. The single greatest source of acid rain in the United States is coal-fired power plants, followed by ore smelters and steel mills.

When these and other industries burn fuels, the sulfur and nitrogen in the emissions combine with the oxygen and sunlight in the air to become sulfur dioxide and nitrogen oxides (precursors of sulfuric acid and nitric acids, respectively). Small acid particles are then carried by the wind and combine with moisture to produce acidic rain or snow. Because of higher concentrations of sunlight in the summer months, rain is more strongly acidic in the summertime. Additionally, the rain or snow that falls at the beginning of a storm is more acidic than that which falls later. The ability of a lake to cleanse itself and neutralize its acidity depends on several factors, the most critical of which is bedrock geology.

▶ *Effects of Acid Rain*   The damage caused to lake and pond habitats is not the worst of the problems created by acid rain. Each year, it is responsible for the destruction of millions of trees in forests in Europe and North America. Scientists have concluded that 75 percent of Europe's forests are now experiencing damaging levels of sulfur deposition by acid rain. Forests in every country on the continent are affected.[16]

Doctors believe that acid rain also aggravates and may even cause bronchitis, asthma, and other respiratory problems. People with emphysema and those with a history of heart disease may also suffer from exposure to acid rain. In addition, it may be hazardous to a pregnant woman's unborn child.

Acidic precipitation can cause metals such as aluminum, cadmium, lead, and mercury to **leach** (dissolve and filter) out of the soil. If these metals make their way into water or food supplies (particularly fish), they can cause cancer in humans who consume them.

Acid rain is also responsible for crop damage, which, in turn, contributes to world hunger. Laboratory experiments showed that acid rain can reduce seed yield by up to 23 percent. Actual crop losses are being reported with increasing frequency. A final consequence of acid rain is the destruction of public monuments and structures, with billions of dollars in projected building damage each year.

Indoor Air Pollution

Combating the problems associated with air pollution begins at home. Indoor air can be 10 to 40 times more hazardous than outdoor air. There are between 20 and 100 potentially dangerous chemical compounds in the average American home. Indoor air pollution comes primarily from six sources: woodstoves, furnaces, asbestos, passive smoke, formaldehyde, and radon.

Sulfur dioxide   A yellowish-brown gaseous by-product of the burning of fossil fuels.

Particulates   Nongaseous air pollutants.

Carbon monoxide   An odorless, colorless gas that originates primarily from motor vehicle emissions.

Nitrogen dioxide   An amber-colored gas found in smog; can cause eye and respiratory irritations.

Ozone   A gas formed when nitrogen dioxide interacts with hydrogen chloride.

Lead   A metal found in the exhaust of motor vehicles powered by fuel containing lead and in emissions from lead smelters and processing plants.

Hydrocarbons   Chemical compounds that contain carbon and hydrogen.

Photochemical smog   The brownish-yellow haze resulting from the combination of hydrocarbons and nitrogen oxides.

Temperature inversion   A weather condition occurring when a layer of cool air is trapped under a layer of warmer air.

Acid rain   Precipitation contaminated with acidic pollutants.

Leach   A process by which chemicals dissolve and filter through soil.

Woodstove Smoke Woodstoves emit significant levels of particulates and carbon monoxide in addition to other pollutants, such as sulfur dioxide. If you rely on wood for heating, you should make sure that your stove is properly installed, vented, and maintained. Burning properly seasoned wood reduces the amount of particulates released into the air.

Furnace Emissions People who rely on oil- or gas-fired furnaces also need to make sure that these appliances are properly installed, ventilated, and maintained. Inadequate cleaning and maintenance can lead to a buildup of carbon monoxide in the home, which can be deadly.

Asbestos **Asbestos** is another indoor air pollutant that poses serious threats to human health. Asbestos is a mineral that was commonly used in insulating materials in buildings constructed before 1970. When bonded to other materials, asbestos is relatively harmless, but if its tiny fibers become loosened and airborne, they can embed themselves in the lungs and cannot be expelled. Their presence leads to cancer of the lungs, stomach, and chest lining, and is the cause of a fatal lung disease called mesothelioma.

Formaldehyde **Formaldehyde** is a colorless, strong-smelling gas present in some carpets, draperies, furniture, particle board, plywood, wood paneling, countertops, and many adhesives. It is released into the air in a process called *outgassing*. Outgassing is highest in new products, but the process can continue for many years.

Exposure to formaldehyde can cause respiratory problems, dizziness, fatigue, nausea, and rashes. Long-term exposure can lead to central nervous system disorders and cancer.

To reduce your exposure to formaldehyde, ask about the formaldehyde content of products you purchase and avoid those that contain this gas. Some house-plants, such as philodendrons and spider plants, help clean formaldehyde from the air. If you experience symptoms of formaldehyde exposure, have your home tested by a city, county, or state health agency.

Radon **Radon** is one of the most serious forms of indoor air pollution. This odorless, colorless gas is the natural by-product of the decay of uranium and radium in the soil. Radon penetrates homes through cracks, pipes, sump pits, and other openings in the foundation. An estimated 30,000 cancer deaths per year have been attributed to radon, making it second only to smoking as the leading cause of lung cancer.[17]

The EPA estimates that 1 in 15 American homes has an elevated radon level. A home-testing kit from a hardware store will enable you to test your home yourself. "Alpha track" detectors are commonly used for this type of short-term testing. They must remain in your home for 2 to 90 days, depending on the device.

Household Chemicals When you use cleansers and other cleaning products, do so in a well-ventilated room, and be conservative in their use. All those caustic chemicals that zap mildew, grease, and other household annoyances cause a major risk to water and the environment. Avoid build-up. Regular cleanings will reduce the need to use potentially harmful substances. Cut down on dry cleaning, as the chemicals used by many cleaners can cause cancer. If your newly cleaned clothes smell of dry-cleaning chemicals, either return them to the cleaner or hang them in the open air until the smell is gone. Avoid the use of household air freshener products containing the carcinogenic agent *dichlorobenzene*.

WHAT DO YOU THINK?

Has the United States government taken strong enough environmental measures to protect citizens? What is the obligation of developing and developed countries regarding the use of fossil fuels? Should the responsibility for curbing their use be equally shared despite disparities in wealth?

Ozone Layer Depletion

We earlier defined *ozone* as a chemical that is produced when oxygen interacts with sunlight. Close to the earth, ozone poses health problems such as respiratory distress. Farther away from the earth, it forms a protective membrane-like layer in the earth's stratosphere—the highest level of the earth's atmosphere, located from 12 to 30 miles above the earth's surface. The ozone layer in the stratosphere protects our planet and its inhabitants from ultraviolet B (UV-B) radiation, a primary cause of skin cancer. Ultraviolet B radiation may also damage DNA and may be linked to weakened immune systems in both humans and animals. Thus, the ozone layer is crucial to life on the planet's surface, and its depletion threatens future generations.

In the early 1970s, scientists began to warn of a depletion of the earth's ozone layer. Special instruments developed to test atmospheric contents indicated that specific chemicals used on earth were contributing to the rapid depletion of this vital protective layer. These chemicals are called **chlorofluorocarbons (CFCs)**.

Asbestos A substance that separates into stringy fibers and lodges in lungs, where it can cause various diseases.

Formaldehyde A colorless, strong-smelling gas released through outgassing; causes respiratory and other health problems.

Radon A naturally occurring radioactive gas resulting from the decay of certain radioactive elements.

Chlorofluorocarbons (CFCs) Chemicals that contribute to the depletion of the ozone layer.

Greenhouse gases Gases that contribute to global warming by trapping heat near the earth's surface.

Chlorofluorocarbons were first believed to be miracle chemicals. They were used as refrigerants (Freon), as aerosol propellants in products such as hairsprays and deodorants, as cleaning solvents, and in medical sterilizers, rigid foam insulation, and Styrofoam. But, along with halons (found in many fire extinguishers), methyl chloroform, and carbon tetrachloride (cleaning solvents), CFCs were eventually found to be a major cause of depletion of the ozone layer. When released into the air through spraying or outgassing, CFCs migrate upward toward the ozone layer, where they decompose and release chlorine atoms. These atoms cause ozone molecules to break apart (see Figure 15.1).

In the early 1970s, the U.S. government banned the use of aerosol sprays containing CFCs in an effort to reduce ozone depletion. The discovery of the "ozone hole" over the Antarctic led to the 1987 Montreal Protocol treaty, whereby the United States and other nations agreed to reduce the use of

CFCs and other ozone-depleting chemicals. The treaty was amended in 1995 to ban CFC production in developed countries. Today, over 160 countries have signed the treaty, and the international community strives to discontinue the depletion of the ozone layer.[18]

Global Warming

More than 100 years ago, scientists theorized that carbon dioxide emissions from fossil-fuel burning would create a buildup of greenhouse gases in the earth's atmosphere and that this accumulation would have a warming effect on the earth's surface. The century-old predictions are now coming true, with alarming effects. Average global temperatures are higher today than at any time since global temperatures were first recorded, and the change in atmospheric temperature may be taking a heavy toll on human beings and crops.

Greenhouse gases include carbon dioxide, CFCs, ground-level ozone, nitrous oxide, and methane. They become part of a gaseous layer that encircles the earth, allowing solar heat to pass through and then trapping that heat close to the earth's surface. The most predominant of these gases is carbon dioxide, which accounts for 49 percent of all greenhouse gases. Eastern Europe and North America are responsible for approximately half of all carbon dioxide emissions. Since the late nineteenth century, carbon dioxide concentrations in the atmosphere have increased 25 percent, with half of this increase occurring since the 1950s. Carbon emissions from the burning of oil, coal, and gas continue to climb. In 1997, carbon dioxide concentrations in the atmosphere reached their highest levels in 160,000 years.[19]

Rapid deforestation of the tropical rain forests of Central and South America, Africa, and Southeast Asia is also contributing to the rapid rise in the presence of greenhouse gases. Trees take in carbon dioxide, transform it, store the carbon for food, and then release oxygen into the air. As we lose forests, at the rate of hundreds of acres per hour, we are losing the capacity to dissipate carbon dioxide. The forest fires in Indonesia in 1997 propelled more greenhouse gases into the atmosphere in a few months than all of Europe's industrial activity in a year.[20]

The potential consequences of global warming are dire. The rising atmospheric concentration of greenhouse gases may be the most economically disruptive and costly change set in motion by our modern industrial society.

Reducing Air Pollution

Our national air pollution problems are rooted in our energy, transportation, and industrial practices. We must develop comprehensive national strategies to address the problem of air pollution in order to clean the air for the future. We must support policies that encourage the use of renewable resources such as solar, wind, and water power

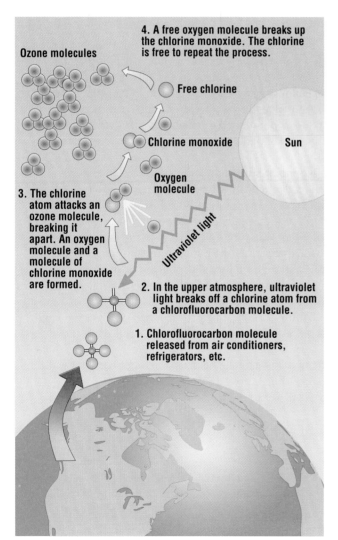

Figure 15.1
The diagram shows how the ozone layer is being depleted.

TABLE 15.1	
Global Trends in Energy Use, by Source, 1990–1997	
ENERGY SOURCE	**ANNUAL RATE OF GROWTH (%)**
Wind power	25.7
Solar power	16.8
Geothermal power	3.0
Natural gas	2.1
Hydroelectric power	1.6
Oil	1.4
Nuclear power	0.6

Source: C. Flavin and S. Dunn, Vital Signs Brief 98–6: Merger Signals Beginning of Geriatric Era for Oil Industry *(Washington, D.C.: Worldwatch Institute, 1998).*

as the providers of most of the world's energy. Table 15.1 indicates that we are started in the right direction.

Most experts agree that shifting away from automobiles as the primary source of transportation is the only way to reduce air pollution significantly. Many cities have taken steps in this direction by setting high parking fees, imposing bans on city driving, and establishing high road-usage tolls. Community governments should be encouraged to provide convenient, inexpensive, and easily accessible public transportation for citizens.

Automakers must be encouraged to manufacture automobiles that provide good fuel economy and low rates of toxic emissions. Incentives given to manufacturers to produce such cars, tax breaks for purchasers who buy them, and gas-guzzler-taxes on inefficient vehicles are three promising measures in this area. Another promising response to the automobile-caused traffic congestion and air pollution is "bicycle power." The production and use of bicycles as transportation has gained in popularity in many parts of the world: over 100 million bicycles were produced in 1997, compared with less than 40 million automobiles.[21] Currently, China leads the world in bicycle use, followed by India. In Germany, bicycle use has increased by 50 percent, and England has a plan to quadruple bicycle use by the year 2012.[22]

········ **WHAT DO YOU THINK?**

What products would you be willing to stop using in order to protect the ozone layer? What alternatives are available to replace those products that contain CFCs? What motivations lead to deforestation of the rain forests? What are some measures that might address these problems?

WATER POLLUTION

Seventy-five percent of the earth is covered with water in the form of oceans, seas, lakes, rivers, streams, and wetlands. Beneath the landmass are reservoirs of groundwater. We draw our drinking water from either this underground source or from surface freshwater sources. The status of our water supply reflects the pollution level of our communities and, ultimately, of the whole earth.

Water Contamination

Any substance that gets into the soil has the potential to get into the water supply. Contaminants from industrial air pollution and acid rain eventually work their way into the soil and then into the groundwater. Pesticides sprayed on crops wash through the soil into the groundwater. Spills of oil and other hazardous wastes flow into local rivers and streams. Underground storage tanks for gasoline may develop leaks. The list continues.

Pollutants can enter waterways by a number of different routes. Congress has coined two terms, *point source* and *nonpoint source,* to refer to the two general sources of water pollution. Pollutants that enter a waterway at a specific point through a pipe, ditch, culvert, or other such conduit are referred to as **point source pollutants.** The two major sources of this type of pollution are sewage treatment plants and industrial facilities.

Nonpoint source pollutants—commonly known as *runoff* and *sedimentation*—run off or seep into waterways from broad areas of land rather than through a discrete pipe or conduit. It is currently estimated that 99 percent of the sediment in our waterways, 98 percent of the bacterial contaminants, 84 percent of the phosphorus, and 82 percent of the nitrogen come from nonpoint sources.[23] Nonpoint pollution results from a variety of human land use practices. It includes soil erosion and sedimentation, construction wastes, pesticide and fertilizer runoff, urban street runoff, wastes from engineering projects, acid mine drainage, leakage from septic tanks, and sewage sludge.[24] (See Figure 15.2.) To learn about some of the potentially devastating effects, see the Health Headlines box on page 384.

Point source pollutants Pollutants that enter waterways at a specific point.

Nonpoint source pollutants Pollutants that run off or seep into waterways from broad areas of land.

Leachate A liquid consisting of soluble chemicals that come from garbage and industrial waste that seeps into the water supply from landfills and dumps.

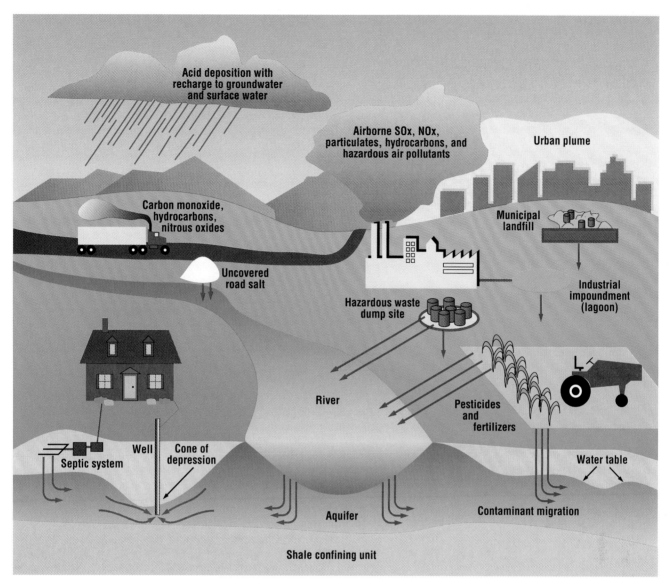

Figure 15.2
Sources of Groundwater Contamination

▶ *Septic Systems*   Bacteria from human waste can leach into the water supply from improperly installed septic systems. Toxic chemicals that are disposed of by being dumped into septic systems can also get into the groundwater supply.

▶ *Landfills*   Landfills and dumps generate a liquid called **leachate,** a mixture of soluble chemicals that come from household garbage, office waste, biological waste, and industrial waste. If a landfill has not been properly lined, leachate trickles through its layers of garbage and eventually into the water supply as acid and into the atmosphere as methane gas.

▶ *Gasoline and Petroleum Products*   In the United States, there are more than 2 million underground storage tanks for gasoline and petroleum products, most of which are located at

gasoline filling stations. One-quarter of these underground tanks are thought to be leaking.[25]

Most of these tanks were installed 25 to 30 years ago. They were made of fabricated steel that was unprotected from corrosion. Over time, pinpoint holes develop in the steel and the petroleum products stored in the tanks leak into the groundwater. The most common way to detect the presence of petroleum products in the water supply is to test for benzene, a component of oil and gasoline. Benzene is highly toxic and is associated with the development of cancer.

Chemical Contaminants

Most chemicals designed to dissolve grease and oil are called *organic solvents.* These extremely toxic substances, such as

Bottled Water: Clean Water in Scarce Supply

Consider the following: Water covers 71 percent of the globe's surface; 98 percent of that water is too salty for human consumption without using extremely costly purification methods. That leaves just 2 percent available for us to drink, and that 2 percent is unevenly distributed around the world, with 60% of it located in just 10 countries. In addition, industrialized countries use far greater amounts than do other nations. As a result, fresh water is becoming a frighteningly scarce commodity. Today about 1.2 billion people lack access to clean water and another 5 to 10 million (mostly women and children) die of illnesses related to water contaminated with solid waste, chemicals, and other water-borne pathogens.

People in the United States are among the worst consumers of water, utilizing an average of 150 gallons a day compared with 50 gallons by Europeans and 7.5 gallons by Africans. Whether it is used to water lawns, wash cars, or for the simple luxury of a daily bath, Americans often take water for granted. Yet, we do seem to be aware that *clean* water is a relatively rare commodity. A growing number of communities across the country have begun to raise objections over the chlorination and fluoridation of public drinking water. In our quest to find the best, most pure drinking water, we are moving increasingly to bottled water that promises to be from pristine wells springing from deep recesses in the Earth's crust. With its designer labels and thirst-quenching names, bottled water has become associated with status, wealth, and a health-conscious society.

But is that $2 bottle of "pure wonder" any better than the water that comes from your municipal system? Is it more likely to be chemical-free, pest-free, and pure, as many of the labels claim? Recent studies of bottled water have shown that, indeed, most are perfectly safe for human consumption and that it is typically free of disease-causing agents. But while indeed safe and fairly free of particulate matter, a great deal of bottled water may in fact come from the same source as the water you get every time you turn on the faucet. Like your tap water, such bottled water has merely been filtered or chlorinated to help make it safe for consumption. In response to consumer demand to clarify some of the misperceptions about bottled water, in recent years the Food and Drug Administration tightened its rules for label claims regarding the sources of bottled water. Now, for bottled water to be called *spring water,* it must truly come from an underground spring, and *sparkling water* has to be carbonated. But those labels with claims of *alpine, crystal clear, fresh,* and *glacial* are only advertising ploys.

While the water initially put in the bottle may be safe, what about the last dregs of water in the bottle that is left to sit in a student backpack, or a bottle that is refilled and drunk throughout the day? Saliva backwash and bacteria from the lips and hands result in a warm, moist, unsterile bottle that provides a vastly different portrait of cleanliness and crystal-clear clarity than the bottle you opened fresh from the store. So, is bottled water worth the extra cost? Most experts say no.

Bottom line? Yes, the world's water supply is becoming increasingly unsafe. However, rather than buying expensive bottled alternatives, you would be well advised to check on the quality of the water coming from public sources in your community. Also, sink-mounted, reverse-osmosis systems are now available that, when added to the purification capability of your municipal system, might be far better investments over time.

STUDENTS SPEAK UP:

Have you checked out the safety of the water supply on your campus? Why might people be concerned over chlorinated and fluoridated water? Is the bottle in your backpack safer?

---

carbon tetrachloride, tetrachloroethylene, and trichloroethylene (TCE), are used to clean clothing, painting equipment, plastics, and metal parts. Many household products, such as stain and spot removers, degreasers, drain cleaners, septic system cleaners, and paint removers, also contain these toxic chemicals.

Organic solvents work their way into the water supply in different ways. Consumers often dump leftover products into the toilet or into street drains. Industries pour leftovers into large barrels, which are then buried. After a while, the chemicals eat their way out of the barrels and leach into the groundwater system.

A related group of toxic substances contains chlorinated hydrocarbons. The most notorious of these substances are the **polychlorinated biphenyls (PCBs),** their cousins the *polybromated biphenyls (PBBs),* and the *dioxins.*

▶ *PCBs* PCBs are fire-resistant and stable at high temperatures and were therefore used for many years as insulating materials in high-voltage electrical equipment such as transformers. PCBs bioaccumulate, meaning that the body does not excrete them but rather stores them in fatty tissues and the liver. PCBs are associated with birth defects, and exposure to them is known to cause cancer. The manufacture of PCBs was discontinued in the United States in 1977, but approximately 500 million pounds of PCBs have been dumped into landfills and waterways, where they continue to pose an environmental threat.[26]

▶ *Dioxins* **Dioxins** are chlorinated hydrocarbons that are contained in herbicides (chemicals that are used to kill vegetation) and produced during certain industrial processes. Dioxins have the ability to bioaccumulate and are much more toxic than PCBs.

The long-term effects of bioaccumulation of these toxic substances include possible damage to the immune system, increased risk of infection, and elevated risk for cancer. Exposure to high concentrations of PCBs or dioxins for a short period of time can also have severe consequences, including nausea, vomiting, diarrhea, painful rashes and sores, and chloracne, an ailment in which the skin develops hard, black, painful pimples that may never go away.

▶ *Pesticides* **Pesticides** are chemicals that are designed to kill insects, rodents, plants, and fungi. Americans use more than 1.2 billion pounds of pesticides each year, but only 10 percent actually reach the targeted organisms. The remaining 1.1 billion pounds of pesticides settle on the land and in our water supplies. Pesticide residues also cling to many fresh fruits and vegetables and are ingested when people eat these items.

Most pesticides remain in the environment and accumulate in the body. A recent study found a correlation between breast cancer and Dieldrin, a popular pesticide used until the 1970s.[27] The women in the study who had the highest traces of Dieldrin in their blood were twice as likely as women with the lowest levels to develop breast cancer. Other potential hazards associated with exposure to pesticides include birth defects, cancer, liver and kidney damage, and nervous system disorders.

▶ *Lead* The Environmental Protection Agency has issued new standards intended to reduce dramatically the levels of lead in U.S. drinking water. These standards are already in place in many municipalities and will eventually reduce lead exposure for approximately 130 million people. The new rules stipulate that tap water lead values must not exceed 15 parts per billion (the previous standard allowed an average lead level of 50 parts per billion). When water suppliers identify problem areas, they will have to lower the water's acidity with chemical treatment because acidity increases water's ability to leach lead from the pipes through which it passes, or they will have to replace old lead plumbing in the service lines.

Polychlorinated biphenyls (PCBs) Toxic chemicals that were once used as insulating materials in high-voltage electrical equipment.

Dioxins Highly toxic chlorinated hydrocarbons contained in herbicides and produced during certain industrial processes.

Pesticides Chemicals that kill pests.

One way to reduce the possibility of ingesting lead if it does exist in your home's water system is to run the tap water several minutes before taking a drink or cooking with it to flush out water that has been standing overnight in lead-contaminated lines. Although leaded paints and ceramic glazes used to pose health risks, particularly for small children who put painted toys in their mouths, the use of leads in such products has been effectively reduced in recent years.

········· **WHAT DO YOU THINK?**

What can you do to ensure clean water? What personal actions can you take to conserve water? What measures can you take to avoid excessive exposure to pesticides?

NOISE POLLUTION

Loud noise has become commonplace. We are often painfully aware of construction crews in our streets, jet airplanes roaring overhead, stereos blaring next door, and trucks rumbling down nearby freeways. Our bodies have definite physiological responses to noise, and noise can become a source of physical or mental distress.

Prolonged exposure to some noises results in hearing loss. Short-term exposure reduces productivity, concentration levels, and attention spans, and may affect mental and emotional health. Symptoms of noise-related distress include disturbed sleep patterns, headaches, and tension. Physically, our bodies respond to noises in a variety of ways. Blood pressure increases, blood vessels in the brain dilate, and vessels in other parts of the body constrict. The pupils of the eye dilate. Cholesterol levels in the blood rise, and some endocrine glands secrete additional stimulating hormones, such as adrenaline, into the bloodstream.

Unfortunately, despite gradually increasing awareness that noise pollution is more than just a nuisance, noise control programs at federal, state, and local levels have been given a low budgetary priority. In order to prevent hearing loss, it is important that you take it upon yourself to avoid voluntary and involuntary exposure to excessive noise. Playing stereos in your car and home at reasonable levels, wearing ear plugs when you use power equipment, and establishing barriers (closed windows, etc.) between you and noise will help you keep your hearing intact.

········· **WHAT DO YOU THINK?**

What do you currently do that places your hearing at risk? What changes can you make in your lifestyle to change these risks?

LAND POLLUTION

Many areas of the United States currently face serious problems concerning safe and effective management of their garbage. As a nation, we are generating more trash than ever before.

Solid Waste

Each day, every person in the United States generates about 4 pounds of **municipal solid waste.** By the year 2000, solid waste generation is projected to reach 216 million tons daily, or 4.2 pounds per person.[28] Approximately 73 percent of this waste is buried in landfills. Cities and smaller communities throughout the country are in danger of exhausting their landfill space.

As communities run out of landfill space, it is becoming more common to haul garbage out to sea to dump it or to ship it to landfills in developing countries for dumping. Figure 15.3 shows the composition of our trash and what happens to our

Many communities now provide special programs where their residents can drop off any kind of hazardous waste for safe disposal.

garbage after disposal. Recycling now accounts for only 13 percent of garbage treatment. Experts believe that as much as 90 percent of our trash is ultimately recyclable. Recycling is not a new word or concept in the United States. During World War I, the Depression, and World War II, scrap materials, bottles, clothing, and other goods were recycled regularly because of scarcities. In today's throwaway society, we need to become aware of the amount of waste we generate every day and to look for ways to recycle, reuse, and—most desirable of all— reduce the products we use. The Skills for Behavior Change box on the following page discusses ways to become a better recycler through better shopping practices.

Hazardous Waste

The community of Love Canal, New York, has come to symbolize **hazardous waste** dump sites. Love Canal was an abandoned canal that was first used as a chemical dump site by the Hooker Chemical Company in the 1920s. Dumping continued for nearly 30 years. Then the area

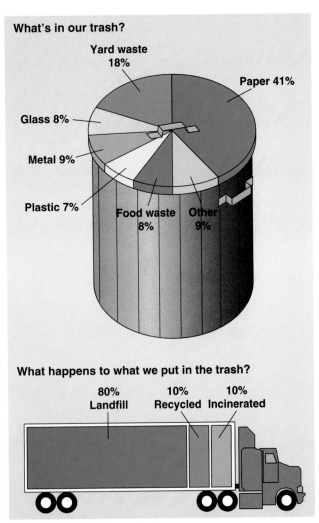

What's in our trash?

Yard waste 18%

Paper 41%

Glass 8%

Metal 9%

Plastic 7%

Food waste 8%

Other 9%

What happens to what we put in the trash?

80% Landfill   10% Recycled   10% Incinerated

Figure 15.3

The Composition and Disposition of Our Trash

Municipal solid waste   Includes such wastes as durable goods, nondurable goods, containers and packaging, food wastes, yard wastes, and miscellaneous wastes from residential, commercial, institutional, and industrial sources.

Hazardous waste   Solid waste that, due to its toxic properties, poses a hazard to humans or to the environment.

Superfund   Fund established under the Comprehensive Environmental Response Compensation and Liability Act to be used for cleaning up toxic waste dumps.

was filled in by land developers and built up with homes and schools.

In 1976, homeowners began noticing strange seepage in their basements and strong, chemical odors. Babies were born with abnormal hearts and kidneys, two sets of teeth, mental handicaps, epilepsy, liver disease, and abnormal rectal bleeding. The rate of miscarriages was far above normal. Cancer rates were also above normal.

In response to these reports, the New York State Department of Health investigated the area of Love Canal. High concentrations of PCBs were found in the storm sewers near the old canal, but it took the department another two years to order the evacuation of the Love Canal homes. Over 900 families were evacuated, and the state purchased their homes. Finally, in 1978, the expensive process of cleaning up the waste dump began. Many lawsuits for damages are still being litigated.

In 1980, the Comprehensive Environmental Response Compensation and Liability Act (**Superfund**) was enacted to provide funds for cleaning up chemical dump sites that endanger public health and land. This fund is financed through taxes on the chemical and petroleum industries (87 percent) and through general federal tax revenues (13 percent). The 1980 allocation was $1.6 billion. By 1984, the EPA estimated that an additional $8 to $23 billion was needed to finish the cleanup.[29] Cleanup cost estimates from the year 1990 through 2020 range from $106 billion to as high as $500 billion.[30]

To date, 32,500 potentially hazardous waste sites have been identified across the nation. After initial investigation, 17,800 of these sites were determined to require no further action. But about 1,300 sites are listed on the National Priorities List (NPL) and 46 percent of the sites assessed from 1992 through 1996 are a hazard to human health.[31]

HEALTH IN A DIVERSE WORLD

Environmental Responsibility Should Begin at Home

In November 1999, a *Boston Globe* exposé revealed that U.S. military presence in over 140 countries has been responsible for hazardous waste contamination in and around the areas of occupation. Even in the United States, it is estimated that 50 million acres of land have been contaminated. To clean up just 5 percent of that land would cost an estimated $15 billion, according to a Pentagon Advisory Group. This is meager, however, when compared with the damage that has occurred around the world.

Controversial reports suggest that irresponsible treatment of the land has resulted in a great deal of illnesses left in the military's wake. There are reports of once healthy children who moved onto contaminated land, only to drink and bathe in water so filled with toxins that it caused a number of disabling conditions and severely retarded their development.

The barracks at Clark Air Force in the Philippines, for instance, once housed U.S. troops, but later became homes for Philippine families. These families planted crops next to the Air Force runway, unaware that the residue from toxic chemicals, insecticides, and hazardous waste had contaminated the soil. In time, these families and their friends were stricken by disease and a wide array of illnesses, including those that compromised their immune and nervous systems.

The Philippines is just one example of U.S.-caused devastation; similar situations can be found worldwide. What is the United States doing to address this devastation? Clearly, not enough. In fact, *The Boston Globe* reported, "The military has polluted in ways that would be illegal and subject to criminal prosecution in the United States," yet the U.S. government claims that complaints abroad are "out of hand." In addition, for 1999, Congress allotted a mere $17 million for clean-up abroad, which is 0.0001 percent of what it spends for military base clean-up in the United States. The Pentagon plans to spend $165 million on overseas projects. This is in comparison with the $1.72 billion being spent on cleaning up the U.S. contaminated sites.

Although the General Accounting Office (GAO), the government watchdog agency that holds government agencies accountable for their actions, has found the United States not in compliance with environmental regulations, there is one catch. Overseas regulations are not always clear and the Environmental Protection Agency (EPA) has no authority to influence the actions of the military. A 1991 GAO audit revealed that even the environmental officials stationed overseas did not know what local regulations were. Without this basic knowledge, compliance with standards is unachievable.

Countries around the world are asking the United States to act responsibly. The United States is seemingly indifferent. Some may wonder why this is even a point of contention. As Gary Vest, the principal assistant deputy undersecretary of defense for environmental security states, "The policy and standards are clear, . . . You do not contaminate ground water or soil with current operations. And if there is a spill, you clean it up." In the current global society, environmental responsibility has to extend beyond just acting locally. It's time for global action as well.

Source: D. Armstrong, "Environmental Injustice: Overseas Dumping," *The Boston Globe,* November 15, 1999, pps. 1, 10, 11.

The large number of hazardous waste dump sites in the United States indicates the severity of our toxic chemical problem. American manufacturers generate more than 1 ton of chemical waste per person per year (approximately 275 million tons). The *Agency for Toxic Substances and Disease Registry* (ATSDR) and the *EPA* evaluate and rank the chemicals that are considered hazardous substances. Table 15.2 shows the 1997 top 20 hazardous substances.

The EPA and the states have undertaken a "cradle-to-grave" program to manage hazardous wastes by monitoring their generation, transportation, storage, treatment, and final disposal. The EPA is exploring ways to create economic incentives to encourage ingenuity in waste minimization practices and recycling.[32]

RADIATION

A substance is said to be radioactive when it emits high-energy particles from the nuclei of its atoms. There are three types of radiation: alpha particles, beta particles, and gamma rays. *Alpha* particles are relatively massive particles and are not capable of penetrating human skin. They pose health hazards only when inhaled or ingested. *Beta* particles are capable of slight penetration of the skin and are harmful if ingested or inhaled. *Gamma* rays are the most dangerous radioactive particles because they can pass straight through the skin, causing serious damage to organs and other vital structures.

TABLE 15.2

Top 20 Hazardous Substances: ATSDR/EPA Priority List for 1997

1. Arsenic	11. Chloroform
2. Lead	12. Aroclor 1254
3. Mercury, metallic	13. DDT, P'P'-
4. Vinyl chloride	14. Aroclor 1260
5. Benzene	15. Trichloroethylene
6. Polychlorinated biphenyls (PCBs)	16. Chromium (+6)
7. Cadmium	17. Dibenz[a,h]anthracene
8. Benzo(a)pyrene	18. Dieldrin
9. Benzo(b)fluoranthene	19. Hexachlorobutadiene
10. Polycyclic aromatic hydrocarbons	20. Chlordane

Source: U.S. Environmental Protection Agency, The Prioritized Chemical List. *(Washington, D.C.: USEPA, Solid Waste and Emergency Response, 1998).*

Ionizing Radiation

Exposure to ionizing radiation is an inescapable part of life on this planet. **Ionizing radiation** is caused by the release of particles and electromagnetic rays from atomic nuclei during the normal process of disintegration. Some naturally occurring elements, such as uranium, emit radiation. Radiation can wreak havoc on human cells, leading to mutations, cancer, miscarriages, and other problems.

Reactions to radiation differ from person to person. Exposure is measured in **radiation absorbed doses,** or **rads** (also called roentgens). Recommended maximum "safe" dosages range from 0.5 rads to 5 rads per year. Approximately 50 percent of the radiation to which we are exposed comes from natural sources, such as building materials. Another 45 percent comes from medical and dental X-rays. The remaining 5 percent comes from computer display screens, microwave ovens, television sets, luminous watch dials, and radar screens and waves. Most of us are exposed to far less radiation than the "safe" maximum dosage per year.

Radiation can cause damage at dosages as low as 100 to 200 rads. At this level, signs of radiation sickness include nau-

Ionizing radiation Radiation produced by photons having high enough energy to ionize atoms.

Radiation absorbed doses (rads) Units that measure exposure to radioactivity.

ACCESSING YOUR HEALTH ON THE INTERNET

Check out the following Internet sites related to environmental health.

1. *Agency for Toxic Substances and Disease.* Public health statements containing easily understood warnings and descriptions concerning toxic chemicals. The statements do not present any numerical scientific data or cite any references.

   http://www.atsdr.cdc.gov/cx.html

2. *Environmental Protection Agency.* Government agency that oversees all environmental issues. This site provides a wealth of information, as well as links to other environmental and safety resources.

   http://www.epa.gov/

3. *National Institute of Environmental Health Sciences (NIEHS).* Contains articles, announcements, and government reports on issues examining the environment and relationships among poverty, pollution, and health status.

   http://www.niehs.nih.gov

sea, diarrhea, fatigue, anemia, sore throat, and hair loss. Death is unlikely at this dosage. At 350 to 500 rads, all these symptoms become more severe, and death may result because the radiation hinders bone marrow production of the white blood cells we need to protect us from disease. Dosages above 600 to 700 rads are invariably fatal. The effects of long-term exposure to relatively low levels of radiation are unknown. Some scientists believe that such exposure can cause lung cancer, leukemia, skin cancer, bone cancer, and skeletal deformities.

WHAT DO YOU THINK?

What do you currently recycle? What are some of the reasons you do not recycle? What concerns would you have about living near a landfill or hazardous waste production or disposal site?

EMFs: Emerging Risks?

If you believe what you hear on T.V. or read in the papers, electric and magnetic fields (EMFs) generated by electric power delivery systems are responsible for risks for cancer (particularly among children), reproductive dysfunction, birth

CONSUMER HEALTH

Speaking Out on the Environment

There are many ways for individuals to get involved in the crusade against environmental pollution. Here are eight.

- *Monitor legislation.* All of the key environmental organizations keep tabs on state and national laws being considered in order to offer testimony and to generate letterwriting campaigns on behalf of (or against) proposed laws. [You can ask them for information.] . . .
- *Write letters.* It may not seem like a potent weapon, but letters to state and federal legislators on pending bills *do* influence their opinions. When writing to any public official, keep your letter simple. Focus on one subject and identify a particular piece of legislation. . . . Request a specific action . . . and state your reasons for taking your position. If you live or work in the legislator's district, make sure to say so. . . .

Keep the letter to one or two paragraphs, and never write more than one page. [You can send your letters to:]

Hon. _____
House Office Building
Washington, D.C. 20515

Senator _____
Senate Office Building
Washington, D.C. 20515

- *Fill out customer comment cards and/or phone toll free numbers on packages* [to let companies know your concerns].
- *Educate others.* You can do this in a variety of ways, from talking to your friends, co-workers, and neighbors to organizing an educational activity. . . .
- *Campaign for environmental candidates.* Don't just be concerned about someone claiming to be an "environmental president." Look at the environmental positions of candidates at all levels of government. . . .
- *Launch a campaign at school or work.* At Rutgers University, for example, members of the law association decided to target the use of plastic foam in the cafeterias. After creating a multistep, long-term strategy, the students first approached the food services department. The director of food services readily agreed to get

rid of foam cups in a matter of days, and the foam food containers as soon as current inventory was depleted. . . . Sometimes all you have to do is ask.

- *Invite speakers to your organization.* Most environmental organizations offer speakers on a wide range of topics who will speak at no charge to your civic, school, religious, or social organization. . . . For maximum impact, consider scheduling a debate or panel discussion among representatives of environmental groups, government agencies, and industry.
- *Get involved with government.* Most communities offer a variety of boards, commissions, and committees that deal with environmental issues: planning commissions, zoning and land-use commissions, parks commissions, transit boards, and so on. Each can play a role in setting policies that affect the quality of the environment in your area.

Source: Except for the first paragraph and the bracketed material, from *The Green Consumer Supermarket Guide,* 260–264, by Joel Makower, J. Elkington, and J. Hailes. Copyright © 1991 by John Elkington, Julia Hailes, and Viking Penguin. Used by permission of Viking Penguin, a division of Penguin Books USA Inc; and Victor Gollanez Ltd.

---

defects, neurological disorders, Alzheimer's disease, and other ailments. Based on the small devices with which school children are running around monitoring so-called emissions, all of the fuss about EMFs has surfaced as something that is not only believable, but highly profitable for some innovative companies. But, does the research support these EMF risks? While many believe that the threat is legitimate, others point to major discrepancies and inconsistencies in the research. In spite of many questions, fears have increased, and there is probably more potential for exploitation than real hazard to health from this nonionizing form of exposure.

Nuclear Power Plants

One source of radioactive emissions is nuclear power plants. At present, these plants account for less than 1 percent of the total radiation to which we are exposed. Radioactive wastes are produced not only by nuclear power plants but also by medical facilities that use radioactive materials as treatment and diagnostic tools and by nuclear weapons production facilities.

Proponents of nuclear energy believe that it is a safe and efficient way to generate electricity. Initial costs of building

Although cell phones are more common every day, recent research has called into question the health risks of prolonged cell phone use.

nuclear power plants are high, but actual power generation is relatively inexpensive. A 1,000-megawatt reactor produces enough energy for 650,000 homes and saves 420 million gallons of fossil fuels each year. In some areas where nuclear power plants were decommissioned, electricity bills tripled when power companies turned to hydroelectric or fossil fuel sources to generate electricity.

Nuclear reactors also discharge fewer carbon oxides into the air than do fossil-fuel powered generators. Advocates believe that conversion to nuclear power could help slow the global warming trend. Over the past 15 years, carbon emissions were reduced by 298 million tons, or 5 percent.

All these advantages of nuclear energy must be weighed against the disadvantages. First, disposal of nuclear wastes is extremely problematic for the entire world. Additionally, the chances of a reactor core meltdown pose serious threats to a plant's immediate environment and to the world in general.

A **meltdown** occurs when the temperature in the core of a nuclear reactor increases enough to melt both the nuclear fuel and the containment vessel that holds it. Most modern facilities seal their reactors and containment vessels in concrete buildings having pools of cold water on the bottom. If a meltdown occurs, the building and the pool are supposed to prevent the escape of radioactivity.

Two serious nuclear accidents within seven years of one another caused a steep decline in public support for nuclear energy. The first occurred in 1979 at Three Mile Island near Harrisburg, Pennsylvania, when a mechanical failure caused a partial meltdown of one reactor core and small amounts of radioactive steam were released into the atmosphere. No loss of human life was reported, although residents in the area were evacuated. Miscarriages, birth defects, and cancer rates in the area are reported to have increased, but no public health statistics have been released.

Human error and mechanical failure were the reported causes of the April 1986 reactor core fire and explosion at the Chernobyl nuclear power plant in the Soviet Union. In just 4.5 seconds, the temperature in the reactor rose to 120 times normal, causing the explosion. Eighteen people were killed immediately, 30 workers died later from radiation sickness, and 200 other workers were hospitalized for severe radiation sickness. Soviet officials evacuated towns and villages near the plant. Some medical workers estimate that the eventual death toll from Chernobyl could top 100,000 from radiation-induced cancers.

Radioactive fallout from the Chernobyl disaster spread over most of the northern hemisphere. Milk, meat, and vegetables in Scandinavian countries were contaminated with radioactive iodine and cesium and were declared unfit for human consumption. Thousands of reindeer in Lapland were declared contaminated and were destroyed. In Great Britain, thousands of sheep had to be destroyed because they were contaminated, and three years after the disaster, sheep in the northern regions of the country were still found to be contaminated. Direct costs of the disaster totaled more than $13 billion, including lost agricultural output and the cost of replacing the power plant. Nuclear accidents continue to pose risks to human health, even in well-controlled settings.

WHAT DO YOU THINK?

How much exposure do you have to ionizing and nonionizing radiation a year? What measures could you take to reduce this exposure? Do you feel the advantages outweigh the disadvantages of nuclear power? Explain why or why not.

Meltdown An accident that results when the temperature in the core of a nuclear reactor increases enough to melt the nuclear fuel and the containment vessel housing it.

Taking Charge ....

Managing Environmental Pollution

The next decade will be a critical period in environmental protection. Only through prudent action, responsible practices, and courageous leadership will our nation's vast resources be protected. Individual efforts to preserve and protect the environment and to elect leaders who make the environment a priority will give the planet a fighting chance. Do you consider yourself environmentally sound? Do you feel you "do your part"? Could you do more? As a student on a tight budget, are you willing to pay 30 to 50 percent more for products such as safer soap and laundry detergent? If not, are you willing to buy a less environmentally friendly product? While it's not likely that you can increase your budget enough to buy all environmentally safe products, you can get a start now. Following are some guidelines for making environmentally sound decisions.

CHECKLIST FOR CHANGE

MAKING PERSONAL CHOICES

✓ Do you know the difference between rhetoric and reality when it comes to the environment?

✓ Do you conserve water? Fix leaky faucets quickly. Run washers only with full loads.

✓ Do you think before you buy? Do you buy products in recyclable packaging? Do you reuse containers rather than buy new ones?

✓ Do you think before you throw away household chemicals? Make sure you use them up, give them away, or save them for a household hazardous waste collection instead. Consider nonhazardous substitutes.

✓ Do you recycle used oil? Oil dumped down storm drains or on the ground can pollute the groundwater.

✓ Do you recycle tin cans, glass, newspaper, paper, plastic, and cardboard?

✓ Have you considered walking, riding the bus, using your bike, and/or carpooling whenever possible?

✓ Always use low-phosphorous fertilizers.

✓ Do you buy used and rebuilt products whenever possible? Do you resell your unused items at yard or garage sales or donate them to charities?

✓ Do you compost leaves, clippings, and kitchen scraps?

MAKING COMMUNITY CHOICES

✓ Do you work in your community to help create and enforce laws that protect drinking water and that prohibit the manufacture, use, storage, transport, or disposal of hazardous substances in your water supply area?

✓ Do you volunteer to take part in clean-up activities in your community?

✓ Does your community have a hazardous materials policy?

SUMMARY

- Population growth is the single largest factor affecting the demands made on the environment. Demand for more food, products, and energy—as well as places to dispose of waste—places great strains on the earth's resources.

- The primary constituents of air pollution are sulfur dioxide, particulate matter, carbon monoxide, nitrogen dioxide, ozone, lead, and hydrocarbons. Air pollution takes the forms of photochemical smog and acid rain, among others. Indoor air pollution is caused primarily by woodstove smoke, furnace emissions, asbestos, passive smoke, formaldehyde, and radon. Pollution is depleting the earth's protective ozone layer, causing global warming.

- Water pollution can be caused by either point (direct entry through a pipeline, ditch, etc.) or nonpoint (runoff or seepage from a broad area of land) sources. Chemicals that are major contributors to water pollution include dioxins, pesticides, trihalomethanes, and lead.

- Noise pollution affects our hearing and produces other symptoms such as reduced productivity, reduced concentration, headaches, and tension.

- Solid waste pollution includes household trash, plastics, glass, metal products, and paper; limited landfill space creates problems. Hazardous waste is toxic; its improper disposal creates health hazards for those in surrounding communities.

- Ionizing radiation results from the natural erosion of atomic nuclei. Nonionizing radiation is caused by the electric and magnetic fields around power lines and household appliances, among other sources. The disposal and storage of radioactive wastes from nuclear power plants and weapons production pose serious potential problems for public health.

DISCUSSION QUESTIONS

1. Explain the ways in which the expanding global population affects the environment.
2. List the primary sources of air pollution, acid rain, and indoor air pollution. What can be done to reduce each type of pollution?
3. What are the environmental consequences of global warming? What can we as U.S. citizens do to help slow the deforestation of tropical rain forests?
4. Explain point and nonpoint sources of water pollution. Discuss how water pollution can be reduced or prevented altogether. What personal actions can you as a student take?
5. List the loudest sounds you have encountered in the last week (rock concert, construction, airplanes, etc.). What could be done to ease the strain of the unavoidable noises?
6. Given all the open land in the United States, why do you think solid waste disposal is a problem?
7. Are the advantages of nuclear power worth the risks involved with storing nuclear waste? Put another way, if you live near a nuclear power plant, would you be willing to pay two or three times as much for electricity in order to have the nuclear power plant closed? Explain why or why not.

APPLICATION EXERCISE

Reread the *What Do You Think?* scenario at the beginning of the chapter and answer the following questions.

1. Why do otherwise rational people tend to vote against environmental initiatives designed to protect the environment at all costs?
2. How much progress can be made in the fight against environmental polluters by community action? What barriers might selected minorities face as they try to fight industrial pollutors?
3. What are an industry's responsibilities to its neighbors? Are employee jobs a viable reason for keeping a factory in operation, even when it pollutes the environment or destroys a natural resource?

16

Consumerism

Selecting Health-Care Products and Services

OBJECTIVES

▶ Discuss the methods advertisers use to attract, switch, and maintain customers.

▶ Explain when self-diagnosis and self-care are appropriate, when you should seek traditional or nontraditional health care, and how to assess health-care professionals.

▶ Compare and contrast allopathic and nonallopathic medicine, including the types of treatments that fall into each category.

▶ Discuss the types of health care available, including types of health-care practices, hospitals, and clinics.

▶ Examine the current problems associated with our healthcare system, including cost, access, choice of treatment modality, and quality.

▶ Describe health insurance options, including private insurance coverage, Medicare, Medicaid, and managed care choices (HMOs and PPOs).

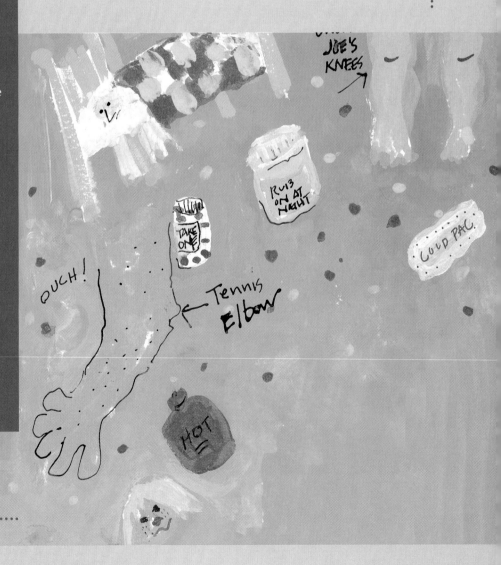

THERE ARE MANY REASONS for you to be an informed health-care consumer. Most importantly, you have only one body and if you don't treat it with care, you will pay a major price in terms of actual costs and health consequences. Doing everything you can to prevent illness, stay healthy, and to recover rapidly when you do get sick will enhance every other part of your life. Our society generally treats health care as a private-consumption good or service to be bought and sold rather than as a social good to which everyone is entitled. Therefore, you need to be not only informed but also assertive in order to obtain high-quality health care at an affordable cost.

This chapter will help you to become more proactive in making decisions that affect your health and health care. Our health-care system is a maze of health-care providers, payers (insurance, government, and individuals), and products, and many of us find it hard to thread our way through it. Health care is the fifth-largest industry in our country, accounting for over 10 percent of our workforce, and many different companies aggressively market health products and services to the public. Increasingly, health-care organizations are "for profit" businesses, sold and traded on the stock market and having profit as the bottom line. Medical professionals report that they too feel overwhelmed, confused, and frustrated by the multitude of choices, seemingly divergent interests, and lack of coordination in our system. Although you are not alone in your feelings of frustration or anxiety about the health industry, there are many things you can do to avoid feeling victimized.

RESPONSIBLE CONSUMERISM
Choices and Challenges

Perhaps the single greatest difficulty that we face as health consumers is the sheer magnitude of choices available to us. If you try to select a general practitioner from the telephone book when you are sick, you may have to thumb through dozens of pages of specialists. When going to the drugstore for a bottle of cough syrup, you may have to choose from hundreds of options, each claiming to do more for you than the brand next to it. Even trained pharmacists sometimes find it impossible to keep up with the explosion of new drugs and health-related products.

Because there are so many profit-seekers competing for a share of the lucrative health market and because misinformation is so common, wise health consumers use every means at their disposal to ensure that they are acting responsibly and economically in their own health choices.

Attracting Consumers' Dollars

Today's marketing specialists can identify a target audience for a given product and carefully go after it with a whole arsenal of gimmicks, subtle persuaders, and sophisticated strategies. Different techniques are used to attract new customers, maintain existing customers, and encourage consumers of the product to switch to another brand. Many ads play on your inner fears and insecurities, causing you to wonder whether your deodorant is working, your breath is bad, or your skin is greasy.

Whatever your desires, countless products and services are available to meet them. Although some marketing tactics are obvious, others are much more subtle and difficult to discern. Perfume advertisements that depict passionate embraces and automobile ads that feature expensive sports cars with beautiful young men and women are common. The implied message is that if you purchase a given perfume, your love life will improve, and if you buy that flashy car, attractive people will flock to you.

Many other marketing strategies revolve around "trendy" news items. A good example of this is the current fascination with the use of herbs to treat the common cold, and wearable magnets to treat arthritis and painful joints.

Putting Cure into Better Perspective

People often fall victim to false health claims because they mistakenly believe that a product or provider has helped them. This belief often arises from two conditions: spontaneous remission and the placebo effect.

▶ *Spontaneous Remission*   It is commonly said that if you treat a cold, it will disappear in a week, but if you leave it alone, it will last seven days. A **spontaneous remission** from an ailment refers to the disappearance of symptoms without any apparent cause or treatment. Many illnesses, like the common cold and even back strain, are self-limiting and will improve in time, with or without treatment. Other illnesses, such as multiple sclerosis and some cancers, are characterized by alternating periods of severe symptoms and sudden remissions. People experiencing spontaneous remissions can easily attribute their "cure" to a treatment, drug, or provider that had no real effect on the disease or condition. On the other hand, there is little scientific evidence that new, unusual, or ancient treatments offer no benefit to the consumer.

▶ *Placebo Effect*   The **placebo effect** is an apparent cure or improved state of health brought about by a substance, product, or procedure that has no generally recognized therapeutic value. It is not uncommon for patients to report improvements based on what they expect, desire, or were told would happen after taking simple sugar pills that they believed were powerful drugs. About 10 percent of the population is believed to be exceptionally susceptible to the power of suggestion and may be taken advantage of by the aggressive marketing of products and services. Although the placebo effect is generally harmless,

Spontaneous remission   The disappearance of symptoms without any apparent cause or treatment.

Placebo effect   An apparent cure or improved state of health brought about by a substance or product that has no medicinal value.

it does account for the expenditure of millions of dollars on health products and services every year. People who mistakenly use placebos when medical treatment is urgently needed increase their risk for health problems; however, those who use low-cost, no-risk placebos and find relief, even for just a short time, should not be criticized.

ACCEPTING RESPONSIBILITY FOR YOUR HEALTH CARE

As the health-care industry has become more sophisticated about seeking your business, so must you become more sophisticated about purchasing its products and services. You need to learn how, when, and where to enter the massive technological maze that is our health-care system without incurring unnecessary risk and expense. Acting responsibly in times of illness can be difficult, but the person best able to act on your behalf is you.

If you are feeling ill, you must decide whether you need to seek outside medical advice and/or care. Not that long ago, as many as 70 percent of all trips to the doctor and nearly half of all hospital stays were unnecessary and potentially harmful.[1] These figures have been reduced considerably, however, with the advent of managed care, which carries with it a degree of out-of-pocket shared costs. Managed care involves a number of measures designed to keep people out of the hospitals and emergency rooms.[2] Although there are no exact figures, respected sources indicate that the number of emergency room visits have decreased dramatically and that the cost of emergency room care for nonemergencies has declined as well.[3] All said, not seeking treatment, whether due to high costs or a limiting coverage, has inherent risks. Being knowledgeable about the benefits of and limits to self-care is critical for responsible consumerism.

We all practice some level of self-care. The challenge is knowing when it's time to seek professional help.

Self-Help or Self-Care

A recent concept in health consumerism is that the patient is the primary health-care provider or first line of defense in health. Patients can practice behaviors that promote health, prevent disease, and minimize reliance on the formal medical system. They can also interpret basic changes in their own physical and emotional health and treat minor afflictions without seeking professional help. Self-care consists of knowing your body, paying attention to its signals, and taking appropriate action to stop the progression of illness or injury or to improve your overall health.

When to Seek Help

Effective self-care requires understanding when you should seek professional medical attention rather than treat a condition by yourself. Generally, you should consult a physician if you experience any of the following:

- A serious accident or injury.
- Sudden or severe chest pains causing breathing difficulties.
- Trauma to the head or spine accompanied by persistent headache, blurred vision, loss of consciousness, vomiting, convulsions, or paralysis.
- Sudden high fever or recurring high temperature (over 102°F for adults and 103°F for children) and/or sweats.
- Tingling sensation in the arm accompanied by slurred speech or impaired thought processes.
- Adverse reactions to a drug or insect bite (shortness of breath, severe swelling, dizziness).
- Unexplained bleeding or loss of bodily fluid from any body opening.
- Unexplained sudden weight loss.
- Persistent or recurrent diarrhea or vomiting.
- Blue-colored lips, eyelids, or nail beds.
- Any lump, swelling, thickness, or sore that does not subside or that grows for over a month.
- Any marked change in or pain accompanying bowel or bladder habits.
- Yellowing of the skin or the whites of the eyes.
- Any symptom that is unusual and recurs over time.
- If you are pregnant.

With the vast array of home diagnostic devices currently available, it appears to be relatively easy for most people to take care of themselves. But some caution is in order here: Although many of these devices are valuable for making an initial diagnosis, home health tests cannot fully substitute for regular, complete examinations by a trained practitioner. The Skills for Behavior Change box offers valuable information about taking an active part in your own health care.

Assessing Health Professionals

Suppose you decide that you do need medical help. You must then identify what type of help you need and find out where to obtain it. Initially, selecting a provider may seem a simple matter, yet many people have no idea how to assess the qualifications of a health-care provider.

Knowledge of both traditional medical specialties and alternative, or "complementary," medical treatment is critical to making an intelligent selection. You also need to be aware of your own criteria for evaluating a health professional. Several studies have pointed to bedside manner and interactions with doctors as key to patient satisfaction. In a survey of HMO members, it was shown that even in a setting of limited physician choice, the opportunity to select one's personal physician had a positive influence on patient satisfaction with that physician.[4] Regardless of your criteria for evaluating a health-care provider, you should fully understand your coverage options when selecting from a panel or network of health-care providers. Carefully consider the following factors about all prospective health-care providers:

- What professional educational training have they had? What license or board certification do they hold? Note that there is a difference between "board eligible" and "board certified." *Board certified* indicates that they have passed the national board examination for their specialty (e.g., pediatrics) and have been certified as competent in that specialty. In contrast, *board eligible* merely means that they are eligible to take the specialty board's exam or that they may have failed the exam.
- Are traditional medical providers affiliated with an accredited medical facility or institution? The Joint Commission on the Accreditation of Healthcare Organizations (JCAHO) requires these institutions to verify all education, licensing, and training claims of their affiliated practitioners. What other doctors are in their group, and who will assist in my treatment?
- Do they indicate clearly how long a given treatment may last, what side effects might be expected from treatment, and what things to be aware of?
- Do their diagnoses, treatments, and general statements appear to be consistent with established scientific theory and practice?
- Does this procedure require an overnight stay at a hospital or can it be performed in a doctor's office?
- Who will be responsible for my care when the doctor is on vacation or off call?
- Why has this test been ordered? What is the doctor trying to find or exclude?
- Do they listen to me, and appear to respect me as an individual, and give me time to ask questions? Do they return my calls, and are they available to answer questions?
- How often has the doctor performed this test, surgery, or procedure, and with what proportion of successful outcome?
- Are the risks from the treatment greater than the risks from the condition?
- Is a second opinion necessary before my insurance company will pay the costs? If not, if I request a second opinion, will my insurance cover the cost?

Being Proactive in Your Health Care

Taking a proactive approach to practicing preventive behaviors can go a long way toward giving you a long and healthy life. Sometimes, however, regardless of the steps you take to care for yourself, you still get sick. At such a time, it is important that you continue to be actively involved in your care. The more you know about your own body and about factors that can affect your health, the better able you will be to communicate complete information to your doctor. It also helps you to make informed decisions and to recognize when a certain treatment may not be right for you. The following points can help:

- Know your own and your family's medical history.
- Be knowledgeable about your condition—causes, physiological effects, possible treatments, prognosis. Don't rely on the doctor for all this information. Do some research on your own.
- Take a friend or relative along for medical visits to help you review what the doctor says. Or, take notes if you go alone.
- Ask the practitioner to explain the problem and possible treatments, tests, and drugs in a clear and understandable way.

- If the doctor prescribes any medications, ask for their generic names so that you can pay less for them.
- Ask for a written summary of the results of your visit and any lab tests.
- If you have any doubt about the doctor's recommended treatment, seek a second opinion.
- If you will need to take a prescription medication for an extended time, ask for the maximum number of doses allowed by your plan if you have a small pharmacy co-payment.

Afterward,

- Write down an accurate account of what happened and what was said. Be sure to include the names of the doctor and all other people involved in your care, the date, and the place.
- Shop around drugstores for the best prices.
- When filling prescriptions, ask to see the pharmacist's package inserts that list medical considerations concerning the medicines. Request detailed information about any potential drug interactions.
- Have clear instructions written on the label to avoid risk to others who may take the drug in error.

Just like you, doctors are human. Their decisions are based on the best information they have available to them and may be influenced by a number of factors—workload, limited information, personal views. Therefore, in addition to following the practical steps listed above, being proactively involved in your health care also means that you should be aware of your rights as a patient. The following are the basic rights of all individuals seeking care from a health-care professional.

1. The right of informed consent. Before receiving any care, you have the right to be fully informed of what is being planned, the risks and potential benefits, and possible alternative forms of treatment, including the option of no treatment. Your consent must be voluntary and without any form of coercion. It is critical that you read any consent forms carefully and amend them as necessary before signing.
2. You have the right to know whether the treatment you are receiving is standard or experimental. In experimental conditions, you have the legal and ethical right to know if the study is one in which some people receive treatment while others do not in order to compare the results and if any drug is being used in the research project for a purpose not approved by the Food and Drug Administration (FDA).
3. You have the right to privacy, which includes the source of payment for treatment and care. It also includes protecting your right to make personal decisions concerning all reproductive matters.
4. You have the legal right to refuse treatment at any time and to cease treatment at any time during the course of care.
5. You have the right to receive care.
6. You have the right to access all your medical records and to confidentiality of your records.
7. You have the right to seek the opinions of other health-care professionals regarding your condition.

- Are these medications necessary? What are their possible side effects? What alternatives are available? Is there a generic version that costs less?

Asking the right questions at the right time may save you personal suffering and expense. Many patients find that writing their questions down ahead of time helps them to get all their inquiries answered. You should not accept a defensive or hostile response; asking questions is your right as a patient.

········· **WHAT DO YOU THINK?**

Are you comfortable allowing your primary care physician to direct *all* of your health care? (Including the specialists you may need to see?) Does your physician consider any nontraditional medical treatment valid?

Doc.com Surfer Beware

Mary, an avid health and fitness proponent with no formal academic training in health, took her first web page–building class in August. Today, because of her interest and enthusiasm for health topics, she has a comprehensive health and medical advice website on which she talks with great authority about a variety of interesting health topics. It includes self-assessment exercises and numerous links to other health sites. But, does her glitzy, interactive page provide accurate, well-researched advice? Or is she just picking up a variety of bits and pieces of information from the same, often questionable sites to which we all have access? In most cases, Mary is just as vulnerable to bad information as the rest of us. She may not even know that her information may be based on weak science. So, while she has no ulterior motives and is well intended, Mary's advice has the potential to harm others seriously.

Although Mary is a fictional character, invented to make a point, such a scenario is more than possible. A great many "Marys" abound on the Internet today, because anyone capable of creating a web page has the tools to put up anything he or she wants. Sometimes, what is put online for the world to see is without the backing of reputable scientists, medical and health care groups, or educational counsel, and can be misleading and may even be harmful to others. This is certainly the case with the surge of sites devoted to health and medical information. The World Wide Web is filled with self-appointed health experts, with legitimate professional health agencies, and, more recently, with what has come to be known as Doc.coms—websites that provide everything from online diagnoses, chat room support groups, and detailed information on conditions and procedures, to opportunities to watch surgical procedures. Today, millions of people throughout the world have information at their fingertips and often turn to that source for help with the self-diagnosis of symptoms. While this is another step in encouraging people to be more proactive in their own care, the potential for harm should make us proceed with caution.

In an article for *The Wall Street Journal,* columnist Marilyn Chase reported her experiences seeking information on the Internet about headaches. Her search focused on finding chat rooms and doctors online offering information. Her conclusion? "In short, browsers in the e-marketplace of medical information will find that the quality is very diverse. Some sites offer depth of data, with credentials to back them up. Others display nice site design or easy access but have thin content. Randomly [hopping] from link to link can leave you with a handful of commercial pitches or fringe benefits."

Although advice on protecting yourself from Internet misinformation and scams also abounds, it is unlikely that you can totally avoid bad information. What you can do is reduce your risk. The following strategies should help.

CHOICES OF MEDICAL CARE

Familiarizing yourself with the various health professions and health subspecialties will help you choose the right provider for your needs. While **allopathic medicine,** or traditional, Western medical practice, is based on scientifically validated methods, there are also a number of allopathic treatments and procedures still under scientific review and considered experimental. Medical practitioners who adhere to allopathic principles are bound by a professional code of ethics.

Traditional Western (Allopathic) Medicine

Selecting a **primary care practitioner**—a medical practitioner whom you can go to for routine ailments, preventive care, general medical advice, and appropriate referrals—is not an easy task. The primary care practitioner for most people is either a family practitioner, an internist, a pediatrician, or an obstetrician/gynecologist. Many people routinely see nurse practitioners or physician assistants who work for an individual doctor or a medical group; others use nontraditional providers as their primary source of care.

Active participation in your own treatment is the only sensible course in a health-care environment that encourages "defensive medicine." That is, physicians will frequently order tests to rule out rare or unlikely diagnoses simply because they are worried about possible malpractice suits. Researchers have documented that this practice often leads to unnecessary tests and overtreatment. By some estimates, between 20 and 70 percent of what is done in medicine either does not improve health outcomes or creates iatrogenic disease (illness caused by the medical process itself). *Informed consent* refers to your right to have explained to you—in nontechnical language you can understand—all possible side effects, benefits, and consequences of a specific procedure and treatment regimen as well as available alternatives to it. It also means that you have the right to refuse a specific treatment or to seek a second or even third opinion from unbiased, noninvolved providers.[5]

- Don't forget the wealth of information at your school's library. Ask the reference librarian at your school to which health-related information data bank the school subscribes. Institutions of higher education generally subscribe to peer-reviewed journals, which are written by professionals and reviewed by the writers' peers. In addition, universities often subscribe to services that compile journal articles from the social and health sciences and meet the criteria for peer review. Many of these publications are online. Those that are not will probably be on your library's shelves.
- Seek information from several different types of sources. Check author credentials and cross-check information from different sources to see where there is the greatest consensus. Taking information from only one source and assuming it to be true is a bad idea.
- Reputable information in the health area often includes complete references. Find out if the site is professionally managed, peer-reviewed, and updated regularly.

- Professional and nationally recognized agencies, including government agencies, are good places to start. Although still possessing inaccuracies, many of these sites include the latest data-based statistics from randomized, clinical trials.
- Remember that just because a site is "linked" to a government source, doesn't mean that the government source is aware of the initial site or endorses it.
- Look at the credentials of the authors of any papers posted online. With what organizations, if any, are they affiliated?
- Avoid online health professionals who will diagnose or make blanket statements about your health without requiring a formal examination or referring you to others.
- Look at the advertisements on the page. If they are part of the text or if they appear to promise quick cures or easy solutions, beware.
- Note the date of the article and all references. Citations that are more than a couple of years old are too old.

- If the site is from a reputable institution of higher education, determine if it is managed by faculty, students, or laboratories on campus.
- Look to see if the site provides both sides of controversial issues, including references. Reputable sites don't try to force you into buying their product or endorsing their view so much as they want you to consider your options.
- Use caution when purchasing health products and services over the Internet. Check out your options, consider the costs and the benefits, and proceed with caution.
- For personal health issues, weigh all the information you gather off the Internet with what your health-care provider has told you. Your health-care providers are still some of the best resources at your disposal.

STUDENTS SPEAK UP:

What are some inherent dangers of relying on health information found over the Internet?

······· **WHAT DO YOU THINK?**

Have you ever opted for a treatment other than what was recommended by your allopathic medical provider? What was the response? Did your health insurer cooperate fully and pay the bill?

Allopathic medicine Traditional, Western medical practice; in theory, based on scientifically validated methods and procedures.

Primary care practitioner A medical practitioner who treats routine ailments, advises on preventive care, gives general medical advice, and makes appropriate referrals when necessary.

Nurse Health practitioner who provides many services for patients and who may work in a variety of settings.

Allied Professionals

Nurses are highly trained and strictly regulated health practitioners who provide a wide range of services for patients and their families, including patient education, counseling, community health and disease prevention information, and administration of medications.

Nurses may today choose from several training options. There are over 2.4 million licensed registered nurses (R.N.) in the United States who have completed either a four-year program leading to a bachelor of science in nursing (B.S.N.) degree or a two-year associate degree program. More than .5 million lower-level licensed practical or vocational nurses (L.P.N. or L.V.N) have completed a one- to two-year training program, which may have been community college-based or hospital-based.

Nurse practitioners (N.P.) are professional nurses having advanced training obtained through either a master's degree program or a specialized nurse practitioner program. Nurse practitioners have the training and authority to conduct diagnostic tests and prescribe medications (in some states). They work in a variety of settings, particularly in HMOs, clinics, and student health centers. Nurses may also earn the clinical doctor of nursing degree (N.D.) or a doctorate of nursing science (D.N.S. and D.N.Sc.), or a research-based Ph.D. in nursing.

More than 30,000 **physician assistants** (P.A.) currently practice in the United States. Most of these are in office-based practices, including school health centers, but approximately 40 percent practice in areas where physicians are in short supply. Studies have shown that this relatively new class of midlevel practitioners may competently care for the majority of patients seeking primary care. All physician assistants must work under the supervision of a licensed physician, but most states do allow physician assistants to prescribe drugs.[6]

Nonallopathic "Complementary" Medicine

While people in other nations consider nonallopathic medicine the "traditional" form of treatment, in the United States we tend to think of **nonallopathic medicine** as "alternative medicine." A newer term for alternative medicine is complementary/alternative medicine (CAM). According to the National Center for Complementary and Alternative Medicine in the National Institutes of Health, nonallopathic medicine includes any medical intervention that hasn't had sufficient documentation in the United States to show that it is safe and effective; that is generally not taught in medical schools; and that generally is not reimbursed by third-party insurance. The intent of the office is to facilitate the evaluation of alternative medical treatments for the purpose of determining their effectiveness and to help integrate effective treatment into mainstream medical practice.

In a study recently published in the *Journal of the American Medical Association,* results revealed that in 1991 more than one-third of U.S. households had used complementary therapies during the previous year. When the same investigators repeated the survey in 1997, they found that 42 percent of the respondents reported using at least one of 16 different CAM therapies during the previous year—a 34 percent increase from the earlier survey. Complementary/alternative medicine use was more common among women than men and among those aged 35 to 49. The most popular therapies were herbal medicine, massage, megavitamins, self-help groups, folk remedies, energy healing, and homeopathy.[7] Although some complementary medical therapies are controversial and may be considered high risk or dangerous by some, many offer significant benefits at a relatively low cost. Interestingly, the users of unconventional therapies tend to have above-average incomes and high levels of education.

▶ *Chiropractic Treatment* **Chiropractic medicine** has been practiced for over 100 years. Allopathic medicine and chiropractic medicine were in direct competition over a century ago.[8] But today, many managed care organizations work closely with chiropractors. Many insurance companies will now pay for chiropractic treatment if a medical doctor recommends it. More than 20 million Americans now visit chiropractors each year.

Chiropractic medicine is based on the idea that a life-giving energy flows through the spine via the nervous system. If the spine is subluxated (partly misaligned or dislocated), that force is disrupted. Chiropractors use a variety of techniques to manipulate the spine back into proper alignment so the life-giving energy can flow unimpeded through the nervous system. It has been established that their treatment can be effective for back pain, neck pain, and headaches.

The average chiropractic training program requires four years of intensive courses in biochemistry, anatomy, physiology, diagnostics, pathology, nutrition, and so forth, combined with hands-on clinical training. Moreover, many chiropractors continue their training to obtain specialization certification, for instance, in women's health, gerontology, or pediatrics. Like allopathic physicians, chiropractors are licensed and regulated by the states in which they practice.

▶ *Acupuncture* Chinese medical treatments are growing in popularity and offer an important alternative or complement to traditional Western biomedical care. Although little is known about who in the United States uses Chinese medicine or why, one study indicates that users are typically middle-aged, well-educated, employed, and middle-income. Acupuncture, one of the more popular forms of Chinese medicine among Americans, is sought for a wide variety of health conditions, including musculoskeletal dysfunction, mood enhancement, and wellness promotion. Following acupuncture, most respondents report high satisfaction with the treatment, improved quality of life, improvement or cure in their condition, and reduced reliance on prescription drugs and surgery.[9]

Acupuncturists in the United States are state-licensed and each state has specific requirements regarding training programs. Most acupuncturists have either completed a two- to three-year postgraduate program to obtain a master of traditional Oriental medicine (M.T.O.M.) degree or attended a shorter certification program either here or in Asia. Acupuncturists may be licensed in multiple areas—for example, the M.T.O.M. is also trained in the use of herbs and moxabustion (the application of a heated herbal moxa stick). Some licensed M.D.s and chiropractors have trained in acupuncture and obtained certification to use this treatment.

Acupressure is similar to acupuncture, but does not use needles. Instead, the practitioner applies pressure to points critical to balancing yin and yang. Practitioners must have the same basic understanding of energy pathways as do acupuncturists. Acupressure should not be applied by an untrained person to pregnant women or to anyone having a chronic condition.

▶ *Herbalists and Homeopaths* Herbalists practice herbal medicine, which is based on the medicinal qualities of plants or herbs. Homeopaths also use herbal medicine (as well as minerals and chemicals), but at the root of their practice is the theory that the administration of extremely diluted doses of potent natural agents that produce disease symptoms in healthy persons will cure the disease in the sick.

Although plants have been used for medicinal purposes for centuries and form the basis of many modern "wonder drugs," herbal medicine is not to be taken lightly. Because something is natural does not necessarily mean that it is safe. Many plants are poisonous, and others can be toxic if used in high doses. One potential danger with this kind of therapy is that practitioners who mix their own tonics may not use standardized measures, and regulation of commercially prepared herbal therapies is rather weak in the United States because they are considered foods rather than drugs.

Many practitioners have received graduate-level training as herbalists in special programs such as herbal nutrition or traditional Oriental medicine. These practitioners have been trained in diagnosis; in mixing herbs, titrations, and dosages; and in the follow-up of patients. Unfortunately, there are some unskilled and untrained people who do not fully understand the potential chemical interactions of their preparations are treating patients. It is therefore imperative that you carefully investigate the chemical properties of herbs yourself before you ingest them.

▶ *Naturopathy* Naturopaths believe that illness results from violations of natural principles of life in modern societies. They view diseases as the body's effort to ward off impurities and harmful substances from the environment. Naturopathic treatment uses substances and forces found in nature: water, magnets, gravity, heat, crystals and minerals, herbs, and even the sun. Practitioners argue that returning to a natural, purified state will restore health.

Thorough training is provided at three naturopathic medical schools in the United States and Canada, and those who receive a naturopathic doctor (N.D.) degree from one of these schools have been through a four-year graduate program that emphasizes humanistically oriented family medicine. As with all practitioners, N.D.s should be checked out.

▶ *Other Complementary/Alternative Therapies* Many other therapies exist, including reflexology, iridology (light therapy), aromatherapy, and auramassage, to name a few. (See Appendix B: Complementary and Alternative Medicine.) Because

of an historical bias in the United States *against* nonallopathic medical treatments along with a general bias *toward* traditional Western medicine, little has been known about the effectiveness of CAM treatments. This is changing, however, as public interest in CAM therapies increases and a growing number of scientifically controlled studies examine alternate interventions for common clinical problems. Some of the studies have looked at the treatment of tension headache with chiropractic, deep massage, and acupuncture; the treatment of nicotine withdrawal with electroacupuncture; the treatment of Alzheimer's disease with extract of ginkgo biloba; the treatment of cardiovascular disease with garlic-extract therapy; the treatment of the common cold with two echinacea extracts; and the self-treatment of HIV with varying complementary medical strategies. Although many of the new strategies have been shown to be ineffective, some have been shown to be very useful, for example, the use of echinacea extract for the reduction of upper respiratory tract infections.[10] Someone considering CAM treatments should maintain a balance of informed consumerism and some skepticism, all the while remaining open to new possibilities.

········· **WHAT DO YOU THINK?**

Why do you think many people are skeptical about CAM therapies? What are the potential risks of choosing a complementary/alternative treatment? What types of controls are reasonable to regulate the quality and consistency of foreign-trained health-care providers? Why do you think more and more people are opting for complementary/alternative treatments?

HEALTH-CARE ORGANIZATIONS, PROGRAMS, AND FACILITIES

Today, managed care is the dominant health payer system in the United States. Because of this, many people are restricted in their choice of a health-care provider. Selective contracting between insurers or employers and health providers has limited the freedom of choice that some Americans previously enjoyed under a fee-for-service system. Two critical decisions you may have to make are (1) choosing an insurance carrier or type of plan and then (2) choosing from among the health-care providers who participate in that plan. This section lists the most common choices.

Types of Medical Practices

In the highly competitive market for patients, many health-care providers have found it essential to combine resources into a **group practice,** which can be single- or

---

Physician assistant A midlevel practitioner trained to handle most standard cases of care.

Nonallopathic medicine Medical alternatives to traditional, allopathic medicine.

Chiropractic medicine A form of medical treatment that emphasizes the manipulation of the spinal column.

Group practice A group of physicians who combine resources, sharing offices, equipment, and staff costs, to render care to patients.

multispecialty. Physicians share their offices, equipment, utility bills, and staff costs. Besides sharing costs, they may also share profits. Proponents of group practice maintain that it provides better coordination of care, reduces unnecessary duplication of equipment, and improves the quality of health care through peer review. Critics argue that group practice may limit competition and patients' access points to services.

Solo practitioners are medical providers who practice independently of other practitioners. It is hard for solo practitioners to survive in today's high-cost, high-technology health-care market. Additionally, solo practitioners often have little time away from their offices, and have to trade on-call hours with other doctors. For these reasons, there are far fewer solo practices today than in the past. Most solo practitioners are doctors who established their practices years ago, have a specialty that's in high demand, or are in a rural or underserved area.

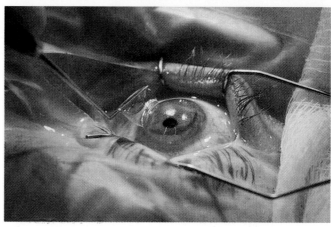

Modern technology has vastly improved the techniques available for treating many illnesses or disorders, but it has also played a major role in the escalating costs of medical care now facing consumers.

Integrated Health-Care Organizations

Both hospitals and clinics provide a range of health-care services, including emergency treatment, diagnostic tests, and inpatient and outpatient (ambulatory) care. Your selection of a hospital or clinic will depend on your particular needs, your income, your insurance coverage, and the availability of services in your community. As the number of hospitals has decreased in recent years due to an oversupply of hospital beds, a decreasing need for inpatient care, and an increase in competition, the number of hospital-based outpatient clinics has grown. These integrated health-care organizations run from groups of loosely affiliated health-service organizations and hospitals to HMOs that control their own very tightly joined hospitals, clinics, pharmacies, and even home health agencies.

There are several ways to classify hospitals: by profit status (nonprofit or for-profit), by ownership (private, city, county, state, federal), by specialty (children's, maternity, chronic care, psychiatric, general acute), by teaching status (teaching-affiliated or not), by size, and by whether they are part of a chain of hospitals. **Nonprofit (voluntary) hospitals** have traditionally been run by religious or other humanitarian groups. Earnings have generally been reinvested in the hospital for purposes of improving health care. These hospitals have often cared for patients whether they could pay or not.

The number of **for-profit (proprietary) hospitals** has been multiplying over the past two decades. Today they constitute over 20 percent of nongovernmental acute-care hospitals. For-profit hospitals, which do not receive tax breaks, are not compelled to operate as a charity and typically provide fewer free services to the community than do nonprofit hospitals. Historically, some for-profit hospitals quickly transferred indigent (poor) or uninsured patients to public hospitals (those that are not heavily supported by taxes) or to nonprofit hospitals.[11] This practice, known as *patient dumping,* was prohibited by federal law in 1986. Today, all hospital emergency rooms are required to perform a screening medical exam on all patients, regardless of their ability to pay. Patients must be determined to be "medically stable" before they can be transferred to another facility or discharged from the emergency room.

More treatments or services, including surgery, are being delivered on an **outpatient (ambulatory) care** basis (care which does not involve an overnight stay) by hospitals, traditional clinics, student health clinics, and nontraditional clinical centers. One type of ambulatory facility that is becoming common is the *surgicenter*—a place where minor, low-risk procedures such as vasectomies, tubal ligations, tissue biopsies, cosmetic surgery, abortions, and minor eye operations are performed. In 1982, nearly 85 percent of all surgeries in the United States involved an overnight hospital stay; by 2000, less than 30 percent of surgeries will have done so.

To reduce the distance patients have to travel, many hospitals are locating satellite clinics in cities' outlying areas, sometimes in large shopping centers. A few hospitals have designated their satellites as freestanding emergency centers, or surgicenters, that function like hospital emergency rooms for uncomplicated immediate-care cases but have lower operating costs. Some consumers have begun to refer to these as "doc-in-the-box" centers.

Many hospitals and group practices now have freestanding imaging and diagnostic laboratory centers affiliated with them through either direct ownership or other profit-sharing arrangements. Significant debate surrounds this practice because research has found that when doctors own the diagnostic and laboratory services to which they refer patients, they tend to order an excessive number of tests. Today, these practices are prohibited by anti-kickback legislation.

The majority of health clinics were once located within hospitals. Today they are more likely to be independent facilities run by medical practitioners. Other health clinics are run by county health departments; these offer low-cost diagnosis and treatment for financially needy patients. Additionally, some 1,500 college campuses have student health centers that, along with county, city, or community clinics, supply low-cost family planning, sexually transmitted disease, gynecological, and vaccination services.

Consumers who are considering using a hospital or clinic should scrutinize the facility's accreditation. Accredited hospitals have met rigorous standards set by the Joint Commission on the Accreditation of Healthcare Organizations (JCAHO). If you use an institution having this form of accreditation, you have a high likelihood of obtaining quality care.

With the growth of managed care organizations, there are new and legitimate concerns about the quality of care under this type of payment system. These concerns compelled consumer groups and public health organizations to require managed care insurers to compile quality care "report cards," known as HEDIS Reports (Health Employer Data Information Set), so that health outcomes could be compared across different plans. Some of the quality measures include preventive services (childhood immunizations, Pap smears, mammograms), disease indicators (eye exams and glucose control tests for diabetics), and screening exams (routine physical exams, including gynecological exams). These reports are available from most managed care health plans on request.

Additional information regarding prior provider malpractice insurance or sanctions may be available to the consumer from state licensure boards and the National Practitioner Data Bank, on request. It is the responsibility of every health-care consumer to report concerns about their health-care providers to local or state medical societies or licensing agencies for investigation. If consumers have specific concerns about billing-related fraud or abuse, these concerns may be reported directly to the Health Care Finance Administration (HCFA).

Solo practitioner   Physician who renders care to patients independently of other practitioners.

Nonprofit (voluntary) hospitals   Hospitals run by religious or other humanitarian groups that reinvest their earnings in the hospital to improve health care.

For-profit (proprietary) hospitals   Hospitals that provide a return on earnings to the investors who own them.

Outpatient (ambulatory) care   Treatment that does not involve an overnight stay in a hospital.

ISSUES FACING TODAY'S HEALTH-CARE SYSTEM

Many Americans believe that our health-care system needs fundamental reform. What are the problems that have brought us to this point? Cost, access, malpractice, restriction of provider and treatment modality choice, unnecessary procedures, complicated and cumbersome insurance rules, and dramatic ranges in quality are the issues involved in typical criticisms. One of the most frequently voiced criticisms concerns lack of access to adequate health insurance, as many Americans have had increasing difficulty obtaining comprehensive coverage from their employers. Until recently, insurance benefits were often lost when employees changed jobs, causing many to remain in undesirable positions in order to avoid losing health benefits. This phenomena, known as *job lock,* led the federal government to pass legislation mandating the "portablity" of health insurance benefits from one job to the next, thereby guaranteeing coverage during the transition.

Cost

Both per capita and as a percent of gross domestic product (GDP), we spend more on health care than does any other nation, yet, unlike the rest of the industrialized world, we do not provide access for our entire population. In 1996, we spent over $1 trillion, or nearly 15 percent of our GDP on health care. This is up from 5 percent of GDP in 1960. There are a variety of theories as to why health care costs continue to spiral upward. Most explanations are multifactorial and include at least the following: excess administrative costs; duplication of services; an aging population; growth, use, and demand for new diagnostic and treatment technologies; an emphasis on crisis-oriented care instead of preventive care; inappropriate utilization of services by consumers; and related factors.

Our system has more than 2,000 health insurance companies, each with different coverage benefit structures and different administrative requirements. This lack of uniformity prevents our system from achieving the *economies of scale* (bulk purchasing at a reduced cost) and elimination of administrative waste realized in countries where there is a single-payer health-care delivery system. The Health Insurance Association of America (HIAA) has stated that commercial insurance companies commonly experience administrative costs greater than 10 percent of the total health-care insurance premium, whereas the administrative cost of the government's Medicare program experiences less than 4 percent. The expenses related to administrative waste in the private sector contributes to the overall high cost of health care and is forcing companies to require employees to share more of the costs, to cut back on benefits, and to drop some benefits altogether. These costs are largely passed on to consumers in the form of higher prices for goods and services.

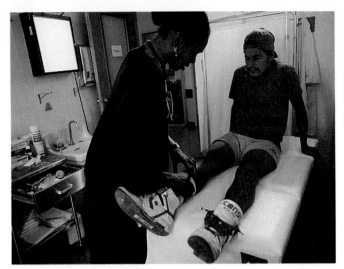

Students frequently turn to health centers, clinics, and hospital emergency rooms for treatment when needed, but those who rely solely on these settings miss out on the benefits of continuity of care by a primary care physician.

The declining availability of health insurance coverage has led to a rise in the number of Americans who are uninsured or underinsured. These people are unable to access preventive care and seek care only in the event of an emergency or crisis. Since the cost of emergency care is extraordinarily high, these individuals often are unable to pay, and the cost is absorbed by those who *can* pay—the insured or taxpayers. This is a process known as *cost-shifting*.

Access

Your access to health care is determined by numerous factors. Under managed care health plans, access is determined on the basis of the participating provider network, the health plan benefits, and the administrative rules. Often this means that consumers do not have the freedom to choose specialists, facilities, or treatment options beyond those specifically contracted with the health plan and recommended by their primary care provider (gatekeeper). In the United States, consumer demand has led to an expansion of benefits to include CAM therapies such as chiropractic and acupuncture. Most CAM therapies are generally not accessible to most people, even to a limited degree, through the available health plans.

Quality and Malpractice

The U.S. health-care system employs several mechanisms for assuring quality services overall: education, licensure, certification/registration, accreditation, peer review, and, as a last resort, the legal system of malpractice litigation. Some of these mechanisms are mandatory before a professional or organization may provide care, while others are purely voluntary. (Consumers should note that licensure, although state

mandated for some practitioners and facilities, is only a minimum guarantee of quality.) Insurance companies and government payers may also require a higher level of quality by linking payment to whether a practitioner is board certified or a facility is accredited by the appropriate agency. In addition, most insurance plans now require prior authorization and/or second opinions as means not only to reduce costs but also to improve quality of care.

Many people believe that malpractice is a leading cause of our health care crisis. Yet the U.S. Department of Health and Human Services estimates that the total cost of malpractice is less than 1 percent of total health outlays. However, these figures do not account for the previously described practice of "defensive medicine." Defensive medicine not only costs money and places patients at additional risk, it has also changed the standards of care in that people have come to expect these extra, but unnecessary, tests and procedures.

THIRD-PARTY PAYERS

The fundamental principal of insurance underwriting is that the cost of health care can be predicted for large populations. This is the principal by which health-care premiums (payments) are determined. Policyholders pay premiums into a pool, which fills as reserves until needed. When you are sick or injured, the insurance company pays out of the pool, regardless of your total amount of contribution. Depending on circumstances, you may never pay for what your medical care costs or you may pay much more for insurance than your medical bills ever total. The idea is that you pay in affordable premiums so that you never have to face catastrophic bills.

Unfortunately, almost 40 million Americans are uninsured at any given point in time—that is, they have no private health insurance and are not eligible for Medicare, Medicaid, or any other health program that would cover the cost of their care. The number of the uninsured has been growing since the late 1970s. Lack of health insurance has been associated with delayed health care and increased mortality. Under-insurance (i.e., the inability to pay out-of-pocket expenses despite having insurance) also may result in adverse health consequences. Findings from the CDC's latest Behavior Risk Factor Surveillance System (BRFSS) indicate that a large proportion of all adults are either uninsured or underinsured. People lacking any type of health insurance make up nearly 17 percent of the nonelderly population, or 15 percent of the total population. Another 20 to 40 million Americans are estimated to be *underinsured* (at risk for spending more than 10 percent of their income on medical care because their insurance is inadequate).[12]

Contrary to the common belief that the uninsured are unemployed, 75 percent of the uninsured are either workers or the dependents of workers. One-quarter of all the uninsured are children under the age of 16. College students are one of the largest groups of the uninsured not in the labor force.

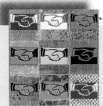
Establishing Goals for Erasing Racial and Ethnic Disparities in Health by 2010

At the beginning of this text, you read about *Healthy People 2000* and *2010* objectives, which are the goals for the nation's health. In a February 21, 1998, radio speech, President Clinton proposed another goal for the year 2010: to eliminate ethnic and racial disparities in health in the United States. As a first course of action, he assembled a group with the resources and expertise within the federal government, private sector, local communities, and higher education to push forward a course of action.

In September 1998, a conference consisting of representatives from these groups, was held to launch a plan. Six key areas, determined by the Department of Health and Human Services (HHS), were established, in which participants were to concentrate their efforts. Racial and ethnic disparities were to be eliminated in cancer screening and management, cardiovascular disease, child and adult immunizations, diabetes, HIV infections/AIDs, and infant mortality.

The harsh reality is that disparities cross racial, ethnic, and socioeconomic conditions. Consider that an African American baby born today is 2.5 times more likely to die than a White baby during the first year of life; or that Native American babies are 1.5 times more likely to die; or that Hispanic babies are two times more likely to die than White babies. Additionally, Native Americans have a rate of diabetes that is three to five times higher than in other ethnic groups. Meanwhile, Asian American men are three to five times more likely than men in other groups to be afflicted with liver cancer, while Vietnamese American women are five times more likely than women of other ethnicities to suffer from cervical cancer. These and other such disparities are a small sample of those that must be eliminated.

Among the key recommendations that came out of this conference were:

- Making the elimination of racial and ethnic disparities a national priority, with leaders at all levels of government and community working to help each other understand that all people deserve to be healthy and have access to adequate health care
- Recognizing the diversity of America's racial and ethnic communities and their diverse needs
- Helping to get the word out by developing messages that everyone can rally behind, by educating the general public, public officials, and community leaders; and by partnering with the media to disseminate prevention messages and positive messages to the community
- Driving changes in communities themselves by building infrastructures that empower these communities to meet their own needs
- Improving the uses of data to document problems and measure progress in finding solutions
- Developing and articulating a plan of action specific enough to ensure that those affected believe in and are committed to the implementation and success of the plan

As we enter the next century, we can pull out our score cards to see whether the *Healthy People 2000* objectives were achieved. Likewise, the success of reaching these goals of equality for all, at this point, is still to be realized. But, as U.S. Surgeon General, Dr. David Satcher, stated, quoting one of his college professors, Dr. Bejamin E. Mays, "Touch the lives of others, then be sure that you leave them better than you found them." It's a place to start.

Source: "Call to Action: Eliminating Racial and Ethnic Disparities in Health," Conference Proceedings, Prepared for the U.S. Department of Health and Human Services and Grantmaking in Health by Health Systems Research, Inc., 1998, http://raceandhealth.hhs.gov/sidebars/report.htm

---

This presents a difficult dilemma for both universities and students when they must seek care because most university insurance plans are designed as short-term, noncatastrophic plans having low upper limits of benefits. As a full-time student, you should consider purchasing a higher level catastrophic plan to protect yourself in the event of a rare, but very costly, illness or accident.

People without health-care coverage are less likely than other Americans to have their children immunized, to seek early prenatal care, to obtain annual blood pressure checks, and to seek care for serious symptoms of illness. Many experts believe that this ultimately leads to higher system costs because the conditions of these people deteriorate to a more debilitating and costly stage before they are forced to seek help.

Early Private Health Insurance

Our current health system began in the last century and its growth accelerated in the post-World War II era to its current massive, complex web. Hospitals became the engines of medicine during the middle of this century. Doctors became the drivers or conductors of this rapidly moving system. The system was fueled by a variety of funding sources but, chiefly, first by the growth of tax-exempt nonprofit private insurance companies established in the 1940s and later by the growth of for-profit insurance companies.

Private insurance companies have increasingly employed several mechanisms to control consumers' use of insurance and to limit the companies' potential losses. These mecha-

ACCESSING YOUR HEALTH ON THE INTERNET

Check out the following Internet sites related to consumer health.

1. *National Committee for Quality Assurance.* The NCQA assesses and reports on the quality of managed care plans, including health maintenance organizations (HMOs).

   http://www.ncqa.org/

2. *Agency for Health Care Policy and Research.* Serves as a gateway to consumer health information, providing links to sites that can assist with answering health-care concerns, as well as providing general information on questions to ask, what to look for, and what you should know when making critical decisions about personal care.

   http://www.ahcpr.gov/consumer/

nisms include cost-sharing (in the form of deductibles, copayments, and coinsurance), exclusions, "preexisting condition" clauses, waiting periods, and upper limits on payments. *Deductibles* are front-end payments (commonly $250 to $1,000) that you must make to your provider before your insurance company will start paying for any services you use. *Copayments* are set amounts that you pay per service received regardless of the cost of the services (e.g., $5 per doctor visit or $10 per prescription). *Coinsurance* is the percentage of the bill that you must pay throughout the course of treatment (e.g., 20 percent of whatever the total is). *Preexisting condition clauses* limit the insurance company's liability for medical conditions that a consumer had before obtaining insurance coverage (i.e., the insurance company will cover everything except "normal pregnancy" for a woman who takes out coverage when she is pregnant; however, pregnancy complications and infant care are covered). Because many insurance companies use a combination of these mechanisms, keeping track of the portion of costs you are responsible for can become very difficult.

Group plans of large employers (government agencies, school districts, or corporations, for example) generally do not have preexisting condition clauses in their plans. But smaller group plans (a group may be as small as two) often do. Some plans will never cover services for preexisting conditions, while others specify a waiting period (such as six months) before they will provide coverage. All insurers set some limits on the types of services they will cover (e.g., most exclude cosmetic surgery, private rooms, and experimental procedures). Some insurance plans may also include an upper or lifetime limit, after which your coverage will end. Although

$250,000 many seem like an enormous sum, medical bills for a sick child or chronic disease can easily run this high within a few years.

Medicare and Medicaid (Social Insurance versus Welfare)

After years of debate about whether we should have a national health program like those of most other industrialized countries, the U.S. government directed the system toward a less-than-universal mixed private and public approach in the 1960s. Most Americans obtained their health insurance through their employers. But this meant that two groups—the nonworking poor and the aged—were left out. To take care of these groups, in 1965 Medicare and Medicaid were established by amendments to the 1935 Social Security Act. Although enacted simultaneously, these programs were vastly different. **Medicare,** basically a federal social insurance covering 99 percent of the elderly over 65 years of age, all totally and permanently disabled people (after a waiting period), and all people with end-stage renal failure, is a universal program that covers a broad range of services except long-term care and pharmaceuticals. It currently covers 36 million people. Medicare is widely accepted by physicians and hospitals and has relatively low administrative costs.

On the other hand, **Medicaid,** covering approximately 35 million people, is a federal-state matching-funds welfare program for the categorically eligible poor (blind, disabled, aged, or receiving Aid to Families with Dependent Children). Because each state determines income eligibility levels and payments to providers, there are vast differences in the way Medicaid operates from state to state.

In order to control hospital costs, beginning in 1983 the federal government set up a prospective payment system based on **diagnosis related groups (DRGs)** for Medicare. Using a complicated formula, nearly 500 groupings of diagnoses were created to establish in advance how much a hospital would be reimbursed for a particular patient. If a hospital can treat the patient for less than that amount, it can keep the difference. However, if a patient's care costs more than the set amount, the hospital must absorb the difference (with a few exceptions that must be reviewed by a panel). This system gives hospitals the incentive to discharge patients quickly after doing as little as possible for them, to provide more ambulatory care, and to admit only patients with favorable (profitable) DRGs. Many private health insurance companies have followed the federal government in adopting this type of reimbursement. In 1998, the federal HCFA expanded the prospective payment system to include payment for outpatient surgery and skilled nursing care. Phasing in of these new payment systems was to continue through the year 2000.

In its continued efforts to control rising costs, HCFA has encouraged the growth of prepaid HMO senior plans for Medicare-eligible persons. Under this system, commercial managed care insurance plans receive a fixed per-capita premium from HCFA and then offer more preventive services with lower out-of-pocket copayments. These managed care plans encourage providers and patients to utilize health-care resources under administrative rules similar to commercial HMO plans. Similarly, states have encouraged the growth of managed Medicaid programs.

Managed Care

Managed care describes a health-care delivery system comprised of the following elements:

1. A budget based on an estimate of the annual cost of delivering health care for a given population
2. A network of physicians, hospitals, and other providers and facilities linked contractually to deliver comprehensive health benefits within that predetermined budget, sharing economic risk for any budget deficit or surplus
3. An established set of administrative rules requiring patients to follow the advice of the participating health-care providers in order to have their health-care paid for under the terms of the health plan

Many such plans pay their contracted health-care providers through **capitation,** that is, prepayment of a fixed monthly amount for each patient without regard of the type or number of health services provided. Some plans pay health-care providers' salaries and some are still fee-for-service plans. Much as with other insurance plans, enrollees are members of a risk pool, and it is expected that some persons will use no services, some will use a modest amount of services, and others will have high-cost utilization over a given year. Doctors have the incentive to keep their patient pool healthy and avoid the catastrophic ailments that are preventable; usually such incentives come back in terms of increased salaries, bonuses, and other benefits.

Managed care plans have grown steadily over the past decade with a proportionate declining of enrollment in traditional indemnity insurance plans. The reason for this shift is that indemnity insurance, which pays providers and hospitals on a fee-for-service basis with no built-in incentives to control health-care costs, has become unaffordable for most Americans.

Today, managed care plans are sweeping the nation, with over 60 million Americans enrolled in one type of plan, the Health Maintenance Organization, and another 90 million in other types of managed care. Four million beneficiaries are in Medicare HMOs, with enrollment growing by about 80,000 people a month.[13] A breakdown of each type of managed care plan follows.

▌ *Health Maintenance Organizations (HMOs)*   HMOs provide a wide range of covered health benefits (such as check-ups, surgery, doctor visits, lab tests) for a fixed amount prepaid by you, the employer, Medicaid, or Medicare.[14] Usually, HMO premiums are the least expensive (saving between 10 and 40 percent more than other plans), but HMOs are the most restrictive type of managed care. These premiums are 8 to 10 percent lower than traditional plans, there are low or no deductibles or coinsurance payments, and copayments are $5 to $10 per office visit. HMOs contract with providers to supply health services for enrollees through various systems,[15] such as:

- *The Staff Model:* You receive care from salaried staff doctors at the HMOs' only facility.
- *The Group Network Model:* The HMO contracts with one or several groups of doctors who provide care for a fixed amount per plan member. Groups often practice in one facility.
- *The Independent Practice Association (IPA):* Doctors in private practice form an association that contracts with HMOs. The physicians generally work in their own offices.

The downside of these plans is that often you are limited to using the plan's doctors and hospitals and must get approval from your "gatekeeper" or primary care physician for treatment and referrals. Although more and more people are opting for HMOs, some people continue to be skeptical. Concerns leveled against HMOs include issues such as:

- Are patients denied costly diagnostic tests because such tests cut into bottom-line profits? Are some tests given too late because of concerns over costs?
- Are HMOs really focused on prevention or intervention? Evidence exists that the fee structure of many HMOs actually discourages basic preventive services, such as immunizations.
- Do policies and profit-motivated concerns interfere with the doctors' roles as advocates for their patients?
- Are the obstacles imposed by HMOs too daunting for patients in need of urgent care?
- Do HMO cost-saving policies force patients out of hospitals and treatment centers too early?

▌ *Point of Service (POS)*   This option often provides a more acceptable form of managed care for those used to the traditional indemnity plan of insurance, which probably explains the fact that it is among the fastest growing of the managed care

---

Medicare   Federal health insurance program for the elderly and the permanently disabled.

Medicaid   Federal-state health insurance program for the poor.

Diagnosis related groups (DRGs)   Diagnostic categories established by the federal government to determine in advance how much hospitals will be reimbursed for the care of a particular Medicare patient.

Managed care   Cost-control procedures used by health insurers to coordinate treatment.

Capitation   Prepayment of a fixed monthly amount without regard to the type or number of services provided.

CONSUMER HEALTH

Choosing the Right HMO

Oh, for the simple days, when you would go to the doctor of your choice and either you or the doctor would submit a bill to your insurance company, which would pay most of the charges without question. Today, finding a good doctor and then sifting through the rules and regulations to determine if you can even go to him or her is a seemingly daunting task. Indemnity plans, managed care plans, preferred provider groups, HMOs, and a host of "medic-speak" terms leave even the strongest of heart with higher blood pressure. What's a person to do?

First and foremost, remember that not all managed care groups are created equal. They vary widely in cost, quality, and services and range from being downright unacceptable to excellent. Before even thinking about which plan is right for you, consider your personal priorities. Is total choice in which doctor or facility you go to a high priority? Is location an issue? What about out-of-pocket expenses? Coverage of preexisting conditions? Alternative care? Mental health services? Prescriptions? At the very least, begin by asking questions. Talk with

your state Health Insurance Counseling and Assistance Program. Ask to see the plan's brochures and find out the following information:

- What services are covered? Be sure that the ones you need or think you'll need are there.
- Is the plan accredited? Find out if the plan has been reviewed and, if so, whether it was approved by the National Committee on Quality Assurance or the Joint Commission on the Accreditation of Healthcare Organizations.
- Does the plan survey patient satisfaction, and what are the results? Are they verifiable by an outside source?
- How many members decided to leave the HMO in the past year? Did they return to fee-for-service plans or go to another HMO?
- Who are the plan's doctors? Are they board-certified, and how often are they reviewed?
- How many doctors leave the plan each year? (The current average is about 4 percent.)
- How much flexibility is there in choosing a doctor? Can you switch if you don't like yours? Can you go back to your original one if you switch or go elsewhere and don't like the alternatives?
- How are doctors paid? Do they receive bonuses if they make fewer referrals to specialists? Are they

paid on a salary or per-person basis?
- What is the level of preventive care? Does the plan cover flu shots, Pap smears, mammograms, and screening for various cancers or cholesterol levels?
- What prescription drugs are covered?
- How does the plan define *medical emergency?* Under what conditions can it refuse to pay?
- How are chronic ailments handled? What if your HMO does not have the type of specialist you need, or you are not comfortable with their skill levels?
- Which hospitals are in the plan? What conditions are considered serious enough to warrant hospitalization?
- Will you be covered while you are traveling outside of your area?
- How long does it take to get an appointment?
- How flexible is the plan overall in doctor choices? If it is not, a preferred provider group or point-of-service plan might be more acceptable. Or, the traditional indemnity or fee-for-service plans still exist and offer a chance to maintain the health-care benefits of which you may have grown fond.

Source: Adapted from "A Variety of Plans and How to Choose One," *AARP Special Bulletin on Managed Care,* vol. 37, no. 10 (November 1996): 11. Reprinted with the permission of the American Association of Retired Persons.

plans. Under POS, patients can go to providers outside of their HMO for care but must pay for the extra cost. Usually this is a reasonable alternative for middle class or wealthy Americans who are willing to pay the extra cost for choices in care.[16]

▶ *Preferred Provider Organization (PPO)* PPOs are networks of independent doctors and hospitals that contract to provide care at discounted rates. Although they offer greater choices in doctors than HMOs, they are less likely to coordinate your care. In addition, while members have a choice of seeing doctors who are not on the preferred list, this choice may come at considerable cost (such as having to pay 30 percent of the

charges out of pocket, rather than 10 to 20 percent for PPO doctors and services.)[17]

WHAT DO YOU THINK?

Why is it important that private insurance cover preventive or lower-level care as well as hospitalization and high-technology interventions? What kinds of incentives cause you to seek early care rather than to delay care?

Taking Charge ....
Managing Your Health-Care Needs

Throughout this text, we have emphasized behaviors important to keeping you healthy. But now you need to turn your attention to your potential behavior when you need medical attention. Most people wait until a problem arises to seek medical care and take the first available physician or medical facility. But by looking ahead to future needs, you can take charge of your choices and make positive moves toward getting better health care.

Many health-care decisions are dictated by physicians, insurance companies, and government agencies. But many decisions still rest with you. Are you a good health consumer? Start by learning about your own insurance protection. What coverage do you currently have? If none, how would you pay for a medical emergency (i.e., an accident)? What coverage is available to you as a student? Once you establish your protection, find out what you have control over. Do you have your choice of physicians or hospitals? How can you best make your choices? Consider some of the following questions.

CHECKLIST FOR CHANGE

MAKING PERSONAL CHOICES

✓ Do you feel comfortable discussing your problems with your health-care provider?

✓ Are you confident that your doctor knows what he or she is talking about?

✓ Is the doctor willing to talk about issues such as credentials, hospital affiliations, qualifications of referrals for special problems, and fees?

✓ Are you able to understand answers to your questions? Does the doctor seem interested in whether you understand? Is he or she willing to answer questions?

✓ Does the physician tell you why one test is being given rather than another? About risks of the test? About preparation for the tests? About what to expect concerning certain results?

✓ Is the physician willing to refer you to a nongroup specialist in a location of your choice?

✓ Does the doctor support your obtaining a second opinion, or does he or she seem irritated with such a request?

✓ If you became seriously ill and had to see a lot of this doctor, would you feel comfortable with him or her, or would you rather have someone else?

MAKING COMMUNITY CHOICES

✓ How long has your doctor been in your community?

✓ How many hospitals are within a 30-minute drive from your home? Are any of them teaching hospitals?

✓ What percentage of people in your community don't have health insurance?

✓ What services are available in your community to help people who are under- or uninsured?

✓ What are the policies of local hospitals concerning the treatment of uninsured individuals who need care?

✓ Have you written your congressional leaders concerning your views about health-care legislation?

SUMMARY

• Advertisers of health-care products and services use sophisticated tactics to attract your attention and get your business. Advertising claims sometimes appear to be supported by spontaneous remission (symptoms disappearing without any apparent cause) or the placebo effect (symptoms disappearing because you think they should).

• Self-care and individual responsibility are key factors involved in reducing rising health-care costs and improving health status. But you need to seek health-care treatment in situations that are unfamiliar to you or that are emergencies. You should assess health professionals using their qualifications, their record of treating your specific problem, and their ability to work with you.

• In theory, allopathic ("traditional") medicine is based on scientifically validated methods and procedures. Medical doctors, specialists of various kinds, nurses, physician assistants, and other health professionals practice allopathic medicine. Many nonallopathic (complementary/alternative medicine, or CAMs) forms of health service—including chiropractic treatment, acupuncture, herbalists and homeopaths, and naturopathy—are used by approximately half of the people in the United States. Some managed care plans are including CAM therapies as covered benefits to plan members.

- Health-care providers may provide services as solo practitioners or in group practices (in which overhead is shared). Hospitals and clinics are classified by profit status, ownership, specialty, and teaching status.

- Problems experienced in the U.S. health-care system concern cost, access, choice of treatment modality, quality and malpractice, and fraud and abuse.

- Health insurance is based on the concept of spreading risk. Insurance is provided by private insurance companies (who charge premiums) and the government Medicare and Medicaid programs (funded by taxes). Managed care (in the form of HMOs, PPOs, etc.) attempts to keep costs lower by streamlining administrative procedures and stressing preventive care (among other initiatives).

DISCUSSION QUESTIONS

1. What types of claims do marketers use to get us to try their health-related products? Why are consumers susceptible to such ploys? What could be done to increase the accuracy/truth of health product messaging?

2. List some conditions (resulting from illness or accident) for which you don't need to seek medical help. When would you consider each condition to be bad enough to require medical attention? How do you decide to whom and where to go for treatment?

3. What are the differences in education between M.D.s and chiropractors? Under what circumstances would you seek treatment from a complementary/alternative medical practitioner? Which types of nonallopathic medicine seem valid to you? Which seem like they should undergo more scientific research?

4. What are the pros and cons of group practices? Of nonprofit and for-profit hospitals? If you had health insurance, where do you believe you would get the best care? On what do you base your choice?

5. What are the inherent benefits and risks of managed care organizations?

6. Discuss the problems of the U.S. health-care system. If you were president, what would you propose as a solution? Which groups might oppose your plan? Which groups might support it?

7. Explain the differences between traditional indemnity insurance and managed health care. Which would you feel more comfortable with? Should insurance companies dictate rates for various medical tests and procedures in an attempt to keep prices down?

APPLICATION EXERCISE

Reread the *What Do You Think?* scenario at the beginning of the chapter and answer the following questions.

1. What are the advantages and disadvantages of being able to choose your modality of health care (CAM vs. traditional Western)?

2. What, if any, alternatives are available to Polly? What would you do?

Appendix A

Injury Prevention and Emergency Care

Unintentional injuries are one of the major public health problems facing the United States today. On an average day, more than a million people will suffer a nonfatal injury; 70,000 will die as a result of unintentional injuries. Unintentional injuries are the leading cause of death for Americans under the age of 44. In the United States, unintentional injuries are the fourth leading cause of death, after heart disease, cancer, and stroke.

Vehicle Safety

The risk of dying in an auto crash is related to age. Young drivers (16–24) have the highest death rate, owing to their inexperience and immaturity. Each year 41,000 Americans die in automobile crashes and another 1.6 million are disabled, 140,000 permanently. Most of these car crashes were avoidable. The best line of prevention against car crashes is to practice risk management driving, accident-avoidance techniques, and to be aware of safety technology when purchasing your car.

▶ **Risk Management Driving** Practicing risk driving management techniques when you drive helps reduce your chances of being involved in a collision. Techniques include:

- **Surround your car with a bubble space.** The rear bumper of the car ahead of you should be three seconds away. To measure your safety bubble, choose a roadside landmark such as a signpost or light pole as a reference point. When the car in front of you passes this point, count "one-one-thousand, two-one-thousand." Make sure you are not passing the reference point before you've finished saying "three-one-thousand."
- **Scan the road ahead of you and to both sides.**
- **Drive with your low beam headlights on.** Being seen is an important safety factor. Driving with your low beam

headlights on *day or night* makes you more visible to other drivers.

In addition:

- Anticipate other drivers' actions.
- Drive refreshed.
- Drive sober.
- Obey all traffic laws.
- Use safety belts.

▶ **Accident-Avoidance Techniques** Sometimes when driving you need to react instantly to a situation. To avoid a more severe accident you may need to steer into another less severe collision. The point of accident evasion is to save lives. Here are AAA's rules for accident avoidance:

1. Generally veer to the right.
2. Steer, don't skid, off the road.
3. If you have to hit a vehicle, hit one moving in the same direction as your own.
4. If you have to hit a stationary object, try to hit a soft one (bushes, small trees, etc.) rather than a hard one (boulders, brick walls, giant oaks).
5. If you have to hit a hard object, hit it with a glancing blow.
6. Avoid hitting pedestrians, motorcyclists, and bicyclists at all costs.
7. Try never to be involved in a head-on collision.

▶ **Safety Technology** The last line of defense against a collision is the car itself. How a car is equipped can mean the difference between life and death. When purchasing a car, look for the following features:

- Does the car have airbags? Remember airbags do not eliminate the need for everyone to wear safety belts. Airbags inflate only in the case of frontal crashes.
- Does the car have antilock brakes? Antilock brakes help pump the brakes and prevent them from locking up and, hence, the car from skidding.

- Does the car have impact-absorbing crumple zones?
- Are there strengthened passenger compartment side walls?
- Is there a strong roof support? (The center door post on four-door models gives you an extra roof pillar.)

(Source: Insurance Institute for Highway Safety)

What should I do if my car breaks down?

- Try to get off the road as far as possible.
- Turn on your car's emergency flashers and raise the hood. Set out flares or reflective triangles.
- Stay in the car until a law enforcement officer arrives. If others stop to help, ask them to contact the police, sheriff's office, or the State Patrol.
- If you must leave your car, leave a note with the car explaining the problem (as best you can), the time and date, your name, the direction in which you are walking, and what you are wearing. This information will help them look for you if necessary.
- Remove all valuables from the car if you must leave it.

Pedestrian Safety

Each year approximately 13 percent of all motor vehicle deaths involve pedestrians, and another 82,000 pedestrians are injured each year. The highest death rates involving pedestrians occur in the very young and elderly population. Pedestrian injuries occur most frequently after dark, in urban settings primarily in intersections where pedestrians may walk or dart into traffic. It is not uncommon for alcohol to play a role in the death or injury of a pedestrian. How can you protect yourself from being injured or becoming a fatality? AAA has the following suggestions for joggers and walkers:

- Carry or wear reflective material at night to help drivers see you.
- Cross only at crosswalks. Keep to the right in crosswalks.
- Before crossing, look both ways. Be sure the way is clear before you cross.
- Cross only on the proper signal.
- Watch for turning cars.
- Never go into the roadway from between parked cars.
- Where there is no sidewalk, and it is necessary to walk in a roadway, walk on the left side facing traffic.
- Don't wear headphones for a radio or tape player. These may interfere with your ability to hear sounds of motor vehicles.

Cycling Safety

Currently over 63 million Americans of all ages ride bicycles for transportation, recreation, and fitness. The Consumer Product Safety Commission reports about 800 deaths per year from cycling accidents. The biggest risk factors are failure to wear a helmet, being male, and riding after dark. Children age

10 to 14 also are at higher risk for injury. Motorists can't be blamed for many of these fatalities as approximately 87% of the collisions were due to cyclists' errors, usually failure to yield at intersections. Alcohol also plays a significant role in bicycle deaths and injuries. The following are suggestions cyclists should consider following to reduce their risk of injury or death.

- Wear a helmet. It should be ANSI or Snell approved. This can reduce head injuries by 85%.
- Don't drink and ride.
- Respect traffic.
- Wear light reflective clothing that is easily seen at night and during the day.
- Avoid riding after dark.
- Ride with the flow of traffic.
- Know and use proper hand signals.
- Maintain the operating condition of the bike.
- Use bike paths whenever possible.
- Stop at stop signs and traffic lights.

Water Safety

Drowning is the third most common cause of accidental death in the United States, according to the National Safety Council. About 85% of drowning victims are teenage males. Many drowned swimmers are strong swimmers. Alcohol plays a significant role in many drowning cases. Most drownings occur in unorganized or supervised facilities, such as ponds, or pools with no lifeguards present. Swimmers should take the following precautions:

- Don't drink alcohol before or while swimming.
- Don't enter the water unless you can swim at least fifty feet unassisted.
- Know your limitations; get out of the water as soon as you start to feel even slightly fatigued.
- Never swim alone, even if you are a skilled swimmer. You never know what might happen.
- Never leave a child unattended, even in extremely shallow water or wading pools.
- Before entering the water, check the depth. Most neck and back injuries result from diving into water that is too shallow.
- Never swim in muddy or dirty water that obstructs your view of the bottom.
- Never swim in a river with currents too swift for easy, relaxed swimming.

Alcohol Poisoning

Alcohol overdose is considered a medical emergency when one or both of the following occur: an irregular heartbeat or the person is in a coma. The two immediate causes of death in such cases are cardiac arrhythmia and respiratory depression. If a person is seriously uncoordinated and has possibly also taken a depressant, the risk of respiratory failure is serious enough that a physician should be contacted. When dealing with someone who is drunk,

1. Stay calm. Assess the situation.
2. Keep the person still and comfortable.
3. Stay with the person if she/he is vomiting. When lying him/her down, turn their head to the side to prevent the head from falling back. This helps to keep the person from choking on the vomit.
4. Monitor the person's breathing.
5. Keep your distance. Before approaching or touching the person, explain what you intend to do.
6. Speak in a clear, firm, reassuring manner.

EMERGENCY CARE

In certain situations, it may be necessary to administer first aid. Ideally, first-aid procedures should be performed by someone who has received formal training from the American Red Cross or some other reputable institution. If you do not have such training, contact your physician or call your local emergency medical service (EMS) by dialing 911 or your local emergency number. In life-threatening situations, however, you may not have time to call for outside assistance.

In cases of serious injury or sudden illness, you may need to begin first aid immediately and continue until help arrives. The remainder of this appendix contains basic information and general steps to follow for various emergency situations. Simply reading these directions, however, may not prepare you fully to handle these situations. For this reason, you may want to enroll in a first-aid course.

Calling for Emergency Assistance

When calling for emergency assistance, be prepared to give exact details. Be clear and thorough, and do not panic. Never hang up until the dispatcher has all the information needed. Be ready to answer the following questions:

1. Where are you and the victim located? This is the most important information the EMS will need.
2. What is your phone number and name?
3. What has happened? Was there an accident or is the victim ill?
4. How many people need help?
5. What is the nature of the emergency? What is the victim's apparent condition?
6. Are there any life threatening situations that the EMS should know about (for example, fires, explosions, or fallen electrical lines)?
7. Is the victim wearing a medic-alert tag (a tag indicating a specific medical problem such as diabetes)?

Are You Liable?

According to the laws in most states, you are not required to administer first aid unless you have a special obligation to the victim. For example, parents must provide first aid for their children, and a lifeguard must provide aid to a swimmer.

Before administering first aid, you should obtain the victim's consent. If the victim refuses aid, you must respect that person's rights. However, you should make every reasonable effort to persuade the victim to accept your help. In emergency situations, consent is *implied* if the victim is unconscious.

Once you begin to administer first aid, you are required by law to continue. You must remain with the victim until someone of equal or greater competence takes over.

Can you be held liable if you fail to provide adequate care or if the victim is further injured? To help protect people who render first aid, most states have "Good Samaritan" laws. These laws grant immunity (protection from civil liability) if you act in good faith to provide care to the best of your ability, according to your level of training. Because these laws vary from state to state, you should become familiar with the Good Samaritan laws in your state.

When Someone Stops Breathing

If someone has stopped breathing, you should perform mouth-to-mouth resuscitation. This involves the following steps:

1. Check for responsiveness by gently tapping or shaking the victim. Ask loudly, "Are you OK?"
2. Call the local EMS for help (usually 911).
3. Gently roll the victim onto his or her back.
4. Open the airway by tilting the victim's head back; placing your hand nearest the victim's head on the victim's forehead, and applying backward pressure to tilt head back and lift the chin.
5. Check for breathing (3 to 5 seconds): look, listen, and feel for breathing.
6. Give 2 slow breaths.
   - Keep victim's head tilted back.
   - Pinch the victim's nose shut.
   - Seal your lips tightly around the victim's mouth.
   - Give 2 slow breaths, each lasting 1½ to 2 seconds.
7. Check for pulse at side of neck; feel for pulse for 5 to 10 seconds.
8. Begin rescue breathing.
   - Keep victim's head tilted back.
   - Pinch the victim's nose shut.
   - Give 1 breath every 5 to 6 seconds.
   - Look, listen, and feel for breathing between breaths.
9. Recheck pulse every minute.
   - Keep victim's head tilted back.
   - Feel for pulse for 5 to 10 seconds.
   - If the victim has a pulse but is not breathing, continue rescue breathing. If there is no pulse, begin CPR.

There are some variations when performing this procedure on infants and children. For children ages 1 to 8, at step 8, give one slow breath every 4 seconds. For infants, you should not pinch the nose. Instead, seal your lips tightly around the infant's nose and mouth. Also, at step 8, you should give one slow breath every 3 seconds.

In cases in which the victim has no pulse, cardiopulmonary resuscitation (CPR) should be performed. This technique involves a combination of artificial respiration and chest compressions. You should not perform CPR unless you have received training in it. You cannot learn CPR simply by reading directions, and without training, you could cause further injury to the victim. The American Red Cross offers courses in mouth-to-mouth resuscitation and CPR as well as general first aid. If you have taken a CPR course in the past, you should be aware that certain changes have been made in the procedure. You should, therefore, consider taking a refresher course.

When Someone Is Choking

Choking occurs when an object obstructs the trachea (windpipe), thus preventing normal breathing. Failure to expel the object and restore breathing can lead to death within 6 minutes. The universal signal of distress related to choking is the clasping of the throat with one or both hands. Other signs of choking include not being able to talk and/or noisy and difficult breathing. If a victim can cough or speak, do not interfere. The most effective method for assisting choking victims is the Heimlich maneuver, which involves the application of pressure to the victim's abdominal area to expel the foreign object.

The Heimlich maneuver involves the following steps: If the victim is standing or seated:

1. Recognize that the victim is choking.
2. Wrap your arms around the victim's waist, making a fist with one hand.
3. Place the thumb side of the fist on the middle of the victim's abdomen, just above the navel and well below the tip of the sternum.
4. Cover your fist with your other hand.
5. Press fist into victim's abdomen, with up to 5 quick upward thrusts.
6. After every 5 abdominal thrusts, check the victim and your technique.
7. If the victim becomes unconscious, gently lower him or her to the ground.
8. Try to clear the airway by using your finger to sweep the object from the victim's mouth or throat.
9. Give 2 rescue breaths. If the passage is still blocked and air will not go in, proceed with the Heimlich maneuver.

If the victim is lying down:

10. Facing the person, kneel with your legs astride the victim's hips. Place the heel of one hand against the abdomen, slightly above the navel and well below the tip of the sternum. Put the other hand on top of the first hand.
11. Press inward and upward using both hands with up to 5 quick abdominal thrusts.
12. Repeat the following steps in this sequence until the airway becomes clear or the EMS arrives:
    a.   Finger sweep.
    b.   Give 2 rescue breaths.
    c.   Do up to 5 abdominal thrusts.

Controlling Bleeding

▶ **External Bleeding**   Control of external bleeding is an important part of emergency care. Survival is threatened by the loss of 1 quart of blood or more. There are three major procedures for the control of external bleeding.

DIRECT PRESSURE.   The best method is to apply firm pressure by covering the wound with a sterile dressing, bandage, or clean cloth. Wearing disposable latex gloves or an equally protective barrier, apply pressure for 5 to 10 minutes to stop bleeding.

ELEVATION.   Elevate the wounded section of the body to slow bleeding. For example, a wounded arm or leg should be raised above the level of the victim's heart.

PRESSURE POINTS.   Pressure points are sites where an artery that is close to the body's surface lies directly over a bone. Pressing the artery against the bone can limit the flow of blood to the injury. This technique should be used only as a last resort when direct pressure and elevation have failed to stop bleeding.

Knowing where to apply pressure to stop bleeding is critical (see Figure A.1). For serious wounds, seek medical attention immediately.

▶ **Internal Bleeding**   Although internal bleeding may not be immediately obvious, you should be aware of the following signs and symptoms:

• Symptoms of shock (discussed later in this appendix)
• Coughing up or vomiting blood
• Bruises or contusions of the skin
• Bruises on chest or fractured ribs
• Black, tarlike stools
• Abdominal discomfort or pain (rigidity or spasms)

In some cases, a person who has suffered an injury (such as a blow to the head, chest, or abdomen) that does not cause external bleeding may experience internal bleeding. If you suspect that someone is suffering from internal bleeding, follow these steps:

1. Have the person lie on a flat surface with knees bent.
2. Treat for shock. Keep the victim warm. Cover the person with a blanket, if possible.

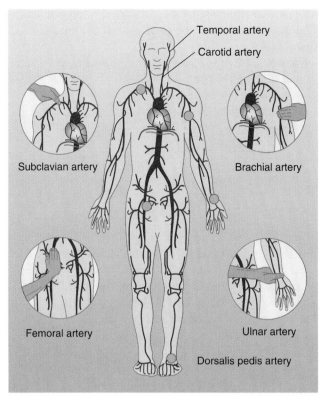

Figure A.1

This figure shows pressure points; the points at which pressure can be applied to stop bleeding. Unless absolutely necessary, you should avoid applying pressure to the carotid arteries, which supply blood to the brain. Also, never apply pressure to both carotid arteries at the same time.

3. Expect vomiting. If vomiting occurs, keep the victim on his or her side for drainage, to prevent inhalation of vomit, and to prevent expulsion of vomit from the stomach.
4. Do *not* give the victim any medications or fluids.
5. Send someone to call for emergency medical help immediately.

▶   *Nosebleeds*   To control a nosebleed, follow these steps:

1. Have the victim sit down and lean slightly forward to prevent blood from running into the throat. If you do not suspect a fracture, pinch the person's nose firmly closed using the thumb and forefinger. Keep the nose pinched for at least 5 minutes.
2. While the nose is pinched, apply a cold compress to the surrounding area.
3. If pinching does not work, gently pack the nostril with gauze or a clean strip of cloth. Do not use absorbent cotton, which will stick. Be sure that the ends of the gauze or cloth hang out so that it can be easily removed later. Once the nose is packed with gauze, pinch it closed again for another 5 minutes.
4. If the bleeding persists, seek medical attention.

Treatment for Burns

▶   *Minor Burns*   For minor burns caused by fire or scalding water, apply running cold water or cold compresses for 20 to 30 minutes. Never put butter, grease, salt water, aloe vera, or topical burn ointments or sprays on burned skin. If the burned area is dirty, gently wash it with soap and water and blot it dry with a sterile dressing.

▶   *Major Burns*   For major burn injuries, call for help immediately. Wrap the victim in a dry sheet. Do not clean the burns or try to remove any clothing attached to burned skin. Remove jewelry near the burned skin immediately, if possible. Keep the victim lying down and calm.

▶   *Chemical Burns*   Remove clothing surrounding the burn. Wash skin that has been burned by chemicals by flushing with water for at least 20 minutes. Seek medical assistance as soon as possible.

Shock

Shock is a condition in which the cardiovascular system fails to provide sufficient blood circulation to all parts of the body. Victims of shock display the following symptoms:

- Dilated pupils
- Cool, moist skin
- Weak, rapid pulse
- Vomiting
- Delayed or unrelated responses to questions

All injuries result in some degree of shock. Therefore, treatment for shock should be given after every major injury. The following are basic steps for treating shock:

1. Have the victim lie flat with his or her feet elevated approximately 8 to 12 inches. (In the case of chest injuries, difficulty breathing, or severe pain, the victim's head should be slightly elevated if there is no sign of spinal injury.)
2. Keep the victim warm. If possible, wrap him or her in blankets or other material. Also, keep the victim calm and reassured.
3. Seek medical help.

Electrical Shock

Do not touch a victim of electrical shock until the power source has been turned off. Approach the scene carefully, avoiding any live wires or electrical power lines. Pay attention to the following:

1. If the victim is holding on to the live electrical wire, do not remove it unless the power has been shut off at the plug, circuit breaker, or fuse box.

2. Check the victim's breathing and pulse. Electrical current can paralyze the nerves and muscles that control breathing and heartbeat. If necessary, give mouth-to-mouth resuscitation. If there is no pulse, CPR might be necessary. (Remember that only trained people should perform CPR.)
3. Keep the victim warm and treat for shock. Once the person is breathing and stable, seek medical help or send someone else for help.

Poisoning

Of the 1 million cases of poisoning reported in the United States each year, about 75 percent occur in children under age 5, and the majority are caused by household products. Most cases of poisoning involving adults are attempted suicides or attempted murders.

You should have emergency telephone numbers for the poison control center and the local EMS ready. Many people keep these numbers on labels on their telephones. Check the front of your telephone book for these numbers. The National Safety Council recommends that you be prepared to give the following information when calling for help:

- What was ingested? Have the container of the product and the remaining contents ready so you can describe it. You should also bring the container to the emergency room with you.
- When was the substance taken?
- How much was taken?
- Has vomiting occurred? If the person has vomited, save a sample to take to the hospital.
- Are there any other symptoms?
- How long will it take to get to the nearest emergency room?

When caring for a person who has ingested a poison, keep these basic principles in mind:

1. Maintain an open airway. Make sure the person is breathing.
2. Call the local poison control center. Follow their advice for neutralizing the poison.
3. If the poison control center or another medical authority advises inducing vomiting, then do so.
4. If a corrosive or caustic (i.e., acid or alkali) substance was swallowed, immediately dilute it by having the victim drink at least one or two 8-ounce glasses of cold water or milk.
5. Place the victim on his or her left side. This position will delay advancement of the poison into the small intestine, where absorption into the victim's circulatory system is faster.

Injuries of Joints, Muscles, and Bones

▶ **Sprains** Sprains result when ligaments and other tissues around a joint are stretched or torn. The following steps should be taken to treat sprains:

1. Elevate the injured joint to a comfortable position.
2. Apply an ice pack or cold compress to reduce pain and swelling.
3. Wrap the joint firmly with a (roller) bandage.
4. Check the fingers or toes periodically to ensure that blood circulation has not been obstructed. If the bandage is too tight, loosen it.
5. Keep the injured area elevated, and continue ice treatment for 24 hours.
6. Apply heat to the injury after 48 hours if there is no further swelling.
7. If pain and swelling continue or if a fracture is suspected, seek medical attention.

▶ **Fractures** Any deformity of an injured body part usually indicates a fracture. A fracture is any break in a bone, including chips, cracks, splinters, and complete breaks. Minor fractures (such as hairline cracks) might be difficult to detect and might be confused with sprains. If there is doubt, treat the injury as a fracture until X-rays have been taken.

Do not move the victim if a fracture of the neck or back is suspected because this could result in a spinal cord injury. If the victim must be moved, splints should be applied to immobilize the fracture, to prevent further damage, and to decrease pain. Following are some basic steps for treating fractures and applying splints to broken limbs:

1. If the person is bleeding, apply direct pressure above the site of the wound.
2. If a broken bone is exposed, do not try to move it back into the wound. This can cause contamination and further injury.
3. Do not try to straighten out a broken limb. Splint the limb as it lies.
4. The following materials are needed for splinting:
   - Splint: wooden board, pillow, or rolled up magazines and newspapers
   - Padding: towels, blankets, socks, or cloth
   - Ties: cloth, rope, or tape
5. Place splints and padding above and below the joint. Never put padding directly over the break. Padding should protect bony areas and the soft tissue of the limb.
6. Tie splints and padding into place.
7. Check the tightness of the splints periodically. Pay attention to the skin color, temperature, and pulse below the fracture to make sure the blood flow is adequate.
8. Elevate the fracture and apply ice packs to prevent swelling and reduce pain.

Head Injuries

A head injury can result from an auto accident, a fall, an assault, or a blow from a blunt object. All head injuries can potentially lead to brain damage, which may result in a cessation of breathing and pulse.

For minor head injuries:

1. For a minor bump on the head resulting in a bruise without bleeding, apply ice to decrease the swelling.
2. If there is bleeding, apply even, moderate pressure. Because there is always the danger that the skull may be fractured, excessive pressure should not be used.
3. Observe the victim for a change in consciousness. Observe the size of pupils and note signs of inability to think clearly. Check for any signs of numbness or paralysis. Allow the victim to sleep, but wake him or her periodically to check for awareness.

For severe head injuries:

1. If the victim is unconscious, check the airway for breathing. If necessary, perform mouth-to-mouth resuscitation.
2. If the victim is breathing, check the pulse. If it is less than 55 or more than 125 beats per minute, the victim may be in danger.
3. Check for bleeding. If fluid is flowing from the ears or nose, do not stop it.
4. Do not remove any objects embedded in the victim's skull.
5. Cover the victim with blankets to maintain body temperature, but guard against overheating.
6. Seek medical help as soon as possible.

Temperature-Related Emergencies

▶ **Frostbite**   Frostbite is damage to body tissues caused by intense cold. Frostbite generally occurs at temperatures below 32°F. The body parts most likely to suffer frostbite are the toes, ears, fingers, nose, and cheeks. When skin is exposed to the cold, ice crystals form beneath the skin. Avoid rubbing frostbitten tissue, because the ice crystals can scrape and break blood vessels.

To treat frostbite, follow these steps:

1. Bring the victim to a health facility as soon as possible.
2. Cover and protect the frostbitten area. If possible, apply a steady source of external warmth, such as a warm compress. The victim should avoid walking if the feet are frostbitten.
3. If the victim cannot be transported, you must rewarm the body part by immersing it in warm water (100°F to 105°F). Continue to rewarm until the frostbitten area is warm to the touch when removed from the bath. Do not allow the body part to touch the sides or bottom of the water container. After rewarming, dry gently and wrap the body part in bandages to protect from refreezing.

▶ **Hypothermia**   Hypothermia is a temperature-related emergency that can be prevented with proper precautions. Hypothermia is a condition of generalized cooling of the body resulting from exposure to cold temperatures or immersion in cold water. It can occur at any temperature below 65°F and

can be made more severe by wind chill and moisture. The following are key symptoms of hypothermia:

- Shivering
- Vague, slow, slurred speech
- Poor judgment
- A cool abdomen
- Lethargy, or extreme exhaustion
- Slowed breathing and heartbeat
- Numbness and loss of feeling in extremities

After contacting EMS, you should take the following steps to provide first aid to a victim of hypothermia:

1. Get the victim out of the cold.
2. Keep the victim in a flat position. Do not raise the legs.
3. Squeeze as much water from wet clothing, and layer dry clothing over wet clothing. Removal of clothing may jostle victim and lead to other problems.
4. Give the victim warm drinks only if he or she is able to swallow. Do not give the victim alcohol or caffeinated beverages, and do not allow the victim to smoke.
5. Do not allow the victim to exercise.

Temperature-related problems common in the summer months include heatstroke, heat exhaustion, and heat cramps. These conditions result from prolonged exertion or exposure to high temperatures and humidity.

▶ **Heatstroke**   Heatstroke, the most serious heat-related disorder, results from the failure of the brain's heat-regulating mechanism (the hypothalamus) to cool the body. The following are signs and symptoms of heatstroke:

- Rapid pulse
- Hot, dry, flushed skin (absence of sweating)
- Disorientation leading to unconsciousness
- High body temperature

As soon as these symptoms are noticed, the body temperature should be reduced as quickly as possible. The victim should be immersed in a cool bath, lake, or stream. If there is no water nearby, a fan should be used to help lower the victim's body temperature.

▶ **Heat Exhaustion**   Heat exhaustion results from excessive loss of salt and water. The onset is gradual, with the following symptoms:

- Fatigue and weakness
- Anxiety
- Nausea
- Profuse sweating
- Clammy skin
- Normal body temperature

To treat heat exhaustion, move the victim to a cool place. Have the victim lie down flat, with feet elevated 8 to 12 inches. Replace lost fluids slowly and steadily. Sponge or fan victim.

▶ Heat Cramps Heat cramps result from excessive sweating, resulting in an excessive loss of salt and water. Although heat cramps are the least serious heat-related emergency, they are the most painful. The symptoms include muscle cramps, usually starting in the arms and legs. To relieve symptoms, the victim should drink electrolyte-rich beverages or a light salt-water solution or eat salty foods.

First-Aid Supplies

Every home, car, or boat should be supplied with a basic first-aid kit. In order to respond effectively to emergencies, you must have the basic equipment. This kit should be stored in a convenient place, but it should be kept out of the reach of children. Following is a list of supplies that should be included:

- Bandages, including triangular bandages (36 inches by 36 inches), butterfly bandages, a roller bandage, rolled white gauze bandages (2- and 3-inch widths), adhesive bandages

- Sterile gauze pads and absorbent pads
- Adhesive tape (2- and 3-inch widths)
- Cotton-tip applicators
- Scissors
- Thermometer
- Antibiotic ointments
- Syrup of Ipecac (to induce vomiting)
- Aspirin
- Calamine lotion
- Antiseptic cream or petroleum jelly
- Safety pins
- Tweezers
- Flashlight
- Paper cups
- Blanket

You cannot be prepared for every medical emergency. Yet these essential tools and a knowledge of basic first aid will help you cope with many emergency situations.

Appendix B

Complementary and Alternative Medicine
New Choices, New Responsibilities

You see it on TV. You see it in magazines. You hear your friends talking about it; you hear your parents bring it up. What is *it*? We're talking about **complementary and alternative medicine,** often referred to simply as **CAM.** No doubt you're familiar with some form of therapy or treatment that as recently as 10 years ago would have been considered as a form of quackery by many. Not that long ago, anyone who utilized unorthodox treatment was considered, well, unorthodox in his or her own right. Today, however, such choices are becoming more and more mainstream as cultural traditions become more familiar to the masses and as people search for options that are less invasive and less expensive than traditional care but also allow them the opportunity to maintain control over their own health. This has led to a remarkable growth in interest in complementary and alternative medicine and has spawned a multibillion-dollar cottage industry with few regulations. With a great many questions about CAM floating around, this special section reflects our best attempt to provide you with a research-based and unbiased perspective on the modern CAM movement

THE LURE OF COMPLEMENTARY AND ALTERNATIVE MEDICINE

If you're thinking that CAM is something of a fad, reserved for those people who live on the fringes of society, you are in for a surprise. Today, Americans are increasingly likely to try therapies once considered to be exotic or strange. Referred to as *CAM (integrative, unconventional,* or *alternative* therapies) and defined as "neither being taught widely in U.S. medical schools nor generally available in U.S. hospitals during the previous year,"[1] and used either singly, additively, or exclusively, these alternatives seem to vary widely in terms of the nature of the treatment, the extent of therapy, and the types of problems for which Americans seek help. Typically, these therapies are compared with the more traditional, allopathic treatments offered by individuals who graduate from U.S.-sanctioned schools of medicine or are licensed medical practitioners recognized by the American Medical Association and its governing board.[2,3]

CAM in the United States Today

In 1993, David Eisenberg and colleagues conducted a ground-breaking study analyzing the patterns of use of alternative medicine in America. The study cast light on a major shift taking place in American behavior when seeking health care. Eisenberg and colleagues found that one in three Americans sought some form of alternative care.[4] In a follow-up study five years later, Eisenberg found that 47 percent of Americans reported using some form of alternative health care in the previous year. In 1998, they actually were more likely to seek out and use some form of alternative care than they were to seek out and use a form of what we've long regarded as traditional medicine. Although exact numbers are difficult to assess, estimated expenditures in the United States for alternative medical services alone indicates a 47.3 percent increase in total visits to alternative medicine practitioners, from 427 million visits in 1990 to 629 million visits in 1997. Total 1997 out-of-pocket expenditures relating to alternative care were conservatively estimated at $27 billion dollars, which is comparable to the out-of-pocket expenditures for all U.S. physician services. Additionally, an estimated 15 million Americans took prescription medications concurrently with herbal remedies or high-dose vitamins and supplements, which are not considered in these service estimates.[5] Such numbers have caused a ground swell of interest in understanding just what is happening in the world of complementary and alternative medicine, and they raise a host of largely unanswered questions—questions that seek to determine who is using CAM and why.

Although it is widely assumed that increasing numbers of us are using various forms of alternative care options, little has been known about the nature and extent of CAM use until fairly recently. In his 1993 and 1998 studies, Eisenberg and others[6] indicated that the most frequently used alternatives to conventional medicine were

- Relaxation techniques (16.9% of the respondents)
- Chiropractic (31 percent)
- Massage (18 percent)
- Self-help (13 percent)
- Energy healing (6 percent)
- Other forms of therapies (16 percent)

In addition to these, other alternative health care therapies used by Americans included acupuncture, homeopathy, herbal therapies and supplements, exercise-movement used to treat particular physical problems, high-dose megavitamin use, spiritual healing, lifestyle diet (such as cutting down on fats to improve heart health), imagery, folk remedies, biofeedback, hypnosis, and art/music therapy. Many of these alternatives are discussed in other parts of this book, and it would be impossible to do justice to them all; therefore, a major part of our focus here is to examine some of the alternatives in which interest has grown considerably in recent years, particularly the array of supplements and functional foods.

Although not specifically assessed in Eisenberg's research, it also has been widely documented that many Americans rely on what are known as **functional foods,** or foods or supplements designed to improve some aspect of physical or mental functioning. Sometimes also referred to as **neutraceuticals,** for the combined nutritional and pharmaceutical benefit to be derived from these products, several are believed to actually work in much the same way as pharmaceutical drugs in making a person well or bolstering the immune system.

▶ **A Historical Perspective**   America's zeal for the healing power of herbs and plant medicines marks a return to a simpler life. In fact, it takes us back thousands of years. Poppy extract was used to quiet crying children in the time of the pharaohs, eons before the medical use of opiates. Ephedra, the main ingredient of some over-the-counter asthma treatments, has relieved breathing problems in China for 5,000 years. Although the United States has been somewhat slow in accepting plant remedies as standard treatment, it should be noted that an estimated 25 percent of all modern pharmaceutical drugs are derived from herbs, including aspirin (from white willow bark), the heart medication digitalis (foxglove); and the cancer treatment Taxol (Pacific yew tree).

Prior to World War II, much of the doctor's medicine bag consisted of plant-based products and "folklore" treatments. However, with the emergence of the major pharmaceutical houses of the world, the advent of synthetic drugs and antibiotics, and a growing pride in the power of U.S. ingenuity and science, a perception took hold that the "best" and safest treatments were those that had been thoroughly tested by the new U.S. consumer protection agency—the U.S. Food and Drug Administration (FDA).[7] As the FDA garnered more clout in testing, regulating and ensuring the safety of pharmaceutical products, many lesser known products and home remedies were put back on the shelf or banned from the market in favor of the highly advertised modern drug regimens. A symbol of wealth, education, and science was the newer, FDA-approved drug of the twentieth century. In contrast, nontraditional treatments fell out of favor among all but a few segments of the U.S. population and became symbols of the undeveloped and impoverished parts of the world, and therefore had no legitimate place in our modern-day, disease-fighting arsenal. After decades of languishing, however, and with a growing dissatisfaction of the populace with the techno-wizardry of late twentieth- and early twenty-first-century U.S. medicine, many of these nontraditional treatments appear to be making a reemergence in treatment arsenals.

▶ **Current Patterns**   Researchers have found that the most frequently cited health problems treated with alternative therapies today are chronic pain (37 percent); anxiety, chronic fatigue syndrome, and other health conditions (31 percent each); sprains and strains (26 percent); addictive problems and arthritis (both 25 percent each); and headaches (24 percent). Other common problems for which people seek alternative care are depression, digestive problems, and diabetes (each over 20 percent).[8] What do all of these conditions have in common? The most obvious similarities include the following[9,10]:

- *An unrelenting form of chronicity,* in which any chance of complete cure or remediation of symptoms is limited

- *A large measure of discomfort or pain* that causes the patient to be largely focused on his or her disease on a daily basis, rather than focusing on health
- *The need for traditional medications that carry substantial risks of side effects or contraindications* if used for long periods of time
- *Symptoms that affect activities of daily living* or interfere with normal daily tasks
- *The need for help from health care specialists* for the health problem in question.

To better understand why Americans behave as they do when confronted with an illness or disorder, it is necessary to understand more about our fears, concerns, and areas that allow us to be hopeful of a positive outcome when we become sick. All too many of us have a powerful distrust of traditional medical practice. Through either direct experience or media portrayals of problems with today's health care system, many people believe that when they are sick, the worst place for them to be is in a hospital or health care setting. The box, "Consumer Fears about Medical Treatment Grow," (page 424) discusses some of the very real threats to health in many of our traditional medical treatments.

CAM Outside the United States

In the midst of a fear of technology, concern over threats from hazardous chemicals and high cost, multiple side effects, prescription drugs, and distaste for the depersonalized treatment in today's health care settings, many Americans are in search of something better, which usually means lower in cost, less risky, and with positive outcomes. The shift to alternatives is not surprising, considering what has happened in other regions of the world. Reports of miracle cures from ancient remedies, more gentle and holistic means of treatment, and positive outcomes from alternative treatments have led many to seek answers from other cultures. In fact, a number of our recent pharmacological advances have their roots in the herbal remedies utilized in cultures throughout the world. For example, there might have been no sexual revolution in the United States without the birth-control pill, derived from the Mexican yam.[11] Although the influence of numerous cultures is at the root of many alternative treatments, Eastern medicine, in particular, has been very influential in today's alternative therapies. Chinese medicine and some of the world's ancient healing practices provide reasonable alternatives to traditional treatment. In particular, traditional Chinese and Ayurvedic therapies seem to offer the more "natural" form of healing that has widespread appeal for many.

Much of our knowledge of ancient remedies stems from teachings of **Ayurvedic medicine,** a method of treatment derived greatly from ancient India, in which practitioners diagnose largely by observation and touch and then assign patients to one of three major constitutional types and to a variety of subtypes. Once classified, patients are treated mostly through dietary modifications and remedies that are primarily herbal and draw on the vast botanical wealth of the Indian subcontinent, but may include animal and mineral ingredients, even powdered gemstones. Other Ayurvedic treatments include steam baths and oil massages.[12]

In addition to Ayurvedic medicine, our interest in alternatives is largely a result of teachings brought forward from Eastern medicine, particularly **traditional Chinese medicine (TCM),** a comprehensive system of diagnosis and treatment that is provided by Chinese immigrants and Westerners trained in China or numerous schools in other countries. In TCM, diagnosis is based on history, on observation of the body (especially the tongue), on palpation, and on pulse diagnosis, an elaborate procedure requiring considerable skill and experience. Treatment includes dietary change, massage, medicinal teas, and other preparations primarily from herbs, but also including animal ingredients and acupuncture.[13] Many Chinese herbal therapies are being studied in clinical trials throughout the United States today, as American medical personnel search for treatments that seem to defy our ready arsenals of prescription drugs. Practiced for centuries and having widespread international appeal, parts of TCM have now gained acceptance in many areas of traditional medicine.

National surveys performed outside of the United States suggest that alternative medicine is popular throughout the industrialized world, and has been for some time. Public opinion polls and consumer surveys in Europe and the United Kingdom suggest a high prevalence rate. Italy, France, Denmark, Finland, and Australia have been significant users of CAM for decades, as have Asian cultures.[14–17] Studies in the United States and abroad support the prevalent use of alternative health care. For example, a 1994 survey of physicians from a wide array of medical specialties in Washington state, New Mexico, and Israel revealed that more than 60 percent had recommended alternative therapies to their patients at least once in the preceding year, while 38 percent had done so in the previous month. These surveys are typical of many others that confirm high usage patterns throughout the world.

Nonindustrialized cultures of the world have had a rich and varied history of folk medicines, alternative therapies, and various "healing modalities" since the earliest beginnings of humanity. So, why so much interest in the United States now? Why do

Consumer Fears About Medical Treatment Grow

Just when you thought you were in the capable hands of a hand-picked allopathic physician, you probably experienced a tinge of anxiety in November 1999, when the Institute of Medicine proclaimed to the world that if we were to count them, the numbers of deadly medical mistakes in the United States would surpass death rates for breast cancer, traffic accidents, and AIDS, making medical error the eighth leading cause of death for Americans. In fact, the report indicated that "medical mistakes are a stunningly huge problem, causing between 44,000 and 98,000 deaths among hospital patients each year."

After making most of us more than a little concerned, the report went on to say that although "to err is human," patients who exercise their rights as consumers will have much better outcomes when nature necessitates a visit to the doctor. The report also recommended major changes in the national health care system that will set a minimum goal of a 50 percent reduction in medical mistakes within five years. This announcement prompted President Clinton to appoint a special task force to develop standards to help protect consumers from mistreatment. Congress has also passed legislation ordering the Agency for Health Care Policy and Research (AHCPR) to seek out strategies designed to reduce patient risk.

According to William Richardson, president of the W. K. Kellogg Foundation, who co-authored the Institute of Medicine report, "Errors can be prevented by designing systems that make it hard for people to do the wrong thing and easy for people to do the right thing." These "people" refer to both consumers and to the health care professionals charged with their care. As such, the Institute of Medicine report recommends the following actions:

- The establishment of a well-funded Federal Center for Patient Safety—$35 million to start and $100 million a year for research. (This represents just a fraction of the $8.8 billion spent per year as a result of medical mistakes.)
- Setting requirements that hospitals and eventually other health organizations report all serious mistakes to state agencies, so experts can detect patterns of problems and take action. Currently, 20 states require error reporting, but the penalties levied vary greatly. In addition, little is being done to avoid cover-ups of potentially costly malpractice claims.
- The establishment of state licensing boards and medical accreditors who periodically reexamine health practitioners for competence, stressing safety practices. Standardized medical equipment and treatment guidelines can help doctors keep up.
- Change the "culture of secrecy" that surrounds medical mistakes, encouraging doctors to discuss errors as well as near-misses, so problems can be fixed.

Other areas in need of improvement include

- Reducing errors caused by the poor handwriting of doctors. Errors in dispensing of drugs can be reduced significantly if doctors take the time to write legibly or use computerized labeling systems to write for them.
- Better training in new technology that often leaves superb doctors fumbling to figure out how a machine works, or relying on short seminars taught by equipment specialists or sales personnel who tell them how to do a procedure
- Regular testing for retention of licenses. Is a physician practicing with knowledge and expertise from 10 to 20 years ago knowledgeable of today's technologically advanced techniques?
- Monitoring doctors' records across state lines. Today, changes in residence have been difficult to monitor, meaning that malpracticing physicians often can find lucrative employment in another state, without repercussions.

As a consumer, there are many things that you can do to protect yourself:

- Know what is wrong with you. Ask questions and seek second opinions from physicians outside of the health group that you routinely visit.
- Know what medications you are taking. Review the contraindications and possible side effects found in a current *Physician's Desk Reference* (PDR). Ask doctors why they are prescribing this drug and whether there are alternatives that may have fewer side effects.
- Monitor all changes in your body while you are taking a prescription drug. Actually, monitor your body prior to ever going to the doctor, so you can be as precise as possible when discussing what is wrong with you.
- Know what lab tests are being requested, why they are being requested, and possible alternatives. Ask about the costs of the tests and whether this is the best test possible. Know the risk of all tests and procedures. When you get lab results, ask that they be explained in detail.
- Have a patient advocate with you at all times. If you don't have one, hire one. When things are not going well, they must be assertive enough to force action by health care providers, either by bringing in another specialist, by making changes in medications and procedures, or through other actions. They should be willing to question the nurses and doctors about medications, and receive information about your vital signs and any problems while you are unconscious or unable to act for yourself.
- Broaden your perspective. There are many alternatives available today, both in terms of practitioners and medications. Don't be afraid to branch out and seek options from others, particularly those options that are less invasive and less harmful. Read widely, seek opinions, and question apparent successes. In short, be a responsible and active participant in your health care— seeking behaviors.

some of us embrace CAM and others have tremendous anxiety and fear about using any or all of these treatments?

PROFILE OF THE CAM CONSUMER

Contrary to popular thinking, decisions to use complementary and alternative medicine tend not to be made on a whim. Those people who seek alternative medical care or a combination of alternative and traditional care tend to be more educated than those who seek care solely from traditional allopathic physicians. In addition, they are more likely to be middle-aged and have a middle-class socioeconomic status.[18,19] In a randomized study of several thousand patients seeking care for low back pain through traditional, allopathic providers versus chiropractic providers, those seeking chiropractic care for low back pain also tended to be more likely to question their providers about the nature and extent of recommended treatments.[20]

Health Behavior

Experts in health care decision making categorize those who seek information or treatment for real and suspected health problems according to three types of health behaviors. People said to engage in **illness behavior** are those who are well at the time of their decision. They are often described as the "worried well," in that, although they do not actually have symptoms, they actively seek information about how to stay well and avoid real or suspected risks. They may read widely, ask their friends or relatives for advice on what to do, seek information on the Internet, or seek advice from alternative and traditional health care sources. In many cases, they may have nagging worries about something that is "not quite right," but they have not actually gone to a medical practitioner for treatment.

On the other end of the continuum are those making decisions about health when they have already been diagnosed as being sick. Termed **sick-role behavior,** this behavior relates to decisions a person makes after he or she is diagnosed with an illness or medical condition. Sick-role behaviors include such things as complying with doctors orders for medications or making surgical decisions. They may include patient advocacy or seeking second opinions for diagnosis and treatment. Sick-role behaviors may either be those

that you control or those that you allow powerful others to control. Hence, you may be an active participant in these decisions, or you may let others whom you respect and trust, or whose authority you trust, make decisions for you.

The third type of health behavior, known as **self-care behavior,** combines elements of both illness and sick-role behaviors and is common among those who use CAM. An individual's actions to engage in self-care may occur when he or she is still extremely healthy and has not even begun to worry about health status (similar to typical wellness activities), when the individual is noting changes or minor problems but is not yet symptomatic ("worried well," similar to illness behavior), or once the person has been diagnosed with a problem (sick-role behavior) (Figure B.1). Regardless of the level of wellness, suspected illness, or diagnosed affliction, the key aspect of self-care is that the individual takes an active, assertive, and informed responsibility for maintaining health and preventing disease, enhancing and protecting health and maintaining normal physical and functional health, and restoring health through the use of appropriate individual, CAM, and traditional medical behaviors.

Seeking Out Alternatives

Most experts in the field have long hypothesized that people who seek out alternatives to traditional medicine do so for one of three reasons[21]:

1. *Dissatisfaction:* Patients are dissatisfied with conventional treatment because it has been ineffective, has produced adverse effects, or is seen as too impersonal, too technologically oriented, or too costly. Many believe that our managed care (managed cost) organizations have pushed people to seek care elsewhere. Typically, these individuals report a significant distrust of the

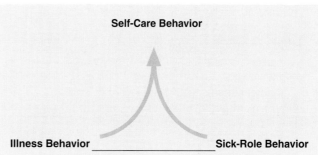

Figure B.1
Self-Care, Illness, and Sick-Role Behaviors in Promoting Health and Preventing Disease

system, either through their own or a loved one's prior experiences in the system. As a result of this distrust and dissatisfaction, they often are highly likely to seek alternatives.

2. *Need for Personal Control:* Individuals seek alternative therapies because they see them as less authoritarian and more empowering, and as offering them more personal autonomy and control over their health care decisions.

3. *Philosophical Congruence:* Alternative therapies are attractive because they are seen as more compatible with patients' values, world views, spiritual and religious philosophies, or beliefs regarding the nature and meaning of health and illness. This is particularly true for people psychologists refer to as **cultural creatives.** These are people who consistently demonstrate the following values: commitment to the environment; commitment to feminism; involvement with esoteric forms of spirituality and personal growth psychology, including self-actualization and self-expression; and love of anything foreign and exotic. These individuals tend to identify with cultural change and innovation and are among those who are most likely to adopt one or more alternative treatment regimens.[22]

Although many of these suggested reasons why people seek CAM, either exclusively or in combination with traditional medicine, were explored in Eisenberg's research, there were some noteworthy differences. Eisenberg et al. noted the following characteristics among respondents:

- They did *not* have a particular negative attitude toward or experiences with traditional medicine that led them to use CAM.
- A need for greater control over their health care experience was not a significant predictor of CAM usage.
- Racial or ethnic differences did *not* predict CAM usage.
- Men and women were equally likely to use CAM.
- People with higher levels of education were most likely to use CAM.
- The poorer an individual's health status, the greater the likelihood he or she would seek a complementary or alternative option.
- Certain conditions, particularly low back pain, chronic pain, anxiety, and urinary tract problems, did predict greater CAM usage.
- Cultural creatives did serve as a predictor of CAM usage. The more spiritual and holistic a person's philosophy, the greater their tendency to use CAM.
- Those who had gone through a transformational experience that had changed their world view were more likely to use CAM.

While there is some variability in determining who is likely to use CAM in general, one glaring fact remains: Increasing numbers of Americans at all ages and stages of life, in all socioeconomic and educational categories, and in all stages of health or illness are turning to alternative remedies as the means to an end. Whether to enhance the body's defenses against disease or disability; ward off the negative effects of aging; enhance memory, performance, or sexual prowess; or boost energy levels, we seem willing to pop pills, drink therapeutic cocktails, and ingest various natural remedies. But are the benefits real? Do we risk harm?

ALTERNATIVES: CLAIMS VERSUS REALITIES

Open any magazine or turn on the television and you are likely to be bombarded with products and services that claim to make you a better you. These ads promise to help us eliminate defects, enhance relationships, provide extra "zip," and help ward off many of the bacterial and viral diseases lurking out in the "cruel world." Fueled by personal insecurities and anxieties and a health care system that appears to be more focused on saving money than on helping people feel valued and worthwhile, it is little wonder that the health alternative industry is well-positioned to capture more and more of our dollars in the days ahead. More important, with each day's growth in products and services and each new claim, consumers are faced with increasing numbers of choices, and few resources to determine what is fact and what is fantasy. Some are identified in Table B.1; others are discussed here. If all of the hype seems too good to be true, it very well may be. But how do we know? One look at the array of alternatives available provides some insight into the challenges facing the average consumer.

Herbal Remedies

Largely derived from Ayurvedic or traditional Chinese medicine, herbal medications now fill supermarket and pharmacy shelves across America. Fueled by mass advertising and promoted as part of multiple vitamin and mineral regimens by major drug manufacturers, herbal supplements represent the hottest trend in the health market. But do they have real benefits? We know that over-the-counter medications have been through rigorous testing to show effectiveness. Herbal supplements, on the other hand, have not undergone the same rigors of efficacy. So, how do we know if the purported benefits are real?

TABLE B.1
Common Herbal, Vitamin, and Mineral Supplements: Benefits vs. Risks

SUPPLEMENT	USE	CLAIMS OF BENEFITS	RISKS
Ephedra (*ma huang, epitonin,* and *sida cordifolia*)	Serves as a stimulant and bronchiodilator	Natural source of ephedrine for use as bronchiodilator in asthmatic attack	Numerous reports of side effects including heart palpitations and psychosis, heart attacks and strokes; banned in several states TOXIC
Chaparral	Sold as teas and pills	Fight cancer and purify blood	Linked to serious liver damage
Comfrey	Originated as a poultice to reduce swelling, but later used internally	Wound healing, infection control	Contains alkaloids toxic to the liver, and animal studies suggest it is carcinogenic
Melatonin	"Clock hormone"	Role in regulating circadian rhythms and sleep patterns	Anti-aging claims unfounded
DHEA	Hormone that turns into estrogen and testosterone in the body	Fights aging, boosts immunity, strengthens bones; and improves brain functioning	No anti-aging benefits proven; could increase cancer risk and lead to liver damage, even when taken briefly
Dieter's Teas	Herbal blends containing senna, aloe, rhubarb root buckthorn, cascara, and castor oil	Act as laxatives	Can disrupt potassium levels and cause heart arrythmias; linked to diarrhea, vomiting, chronic constipation, fainting and death
Pennyroyal	Member of the mint family	Soothing effect in teas	Pregnancy-related complications, heart arrythmias, death
Sassafras	Once a flavoring in root beer; used in tonics and teas	No real claims	Shown to cause liver cancer in animals
Flax Seeds	Produce linseed oil	Omega-3 fatty acid benefits	Delay absorption of medicine
Kava Kava			Increase the effects of alcohol and other drugs
High-Dose Vitamin E	Antioxidants	Reduce risk of heart disease; better survivability after heart attack	Cause bleeding when taking blood thinners
Vitamin C	Antioxidant, manufactures collagen, wound repair, nerve transmission	Improves blood vessel relaxation in people with CVD, diabetes, hypertension, and other problems; can relieve pain of angina pectoris	
l-Carnitine	Amino acid	Improves metabolism in heart muscle, purported to increase fat burning enzymes	Heart palpitations, arrythmias, sudden death; claims largely unsubtantiated
Licorice Root		None proven	Speeds potassium loss
Niacin (vitamin B3)	Reduces serum lipids, vasodilation, and increased blood flow		Skin flushing, gastrointestinal distress, stomach pain, nausea and vomiting
Chondroitin	Shark Cartilage or sea cucumber	Improve osteoporosis and arthritis by improving cartilage function	Fewer benefits than glucosamine; benefits still unproven

To be a wise consumer of the great variety of herbal remedies available in health food stores and supermarkets, there are a few things you should know. **Tinctures** (alcoholic extracts of fresh or dried plants) usually contain a high percentage of grain alcohol to prevent spoilage and are among the best herbal options. Freeze-dried extracts are also very stable and offer good value for your money. Standardized extracts are also among the more reliable forms of herbal preparations. In general, herbal medicines tend to be milder than chemical drugs and produce their effects more slowly; they also are much less likely to cause toxicity, because they are diluted forms of drugs rather than concentrated forms.[23] It is important to note, however, that too much of even the most seemingly harmless herb may cause problems, particularly those from nonstandardized extracts. Remember that herbals are drugs and should not be taken casually, any more than you would take over-the-counter or prescription drugs without really needing them or knowing their side effects. Whether or not you get comfort from hearing that they are *natural,* remember that they have the many of the same chemicals as their synthetic prescription relatives.

Perhaps most important, remember that even though herbal supplements are growing in popularity, herbs are not panaceas. Some of them work; many do not. Unfortunately, because herbs are classified by the government as foods, not drugs, they are not subject to the same rigorous evaluation and testing that the FDA completes for virtually every medicine on the market. The following discussion, though not at all inclusive, provides an overview of some of the most common herbal supplements on the market.

▶ **Ginkgo Biloba** If you're like many people, you have probably heard of the reported "miracle memory-enhancing" qualities of ginkgo biloba. Ginkgo biloba is actually an extract from the leaves of a deciduous tree that lives up to 1,000 years, making it the world's oldest living tree species, one that can be traced back more than 200 million years. The ginkgo was almost destroyed during the Ice Age in all regions of the world except China, where it is considered to be a sacred tree with ancient medicinal qualities.[24] Today, ginkgo leaf extracts are among the leading prescription medicines in both Germany and France, where they account for nearly 2 percent of total prescription sales.[25]

Purported benefits are many, and include such things as improvements in depression; impotence; premenstrual syndrome; diseases of the eye, such as retinopathy and macular degeneration; and general vascular disease. In particular, it has been shown to improve short-term memory and concentration in those individuals who have impaired blood flow to the brain due to narrowing of vessels or clogging of key arteries. A Harvard-based study of 202 men and women with mild to moderately severe dementia caused by stroke or Alzheimer's disease was among the first to promote ginkgo in the United States. After 1 year, the group receiving ginkgo experienced significant improvement in cognitive performance (memory, learning, reading) and had better social functioning (carrying on conversations, recognizing familiar faces) than those in the placebo (non-ginkgo) group.[26] Much of this improvement was believed to be due to the antioxidant properties of the herb, as well as to the blood-thinning properties that seem to improve blood and oxygen flow to clogged blood vessels. Whether this herb works for people with normal blood flow remains largely unexplored. Claims that ginkgo will improve short- and long-term memory in the typical person are not scientifically based.

Most nutritional experts and physicians recommend that people who are considering using this herb take a 40-milligram tablet three times a day for a month or so to determine whether there is any improvement. If there is none, continuing to take this supplement is largely unwarranted. Also, remember that disturbing memory loss or difficulty thinking, regardless of age, should be checked by a doctor to determine underlying causes.

Because the main action of ginkgo appears to be as a blood thinner, it should not be taken with other blood-thinning agents, such as aspirin, vitamin E, garlic, ginger, the prescription drug warfarin (trade name, Coumadin), or any other medications that list thinning of the blood as a potential side effect.[27] Doing so could increase your risk of severe hemorrhage in cases of accidents or emergency surgeries or in the event of a stroke or aneurysm. Other reported side effects in a very small number of patients include stomach upset, headache, and dizziness, as well as allergic reactions.

▶ **St. John's Wort** The bright yellow, star-shaped flowers of St. John's Wort (SJW) have had a rich and varied history of use in Europe, Asia, and Africa. The name for this herb is believed to date back to Christian times and relates to the red oil that is secreted by special glands in the flowers of SJW when they are pinched or cut. Christians believed that the flowers secreted this blood-red oil on August 29, the anniversary of the beheading of St. John the Baptist, and that they bloomed on June 24, St. John's birthday. The term *wort* is Old English for "plant." In addition, John the Baptist represents light, and the flowers themselves seemed to represent the bright yellow light of the sun.[28] Colonists to the United States brought SJW with them, only to find that native Americans were already using it for everything from snake bite to a general health enhancer. In the United States, SJW grows in abundance in northern California and southern Oregon and is also referred to as *klammath weed*.[29]

Today, SJW enjoys a global popularity that finds it the favored therapy for depression in a number of countries around the world, including Germany, actually surpassing most standard antidepressants as the first mode of treatment for clinical depression. German researchers report that it is decidedly better than placebos in medical trials and at least as good as some prescription antidepressants for treatment of the milder forms of depression. It is also cheaper and appears to cause fewer side effects than drugs such as Prozac, Paxil, and Zoloft.[30,31] SJW is also believed to

- Act as a positive mood enhancer by helping maintain serotonin levels, and as natural neurotransmitters that help brain function and calm the body[32]
- Help as a sleep enhancer for those having difficulty sleeping[33]
- Support immune functioning by suppressing the release of interleukin-6, a protein that controls certain aspects of the immune response[34]

A review of 23 well-designed clinical trials published in *The British Medical Journal* concluded that extracts of SJW "are more effective than placebo for the treatment of mild to moderately severe depressive disorders." This review also found evidence from eight other studies that SJW may work as well as some other drugs in countering mild depression. However, noting that most of the studies done to date did not control rigidly for levels of depression, that they varied the dosage and method of delivery, and that the trials were all less than 8 weeks in length, the research team called for more rigorously controlled, larger sample-sized studies comparing this herb with prescription doses of Prozac.[35] Like most antidepressants, SJW's benefits are not even felt for about 4 weeks. With the trials so short in nature, and the variability of other factors, few conclusions may be made about short- or long-term effectiveness. While some improvements in participants' depression were noted, the efficacy of subjecting people to higher doses, longer time periods, and other variables pose important questions about long-term risks for use that have been largely unanswered.

Like other plants, SJW contains a number of different chemicals, many of which are not clearly understood. Why it seems to improve depression and to have antiviral properties remains largely unknown. Taking any drug that has not been thoroughly tested and for which safe and effective doses are not clear will have risks. What we *do* know is that there is more to SJW than myth and the simplistic explanations that many health food stores tend to give to consumers.

Unfortunately, rigorous testing has not been done in the United States because the herb is sold as a dietary supplement, which does not fall under the watchful eye of the FDA. What side effects have been noted? Most have been more bothersome than severe and range from slight gastrointestinal upset to fatigue, dry mouth, dizziness, skin rashes, and itching. Some people have noted some sensitivity to sunlight. Most of these side effects are minor, however, when compared with those of major antidepressant medicines.

In spite of the apparent positive news about SJW, consumers should proceed with caution when considering its use. First, little is known about the herb and its compounds. Second, for more severe forms of depression, SJW may not be enough to prevent potentially negative outcomes. Anyone suffering from clinical depression should be under a psychologist's care and should be monitored for progress or difficulties. In fact, the combination of therapy and medications is typically the most effective way to achieve any improvement.

In addition, SJW should never be taken in combination with prescription antidepressants. When combined with other serotonin-enhancing drugs, such as Prozac, SJW may result in serotonin overload, leading to tremors, agitation, or convulsions. SJW also should not be used by pregnant women or women who are nursing, by young children, or by the frail elderly, because the safety margins have not been established.

▶ **Echinacea** Echinacea, or the *purple coneflower*, is found primarily in the Midwest and the prairie regions of the United States. Two of the nine species of Echinacea in the United States are now on the federal endangered species list, a cause of growing concern for many environmentalists as the herb's popularity has grown. Believed to be used extensively by Native Americans for centuries, Echinacea eventually gained widespread acceptance in the United States before being shipped to Europe, where its use grew gradually over the eighteenth and nineteenth centuries. Today, Echinacea has emerged as the best-selling herb in health and natural food stores in the United States and is widely used throughout most of the world. It is said to stimulate the immune system and, more specifically, to increase the effectiveness of the white blood cells that attack bacteria and viruses. Many people believe it to be helpful in preventing and treating the symptoms of a cold or flu. In spite of many studies in Europe that have provided preliminary evidence of Echinacea's effectiveness, however, there remains a great deal of skepticism and controversy about it. Recent controlled trials in the United States indicate that Echinacea is no more effective in preventing a cold than is a placebo.[36]

As with many of the herbal treatments, little research has been conducted on the benefits and risks of Echinacea. Preliminary findings indicate there are certain situations when you should not be taking this herb. Because Echinacea can affect the immune system, people with autoimmune diseases such as arthritis should not take it. Pregnant women and those with diabetes or multiple sclerosis also should abstain from taking Echinacea, as should anyone allergic to the Asteraceae, or daisy family, of plants.[37] Until more is known about Echinacea, rest and vitamin C may still be your best bets in warding off a cold.

Special Supplements

A dietary supplement is defined as "products (other than tobacco) that are intended to supplement or add to the diet and contain one or more of the following ingredients: vitamins, minerals, amino acids, herbs or other substance that increases total dietary intake; and is intended for ingestion in the form of a capsule, powder, soft gel, or gelcap and is not represented as a conventional food or as a sole item" (Dietary Supplement Health and Education Act). Typically, these supplements are taken to enhance health, prevent disease, or enhance mood. In recent years, we've heard increasing reports on the health benefits of a number of vitamins and minerals.

When taken to increase work or the potential for work, dietary supplements are labeled as **ergogenic aids.** Compounds such as bee pollen, caffeine, glycine, carnitine, lecithin, brewer's yeast, and gelatin are typical forms of ergogenic aids. In recent years, a new generation of performance-enhancing ergogenic aids has hit the market. Many of these are designed to attract young, athletic adults with claims of increasing muscular strength and performance. Others are designed to attract people of all ages who are seeking improvements in physical functioning, increased energy, and better resistance to disease. This section looks at both health-enhancing supplements and ergogenic aids.

▶ Muscle Enhancers In 1998, Mark McGwire made headline news for his home run records. At the same time, he also made news for his open admission that he was a regular user of the diet supplement androstenedione, a substance found naturally in meat and some plants and which is also produced in the human body by the adrenal glands and gonads. The synthetic version, sold in concentrated form, is known in locker room talk as "andro," a precursor to the human hormone testosterone. In other words,

the body converts andro directly into testosterone, which enables an athlete to train harder and recover more quickly. Ironically, although the NCAA, the NFL, and the International Olympic Committee have banned andro, it is available over the counter as a "natural" performance supplement. The attention brought to androstenedione raised a great many questions about its true benefits, but little was known about it. The controversy over the McGwire home run race encouraged some new research into the compound. Early results indicate that andro has a chemical structure that is very similar to anabolic steroids, which may result in long-term risks similar to those of the illegal androgens.[38]

Creatine is a naturally occurring compound found primarily in skeletal muscle that helps to optimize the muscles' energy levels. In recent years, the use of creatine supplements has increased dramatically in an effort to increase muscle energy and allow a person to work harder with less muscle fatigue and, thus, increase muscle mass with less effort. Reports of creatine's benefits, however, appear exaggerated. Over one-third of those taking creatine are unable to absorb it in the muscles and achieve no benefit. Side effects include muscle cramping, muscle strains, and possible liver and kidney damage.[39]

▶ Ginseng Grown commercially throughout many regions of the United States, ginseng is much prized for its reported sexual restorative value. It is believed that ginseng affects the pituitary gland, increasing resistance to stress, affecting metabolism, aiding skin and muscle tone, and providing the hormonal balance necessary for a healthy sex life. Other purported benefits include increased endurance, increased muscle strength, improved recovery from exercise, improved oxygen metabolism during exercise, improved auditory and visual reaction time, and improved mental concentration.[40] Studies of the effectiveness of ginseng, however, have simply raised more questions about it: primarily about appropriate dosages and how long it should be taken to realize benefits. Because the potency of plants varies considerably, dosage is difficult to control and side effects are fairly common. Noteworthy side effects of high usage include nervousness, insomnia, high blood pressure, headaches, skin eruptions, chest pain, depression, and abnormal vaginal bleeding.[41]

▶ Glucosamine Glucosamine is a substance manufactured by the body that plays a key role in the growth and development of cartilage. When present in sufficient amounts, it stimulates the manufacture of substances necessary for proper joint function and joint repair. It is manufactured commercially and is sold under the a variety of different names, with glucosamine sulfate being the preferred product. To date, glucosamine has been shown to be effective in the treatment of osteoarthritis and related degenerative joint diseases and appears to relieve swelling and decrease pain. Unlike many other supplements that are available, glucosamine sulfate has an excellent safety record with few noteworthy side effects.[42]

▶ **Chromium Picolinate**   A few years ago, chromium picolinate was believed to be the new miracle for anyone interested in weight loss. Since then, at least two major studies at the U.S. Department of Agriculture Human Nutrition Research Center have shown no benefit.[43]

▶ **SAMe**   Touted as yet another in a growing list of "natural" antidepressants, SAMe (pronounced "Sammy") is the nickname for *S*-adenosyl-methionine, a compound produced biochemically in all humans to help form some 40 functions in the body, including everything from bone preservation (hence its purported osteoarthritis benefits) to DNA replication.

Although no one is quite sure how it works, SAMe has been reported to have a significant effect on mild-to-moderate depression without many of the typical side effects of prescription medications, such as sexual dysfunction, weight gain, and sleep disturbance. Scientists speculate that SAMe somehow affects brain levels of the neurotransmitters noradrenaline, serotonin, and, possibly, dopamine, all of which are related to the human stress response and to the origins of depression in the body.[44]

While there has been much ado about the wonders of this natural antidepressant, much of the hype has not been substantiated in large, randomized clinical trials, the type of research necessary to validate drug claims. Also, the research has been of short duration, meaning that little is known of any long-term side effects such as toxicity to the liver or carcinogenic properties. In addition, questions exist over how much SAMe a person should take and in what form it should be administered.

Anyone considering using SAMe should consider these factors:[45,46]

- While preliminary evidence suggests that SAMe may promote joint health and enhance mood, there have been no large-scale, scientifically controlled studies in the United States that have verified such claims.
- Without conclusive evidence of real benefits, many question the high cost of SAMe (between $15 and $35 or higher for 20 pills).
- Serious depression requires something more than just treatment with SAMe or the popular herb SJW. Any major depression episode should

receive more than just pharmaceutical or natural remedies. The best long-term outcomes for depression occur during careful analysis of the person's health, environmental contributors, and a combination of chemical and counseling therapy.
- People with a family history of heart disease should not take SAMe, due to preliminary indications that it may trigger coronary events.

Although it is a supplement, anyone deciding to try SAMe should check first with his or her doctor. Under no circumstances should SAMe be taken by anyone on prescription antidepressants, and the time lag between taking the prescription and beginning SAMe, and vice versa, should be carefully considered.[47]

▶ **Antioxidants**   Although covered in depth in the "Nutrition" chapter of this text (see Chapter 9), it should be noted that antioxidants are among the most sought-after forms of supplements on the market. Primary antioxidants include betacarotene, selenium, vitamin C, and vitamin E.

Foods as Healing Agents

Although all of the previously mentioned supplements may arguably fit the definition of "health enhancers" and "healing agents," some products are emerging as part of a new generation of health-promoting agents. Some combine the elements of foods with the healing aspects of chemicals and emerge as "neutraceuticals." Others are known for their stand-alone benefits. Although we have long known that many foods are natural sources of all the essential vitamins and minerals and have known about their benefits in building "strong bones and healthy bodies," today we know more about the foods we eat than ever before. Numerous books and diet plans exhort the preventative or curative natures of certain foods that provide people with options more natural than popping a pill or drinking an elixir. Foods contain many different "nonnutrient" active ingredients that can affect us in different ways. For example, chili peppers contain ingredients that may cause our eyes to water and our sinuses to clear. Many of these active ingredients, or constituents, can be used to promote good health. A number of foods, such as sweet potatoes, tangerines, and red peppers, are recognized as excellent sources of antioxidants. Onion and garlic contain allium compounds that reduce blood clotting. Others have natural digestive or antiinflammatory properties. Others are what is sometimes called *prebiotics*, foods that promote good bacteria in the body that may help to fight off infection.[45] Some of the most common

Mixing Foods and Medicines

If you are like most Americans who take prescription drugs, you probably aren't aware that you could be playing Russian roulette with your medications. Sure, you know you shouldn't take medications with alcohol or in certain combinations. But, did you know that certain foods can cause serious reactions when combined with some medications? According to a National Consumer alert from the Food and Drug Administration, there are some things that you should avoid. For example:

- Never drink grapefruit juice less than two hours before or five hours after taking heart drugs called calcium channel blockers, such as Procardia. This combination can kill.

- Grapefruit juice taken with cyclosporin, which fights organ rejection in transplant recipients, can cause confusion and trembling.
- High doses of vitamin E thin the blood. If taken by heart patients along with the popular blood thinner Coumadin, the risk of serious bleeding increases.
- Foods high in Vitamin K, such as broccoli, spinach, and turnip greens, can reduce the effectiveness of Coumadin.
- Antidepressants called MAO inhibitors can cause a potentially fatal blood pressure rise when taken with foods high in chemical tyramine, such as cheese and sausage.
- Drinking coffee or colas with certain antibiotics, such as Cipro, or the ulcer drugs Tagamet, Zantac, and Pepcid can increase caffeine

levels, causing the jitters and stomach irritation.
- Consumption of bananas or potassium supplements along with heart drugs called ACE inhibitors, such as Capoten and Vasotec, can cause harmful potassium buildup if not monitored carefully.
- The combination of grapefruit juice and antihistamines, either prescription versions, such as Claritin and Allegra, or over-the-counter types, such as Benadryl, can cause serious heart problems.

Source: Food and Drug Interactions. Food and Drug Administration. 1998. For a free copy, call 1-800-639-8140, or visit the Internet site: www.nclnet.org

---

healthful foods, and their purported benefits, include the following:

- Plant stanol: Can lower "bad" LDL cholesterol
- Oat fiber: Can lower "bad" LDL cholesterol; serves as a natural soother of nerves; stabilizes blood sugar levels
- Sunflower: Can lower risk of heart disease; may prevent angina
- Soy protein: May lower heart disease risk; provides protective phytoestrogen effect; may reduce risk from certain cancers
- Red meats and dark green, leafy vegetables: Contain B vitamins (B6, B12, folate), which can lower levels of homocysteine, an amino acid associated with heart disease
- Garlic: Lowers cholesterol and reduces clotting tendency of blood; lowers blood pressure; may serve as form of antibiotic
- Japanese green tea: Lowers cholesterol; may have a role in fighting certain cancers
- Ginger: Fights motion sickness, stomach pain and upset; discourages blood clots; may relieve rheumatism
- Yogurt: Untreated, nonpasteurized yogurt contains active, friendly bacteria that can fight off infections

As interest in and demand for "healthy" foods have grown, people have turned to foods labeled as

organic, expecting them to contain only the health-promoting substances they seek. But is the label of *organic* a guarantee of safety? Today, when something is labeled as *organic,* it doesn't necessarily mean that it is free of anything. Even though the Organic Foods Production Act (OFPA) of 1990 established a national certification process to assure consumer safety, few states consistently apply the standards defined in that legislation. Going to your local farmer's market and paying a premium price for organic produce is still no guarantee that the produce meets any consistent levels of toxin acceptability. The need for a certifying process to ensure consumer protection is warranted.[49]

Practitioners and Treatments

Just as there has been tremendous growth in the numbers of supplements and related alternatives that are designed to promote health and prevent disease, there has also been exponential growth in the numbers of alternative therapists, treatment modalities, and avenues for health care services. The most common of these are listed in Table B.2. As several of these have been discussed in the "Consumer Health" chapter of this text (Chapter 16), discussion here is limited to special exercise programs that have been of particular interest to modern consumers and that are designed to help people work on themselves

---

TABLE B.2
Complementary Medicine

There is an emerging prominence of complementary/alternative medicine (CAM) strategies and services available to U.S. health-care consumers. Below is a list of some of the most popular CAMs, with a brief explanation of each.

Energy healing	Different therapies based on the philosophy that humans produce waves of energy that are disrupted during illness.
Food therapy	Treatment is based on the belief that many disorders are based on allergies and toxic synergism among food combinations. Naturopaths test for and treat food allergies, and assign special diets designed to produce nutritional balance.
Homeopathy	Treatment of disease with small doses of a substance that would, in healthy persons, produce symptoms of the disease.
Hypnosis	The treatment of disease with suggestion while the patient is in an hypnotic trance.
Relaxation techniques	The goal is to remove stress and promote healing. Techniques include yoga, meditation, breathing and posture exercises, and visualization.
Acupuncture	Piercing the body with long, thin needles and wires at specific points, or medians, to prevent disease, relieve pain, and promote health.
Chiropractic	A practice based on the belief that disease results from malalignment of the spinal column, which reduces normal nerve function. Practice uses manipulation and adjustment of the spinal column.
Herbal medicine	Using a wide assortment of herbs to treat health problems ranging from insomnia to heart disease.
Megavitamins	The promotion of the consumption of large doses of common essential vitamins and minerals to prevent disease and heal illness.
Massage	Rubbing, stroking, kneading, or lightly pounding the body with the hands or other instruments.

from a more metaphysical perspective—from the inside out.

▶ **Yoga** Once relegated to out-of-the-way locations or even private homes, yoga is one of the most popular alternative fitness programs available, offered at the vast majority of up-scale fitness centers. Focusing on the mindful aspects of fitness, the contemplative and meditative components, this ancient breathing and focusing program enhances flexibility, calms the spirit, reduces stress, strengthens the back, reduces the pain of arthritis, and provides a powerful element of personal control. Although recognized for its potential for good, yoga can also have risks if practiced incorrectly. A typical yoga class starts with some breath-control exercises, called *pranayama,* and then moves to a series of yoga positions designed to move the spine through a full range of movement. Finding a yoga class that is best for you will be easy if you follow these recommendations[50]:

- Watch a few classes first. Observe the instructor and his or her techniques. The more experienced the instructor, the better.
- Get permission from your doctor, particularly if you are out of shape or are recovering from an illness.
- If you are pregnant and/or have high blood pressure, asthma, or glaucoma, talk to your instructor about the breathing techniques being used.
- Allow at least 2 hours between your last meal and your class.
- Start slowly and go gently. Stop if you feel any major discomfort.

▶ **Tai Chi** If you see a group of people engaged in graceful, slow, controlled movements, you're probably observing a Tai Chi class, an ancient exercise program that has been called "moving meditation." Today's Tai Chi classes are full of young and old alike who are trying to improve balance, fitness, and bodily control. Programs in Tai Chi have been reported to improve balance and reduce falls in the elderly and to lower blood pressure among the chronically ill. As a low-impact exercise that involves a series of slow movements or forms, even those who are not fit are able to participate. Surprisingly, Tai Chi provides participants with a vigorous workout without appearing to do so. Virtually any ambulatory person can get involved. The only exception is someone who has problems with the knee or ankle.

▶ **Body Work** Body work actually consists of several different forms of exercise. *Feldenkrais* work is a system of movements, floor exercises, and body work designed to retrain the central nervous system to help it find new pathways around any areas of blockage or damage. It is gentle and effective in rehabilitating trauma victims. *Rolfing* is a more invasive form of body work and aims at restructuring the musculoskeletal system by working on patterns of tension held in deep tissue. The therapist applies firm pressure to different areas of the body, and this pressure may be painful. Rolfing can release repressed emotions as well as dissipate muscle tension. *Shiatsu* is a traditional healing art from Japan that makes use of firm finger pressure applied to specified points on the body and is intended to increase the circulation of vital energy. The client lies on the floor, with the therapist seated alongside. *Trager work* is one of the least invasive forms of body work, using gentle rocking and bouncing motions to induce states of deep, pleasant relaxation.[51]

Who Is Protecting Consumers and Regulating Claims?

While the frantic rush to use alternative therapies, foods, and supplements continues, this movement is not without its risks for consumers. Most products are not regulated in the United States nearly as strictly as are over-the-counter drugs or even foods. This is in sharp contrast to countries such as Germany, where the government holds companies to strict standards for ingredients and manufacturing. In all too many instances, products such as nutritional supplements and genetically engineered and organic foods have had a long history of unregulated growth. With that growth has come an abundance of claims and testimonials about the medicinal qualities of some and the health-enhancing claims of others. In the get-rich-quick mania, many charlatans have jumped into the health food and CAM market. As profits soar, more and more companies enter the market. Unfortunately, what this also means is that issues related to consumer safety and

protection from fraudulent claims will also rise and continue to raise serious questions about our current regulatory system.

Protecting Consumers and Regulating Claims

Like many other CAM practices, the burgeoning practice of using herbs, roots, and natural remedies to enhance moods, prevent colds, and boost energy has taken a new turn with the introduction of neutraceuticals or functional foods. According to National Institutes of Health (NIH) nutritional biochemist and NIH Office of Dietary Supplements spokesperson, Dr. Terry Krakower, "NIH does have some concerns about them and we are looking into them, especially the potential for interaction with other medications. We advise anyone who uses them to talk to their physician. [Functional foods] are so new we don't know yet if they are good, bad, or indifferent. [Much] of the herb content in these food products is so small that it's probably ineffective, and if it were included in large amounts, it could be harmful. Anyone taking these supplements, whether in pill form or in foods, should do their homework and thoroughly research them rather than relying on health claims made by manufacturers."[52] Although touted as having health benefits, herbal supplements and functional foods have not been labeled with the precise amount of chemicals in the product, are available without a prescription, and often provide little guidance on how they should be used. This poses risks for unsuspecting consumers at all levels, raising issues of consumer safety to new levels.

More important, by legal definition, they are neither prescription drugs nor over-the-counter medications. Instead, classified as food supplements, they can be sold without approval of the FDA, but they are not supposed to be accompanied by claims of therapeutic benefit, even though they often are. Faced with increasing claims, growing risks, and the potential for serious health effects, consumer groups, members of the scientific community, and government officials are calling for action. Increasingly, pressure is mounting to have consistent standards, similar to those used in Germany and other countries of the world. Many are calling for a more stringent FDA approval process for virtually all supplements sold in the United States.

The German Commission E

The German Commission E is among the most noteworthy of the international groups attempting to regulate the sale of alternative medicines and supple-

regulate the sale of alternative medicines and supplements. Consisting of an expert panel established in 1970, its mission was to conduct a formal evaluation of the hundreds of herbal remedies that have been part of traditional German medicine for centuries. The members of the commission carefully analyzed data from clinical trials, observational studies, biologic experiments, and chemical analyses, and between 1983 and 1996, evaluated 383 herbal remedies, approving nearly two-thirds of them for use, but discounting nearly another one-third, some of which continue to be sold in America as herbal supplements.[53]

Essentially, the German Commission E analyzed a growing list of **phytomedicines,** another name for medicinal herbs, many of which are sold over the counter in Europe. Typically, these medicinal herbs are integrated into conventional medical practice and are prepared in several different ways, usually as tablets or ground into powders.[54] Many are sold in much the same way as cough medicines and other over-the-counter remedies in the United States.

Looking to Science for More Answers

Clearly, CAM is fast gaining popularity and respect among the highest levels of government, scientific and medical communities, and the population at large. However, it is important to note that while some CAM treatments are gaining credibility, this credibility must be tempered with good science. Testimonials, spontaneous remissions of disease, and claims by professionals with professional credentials and pseudocredentials are only as good as the research that support the claims. Although slow in coming, the federal government and legislators have pushed for better science, increased funding, and an agency designed to help garner information useful to consumers. In 1993 Congress paid heed by establishing the Office of Alternative Medicine (OAM) at the NIH. Recently renamed the National Center for Complementary and Alternative Medicine (NCCAM) and with a budget of nearly $50 million dollars, it now is able to fund its own projects and has established research centers at universities and other institutions throughout the United States, where many clinical trials are being conducted[55–57] (Table B.3 on page 438). In addition, numerous other studies into alternative treatments for ailments from arthritis to depression to high blood cholesterol are taking place at institutions across the United States. One of the most promising aspects of this research is the enthusiastic support of professionals who have the training and laboratory expertise to actually measure the efficacy of current market-driven claims and ask the right questions of manufacturers.

FUTURE DIRECTIONS: NEW THERAPIES IN THE NEW MILLENNIUM

Although we may not agree with all of the alternative remedies discussed in this special section, one thing must be acknowledged: Regardless of form or marketing ploy, CAM is here to stay. It appears to serve a very real need of consumers, and the potential benefits seem to outweigh any projected risk. While consumers are making the adjustment to CAM in record numbers, members of the health care delivery system seem slow to act. Although progress has been noted, there is still a long way to go before CAM becomes fully accepted in tomorrow's mainstream medical practice.

How Tomorrow's Health Care Providers and Insurers May React

As pressure mounts from consumer groups interested in utilizing alternative practitioners and having their insurance plans pay for it, more and more insurers are hiring alternative practitioners on their staffs or covering alternative care as a routine benefit, at least to some degree. This is especially true as criticisms of managed care increase and government agencies get involved.

In 1999, over 60 health maintenance groups throughout the United States covered some form of alternative care, nearly three times the numbers covered in 1994. In some cases, consumers are offered the option of having a special "extra-cost" rider on their insurance policy, through which they may choose to see one of several categories of alternative practitioners for a higher premium and co-pay agreement. For many consumers, just knowing they have a choice seems to be worth the extra cost. Usually the cost of these added practitioners to the treatment pools adds anywhere from $3 to $9 dollars per patient to the monthly premium.[58]

As insurers open up their coverage to CAMs, support from professional organizations, such as the American Medical Association (AMA), is also increasing, as more and more physician training programs require or offer electives in alternative treatment modalities. In some cases, medical schools are educating a new generation of young medical doctors to be better prepared to advise their patients about the pros and cons of alternative treatments, and more comprehensive studies are examining the efficacy of alternative strategies compared with traditional treatments.[59–61] Although alternative medicine is becoming increasingly integrated into today's health care programs and plans, there is still a long way to go. As we learn more, we will be

COMPLEMENTARY and ALTERNATIVE MEDICINE

TABLE B.3
NCCAM-Funded Centers of Research on Alternative Medicine

INSTITUTION NAME	NAME OF CENTER	SPECIALTY OF CENTER
Bastyr University, Kenmore, WA	Bastyr University AIDS Research Center: www.bastyr.edu/research/buarc	HIV/AIDS
Columbia University, New York	Center for CAM and Research in Aging: cpmcnet.columbia.edu/dept/rosenthal	Aging and Women's Health Issues
Harvard Medical School, Beth Israel Deaconess Medical Center, Boston, MA	Center for Alternative Medicine Research: www.bidmc.harvard.edu/medicine/camr	General Medical Outcomes
Kessler Institute for Rehabilitation, Newark, NJ	Center for Research in Complementary and Alternative Medicine for Stroke and Neurological Disorders: www.umdnj.edu/altmdweb/web	Stroke and Neurological Conditions
Palmer Center for Chiropractic Research, Davenport, IA	Consortial Center for Chiropractic Research: www.palmer.edu	Chiropractic
Stanford University, Palo Alto, CA	Complementary and Alternative Medicine Program at Stanford: http://scrdp.standford.edu/camps.html	Aging
University of Arizona, Health Sciences Center, Tucson, AZ	Pediatric Center for Complementary and Alternative Medicine	Pediatric Conditions
University of California, Davis, Davis, CA	Center for Alternative Medicine Research in Asthma and Immunology: www-camra.ucdavis.edu	Asthma, Allergy and Immunology
University of Maryland, School of Medicine, Baltimore	Center for Alternative Medicine Research on Arthritis: www.compmed.umaryland.edu	Arthritis
University of Michigan, Taubman Health Care Center, Ann Arbor, MI	Center for Complementary and Alternative Medicine Research for CVD	Cardiovascular Disease
Minneapolis Medical Research Foundation, Minneapolis, MN	Center for Addiction and Alternative Medicine Research (CAAMR): www.mmrfweb.org/caamrpages/caamcover.html	Addiction
University of Texas–Houston, Houston, TX	University of Texas Center for Alternative Medicine: www.sph.uth.tmc.edu/utcam	Cancer
University of Virginia School of Nursing, Charlottesville, VA	Center for the Study of Complementary and Alternative Therapies: www.nursing.virginia.edu/centers/altrther.html	Pain
Maharishi University of Management, Fairfield, IA	Center for Natural Medicine and Prevention	Cardiovascular Disease and Aging in African Americans
Kaiser Foundation Hospitals, Portland, OR	Center for Complementary and Alternative Medicine Research in Craniofacial Disorders	Craniofacial Disorders
Oregon Health Sciences University, Portland, OR	Oregon Center for Complementary and Alternative Medicine in Neurological Disorders	Neurological Disorders

Sources: Marwick, Charles, "Alterations Are Ahead at the OAM," *Journal of the American Medical Association* 280 (1998): 1553–1554. "CAM Centers of Research," 2000. National Center for Complementary & Alternative Medicine. Web site: http://nccam.nih.gov/nccam/research/centers.html. Bethesda, MD.

better able to justify decisions for traditional and alternative care based on facts rather than speculation.

Self-Care: Protecting Yourself

CAM certainly provides us all with new options for taking control of our own health care. But it is still a relatively new path, strewn with many obstacles and dimly lit. With a few notable exceptions, much of what you read on the Internet about functional foods, herbal medicines, and CAM, in general, is unreliable. Several reliable texts are available, however, including an English version of the *Complete German Commission E Monographs,* a 685-page scientific treatise published by the American Botanical Council, and the *American Pharmaceutical Association Practical Guide to Natural Medicines* and a *PDR for herbal medicines.* Also, the government agencies cited in this special section offer sensible and reliable information for consumers. When considering alternative treatment, do your homework and keep the following in mind:[62]

- Remember that, when it comes to herbals and other supplements, *natural* doesn't necessarily mean *safe.* Many people have actually had serious reactions to the e seemingly harmless products. For example, some have suffered serious liver damage from sipping teas brewed with comfrey, an herb that is used in poultices and ointments to treat sprains and bruises and that should not be taken internally. Pregnant women face special risks from herbs such as Echinacea, senna, comfrey and licorice.
- Realize that no one is closely monitoring whether herbals are pure. In May 1998, the FDA verified industry reports that certain shipments of ginseng were contaminated with high levels of fungicides. Other problems with imported herbs and remedies have been noted.
- Recognize that dosage levels in many herbal products are not regulated. German manufacturers produce identical batches of herbal remedies, as required by law. U.S. Pharmacopeia, a nonprofit organization, publishes standards for several herbs. Look for reputable manufacturers and remember that price doesn't necessarily mean quality.
- Remember to tell your doctor if you are taking herbal medications. Several of them may interact with medicines that you are taking or cause unusual side effects.
- It is unlikely that any herbal medicine will completely cure a serious disease, just as many prescription medications tend to relieve symptoms but don't cure underlying problems. Monitor all illnesses carefully. Be careful about running right out to the health food store for an herb after self-diagnosing an illness. Pay attention to your body and bodily reactions when you are taking any medications. If problems persist, or if you notice any unusual results, consult with your doctor or licensed health provider.
- Always look for the word *standardized* on any herbal product you plan to buy.

Although efforts will undoubtedly be focused on developing regulations that will help protect you, your best mode of protection is to be an informed consumer. As the numbers of products and services increase, there will be increasing challenges to stay informed and to use prudence when using any untested product or service. Technological advances and scientific breakthroughs will help answer many of the nagging questions that surround CAM today. Results of national clinical trials should provide much-needed information for consumers and policy makers. We are entering a new era of medicine; one in which what you do for yourself may be as important as what the health care establishment may be able to do for you. By using the information presented here and accessing the resources that are recommended, you will be well on your way toward safe and responsible CAM use in the days ahead.

CAM Review

GENERAL REVIEW

1. What are some of the potential benefits of alternative medicine?
2. What is the FDA able to do to regulate herbal supplements and alternative therapies?
3. What are some possible reasons for the recent growth in popularity of CAM and related and therapies?

4. What is the name of the federal agency that oversees CAM in the United States?
5. What was the goal of the German Commission E?

APPLICATION

For over a year now, Maia has been suffering from chronic knee pain. Expecting a diagnosis of torn cartilage, Maia prepared herself for minor knee surgery intended to clean out the damaged joint, a brief period of rehabilitation, and then a return to normal activity. She was surprised, however, when an MRI indicated no structural damage to the knee, which also ruled out surgery. The orthopedist did indicate the beginning of osteoarthritis and prescribed a course of action that included an over-the-counter anti-inflammatory medicine, physical therapy, and a possible injection of cortisone. In the meantime, Maia's chiropractor, whom she'd been seeing as part of a regular wellness program, suggested joint manipulation to improve motion in the joint and increase blood flow to the damaged area, thereby reducing inflammation and pain. Maia's best friend told her she'd heard good things about the benefits of taking chondroitin and glucosamine as a means of rebuilding the cartilage in the damaged joint. Maia, herself, had recently seen commercials on TV advertising remarkable new arthritis medications "for the most common form of arthritis—osteoarthritis" that "guaranteed" she'd be bounding up stairs in no time. Finally, her mother gave her a copy of the latest "best seller" extolling the virtues of "foods that heal." Needless to say, Maia's head was spinning!

What Do You Think?

Why is Maia's head spinning? Which of the suggested options would qualify as complementary and alternative therapies or treatments? What are the potential benefits of each option? Can Maia try all of the options? Are there any potential interactions of combining treatments? What would you do if you were Maia?

COMPLEMENTARY AND ALTERNATIVE WEBSITES

The National Center for Complementary and Alternative Medicines   A new division of the National Institutes of Health dedicated to providing the latest information on complementary and alternative practices.

http://altmed.od.nih.gov/nccam/

National Institutes of Health, Office of Dietary Supplements   Check out any questions you have on dietary supplements on this web site.

http://dietary-supplements.info.nih.gov

FURTHER READING

Hiroyuki Ageta, Norio Aimi, Yutaka Ebizuka, Testuro Fujita and Gisho Honda (eds). *Towards Natural Medicine Research in the 21st Century* (Symposium, Kyoto, Japan, October 1997). (New York: Elsevier, 1998).

N. Barnard. *Foods That Fight Pain: Revolutionary New Strategies for Maximum Pain Relief* (New York: Harmony Books, 1998).

Barrie R. Cassileth. *The Alternative Medicine Handbook: The Complete Reference Guide to Alternative and Complementary Therapies* (New York: WW Norton & Co. 1998).

James Dillard and Terra Ziporyn. *Alternative Medicine for Dummies* (Chicago: IDG Books Worldwide, 1998).

Wayne B. Jonas and Jeffrey S. Levin (eds). *Essentials of Complementary and Alternative Medicine* (Philadelphia: Lippincott Williams & Wilkins, 1999).

Ross Turchaninov and Connie A. Cox. *Medical Massage* (Scottsdale, AZ: Stress Less Publishing and Phoenix: Aesculapius Books, 1998).

Peter Uhlmann. *Flowing the Tai Chi Way: A Voyage of Discovery by a Tai Chi Master and His Student* (Powell River, BC, Canada: China Books and Periodicals, 1998).

2. University of Southern California School of Medicine, "Noncontraceptive Health Benefits," *Dialogues in Contraception* 3 (1990): 2.

3. D. E. Greydanus and R. B. Shearin, *Adolescent Sexuality and Gynecology* (Philadelphia: Lea & Febiger, 1990), 107.

4. U.S. Department of Health and Human Services, *FDA Talk Paper: FDA Approves Application for Preven Emergency Contraceptive Kit,* September 2, 1998.

5. "FDA Approves Emergency Contraception Kit," *College Health Report* 1 (1998): 8.

6. P. Silva and K. E. Glasser, "Update on Subdermal Contraceptive Implants," *The Female Patient* 17 (1992): 34–45.

7. R. Hatcher, J. Trussell, F. Stewart, W. Cates, G. Stewart, F. Guess and D. Kowal, *Contraceptive Technology,* 17th rev. ed. (New York: Ardent Media, Inc., 1998): 619.

8. Ibid., 620.

9. National Center for Health Statistics, "Fertility, Family Planning and Women's Health," 23 (1997): 19.

10. Boston Women's Health Collective, *The New Our Body, Ourselves* (New York: Simon and Schuster, 1996).

11. P. Gober, "The Role of Access in Explaining State Abortion Rates," *Social Science & Medicine* 44 (1997): 7.

12. Hatcher et al., op. cit., 681.

13. R. Lacayo, "Abortion: The Future Is Already Here," *Time,* May 4, 1992, 8.

14. D. A. Grimes and R. J. Cook, "Mifepristone (RU-486)—An Abortifacient to Prevent Abortion?" *The New England Journal of Medicine,* 8 October 1992, 1041–1044.

15. K. Schmidt, "The Dark Legacy of Fatherhood," *U.S. News and World Report,* 14 December 1992, 94–95.

16. U.S. Department of Health and Human Services, *The Health Benefits of Smoking Cessation: A Report of the Surgeon General,* 1990.

17. H. Klonoff-Cohen et al., "The Effects of Passive Smoking and Tobacco Exposure through Breast Milk or Sudden Infant Death Syndrome." *Journal of the American Medical Association,* 273 (1995), 795–798.

18. American College of Obstetricians and Gynecologists, "Nutrition During Pregnancy," *Patient Education Pamphlet* (AP001), March 1996.

19. National Down Syndrome Society (1998): http://www.ndss.org/.

20. A. Curtin, "Rates of Caesarian Birth and Vaginal Birth after Caesarian." 1991–1995. *Monthly Vital Statistics Report,* 45 (1997): 11.

21. Hatcher et al., op. cit., 204.

22. C. O. Byer, L. W. Shainberg, G. Galliano, *Dimensions of Human Sexuality* (Boston, MA: McGraw-Hill, 1999), 196.

CHAPTER 7

1. H. F. Doweiko, *Concepts of Chemical Dependency* (Pacific Grove, CA: Brooks/Cole, 1993), 9.

2. C. Nakken, *The Addictive Personality* (Center City, MN: Hazelden, 1996), 24.

3. *Physicians' Desk Reference,* 51st ed. (Oradell, NJ: Medical Economics Data, 1997).

4. S. Greenberg, *Physician's Desk Reference for Nonprescription Drugs,* 17th ed. (Oradell, NJ: Medical Economics Data, 1996).

5. "Top 200 Drugs of 1995," *Pharmacy Times* 62 (1996): 29.

6. J. Shuster, "Insomnia: Understanding Its Pharmacological Treatment Options," *Pharmacy Times* 62 (1996): 67–76.

7. J. Foreman, "Ginseng: $350 Million for Not Much," *Boston Globe* 3 February 1997, C4.

8. G. Cowley, "Herbal Warning," *Newsweek* 6 May 1996, 61–68.

9. Ibid.

10. "New York County Bans Herbal Stimulant," *Pharmacy Times* 62 (1996): 8.

11. National Institute on Drug Abuse (NIDA), "Research on Drugs and the Workplace" *Capsules* (Rockville, MD: U.S. Department of Health and Human Services, June 1995).

12. U.S. Department of Health and Human Services, 1996 National Household Survey on Drug Abuse, 1997.

13. Ibid.

14. National Institute on Drug Abuse, "National Survey Results on Drug Use from Monitoring the Future Study 1975–1995," *NIDA Capsule,* 1996.

15. 1998 National Household Survey on Drug Abuse, *www.samhsa.gov/Press*

16. Ibid.

17. National Institute on Drug Abuse. National Trends. Cocaine, 041, 1996, 1.

18. M. Fishman and C. Johanson, "Cocaine," in *Pharmacological Aspects of Drug Dependence: Towards an Integrated Neurobehavior Approach (Handbook of Experiemental Pharmacology),* C. Schuster and M. Kuhar, eds. (Hamburg: Springer Verlag, 1996), 159–195.

19. Ibid.

20. National Institute on Drug Abuse, "Cocaine Abuse," *NIDA Capsule,* 1996.

21. National Institute on Drug Abuse, *Capsules,* 1996.

22. J. Reno (U.S. Attorney General), "National Methamphetamine Strategy" (message to the President of the United States). U.S. Department of Justice, Office of the Attorney General (April 1996).

23. National Institute on Drug Abuse. "Methamphetamines, 016" Infofax, 1998, 1.

24. U.S. Department of Health and Human Services, "1998 National Household Survey on Drug Abuse," 1998.

25. National Institute on Drug Abuse, "National Survey Results on Drug Use from Monitoring the Future Study 1975–1996," *NIDA Capsule,* 1996.

26. L. Morrow, "Kids and Pot." *Time,* 9 December 1996, 36.

27. "Your Health: Marijuana as Medicine," *Consumer Reports,* May 1997, 1–4.

28. Downloaded from Join Together on Line, on 11/11/98. *Latest News: New Image Helps Medical Marijuana Passage,* 1998.

29. R. Mathias, "Marijuana Impairs Driving-Related Skills and Workplace Performance," NIDA Notes 11, no. 1 (January/February 1996): 6.

30. National Institute on Drug Abuse, "Heroin, 0–12" Infofax, 1998, 1.

31. National Institute on Drug Abuse, "National Survey Results on Drug Use from Monitoring the Future Study 1975–1996," *NIDA Capsules.* 1996.

32. National Institute on Drug Abuse. *NIDA Capsules:* "Designer Drugs," September 1997.

33. Ibid.

34. National Institute on Drug Abuse, MDMA (Ecstasy), *NIDA Capsules,* 1998.

35. Ibid.

36. "The History of Synthetic Testosterone," *Scientific American,* February 1995, 80.

37. National Institute on Drug Abuse, "Costs to Society," *NIDA Infofax,* 1998.

38. National Institute on Drug Abuse. "Monitoring the Future: Women and Drug Abuse," *NIDA Capsules,* 1997.

39. Ibid.

40. National Institute on Drug Abuse (NIDA), "Research on Drugs and the Workplace," *Capsules* (Rockville, MD: U.S. Department of Health and Human Services, June 1995).

41. Ibid.

42. R. Tricker and D. L. Crook, *Athletes at Risk: Drugs and Sport* (Dubuque, IA: Wm. C. Brown, 1990), 47.

CHAPTER 8

1. C. A. Presley, P. W. Meilman, J. R. Cashin, and R. Lyerla. *Alcohol and Drugs on American College Campuses: Use, Consequences, and Perceptions of the Campus Environment*, Vol. IV: 1992–94 (Carbondale, IL: Core Institute, 1996).

2. Ibid.

3. A. Cohen, "Battle of the Binge," *Time*, 8 September 1997.

4. H. Wechsler, et al., "Changes in Binge Drinking and Related Problems Among American College Students Between 1993 and 1997," *Journal of American College Health* 47 (1998): 61.

5. L. D. Johnson, P. M. O'Malley, and J. G. Bachman, *The Monitoring the Future Study*, 1975–1994, Vol. II (Rockville, MD: NIDA, 1996), 185.

6. Wechsler et al., op. cit., 57–68.

7. Ibid.

8. H. Wechsler, "Health and Behavioral Consequences of Binge Drinking in College," *JAMA* 272 (1994): 1672–1677.

9. T. Katsouyanni, et al., "Ethanol and Breast Cancer: An Association That May Be Both Confounded and Causal." *International Journal of Cancer* 58 (1994): 356–361.

10. National Highway Traffic Safety Administration, Fatal Accident Reporting System, 1997.

11. Ibid.

12. Wechsler et al., op. cit., 57–68.

13. National Highway Traffic Safety Administration, "Traffic Safety Facts 1996: Alcohol, Washington D.C.: National Center for Statistics and Analysis, 1997.

14. Ibid.

15. Insurance Institute for Highway Safety. Fact Sheet, Arlington, VA: 1998.

16. National Highway Traffic Safety Administration, op. cit.

17. F. K. Goodwin and E. M. Gause, "Alcohol, Drug Abuse, and Mental Health Administration," *Prevention Pipeline* 3 (1990): 19.

18. S. I. Benowitz, "Studies Help Scientists Home in on Genetics of Alcoholism," *Science News*, 29 September 1984, 17.

19. O. Ray and C. Ksir, *Drugs, Society, and Human Behavior* (St. Louis: Times Mirror/Mosby, 1990).

20. U.S. Department of Health and Human Services, *Ninth Special Report to the U.S. Congress on Alcohol and Health* (1997), 261.

21. E. Gomberg, in "Women and Alcohol: Issues for Prevention Research," *National Institute on Alcohol Abuse and Alcoholism Research Monograph* 32 (1996): 185–214.

22. L. Timnick, "A Sobering Finding, No Social Drinks for the Alcoholic," *Social Resources Issues* 3 (1982): Article 2.

23. J. M. McGinnis and W. H. Foege, "Actual Causes of Death in the United States," *Journal of the American Medical Association* 270 (1993): 2207–2212.

24. American Lung Association, "Trends in Cigarette Smoking," February 1998.

25. "1998 SAMHSA Fact Sheet, National Household Survey on Drug Abuse," Substance Abuse and Mental Health Services Administration, Rockville, MD.

26. Centers for Disease Control and Prevention, "Tobacco Use Among High School Students," *Morbidity and Mortality Weekly* 47 (1998): 229–233.

27. *Smoking and Health: National Health Status Report* (Rockville, MD: U.S. Department of Health and Human Services, 1992).

28. K. Turnquist, "Scions of Joe Camel Aren't Just Blowing Smoke," *The San Diego Tribune*, 7 June 1998, D5.

29. United States Department of Health and Human Services, "Targeting Tobacco Use: The Nation's Leading Cause of Death," Centers for Disease Control and Prevention, 1998, 2.

30. A. Thorndike, N. Rigotti, et al. "National Patterns in the Treatment of Smokers by Physicians." *Journal of the American Medical Association* (1998) 279: 604–608.

31. L. Brown, ed., *The State of the World, 1990* (New York: Norton, 1990), 100–102.

32. American Cancer Society. Tobacco Information: Cigar Smoking and Cancer. 1998.

33. American Lung Association, op. cit.

34. American Cancer Society, "Cancer Facts and Figures," 1997, 18.

35. "Study Links Smoking to Pancreatic Cancer," *Science New*, 22 October 1994, 261.

36. American Cancer Society, op. cit.

37. Ibid.

38. WHO Collaborative Study of Cardiovascular Disease and Steroid Hormone Contraception, "Acute Myocardial Infarction and Combined Oral Contraceptives: Results of an International Multicentre Case-Control Study," *The Lancet*, 26 April 1997: 1202–1209.

39. American Cancer Society, op. cit.

40. C. Sears, "Three More Reasons Not to Smoke," *American Health*, June 1990, 42.

41. NIDA Notes, "Nicotine Conference Highlights Research Accomplishments and Challenges," Sept/Oct 1995, 11–12.

42. National Institutes of Health, *Smokeless Tobacco or Health*, Monograph 2, May 1993, 3.

43. Centers for Disease Control and Prevention, "Exposure to Secondhand Smoke Widespread," *Tobacco Information and Prevention Source*, 1997.

44. Centers for Disease Control and Prevention. "Tobacco Use and Prevention Program," *Tobacco Information and Prevention Source*, 1998.

45. K. Steenland, "Passive Smoking and the Risk of Heart Disease," *Journal of the American Medical Association* 267 (1992): 94–99.

46. P. Hilts, "Wide Peril Is Seen in Passive Smoking," *New York Times*, 9 May 1990, A25.

47. Centers for Disease Control and Prevention, "Fact Sheet: Smoking Prevalence and Exposure to Tobacco Smoke Among Children," 1997.

48. D. Mannino, "Children Exposed to ETS Miss More School," *Tobacco Control*, May 1996.

49. Centers for Disease Control, *Morbidity and Mortality Weekly*, 41 (1992): 2.

50. C. Failey and A. Toufexis, "The Butt Stops Here," *Time*, 18 April 1994, 58.

51. ABC News, "Tobacco Deal Near," Online at *http://abcnews.com/*. Downloaded 11/12/98.

52. "Action on Smoking and Health: Detailed Outline of Proposed Agreement." Downloaded 11/13/98. *http://ash.org*.

53. "Tobacco Settlement Proceeds to be Released to States." *News Release*, November, 12, 1999. National Association of Attorneys General, *http://www.naag.org*

54. "Nicotine Patches Seen to Help Smokers Quit," *Boston Globe*, 23 June 1994, 3.

55. "Grounds for Breaking the Coffee Habit?" *Tufts University Diet and Nutrition Newsletter* 7 (1990): 4.

56. "Fetal Loss Associated with Caffeine." *Fact and Comparisons Drug Newsletter* 13 (March 1994): 39.

CHAPTER 9

1. Janet Beary and Rebecca Donatelle, Unpublished Doctoral Dissertation, 1994, Oregon State University.
2. Constance Georgiou, Nancy Betts, Sharon Hoerr, Kathryn Keim, Paula Peters, Beth Stewart, and Jane Voichick, "Among Young Adults, College Students and Graduates Practiced More Healthful Habits and Made More Healthful Food Choices than Did Nonstudents," *Journal of the American Dietetic Association* 97 (1997): 754–762.
3. Harvard Women's Health Watch, "Protein," 5 (1998): 4.
4. Ibid., 4.
5. R. B. Kanarch and R. Kaufman, *Nutrition and Behavior* (New York: Van Nostrand Reinhold, 1991).
6. *Food, Nutrition and the Prevention of Cancer: A Global Perspective,* World Cancer Research Fund and the American Institute for Cancer Research, 1997.
7. Charles Fuchs, Edward Giovannucci, Graham Colditz, David Hunter, Meier Stampfer, Bernard Rosner, Frank Speizer, and Walter Willet, "Dietary Fiber and the Risk of Colorectal Cancer and Adenoma in Women," *New England Journal of Medicine* 340 (1999): 169–176.
8. Ibid., 170.
9. R. Mensink and M. Katan, "Effect of Dietary Trans-Fatty Acids on High-Density and Low-Density Lipoprotein and Cholesterol Levels in Healthy Subjects," *New England Journal of Medicine* 16 August 1990.
10. G. Ruoff, "Reducing Fat Intake with Fat Substitutes," *American Family Physician* 43 (1991): 1235–1242.
11. *Food, Nutrition and the Prevention of Cancer,* op. cit.
12. Ibid., 532.
13. Walter Willet and Albert Ascherio, "Trans Fatty Acids: Are the Effects Only Marginal?" *American Journal of Public Health* 84 (1994): 722–724.
14. Julian Midgley, Andrew Matthew, Celia Greenwood, and Alexander Logan, "Effect of Reduced Dietary Sodium on Blood Pressure: A Meta-Analysis of Randomized Controlled Trials," *Journal of the American Medical Association* 275 (1996): 1590–1598.
15. Haas, *Staying Healthy with Nutrition* (Berkeley, CA: Celestial Arts, 1992), 470–471; J. Solonen et al., "Iron and Your Heart," *Circulation,* September, 1992.
16. "Food as Medicine," *Harvard Women's Health Watch* 5 (1998): 4–5.
17. Ibid., 4.
18. Ibid., 4.
19. Ibid., 5.
20. John Smythies, *Every Person's Guide to Antioxidants* (Newark, N.J.: Rutgers University Press, 1998).
21. Ibid., 35.
22. Balz Frie, OSU Linus Pauling Institute Seminar Series, February 1999.
23. Ibid.
24. Ibid.
25. Ibid.
26. "Dietary Guidelines, 1998," U.S. Department of Agriculture. Available from the Superintendent of Documents, Consumer Information Center, Department 378-C, Pueblo, Colorado or at the USDA web site.
27. Joan Stephenson, "Public Health Experts Take Aim at a Moving Target: Foodborne Infections," *Journal of the American Medical Association* 277 (1997): 97–102.
28. Ibid., 97.
29. Ibid., 98.
30. Ibid., 98.
31. Ibid., 99.
32. Morris Potter, Motarjemi Yasmin, and Fritz Kaferstein, "Emerging Foodborne Diseases," *World Health* 50 (1997): 16–22.
33. L. Katzenstein, "Food Irradiation: The Story behind the Scare," *American Health* 60–80.
34. "Diagnosing Food Allergies," *University of California at Berkeley Wellness Letter,* May 1992, 7.
35. Ibid., 7.
36. Ibid., 7.

CHAPTER 10

1. R. J. Kuczmarski, K. M. Flegal, S. M. Campbell, and C. L. Johnson, "Increasing Prevalence of Overweight among US Adults: The National Health and Nutrition Examination Surveys, 1960–1991," *Journal of the American Medical Association* (1994) 272: 205–211.
2. Ellen Fuller and Jan Stanton, "Lifesteps versus "Weighing the Options: Criteria: An Evaluation of a Nonclinical Weight Management Program," *Nutrition Today* 31 (1998): 198–205.
3. Sachiko St. Jeor, "New Trends in Weight Management," *Journal of the American Dietetic Association* 97 (1997): 1096–2003.
4. Department of Health and Human Services, *Healthy People 2010, National Health Promotion and Disease Prevention Objectives,* Washington, D.C., 1999.
5. Anne Novitt-Morena, "Obesity: What's the Genetic Connection?" *Current Health* 24 (1998): 18–23.
6. St. Jeor, op. cit., 1098.
7. A. M. Wolf, G. A. Colditz, "The Cost of Obesity: The US Perspective," *Pharmacoeconomics* 5 (1994): 34–38.
8. St. Jeor, op. cit., 2000.
9. Ibid., 2000.
10. Food and Nutrition Board, Institute of Medicine, P. R. Thomas, (ed.), "Weighing the Options: Criteria for Evaluating Weight Management Programs Committee to Develop Criteria for Evaluating the Outcomes of Approaches to Prevent and Treat Obesity," Washington, D.C.: National Academy Press, 1995.
11. Position of the American Dietetic Association: Women's Health and Nutrition. *Journal of the American Dietetic Association* 95 (1995): 362–366.
12. ADA Position adopted by the House of Delegates, October 20, 1996. ADA headquarters at (800) 877-1600, ext. 4896.
13. Sue Cummings, Ken Goodrick, and John Foreyt, Position of the American Dietetic Association: Weight Management. 97 (1997): 71–75.
14. J. G. Meisler and S. St. Jeor, "Summary and Recommendations from the American Health Foundation's Expert Panel on Healthy Weight," *American Journal of Clinical Nutrition* 63 (1996): 474S–477S.
15. Cummings, op. cit., 72.
16. Hwang, Mi Young, "Are You Obese?" *The Journal of the American Medical Association,* 282 (1999): 1596.
17. Albert Stunkard et al., "The Body Mass Index of Twins Who Have Been Raised Apart," *New England Journal of Medicine* 322 (1990): 1477–1482.
18. Claude Bouchard et al., "The Response to Long-Term Overfeeding in Identical Twins," *New England Journal of Medicine* 322 (1990): 1483–1487.
19. Ibid.
20. Cummings, op. cit., 73.

21. P. Jaret, "The Way to Lose Weight," *Health,* January/February 1995, 52–59.
22. Novitt-Morena, op. cit.
23. "Genes and Appetite," *Harvard Women's Health Watch,* January 1996.
24. L. Tartaglia et al., "Identification and Expression Cloning of a Leptin Receptor," *Cell* 83 (1995): 1263–1271.
25. M. Turton, D. O'Shea, I. Gunn, et al., "A Role for Glucagon-like Peptide 1 in the Central Regulation of Feeding," *Nature* 379 (1996): 69–72.
26. F. Katch and W. McArdle, *Introduction to Nutrition, Exercise, and Health,* 4th ed. (Philadelphia: Lea and Febiger, 1992), 53.
27. Phillip Elmer-Dewitt, "Fat Times" *Time,* January 16, 1995, 60.
28. Ibid., 61.
29. Ibid., 61.
30. Kelly Brownell, "Comments on the Latest Study on Yo-Yo Diets by Steven Blair of the Institute for Aerobics Research" (paper originally presented in 1993, newer report at paper presented at Oregon State University by Steven Blair, Fall, 1998).
31. Elmer-DeWitt, op. cit., 64.
32. Nancy Diehl, Courtney Johnson, and Rebecca Rogers, "Social Physique Anxiety and Disordered Eating: What's the Connection?" *Addictive Behaviors* 23 (1998): 1–16.
33. G. K. Goodrick and J. P. Foreyt, "Why Treatments for Obesity Don't Last," *Journal of the American Dietetic Association* 91 (1991): 1243–1247.
34. C. F. Telch and W. S. Agras, "The Effects of Very Low Calorie Diet on Binge Eating," *Behavior Therapy* 24 (1993): 177–193.
35. Cummings, op. cit., 75.
36. "Eating Disorders," *Harvard Mental Health Letter* 14 (1997): 1–5.
37. Ibid., 4.
38. "Treating Eating Disorders," *Harvard Women's Health Watch,* May 1996, 4–5.

CHAPTER 11

1. B. A. Dennison, J. H. Straus, E. D. Mellits et al., "Childhood Physical Fitness Tests: Predictor of Adult Physical Activity Levels?" *Pediatrics* 82 (1988): 324–330; and K. E. Powell and W. Dysinger, "Childhood Participation in Organized School Sports and Physical Education as Precursors of Adult Physical Activity," *American Journal of Preventive Medicine* 3 (1987): 276–281.
2. U.S. Department of Health and Human Services, *Physical Activity and Health: A Report of the Surgeon General.* Atlanta: U.S. Department of Health and Human Services, Centers for Disease Control and Prevention, National Center for Chronic Disease Prevention and Health Promotion, 1996.
3. R. Gates, "Fitness Is Changing the World: For Women," *IDEA Today* July-August 1992, 58.
4. C. J. Caspersen, K. E. Powell, and G. M. Christianson, "Physical Activity, Exercise, and Physical Fitness: Definitions and Distinctions for Health-Related Research, *Public Health Report* 100 (1985): 126–131.
5. L. J. Ransdell and C. L. Wells, "Physical Activity in Urban, African-American, and Mexican-American Women," *Medicine and Science in Sports and Exercise* 30 (1998): 1608–1615.
6. DHHS, *Physical Activity and Health: A Report of the Surgeon General,* op. cit.
7. T. Baranowski, C. Bouchard, O. Bar-Or et al., "Assessment, Prevalence, and Cardiovascular Benefits of Physical Activity and Fitness in Youth," *Medicine and Science in Sports and Exercise* 24 (6) Supplement: (1992): S237–S247.

8. M. Artal and C. Sherman, "Exercise Against Depression," *The Physician and Sportsmedicine* 26 (1998): 55–60; and S. J. Petruzello, D. M. Landers, B. D. Hatfield et al., "Effects of Exercise on Anxiety and Mood," *Sports Medicine* 11 (1991): 143–182.
9. L. Bernstein et al. "Adolescent Exercise Reduces Risk of Breast Cancer in Younger Women," *Journal of the National Cancer Institute,* September 1994.
10. Baranowski et al., op. cit.
11. G. S. Berenson, C. A. McMahon, A. W. Voors et al., *Cardiovascular Risk Factors in Children: The Early Natural History of Atherosclerosis and Essential Hypertension* (New York: Oxford University Press, 1980).
12. DHHS, *Physical Activity and Health: A Report of the Surgeon General,* op. cit.
13. A. Lubell, "Can Exercise Help Treat Hypertension in Black Americans?" *The Physician and Sportsmedicine* 16 (September 1988): 165–168.
14. V. H. Heyward, *Advanced Fitness Assessment and Exercise Prescription,* 2nd ed. (Champaign, IL: Human Kinetics Publishers, 1991).
15. W. L. Haskell, A. S. Leon, C. J. Caspersen et al., "Cardiovascular Benefits and Assessment of Physical Activity and Physical Fitness in Adults," *Medicine and Science in Sports and Exercise* 24 (6) Supplement (1992): S201–S220.
16. Ibid.
17. DHHS, *Physical Activity and Health: A Report of the Surgeon General,* op. cit.
18. P. A. Kovar, J. P. Allegrante, C. R. MacKenzie et al., "Supervised Fitness Walking in Patients with Osteoarthritis of the Knee: A Randomized, Controlled Trial," *Annals of Internal Medicine* 116 (1992): 529–534; and D. T. Felson, Y. Zhang, J. M. Anthony et al., "Weight Loss Reduces the Risk of Symptomatic Knee Osteoarthritis in Women: The Framingham Study," *Annals of Internal Medicine* 116 (1992): 535–539.
19. H. M. Frost, "Skeletal Structural Adaptations to Mechanical Usage (SATMU)—1. Redefining Wolff's Law: The Bone Remodeling Problem," *The Anatomical Record* 226 (1990): 403–413.
20. C. M. Snow, J. M. Shaw, and C. C. Matkin, "Physical Activity and Risk for Osteoporosis," in *Osteoporosis,* eds. R. Marcus, D. Feldman, J. Kelsey (San Diego: Academic Press, 1996), 511–528.
21. American College of Sports Medicine, *ACSM's Guidelines for Exercise Testing and Prescription,* 5th ed. (Philadelphia: Lea and Febiger, 1995).
22. M. I. Harris, "Classification, Diagnostic Criteria, and Screening for Diabetes," in *Diabetes in America,* eds. M. I. Harris, C. C. Cowie, M. P. Stern, E. J. Boyko, G. E. Reiber, and P. H. Bennett, eds. (Bethesda, MD: National Institutes of Health, National Institute of Diabetes and Digestive and Kidney Diseases, NIN Publication no. 95–1468, 1995), 15–36.
23. National Institutes of Health, "Consensus Development Conference Statement on Diet and Exercise in Non-Insulin Dependent Diabetes Mellitus," *Diabetes Care* 10 (1987): 639–644.
24. S. P Helmrich, D. R. Ragland, and R. S. Paffenbarger, Jr., "Prevention of Non-Insulin Dependent Diabetes Mellitus with Physical Activity," *Medicine and Science in Sports and Exercise* 26 (1994): 824–830.
25. S. N. Blair, H. W. Kohl III, R. S. Paffenbarger Jr., et al., "Physical Fitness and All-Cause Mortality: A Prospective Study of Healthy Men and Women," *Journal of the American Medical Association* 262 (1989): 2395–2401.
26. E. R. Eichner, "Infection, Immunity, and Exercise: What To Tell Patients?" *The Physician and Sportsmedicine* 21 (January 1993): 125–135.

27. W. A. Primos, Jr., "Sports and Exercise During Acute Illness: Recommending the Right Course for Patients," *The Physician and Sportsmedicine* 24 (January 1996): 44–53.

28. D. C. Nieman, L. M. Johanssen, J. W. Lee, et al., "Infectious Episodes in Runners Before and After the Los Angeles Marathon," *Journal of Sports Medicine and Physical Fitness* 30 (1990): 316–328.

29. Eichner, op. cit.

30. Ibid.

31. Gates, op. cit.

32. American College of Sports Medicine, "ACSM Position Stand on the Recommended Quantity and Quality of Exercise for Developing and Maintaining Cardiorespiratory and Muscular Fitness and Flexibility in Adults," *Medicine and Science in Sports and Exercise* 30 (1998): 975–991.

33. *ACSM Guidelines for Exercise Testing and Prescription,* op. cit.

34. DHHS, *Physical Activity and Health: A Report of the Surgeon General,* op. cit.

35. American College of Sports Medicine, op. cit.

36. B. Stamford, "Tracking Your Heart Rate for Fitness," *The Physician and Sportsmedicine* 21 (March 1993): 227–228.

37. U.S. Centers for Disease Control and Prevention and American College of Sports Medicine: "Summary Statement: Workshop on Physical Activity and Public Health," *Sports Medicine Bulletin* 28(4) (1993): 7.

38. G. A. Klug and J. Lettunich, *Wellness: Exercise and Physical Fitness* (Guilford, CT: Dushkin Publishing Group, 1992).

39. P. D. Wood, "Physical Activity, Diet, and Health: Independent and Interactive Effects," *Medicine and Science in Sports and Exercise* 26 (1994): 838–843.

40. American College of Sports Medicine, op. cit.

41. M. Cyphers, "Flexibility," in *Personal Trainer Manual,* 2nd ed. (San Diego: American Council on Exercise, 1996), 291–308.

42. American College of Sports Medicine, op. cit.

43. Ibid.

44. P. A. Sienna, *One Rep Max: A Guide to Beginning Weight Training* (Indianapolis: Benchmark Press, 1989).

45. G. A. Brooks, T. D. Fahey, and T. P. White, "Gender Differences in Physical Performance," in *Exercise Physiology: Human Bioenergetics and Its Applications,* 2nd ed. (Mountain View, CA: Mayfield, 1996), 644–665.

46. M. S. Feigenbaum and M. L. Pollock, "Prescription of Resistance Training for Health and Disease," *Medicine and Science in Sports and Exercise* 31 (1999): 38–45.

47. M. L. Pollock and W. J. Evans, "Resistance Training for Health and Disease: Introduction," *Medicine and Science in Sports and Exercise* 31 (1999): 10–11.

48. American College of Sports Medicine, op. cit.

49. C. L. Wells, *Women, Sport, and Performance: A Physiological Perspective,* 2nd ed. (Champaign, IL: Human Kinetics, 1991).

50. American College of Sports Medicine, op. cit.

51. W. C. Whiting and R. F. Zernicke, *Biomechanics of Musculoskeletal Injury* (Champaign, IL: Human Kinetics, 1998).

52. D. M. Brody, "Running Injuries: Prevention and Management," *Clinical Symposia* 39 (1987).

53. J. C. Erie, "Eye Injuries: Prevention, Evaluation, and Treatment," *The Physician and Sportsmedicine* 19 (November 1991): 108–122.

54. J. G. Stock and M. F. Cornell, "Prevention of Sports-Related Eye Injury," *American Family Practice* 44 (August 1991): 515–520.

55. R. C. Wasserman and R. V. Buccini, "Helmet Protection from Head Injuries Among Recreational Bicyclists," *American Journal of Sports Medicine* 18 (1990): 96–97.

56. S. M. Simons, "Foot Injuries of the Recreational Athlete," *The Physician and Sportsmedicine* 27 (January 1999): 57–70.

57. J. Andrish and J. A. Work, "How I Manage Shin Splints," *The Physician and Sportsmedicine* 18 (December 1990): 113–114.

58. E. A. Arendt, "Common Musculoskeletal Injuries in Women," *The Physician and Sportsmedicine* 24 (July 1996): 39–48.

59. American Academy of Orthopaedic Surgeons, *Athletic Training and Sports Medicine,* 2nd ed. (Park Ridge, IL: AAOS, 1991).

60. B. Q. Hafen and K. J. Karren, *Prehospital Emergency Care and Crisis Intervention,* 4th ed. (Englewood Cliffs, NJ: Prentice-Hall, 1992).

61. American College of Sports Medicine, "Position Stand—Heat and Cold Illnesses During Distance Running," *Medicine and Science in Sports and Exercise* 28 (December 1996): i–x.

62. American College of Sports Medicine, "Position Stand—Exercise and Fluid Replacement," *Medicine and Science in Sports and Exercise* 28 (January 1996): i–vii.

63. P. R. Below, P. Mora-Rodriguez, J. Gonzalez-Alonso, and F. F. Coyle, "Fluid and Carbohydrate Ingestion Independently Improve Performance During 1 Hr of Intense Exercise," *Medicine and Science in Sports and Exercise* 27 (1995): 200–210.

64. J. S. Thornton, "Hypothermia Shouldn't Freeze Out Cold-Weather Athletes," *The Physician and Sportsmedicine* 18 (January 1990): 109–113.

65. American College of Sports Medicine, "Position Stand—Heat and Cold Illnesses During Distance Running," op. cit.

CHAPTER 12

1. Center for Science in the Public Interest, *Nutrition Action Health Letter* 22 (1995): 4.

2. Ibid., 2.

3. Ibid., 2.

4. American Cancer Society, *Cancer Facts and Figures: 1999* (American Cancer Society, 1999).

5. Ibid., 6.

6. Ibid., 6.

7. Russell Ross, "Atherosclerosis—An Inflammatory Disease," *New England Journal of Medicine* 340 (1999): 115–126.

8. C. Napoli, F. P. D'Armiento, F. P. Mancini, et al., "Fatty Streak Formation Occurs in Human Fetal Aortas and Is Greatly Enhanced by Maternal Hypercholesterolemia: Intimal Accumulation of Low Density Lipoprotein and Its Oxidative Precede Monocyte Recruitment into Early Atherosclerotic Lesions." *Journal of Clinical Investigation* 100 (1997): 2680–2690.

9. J. L. Breslow, "Cardiovascular Disease Burden Increases, NIH Funding Decreases," *Nature Medicine* 3 (1997): 6000–6009.

10. Ross, op. cit., 115.

11. J. Danesh, R. Collins, and R. Peto, "Chronic Infections and Coronary Heart Disease: Is There a Link?" *Lancet* 350 (1997): 430–436.

12. Braunwald E. Shattuck Lecture, "Cardiovascular Medicine at the Turn of the Millennium: Triumphs, Concerns and Opportunities," *New England Journal of Medicine* 337 (1997): 1360–1369.

13. Ross, op. cit., 122.

14. American Heart Association, op. cit., 5.

15. Ibid., 12.

16. Ibid., 6.

17. Ibid., 14.

18. Ibid., 13.

19. Ibid., 15.

20. Ibid., 15.

21. Christopher R. Cole, Eugene H. Blackstone, Fredric J. Pashkow, Claire E. Snader, Michael S. Lauer, "Heart-Rate Recovery Immediately after Exercise as a Predictor of Mortality," *New England Journal of Medicine,* 340 (1999): 1351–1357.
22. American Heart Association, op. cit., 22.
23. Ibid., 24
24. Ibid., 24.
25. Ross, op. cit. 116.
26. A. G. Boston, et al., "Elevated Plasma Lipoprotein (a) and Coronary Heart Disease in Men Aged 55 Years and Younger: A Prospective Study," *Journal of the American Medical Association* 276 (1996): 555–558.
27. Ibid., 556.
28. Braunwald Shattuck Lecture, op. cit., 1362.
29. American Heart Association, op. cit., 14.
30. U.S. Department of Health and Human Services, *Surgeon General's Report on Physical Activity: 1996.*
31. American Heart Association, op. cit., 10.
32. Ibid., 6.
33. Center for Science in the Public Interest, op. cit., 6.
34. Ross, op. cit., 117.
35. R. Eliot, "Changing Behavior: A New Comprehensive and Quantitative Approach" (keynote address at the annual meeting of the American College of Cardiology on stress and the heart, Jackson Hole, WY, July 3, 1987).
36. American Heart Association, op. cit., 2.
37. Boston et al., op. cit., 555.
38. Ibid., 556.
39. Ibid., 556.
40. National Heart, Lung and Blood Institute, *Heart Memo: The Cardiovascular Health of Women,* 1995, 5.
41. Ibid., 5.
42. Jersey Chen, Martha Radford, Yun Wang, Thomas Marciniak, and Harlan Krumholz, "Do America's Best Hospitals Perform Better for Acute Myocardial Infarction?" *New England Journal of Medicine* 340 (1999): 286–290.
43. Ibid., 288.
44. J. E. Willard, R. A. Lange, and D. L. Hillis, "The Use of Aspirin in Ischemic Heart Disease," *New England Journal of Medicine* 327 (1992): 175–179.
45. Agency for Health Care Policy and Research, "Cardiac Rehabilitation: Exercise Training, Education, Counseling, and Behavioral Interventions," Publication #96-0672, 1996.
46. American Cancer Society, *Cancer Facts and Figures 1998* (Atlanta: American Cancer Society, 1998).
47. American Cancer Society, *Cancer Facts and Figures 1999* (Atlanta: American Cancer Society, 1999).
48. Larissa Remennick, "The Cancer Problem in the Context of Modernity, Sociology, Demography, and Politics," *Current Sociology* 46 (1998): 144.
49. Michael Osborne, Peter Boyle, and Martin Lipkin, "Cancer Prevention," *The Lancet* 349 (1997): 1–8 (special oncology supplement).
50. Ibid., 1–29.
51. Ibid., 1–29.
52. Ibid., 30.
53. Ibid., 30.
54. Ibid., 25–27.
55. M. Osborne, "Cancer Causing Viruses," *The Lancet* 349 (1997): 2.
56. American Cancer Society, op. cit., 12.
57. Ibid., 25–27.
58. Ibid., 8–9.

59. American Cancer Society, op. cit. "Percentage of Population (Probability) Developing Invasive Cancers at Certain Ages by Sex, US, 1992–1994" p. 17.
60. Ibid., 8–9.
61. Ibid., 9.
62. Ibid., 10.
63. Fuchs, C. S. et al. "Dietary Fiber and the Risk of Colorectal Cancer and Adenoma in Women," *New England Journal of Medicine* 340 (1991): 169–176.
64. American Cancer Society, op. cit., 10.
65. Ibid., 10.
66. *New England Journal of Medicine,* op. cit., p. 170.
67. National Cancer Institute, CancerNet: Screening for Skin Cancer, 1998: 1.
68. S. H. Landis, T. Murray, S. Bolden et al., "Cancer Statistics, 1998," *Cancer Journal for Clinicians* 48 (1998): 6–29.
69. NCI, CancerNet, op. cit., 3.
70. American Cancer Society, op. cit., 9.
71. Ibid., 13.
72. A. Harvey, Meera Jain Risch, Loraine D. Marrett, and Geoffrey R. Howe, "Dietary Fat Intake and Risk of Epithelial Ovarian Cancer," *Journal of the National Cancer Institute* 86 (1994): 21.
73. American Cancer Society, op. cit., 9.
74. Ibid., 11.
75. Ibid., 11.
76. Ibid., 11.
77. Ibid., 12.
78. Ibid., 11.
79. Ibid., 12.
80. Ibid., 12.
81. Ibid., 1–30.

CHAPTER 13

1. A. Benenson, *Control of Communicable Diseases in Man* (Washington D.C.: American Public Health Association, 1995).
2. A. Evans, and R. Kaslow, *Viral Infections in Humans: Epidemiology and Control,* 4th ed. (New York: Plenum Publishing, 1997), 6–11.
3. "Preventing Emerging Infectious Diseases: A Strategy for the 21st Century," U.S. Department of Health and Human Services, Centers for Disease Control and Prevention, Atlanta, 1998.
4. A. Evans, and P. Brachman, *Bacterial Infections of Humans: Epidemiology and Control,* 3rd ed. (Atlanta, Plenum Publishing, 1998).
5. Ibid., 425.
6. Evans Kaslow, op. cit. 623.
7. Ibid., 535.
8. Anita Manning, "Tiny Microbes Have Become a Large World Problem," *USA Today,* 21 May 1996, 8D.
9. Ibid.
10. J. Lederberg, "Emerging and Resurgent Infectious Diseases: Challenges to Public Health Health," Keynote address: American Public Health Association's Annual Meeting, November 1996, New York.
11. Manning, op. cit., 8D.
12. Kim Painter, "STI rate higher than previously believed," *USA Today,* 3 December 1998, section D, page 1 (taken from CDC December 1998 report)
13. "Preventing Emerging Infectious Diseases," op. cit.
14. "PID: Guidelines for Prevention, Detection, and Management," *Clinical Courier* 10 (1992): 1–5.
15. Evans and Brachman, op. cit., 285.

16. Evans and Kaslow, op. cit., 419–446.
17. "1998 World AIDS DAY Report," United Nations Joint Commission on AIDS (UNAIDS), November 30, 1998.
18. "HIV/AIDS Surveillance Report—1997," U.S. Department of Health and Human Services, Centers for Disease Control and Prevention, Atlanta, 1998.
19. "Report on the Global HIV/AIDS Epidemic," United Nations Joint Commission on AIDS (UNAIDS), June 30, 1998.
20. "HIV-AIDS Surveillance Report—1997," op. cit.
21. "HIV Reporting in the United States," Health Policy Tracking Service, National Conference of State Legislatures, September 1998.
22. "CDC Update: Critical Need to Pay Attention to HIV Prevention for Women," Centers for Disease Control and Prevention, July 24, 1998.
23. "Women and HIV," National Institute of Allergy and Infectious Disease, April 1997.
24. "Births and Deaths—U.S. 1997," National Center for Health Statistics, U.S. Department of Health and Human Services, December 1998 Web Facts.
25. R. Brownson, P. Remington, and J. Davis, eds., *Chronic Disease Epidemiology and Control.* (Washington, D.C.: American Public Health Association, 1998), 379–382.
26. Ibid., 389.
27. Ibid., 401.
28. Ibid., 516.
29. J. Adler, and A. Rogers. "The New War Against Migraines," *Newsweek,* 11 January 1999, 46–55.
30. Ibid., 48.
31. Ibid., 49.
32. Adler and Rogers, op. cit., 52.
33. Brownson et al., op. cit., 424.
34. Ibid.
35. *The Back Letter.* "Prevalence of Low Back Pain in the United States: New Estimates." Lippincott, Williams & Wilkins, Philadelphia (1998).
36. S. Straus, "Chronic Fatigue Syndrome: Biopsychosocial Approach May Be Difficult," *The British Medical Journal* 313 (1996): 831.
37. A. J. Barsky, "The Paradox of Health," *New England Journal of Medicine* 318 (1988): 414–418.

CHAPTER 14

1. John Kavenaugh, *Adult Development and Aging* (Pacific Grove, CA: BrooksCole/ITP, 1996), 45.
2. U.S. Census Bureau, 1996, as reported in *Profile on Aging, 1998,* American Associaton of Retired Persons.
3. Ibid.
4. H. Nasser and A. Stone. Study, "2020 Begins Age of the Elderly," *USA Today,* 21 May 1996, 4A.
5. Ibid.
6. *Health United States, 1998,* U.S. Department of Health and Human Services, 1998, 27.
7. National Center for Health Statistics, "An Overview of Nursing Homes and Their Current Residents: Data from the 1995 National Nursing Home Survey," January 23, 1997.
8. National Osteoporosis Foundation, *Physicians Resource Manual on Osteoporosis: A Decision-Making Guide,* 2nd ed. (National Osteoporosis Foundation, 1991), and National Dairy Council, "Calcium and Osteoporosis: New Insights," *Dairy Council Digest* 63 (1992): 1–6.
9. Tom Hickey, Margorie Speers, Thomas Prochaska. *Public Health and Aging.* (Baltimore: Johns Hopkins University Press, 1997).

10. Ibid., 69–71.
11. Ibid., 137–138.
12. National Council on Aging, Press Release, "Half of Older Americans Report They Are Sexually Active; 4 in 10 Want More Sex, Says New Survey," September 28, 1998. Weblink: http://ncoa.org/news/archives/sexsurvey.htm
13. The Alzheimer's Association, "Understanding Alzheimers: Statistics and Prevalence" Chicago (1998).
14. T. Brubaker and K. Roberto, "Family Life Education for the Later Years," *Family Relations,* 1993, 213.
15. *Oxford English Dictionary* (Oxford: Oxford University Press, 1969), 72, 334, 735.
16. President's Commission for the Study of Ethical Problems in Medicine and Biomedical and Behavioral Research, *Deciding to Forgo Life-Sustaining Treatment* (New York: Concern for Dying, 1983), 9.
17. Ad Hoc Committee of the Harvard Medical School to Examine the Definition of Brain Death, "A Definition of Irreversible Coma," *JAMA,* 205 (1968), 377.
18. Lewis R. Aiken, *Dying, Death, and Bereavement,* 3rd ed. (Boston: Allyn and Bacon, 1994), 4.
19. Elisabeth Kübler-Ross, *On Death and Dying* (New York: Macmillan, 1969), 113.
20. Robert J. Kastenbaum, *Death, Society, and Human Experience,* 6th ed. (Boston: Allyn and Bacon, 1998), 95.
21. K. J. Doka, ed., *Disenfranchised Grief: Recognizing Hidden Sorrow* (Lexington, MA: Lexington Books, 1989).
22. Kastenbaum, 6th ed., op. cit., 336–337.
23. The term *quasi-death experience* was coined by J. B. Kamerman; see ibid., 71.
24. "Last Rights: Why a 'Living Will' Is Not Enough," *Consumer Reports on Health,* September 1993, 5, 9.
25. Jerald G. Bachman, Kirsten H. Alcser, David J. Doukas, Richard L. Lichtenstein, Amy D. Corning, and Howard Brody, "Attitudes of Michigan Physicians and the Public Toward Legalizing Physician-assisted Suicide and Voluntary Euthanasia," *New England Journal of Medicine* 334 (1996): 303.
26. M. A. Lee, H. D. Nelxon, V. P. Tilden, L. Ganzini, T. A. Schmidt, and S. W. Tolle, "Legalizing Assisted Suicide: Views of Physicians in Oregon," *New England Journal of Medicine* 334 (1996): 310–315.

CHAPTER 15

1. G. Paeth, "ABC Reports on Apocalypse and Gore," *The Cincinnati Post,* 1998, 7C.
2. M. Renner, "Economic Features," *Vital Signs 1997: The Environmental Trends that Are Shaping our Future* (New York: W. W. Norton & Co., 1997).
3. R. Caplan, *Our Earth, Ourselves* (New York: Bantam, 1990), 247.
4. United Nations, *Global Population Policy Database* (New York: UN Population Division, 1995).
5. J. Abramovitz and S. Dunn, "Record Year for Weather-Related Disasters," in *Vital Signs Brief 98-5* (Washington, D.C.: Worldwatch Institute, 1998).
6. L. R. Brown, M. Renner, C. Flavin, *Vital Signs 1998: The Environmental Trends that Are Shaping our Future* (New York: W. W. Norton & Co., 1998).
7. M. Lowe, "Shaping Cities," in *State of the World, 1992,* Lester Brown, ed. (New York: W. W. Norton, & Co., 1992).
8. Brown, Renner, and Flavin, op. cit.
9. Larry Gordon, "Environmental Health and Protection: Century 21 Challenges," *Journal of Environmental Health* 57 (1995): 28–34.

10. L. R. Brown, G. Gardner, B. Halweil, *Beyond Malthus: Sixteen Dimensions of the Population Problem* (Washington, D.C.: Worldwatch Institute, 1998).

11. Ibid.

12. Lester Brown, "The Illusion of Progress," in *State of the World, 1990,* Lester Brown, ed. (New York, W. W. Norton Co., 1990), 11.

13. L. Brown, H. Kane, and D. Roodman, *Vital Signs 1995* (Washington, D.C.: Worldwatch Institute, 1996), 20.

14. J. Schwartz, "Health Effects of Particulate Air Pollution," *The Center for Environmental Health Newsletter,* 7 (1998) (University of Connecticut, College of Agriculture & Natural Resources).

15. National Center for Environmental Health, *Screening Young Children for Lead Poisoning: Guidance for State and Local Public Health Officials.* (Atlanta: Centers for Disease Control and Prevention, U.S. Public Health Service, 1997).

16. Lester Brown, "A New Era Unfolds," in *State of the World, 1993,* Lester Brown, ed. (New York: W. W. Norton Co., 1993), 107

17. K. E. Warner, D. Mendez, and P. N. Courant, "Toward a More Realistic Appraisal of the Lung Cancer Risk from Radon," *American Journal of Public Health* 86 (1996): 1222–1227.

18. U.S. Environmental Protection Agency, *Questions and Answers on Ozone Depletion* (Washington, D.C.: Stratospheric Protection Division, 1998).

19. Brown, Renner, and Flavin, op. cit.

20. J. Abramovitz, *Taking a Stand: Cultivating a New Relationship with the World's Forests* (Washington, D.C.: Worldwatch Institute, 1998).

21. Brown, Renner, and Flavin, op. cit.

22. Ibid.

23. U.S. Environmental Protection Agency, *Water on Tap: A Consumer's Guide to the Nation's Drinking Water* (Washington, D.C.: Safe Drinking Water Information System, 1997).

24. Ibid.

25. Ibid.

26. Brown, Renner, and Flavin, op. cit.

27. A. Hoyer, "Organochlorine Exposure and Risk of Breast Cancer," *Lancet* 352 (1998): 1816–1831.

28. B. L. Johnson, and C. T. DeRosa, "The Toxicologic Hazard of Superfund Hazardous Waste Sites," *Environmental Health* 12 (1997): 235–251.

29. Ibid., 238.

30. Ibid., 242.

31. Ibid., 243.

32. U.S. Environmental Protection Agency, *Meeting the Environmental Challenge: EPA's Review of Progress and New Directions in Environmental Protection* (EPA Publication No. 21K-2001, 1990), 4.

CHAPTER 16

1. L. C. Baker and L. S. Baker, "Excess Cost of Emergency Department Visits for Nonurgent Care," *Health Affairs* Winter 1994: 162–180.

2. Hospital Health Network, "Emergency Care: The Number of Visits to U.S. Hospital Emergency Departments Has Declined," *Hospital Health Network* 70 (1996): 14.

3. R. M. Williams, "The Costs of Visits to Emergency Departments," *New England Journal of Medicine,* 334 (1996): 642–646.

4. J. Schmittdiel, J. V. Selby, K. Grumbach, and C. P. Quesenberry, "Choice of a Personal Physician and Patient Satisfaction in a Health Maintenance Organization," *Journal of the American Medical Association* 278 (1997): 1596–1599.

5. G. Annas, *The Rights of Patients: The Basic ACLU Guide to Patient Rights,* 2nd ed. (Chicago: Southern Illinois University Press, 1989), 105.

6. Pennsylvania Medicine, "Use of Non-Physician Practitioners." *Pennsylvania Medicine* 101 (1998): 17–19.

7. D. M. Eisenberg et al., "Trends in Alternative Medicine Use in the United States, 1990–1997," *Journal of the American Medical Association* 280 (1997): 1569–1575.

8. P. Starr, *The Social Transformation of American Medicine* (New York: Basic Books, 1982), 127–229.

9. C. M. Cassidy, "Chinese Medicine Users in the United States, Part 1: Utilization, Satisfaction, Medical Plurality," *Altern Complement Med* 4 (1998): 17–27.

10. A. S. Brett and R. Dall, "Emerging Literature on Alternative Medicine." *Journal Watch* 18 (1998): 192–193.

11. C. Hafner-Eaton, "Patterns of Hospital and Physician Utilization Among the Uninsured," *Journal of Health Care for the Poor and Underserved* 5 (1994): 297–315.

12. Centers for Disease Control and Prevention, *Morbidity and Mortality Weekly Report,* 47 (1998): 529–532.

13. *Medical Group Practice Digest: Managed Care Digest Series 1998* (Kansas City: Hoechst Marion Roussel, Inc., 1998).

14. Ibid.

15. Ibid.

16. Ibid.

17. Ibid.

APPENDIX B

1. D. Eisenberg, et al., "Trends in Alternative Medicine Use in the United States, 1990–1997: Results of a Follow Up National Study," *Journal of the American Medical Association* 280 (1998): 1569–1579.

2. L. C. Paramore, 1997. Use of Alternative Therapies. *Journal of Pain and Symptom Management* 13 (1997): 83–89.

3. Landmark Healthcare. *The Landmark Report on Public Perceptions of Alternative Care* (Sacramento, CA: Landmark Healthcare, 1998).

4. D. M. Eisenberg, R. C. Kessler, C. Foster, et al. "Unconventional Medicine in the United States," *New England Journal of Medicine* 328 (1993): 246–252.

5. Eisenberg, 1993, 247; Eisenberg, 1998, 1570.

6. Ibid., 1993, 247; 1998, 1570.

7. John Greenwald, "Herbal Healing," *Time* November 23 (1998): 63–65.

8. John Astin, "Why Patients Use Alternative Medicine: Results of a National Study, *Journal of the American Medical Association* 279 (1998): 1548–1552.

9. Ibid., 1553.

10. M. Angell and J. P. Kassirer, "Alternative Medicine—The Risks of Untested and Unregulated Remedies," *New England Journal of Medicine* 339 (1998):839–841.

11. Greenwald, op. cit., 64.

12. Andrew Weil, *Spontaneous Healing* (New York: Fawcett Columbine, 1995:233).

13. Ibid., 239–241.

14. N. Rasmussen and J. Morgall, "The Use of Alternative Treatments in the Danish Adult Population," *Complementary Medicine Research* 4 (1990):16–22.

15. A. MacLennan, D. Wilson and A. Taylor, "Prevalence and Cost of Alternative Medicine in Australia," *The Lancet* 347 (1996): 569–573.

16. P. Fisher and A. Ward, "Complementary Medicine in Europe," *British Medical Journal* 309 (1994): 107–111.

17. W. Millar, "Use of Alternative Health Care Practitioners by Canadians," *Canadian Journal of Public Health* 88 (1997): 154–158.

18. Astin, 1999, 1550.
19. Eisenberg, 1998, 1571.
20. R. Donatelle, J. Nyiendo and M. Haas. "Health Care Decision-Making Among Those Seeking Care for Low Back Pain from Traditional Medical and Chiropractic Physicians." Paper presented at the American Public Health Association's annual meeting, 1998.
21. Astin, 1999, 1552.
22. P. H. Ray, 1997. "The Emerging Culture," American Demographics. Available at http://www.demographics.com, Intertec Publishing.
23. Weil, op. cit., 243.
24. J. Kleignen and P. Knipschild, "Gingko Biloba," The Lancet 340 (1992): 1136–1139.
25. M. Murray. 1998. "Gingko Biloba Extract and Ginkgo Phytosome." Ask the Doctor. Vital Communications.
26. P. L. LeBars, et. al. "A Placebo-Controlled, Double Blind, Randomized Trial of an Extract of Gingko Biloba for Dementia," Journal of the American Medical Association 278 (1997): 1327–1332.
27. "The Pill that Helps You Think?" Tufts University Health and Nutrition Letter 15 (1997): 8–10.
28. "St. John's Wort." 1998. Nature's Life brochure.
29. H. Schultz, "St. John's Wort for Depression," British Medical Journal 7052 (1996): 313–319.
30. K. D. Hansgen, et al. "Multicenter Double Blind Study Examining the Anti-depressant Effectiveness of the Hypericum Extract LI160," Journal of Psychiatric Neurology October 7. Supplement 1 (1994): s15–18.
31. H. Schultz, et al. "Effects of Hypericum Extract on the Sleep EEG in Older Volunteers," American Journal of Geriatric Psychiatry Suppl.1 (1994): s65–68.
32. Ibid., 66.
33. Ibid., 66.
34. H. Martin, "St. John's Wort vs Tricyclic Antidepressants," American Journal of Naturopathic Medicine 2 (1995): 42.
35. Schultz, 1996, 314.
36. J. Blair, "Echinacea—New Wonder Drug?" Archives of Family Medicine November, 24 (1998): 1332–1339.
37. "Echinacea For What Ails You? Weighing the Evidence for a Popular Herb," Tufts University Health and Nutrition Letter 9 (1997): 8–9
38. "New Guides in Herbal Remedies," Harvard Women's Health Watch 41 (1999): 6–8.
39. P. A. DeSmet, "Health Risks of Herbal Remedies," Drug Safety 13 (1996): 81–93.
40. E. Ernst, "Harmless Herbs," American Journal of Medicine 104 (1998): 170–178.
41. Harvard Women's Health Watch, 1999, 7.
42. Ernst, op. cit., 172.
43. Ernst, op. cit., 173.
44. Astin, 1553.
45. Charles Marwick, "Medical News and Perspectives: Alternatives Are Ahead of the OAM," Journal of the American Medical Association 280 (1998): 1553–1554.
46. Dru Wilson, "Health Food Masquerade." Corvallis Gazette Times August 11 (1999): C-4.
47. Tufts Nutrition Letter, op. cit.
48. M. Polunin, Healing Foods: A Practical Guide to Key Foods for Good Health (New York: DK Publishing, 1997).
49. FDA Guide to Dietary Supplements. U.S. Food and Drug Administration, 1998: 1–14.
50. Weil, 1995, 205.
51. Ibid., 241.
52. Wilson, op. cit.
53. Greenwald, op. cit., 64.
54. Ibid., 65.
55. Marwick, op. cit.
56. M. Angell and J. P. Kassirer, "Alternative Medicine—The Risks of Untested and Unregulated Remedies," New England Journal of Medicine 339 (1998): 839–841.
57. "CAM Centers of Research: Overview of the Specialty Centers," 2000 National Center for Complementary & Alternative Medicine. Website: http://nccam.nih.gov/nccam/research/centers.html
58. Astin, 1550.
59. D. Eskinazi, 1998. Policy Perspectives: Factors that Shape Alternative Medicine 280(18): 1621.
60. "Clinical Practice Guidelines in Complementary and Alternative Medicine: An Analysis of Opportunities and Obstacles," 1997 Practice and Policy Guidelines Panel. National Institutes of Health, Office of Alternative Medicine. Archives of Family Medicine 6 (1997): 149–154.
61. D. M. Studdert, D. M. Eisenberg, F. H. Miller, et al. "Medical Malpractice Implications of Alternative Medicine," Journal of the American Medical Association 280 (1998): 1610–1615.
62. Greenwald, op. cit., 66.

Index